ALIEN *IN THE*
MIRROR

ALIEN IN THE MIRROR

Extraterrestrial Contact
Theories & Evidence

Randall Fitzgerald

Foreword by Jacques F. Vallée

Waterside Productions

Cover design by Ken Fraser
Typesetting and interior design by Josh Freel
Index by Kenneth Kales

First Printing, 2022

ISBN-13: 978-1-957807-00-3 print edition
ISBN-13: 978-1-957807-01-0 ebook edition

Waterside Productions
2055 Oxford Ave
Cardiff, CA 92007
www.waterside.com

What Reviewers Said About *Cosmic Test Tube*

Richard Dolan, historian and author of *UFOS and the National Security State*, writing in *Phenomena* magazine:

I consider *Cosmic Test Tube* to be one of the most important books in the UFO genre. In a way, it is itself the ultimate book review. What Randall Fitzgerald did was to provide clear, clean reviews of more than 150 books dealing with this topic of UFOs and alien visitation, essentially published during the second half of the 20th century. Everything, it seems—the pro, the con, the good, the bad, the ugly—is covered. The breadth of topics is impressive, as is Fitzgerald's organization of the material.

He divides these books within five basic sections: ancient astronauts, UFOs and UFO occupants, contactees and abductees, debunkers and skeptics, and the scientific approach to contacting extraterrestrial intelligence. The books within each section are then organized chronologically, and he usually devotes two or three pages for each entry.

This book is especially useful to serious researchers. I wish I had a copy when I was writing my own book, dealing with the history of UFOs and the U.S. military-intelligence community. There were many times during my work that I wanted to read a concise description of the contents of a particular book, or even learn which books I needed to be reading. Fitzgerald's resource would have been very useful.

What is perhaps most impressive about this book is Fitzgerald's uncanny ability to remove himself from the equation. At times, I find it frustrating that he absolutely refuses to provide a critique of the merits and flaws of particular book. In other words, Fitzgerald does not critique, pontificate, or grandstand in any way. What he does is *describe*. And when you think about the tangle of a topic that is the UFO phenomenon, perhaps this is quite enough. Besides, each major section of the book has a solid introduction, providing useful background that lays out the key issues and problems for the reader.

Although the book is to be coveted by serious researchers, I think any intelligent layperson would find it to be worthwhile, especially those people seeking a well-balanced introduction to this field. It certainly helps that Fitzgerald is so very easy to read. His style is always graceful and—among writers on the edge—he is one of the leading exponents of what one may call classic-style prose.

For that reason, this book is an education not only in the subject of UFOs, but in how to write about them.

Victor Marchetti, former CIA official and co-author of *The CIA And The Cult of Intelligence* wrote: "A fascinating and informative book. Fitzgerald's penetrating insights are illuminating."

The *Los Angeles Times* described *Cosmic Test Tube* as "A skillful blend of Fitzgerald's veritable research talents and his own insights."

MSN, **the Microsoft Internet** network, gave it a rating of five out of a possible five, calling it "brilliant" and "indispensable."

Associatedcontent.com headlined its review, **"Five of the Best UFO Books for Veterans or Novices Alike,"** April 23, 2008, by **Will Stape**:

> *Cosmic Test Tube* Stands Out from UFO Book Crowd. Part historical guidebook, with clear analysis and also a UFO bibliography, *Cosmic Test Tube* impresses as one of the best UFO reference guides. Describing all major UFO books printed up until the time of publication (1998), Fitzgerald covers everything from the ancient astronauts of Erich Von Daniken's *Chariots of the Gods*, to the famous Betty and Barney Hill alien abduction case to the celebrated incident at Roswell, New Mexico. Unlike some dry pure reference guide or quick listing of sources, Fitzgerald prefaces each comprehensive section with anecdotes and thoughtful observations about the material he's collated. This is one book which deserves to be updated periodically as new ones come along worth of inclusion.

From ***Library Journal***: This is a greatly expanded edition of the author's *Complete Book of Extraterrestrial Encounters* (LJ 11/15/79).

> Fitzgerald, a journalist, provides descriptive summaries of over 150 books on ancient astronauts, UFO contactees/abductees, debunkers and skeptics, and the search for radio signals from space. Publication dates range from 1919 to 1997. Fitzgerald provides introductory context for each of the five

topic areas. Books were selected based on their impact on public debate, their contribution to scientific understanding, or their thought-provoking content. Well-known authors such as Charles Fort, Eric von Daniken, and Carl Sagan are found here, along with those only UFO buffs will recognize. Added features include a "Guide to Books" with one-sentence descriptions of the titles summarized, an eight-page bibliography, and a detailed index. This selective guide to books on UFOs and related phenomena will help interested readers sort out a very complex topic. Highly recommended for most libraries, especially those having the earlier edition.

Gary D. Barber, SUNY at Fredonia Library

Contents

Foreword by Jacques F. Vallée

As this book goes to press, the public is learning about stunning developments in the field of "ufology," the study of unidentified flying objects. Most remarkably, the US Government has now admitted that it did not understand the phenomenon after all.

More than seventy years of erratic investigation, the funding of studies at taxpayers' expense (several of them still secret) and the occasional collection of physical traces, have led nowhere.

The possible recovery of material and biological samples by the military and a few private groups, under classified conditions, is very much a part of the new equation. So is the persistent claim that some of the old UFO information was misused, planted, or simply repurposed, as part of what should be called "active measures," inherited or inspired in the long shadow of MK-ULTRA, confusing everybody except the Russians. Yet unassailable evidence of a truly unknown phenomenon with its own internal logic also kept accumulating. These facts are likely to make the next phase of study not more open and accessible to the public but even more secretive and esoteric, unless the lessons of the last decades are remembered and used.

Back in 1968, an expensive review of the available data by the University of Colorado concluded that the cases in the Air force files and other records were of little or no interest to science, prompting many specialists to drop their budding investigations. Important reports, formal or informal, continued to come through private and public channels. They were colorful, remarkably complex, and occasionally threatening, like the overflight of the aircraft carrier Nimitz and the ships of the Pacific Fleet in the first decade of the present century, which couldn't be swept under the same rug as mirages, sun dogs or that favorite of skeptical academics: temperature inversions!

They forced a painful re-appraisal once the data was leaked.

Reappraisal of WHAT? The new data provides welcome measurement (time, speed, energy, temperature, photographs, frequency, distance, etc.) where earlier reports had rarely based on reliable instruments beyond a compass and occasionally, a radiation probe. But there is bias in that new data in its own context, and we can only make sense of it by placing it within the much larger universe of the accumulated sightings over half a century of worldwide observation, some of it extremely good, and recorded in a few dozen valuable books.

What was needed was a reappraisal of the literature, such as the material in this volume.

The available information is enormous, even if one only lists the actual books, ignoring articles, bits and pieces of reports, or occasional notes. Prominent scholars have done such work before, like George M. Eberhart in his two-volume bibliography of "UFOs and the Extraterrestrial Contact Movement" (Scarecrow Press, 1986). That work fairly cited many of its predecessors, from Lynn Catoe's study at the Library of Congress in the 1960s to the Condon Report in 1969. But a major gap remained to bridge the research to the present time, when American officials are reviewing and re-framing the entire field.

Pointedly re-naming the problem under the label of "unidentified *aerial phenomena*" to make it appear less threatening and of more immediate interest to natural scientists, officials of the Intelligence community, Congress, NASA and even prominent members of the cloth, have now reversed their negative assessment and removed much of the stigma. Years of lies, ridicule and fake official "explanations" for what good citizens had the intelligence to observe and the guts to report in the face of scientific contempt and journalistic titillation, not to mention family disrepute and scandal, has been erased.

Major universities are gearing up to restart the studies from scratch, using combinations of private and public funds.

Whenever money becomes available, brains suddenly start shining over campuses with renewed brilliance: a new generation of scientists, philosophers, sociologists and good investigators has now emerged, taking active interest in good old flying saucers.

In the process, wheels are re-invented and inevitably, decades of well-meaning, underfunded investigation – the dubious stuff of amateurish passion — are pushed aside or ignored. This is not unheard of in the history of knowledge: once you discover America, its vast lands and high mountains, you no longer need those beautiful ancient maps of vast empty oceans only showing the horrible heads of a few emerging sea monsters, except to hang them in a museum.

Most of the researchers of my generation are delighted to welcome this change. We feel vindicated. We've worked for it for a long time. Yet the challenge is intact: new hope is there, but most of the data hasn't been re-examined. Nobody has discovered a new America yet, and it's appropriate to yell: *Not so fast!* This vast and complex phenomenon, loaded and enriched by decades, if not centuries of extraordinary exposure, has not capitulated just because of a speech by the director of the CIA, a statement by the Pope or a new truckload of dollars from Congress.

What was unexplained in 1945, when an avocado-shaped object weighing several tons and carrying strange biological entities crashed at the Trinity site, a few days after the first atomic bomb, remains a tantalizing mystery today; so do the close-range observations by competent witnesses of similar objects that touched the ground at places like Socorro (New Mexico, 1964) and Valensole (France, 1965) for which extensive government investigation files exist. Hundreds of such reports sleep in dusty files, unexamined and unsolved. Few of the witnesses are still alive, and the scientists who did the studies have moved on in their careers, or retired. Or died.

What remains is the literature.

And what a literature it is! You will find it summarized here, repurposed and reorganized rationally by an author of long experience in the field. Randall Fitzgerald has carefully compiled it for the benefit of new researchers seeking a quick overview of the field they are entering. It can save them valuable time and much money that might have been wasted on the reassessment of wild-goose chases. It can even provide the basis of a cross-index for the most cogent data gathered in past decades. It is a tool for research. But above all, it will stand as testimony to a well-travelled road of investigation and wonder. We should acknowledge it with gratitude, not only for its neat classification of complex events, but for the hope it gives us of a long-delayed, much welcome re-awakening of the true spirit of science after seventy years of slumber.

· · ·

Jacques F. Vallée has written several dozen highly regarded books on various aspects of the UFO phenomenon, along with five books on technology and finance, and five novels, one of which received the Jules Verne prize in France. He received a Ph.D. in artificial intelligence and a master's degree in astrophysics, and coded the first computer-based map of Mars for NASA. As a Silicon Valley entrepreneur, he founded numerous venture funds, including NASA's 'Red Planet Capital'. He was the real-life model for the character portrayed by Francois Truffaut in the Steven Spielberg movie, *Close Encounters of the Third Kind.* (Learn more at: www.jacquesvallee.net)

Introduction: Why Are We Being Manipulated?

"Why haven't you asked me to write for your magazine?" the man demanded to know, after I had staggered out of bed early one morning in the Spring of 1979, to answer my apartment phone in suburban Washington, D.C.

"Who is this?" I replied, thinking a friend was playing a lame joke.

"Stanton Friedman, nuclear physicist," the caller announced.

My mind cycled through names and titles until a mental index card popped up. Stanton Friedman, the bearded conference-circuit showman who billed himself in his lecture series, "Flying Saucers Are Real," as the world's only nuclear physicist investigating the UFO phenomenon fulltime.

"Maybe we just haven't gotten around to asking you for an article yet." I was trying to be diplomatic because we were a new, under-funded monthly magazine, reporting on life's mysteries. We couldn't yet afford to alienate anyone.

"Where do you stand on alien visitation?" Friedman inquired.

I explained how the other editor, British author Robert Temple, and I, were both agnostics about whether UFOs were extraterrestrial in origin. We wanted to provide a forum with our magazine, *Second Look*, for both believers and skeptics of alien visitation to present the facts and debate the quality of evidence.

That answer seemed to satisfy Friedman and he asked me whether I had heard about the crash of a flying saucer in Roswell, New Mexico, back in 1947. "This is a cosmic Watergate," he declared, "and anyone who breaks this story will get a Pulitzer Prize."

The alleged saucer crash incident sounded familiar because I had received some Roswell-related information in the mail just a month earlier. My correspondent had been Leonard Stringfield, an Ohio corporate executive who worked as a volunteer with a civilian UFO investigative group, NICAP, whose newsletter I had subscribed to as a teenager in Texas during mid-1960s. This sort of material fell well within the purview of what *Second Look* had been founded to explore, but I suspected doing an adequate investigation would take resources that we didn't possess.

After my interactions with Friedman and Stringfield, I decided to investigate what happened at Roswell by proposing an article to the editors of *The Washington Post* Sunday magazine, for which I had written a cover story a month earlier chronicling some of my findings about the tabloid newspaper, *The National Enquirer,* and how it manipulated members of the U.S. Congress to do its bidding. Two of the Post editors I worked with,

William Mackaye and Richard Harwood, seemed intrigued by the crashed saucer conspiracy idea and gave me an assignment to produce a lengthy article.

My interviews began with one of the primary witnesses to the Roswell incident, Major Jesse Marcel, a Roswell Army Air Field intelligence officer sent out in June 1947, to examine the purported crash debris on a ranch north of Roswell, New Mexico. Marcel had subsequently retired from the Air Force to the small town of Houma, Louisiana. Though he had been ordered by a superior officer to keep quiet about the incident, he indicated that he had decided to become a whistleblower because he felt the truth should come out before he and other witnesses passed away. He proceeded to tell me the outline of an incredible story that is now probably familiar to most people on the planet.

Stringfield provided me with copies of several FBI documents making references to the recovery of crashed saucers in the southwestern desert, something that FBI Director J. Edgar Hoover had apparently taken a personal interest in. Stringfield also sent me photographs of an alleged alien body in a burnt craft that he implied had been taken at Roswell, though I was never able to verify its origin.

It's worth taking a brief tour of the rugged and confusing UFO terrain that existed when I began my 1979 investigation. Since the news media began mirroring widespread public interest in the subject, beginning in 1947, UFOs had been variously identified as swamp gas, ball lightning, secret government spy craft, illusions, hoaxes, natural and human-made phenomena, psychic projections, holograms, time travelers, plasma life in our atmosphere, and extraterrestrial spaceships. Occupants of the UFOs had been variously described as dwarfs, giants, angels, demons, Nazis, 2-inch-long bees, evolved reptiles, human beings from the future, or 'tulpas' created by pure mind energy.

Rumors of crashed saucers and little gray men, though not explicitly labeled as being from Roswell, had been in circulation since October 1949, when *Variety* entertainment writer Frank Scully published a column about the alleged military retrieval of 16 dwarfish gray aliens who died in the crash of their 100-foot-diameter saucer in the New Mexico desert. *Time* magazine took notice in a January 9, 1950 issue by reporting how these rumors had taken on a life of their own, being repeated in Los Angeles "from mouth to mouth with amplification and new twists," which included the revelation that one interplanetary visitor was "three feet tall and a bit primitive, even monkeylike in appearance," having survived the crash and been "rushed to the Rosenwald Foundation in Chicago for expert examination."

Scully later wrote a book, released in 1950, detailing the New Mexico crash story and alleging that the U.S. Air Force kept the alien bodies stored at Wright-Patterson

Field in Ohio. After Scully's two sources were apparently exposed as conmen, and a 1952 *True* magazine investigation labeled Scully's book "one of the greatest scientific hoaxes of this century," his tale fell into disrepute as a bizarre footnote in UFO history. (Scully's book may actually have been based on some truths, at least as he learned them at the time; his image is now being rehabilitated in light of the prospect that he may have been manipulated as part of a U.S. Air Force and CIA disinformation campaign.)

Still the rumors persisted. Syndicated columnist Dorothy Kilgallen reported from London in 1955 how British scientists had allegedly been allowed to examine the wreckage of an alien spacecraft in American military hands. She named none of her sources. When former atomic physicist Leon Davidson checked into these rumors, he claimed to have found evidence of a CIA program to exploit the UFO phenomenon to serve some unspecified purpose in the Cold War. He revealed how the CIA had used "secret flights of U.S. aircraft," combined with hoaxes played on unsuspecting persons and "the release of planted information," to condition the American public to believe in flying saucers and little gray men.

Partial confirmation of Davidson's suspicions came unexpectedly, decades later, in 1997, with release of an unclassified version of a study from the secret CIA journal, *Studies In Intelligence*, examining the CIA and U.S. Air Force roles in deceiving the American public about the true nature of some UFOs reported in the 1950s and 1960s. Many were allegedly U-2 and SR-71 spy planes being flown from bases in Nevada and California on overseas surveillance missions. False stories were planted in the media claiming the sightings were of common atmospheric phenomena. "Leon Davidson was closer to the truth than he suspected," commented the CIA study, which went on to describe instances where CIA officers, working undercover wearing Air Force uniforms, contacted Davidson and other UFO researchers and witnesses "to monitor UFO sightings," sometimes feeding them disinformation to evaluate how the agency might "use the UFO phenomenon in connection with U.S. psychological warfare efforts." It was a startling and frank admission about government manipulation and deception and it further fed conspiracy theorizing.

The next media flash frenzy about crashed saucers came in 1974, when Robert Carr of Clearwater, Fla., a former Director of Educational Research for Walt Disney Studios, held a press conference to declare that he had evidence the Air Force recovered two spacecraft with alien crews in New Mexico during 1948. He described the 12 alien beings who died of 'decompression' as four feet in height, light brownish hair, fair skinned with blue eyes, who could "pass unnoticed on the streets of Tampa as small men or as children." One body was autopsied by six government physicians as a motion picture cameraman recorded the event. Carr claimed the bodies and saucer debris were being stored at Wright-Patterson Air Force Base in Hangar 18, a revelation which triggered nearly 100 news media inquiries to the base, prompting the Air Force to conduct public tours and inspections for the media at every building associated with the number 18.

After Carr died in 1994, at age 85, his son published an article calling his father delusional and apologizing to investigators who had spent years trying to track down his tales of crashed saucers and alien bodies. "His imaginary world was more real to him than the real world," confessed Timothy Spencer Carr, a Ph.D. in social psychology. "The myth/legend of the 'alien autopsy' and UFO at Wright-Patterson is nothing but total fantasy."

By 1978 the rumors of crashed saucers and alien bodies had once again become a fleeting fixture of mainstream media speculation. On television's Merv Griffin Show, host Griffin and former NASA astronaut Gordon Cooper of Mercury 9 and Gemini 5 fame, became immersed in a discussion about alien visitation. In a confidential tone Griffin related having heard about a spaceship crash which had occurred somewhere in North America after World War II. "There have been stories there were occupants," Griffin half-whispered, "and that our government was able to keep one alive."

"I think it's credible," Cooper replied matter-of-factly.

In subsequent interviews with newspaper reporters Cooper revealed how several of his friends claimed to have been involved in the mission to salvage the spaceship and its alien passengers. "I must say there is a good possibility that this thing exists. That the incident took place."

The 'incident' Cooper referred to had by now multiplied into vague rumors describing at least five separate crash scenarios. These accounts all had in common the military retrieval of crashed disks and tiny humanoid bodies. All occurred within the same general time frame of 1947-53, and the stories were concentrated in New Mexico, Arizona, and western Texas, an area surrounding what then constituted the nation's most secret nuclear test sites.

Rumors of conspiracy thrive in an atmosphere shrouded in secrecy. New Mexico in 1947 was the official secrets capital of America, if not the world, with White Sands, Alamogordo and Roswell constituting ground zero of the U.S. nuclear arsenal and weapons testing research. Southern New Mexico, at White Sands Proving Ground, had been where the first atomic bomb was exploded and where captured German V-2 rockets were tested, and Roswell Army Air Field had been where the world's first atomic bomber squadron was stationed. Foreign spies, both real and imaginary, lurked everywhere in the shadows, which made secrecy essential to cloak military activities. During the second half of 1947, the Army Air Force was separated into distinct Army and Air Force services, the Central Intelligence Agency was created, the Soviets were close to exploding their first atomic weapon igniting the nuclear arms race, and flying saucer sightings became an almost daily feature of American newspapers and radio broadcasts. The stage was set for crashed saucer stories and the most enduring legend of all, Roswell.

Rumors of crashed saucers eventually concentrated into these scenarios:

Early July, 1947—A ranch foreman northwest of Roswell reports finding unusual aerial wreckage scattered in a pasture, prompting an investigation by Air Force officers and a press release in which Roswell Army Air Field announces the capture of a flying saucer, a claim later retracted and explained away as a weather balloon.

Spring, 1948—Outside Aztec, New Mexico, a disk 99 feet in diameter allegedly crashed with 16 to 18 alien humanoids aboard, which became the basis for the magazine columns and the book produced by Frank Scully.

July, 1948—Thirty miles south of Laredo, Texas, a disk-shaped craft supposedly crashed with several humanoids less than four feet tall aboard; a U.S. Navy photographer claimed to have taken 40 photos of their burned bodies amid the wreckage.

Spring, 1950—Near Del Rio, Texas, a crashed disk was reportedly seen with several dead four-foot-tall aliens, a retrieval allegedly witnessed by two Air Force colonels who described the incident in signed affidavits given to an Arizona aerospace engineer, William Spaulding.

July, 1952—During a Chamber of Commerce luncheon in Pueblo, Colo., the speaker, Joseph Rohrer, president of Pike's Peak Broadcasting Company, told the audience that during 1942, he had been inside one of seven crashed flying saucers, which used magnetic propulsion, that were being stored at a U.S. government facility. He claimed that a three-foot tall alien pilot of one saucer had survived a Montana crash and had been kept alive.

May, 1953—In Arizona a project engineer for the Atomic Energy Commission, Fritz A. Werner, claimed he and 15 other specialists were sent to inspect a 30-foot diameter crashed disk that had one or two small alien bodies on board.

An organization called Ground Saucer Watch, co-founded by the aerospace engineer William Spaulding, filed a lawsuit against the CIA in 1977, under the Freedom of Information Act, seeking documents the CIA might possess concerning UFOs and the retrieval of crashed saucer debris. Spaulding won the lawsuit and the CIA released about 1,000 pages of documents which showed "the Government has been lying to us all these years," declared Spaulding, an engineer for AiResearch, a producer of aerospace components based in Phoenix. The documents revealed that U.S. embassies around the world had been directed to gather UFO sighting information and forward it to the CIA and the National Security Agency, despite claims by these agencies of having no interest in the UFO phenomenon.

When I interviewed Spaulding for my *Post* article in 1979, he told me the following, based on his analysis of the CIA documents: "We believe UFOs exist, but they are not from outer space. We believe the CIA is motivating and manipulating the phenomenon. We found two cases of crashed discs that most likely involved government experimental vehicles which crashed with monkeys aboard. Two Air Force colonels have signed affidavits about a crash that occurred near Del Rio, Texas, in 1950. Our theory is that during the period 1947-53 some experiments overshot White Sands and crashed with monkeys inside."

More than any other single researcher, Leonard Stringfield deserves the credit— or blame, depending on your perspective—for having set in motion the avalanche of articles, books, and films which created what came to be known as the Roswell case. A public relations executive for DuBois Chemical Company in Cincinnati, Ohio, Stringfield's consuming hobby since 1953 had been investigating UFOs and writing monograms and books about his findings. Because of his prominence, and perhaps due to his proximity to Wright-Patterson Air Force Base in nearby Dayton, he became a magnet for current and former military personnel who claimed to have seen evidence or heard stories of crashed spacecraft and alien bodies.

When I first interviewed Stringfield for the *Post* article, he described having 60 informants attesting to firsthand, secondhand, and thirdhand knowledge of crash incidents concentrated in the 1947-53 period. Fifteen of these sources were said to be firsthand witnesses—nine Air Force, two Army, one Navy, one CIA, and two physicians of whom one allegedly performed an autopsy on an alien corpse. All had supposedly signed government secrecy oaths not to reveal what they had seen. As a consequence, Stringfield refused to release their names publicly except to congressional investigators who would grant the witnesses immunity from prosecution.

The only source Stringfield provided me was Jesse Marcel, the former Air Force intelligence officer who seemed to no longer fear prosecution for disobeying secrecy orders. Here are excerpts of what Marcel told me: "It was sometime in July 1947. I was a major in Air Force Intelligence. A rancher had reported finding something unusual crashed on his farm. A Counter Intelligence Corps officer, a Mr. Cavitt, and I drove out to the ranch 35 miles northwest of Roswell, New Mexico. The crash site was a mile long stretch of debris. Something had exploded in the air overhead. We picked up a large amount of porous material and metal. The largest piece was three or four feet long. It was not a rocket. I knew it hadn't come from White Sands because I knew what they were testing there. We sent the pieces to Wright Patterson for analysis. I was ordered not to say anything about what I had seen."

Marcel mentioned nothing to me about the retrieval of bodies from the wreckage, but my curiosity was aroused by a recurrent theme in saucer crash reports linking the wreckage to a storage and analysis facility at Wright-Patterson. Over the previous decade I had heard a rumor in conservative political circles that U.S. Sen. Barry Goldwater of Arizona had been denied entry in the early 1960s to this secret section of the Wright-Patterson base where the UFO wreckage and alien bodies were allegedly kept. I knew he had an interest in the UFO subjects because I had discussed it with him in his office in the summer of 1970, when I had been a young intern. Though he declined my request to be directly interviewed about Roswell or crashed UFOs for the *Post* article, presumably because he then served on the Senate Intelligence Committee, Sen. Goldwater did craft a statement which he released to me through Charles Lombard, a former CIA employee who worked as Goldwater's special assistant for science.

Said Goldwater: "I asked General Curtis LeMay (head of the Strategic Air Command) if I could go in a room there at Wright-Patterson that was called either the Green Room or the Blue Room, because I thought that was where they kept UFO records. And Curtis LeMay said, 'you can't go in there and I can't go in there.' But he would never say what was in the room. LeMay never affirmed or denied that UFO records or material were in the room." In a subsequent interview, Lombard told me the incident remained puzzling. "We don't know why the senator was refused admittance," Lombard said. "He has a Top Secret clearance. If there is a departmental clearance for UFOs, I've never heard of it." Lombard scoffed at stories that the room at Wright-Patterson might hold the bodies of aliens from the Roswell crash. "General LeMay never said it had to do with little men. We don't believe there is a government conspiracy. But we have reports in NICAP files of radar locks on UFOS simultaneous with visual sightings, and 10 to 15 percent of sightings are unexplained, so we can't pooh pooh the UFO phenomenon."

Lombard served as an investigative staffer on the Church Committee, a U.S. Senate investigation of CIA excesses and abuses in the mid-1970s, that according to Lombard, "briefly got involved with studying UFOs." Since Lombard was both a member of NICAP and a former CIA employee, as was then NICAP executive director Alan Hall, and many CIA officials were involved in the founding of NICAP, I was naturally curious about the CIA-UFO link and asked Lombard about it. He smiled and shrugged: "Most of my friends in this city were once associated with the intelligence agencies."

"Are most of your friends also interested in the UFO phenomenon?" I pressed him.

"Yes, you could say that," replied Lombard.

For well over a year after finishing my *Washington Post* article about crashed saucer conspiracies, I kept getting the run-around from editors about a publication date. The first book on Roswell had by now appeared, in 1980, *The Roswell Incident*, by Charles Berlitz and William Moore, using some research by Stanton Friedman. It wasn't until early 1981 that I finally received word that my article had been unceremoniously killed by Richard Harwood, then the number two editor of *The Post*. As another editor relayed his reasoning to me, merely by writing about an alleged conspiracy of this nature, especially since I had adopted a neutral tone without conclusions, rather than engaging in dismissive debunking and ridicule, might in itself further encourage the spread of fevered conspiracy speculations. When I requested that the alleged crash victim photos and FBI documents that I had provided be returned, I was told the material could not be found. Why the editors waited nearly two years to inform me of having killed the article remains a mystery.

The Genesis of *Second Look*

While on a magazine assignment at a 1975 UFO convention in Fort Smith, Arkansas, I met the two men who then held opposing polarities in the debate about alien visitation—the astronomer and former Project Blue Book adviser J. Allen Hynek, who had evolved from a skeptic into a believer, and Philip J. Klass, an aerospace magazine editor who specialized in debunking UFO reports. Around each man a cadre of supporters had coalesced into enemy camps hurling shrill invective. I never felt comfortable being allied with either camp, believers or debunkers, because both seemed more intent on fitting UFO reports and evidence into preconceived theories, more interested in proving themselves right and others wrong, than in being open to the possibility of this phenomenon—whatever it is—posing a challenge beyond our power to explain. (I always made an exception in the case of Hynek, who I found to be fair-minded; Phil Klass was another character study entirely!)

As useful and necessary a role for critical thinking that many debunkers play, it became my experience that most weren't really skeptics in the sense of a Webster's dictionary definition: "the method of suspended judgment; the doctrine that true knowledge in a particular area is uncertain." Most debunkers came across as cynics projecting a sniveling disbelief instead of doubt, who were unable or unwilling to accept the very prospect of alien visitation, and whose rigid mindset compelled them to campaign against 'irrationality' with a missionary zeal often characterized by scathing mean-spirited ridicule and character assassination.

At the other extreme, among alien visitation believers I found a widespread and disturbing gullibility. Many cultivated stubborn evangelical attachments to pet theories about the nature of the phenomenon, rendering them eager to accept just about any claim, no matter how preposterous, if it supported their point of view. As a result, a continuous dribble of faked UFO photos, bogus alien body autopsy films, crashed saucer stories, fabricated alien artifacts, and banal alien 'channeled' messages had seeped into mainstream awareness without consistent critical challenge, making it easier for conventional scientists and media institutions to dismiss the entire area of inquiry as a veritable toxic waste dump.

Another concern of mine revolved around the way human genius and achievement got discounted and demeaned in the frenzied rush to prove that alien visitation occurred in ancient times. While at a convention of the Ancient Astronaut Society in Chicago during the late 1970's, I heard Erich von Daniken, author of *Chariots of the Gods*, rattle off a long list of suspected extraterrestrial constructions—Stonehenge, the Great Pyramids, Easter Island statues, the Nazca lines in Peru—as hundreds of heads throughout the ballroom bobbed in unison without a murmur of dissent. To accept as gospel what I heard that weekend would have been to render the human species as little more than a clueless marionette, lacking ingenuity and intellectual capacity, dependent on outside assistance from superior beings for its evolutionary heritage. (Though I must confess, I have always intuitively felt there might be some validity to aspects of the ancient astronaut theory based on the nature and origin of religious myths, legends and folktales.)

To help establish a middle ground and a dialogue between believers and debunkers, I secured modest financial backing and started *Second Look* magazine in early 1978, which I co-edited for two years with Robert K.G. Temple, a Fellow of the Royal Astronomical Society in England, and author of the international bestseller, *The Sirius Mystery*. Our three areas of inquiry (which we believed to be interconnected) were the origins of civilization, the nature of consciousness, and the search for other intelligent life in the universe. The first issue featured an article by science fiction author Isaac Asimov, titled "Is it wise to contact advanced civilizations?" Subsequent issues contained articles by Colin Wilson, Jacques Vallée (serializing his *Messengers of Deception* book), Erich von Daniken, Robert Anton Wilson, J. Allen Hynek, Stanislaw Lem, the debunkers Robert Sheaffer and James Oberg, and the physicists and astronomers Sir Fred Hoyle, Paul Davies, T.B.H. Kuiper and Sir Roger Penrose. In each issue, we featured 'A Chronology of the UFO Phenomenon' in which daily sightings from the previous month were culled from local newspapers nationwide and the details were contrasted to delineate evolving trends.

Our magazine brought us into contact with numerous people who believed they had been abducted by alien visitors. *Second Look* acted as a magnet for such persons partly because we operated out of offices on Capitol Hill in Washington, D.C., which made us accessible to a surprising range of abductees and UFO enthusiasts who held responsible positions in the federal government and the news media. Just off Dupont Circle, within a dozen blocks of the White House, I periodically visited a restaurant called The Planet, co-owned by a woman named Valerie, who I met through the magazine. Valerie had been an employee of the White House press office during Gerald Ford's administration. She claimed that she and her boyfriend were abducted by aliens while sleeping in a motel along a Florida beach. After she and two friends opened The Planet in 1979, it became a hangout for other abductees, along with political appointees of then-President Jimmy Carter, who himself had sighted a UFO and filed a report on it while Governor of Georgia. Through Valerie I met numerous closet abductees who were public figures, among them a high-profile male CBS News television correspondent, the daughter of a prominent Republican U.S. Senator from Tennessee, and a memorably wild woman named Cindy, the heiress to a pharmaceutical fortune, who sought out my co-editor in England and then me in D.C. because she wanted us to help her birth a 'star baby'.

What initially struck me about most of these self-described abductees was their apparent sincerity. Few seemed interested in ego massage or any financial gain from confiding in me. They appeared genuinely confused yet still casually accepting of their experiences. My attitude about their stories mixed compassion with some degree of caution. Something traumatic and life-altering had obviously affected these people, but my journalistic radar picked up signals which left me feeling that all of them possessed enough capacity for confabulation and self-delusion to explain what might have happened to them based on the powers of their own consciousness, not necessarily due to physical intervention by extraterrestrials. The on-going tension between doubt and belief sometimes left me struggling to keep an open mind, yet never so open that my brains oozed out.

Though we never exceeded 10,000 subscribers—a readership built entirely on direct mail marketing—several dozen copies went to subscribers each month at the U.S. State Department, which seemed strange to me until a friend who had served at high levels of the CIA explained how the State Department was often used as a 'front' by the Agency to conceal the true identities of mail recipients. These government readers of *Second Look* apparently worked in both the CIA clandestine services and the CIA's Directorate of Science and Technology, a clue that the Agency had a standing professional curiosity about the magazine's subject matter, perhaps because our contributors included current and former government officials and many prominent scientists, including several from the Soviet Union.

Why We Were Manipulated

The role played by the various agencies of government in the UFO phenomenon continually perplexed me, though it became abundantly clear that the public was either being psychologically manipulated by the phenomenon, whatever it is, or that our perceptions and opinions were being manipulated by elements of the military and intelligence arms of government to serve some hidden agenda, perhaps connected to the Cold War and the Soviets. Oftentimes it seemed to be a mixture of both. Trying to disentangle fact from fiction, separating willful bureaucratic ignorance from intentional disinformation, proved to be problematic exercise for all of us as researchers, a bit like trying to scuba dive in muddied waters wearing fogged up goggles.

We now know that an intentional program of psychological manipulation of the public began systematically in earnest after the July 1952 visual and radar sightings of up to 10 UFOs over Washington, D.C., an event that historian Richard Dolan, in his book, *UFOs and the National Security State*, described as having greatly shocked and alarmed CIA and Pentagon officials because the UFO problem "threatened to overwhelm the military in every way: by causing a mass panic, by clogging military communications, by presenting the Soviet Union with an opportunity to make mischief or worse, by causing dissension among the various services and within the ranks, by the air force's continued inability to stop UFOs from trespassing over restricted airspace."

To get control of the situation the CIA and Pentagon decided to calm public fears—and confuse the Soviets about what the U.S. really knew—by colluding on a campaign of public disinformation and ridicule of persons reporting UFOs. As Captain Edward Ruppelt eventually confessed, after having managed the Air Force's Project Blue Book investigation of UFOs, he and other Blue Book officers had been directed by the CIA to engage in a national debunking campaign. "We're ordered to hide {UFO}sightings, when possible, but if a strong report does get out, we have to publish a fast explanation—make up something to kill the report in a hurry, and also ridicule the witness, especially if we can't figure out a plausible answer. We even have to discredit our own pilots. The whole thing makes me sick," Captain Ruppelt was quoted as telling associates.

UFO investigators like Leon Davidson, who attempted to expose this coverup and disinformation campaign, received a vicious treatment in public and private from scientists, government officials, and much of the news media, derisively dismissing him and others as delusional conspiracy theorists. Revelations in the 1997 declassified CIA study, as mentioned earlier, underscore how determined and effective this smear campaign turned out to be, a Cold War relic with a lasting toxic legacy. It inflicted damage to the reputations of countless UFO witnesses over six decades—from airline and military pilots to ordinary citizens—who were publicly ridiculed or condemned as liars or incompetents. Few if any of these victimized people ever received the proper and overdue apology they were due from their accusers or from the institutions that harbored the villifiers.

A case can also be made that another lasting legacy consequence of the government UFO-related campaign to sow mistrust and disinformation is a condition we see afflicting society today—a cynical disbelief in public institutions and their credibility and a widening firestorm of conspiracy theorizing about everything from whether humans ever walked on the moon to whether the Holocaust ever really happened. No longer willing to believe anything from authority figures, a growing segment of society has become willing to believe anything that their own worst fears, instincts, and suspicions can conjure up.

Finally, as if trying to clear the historical air of toxic fumes by doing what some would call 'a limited hangout', the Pentagon released, in June 2021, a report on 143 UFO sightings by military aviators that had remained unexplained since 2004, and offering five possible explanations about the origin of the observed objects. One explanation 'did not rule out' the extraterrestrial visitation hypothesis, which represented an unprecedented declaration by the Pentagon. Compared to the previous six decades of disinformation, manipulation and constant ridicule in a campaign that debunked extraterrestrial explanations for UFOs, this admission seemed to represent a cathartic release—or perhaps just a burp—as a milestone in the annals of disclosure. Still another small step forward, also in 2021, came when NASA administrator Bill Nelson confessed there may be an extraterrestrial explanation for some UFO sightings, a conclusion he came to after reading a classified government report on the military UFO encounters that caused "the hair to stand up on the back of my neck." And just a few weeks later, the U.S. Director of National Intelligence, Avril Haines, who oversaw the CIA, NSA and DIA, admitted the intelligence community had opened up to the prospect that the answer to UFOs "might come extraterrestrially."

All of these developments signaled to me that it was time to prepare and trot out a new version of my 1979 book, *The Complete Book of Extraterrestrial Encounters*, which morphed in expanded form 20 years later into *Cosmic Test Tube*, and now more than 20 more years later, morphs again in expanded form into *Alien in the Mirror*. It has been written for readers who want to access and evaluate the full range of possible theories and supporting evidence about the true nature of this phenomenon, going back one hundred years. Consider it a third-generation book in which I summarize not just the most important books published over more than a century, but have interspersed each section with accounts of my own investigations of various UFO related incidents, such as the 'Arizona Lights'.

Because theorists and researchers are usually influenced by their predecessors, book sections are organized chronologically by date of publication to help track the emergence and cross-fertilization of ideas, theories, and evidence. Books were selected in each of the five sections based on their relative enduring impact on public debate, their contribution to advancing scientific understanding, or the thought-provoking quality of their content. Sometimes books were included simply because their appearance heralded the evolution of a cultural trend or even something resembling the occult, which is unavoidable since the search for evidence of extraterrestrial life on Earth periodically veers off into mysticism, parapsychology, and other fringes of conventional science that eventually float like flotsam into the mainstream.

By all appearances we do live in a metaphorical cosmic test tube—perhaps even in a literal one—and our human species continues to be an evolving genetic experiment. Whether a higher intelligence played a role and continues to do so may always remain an open question, despite our best efforts to discover the truth, if only because the *Alien in the Mirror* who stares back at us often seems as strange and as mysterious as the superior beings we dream of encountering. Picture the black monolith featured in Stanley Kubrick's *2001: A Space Odyssey* as if it were a cinema screen onto which humankind projects its collective unconscious and which mirrors back all of our hopes and fears and sense of wonder about our rightful place in the universe's great chain of being. That too, reveals to us the identity of an *Alien in the Mirror*!

SECTION ONE

Ancient Astronauts...

Were They 'Angels' Who Bestowed Civilization?

Ancient astronaut theorists seek to radically revise our collective perceptions of human origins by raising an endless series of provocative questions. Are legends and religious myths simply tales from human imagination, or might they be species memories and fossils of history telling an alien visitation story? Were the angels of the Bible extraterrestrial missionaries, or might they have been genetic engineers on a mission to accelerate human evolution?

Watch any episode of the History Channel's *Ancient Astronauts* series and you confront steady starbursts of questions left floating in a speculative fog. If humankind reflexively wove philosophy, mysticism and storytelling around the memory of our 'god's' exploits, did religions transform space visitors individually into angels and collectively into God? Were these visitors benign and benevolent, traders of knowledge for minerals, or did a supercivilization of celestial breeders accelerate our evolution as an exploitative gesture, like the wicked witch who fattened up Hansel and Gretel before killing them? If Earth is a garden that galactic gardeners have been tending off and on since life evolved here, are UFOs in our skies still their mode of travel? Could aliens be a projection from another dimension, or even from our own collective unconscious, playing the role of Cosmic Trickster to condition us with mind twisting drama traumas and unsolvable riddles as a teaching tool?

My own most provocative lingering question has always concerned Berossus, a Babylonian scholar living in Greece during the reign of Alexander the Great, who may have been the first historian attempting to document alien visitation based on the oral and written accounts available to him. He described the beings given credit for bestowing civilization on Sumer before 3000 B.C. as "animals endowed with reason." Never did the Sumerians, or the Babylonians who inherited their culture, apparently refer to these beings as gods. They said the creatures were "disgusting abominations," a rather strange way for superstitious people to treat a god, but not so unusual if their visitors really were abhorrent to look at and who inspired fear and veneration in equal measure.

At the mid-point of his life in 1966, the celebrity astronomer Carl Sagan speculated how "it seems possible that the Earth has been visited by various Galactic civilizations many times during geological time," and as a result, "it is not out of the question that artifacts of these visits still exist or even that some kind of base is maintained within the solar system to provide continuity for successive expeditions." Until his death in 1996, Sagan voiced skepticism that any evidence of alien inspired or created artifacts had been located to satisfy his rigorous standards of proof. There were *two possible exceptions*, however, which he conceded were deserving of more serious investigation.

The first possible exception that Sagan found intriguing involved photographs taken in 1976, by the Viking 1 Orbiter space probe, showing features of Mars which resembled artificial structures, including a human-looking face, two-kilometers wide, in an area of Mars called Cydonia. Subsequent more detailed photographic surveys of the planet in the late 1990s and early 2000s showed The Face to be a naturally weathered mesa. A series of robotic landers also failed to find proof for any artificial Martian structures on the planet's surface and so we can probably dismiss Sagan's 'possible exception' number one, unless and until something new and provably artificial turns up in future explorations.

The second mystery identified by Sagan as overdue for deeper investigation concerned those Sumerian legends of amphibious creatures, discussed by Berossus, who may have instructed humankind on agriculture and sciences, accounts that struck Sagan as raising "the possibility of direct contact with an extraterrestrial civilization." While this isn't meant to insinuate that Sagan's ideas of what constitutes alien visitation evidence represents the 'be all' or the 'end all' measurement for the ancient astronaut theory, it does give us one well-traveled benchmark for evaluating the proposed evidence for visitation. Let's take a closer look at the Sumerian angle.

A Sirius Mystery Explained?

Near the city of Timbuktu in Mali, along a well-worn trade route linking Egypt to West Africa, live the Dogon tribe. From 1931 to 1952, two French anthropologists lived among the Dogon and gained their trust until the tribe allegedly agreed to reveal a secret they said had never before been shared with outsiders. Four tribal elders—two priests, a chief, and a priestess—sat with the anthropologists and described their rituals and ceremonies revolving around specific knowledge about the stars. At the center of their cosmology is Sirius, the brightest star in Earth's night sky, located 8.6 light years away.

Drawing on the ground with sticks, Dogon elders outlined a series of astronomical facts which could not have been observed without the aid of a high-powered telescope, a device the Dogon reportedly had never touched or seen in action. They knew that the Earth rotates around the sun, that orbits are an ellipse rather than a circle, that Jupiter has four major moons, and Saturn has rings. More mysteriously, they knew that Sirius has a companion star, Sirius B, invisible to the naked eye, which revolves around the larger

Sirius in an elliptical orbit that takes 50 years to complete. Furthermore, they described Sirius B as "the star which is considered to be the smallest thing in the sky, is also the heaviest," consisting of a metal so heavy that "all earthly beings combined cannot lift it." That sounds like a fair approximation of what astronomers believe, that Sirius B is a white dwarf, the smallest and heaviest type of star known.

Sirius B's existence had first been hypothesized in 1836, based on perturbations observed in Sirius A's trajectory, but B was not actually seen in a telescope until 1862. Only in 1925 did some astronomers finally conclude that white dwarf stars—small and super dense—were theoretically possible, and that Sirius B was such a star. In 1928 this information received wide Western dissemination in a popular English scientific book by Sir Arthur Eddington. All of which is to say by the time the two French anthropologists got to the Dogon in 1931, an extremely short window of opportunity had passed for this remote tribe to have obtained details about the nature of Sirius B, and to have absorbed those details into their tradition of religious beliefs and rituals surrounding the Sirius star system. So how did the Dogon elders know that the invisible Sirius B exists and it has a 50-year orbit around Sirius A and it is what astronomers call a white dwarf? A search for answers might begin with humankind's long reverence for Sirius A and the place it held in the pantheon of beliefs about Gods in the heavens.

Throughout recorded history Sirius A has been a central player in the cosmology and myths of ancient cultures. Egyptians in 3000 B.C. worshiped Sirius, and no other star, largely because its appearance at certain times of the year heralded the flooding of the Nile River. Babylonian cuneiform texts from 1000 B.C. identify Sirius as the star marking the tip of an arrow in a constellation they described as a bow and arrow. Chinese of the same period placed Sirius as part of a star image called "the dog," at which stars forming the bow and arrow are aiming. Ironically, Sirius has been known since antiquity as the "Dog Star" in the cosmologies of widely separated cultures, evidence which some researchers use to make a case that Chinese, Sumerian, and Egyptian astronomical myths all derive from a common body of knowledge and a single cultural source.

Two M.I.T. professors of the History of Science, Giorgio de Santillana and Hertha von Dechend, wrote a book published in 1969, *Hamlet's Mill*, in which they presented a persuasive case that "the remnants of a preliterate 'code language' of unmistakable co-herence" existed worldwide and could be traced to the Near East, presumably to a time before the Sumerian and Egyptian civilizations arose. This code language evolved in the form of myths which were designed as metaphors to disguise the underlying information and make it accessible only to a self-perpetuating priestly class. "Myth can be used as a vehicle for handing down solid knowledge independently from the degree of insight of the people who do the actual telling of stories," wrote the professors. "In ancient times, moreover it allowed the members of the archaic 'braintrust' to 'talk shop' unaffected by the presence of laymen." The authors do not specifically address Dogon beliefs about Sirius, but they leave no doubt about the ability of a seemingly primitive tribe to retain and protect knowledge thousands of years old, handing it down disguised as myth from one generation of priest initiates to the next without significant alteration in the data content.

Could the Dogon be preserving accurate astronomical data originating in pre-history, perhaps even derived from extraterrestrial visitors? Enter Robert K. G. Temple, an American scholar of Oriental studies living in England, who read the Dogon study by the French anthropologists and felt inspired to undertake eight years of research culminating in a book, *The Sirius Mystery*, examining how the Dogon *might* have obtained their information about Sirius and its companion star. His conclusion: the Dogon *might* be protecting astronomical data handed down from pre-dynastic Egypt—a people the Dogon *might* be descended of, and with whom they engaged in trade—data which in turn *might* have originated in Sumer, where it was first revealed to humankind by those amphibious beings described by Berossus and earlier Sumerian chroniclers. (That word *might* looms large here.)

A *Time* magazine review of Temple's book in 1976 called it "a dizzying patchwork of evidence that tends to support his theory," prompting the reviewer to remark, "why Dogon religious rituals contain information that is uncannily similar to astronomers' findings about Sirius is a genuine mystery."

Dogon elders call the Sirius system the 'land of the fish', from which came the Nommo, a race of amphibious creatures who transported themselves to Earth ages ago in an "ark," which the Dogon represent in their rituals as a basket. According to the Dogon accounts, after these Nommo arrived in their arks accompanied by rushing winds, thunder, and flames, they tried to educate humankind. To Temple this Dogon story sounded remarkably similar to ancient Sumerian tales of amphibious visitors who became our teachers. The more he searched the records of Sumerian, Babylonian, and Egyptian religious history the thicker became the web of connections linking Dogon traditions to these earlier civilizations. For instance, Egyptian priests assigned three goddesses to Sirius in honor of it being a watery paradise. Dogon elders too, teach that Sirius A and Sirius B have yet a third companion, Sirius C, from whose planet the water-loving Nommo came.

Astronomical diagrams drawn by the Dogon show the star Sirius C revolving around

Sirius A in an elliptical orbit, and a planet revolving around Sirius C in its own elongated orbit. "The descriptions by the Dogon tribe of a third star in the Sirius system maintains that it is four times lighter in weight than Sirius B, which in astronomical terms would mean that it is what astronomers call a red dwarf star," Temple reported. Star watchers in antiquity often described Sirius as a red star, which prompted early 20th century astronomers to speculate that Sirius A might have once been a red dwarf. Might the ancients have instead seen Sirius C flare into redness, a celestial event which might have precipitated a migration by any spacefaring civilization living in the region of that star?

By some accounts Sirius C was observed briefly by a few astronomers in the late 1920s, but not after that. This once again raises the question of whether the Dogon could have incorporated speculation about Sirius C, much as they might have done with Sirius B, into their mythology during the three-year period before the French researchers arrived in 1931. Just such a claim was raised by skeptics responding to Temple's book, prominent among them Kenneth Brecher, an M.I.T. theoretical physicist, who read Temple's book and wondered if the Dogon findings were "all just a fake," only to be reassured by colleagues who knew the French anthropologists that they "did scrupulously honest research." Brecher proposed that somebody, probably a Jesuit missionary, must have told the Dogon about the astronomy of Sirius A and B, along with theories that a Sirius C might be found.

During his book research Temple contacted the organization which oversaw missionary visits to the Dogon, learning that no missionaries had been involved with that tribe until 1949, many years after the French researchers had recorded the tribal belief system. Even more compelling, Dogon ceremonies honoring Sirius are held every 50 years or so, marking the 50-year orbit, with ritual masks carved each time to commemorate the event. Carbon dating of these accumulated masks indicates the tradition goes back 600 years, perhaps much longer since many masks had turned to dust.

Brecher's fallback position, ventured in a *Technology Review* article, argued that if cultural transfer turns out to be disproved, Dogon astronomical knowledge must be the result of "coincidences and lucky guesses." NASA scientist James Oberg similarly was troubled that "the Dogon 'Sirius secrets' legend is reminiscent of European Sirius speculations in the late 1920s." Yet Oberg conceded, in an article for *Fate* magazine in 1978, that "evidence for the recent acquisition of the information is entirely circumstantial... the antiquity of the Dogon astronomy is not so obvious as ancient astronaut enthusiasts claim, but neither has it been disproved."

A missing piece of this puzzle had been solid astronomical evidence that a third star, Sirius C, really does exist as the Dogon believe. This Dogon information about the Sirius system, said Temple, gives us "a predictive mechanism: testable predictions made by a possibly extraterrestrial source from the past." In 1980 Temple wrote that "if a Sirius C is ever discovered and found to be a red dwarf, I will conclude that the Dogon information has been fully validated." A huge step toward just such validation came in 1995 when two French astronomers did a thorough historical analysis of all measures of Sirius A and B, searching for behavioral anomalies in their orbits. In findings published in *Astronomy & Astrophysics*, they concluded there is "a 90 percent chance that Sirius C does exist" and perturbs the orbits of Sirius A and B! Furthermore, Sirius C is probably "a dim red dwarf," a star with low mass! These astronomical observations may provide what Temple called in 1997, "splendid confirmation of *The Sirius Mystery* hypothesis by the ultimate scientific method: confirmation of a prediction."

All of this seeming confirmation got thrown into doubt, however, when the 'linch-pin' of the entire Dogon theory—the original French anthropologist's interpretation of Dogon cosmology—received a serious challenge from Belgian anthropologist Walter Van Beek. During the 1990s, Van Beek led a team of researchers to Mali where they interviewed some of the surviving Dogon informants who had reportedly passed on the secret knowledge about Sirius. Not only did Van Beek claim that he didn't find any evidence from them supporting the original report, he discovered the Dogon elders were in disagreement among themselves about which stars are even considered important to the tribe. If Van Beek's account is accurate, Temple's entire book premise involving the Dogon and a link to astronomical information from Egypt and Sumer is threatened with collapse. More research needs to be undertaken to sort out these contradictions.

Weakening mainstream science's resistance to the prospect of visitation by an-cient astronauts will require nothing less than extraordinary, irrefutable evidence of a kind which transcends legend and myth. That evidence might require something unmis-takable and profound, such as a mathematical formula for a futuristic machine being found in the 5,000- year-old ruins of Sumer in modem Iraq, or astronomical data un-known to us today being uncovered etched in stone on the walls of a newly excavated Egyptian tomb. Or better yet, if we were to discover tangible non-terrestrial artifacts and verify them as being from an alien civilization once having had an outpost somewhere in our solar system.

Otherwise, failing that confirmation, the various ancient astronaut theories in cir-culation will always remain fevered speculations that may tantalize our imagination, but leave our critical thinking faculties recoiling with suspicion and doubt.

The Evolution of Ancient Alien Theories and Evidence, 1919 Onward. . .

The Book of the Damned
CHARLES FORT
(1919, Boni & Liveright; 1941, Rinehart & Winston)

Charles Fort has been described as one of the truly original minds of the 20th century. His unorthodox attacks on the blind dogmatism of conventional science involved the cataloguing of unexplained phenomena-culled from newspapers and scientific journals-that the scientists of 1919 could not explain, or chose to ignore. Fort wrote about large stones, red snow, and black rain falling from the sky, sometimes from cloudless skies. He wrote about Roman coins being found hundreds of feet in the ground on the North American continent. He wrote about eerie lights in the heavens, disk-shaped objects seen before the invention of airplanes, cigar-shaped craft seen before the invention of zeppelins. He displays in abundance his pet theories-that Earth has been visited in the past by beings from other planets; that perhaps, like the Native Americans who traded away Manhattan Island, our primitive ancestors bargained with these visitors, and we are now their property.

In this, his first of four books, Fort assembled from 40,000 notes more than 1,000 examples of unexplained phenomena. UFO researchers owe him a great debt. Fort approached UFOs like a scientist, but with an open mind. He erected a general principle of continuity, writing that if "super-vehicles" have traversed the skies, then "there must be mergers between them and terrestrial phenomena: observations upon them must merge away into observations upon clouds and balloons and meteors.

He discusses at length the behavior of clouds, balloons and meteors, ball lightning and birds, then chronicles case after case of observations not fitting those characteristics. For instance, on March 22, 1870, the sailors on board a British vessel, The Lady of the Lake, saw what appeared at first to be a "cloud," a rather remarkable cloud. It was light grey in color, and much lower than all the other clouds. It was circular in shape, with a semicircle inside divided into four distinct parts. For half an hour it was visible, traveling against the wind!

Fort quotes a British astronomer, E.W. Maunder, writing in the Observatory magazine, who described a craft he observed in the skies over the Royal Observatory in November 1881. It was a disk of greenish light, cigar shaped, which sailed for several minutes smoothly across the sky. Maunder said it moved too fast for a cloud and was totally unlike "the rush of a meteor." It had "a definite body," and were the sighting thirty years later, it would have been explained away as a zeppelin.

Cup marks are strings of cuplike impressions in regularly shaped rows on rocks, with rings, or semicircles around them. They occur in enormous numbers all over this planet. Fort proposes two possible solutions: that someone, somewhere, has showered messages on Earth to communicate with "Lost Explorers from Somewhere"; or that receptors, or a polar construction, exists on Earth "upon which for ages have been received messages from some other world," that occasionally go astray. He wonders if someday when these messages are deciphered, they will prove to have been misdirected instructions "to certain esoteric ones" like the Order of the Freemasons, or the Jesuits.

Fort asks whether there might be "vast living things" in the sky that we rarely if ever see. He proposes that "dragnets have often come down," mistaken for waterspouts and whirlwinds, which explain the mysterious disappearances of people and other living things. "I think we're fished for," he writes. Perhaps beings, or "super-things," are engaged in attempts to "investigate phenomena of this earth from above."

Before "proprietorship" was established over this planet, Earth was visited by "inhabitants of a host of other worlds," who came for "hunting, trading, replenishing harems, mining," and founded colonies here. But among the "contesting claimants" an "adjustment has occurred," so that something "now has a legal right to us." Fort speculates that our ownership has been known for ages "to certain ones upon this Earth, a cult or order, members of which function like bellwethers to the rest of us" directing humanity in accordance with instructions sent from our mysterious owners.

UFO and the Bible
MORRIS K. JESSUP
(1956, Citadel Press)

Astronomer M. K. Jessup voices in this slim volume his "growing, profound suspicion" that the UFO may prove to be the missing link, or common denominator, uniting the "miracles" of the Bible with the universal concepts sought by modern science.

Nothing is supernatural, because nothing that exists is outside nature. Miracles seem supernatural only because theologians fail to provide convincing answers to anyone but themselves. Science shares in the blame, "excluding everything which falls outside its cherished mechanistic framework."

Two types of UFO are consistently reported-structures and lights. Throughout the Bible, angels, messengers, voices, and gods appeared as brilliant lights. Jessup cites dozens of verses. He makes a case that "intelligently operated, or innately intelligent" lights are by no means a recent phenomenon. The ascension into the clouds of Elijah and Jesus Christ both involved "some type of levitation" or teleportation into a UFO, which human observers, using the terminology of that era, could only describe as an "odd cloud" or "dazzling light." Later translators further garbled these first-hand observations, yet the references to aerial phenomena are explicit, recorded in sacred and semi-sacred literature, from 1491 B.C. to about 712 B.C., as fiery chariots and revolving wheels in the sky on fire. Isaiah 60:8 asks: "...who are these that fly as a cloud?"

Fundamentalist interpretations of the Bible help to explain the UFO. Jessup says the Bible is a physical record, not just a collection of divine and occult revelations. The Bible means literally what it says, although the miracles of this and all religions invite rational and physical explanation.

Nowhere does the Bible limit humankind to the planet Earth. Many references describe "visitors of humanlike characteristics" coming here from space. In Genesis these "sons of God" arrive and impregnate human females, producing a race of giants. In the thirteenth chapter of St. Mark, as elsewhere, the "Son of Man" is prophesied to return from the clouds. Jessup does not believe that the Son of Man and the Son of God are synonymous. The Son of Man rather embodies descendants, offspring or a branch of humankind, perhaps the children produced by the couplings between humanlike visitors and Earth women. Their "coming in the clouds," says the author, can only refer to the UFO. References to the Son of Man "who left his house" can only mean this planet, to which the Son of Man will one day return. Ezekiel's vision of a great fiery cloud and its humanlike occupants recorded one such visitation.

Jessup thinks of the human race as analogous to a flock of sheep, being tended carefully at times "and not so carefully at others, by a space-dwelling race." These UFO occupants may only be "mere sheep dogs," so to speak, sent here to await the return of their master.

Section One: Ancient Astronauts

The Morning of the Magicians
LOUIS PAUWELS & JACQUES BERGIER
(1960, Editions Gallimard; 1963, Stein & Day)

Although they rely in many instances on theories advanced forty years earlier by Charles Fort, this book by Pauwels and Bergier must rank as a pioneering work on the ancient astronaut theme. They were the first to synthesize evidence of extraterrestrial visitation with the traditions and myths of secret societies to conclude that mutations in intelligence, producing Einsteins and Leonardo da Vincis, may result from extraterrestrial programing or interference in the process of evolution. Intelligence itself, on reaching a certain collective mass, might actually constitute a kind of secret society.

These two Frenchmen-Pauwels was a founder and editor of the magazine Planete, Bergier a nuclear scientist—assembled an array of scientific questions, riddles, and evidence about the origins of civilization that later authors, such as Erich von Daniken, would emulate. For instance, they speculate that the Pyramid of Cheops was constructed in ways "involving instruments for measuring and methods of manipulating matter unlike anything we know " They trace legends that tell of a race of teachers "fallen from the skies," who supervised the sculpting of 593 enormous statues on Easter Island; pre-Incan myths are cited, which relate how the stars are inhabited and the gods came from the constellation of the Pleiades; the authors puzzle over the origin of Mayan astronomical and mathematical knowledge, over designs traced in the plain of Nazca in Peru that can only be seen from the air, over 2,000-year-old electric batteries discovered in Baghdad, and over the Piri Reis map, a sixteenth-century Turkish rendering of the Earth that allegedly rivals in accuracy any map we possess today.

Perhaps in ancient times messages from other intelligent beings were received and interpreted on Earth, through telepathy or actual visitation in spaceships. Perhaps the knowledge imparted by these beings is but a distorted memory to us now. Myths or legends of secrets were entrusted to monks and initiates of secret orders down through the ages, all but a few of whom were "incapable of understanding their full significance." Here the authors delve deeply for answers into the traditions of secret societies. They conclude that alchemy is a relic of a science, a forgotten science, belonging to an advanced civilization which has disappeared. Both the alchemists and the Rosicrucians affirmed that the true object of the science of transmutations "is the transmutation of the human mind itself." Could this mean, the authors ask, that by studying much of what passes for mysticism, we might rediscover powers over nature that humans or their benefactors once exerted?

Adolf Hitler fanatically sought rediscovery of this wisdom. He sent expeditions in search of Atlantis and the Holy Grail. He consulted astrologers. Many of those around him believed in the theory of a hollow Earth. His scientific adviser, an elderly mystic named Hans Horbiger, prophet of a weird mythological cosmogony known as the doctrine of eternal ice, preached how giants had inhabited the Earth for millions of years, enslaving humans before finally being replaced by the gods of mythology who established Atlantis. The authors conclude that Nazi Germany's innovation was "to mix magic with science and technology" in the pursuit of a new "superior" race. They quote Hitler as having told associates toward the end of the war that he had glimpsed this "new man," who "is living amongst us...I was afraid in his presence."

Pauwels and Bergier believe that the "new man" is in our midst, as mutants, "ultra-humans" of superior intelligence, concealing themselves in our cities, communicating only with others of equal intelligence. They are beings, like the extraterrestrials to whom they are related, existing outside our field of sensory perception. They form a society superimposed on our own. They remain camouflaged or hidden in order to escape the hostility that human society throughout history has directed against superior intellect and radical ideas.

The Sky People
BRINSLEY LEPOER TRENCH
(1960, Neville Spearman)

Sky people have been visiting Earth for millions of years. Every culture preserves legends and myths, sacred texts and folklores, associated with that "Golden Age" when the gods mingled with mortals. In the Hebrew version of Genesis, the word "Elohim" for God is plural, referring to a plurality of gods. These are the Sky People who deliberately created, in an artificial environment, a race of human beings.

Genetic engineering occurred in a Garden of Eden established, so reads the King James version, where a river watering the Garden became "four heads," a head being a "prime source." The author interprets this to mean that "four prime sources flowed in four directions." Rivers don't flow that way in nature, he reasons, but canals do. Most ancient sources placed the Garden of Eden in the Underworld, not underground, but rather below or outside Earth's orbit. Trench concludes from this that the planet Mars once sustained the Garden of Eden.

Those people living outside the confines of the Garden, constituting another

13

Galactic race created by the Elohim, were known as the People of the Serpent. Their symbol embodies a concentric figure that represents the two major arms of the spiral galaxy in which we live, at one level the wave-form of energy, and at another level, a sperm-symbol of "life in bodily form." Human women created in the Garden were much-sought after sexual partners among these Serpent People. "Forbidden fruit" offered by serpents, meaning the knowledge that comes of fornication and procreation, resulted in the eventual expulsion of humans from the Garden. Back to Earth they were cast, from whence the initial breeding stock had been taken. Trench also theorizes that the Great Flood may have occurred on Mars, destroying the Garden of Eden and forcing Noah to build a Great Ark, or giant spaceship, in which to escape.

"There are other races of Man spread throughout the Galaxy," says the author. They are not physical in the sense of being composed of cells originating on Earth, but Earth humans do duplicate them, using terrestrial elements. While resembling Galactic man, we are but crude imitations. This superior race possesses a skin pigmentation "the colour of brass," as the prophet Ezekiel described it, a faint golden tint that inspired humankind to represent all gods and heroes as gold idols, which explains the value historically attached to this metal.

Visits by Galactic man to Earth are recorded in the Bible and other ancient texts as appearing to be whirlwinds and clouds. Enoch was carried off on at least two occasions by one of these "whirlwinds," or space vehicles; in a later period, Elijah too traveled in a whirlwind. Certain areas of the Earth, probably Atlantis, were presided over by these Sky People as divine rulers, which gave rise to the divine right of kings.

When Moses saw the burning bush, he probably gazed upon the glowing light emanating from the electric field surrounding a spacecraft used by the Sky People. When Moses ventured too near the bush, the "Lord" warned him to retreat, for the current would disable or kill him.

The Star of Bethlehem may have been a gigantic spaceship. Trench does not think it any coincidence that cases of unusual childbirth, especially among virgins and the barren, have been preceded by appearances of "angels." These angels, or Sky People, influenced reproduction through a juggling of genes and chromosomes, and created Jesus Christ and other prophets so that their teachings might give humans guidance. The struggle on this planet is between those humans dominated by the animal genealogy arising from evolution, and those humans retaining that mixture of divinity and wisdom that resulted from the intermingling of Galactic man with Earth woman in Eden.

"Spaceships, broadcasting information, now patrol the skies of Earth on regular schedules," writes Trench. Contact is usually established with Adam-I dominant-Galactic-man bred-people, like Nikola Tesla, the electrical wizard and Nobel prizewinner, who "was in constant contact with the Sky People." They communicate with us using five methods: telepathic signals in which the receiver writes messages down; paraphrasing, when the receiver puts into his own words the messages; symbolic communication intended to alter the mental machinery; emotional impact, which works especially well for the religious; and conceptual communication, implanting at a subliminal level a concept that will eventually filter down into the consciousness. Contactees unburdened by such emotional baggage as delusions of grandeur are generally selected for this conditioning.

Planet Earth is under a kind of quarantine. The Sky People "will not step in overtly until humans actually project themselves into space so effectively as to become a threat to systemic or galactic order."

One Hundred Thousand Years of Man's Unknown History
ROBERT CHARROUX
(1963, Editions Robert Laffont; 1970, Berkley)

Robert Charroux, a Frenchman and self-described pioneer in 'primohistory,' says it is a near certainty that our prehistory supplanted a more advanced civilization that had mastered space travel. A nuclear cataclysm destroyed this ancient technological civilization.

Borrowing from theories advanced in a Russian magazine in 1960, Charroux proposes that the Atlanteans were a blue-skinned people, lacking oxygen in their blood from high mountain living. This condition supposedly spawned the term "blue bloods" to describe superior persons of noble birth. Most Egyptian gods are represented as blue-skinned because mythology claims that Atlanteans founded the Egyptian civilization.

Venus is known to the ancients as the blue planet. Based on an alleged decoding of the Gate of the Sun, the Incan stone archway at Tiahuanaco in Bolivia, the author interweaves Andean traditions that relate how four-fingered Venusians led by Orejona ("Big Ears") —a woman with a pointed head, large ears, webbed hands, but humanlike breasts and vagina—colonized what is now Bolivia and built Tiahuanaco. Orejona seduced the local male humanoids and established with her offspring the pre-Incan civilization. This new race was apparently not much of an improvement over the Neolithic humans, for Incan legend tells how bearded white men accompanied by beautiful blond women arrived later to bestow knowledge.

Soviet engineer Alexander Kazantsev, who studied the Venusian calendar chiseled into the Gate of the Sun, describes it as the oldest calendar on Earth, with 225 terrestrial days. He points out that a Venusian year is 225 terrestrial days. "How were the ancestors of the Incas able to know the Venusian year?" he asks.

Charroux quotes occult tradition alleging that the legendary lands of Lemuria, Hyperborea, and Atlantis were all destroyed simultaneously; he wonders whether Atlantis wasn't America. He quotes from Sanskrit writings that supposedly tell of an atomic war in India. He contends that secrets revealing the nature of these cataclysms and the science that spawned them are known to initiates of Freemasonry, and to initiates among the popes of the Catholic Church. This 'Conspiracy of Secrets,' as he calls it, is actually intended to withhold from us information about our extraterrestrial origins.

===========================

Gods or Spacemen?
W. RAYMOND DRAKE
(1964, Amherst Press)

Ancient myths from every known civilization are in agreement that "Beings of transcendent wisdom and beauty descended from the skies, usually landing in mountainous regions away from populous cities; sometimes to those holy mountains they summoned chosen Leaders to whom they revealed cosmic mysteries." So writes W. Raymond Drake, in the first of his five books on the ancient astronaut theme.

To illustrate how such myths evolved, Drake relates the history of "Cargo Cult" worship in the New Hebrides Islands of the South Pacific, where the natives have created a primitive religion honoring American GIs who landed there during World War II. These soldiers became "gods" when they descended from the skies in "giant birds," bestowing gifts and technical knowledge, then "soaring back to heaven" but promising to return. "If a South Sea God actually evolves in only a few years from real live airmen who once visited an island, is it not equally likely that the whole pantheon of Gods personified to the unsophisticated ancient peoples the real visitors from other worlds ages before?"

Drake's research indicates that witch doctors in Africa, the shamans of Siberia, the medicine men among American Indians, the lamas of Tibet, the Druids of Stonehenge in Britain, "and the old men in most primitive communities," all preserved in varying degrees of coherence fragments of "a very high theology," which at one time existed worldwide and perhaps included a "universal psychic science." This theology inspired construction of the megaliths, such as Tiahuanaco in the Andes, Stonehenge, Baalbek in Lebanon, the Easter Island statues, Egyptian and Mayan pyramids, and the Nazca lines of Peru, those desert sculptures and astronomical ground patterns visible only from the air, which "appear to have been landing-grounds for ships from space."

Space visitors created a fundamental confusion in theology and Bible history revolving around the conception of God. Surely God the Creator, God the Absolute, cannot have been the same entity that landed on Earth, this tiny grain of dust in the universe, "and took such a partisan interest in the affairs of its ancient peoples"? When the Jews claim to be God's "Chosen People," says Drake, "it can only mean that the early Hebrews were befriended by Spacebeings who promised in return for certain observances to help them against their enemies." Drake argues that it is absurd to think of the Creator of an entire universe lowering itself to become embroiled "in the squabbles of a primitive, nomadic people."

Babylonian accounts as recorded by Berossus, the historian who lived in Greece during Alexander the Great's reign, describe these space visitors as animals endowed with reason, possessing the body of a fish. They were known collectively as Oannes. They taught humankind "insight into letters and science and every kind of art." Drake speculates how the visitors' resemblance to fishes might have been a garbled memory of space suits.

Other traditions spoke of visitors from Venus, ethereal hermaphroditic beings who descended to Earth 18 million years ago and settled in Lemuria, that mythical continent predating Atlantis. After many ages these beings materialized into coarser vibrations, male then separated from female. In the Book of Revelation, Jesus Christ at one point described himself as "the bright and morning star." Was Christ incarnated from Venus, or was Venus the star at his birth? Drake points out that Christ also taught that "In my Father's House are many Mansions," which clearly states that life exists elsewhere on other planets. Buddha preached of countless inhabited worlds, as did many Yogis in their theories of reincarnation.

Space visitors throughout history probably appeared among human beings using the dress and mannerisms of that particular period so as to be indistinguishable from ourselves. Much of what has passed for paranormal phenomena-fairies, witchcraft, apparitions, and the like could be emanating from extraterrestrial sources. Drake says fairies and other mythological creatures "could well be the same as the Spacemen," since the appearances of each are similar, materializing then vanishing as if their bodily frequencies, different from our own, retarded our ability to perceive them.

The Flying Saucer Vision
JOHN MICHELL
(1967, Sidgwick and Jackson)

British author John Michell makes a case that unusual aerial phenomena seen in the sky during ancient times, particularly the flying disc or flying saucer-shaped objects, piloted by entities worshipped as gods, produced the myths and legends handed down to us cloaked in religious and mystical symbolism embraced by all of the world's religious and tribal belief traditions.

We humans have been an object of study by extraterrestrial visitors for many thousands of years and their appearance created our earliest myths. "The earlier the inscription the more explicit is the figure of the god within the circular airship," notes Michell, pointing to ancient Assyrian cylinders showing "the figure of a man, presumably one of the divine race, descending to earth inside a disc."

Michell describes an old and universal belief "that sound can cause levitation" as possibly being connected to the flying saucers using "some great natural current, electro-magnetic fields of force" to account for their ability to move so quickly and change direction, characteristic of sighting reports of discs and 'flying dragons' made by many cultures across the planet. These reports about the vehicles of the gods came from Roman, Greek and Egyptian witnesses who were the first to document the phenomenon using the written word.

A legend that Michell finds compelling is that creatures from flying saucers came to earth "to create a hybrid race, people with the intelligence and knowledge of the extra-terrestrial, but physically adapted to life on earth." Even now, based on UFO reports, Michell suspects men are still being used in genetic experiments by alien visitors.

A more contemporary example of a flying disc sighting comes from the 1917 incident at Fatima in Portugal, where 70,000 people witnessed a "shining, spinning silver disc descend from the sky," brighter than the sun, instantaneously drying out the crowd which had been drenched in a rain shower. Though the event was given religious connotations at the time, Michell discerns all of the characteristics of classic flying saucer reports.

Stone heads attributed to the Olmec in Central America and to the inhabitants of Easter Island represent a race of civilizing gods, writes Michell, and even the Mayan calendar seems to have come from information provided by extraterrestrial visitors because "it seems to have been an integral part of Mayan culture, something which at a certain moment in history emerged fully formed from some hidden stream of knowledge." Even the folklore surrounding the stories of humans being kidnapped by little fairy people might actually represent abductions of humans by a visiting alien race who needed guinea pigs for their experiments.

Many of humankind's "greatest monuments of antiquity," according to Michell, such as Stonehenge in Britain and the Nazca Lines in Peru, were laid out for three reasons: "as instruments for the study of the nature of the gods and the patterns of the universe; secondly, as meeting places with people of the divine race, often on sites where, in the past, the gods had been known to appear. And thirdly, to give by their shape and outline some message, visible and comprehensible only to the gods in the sky."

The sky discs of the gods that were venerated in ancient times became sun worshipping cults once the gods departed and subsequent generations of humans began to lose their knowledge and wisdom. Sun worship in Egypt and elsewhere "was only a corruption of an earlier cult, that of the flying saucer."

Michell ends his book with a cautionary admonition about these objects which resemble ghosts or another order of matter: "Only by analysing the influence of the early knowledge of flying saucers and the gods upon the structure of ancient societies can we find some clue to the probable effects of our confrontation with them in the future."

The Bible and Flying Saucers
BARRY H. DOWNING
(1968, Lippincott; 1973, Sphere Books)

Unlike Erich von Daniken and others who assume that ancient astronauts unintentionally left behind religion as their legacy, Barry Downing believes that biblical teachings were strongly influenced, if not deliberately inspired, by extraterrestrial visitors-those whom we have come to regard as "angels." As pastor of a Presbyterian church in Endwell, New York, Downing brings to the subject matter an approach that seeks a unity, or common denominator, linking flying saucers, the Bible, and Einstein's general theory of relativity.

Downing claims that the Bible clearly identifies UFOs as playing a role in the development of the Hebrew-Christian faith. A realistic interpretation of the Scriptures suggests to Downing that Jesus' Resurrection occurred when he was spirited from this planet on a flying saucer. A literal interpretation of the same material yields references to Jesus being taken in "a cloud." Downing uses a realistic rather than literal approach in evaluating events portrayed in the Bible.

By his standard the "bright cloud" that led the Israelites through the Red Sea, parting the waters and then engulfing the Egyptians, was a space vehicle, which spoke in all its radiance to Moses from the middle of a glowing thicket, and later spoke to Elijah outside the cave, forcing Elijah to shield his eyes because of its brightness. The UFO also took away Christ at the Ascension, and hovered over Paul and his companions on the Damascus Road. The three wise men probably followed a UFO to Bethlehem, since stars do not move or abruptly stop in the manner the Bible described.

Downing uses the Egyptians drowning in the Red Sea, warnings given Moses not to approach too near the burning bush, and warnings given his followers not to approach Mount Sinai, as evidence that UFOs could be hazardous to human health. He points out that when Moses descended from Mount Sinai with two tablets in his hands, Exodus records that the skin of his face shone from talking with God. A parallel exists in the New Testament: Jesus begins to glow when in contact with a bright object on a mountain. When the Tabernacle is built on orders of Moses, the priests serving it are instructed on what clothing to wear, possibly as a necessary precaution against radiation because the UFO hovered like a cloud over the tent enclosing the Tabernacle. Perhaps this precaution spawned the Jewish custom of wearing skull caps into houses of worship. Downing even wonders whether mutations in the growth of biological life caused by radiation could have resulted in the plagues described in Exodus.

He speculates that Einstein's curvature of space theory provides a clue to the "place" where Heaven is located. Jesus may have meant that the kingdom of God or of Heaven quite literally rests in the midst of us, meaning that Heaven is an entirely different universe, invisible to us, but existing parallel to our own and connected by bends or warps in the space-time continuum. It seems clear to Downing that these beings, if they are still watching us, are pursuing a laissez-faire policy, visiting but no longer interfering.

Chariots of the Gods?
ERICH VON DANIKEN
(1968, Econ-Verlag; 1970, G. P. Putnam's Sons)

Though he doesn't yet know who they were, or from which planet they came, those "gods of the dim past"-the extraterrestrial intelligences who visited here and "annihilated part of mankind" to produce Homo sapiens-left behind "countless traces which we can read and decipher today for the first time," contends Erich von Daniken, the onetime Swiss hotelkeeper and foremost popularizer of the ancient astronaut hypothesis.

In this, his first and most widely circulated of many books, von Daniken seizes upon every megalith, every seemingly technical vestige of lost civilizations, practically every known myth or religious tale that mentions gods from the heavens, to make his case that conventional theories of history and archeology cannot possibly explain the evolution of human intelligence. Only the extraterrestrial alternative can. He gives partial credit for his findings to a rediscovery of "knowledge that was hidden in the libraries of secret societies," groups that he does not name, nor mention again beyond the introduction.

God must have been a group of astronauts. Why else would he speak throughout the Bible in the plural "our" and "we"? When sons of God took Earth women, bearing giants into the world, were these offspring our forefathers, "who built the gigantic buildings and effortlessly manhandled the monoliths?"

He finds their handiwork everywhere. At Nazca on the plains of Peru, what can have induced the pre-Inca peoples to build the fantastic lines, the landing strips to be seen only from the air? At the abandoned city of Tiahuanaco in Bolivia he found himself in awe of the stonework, blocks weighing 100 tons used for walls and water conduits. Did "our forefathers at Tiahuanaco (have) nothing better to do than spend years without tools-fashioning water conduits of such precision that our modern concrete conduits seem the work of mere bunglers in comparison?"

Von Daniken asks a lot of questions. Instead of sending radio telescope signals into space, "why don't we first or simultaneously seek the traces of unknown intelligences on our own earth?" How did the ancient Sumerians know that a fixed star has planets? Where did the Babylonians obtain their electric dry batteries which work on the galvanic principle? The answer: "We can imagine that 'gods' appeared who collected semi-savage peoples in the region of Sumer around them and transmitted some of their knowledge to them."

In Egypt, can it really be coincidence that "the height of the pyramid of Cheops multiplied by a thousand million-98 million miles corresponds approximately to the distance between the earth and sun?" Can it be coincidence that "the rocky ground on which the structure stands is carefully and accurately leveled?" Since it is "extremely difficult" for von Daniken to believe in coincidences, the building site had to have been chosen "by beings who knew all about the spherical shape of the earth and the distribution of continents and seas."

As evidence of this geographical knowledge that could only have come from the sky, he cites the Piri Reis map, named after the Turkish naval officer who supposedly owned it in the sixteenth century. It pictures the coasts of North and South America, even the contours of the Antarctic, all drawn "with extreme accuracy." Von Daniken believes a spaceship hovered over Cairo and took photographs, because "everything that is in a radius of about 5,000 miles of Cairo is reproduced correctly."

———————————————

Those Gods Who Made Heaven and Earth
JEAN SENDY
(1969, Editions Robert Laffont; 1972, Berkley)

About 23,500 years ago, according to this version of Creation, a community of thirty or forty scientists, known collectively as the Elohim, utilizing the energy of quark fission, arrived in our solar system inside a large hollow sphere. That spacecraft is Phobos, one of two Martian moons. These Celestials left their home planet, known as Theos, because it had become so perfected as to offer little or no challenge to inquisitive, adventurous minds.

Since "intelligent bipeds are a normal product of evolution on all planets where conditions permit the appearance of life as we know it," writes the Frenchman Jean Sendy, these Celestials resembled our forebears, much as the Bible describes them. Their leader Adonai and his assistant Shaddai were kept frozen throughout the voyage.

On the Bible's "first day," these visitors stabilized the rotation of the Earth's moon so that one side always faced earthward. Cloud cover blanketing Earth was dispersed so that the stars could be seen. Eden became a climate-controlled laboratory, stocked with representative samplings of Earth fauna and other native species. Eden provided optimum conditions for the development of a superior strain of humans, a genetically pure "eternal lineage of immortal Adams." Outside Eden, during the thousands of years comprising each biblical "day," humans remained primitive and ignorant.

Expulsion from Eden apparently occurred when a human mutant discovered that the Celestials were not divine after all. On realizing they were part of an experiment, the control group, composed of specimens of a stabilized human breed produced over thousands of years, "lost its purity, its original ignorance...this meant it was no longer usable, since the goal of the experiment was an intellectual mutation." These mutants were expatriated back among the primitive Homo erectus, whom they soon began to dominate.

Humans sent out as "managers" by the Celestials were easily corrupted by the power of their knowledge, and consented to be venerated as gods. When the Celestials decided to end their experiment and destroy humankind, one of the managers, Noah, succeeded in surviving. Along "'with the seeds of life," probably genetic material, Noah waited out the atomic explosion that destroyed Eden and flooded the planet. Sodom and Gomorrah, a secondary Eden, were later destroyed again by nuclear fuel forgotten by the Celestials. The Celestials left our solar system. It is unlikely they will ever return, at least any time soon.

Had the Celestial experiment succeeded as originally envisioned, argues Sendy, the result would have been "a hereditary monarchial world government in the hands of Celestials reproducing between brothers and sisters, a privilege reserved for genetically pure individuals The mutants of Eden...(would have been placed) in charge of the rest of mankind, who would be left to develop naturally, but under supervision....We would...be living in a state that would correspond to one definition of happiness...bovine happiness." Celestials had wanted to "create cattle," but instead left the Earth swarming "with rats."

―――――――――――

God Drives a Flying Saucer
R.L. DIONE
(1969; 1973, Bantam)

Occupants of flying saucers, argues R. L. Dione, a Connecticut school teacher and former prize fighter, are responsible for the prophecies, Scriptures, and miracles of the Christian religion. God is not supernatural but super-technological, having been rendered immortal by the miracle of technology.

UFOs are God's messengers. They appear and disappear at will in our atmosphere by adjusting "their luminosity and color" like chameleons to resemble the background. That would explain the translucence of some UFOs, and why other invisible UFOs have been tracked on radar. UFOs are attracted to power lines, spending hours hovering over these alternating electrical currents, not to measure or steal the power, contends Dione, but in an attempt to communicate with what they perceive is an intelligent life form speaking in the language of high voltage.

UFOs have healed human beings and accomplished other miracles throughout recorded history. A police officer in 1965, returning from a football game with another officer in Sweeny, Texas, allegedly had his cut index finger healed when a large saucer-shaped object bathed their car in an intense light and heat. Dione says Jesus Christ performed similar "miracles" by using energy beamed to him by extraterrestrial craft hovering within our atmosphere.

The author implies that "divinely inspired writing," for both good and evil, by persons incarcerated or immobilized, is the result of intervention by space visitors beaming programing signals. "Is it coincidence," asks Dione, "that Hitler, while confined in a prison cell [where electromagnetic signals could be beamed at him], wrote Mein Kampf?"

God is portrayed throughout the Old Testament as wielding unlimited power, often in an irrational way. For worshipping the golden calf, God vowed to exterminate the Jews, but Moses talked the Supreme Being out of it. God seems more concerned with human treatment of God than human treatment of humans. "How do we account for a God with human weaknesses unless we admit that He is humanlike?"

---

*Extraterrestrial Visitations from Prehistoric Times to the
Present*
JACQUES BERGIER
(1970, Editions J'ai Lu; 1973, Henry Regnery)

Dinosaurs suddenly disappeared on Earth when radiation from an exploding star bombarded our planet, writes French physicist Jacques Bergier. The explosion was deliberately induced by an advanced civilization to kill all primitive life forms on Earth, setting off the process of evolution that would result in intelligent beings. This series of events will not stop with humans, but will continue until "evolution results in other gods, beings equal to their creators."

Cylindrical objects, apparently made of iron, with intersecting angles, have been found all over our planet. Bergier believes these were data collectors, fed by radiations to store detailed data on everything that has taken place in the past 10 million years. Many data collectors have disappeared from museums, "retrieved by the Intelligences who placed them on earth." These same Intelligences who built and modulated the star that murdered the dinosaurs also regulate "to a hundred billionth the frequency" of pulsars, stars that are used as artificial signaling beacons.

Since humans first began recording history, luminous beings have been reported among us. These Intelligences appeared in great numbers during the thirteenth and fourteenth centuries, simultaneous with "the first manifestations of freemasonry." Because of these luminous appearances, the Freemasons called themselves "Sons of Light." Bergier insinuates that the Masons and Rosicrucians both benefited from "interplanetary connections." These luminous beings, known to us as "demons," shuttled back and forth through history sharing secrets with initiates.

During the eighteenth century, somebody, perhaps a nonhuman or beings passing as human, seeded Europe with important information on chemistry and physics. Messengers spread this information: Saint Germain, Sir Henry Cavendish, Benjamin Franklin, and others. Roger Boscovitch, a Jesuit priest, in 1756 published a treatise in which Bergier finds "a hint of relativity and of the quantum theory" as well as time travel and anti-gravitation. An organization "whose importance we are only now beginning to grasp," known as the Invisible College, decided about 1660 to "reveal to the world a certain number of secrets" through the Royal Society of Science in England.

Several centuries ago, the Intelligences began introducing in our midst unusual humanlike beings to arouse our reactions, which they would then study, like social scientists, much in the way we experiment with rats in mazes. An amnesiac, found in Paris at the beginning of this century, had a map in his pocket of a planet that was not Earth. A woman in England in the eighteenth century claimed to be princess of a country that didn't exist. When no one believed her, she disappeared. People periodically pop up all the time from nowhere, revealing nothing about their identity.

According to police statistics, 2 million persons worldwide disappear each year "without leaving a trace," says Bergier. Those who disappear may eventually reemerge among us brainwashed. False memories might be introduced to puzzle and disconcert us. Bigfoot, the Abominable Snowman, maybe even elves and fairies, are manufactured elsewhere and deposited among us in this experiment. That extraterrestrial intelligences have not directly contacted the human species but continue to experiment on individuals leads Bergier to believe that we are in cosmic quarantine.

We Are Not the First
ANDREW TOMAS
(1971, G. P. Putnam's Sons; 1971, Souvenir Press Ltd.)

Somewhere on this planet, hidden in a cave or within an ancient megalithic structure, there may be "a secret cosmic center of universal science with libraries, museums and laboratories." Historical records and legends supposedly allude to such a treasure trove of information. Australian author Andrew Tomas believes some humans-among them Apollonius of Tyana, a contemporary of Jesus Christ, and comte Saint Germain, an eighteenth-century dabbler in Masonic and Rosicrucian rituals—probably even reached "this fountain of primordial science...and have drunk of its waters."

Technical and esoteric information had been bestowed upon humankind at the dawn of civilization. A superior being descended in the land of the Nile, civilized the dwellers of Egypt, taught them to record ideas, gave them charts of the stars, numbers to count with, and remedies for sickness. Another creature landed on the shores of the Persian Gulf, giving birth to the civilization of Sumer. "This fishlike god, known as Oannes, civilized the savages....His scientific legacy" being that "the people of the Tigris and Euphrates valleys became great astronomers and mathematicians." Another culture bearer in a "winged ship" visited Central America, leaving behind agriculture, architecture, and a code of ethics.

Priests and secret societies preserved the nucleus of this information, although much was apparently misplaced or forgotten. During fourteen centuries-from Ptolemy to Copernicus-no contributions at all were made to human knowledge of astronomy. "Even in Ptolemy's time thinkers looked back to former centuries for knowledge as if there had been a Golden Age of Science in the past."

That galactic civilizations established contact with humankind accounts, says Tomas, for the following "unexplained knowledge in remote antiquity" ...an Egyptian engineer named Heron built a steam engine, embodying principles of "both the turbine and jet propulsion." He also invented a speedometer. Details were apparently lost when Caesar burned the Alexandrian library.

...Mayans computed the length of the year as 365.2420. Our Gregorian calendar computes it to 365.2425. The actual figure is 365.2422 days. How could the Mayans have "had a more precise calendar than we in this Age of Science"?

... The Dogon tribe of Mali has a tradition about the "dark companion of Sirius." The companion star of Sirius is invisible to the eye. How could the Dogon without telescopes have known for thousands of years about the Sirius system?

...The fifteenth book of the ancient Greek Iliad mentions two companions of Mars, Phobos and Deimos. Were the ancients expressing in symbolic form a tradition about Martian moons that was only rediscovered in the nineteenth century?

...In 1939 a German archeologist working near Baghdad discovered numerous earthenware jars containing iron rods encased in copper cylinders. They were electrical batteries from 2000 B.C. How did the Sumerians come to have this technology?

...The corroded fragments of a metallic object, later identified as a computing machine, a forerunner of today's computers, proved to have been used in 65 B.C. by the Greeks to calculate the motions of the sun, moon, and planets. Where did the knowledge to build it originate?

...Stonehenge in Great Britain has been shown to be an astronomical computer built about 2000 B.C. Could men in skins have designed and erected a giant computer in stone?

...The Catholic Church lists 200 saints who allegedly levitated. Did the ancients know how to utilize anti-gravity?

The Legend of the Sons of God
T.C. LETHBRIDGE
(1972, Penguin Group)

British archaeologist and explorer T.C. Lethbridge makes a case that 'the sons of God' referred to in the Old Testament's book of Genesis were advanced extraterrestrial beings who inspired the development of human civilization when they visited earth about 5,000 years ago.

Megalithic monuments scattered across the planet, such as the Easter Island statues and Stonehenge, along with the many stone rings and lines of stones, remind Lethbridge of navigation markers "meant to be seen from the air." A bio-electric force exists within many of these stone circles, as Lethbridge and his wife personally experienced, giving Lethbridge more reason to regard them as navigation beacons erected by ancient humans for extraterrestrial visitors in exchange for education in agriculture and metal-working.

Flying saucers may have been observing humanity for thousands of years, speculates Lethbridge, and as happened in ancient times, saucers are still appearing today and "the casual way in which some people see them while others do not, suggests that they may not be visible to anybody who does not happen to have a high vibrational rate." The visitors might be coming from another higher vibrational dimension. Another option might be they are "the work of people, spoken of today as dead {ghosts}, living in a timeless zone above that of our earth."

Lethbridge relates his own UFO sighting during a rainstorm one summer afternoon, on a remote country road, when he rounded a bend and beheld nearby "a great shining disc or globe" slowly descending to the ground. Until he died this experience remained unexplained and haunted him. What he saw that day reminded him of ancient accounts of 'wheels in the sky' and the curious symbols known as 'sun discs' he had seen carved on stones at Megalithic and Early Bronze Age archaeological sites in western Europe. He suspects these images weren't meant to represent sun discs at all, but rather "to picture the vehicles in which the gods were transported through the heavens."

The Home of the Gods
ANDREW TOMAS
(1972, Editions Robert Laffont; 1974, Berkley)

Andrew Tomas theorizes that the inhabitants of that "mighty empire" Atlantis, once situated somewhere in the Atlantic, may well have had "contacts with other planetary civilizations." This interchange of knowledge resulted in the introduction of unknown plants and fruits to this planet.

After colonizing Europe, Africa, and the Americas, which explains cultural similarities between Egypt and Peru, Atlantean civilization apparently began to decline. Despite a well-regulated socialist state, in which planning was projected over centuries, money was nonexistent, and private property abolished, an atomic missile destroyed Atlantis, causing a global catastrophe. Another strong possibility for its destruction was a geological fluctuation such as a shifting of the Earth's crust, producing an enormous flood that destroyed all the civilizations of the world.

Most Atlanteans attempted to escape by boat. The privileged classes evacuated in aircraft to become the "sky people" who "climbed into the heaven of Anu" as described in the Sumerian Epic of Gilgamesh and other legends. These Atlantean leaders may have orbited the Earth in spacecraft, surveying the damage, or they flew to another planet. Others fled to a network of underground tunnels, chambers, and hidden valleys in the mountain ranges of the world, where they remain today, occasionally emerging to share "their wisdom with those who are ready for it." UFOs may be the airships of this secret colony.

The survivors of the global disaster, scattered and reduced to privation, have regressed into primitive savagery, retaining only memories of "a rich empire destroyed by fire and water...the origins of all myths."

It is unclear what happened between ancient post-Diluvian times and the Renaissance, when "progressive intellectuals...turned their faces towards ancient Romans, Greeks and Egyptians to hear about a forgotten science and its benefits to humanity... the foundation upon which our contemporary civilization is built." Today we are rediscovering what the Atlanteans knew. That knowledge is still accessible, says the author, if we seek out the secret Atlantean colonies, whose hidden vaults contain mechanisms and texts to provide us with the technical and moral means to reestablish Eden. Tomas believes that these "time capsules of Atlantean civilization" can be found in such places as the Sphinx at Giza and the Khufu Pyramid.

The Spaceships of Ezekiel
JOSEF F. BLUMRICH
(1973, Econ-Verlagsgruppe; 1974, Bantam)

Ezekiel, the Jewish priest of Chaldea, claimed to have been contacted four times during a twenty-year period beginning in 593 B.C. by manlike beings who descended in a fiery chariot. He described in detail these beings and their craft, writings that were included after his death in the Old Testament.

Josef F. Blumrich, a NASA engineer and co-builder of the Saturn V rocket, reinterprets Ezekiel's observations to produce an engineering analysis of the "fiery chariot." That analysis finds that the device Ezekiel saw falls within the structural technology available to modem science.

During his first close encounter, at about the age of thirty, Ezekiel watched "a stormy wind" descend from the north, "fire flashing forth continually," and within it he saw the "likeness of four living creatures," each with four wings and, underneath, pairs of human hands. Blumrich interprets this to mean four landing legs, each with four-bladed helicopter and mechanical arm attachments, supporting a conical spacecraft body. The only features that Ezekiel could positively identify were wheels, one at the bottom of each leg, which were capable of moving in any direction "without turning as they went." Blumrich stresses the importance of this observation, for Ezekiel specifically spoke of "a wheel within a wheel," a technique for locomotion that our own space program incorporated into vehicles designed to operate on the surface of other planets. Ezekiel describes the wheels he saw as a light greenish-blue, and the body of the craft as resembling "rock crystal" or "terrible ice," in other words, a bright, shiny surface.

From the craft emerged "the appearance of a man," who had been seated upon "the likeness of a throne." Ezekiel does not interpret what he sees, so he refers to this being as "the glory of the Lord," rather than the Lord. This "likeness of a man," whom Blumrich calls the spacecraft commander, wore a gold or brass-colored suit and demonstrated for Ezekiel an ability to fly from his craft to the ground. When taken for a ride on the craft, Ezekiel described the experience with the words "the spirit lifted me up." When they landed, seven men received the commander. One of them said, "I have done as thou didst command me."

On three other occasions during the next twenty years, Ezekiel observed and described the same vehicle. At the outset of each encounter, the "hand of the Lord was upon me." Blumrich wonders whether this doesn't mean a hypnotic influence. When Ezekiel says "the spirit took hold of me" or "the spirit lifted me up," Blumrich theorizes this might refer to teleportation.

Blumrich speculates that the craft began its descent after separating from a mother ship at 220 miles in altitude. A brief firing of its rockets enabled the helicopter blades to descend the rest of the way and maneuver for a landing. This phase of the flight is what Ezekiel witnessed, mistaking the rocket blasts for lightning and the helicopter blades for rushing wind.

Crews were apparently stationed at several different locations. Ezekiel portrays their actions as highly organized, one of their assignments apparently being able to establish contact with Earth dwellers. Ezekiel was chosen since as a priest he occupied a leadership role among his people. At one point, in his fourth and final encounter with the commander, Ezekiel is admonished to pay close attention to what they tell him, for knowledge or instruction is being conveyed.

Based on Ezekiel's observations, Blumrich assumes these visitors undertook at least three missions for the purpose of exploration, the study of humans, and some sort of intellectual influence on the development of human civilization.

Jesus Christ Heir to the Astronauts
GERHARD R. STEINHAUSER
(1974, Abelard-Schuman)

At some point between 12,000 and 8,000 B.C. a final and conclusive war waged throughout the solar system, resulting in the defeat of the Titans by those colonizers humankind came to refer to as the gods. From these occupying forces, numbering no more than a few hundred scattered over the planet, primitive humans took their knowledge and religion. These gods were not supernatural or lofty beings. Human imagination portrayed them as divine, for humans are notoriously inclined to worship every power, "so long as it is in power."

This German author emphasizes that the gods were in no way magical, enigmatic, or miraculous. Everything they did had a logical explanation. But the wealth of knowledge they left behind "degenerated into religions and superstitions."

When the gods landed on Earth, they immersed their spaceships in the ocean or a lake as a precaution against radiation. Humans emulated them, using the symbolic cleansing in water as a baptism rite of the gods. When the gods refueled their spacecraft, they were seen to oil the vehicles. Thus began the tradition of anointing with oil the human body when near death for a flight into the next world. These gods brought along an arsenal of weapons and vehicles-space gliders, rockets, and flying tanks. Humans regarded these machines as beasts and described them as winged bulls and dragons. Even today that tradition remains, for we call our tanks Tiger, Leopard, and Panther.

Steinhauser says the gods had at their disposal three means of overcoming time and space: spaceships; physical transformation similar to astral projection; and time transport through energy gates. Some of these energy gates still exist as stone monuments. The Gate of the Sun at Tiahuanaco in Bolivia, which apparently never served as an entrance or exit to any building, functioned as one such window in time, connected to another gate elsewhere in the cosmos to form a positive-negative pole. Gates and doors throughout history have provided a source of superstitious folklore-bridegrooms still protectively carry their brides through doorways.

Authors of the Christ "legends," Steinhauser contends, simply built upon earlier cults and myths derived from human interpretations of the gods and their actions. Ascension was practiced by the gods and ascribed to Jesus Christ. According to Luke, on the third day after Christ's death, when some of his followers entered the cave, they saw two men in shining garments, apparently angels or messengers. Steinhauser points out that white-coated messengers and technicians can be found at space launchings in our own age, their presence necessary for any ascension into Heaven. The author dismisses the miracles attributed to Jesus either as a form of mass hypnotism or as myths taken from earlier tales of the gods, their resurrections and powers. Gods of subordinate rank, known as angels to us humans, amused themselves on this planet by fondling the wives of mortals. But this gesture had no divine inspiration.

Gods transmitted their commands to each other and to humans through loudspeaker systems. That is why Moses often reported the voice of the Lord as terribly loud, like "the voice of the trumpet." These speakers were placed within pillars or bushes, and inside robots. The legendary Ark of the Covenant, used by Moses to communicate with the Lord, was only a reproduction, a crude human representation fashioned from wood and gold. It had enough voltage, however, to electrocute a man named Uzzah who touched it when a cart almost dumped it onto the ground.

All forms of belief and all religions based on miracles rather than technological reality, are doomed to die, says Steinhauser. Only when humans no longer hold anything in wonder will we be like gods.

Mystery of the Ancients
ERIC & CRAIG UMLAND
(1974, Walker and Company; 1975, Signet)

Decoding the Mayan hieroglyphs is the goal of a military rivalry between the United States and Russia. Each has spent millions in a crash program to intercept and decipher signals from space intended for a group of stranded Mayan miners and colonists now hiding in underground caverns and beneath Mount Shasta in California, their numbers reduced centuries ago by disease and cataclysms that sank their island kingdoms of Atlantis, Mu, and Lemuria.

Mayans first visited Earth from another solar system 190 million years ago. Using as a base Planet X, a tenth planet between Mars and Jupiter, they mined titanium and iron from the core of Earth's moon, and Earth itself. When Planet X exploded, creating the asteroid belt, the greater part of the Mayan population, their instruments, and all interstellar spacecraft were irreplaceably lost, stranding them in what is now Antarctica.

With the destruction of Planet X came the first Ice Age, forcing the Mayans to settle the continent of Atlantis in the Atlantic, and Mu and Lemuria in the Pacific. From these bases, they launched expeditions throughout the world, teaching Stone Age tribesmen the trappings of civilization. The Mayans built Stonehenge in the British Isles as an astronomical observatory after a flood erased Atlantis, Mu, and Lemuria, leaving them homeless once again. They sought refuge in Central America, among the rain forests and mountains. They built the first pyramids there, as storehouses, passing on this knowledge to the Egyptians whom they assisted in raising the Pyramid of Cheops. From these travels, the Mayans, who used the wheel only as a child's toy, compiled maps later used by all explorers including Christopher Columbus. These came to be known as the Piri Reis map. The Hebrews may have been a group of the original Mayan colonists who still await the Messiah, translated to mean a relief ship. "We know that there were Mayan physicians living in ancient Egypt," claim the authors, so couldn't Moses have been using the Ark of the Covenant to maintain "contact with the Mayan bases in Central America?" Is rescue the reason why the Mayans, in their calendars and astronomical knowledge, seem so obsessed by time?

Catastrophe again struck the Mayans in the form of disease, probably syphilis. As in the H. G. Wells classic, War of the Worlds, microbes and germs accomplished what implements of human destruction couldn't. Those that survived fled underground; the Spanish conquered a dying race. But we should not so easily bury their memory, for already, the authors contend, "there are thousands of people in California who worship the Mayan colony living in Mount Shasta, who believe that these aliens will make the perfect masters for us!"

Obviously, this possibility is a matter of concern to the governments of the world. That explains why America and Russia are cooperating in the exploration of Antarctica and other former Mayan bases, overcoming their differences "to work together in the face of a common threat." Mayan rescue ships already have penetrated our skies, producing the reports of UFOs that so excite and confuse the public. "Our government is well aware of the existence of Maya spacecraft," insist the Umlands, but it keeps this secret to prevent panic. After all, we don't know the intentions of these Mayan rescue ships. Have the Mayans returned as friends or foes? Has our government, or another, already translated the Mayan writings and learned their secrets? If we humans remain divided, will we be conquered like the Incas when the Spaniards landed?

———

The Lost Tribes from Outer Space
MARC DEM
(1974, Editions Alvin Michel; 1977, Bantam)

Why have the Jews been persecuted throughout history? After the first eleven chapters of Genesis, why is the whole of the Old Testament concerned with the Jewish people? Why are the Jews thought of as God's chosen people?

In his unorthodox yet literal interpretation of the Scriptures, French author Marc Dem proposes an answer: Jews are not of this planet. They have always been oppressed by other peoples because oppression "is like the process of rejection that sometimes occurs in organ transplants." They are the product of a selective breeding process, instituted when Yahweh (translated as the Christian Jehovah) discovered on landing here that Stone Age humanoids were an inadequate breeding stock. Genesis is thus a literal truth: Adam was the first Jew, and Adam's rib, his genetic structure, was used to create Eve.

The descendants of Adam and Eve displeased Yahweh by intermingling with the primitive stock already populating the planet. One result was a progressive decline in immortality; Adam lived 930 years, Noah's son Shem only 600 years, and Abraham but 175 years. In Genesis 6:3, Yahweh warned that crossbreeding would lower the life expectancy of the chosen people: "My life-giving spirit shall not remain in man forever; he for his part is mortal flesh." This passage evokes what Plato wrote in Timaeus and Critis, in speaking of the inhabitants of Atlantis, that fabled Garden of Eden, who remained superior until "the divine portion began to fade away, and became diluted too often and too much with the mortal admixture, and the human nature got the upper hand "

As centuries passed and the Jewish race became almost indistinguishable from the peoples who emulated them, Yahweh "submerged and swept away everything that was defective" in a Great Flood, which for a cosmic geneticist was tantamount to simply rinsing out the genetic test tube.

Jesus Christ is explained, quite simply, as an inspired humanitarian Jew who, against Yahweh's wishes, wanted to end segregation between Jew and Gentile and to rebuild the Tower of Babel, thereby ensuring the ascent of Gentiles into the kingdom of Heaven. Jesus deserves the title of savior, writes Dem, because he sought to establish a universal religion that would "save the Gentiles who had been condemned by the extra-terrestrial YHWH...." But Jesus failed.

Dem predicts that one day soon we must negotiate with Yahweh. For that reason, he says, to ensure the survival of us all, there must be unity on this planet between Jew and Gentile. Anti-Semitism will bring on catastrophe. So will the space program. Yahweh fears us as potential competitors, and any further advances in our space capabilities would be enough "to make him inclined to destroy our planet," for Yahweh "was not a God of peace. He made himself responsible for the oppression that would weigh down on his people."

_____

Secret of the Ages: UFOs from Inside the Earth
BRINSLEY LEPOER TRENCH
(1974, Souvenir Press Ltd.; 1977, Pinnacle Books)

Visitors from another planet became the god-kings of Atlantis, erecting the mega-liths and an intricate maze of tunnels intending, so the author theorizes, to protect them-selves from earthquakes, floods, and attacks from outer space. When Atlantis went under, these colonists took refuge in the tunnels that link our planet's surface to the hollow world within; their descendants remain there, venturing out to visit us in flying saucers.

Survivors from the sinking of Poseidonis, the last island of Atlantis, about 9500 B.C., handed down topographical information used by a Turkish admiral in 1513 to draw a map of the world that included the Antarctic continent, not thought to have been dis-covered until 300 years later. This Piri Reis map, as it is known, contains detail that even modern-day cartographers can acquire only with cameras and airplanes.

Trench relies heavily on Erich von Daniken and other authors for information about tunnel systems that exist underneath Ecuador, Peru, and the West Indies, and which allegedly connect Iran with the Caucasus, China, and Tibet. These tunnels lead to the hollow Earth, where the Atlanteans who could not escape catastrophe in their spaceships fled and flourished.

Everything-bones, hair, stalks of plants-is hollow, the author reasons. So why not planets? Like most hollow Earth advocates, Trench says the openings into this inner world can be found at the North and South Poles; the aurora borealis is the reflection of the small sun that shines within the Earth. What else but a hollow interior would explain colored snow in the Arctic region, or why icebergs are composed of fresh water, or why dust accumulates in the northern reaches of the Arctic? Several weather satellite photographs taken in 1967 and 1968 of the North Pole, which is almost perpetually obscured by cloud cover except in these photos, do show what appears to be an immense hole several hundred miles in diameter.

Trench believes that these inner Earth people use the UFOs to confuse us, to make us think the phenomenon has an extraterrestrial or psychic explanation. Their representatives on the surface, acting as fifth column infiltrators, may be the notorious Men in Black, those sinister looking characters who allegedly harass UFO witnesses. Trench points out that an estimated 100,000 people are listed as missing persons each year. "The inner earth people are taking away large numbers of our world population," he writes, "brain-washing and programing them to work for them."

UFOnauts are disturbed by our underground nuclear explosions, which threaten the Underworld by creating radioactive fallout that filters through their tunnel systems. They come to warn us, telling the contactees and those they abduct: Stop nuclear experimentation or else! The first widespread reports of flying saucers in 1947 correspond to our atomic experiments, and to Admiral Byrd's expedition that year to the North Pole when he partially penetrated that inner realm.

Trench admonishes us to beware of the Antichrist from below: "It is my firm view that the ground work has now been prepared for a takeover of this planet by those who live inside it."

Did Spacemen Colonise the Earth?
ROBIN COLLYNS
(1974, Pelham Books)

Did Alexander the Great "study the topographical features of Earth" from a UFO as he planned his world conquest? Are Bigfoot and Sasquatch Neanderthals created by spacemen, or are they the spacemen themselves? Were the aborigines transported to Australia in a UFO? Was the first cabbage artificially developed on another planet? Was a nuclear war fought in North and West Scotland a few thousand years ago? Robin Collyns, a New Zealander who says his theories were influenced by Buddhist philosophy, poses a question in practically every paragraph of this book.

Earth was established as a way station for reincarnated souls from other parts of the universe. This collection of inhabitants explains Earth's linguistic and racial diversity. The universe is the manifestation of a sublime species of radiant, spiritual energy, which also takes the form of individual souls. The souls project physical bodies. Yet in spite of a common spiritual Creator, Collyns says all individual races of modern humans throughout the universe are hostile to one another. Why else, he asks, would disease organisms exist?

Spacemen, as part of a plan to make Earth more habitable for themselves, deposited algae to oxygenate the atmosphere, then, in later stages, brought flowering plants and metazoic animals. Neanderthal and Java man were created simultaneously, the latter as servants to modern man. A nuclear holocaust, just one of many, sank Atlantis, eliminated the dinosaurs, and sent the Neanderthals fleeing to Europe, where they are known as Bigfoot and the Abominable Snowman. Collyns theorizes that the war was between imperialists from another planet who attacked the spacemen on Atlantis with atomic weapons, but lost.

We are even now drawing upon knowledge bequeathed to our ancestors by spacemen, says Collyns, evidenced by American scientists using alchemists' texts as a guidebook to developing nuclear fission. "How did the Chinese of antiquity know that space is black? Did spacemen destroy the Tower of Babel with an atomic missile? Did some Earthlings not wish to live on this planet?" Collyns uses other such questions as evidence that we were the beneficiaries of extraterrestrial knowledge.

He postulates that dreams are "racial memories" of past-life experiences in outer space. Children's nightmares are probably vestiges of this other existence, a fear of punishments meted out by violent spacemen. These space people are not necessarily sadistic in terrorizing helpless children. It is possible that they are simply guilty souls in exile from other planets who were reincarnated here.

Collyns theorizes that Venus, Mars, Jupiter, and Neptune are inhabited, and that our earthly space vehicles do not detect the presence of life there because our satellite photographs are "scrambled," or in some cases, substituted for other less revealing photos by the space intelligences. "Evidence indicates that on several occasions, spacemen may have repaired our malfunctioning satellites, and on one occasion, even captured a Russian satellite and did not return it to its orbit!"

Colony: Earth
RICHARD E. MOONEY
(1974, Stein & Day)

Homo sapiens may not be a species native to this planet, but could have arrived here as colonists from elsewhere in the galaxy. All human civilization developed from the wreckage of an earlier "greater culture," established by colonists or the humans they created, using advanced biological engineering. That earlier culture was destroyed in a cataclysm.

Mooney proposes that these colonizing visitors might have accidentally or deliberately seeded life on this planet with space probes before arriving themselves. A spaceship could have landed here in an emergency and been unable to leave again. Earth could have been a military outpost or communications base. Perhaps a group of homeless immigrants, or a band of criminals expelled from a more civilized society, originally settled on our planet.

Quoting Carl Sagan, who has estimated that ten other civilizations exist within 1,000 light years of Earth, Mooney points to a 1,000-year cycle of UFO activity, which he speculates could be related to Sagan's estimate. UFOs were recorded "in substantial numbers" about 1000 B.C., then followed another wave of sightings during the Christian and Roman era, another wave from A.D. 1000 to 1200, and yet another in our own century.

There is a unanimity in the legends of the Toltec/Aztec region of Mexico, the Maya of Yucatan, and the Incan empire in Bolivia and Peru that revolves around the appearance of "white, bearded gods with remarkable abilities," who brought civilization to the American continent and preached peace and brotherhood. Mooney believes these godlike culture bearers were the survivors of the Great Flood, or a similar catastrophe. While every culture has a flood mythology, strangely the Ice Age is not mentioned in the myths and legends of the human species.

Mooney believes that the flood and "the fall of man" are inextricably connected. Before the flood, according to the Book of Genesis, Adam lived 930 years, Seth 912 years, and Enoch 905 years. Sumerian myths also give long lifetimes to those before the deluge. Both Hebrew and Sumerian legends record a steady decrease in lifespans after the waters had subsided. This leads the author to conclude that "the Garden of Eden was perhaps not so much a specific place as the condition of the world before the catastrophe."

Stonehenge in Great Britain and other megalithic structures were built after the flood "to determine the new orbital position and, accordingly, length of year, and the new axial position of earth following the catastrophe." Stonehenge as an astronomical computer had no moving parts, and once the stones were in place, could not wear out, break down, or make a mistake, unlike our modern computers, which rely on outside energy sources. Higher mathematics and astronomy were credited by early Greek writers to the Hyperboreans, who supposedly inhabited what is now Britain. The Greek historian Diodorus praised the Hyperboreans and "their great round temple," which presumably was Stonehenge.

Construction of the Pyramids of Egypt was also prompted by the same catastrophic events that resulted in the erection of Stonehenge. The Pyramids make little sense as tombs because "in not one instance has the embalmed corpse of one of these rulers been found in any pyramid." Mooney points out that within the first pyramid to be built, the Step Pyramid, 20,000 alabaster jars for food were found. Would Egyptians squander their resources this way on one dead man whose body wasn't even in the tomb? Air shafts were built into each of the chambers of the Great Pyramid of Cheops. A corpse wouldn't need an air supply, but living people would! Mooney proposes that the Pyramids of Egypt were built as shelters, not tombs, to protect the ruling class from other predicted cataclysms.

Atlantis could have been the ancient Cretan Minoan sea empire. Mooney uses the 1500 B.C. date for the volcanic eruption of the Cretan island Thera as the destruction of Atlantis. This date would have corresponded to the twelve plagues of Egypt in the Bible. Red pumice from the eruption would have caused waters to "turn into blood," which would result in frogs leaving the water, dying on the land, bringing plagues of flies and lice to feed on the bodies. Ash would cover and kill plant life, and darken the sky. Polluted drinking water and the lack of food would in turn result in bubonic plague or cholera. The twelfth plague, death of all the firstborn, was "either Hebrew propaganda, or a misunderstanding," Mooney assures us.

The Fire Came By
JOHN BAXTER & THOMAS ATKINS
(1976, Doubleday)

During the early morning hours of June 30, 1908, a huge, shining, cylindrical object flashed across the skies of China and Mongolia, and according to witnesses, maneuvered from an eastward to a westward approach before suddenly exploding over a desolate region of the Siberian plateau, an explosion of such magnitude that it activated seismographs and created eerie nocturnal displays on every continent. Did a meteor, a comet, or a black hole impact? Or was the object a nuclear spacecraft attempting to land?

The authors investigate this "cataclysm greater than any the world had ever known" by chronicling the expeditions, researches, and theories of Russian scientists. Thirteen years had passed before the first scientists arrived at the site. The trip into the wilderness took months; trails had to be hacked, ferocious mosquitoes and the swampy bog of summer permafrost contended with; and the native inhabitants-Tungus tribesmen-refused to cooperate, so stricken were they with fear of the object that had fallen. Initially, the scientists expected to find remains of a meteor and a large crater. But that did not happen.

Evidence emerged pointing toward a nuclear explosion. Aleksander Kazantsev, the Soviet writer and space authority, first proposed this theory publicly in 1958, and later developed it in the book *A Guest from the Cosmos*. He was among a group of Soviet scientists who visited Hiroshima soon after the atomic blast. What he saw there bore remarkable resemblance to the devastation in Siberia.

At least 1,200 square miles of forest had been leveled by the Tunguska explosion, requiring an energy yield of nearly 30 megatons, more than ten times as great as that at Hiroshima. A blinding flash and a mushroom cloud were reported by the Tungus people, just as occurred at Hiroshima. Other similarities abound. The Siberian explosion was in the air, leaving an epicenter of trees standing. Significant radiation was found. The Earth's magnetic and gravitational fields had been disturbed. Dust in the atmosphere from the explosion made night seem like day. Siberian reindeer after the blast contracted scabs, a disease caused by radiation. And, just as at ground zero in Hiroshima, the trees left upright directly beneath the blast experienced accelerated growth.

Two scientists at the University of Texas in 1973 proposed that a compressed "mini" black hole might have struck Siberia, setting off the nuclear explosion, before passing through the Earth on its "rampage through the universe." Soviet authorities rejected this theory because it not fit all the evidence, especially the eyewitness accounts.

No known natural object is capable of carrying out a maneuver like that attributed to this "cylinder." Comets have never been seen to change course, or to deaccelerate when near the planet's surface. Another puzzle was the elliptical contours of the devastation. Apparently, as A. V. Zolotov and other scientists finally concluded, the explosive charge was encased in a container, like an artillery shell, which fanned outward elliptically when it burst.

Felix Zigel, aerodynamics professor at Moscow Institute of Aviation, calculated that the Tunguska body "carried out a maneuver" using a 375-mile arc—a feat he says can be attributable in 1908 only to "an artificial flying craft from some other planet."

===

The Sirius Mystery
ROBERT TEMPLE
(1976, Sidgwick & Jackson; 1977, St. Martin's)

Robert Temple, a Fellow of the Royal Astronomical Society, explores the common derivations of Sumerian and Egyptian astronomy and mathematics, and establishes parallels in the evolution of religious myths. From the outset, Temple disassociates himself from what he describes as the disturbing and unwholesome trend, advanced by von Daniken and others, of encouraging among believers in extraterrestrial life a religious-type zeal.

What Temple has done is to trace the origins of an obscure African tribe in order to determine the source of information they have preserved about the Sirius binary star system some 8.6 light years away. The Dogon, as the tribe is known, are apparently descendants of Egyptians who left Libya centuries ago to settle in Mali, the former French Sudan, south of Timbuktu. These simple tribesmen seem to possess astronomical knowledge handed down in pre-dynastic Egypt, before 3200 B.C. We know this now because four Dogon priests revealed the details of their secret oral traditions to two French anthropologists whom they had come to trust during the late 1940s. Two neighboring tribes, the Bambara and Bozo, also venerate the Sirius system, but retain significantly less information than their cousins the Dogon.

First of all, the Dogon disclosed that Sirius B, central to their myths and worship, is invisible. The first known photograph of that white dwarf star was taken in 1970, twenty years after the Dogon revealed its location to the anthropologists, and 5,000 years after the Dogon claim this knowledge was imparted to them. The Dogon knew that Sirius B took fifty years to revolve around the larger Sirius A. These tribesmen knew that the orbit of planetary bodies is elliptical, or egg-shaped, not circular. Furthermore, Dogon tradition says of Sirius B: "The star which is considered to be the smallest thing in the sky is also the heaviest." How did the Dogon know that Sirius B was a white dwarf, the smallest and heaviest (by virtue of an immense gravitational pull) of all types of known stars? Here the mystery deepens.

Dogon teachings relate how this knowledge was conferred upon humans by a race of amphibious creatures from Sirius. The Dogon call the Sirius system the "land of the fish," from which came the Nommo, or visitors, a word derived from a Dogon term meaning "to make one drink." The landing of the Nommo on Earth is referred to as "the day of the fish." These beings were said to have transported themselves in an ark, whose rushing winds, thunder, and flames, were "red as fire turning white."

On landing, a quadruped resembling a horse appeared and pulled the ark into a hollow, which filled with rainwater. Water insects entered the water, intending to "bite the Nommo's head...but [were] unable to reach the edge of the ark." Humankind is called Ogo, the imperfect ones, who rebelled at their creation and remained unfinished, like Lucifer. Ogo became the galactic pariah.

Temple provides the remaining pieces in this complex puzzle by drawing upon Egyptian, Sumerian, and Babylonian religious history. The creatures credited with founding civilization in the Middle East were described by the Babylonians who worshipped them as being "repulsive abominations." Temple cites this as psychological evidence for his theory: "If ever anything argued the authenticity of their account, it was this Babylonian tradition that the amphibians to whom they owed everything were disgusting, horrible, and loathsome to look upon." One account of these contacts, written by Berossus, the Babylonian scholar living in Athens during the time of Alexander the Great, portrays the amphibians as fishlike, with feet similar to those of man "subjoined to the fish's tail." Babylonian and Assyrian cylinder seals have preserved their likenesses.

The Nommo, known collectively as Oannes by the Babylonians, are revered as "monitor for the universe and guardian of spiritual principles." Nommo is master of the water, dispenser of rain. This water tradition is closely related to the Babylonian god Ea, and to the Sumerian god Enki, both water creatures. The Egyptian goddess Isis, with her fishtail headdress, is connected in worship to Sirius. From her it is said we derive our mermaid legends. The tale of Jason and the Argonauts, "argo" being a word derived from ark, involves fifty oarsmen, or argonauts, which corresponds to the fifty-year orbit of Sirius B. Other connections include the phrase "dog days" to describe a hot, dry summer. Sirius A has always been known as the "Dog Star" and the fifty dog days of summer correspond again to the orbit of Sirius B. Dogon priests say Sirius B is composed of super-heavy "star metal," something the Egyptians described as tcham, the source of power for Anubis, their jackal-headed god patterned after the Dog Star. Astronomers have speculated that dwarf stars like Sirius B may be composed of a heavy metal unknown to our solar system.

The Dogon prophesy that a third star exists in the Sirius system, Sirius C, larger and lighter than Sirius B, and also revolving around Sirius A. Based upon observations of wobbly movements in Sirius A, a few astronomers have theorized such a third as yet unobserved star may exist. Again, connections can seemingly be found in mythology, for the Egyptians assigned three goddesses to the Sirius system, one being Anukis, always pictured holding two jars from which water pours, perhaps symbolizing two watery planets circling Sirius B. Egyptian priests glorified the Sirius system, or "Sothic heavens," as a watery, reed growing Paradise.

Should modern science finally isolate and identify this phantom third star in the Sirius system, we must reassess any lingering doubts about the accuracy of Dogon religious revelations, for the Dogon predict that Nommo will return. These amphibious beings, whose intellect may have given us all the enduring features of civilization, remain curious about our struggle with the brutish nature of ourselves.

The 12th Planet
ZECHARIA SITCHIN
(1976, Stein & Day; 1978, Avon)

Using the original Hebrew version of the Old Testament, supported by more recent translations of Sumerian, Assyrian, and Babylonian texts, the author has pieced together the origins of civilization in Sumer as inspired or originated by the Nefilim, "sons of the deities" mentioned in Genesis as having been "cast down" on this planet before the Great Flood, and who married the daughters of men. From a twelfth as yet undiscovered planet in our solar system, probably a comet circling out beyond Pluto, the Nefilim came to Earth in search of minerals. A byproduct of their enterprise was the emergence of humankind.

To Sumer, beginning about 3800 B.C., we owe the origins of civilization. Sumerians built the first high-rise buildings from architectural plans, molded the first bricks, erected the first ziggurats that were imitated centuries later when the Egyptians built their Pyramids. Sumerians invented writing, printing, and the first movable type-stone stamps impressed in clay known as cylinder seals. Sumeria perfected metallurgy, developed higher mathematics, astronomy, medicine, and the textile industry. Sumerians introduced, long before Hammurabi, a system of laws that included a court made up of judges. To this day, we still don't know who the Sumerians were, where they came from, or how their civilization arose so suddenly and unexpectedly. After thirty years of "assiduous scholarship," Sitchin, a New York City Bible scholar, thinks he has found the answer.

Of all numbers, twelve seemed to be held in genuine reverence among ancient peoples. Hittite deities, like the later Greek, were governed by the Olympian twelve, with lesser gods organized in groups of twelve. The Egyptian god Ra presided over an assembly of gods numbering twelve; twelve was the divine celestial number, just as day and night were divided into twelve hours, and a year divided into twelve months. There were twelve tribes of Israel, twelve Apostles of Jesus, and twelve Greek Titans. All these traditions date back to Sumer, where twelve gods comprised the Great Circle, each representing a heavenly body. Numerous cylinder seals depict a large, ray-emitting star circled by eleven smaller globes. Is it any coincidence, asks the author, that the moons or large satellites of the planets in our solar system add up to twenty-four? The Sumerians claimed our solar system was composed of a sun and eleven planets (counting Earth's moon and another planet, since destroyed), and on the twelfth heavenly body, far into the heavens, lived the Nefilim.

Marduk, as this twelfth planet was known, passes between Mars and Jupiter on its orbit around the sun every 3,600 years. A winged globe, symbol for Marduk, became central to the beliefs and astronomy of the ancient world. The pictographic sign for the twelfth planet became the cross, referring to the Planet of Crossing. This 3,600-year orbital period was written in Sumerian as a circle that also symbolized 360 degrees, a completed cycle. Sitchin believes Marduk is almost certainly a comet.

According to Sitchin, humankind's evolution toward civilization, aided along the way by the Nefilim, passed through three distinct stages: the Mesolithic period of about 11,000 B.C.; the pottery phase of 7400 B.C.; and the emergence of Sumeria in 3800 B.C. Each of these periods is separated by 3,600 years, coinciding with the appearance of Marduk and the Nefilim. This would explain references in Genesis, Chapter 6, that closely parallel Sumerian tales about those who ruled before the Great Flood: in the biblical account, 120 years is referred to as the lifespan granted human-kind. Sitchin reinterprets this to mean 120 shar-a "shar" being 3,600 years-indicating that 432,000 Earth years had passed between the Nefilim first setting foot here and the deluge.

Nefilim landed on Earth in search of minerals, probably platinum, gold, and uranium, all plentiful in southern Africa where modern excavators have discovered many prehistoric mines. Since gold is invaluable to the electronics industry, no wonder it became known as the metal of the gods. Three major river systems and their plains-the

Nile, the Indus in India, and the Tigris-Euphrates-probably were Nefilim bases. Somewhere along the way, through genetic engineering, the Nefilim created humankind from Homo erectus.

Nefilim came to be known among humans as "the people of the shem." A "shem" translates into rocket, or skyborne vehicle. Assyrian cylinder seals clearly show "eagle-men" saluting a shem. Ziggurats consisting of seven stages sloping upward into a pyramidlike form about 300 feet high seem designed to accommodate spacecraft as a sort of launch tower. Symbolically, in Sumerian religious beliefs, they served as the connecting link between the gods and mortals on Earth.

Sitchin contends this interpretation supports the biblical account of the Tower of Babel. Babili literally meant "Gateway of the Gods," he points out, so perhaps humans attempted to erect a shem of their own, first building the launch tower to "High Heaven." One Sumerian seal does depict a confrontation between armed gods, "apparently over the disputed construction by men of a state tower." The shem is portrayed as a conical object. Apparently, humans had both protectors and enemies among the gods, for they destroyed the Tower of Babel with wind, dispersed its builders by confusing their language, but spared them their lives. Such a version would explain the biblical deluge, also recounted in the earlier Sumerian Epic of Gilgamesh, in which humankind is condemned, yet forewarned of destruction. "The decision to destroy and the effort to save are not contradictory acts of the same single Deity," writes Sitchin, "but the acts of different deities."

Should his theory prove accurate-that Nefilim were the "gods" who created humankind and passed on civilization, and that one day we will discover the existence of their heavenly abode-Sitchin poses for us one final question: "Did evolution alone, on the Twelfth Planet, create the Nefilim?"

Paradox: The Case for the Extraterrestrial Origin of Man
JOHN PHILIP COHANE
(1977, Crown)

Irish archeologist John Philip Cohane does not question evolution as a process, only the Darwinian version of that process which teaches that humans evolved from the ape. Human beings and human civilization, he contends, are rather the product of interplanetary colonization.

Prior to the appearance of Cro-Magnon man "suddenly out of nowhere" in about

30,000 B.C., there is a complete absence of fossil records to indicate any relationship whatsoever to the ape family. This absence of fossil records, combined with the consistently high level of civilization which Cohane believes accompanies the earliest traces of modern humans, suggests that Homo sapiens descended directly from extraterrestrial colonists. He also points to humankind's "psychozoatic aspect," which sets us apart from apes, meaning that humans are too spiritually refined to be related to the ape family.

Artifacts reveal that even in furthest antiquity, human civilization possessed technological sophistication. He draws upon Professor Barry Fell's thesis that the American and Australian continents were visited and perhaps settled by travelers from higher civilizations in Asia Minor and Africa. The Pyramid of Cheops at Giza, and Stonehenge in Britain, both built before 2000 B.C., are evidence of complex astrophysical knowledge having been distributed through the ancient world. Megaliths are scattered all over this planet, from the South Sea Islands to Yucatan. He hints that the ancients had an understanding of gravity and how to manipulate it-information that was lost, and has not yet been rediscovered.

Those unsuspecting scientists who uncover and accept artifacts or information lying outside the boundaries of accepted science, for instance, the discovery of "an iron nail in a five-hundred-year-old Andean stratum, or a Central African rock carving which looks remarkably like an astronaut in a space suit, or an inscription in a New Guinea cave that closely resembles ancient Libyan or Egyptian," often find that they are "swiftly consigned to the lunatic fringe."

Cohane sees developments that indicate the imminence of extraterrestrial contact. The population explosion on this planet signifies that the human species is ready to colonize other celestial bodies, perhaps as part of a universal colonizing and evolutionary process. The fact that our planet will one day be uninhabitable, combined with our technological ability to leave, translates into our evolution as an interplanetary creature, continuing the process that made possible the growth of intelligent life on planet Earth.

The Manna Machine
GEORGE SASSOON & RODNEY DALE
(1978, Sidgwick & Jackson)

For forty years, so the Bible tells us, 600 families under the leadership of Moses roamed the wilderness, sustained each day by "manna from Heaven." What was this manna, and where did it really come from are questions not normally asked, if only because most people either have already accepted the Scriptures as literal truth or rejected them as nothing more than imaginative outpourings of folklore.

After several years of research into ancient oral traditions and Jewish spiritual texts, George Sassoon and Rodney Dale have concluded that manna might very well have been a form of alga cultured in a machine and given to the "Chosen People" by extraterrestrial visitors. The authors are probably the first to examine as a technical document those Hebrew traditions encompassing a book known as the "Kabbalah." Included in the text is a detailed description of the manna-making device referred to in the Old Testament. It quickly became apparent to the authors on reading the Kabbalah that it described a machine, not a god, so they undertook a technical translation. Since both men are engineers, and Sassoon a well-known and accomplished linguist, their efforts merit serious consideration.

Each part of the "machine" was named by Moses and his followers according to corresponding parts of the human body. The manna was made from a dew distilled in the upper skull of what became known as the Ancient of Days, and coursed through the body, exiting at the penis, a functional name given to the manna-discharge nozzle. Besides two skulls and a penis, the machine had parts resembling a beard, a nose, and two testicles. The authors point out that human beings can still be found who describe technology in this way. The Apache Indians, for instance, had no words in their language for the mechanical parts of a motorcar, so they called headlights "eyes," the hood a "nose," electrical wiring became "veins," and the radiator hose the "intestine."

By function, the manna-machine apparently had parts that served as a dew-still for water, a light source for energy to grow the algae plants, a culture vessel with ventilating coils, tanks for seed and fertilizer, and a power plant and exhaust to eliminate waste heat. The sugary soup produced by this process, when dried and toasted, became the small, sugary grains described in the Bible. Such a machine could produce about 800 kilograms a day. Every seventh day or so the machine would need to be cleaned and sterilized of bacteria. The authors theorize that a neutron pumped laser, converting nuclear energy into light-probably in the red region of the spectrum since the machine's "face" turned bright red fueled the manna-making process.

Operating this machine were the priests who made its secrets a holy tradition among the tribes of Israel, training successive generations of priests in its use even after the machine fell into disrepair. Secrecy and esoteric references to its uses were made essential by the very nature of its "miracles," for had word leaked out, all the nations in the known world would have made war to acquire it. The Bible relates how it was kept possibly disguised as the Ark of the Covenant, in a screened enclosure or Tabernacle, at a considerable distance from the main camp. Only priests were permitted near it. The Bible also reports that no manna was distributed on the Sabbath, the holy day, holy also meaning clean, which is what the priests did to the manna-machine.

On one occasion, in the wilderness, manna refused to flow. The "penis" of the machine had become clogged. As priests worked to cleanse it, Aaron supposedly ordered all his men who had not yet done so to circumcise themselves. Since that day, "what began as an attempt to restart the flow of 'mercy' [another term for manna]...has now become a ritual branding with the mark of an ancient faith." Other customs directly related to the manna-machine have survived, but explanations for them have long since been forgotten. The Lord's Prayer, based on an earlier Jewish prayer, asks "Give us this day our daily bread," just as Moses and his flock prayed each day for manna-bread from their machine. Even Christian Communion, as evolved from the Last Supper, seems more a reenactment of the manna-distribution ritual, receiving a ration of "Bread of Heaven."

Original technical descriptions of the manna-machine eventually developed into the mystical beliefs of the Kabbalah, which in a companion volume, The Kabbalah Decoded, Sassoon and Dale have reinterpreted. When, after forty years, the machine ceased working, its purpose was forgotten. "It became a mere ritual object." After crossing the Jordan River, carried by priests at the head of the Israelites into their Promised Land, the machine disappeared into oblivion. It became known as the "Ark of Testimony," or "Evidence," the proof that an almighty Lord existed. It was left in a shrine at Shiloh, about 40 kilometers north of Jerusalem, and "no longer occupied a central position in the life of Israel." A dedicated group of priests continued to worship and attend to the machine, their activities producing a mystical society known as the Reapers of the Holy Field, whose rituals and musings the Rosicrucians and other secret societies would later borrow.

When the Philistines defeated Israel on the battlefield, they carried away the sacred "Ark" to Ashdod, their capital, where it was placed in the temple of their god. The Bible relates how a plague of "emerods," or tumors, struck all those Philistines who came in contact with the Ark. The authors remark that unlike the Jewish priests, the Philistines did not know which parts of the machine were safe to touch. Because it remained radioactive, all those who fiddled with it were contaminated.

Sores and ulcers are, of course, two common effects of radiation poisoning. The Scriptures further tell how this plague spread and the Philistines returned the Ark to Israel for fear of it. They placed it on a cart tethered to some cows that pulled it into Beth-Shemesh. Seventy farmers in Beth-Shemesh, fondling the machine before their priests arrived, soon died. When King David brought it to Jerusalem, the Ark almost toppled off a cart, striking dead a man named Uzzah when he tried to right it. According to the Bible, the Ark finally disappeared for good in 587 B.C., when the Babylonians conquered Israel. Jewish texts like the Talmud record how the Ark was hidden by Jeremiah, the prophet, "In a cave on the mountain from which Moses viewed the Promised Land before his death." This would be Mount Nebo, about 26 kilometers southwest of Amman, the capital of Jordan, a likely starting point for properly equipped expeditions to search for radiation leakage that might betray once again the whereabouts of a nuclear-powered machine, the alleged source of manna from Heaven.

The Monuments of Mars
RICHARD C. HOAGLAND
(1987, North Atlantic Books)

When the author studied two 1976 Viking photos of the humanlike face on the Cydonia region of Mars, he realized that either the images were "a complete waste of time, or the most important discovery of the twentieth century if not of our entire existence on Earth." There could be no middle ground, concluded Hoagland, a science writer and former editor of Star & Sky magazine. Either this face, measuring one mile across, is an artificial structure created by ancient astronauts to attract our attention, or it is an unusual but natural mesa shaped by winds.

As he pored over depictions of an area of Cydonia a few miles from the face, Hoagland spotted what appeared to be an immense pyramid one mile by 1.6 miles across-and other structures resembling an entire weather-worn city. At this point he confesses to having crossed over "into the suspension of disbelief," and three extraordinary, possible explanations struck him: (1) An indigenous Martian civilization had built the face and city. (2) The face was a "calling card" designed by extraterrestrial visitors to mark their visit. (3) A previous civilization had developed on Earth, traveled to Mars, and created the monuments.

Eventually Hoagland convinced himself that explanations one and three could not possibly be true. Based on everything we know, or think we know, about the evolution of life on our planet and about the geological and climatological history of Mars, too little time has elapsed for intelligent life to have evolved into a civilization and then to have disappeared on that planet. The patterns of meteorite cratering and geological change on Cydonia seem to indicate these structures-if they are artificial-could be no less than 500,000 years old, a period before Cro-Magnon even emerged on Earth. Nor could Hoagland find any compelling evidence that an advanced civilization might have evolved on Earth 500,000 or more years ago and mastered spaceflight only to disappear without leaving behind traces of their technology on Earth.

That left option number two, the idea of alien visitors on Mars, and the more Hoagland examined The Face the more the Cydonia complex reminded him of the Giza Plateau in Egypt with its Sphinx, Great Pyramid, and other colossal monuments. Could there be a connection between these two areas, a connection with meaning still beckoning to us through the mists of time?

The author began a series of detailed comparisons. "Egyptian temples-even the pyramids themselves-were celestially aligned, some to certain stars, such as Sirius, others to the rising sun." Several researchers pondering Cydonia prior to Hoagland had noted how its huge pyramid ten miles from The Face was aligned to the north, as are the Egyptian pyramids. Hoagland noticed that the Cydonia structures resembling a city were aligned to the sunrise/sunset, and from the center of this complex one could mark the Martian summer solstice as the sun rose directly over the mouth on The Face!

Carl Sagan once stated: "Intelligent life on Earth first reveals itself through the geometrical regularity of its constructions." With this in mind Hoagland began measuring the Cydonia structures for the presence of geometric patterns. First of all, these structures concentrated in this one region of Cydonia were qualitatively and quantitatively different from the rest of Mars. Each structure constitutes an anomaly, "each unusual enough in itself to warrant some kind of explanation beyond 'weird geology.' More than that, however, it was the way these anomalies all 'stuck together' forming a truly inexplicable 'integrated anomaly' on the Martian landscape."

Four unique anomalous structures are within the same 100 square kilometers on a planet with a surface area of 150 million kilometers. (1) The Face, a bisymmetrical resemblance to a human. (2) The Pyramid, a five-sided bisymmetrical colossus. (3) The Cliff, a multi-level sharply defined feature. (4) The Fort, a triangular object with straight walls and an interior containment. Hoagland calculated the odds of randomly finding an association between The Face and The Pyramid on Mars to be "less than one chance in a hundred million." By factoring in the series of alignments connecting all of these structures—one wall of The Fort, for instance, is aimed directly at The Pyramid, while the other wall is aimed at The Face—he concludes there is "an overall probability of less than one chance in 70 trillion that this grouping is the result of merely random forces!"

Did both ancient Sumer and Egypt originate from a common source as evidenced by their wealth of cultural similarities ranging from arcane astrological notations to architectural designs? Could both cultures have taken inspiration and guidance from the builders of the Cydonia complex? The author observes that it may not be just a weird coincidence that Cairo, the site of the Sphinx and Great Pyramid, was originally named El-Kahira from the Arabic El-Kahir, a word which means Mars!

We may have to seriously consider, concludes Hoagland, "that Mars played some crucial role in the formative development of our own species, that we might ultimately be 'the Martians' who, sometime in the last half million years, returned to Earth...and stayed."

The Gods of Eden
WILLIAM BRAMLEY
(1989, Avon Books)

To explain mankind's succession of bloody conflicts and turmoil the author proposes a conspiracy theory of history-we humans are a species of slaves, once a source of labor for an extraterrestrial civilization, and our alien owners have kept us under control for thousands of years by having "bred never-ending conflict between human beings, promoted human spiritual decay, and erected on Earth conditions of unremitting physical hardship." Furthermore, it is possible that ownership of Earth has changed hands over the millennia, passing from one alien group to another.

These "Custodians," as the author calls our extraterrestrial keepers, created Homo sapiens as laborers to carry out building and mining operations on Earth. Select humans who acted as personal servants to the alien rulers became a caste of priests anointed to be intermediaries between the alien "gods" and their human slaves. According to Sumerian and Egyptian accounts, these Custodians were physically humanlike and racially diverse, and exhibited the entire range of human behaviors from that of saints to sinners. When their human slave population grew arrogant and rebellious, the Custodians dispersed them in a great flood, scattered them into a multitude of linguistic groups, and repressed their access to spiritual knowledge.

An early secret society emerged called the Brotherhood of the Snake, a group which sought to disseminate spiritual knowledge and to liberate the human race from Custodial bondage. Their use of the snake-taken from the Garden of Eden's symbol of knowledge-came to symbolize spiritual healing, and in later centuries evolved into the physician's logo for physical healing. But somewhere in its early life the Brotherhood was infiltrated and then "turned under its new Custodial gods into a chilling weapon of spiritual repression and betrayal."

Teachings of the Brotherhood in ancient Egypt were limited to the pharaohs and priests initiated into secretive institutions known as "Mystery Schools." These schools "not only twisted spiritual knowledge, they greatly restricted public access to any theological truths still surviving." It was this Brotherhood, organized into Mystery Schools, which began spreading a "one God" religion with the goal of making it the world's dominant theology. As part of this new monotheism "the Brotherhood began to teach the fiction that members of the Custodial race were the physical manifestations of a Supreme Being."

A series of Hebrew leaders such as Moses were confronted by a being calling itself Jehovah who periodically gave them instructions. Jehovah "appears to have been a succession of Custodial management teams" using their aerial craft over a timespan of many human generations "to perpetuate the lie that they were God." Similar Custodial appearances before Jesus of Nazareth, Mohammed in about 600 A.D., and Joseph Smith in the early 19th century produced the new religions of Christianity, Islam, and Mormonism. These and other Custodially inspired religions were designed to provoke artificial disagreements and armed conflicts that would keep the human race divided and in turmoil.

Through its various mystery school orders—Freemasons, Rosicrucians, the Illuminati, and the monarchies—the Brotherhood has for millennia fomented a reign of terror, revolution, and warfare. Naziism, for instance, "was a powerful new Brotherhood faction steeped in Brotherhood beliefs and symbols," choosing as its emblem the swastika, a symbol thousands of years old connected to the original Brotherhood groups. Members of a Nazi mystical group called The Thule Society actually confessed that their true leadership came from extraterrestrial masters-a race of underground supermen-one of which Adolf Hitler met and before whom Hitler trembled with awe and fear.

Alien Identities
RICHARD L. THOMPSON
(1993, Govardhan Hill)

From the 5th century B.C. to the 9th century A.D., a collection of texts and works of traditions and folklore in India known as the Vedic Accounts were written down in Sanskrit, though the material itself has been traced back to about 3,000 B.C. These stories portray the ancient peoples of India being in regular contact with advanced beings from a host of other worlds who traveled to and around Earth in aerial vehicles resembling modem descriptions of UFOs. In this book mathematician Richard Thompson draws parallels between current UFO sightings, abductions, and alien visitors, and the cosmological literature of India's Vedic culture to make a case these ancient writings may not be mythological after all.

One Vedic text called the Puranas speaks of 400,000 humanlike races of beings living on various planets, with humans on Earth among the least powerful. These extraterrestrial races possess powers called "siddhis," among them: telepathy and thought-reading; levitation or antigravity; invisibility; the ability to shift into different forms; and longdistance hypnotic control of humans. All of these powers have been ascribed to modem space visitors. "There were established diplomatic relationships and satisfying mutual understandings between leading members of human society and representatives of other societies in the cosmic hierarchy."

Vedic literature contains numerous accounts "of sexual relations between humans and members of nonhuman races that give rise to offspring." These stories may be thinly veiled allusions to genetic manipulations or transformations, which supports the Vedic contention that humans descended from higher humanlike beings on other planets. Thompson speculates how these other planets may exist in a parallel to our own three-dimensional space, thus giving alien visitors the appearance of penetrating walls and operating flying vehicles that seem to violate the known laws of physics.

When Time Began
ZECHARIA SITCHIN
(1993, Avon Books)

Stonehenge in England has been described as a computer made of stone, an ancient astronomical observatory, and an enigma wrapped in a mystery. In book five of his Earth Chronicles, Zecharia Sitchin further expands his theory about the extraterrestrial origins of human civilization to propose that Stonehenge was built or inspired by alien visitors who masqueraded as gods, and the megalith was intended to be a solar clock calibrated to Celestial Time and the passage of the zodiacal ages.

Archeologists seem in agreement that Stonehenge was created in three stages-the first about 2900 B.C., the second around 2100 B.C., and the third stage just decades later. The bluestones which compose most of the standing circle weigh up to four tons each and at least 80 had to be cut and transported 250 miles across land and over water to the Salisbury plain. Their alignment was designed to foretell eclipses of the moon and sun, as well as solstices and other time cycles.

Sitchin quotes astronomer and mathematician Sir Fred Hoyle as calling Stonehenge's powers to predict celestial events "an intellectual achievement beyond the capacity of the local Neolithic farmers and herdsmen" and ranking up there with the work of Albert Einstein. This prompts Sitchin to ask: "Who circa 2900 B.C. possessed the knowledge of astronomy (to say nothing of engineering and architecture) to build such a calendrical 'computer,' and circa 2100 B.C. to rearrange the various components thereof and attain a new alignment? And why was such a realignment required or desired?"

An Egyptian temple of astronomical orientation was built in 3100 B.C., two centuries before Stonehenge, but it was square rather than circular like Stonehenge. The oldest phase of a solstitially-oriented temple in Karnak took place about 2100 B.C., "a date coinciding (perhaps not by chance) with the date for the 'remodeling' of Stonehenge." Again, this temple too, was square. Nowhere in Egypt can anything resembling Stonehenge be found. The Sumerians are the only other cultural candidate for building Stonehenge, but they were not stonemasons and used mud bricks, nor did they use a circular shape for observatories. So who were the builders if not the Egyptians and Sumerians?

A clue for Sitchin comes from Ireland and its observatory/burial mound called Newgrange, which was built about 3100 B.C. According to Irish legend this site was known as the House of Oengus, who was the son of An, the chief god of Newgrange's builders. Is it a coincidence that the principal deity of Sumer at this time was named EANNA, and Egypt's principal deity was Anu? The names are too similar for coincidence, says Sitchin. It was not ancient peoples but their ancient gods who created Stonehenge, and these gods were alien visitors called Anunnaki, or An and Anu for short, who splashed down in the Persian Gulf and first became immortalized as deities by the Sumerians.

So why was Stonehenge reoriented in 2100 B.C.? In that year the zodiacal constellation of Taurus, the age of Taurus the Bull, ended after having begun in 4400 B.C., and the new age of Aries the Ram was born. This celestial time served to date major events, while other features of the stone calendar helped "predetermine the precise time of festivals honoring the gods." The calendar thus became a religious device to pay homage to its divine architects, the Anunnaki.

Further developing this theory, Sitchin points to the enigma of why seven was chosen as the number of days to represent the slice of a year known as a week. In Sumerian texts, long before the Bible's Genesis was written, Earth was called "the seventh" and depicted by a symbol of seven dots. The reason is that the Anunnaki, traveling into our solar system, first passed six planets—Pluto, Neptune, Uranus, Saturn, Jupiter, and Mars—before reaching the seventh, our Earth. To commemorate that journey the number seven has been held symbolic by humans ever since, used as seven days for creation in the Bible, seven days of advance warning to Noah before the great flood, Jericho circled seven times before its walls would tumble down, and countless other references.

The Eyes of the Sphinx
ERICH VON DANIKEN
(1996, Berkley Books)

Why did the ancient Egyptians mummify then carefully wrap inside urns and bury in tombs untold millions of birds, dogs, baboons, crocodiles, frogs and fish? Even if they believed the animals that they venerated would need their earthly bodies in the afterlife, why was so much expense and labor dedicated for thousands of years to the preservation of such a wide variety of species and in such huge numbers?

A three-volume history of Egypt written in about 300 B.C. by Manetho, the high priest of holy temples, relates how the gods ruled Egypt for 13,900 years, during which time they created hybrid monsters of all kinds. Humans emerged from these laboratories of the gods possessing two heads, two wings, two genders, or grafted with the legs of horses and goat horns, while all sorts of animals were mixed with each other in equally ghoulish combinations. These hybrid images were supposedly kept in the temple of Belos as a museum to genetic experimentation.

Both the ancient Egyptians and Sumerians produced statues and a wide array of art images depicting hybrid creatures. An engraved cup from 2200 B.C., for instance, shows a creature with the body of a snake, the head of a dragon, and human hands. Even in South and Central America, the Olmec and Mayan cultures featured human-animal monsters on their temple walls and in art representations.

Von Daniken finds only two ways to explain these stories and images. (1) They are the product of early human's collective imagination, spanning cultural separations and differences. (2) Or such hybrid creatures did in fact once exist, a product of genetic design by alien visitors who were worshipped as gods. If the latter is true-and the author strongly insinuates he believes it is-then the Egyptians were simply imitating the actions of their gods when they mummified and stored both animals and humans, expecting that one day the gods would return and desire to begin again their genetic experiments.

Humans are great imitators, especially when it involves imitation of the gods. Another example is the cult of skull deformation that existed in most societies of the ancient world. Young children were selected at an early age and their still growing heads were kept squeezed inside padded boards. Their skulls would end up elongated and terribly deformed. Why was this cruelty inflicted? "The elongated skull is an attribute of the gods depicted in pictures worldwide." Children's skulls were made to resemble the heads of their deities as homage and worship of these divine beings.

The Stargate Conspiracy: The Truth About Extraterrestrial Life and the Mysteries of Ancient Egypt
LYNN PICKNETT & CLIVE PRINCE
(1999, Little, Brown and Company)

British researchers Picknett and Prince believe they have uncovered a "gigantic and complex conspiracy" that links together various proponents of ancient 'lost' advanced civilizations and the ancient astronaut theory and people who claim to channel an alleged extraterrestrial entity called the Council of Nine, which has its origins in ancient Egypt, all of this fitting together in an attempt to create a new religion based on a belief that these extraterrestrials will soon return.

"What we call the stargate conspiracy is the fostering of a belief that extraterrestrial 'gods' created the human race and presided over its civilization—and that those gods are about to return. This belief is being promoted in different ways to different groups of people, but the underlying themes are always the same."

Among the book authors that Picknett and Prince claim are consciously or unconsciously involved in this conspiracy, cross-fertilizing each other's ideas, include: Graham Hancock, Robert Bauval, Robert Temple, Richard Hoagland, Whitley Strieber, James Hurtak, Andrija Puharich, Gene Roddenberry, Alice Bailey, and many others. "We have shown how all of these writers use each other's ideas in support of their own, and consequently not only do they reinforce each other, but the end result is that one large, consistent picture emerges. This is despite the fact that the arguments are often built on very shaky foundations."

Channeled information concerning 'The Nine' first came through a 'stargate' in December 31, 1952, in which the channeled entity claimed to be the collective intelligence of the nine gods of Heliopolis, worshipped in ancient Egypt. The Nine claimed to be extraterrestrials who built the Great Pyramid and the Sphinx. Present at this series of channeling sessions was Andrija Puharich (later mentor to Uri Geller who also channeled The Nine). Also present was Arthur M. Young, the Bell helicopter inventor, who later became the mentor to a 21-year-old Robert Temple, with whom he planted the idea of writing the ancient astronaut book, *The Sirius Mystery*. Picknett and Prince found evidence that the emergence of the Council of Nine actually goes back to the 1930s and the occultists Aleister Crowley and Alice Bailey, who first attached significance to Sirius and Freemasonry and their connections to ancient Egypt.

Puharich also allegedly mentored James Hurtak, an American with a Ph.D. in history, who the authors of this book credit as being the "dedicated myth-maker" who created "the link between the Egyptian side of The Stargate Conspiracy and the New Age." As a UFO researcher, Hurtak promoted a link between UFOs and Nazi Germany. "He claimed that the extraterrestrial that brought civilization to the Middle East many thousands of years ago chose to re-establish contact with the human race in modern time with the Germany of the 1930s" and these extraterrestrials "gave Nazi scientists the secret of how to construct disc-shaped flying craft" which ended up in the hands of the U.S. military after World War II.

Shadowy agents of a covert agenda may be the puppet masters manipulating all of these book authors. "It may be that the stargate conspirators include CIA operatives, Freemasons, politicians and their wealthy backers, who believe they have something to gain by creating this belief system, or fear they have something to lose if it {extraterrestrial visitation} does not happen."

Slave Species of God: The Story of Humankind from the Cradle of Humankind
MICHAEL TELLINGER
(2005, Bear & Company)

South African researcher Michael Tellinger makes a case for "a terrible truth about our human origins" in this book, building upon the nine books of Zecharia Sitchin, showing how the Anunnaki astronauts from the planet Nirbiru created humans using pieces of their own DNA more than 200,000 years ago, making the resulting hybrids into a slave species for mining gold, which began the long human obsession with that precious metal.

It is probably no coincidence, writes Tellinger, that Sumerian tablets claim most of the original ancient astronaut gold mining took place in southern Africa, later identified by scientists as the 'cradle of humankind', the origins of human evolution, which indeed it was, as a result of genetic manipulation by the Anunnaki. They were under the command of Anu, hence the name Anunnaki, and up to 600 of them were present on Earth conducting mining operations using their genetically modified slave labor force to send gold "to help mend their planet Nibiru's failing ozone layer and atmosphere." Nibiru orbits our sun every 3,600 years and each close approach causes geological upheavals on Earth and Mars.

Gold being the property of the Gods became a tradition in many human civilizations, from Sumeria, Egypt, and the Indus Valley of India, to Mesoamerica. "This is very well documented by the conquistadores in Mesoamerica," says Tellinger, who "were repeatedly told by the natives that all the gold 'belonged to the gods.'" Even the Old Testament contains examples of God treating gold as a divine metal which was given as a reward to humans.

Once human civilization began to flourish, under tutelage from the Anunnaki, who taught us agriculture, architecture and construction, writing and mathematics, slavery was institutionalized among humans just as it had been when the Anunnaki needed slave labor and modified our genetic code. In the Old Testament of the Bible there are over 130 references to slaves and slavery, with the entity identified as 'God' speaking approvingly of slavery, if the slaves were not Israelites, the chosen people by God (the Anunnaki), who played favorites among the various types of humans. Slavery and greed were both encoded into our genes.

All of the world's religions were inspired by the Anunnaki to control humans, create dissension between them, and keep them in bondage to a belief in the divinity of the Anunnaki. Religious leaders such as Jesus, whose mother Mary was artificially inseminated by an Anunnkai named Enlil, were programmed to "plant the seeds of obedience but also perpetuate the fear of god."

In the 100 pages of his last chapter, Tellinger presents a narrative, The Story of Humankind, based on Sitchin's translations and interpretations of Sumerian clay tablets. Tellinger links together Sitchin's body of work with more translated Sumerian tablets and stone carvings emerging since the 1970s, which Tellinger says "lead to one simple conclusion…the Sumerian gods who came from distant lands and gave the early humans all their knowledge" were ancient astronauts.

Tellinger suspects that "the ancient 'gods' may still be active among us in ways that we cannot comprehend, not allowing knowledge to spread, keeping their firm grip through religious oppression over their 'slave species'" and waiting patiently for our technological development to reach a level that forces them to intervene again to assert their will and their property rights over us.

———————————

The Ancient Alien Question: An Inquiry into the Existence, Evidence and Influence of Ancient Visitors
PHILIP COPPENS
(2012, Weiser)

A native of Belgium, Philip Coppens became a charter cast member in 2009 of The History Channel's television series, *Ancient Aliens,* and wrote this book as a summation of evidence and ideas he contributed showing that some ancient civilizations had contact with non-human intelligences.

He believes most ancient astronaut theories "have failed in finding proof because their scope was too limited," and many other theories have failed because their underlying premise was faulty, a perspective prompting some theorists to label Coppens as a skeptic. While he believes that ancient contact with aliens was "sporadic at best," he also contends that "civilization was indeed guided by gods, by a nonhuman, extraterrestrial intelligence."

Coppens turns a skeptical eye toward some of the claims for ancient astronauts, such as that visiting aliens constructed structures on Mars, and that the Dogon tribe in Mali preserve ancient astronomical evidence given to humans by visitors from the Sirius star system. In the case of the Mars structures, he points out a series of space probes have failed to find evidence for the existence of such structures and theories for these structures "remain unsupported by evidence."

As for *The Sirius Mystery*, a 1976 bestseller by Robert Temple that claimed the Dogon tribe of Mail possess astronomical knowledge about the Sirius star system passed down to them by extraterrestrials, Coppens quotes anthropologists who visited the Dogon in 1991 and failed to find any oral history supporting them eve possessing any knowledge that couldn't have been gained in recent times. "The evidence to support his {Robert Temple's} claim is lacking," Coppens concluded.

In discussing the ideas of French chemist Joseph Davidovits, who proposed in 1974 that the huge stones of the Great Pyramid of Egypt weren't quarried but had been created using a chemical process known as geopolymerization, Coppens fashions a case showing how this theory makes more logical sense than asserting the ancient Egyptians used copper tools to chisel out and then transport 2.3 million gigantic blocks of granite and limestone weighing up to 80 tons each. He cites chemical analyses indicating the stones didn't come from nearby quarries but had been cast. Credit has been given to an ancient Egyptian engineer named Imhotep as being responsible for inventing the art of construction with cut stones 4,700 years ago. While Coppens argues "that aliens are unlikely to have built" the Great Pyramid, he wonders that since it was built with technology "far ahead of its time" but apparently in Imhotep's possession, was he "given this knowledge" by extraterrestrials.

Other ancient technologies he cites as possibly being inspired by or given by aliens include the Baghdad Battery and the Antikythera Device. The 5-inch pottery jar known as the Battery had been found in Sumerian ruins east of Baghdad in Iraq and contained a copper cylinder with an iron bar at the center; the cylinder was covered by tar, as was its copper base. When a replica of the battery was built by an archaeologist, and filled with freshly pressed grape juice, it generated a 0.87-volt current which would have been useful in electroplating gold onto silver objects. The Antikythera Device had been found in a shipwreck off a Greek island, and the lump of bronze turned out to be an intricate geared mechanism, the first known calculator, that seemed far beyond the knowledge or ability of the ancient Greeks. These out of place technologies prompt Coppens wonder if they had been alien-inspired.

He came to a similar conclusion about an ancient stylized gold artifact, nearly 2,000 years old, resembling a high-speed aircraft that was found in Colombia, one of 18 known to be in museums. Archaeologists claimed it depicted a bee in flight. But Coppens believes a recreation in large scale of the artifact, done by three Germans in 1994, demonstrated it was a model of a flyable airplane. Once a propeller was added to the nose and the wings were outfitted with flaps, it showed a stable flight path and easy takeoffs and landings. A second model using a jet engine design, and resembling a Space Shuttle, also proved aerodynamically sound.

What also makes Coppens wonder about extraterrestrial influence are the ancient Babylonian and Mayan calendars. The Mayan calendar is more than 90 million years long, whereas the Babylonian calendar was at least six million years in length. Were these long cycles of time a result of astronomical observations? Not likely. "Whatever these cycles represent, it is clear that our ancestors held these calendars to be important. It is equally clear that it had to have been a nonhuman intelligence that told our ancestors that a cycle of 90 million years was somehow important, for 90 million years ago there were no humans on this planet!"

His answer to the question 'were we alone' in ancient times is an unequivocal NO!

While he is open to the idea that aliens were physically present on our planet to inspire and educate us, he also finds merit in the idea that our godly benefactors "were not necessarily physically here, and may not *be* physical as such; they could best be described as a nonhuman, otherworldly intelligence that we can contact through a number of means, many of which today would be classified under the label of paranormal, parapsychological, or—a term I prefer—metaphysical."

Two weeks after completing this book, at the age of 41, Coppens died of a rare form of cancer in late 2012, a cancer thought to have been triggered by contact with an unknown toxic chemical substance.

---

*Lost Secrets of the Gods: The Latest Evidence and Revelations
on Ancient Astronauts, Precursor Cultures, and Secret Societies*
MICHAEL PYE & KIRSTEN DALLEY
(2014, Weiser)

This book is composed of a collection of essays from 11 different authors, including three articles directly related to aspects of the ancient astronaut theory.

In the first, Paul Von Ward, a former diplomat in the U.S. State Department, advances what he calls the advanced being intervention theory in which highly advanced beings (ABs) "have colonized and still are colonizing our planet," and "humans have some genes in common with these aliens." Given these genetic links to an un-earthly species, Ward says we humans are also aliens, who "can no longer claim to be the sole native citizens of Earth."

Different periods and events in human evolution, according to Ward, resulted in "anomalous physical characteristics" becoming entrenched in the human genome, as a result of AB manipulation of human evolution. From the Old Testament of the Bible, he pulls examples of extraordinary longevity and 'strange' physical appearances, such as Noah's "blue eyes, curly reddish hair, and pale white skin" so uncharacteristic of his tribe, to make a case for AB-human hybrids, the interbreeding with "daughters of men" accounts that took root in Hebrew and Egyptian traditions.

Stories of 'giants' and people in ancient times living for hundreds or even thousands of years are used by Ward as more evidence for AB interbreeding and genetic engineering. "More advanced beings from elsewhere in the universe have played a significant role in the history of Earth's humans," concludes Ward. "Some of these areas are the origins of language, alphabets and writing. The evidence suggests that human institutions have been significantly shaped by the agenda of advanced beings."

A second article by Ardy Sixkiller Clarke, a professor emeritus at Montana State University, describes her collection of nearly 1,000 stories "from indigenous people throughout the Americas, the South Pacific, New Zealand and Australia about their ancient stories and interactions with star people and encounters with UFOs." Her research has convinced her these stories aren't just myths but that "there must be something more to their legends" about visits from beings that came down from the sky.

She gives numerous specific examples of this Star People belief in oral traditions of indigenous people. Cherokee traditions hold that Star People arrived from another planetary system almost a million years ago; the Aborigines in Australia tell how Sky Gods descended from the heavens and are able to shape-shift; the Maori in New Zealand claim that their ancestors came to Earth from the stars; Star People and Sky God legends can be found among descendants of the Maya in central America. Says the author: "Whereas most anthropologists discard Native legends and stories of so-called primitive people as stories borne of superstitious cultures, this author believes that something happened to cause these legends to come into being."

Finally, the third article, by Texas journalist Jim Marrs, sketches an elaborate conspiracy that links together alien visitors in ancient times as part of a lineage extending all the way to bankers and rich families who control affairs of the world in the present day. These ancient visitors, who the Sumerians referred to as Anunnaki, ruled over humans using a priesthood that became the origins of all the world's religions. This clergy absorbed ruling families of kings and queens who advanced bloodlines that kept the human population under control with a blend of religion and economics, eventually evolving into an international class of money changers and bankers led by the Rothschild family bloodline, who now concentrate much of the planet's wealth.

Aliens and UFOs in Ancient China
YIN ZHE
(2016, CreateSpace)

This author/scholar describes himself as a bilingual Singaporean learned in Old Chinese, a skill which enabled him to translate and interpret ancient Chinese written passages about extraterrestrial visitation that might have otherwise been unavailable to most readers "because Old Chinese have different grammar, pronouns, syntax and word orders, when compared to the modern {Chinese language} vernaculars."

A series of three-meter-tall cliff paintings from the Neolithic age, located at the southern edge of the Eastern Yan Jiao Mountains, receive attention in this book because the "rather strange-looking beings...resemble that of astronauts donning peculiar looking space helmets." These images bring to mind ancient art from cultures throughout the world, described in countless other ancient astronaut theory books, which seem to portray extraterrestrial visitors.

The ancestral king of kings for the Chinese people is Jiang Shi Nian, who "taught the ancient Chinese people farming and agriculture and medicine and the use of herbal drugs." He was said to have a transparent stomach that was used to "monitor the effects of ingested plants." These descriptions seem to have more in common with an alien visitor than with a flesh and blood human being.

Another legendary ruler, known as the Yellow Emperor, was credited with giving the Chinese people "mathematics, music, astronomy, art, watercraft and the first Chinese medical text. All of it "seems to suggest that he was perhaps more than a man," owing to his achievements and the fact that he allegedly ruled for 100 years. Not only that, but his birth seems suspicious. His mother, Fu Bao, "one night witnessed an unusual electrical light which shone upon her," after which she became pregnant. She gave birth to the Yellow Emperor 25 months later. The author speculates all of this indicates a possible extraterrestrial origin.

In the last accounts of his life, the "Yellow Emperor rode on the dragon, together with 70 of his court ministers and maids, and the dragon ascended into the sky." The author of this book suspects the dragon was a spacecraft and not a mythical creature and that it took the Yellow Emperor and his entourage away to another realm, identified as a region of 17 stars in the Leo constellation.

Other ancient accounts from the days of the Qin Emperor describe visits from entities that sound to us today like they have extraterrestrial qualities. These entities did not resemble humans and emerged from craft that came up from underwater and departed the same way. This was the same period when 12 giants arrived, sent from the heavens, creatures that "bore a semblance to the popularly known Nephilims," described in the series of books by Zecharia Sitchin.

Numerous ancient accounts of what we today call UFOs are listed by the author. During the Jin dynasty for instance, a "sun-like thing" landed on the ground, and other reports were made of sun-like objects appearing at night, each time the circular object was only about 10 meters wide.

SECTION TWO

UFOs And UFO Occupants. . .

Are We Specimens in Their Cosmic Test Tube?

A Rohrschach Test Over Arizona

What was arguably the most widely witnessed UFO event in U.S. history occurred March 13, 1997, known to us now as the 'Arizona Lights' incident. A few months after the UFO event occurred, Reader's Digest magazine, at that time the most widely read publication in the world, where I worked as a Roving Editor, gave me the assignment of investigating what happened. The magazine's support enabled me to travel around Arizona and interview in person, or by phone, more than 50 witnesses, including many who would later become fixtures in the media as commentators on the incident.

During the interview process, I was particularly interested in finding three categories of witnesses: airline pilots who were flying that night and came close to the formation of lights, or communicated with them; air traffic controllers on duty that night; and observers who used binoculars to get close-up views of the lights from the ground. I found all three types of witnesses. What follows is a chronology of my findings in which I attempted to answer whether this event was extraterrestrial in origin, an elaborate hoax, misidentification of natural phenomena, or a staged incident as part of a psychological warfare test by the U.S. military.

A crystal-clear night sky over Arizona revealed the panorama of the Milky Way, its multitude of stars visible as a shimmering smudge brushed from one horizon to the other. Against this backdrop on March 13, 1997, the Hale-Bopp comet appeared at the peak of its brilliance, an arc glowing low in the northwestern sky. People not normally curious or prone to sky-watching ventured outside by the thousands, peering up at this awe-inspiring celestial display. The stage was now set for one of the more unusual and widely witnessed UFO events in human history.

To James and Fawn Clemens of Kingman, Az. the fuzzy but bright amber light hanging in the northwest, just to the right of Hale-Bopp, seemed odd and out of place, as if a second comet had materialized. It was 8 p.m. and the couple, both 42 years old, stood in the yard between their house and the taxidermy shop they operate, training their binoculars on the light.

It seemed to be over Nevada's Lake Mead, heading southeast. Instead of one

65

light, magnification from their binoculars enabled them to discern five intense orange orbs flying in a v-shaped formation. In all their years of stargazing they had never seen anything so mystifying before.

Driving along Highway 40 from Flagstaff, Az. to Laughin, Nev., Air Force veteran and pilot Rich Contry spotted the light formation, stopped his car, got out and focused his 10x50 magnification binoculars on them. "As if came towards me," he posted a few days later, on an Internet message board, "I saw five aircraft with their running lights (red and green) and the landing lights (white) on. They were also flying fairly slow and in the delta formation. As they went over me, I could see stars between the aircraft. Their jets were not very loud because of the low throttle setting for flying slow."

As the formation of lights passed near Chino Valley and then over Prescott Valley, sighting reports began streaming into local law enforcement agencies, media outlets, the National UFO Reporting Center phone line in Seattle, Wash., and hotlines throughout Arizona maintained by the Mutual UFO Network (MUFON).

At 8:13 p.m. Dennis Monroe and his wife stopped their car along a residential street in Paulden, Az. when the brightness of the approaching lights attracted their attention. They got out and watched the five peach or light orange-colored orbs fly overhead, traveling south in a kite-shaped formation. Monroe, 47, a former police officer, estimated the entire formation covered a part of the sky about the size of his fist if he held it at arm's length.

"They were the speed of helicopters and soundless. The lights were large and soft, not focused or concentrated. I thought I saw stars between the lights. We had them in sight for five minutes. Over the southern horizon they went out a few at a time, like they weren't 360 degree lights. As a police officer I learned to control my emotions, but this got me pretty excited."

Along Highway 89, about 90 miles north of Phoenix, Ross Nickle and his wife and their three children were driving north as the formation came into view. "They looked like five stars coming toward us," Nickle related to me. "They changed colors from white to red. There was no sound. I'm guessing they were 1,000 feet off the ground."

Not far away in Chino Valley, John Widener observed five white lights in a triangular pattern slowly pass to the north and east of Prescott airport, in the direction of Phoenix. Over Prescott Valley the lights were scrutinized through binoculars by at least two separate groups of comet-watchers. Ann Baker peered directly up at them passing silently above her and could see stars between the lights. "I did not see any solid mass. There were five bright, white lights in a v-shape formation. Then it actually changed formation. It was now in a half-circle with five red, bright lights."

Michael Rainwater and three friends noticed that once they focused their binoculars on the v-formation, "what looked like white lights were actually two lights, red and green, forming one. They appeared to be about 1,000 feet in the air."

Once the formation of lights intersected Interstate 17, they followed the heavily trafficked roadway south, a procedure often used by pilots who fly unfamiliar territory at night and navigate using Interstate highways. By 8:28 p.m., when the only known video of the formation was taped, the lights had traveled 184 miles from Kingman to the northern suburbs of Phoenix and Scottsdale, which translates to a speed of about 400 miles per hour.

A contract employee with the U.S. Department of Defense caught the formation on tape for 43 seconds from his backyard in north Scottsdale. Though poor in quality, the tape does clearly show five white lights in a v-formation, with one light gradually trailing behind the others.

Simultaneous with this video recording, three other clusters of witness reports helped to establish this formation was composed of five or more independent aircraft. MUFON investigator Alan Morey, a 36-year-old machinist, sat on the patio of his Scottsdale home with Pan Am pilot Steve LaChance. As the formation passed overhead they watched through high-powered binoculars.

"At first the lights appeared pale orange in color, but through the binoculars we could see a little red light on the port side of each of the five larger orange lights," Morey told me. "They were five independent objects because we could see stars between them. One light was behind the others in a delta wing configuration. But then the formation tightened. The lights covered an area twice the size of my fist if I extended my arm to the sky."

A few miles away Mitch Stanley, a 20-year-old amateur astronomer, aimed his 10-inch telescope at the v-formation and discerned that each light was actually two lights on aircraft with squared wings. "They were planes," he told the *Arizona Republic*. "There's no way I could have mistaken that."

North of Phoenix over Lake Pleasant, three pilots in the cockpit of an America West 757 airliner, headed to Las Vegas at 17,000 feet, noticed the strange v-formation of five bright lights off to their right and slightly above them in this heavily trafficked airspace. "Hey, there's a UFO!" co-pilot John Middleton kidded pilot Larry Campbell. Puzzled by what they were seeing, Middleton queried the regional air traffic control center in Albuquerque, N.M. A controller radioed back that the formation was a flight of CT-144's at 19,000 feet. Apparently overhearing this exchange, a pilot claiming to be part of the mystery formation spoke up.

"We're Canadian Snowbirds flying Tutors," the mystery pilot radioed Middleton. "We're headed to Davis-Monthan Air Force Base."

An air show performance team, the Snowbirds are pilots of the Canadian Air Force based at Moose Jaw, Saskatchewan, who fly CT-144's, a two-seat training jet nicknamed the Tutor, which has a single landing light in its nose. Normally the Snowbirds perform at North American air shows from April through October each year.

Though this answer satisfied the America West crew, they still found the other pilot's behavior to be unexplainable. Middleton kept wondering, why are they flying in a show formation at night with their landing lights on and pointed downward? Why are they intentionally trying to draw attention to themselves? Based on the radio traffic Middleton overheard, these were questions on the minds of numerous commercial airline crews in the air that night.

As the formation of lights penetrated more deeply into the heavily populated neighborhoods of Phoenix and Scottsdale, the descriptions given by witnesses underwent a profound transformation. No longer were the lights being seen as five independent objects in formation. Dozens of observers on the ground would swear, in interviews and sighting reports made in the weeks afterward, they witnessed a single boomerang or delta shaped craft, bigger than any known plane, flying low, slow, and silent. None of them making this claim, however, examined the object through binoculars.

Five Objects Morphed Into One?

Southwest Airlines pilot Greg Aguirre and his wife were driving home from dinner in north Phoenix when she excitedly blurted, "What are those lights!?" Aguirre stopped the car and jumped out. Five lights in a v-formation passed over him at an altitude he estimated at between 3,000 and 6,000 feet. Two of his fists held at arm's length would cover the formation. No navigation lights were visible and no matter how hard he tried to envision this as a flight of conventional aircraft, his mind recoiled from the awareness that the formation was flying much too slowly for planes, at a speed comparable to blimps. They made absolutely no noise.

"Then the next thing that struck me was why the landing lights would be pointed straight down," Aguirre told me. With 29 years of flying experience, including a stint as an Air Force fighter pilot, Aguirre wasn't used to "looking up in the sky and not being able to figure out what I'm seeing."

The lights so scared Aguirre's wife that she conjured up in her mind visions of the movie *Independence Day*, featuring a giant alien spacecraft ominously hovering over the city. "It gave me such a creepy feeling that I immediately got back into the car and started hugging myself and getting cold chills," she later confessed in an interview. Aguirre remained outside for about five minutes watching the lights disappear over mountains to the south. He has tried to keep an open mind about what he saw that night, yet this conclusion became inescapable: "I think what I saw was one object."

Not far away, 34-year-old real estate consultant Max Saracen and his wife, Shahla, were also driving home through an area with few street lights. They pulled to the side of the street and got out when they spotted the v-shaped formation of white lights overhead. "Oh my God, look at that!" they kept repeating to each other in stunned amazement. It seemed to be about 1,000 feet in altitude, flying silently at 20 or 30 miles per hour. Saracen says two of his fists held up to the sky would have obscured the object. "It was a solid mass of metal, but we saw no structure. It blocked the stars out. My wife saw some humanoid shapes at some of its windows. The movie, *Independence Day*, went through my mind. It was very spooky, this gigantic ship blocking out the stars and silently creeping across the sky. Without a doubt, we believe it was extraterrestrial from another world."

A dozen miles further south the lights passed over a Phoenix neighborhood which is situated at an elevation of about 1,800 feet. Laser printer technician Dana Valentine and his father, an aeronautics engineer, saw the formation over their house at a height they guessed to be no more than 500 feet. "We could see the outline of a mass behind the lights," the younger Valentine claimed. "It was more like a gray and wavy distortion of the night sky. I know it's not a technology the public has heard of before."

Six blocks away in the same residential neighborhood, Tim Ley, his wife Bobbi, and their son and grandson watched in astonished awe from their front yard as the five lights seemed to float straight toward them. "By the time it got about a mile away we decided it was definitely one huge structure, because the lights were so rigidly maintaining their relative positions to each other," Ley, a 54-year-old electronics repair shop manager, later reported. "We also noted that we still had not heard any kind of sounds. Where we live, up in this small mountain valley, we can hear the slightest engine noises from miles away. At this point, especially because of its apparent immense size and slow speed, it began to dawn upon us that this was a real UFO."

Ley described the v-shaped structure as slightly darker than the night sky and so huge that it covered several entire neighborhood blocks, with "the length of the arm passing over us probably about 700 feet long." He estimated that it floated at 30 miles per hour, skimming silently about 100 feet above the roof of their home.

"The kids started jumping up and down talking about how there was no sound and mentioning the movie Independence Day and exhibiting symptoms of hysteria. The kids were out in the street looking up inside in the space between the arms and they pointed out to my wife and I how strangely the stars looked, almost as if looking through a very thick glass with the slight distortion of the light as it passed through. Finally, after about 13 to 15 seconds, the last light on the tip of the right arm passed slowly overhead. The diameter of the light was at least 6 or 7 feet across. As the craft moved away from us towards the southeast the kids started running down the street after the object. The light I was focused on seemed to split into two lights, one above the other. Both lights remained white but took on a slight reddish/amber caste and it seemed that I was seeing the light through a kind of transparent waviness like a mirage.

We watched the object reach the gap through the mountain peaks, passing west of Squaw Peak, which is two miles southeast of our house. It went through the pass (between North Mountain and Squaw Peak) and headed out over the city. At the moment when the craft had just passed over us, I summed up all my immediate perceptions and feelings and thoughts into one conclusion: this craft was not from this world."

To the southeast of Squaw Peak, in a residential area one mile south of Camelback Mountain, the 21-year-old daughter of Sue Watson, a boy's school administrator, noticed the lights seemingly coming straight over the 2,704-foot-tall Camelback. From the front yard she screamed to her mother, "Come quick. You won't believe this!"

Watson dashed outside along with three of her other children. They saw seven bright, whitish lights approaching their home. "We could see the outline of the craft. We couldn't see stars through it. It was boomerang shaped, and going slowly and soundlessly." Watson estimated the craft to be 10 of her fists held up to the sky, its underside lit up in an amberish color. Giddiness from this sudden excitement prompted the entire Watson family to reflexively wave at the object as it went overhead, "disappearing really fast to the south."

A few miles east of Phoenix's Sky Harbor Airport, from his workplace in northwest Tempe, Bree Crownover and four friends noticed red/orange lights in the northern horizon on a flight path intersecting airliners traveling east to west for landing at Sky Harbor. According to Crownover, "the red/orange lights seemed to be lower in altitude and oblivious to the fact they were flying directly toward commercial aircraft traffic. They were in a v-formation, three red/orange lights in front, two red/orange lights behind and to each side. There seemed to be no 'body' to this aircraft, only lights. When directly overhead, it was so large it wouldn't fit into direct vision. I had to shift my eyes to see the entire object. At this time, we realized that this was not one object, it was five or more, with one light in back trailing slightly. The lights moved slowly to the south."

While closing a window in his bedroom, three bright, white lights attracted Mike Fortson's attention. Thinking a plane was about to crash at Sky Harbor Airport, located 23 miles to the northwest of his Chandler home, Fortson grabbed his glasses and yelled to Nannette, his wife, "Get outside, right now!"

From the patio they viewed a boomerang-shaped object—about the size of eight of his fists held up to the sky—moving silently and slowly south. Three bright white beams of light projected from the front, trailed by five solid, non-blinking red/amber lights on the side and rear. All the lights appeared to be angled down at the ground. The craft seemed to pass under a 737 airliner in its landing approach path.

Observed Fortson: "There was a bright bottom quarter moon setting in the west, and as the front of the v-shaped craft entered the light of the moon, this black chevron object became translucent. We could still see the bottom quarter moon through the object, but the moon turned a dingy yellow. As the craft exited the bright moon, it became a solid black object again, and disappeared to our south." The impact of this sighting on Mike, 44, and Nannette, 43, proved life-altering: "This was so profoundly my most significant visual experience ever," Mike marveled in his interview with me, "like the hand of God coming down."

Once beyond the southern suburbs of Phoenix, the formation of lights followed Interstate 10, toward Tucson. Driving north just past Casa Grande, Dr. Bradley Evans had just commented to his wife, Kris, that in 22 years as a psychiatrist and private pilot he had never seen a UFO. Without missing a beat, she replied, "Well, then what is that?!" In the sky ahead of them seven bright reddish-orange glowing orbs could be seen.

As the couple, their teenage daughter, and their daughter's friend watched, the lights changed to a yellowish-white color and moved into a diamond-shaped formation traveling south along I-10. "I had no sense at all that this was a solid object," Dr. Evans later related. "I could see background stars between the lights. In an instant the lights were directly overhead (the car's moon roof was open.) While our car was traveling at about 63 miles per hour, and the lights apparently moving south and east, they seemed to hold directly overhead for about five to 10 minutes, still holding formation. We could hear no aircraft engine noise whatsoever. I thought this was odd since the lights seemed to be at about 1800 feet in height. I could see stars immediately around the lights and within the formation itself. Not one vehicle ever pulled to the side of the highway to watch, including ourselves! And I had no desire at all to take any pictures. Psychologically this is really very strange."

Still further along I-10, about 10 miles south of Casa Grande, Stacey Roads, her mother and daughter, and two friends of the family, all of Tucson, observed three orange-yellow lights heading straight for their car. "What in the hell is that?" exclaimed the car's driver. Both girls stuck their heads out the backseat windows and began screaming, "It's a UFO!"

Roads looked at the car clock and noted the time—8:42 p.m. Here she picks up the narrative. "The object was huge, an immense black shape. It came over the freeway, using I-10 as a map of some sort. We were under its shadow for over two minutes and we were traveling 80 miles per hour in the opposite direction. It was a huge triangular metal mass, with three lights far apart, and seams of metal on the underside. It was only a few thousand feet off the ground and this thing blotted out the stars. This thing was so big you could land planes on it. I could have held open a newspaper to the sky and not been able to block out the object. Like in the movie Independence Day, that's how big the thing was. I couldn't focus my camera to fit it all in, so I didn't get a shot of it. It was headed for Tucson. All five of us are in agreement the thing was not from this planet."

One of the last and southernmost eyewitness reports that evening came from a concrete truck driver, Gary Morris, driving north on I-10 about 80 miles outside Phoenix. "It looked to me like a flock of geese with flashlights in their mouths," he commented.

Later that same night, around 10 p.m., a second unusual aerial event occurred— by coincidence or design—which would complicate attempts to sort out the evening's chronology. Six A-10's from the Maryland Air National Guard, on an annual training mission known as Operation Snowbird, dropped high-intensity illumination flares at 15,000 feet over an Air Force gunnery range 40 miles southwest of Phoenix. Each 1.8 million-candle-power flare was suspended from a parachute, burned for up to 10 minutes, and could be seen clearly for a radius of over 100 miles, creating the impression among Phoenix-area witnesses of nine giant white objects in a chorus line over the mountains. Numerous video camera operators recorded this display and the tapes played repeatedly on Arizona television stations fueling a belief in the minds of many that the v-shaped formation seen earlier in the evening had returned.

Enigmas Inside of a Mystery

Divergent Witness Reports: Both Arizona Governor Fife Symington and Mutual UFO Network field investigator Alan Morey witnessed the lights formation around Phoenix at about the same time, yet they had fundamentally different accounts of what they saw, reflecting the division of opinion that occurred among hundreds of other witnesses.

Here is how Gov. Symington, a former Air Force pilot, described his sighting on the Larry King Live show a decade after the event happened: "I saw a craft…this large sort of delta-shaped, wedge-shaped craft moved silently over the valley, over Squaw Peak, dramatically large, very distinctive leading edge with some enormous lights. And it just went on down to the Southeast Valley…It was definitely not an airplane…I think it was from another world…It was enormous…the lights over Phoenix was a very compelling, dramatic event seen by so many people that you can't just blow that off and say everybody in Phoenix was hallucinating."

By contrast, Morey and his friend Steve, a Pan Am 727 airliner pilot, provided this account: "We were on my patio facing due North at 8:30 pm. We had binoculars and had been watching planes land. We saw a cluster of lights coming from the direction of the comet and moving independently. Extremely bright lights pale orange in color. Through the binoculars we could see five independent objects. We knew they were separate because we could see stars between them. They were in a delta wing configuration headed south. The whole array went over my home. We could hear nothing as they disappeared over South Mountain. My personal view is that it was a military stealth exercise from Nellis Air Force Base in Nevada or Holloman Air Force Base in California."

The Symington and Morey reports best reflect the sharp polarization which emerged among the hundreds of witness accounts from that night. People either thought they saw a gigantic vehicle visiting from another world, or else a formation of planes that was behaving oddly. A few speculated that if the lights were attached to a single huge craft, it might be an experimental military vehicle. Some UFO enthusiasts have even suggested that multiple UFO and other events were happening that night to account for the variety of craft descriptions.

Were there observers in the 'extraterrestrial craft' category of witnesses seeing a single huge object who trained binoculars on the lights that night? If so, I never found them. Everyone I interviewed who studied the lights through binoculars came away insisting that the lights were five separate objects that appeared to be planes.

The only known publicly released video recording of the lights in a v-formation, taken by a Phoenix-area contract employee with the U.S. Department of Defense, is 43 seconds in duration. I have a copy of it and have viewed it many times. It shows five bright white lights. One in the formation falls gradually behind the others, much as planes flying in formation often do.

Were Canadian Pilots Pulling a Hoax? In the radio exchange between the America West airline crew and a pilot claiming to be a part of the lights formation, the mystery pilot said "we're Canadian Snowbirds flying Tutors." From their Canadian Forces Base in Saskatchewan, the Snowbirds, officially known as the 431st Air Demonstration Squadron, tour the North American continent from April through October performing at air shows. They fly the CT114 Tutor, a two-seat trainer. It has a single whitish-colored landing light in its nose that can be pointed downward.

To get more information, I had numerous contacts with Major Jeff Young, Chief Flying Instructor for the Snowbirds. He told me the following: "we could find no record of our jets going cross country in that time frame. We can't find anybody in our operation who could have been responsible for the lights that people saw." Major Young did concede that Tutor planes could have been in Arizona that night flown by pilots other than the Snowbirds performance team.

That view was echoed by Captain Mike Perry, squadron logistics officer for the Snowbirds, who mentioned that out of 100 Tutor planes at their base, it was possible that "some may have been flown to Arizona by pilots from our training school, but it was not our performance team. We don't travel in a v-shaped formation. We travel in threes and we never fly with our landing lights on."

Major Young also gave me these characteristics of the Tutor aircraft. Its maximum cross-country speed is 420 miles per hour, but it can travel as slow as 100 mph before the engine stalls. The fuel tank range is 450 miles, with another 100 miles available by using an extra tank. And most importantly, Tutors have a landing light in the nose of the aircraft that can be pointed downward.

Is it a coincidence that the lights over Arizona traveled the state from northwest to southeast at an average speed of about 400 miles per hour, within the Tutor cruising speed range? Is it a coincidence that the maximum fuel tank range for the Tutor is 550 miles and that distance covers a non-stop flight from the Area 51 military facility in Nevada to the Fort Huachcua military airfield in southern Arizona, south of Tucson?

One other thing worth noting: Snowbird isn't just the name of the Canadian air show team. Operation Snowbird was the name given a military flare drop exercise conducted later that night, after the main sighting event, over the Barry Goldwater Gunnery Range southwest of Phoenix.

Could the mysterious formation of planes have been communicating to the America West crew that they were from Canada and were participating in the Operation Snowbird exercise, if not on that night, then on subsequent nights? Rather than Tutors, might the Canadian military pilots have been flying A-10s, which was the primary aircraft being used in the Operation Snowbird exercise? Did the mystery pilots have their landing lights on and pointed down as a joke, a hoax, just to see what the American reaction would be? Or did they have another motive?

No Radar Identification? Despite having traversed the entire state of Arizona over a nearly one-hour period, no civilian radar sightings of the formation were recorded, or at least released to the public.

Southwest Airlines pilot Greg Aguirre, one of the witnesses who I interviewed, pointed how planes flying above 10,000 feet would be under the jurisdiction of Albuquerque regional controllers, but if they were below 3,000 feet "they wouldn't have to identify themselves to anybody." The formation seemed to spend most of its flight time over Arizona at between 10,000 and 17,000 feet, according to other pilots in the air. Once over Phoenix, witnesses reported the lights to be flying much lower, at one point crossing directly over the flight path of planes landing and taking off from Phoenix Sky Harbor Airport.

A controller on tower duty that night at Phoenix Sky Harbor, Bill Grava, told me that the lights didn't show up on tower radar, nor did controllers visually see the lights, despite the fact that he and other controllers were getting numerous radio requests from other pilots in the air to identify the formation. This seemed quite odd. Furthermore, as Martin Hardy, manager of Sky Harbor Air Traffic Control, explained to me, "We're really not sure what happened that night. Unless it was some sort of military exercise, I don't know what it could be. They didn't show up on our radar. But our tower radar only goes up to 3,000 feet."

Other air traffic control towers in Prescott and elsewhere in the state, whose personnel I queried, claimed not to have observed the lights or registered anything unusual on their radar screens. If the planes had transponders, they apparently were turned off that night because no airport registered them. As air traffic controller Rich McIntosh was quoted as saying, "The Air Traffic System is designed to identify aircraft who want to be identified. It is very easy to elude FAA radar."

My attempt to get answers about flight plans filed for what was in the air that night from officials in Albuquerque, the FAA regional center, proved frustrating. They claimed to have no records of anything unusual. An FAA official in Seattle told me that if the pilots were Canadian, they should have filed a flight plan by computer or radio at their first point of entry into the U.S., which would have been Great Falls, Montana. But there was no such documentation, or at least nothing anyone would release.

Was the formation of lights invisible to radar, much as a formation of stealth fighters might have been? Were the transponders turned off on this formation of five planes? Or was something else even stranger going on involving intentional radar jamming?

Did Fighter Jets Intercept the Lights? There had been reports that fighter jets were scrambled that night to intercept the formation of lights. When I posed this question to officers at Luke Air Force Base in Phoenix, they informed me that F-16s from the base had been sent up that evening "for night training," which they claimed to do routinely almost every night.

Public Affairs spokesman, Senior Airman Petosky, issued this statement in response to my many persistent queries: "I can tell you flat out there was no intercept that night of any lights formation."

But was that completely accurate? On a website called The UFO Chronicles, dated January 26, 2009, an anonymous writer nicknamed Topol-M, claiming to be a former Luke Air Force Base airman, gave a different account of Luke's role in the sighting incident. Since this claimant is coming forward anonymously, we must treat his or her information with some caution. But elements of the story ring true. Here is the provocative claim.

On that March night, Luke scrambled two F-16C's from the 56th Fighter Wing and vectored them towards Tucson. Less than 10 minutes later a second set of F-16Cs were also scrambled. Pilots from the first flight reported by radio that "something odd" was happening, but they didn't give any specifics over the radio.

A radar sighting of the lights formation allegedly occurred north of Casa Grande, Arizona, somewhere below 10,000 feet, but the pair of jets making this contact picked up "radar clutter common to stand-off jamming." Radar at both Luke and Davis-Monthan "were picking up low level 'noise' on several frequencies…this 'noise' was consistent with active wide-spectrum jamming."

One pair of the intercept jets flew all the way to the Mexican border as the lights "passed over the outskirts of Tucson and over Fort Huachuca." This first intercept flight of jets lost contact with the lights "approximately 7 miles south of Tucson."

As I will explain in a moment, if all of any of this is true, it's an important and revealing piece of the puzzle because Fort Huachuca south of Tucson, may hold the key to this entire night of mystery.

The flares that were dropped around 10 pm on the Goldwater training range, this anonymous source related, "was a deception measure" to keep people focused on the sky because "flares were never used that far north of the Goldwater training range...if they were, there would be weekly Phoenix Lights incidents."

Coincidences or Design?

The Light's Flight Origin: When the first UFO sighting reports began coming in that night, the formation of lights were seen coming from the direction of Las Vegas along a commercially trafficked air corridor. Nellis Air Force Base is outside of Las Vegas. When I sent queries to base commanders about whether any planes fitting the light's description had originated there, I was contacted by a Sgt. Covington of the public affairs office who informed me that "all our base had in the air that night were F-18s, F-15s and F-16s over Nevada on training missions. We had nothing over Arizona. But transient aircraft passing through aren't tracked by us."

There is, however, one other military facility in the direction from which the lights were seen coming from—the notorious Area 51 in the Nevada desert, an aircraft development and testing facility so top secret at the time that the U.S. military wouldn't even acknowledge the air base existed to me or anyone else in the media.

The Light's Flight Direction: Was it by coincidence or by design that the formation of lights came from the same general direction as the Hale-Bopp comet that hung brilliantly in the northwestern sky and which had already attracted the attention of thousands of skygazers that night? Numerous witnesses made the statement to me that, "it was as if the lights wanted to be seen by as many people as possible."

The Light's Flight Path: After following Interstate 17 south to Phoenix, the formation of lights then flew along Interstate 10 to Tucson. Does it make sense that an extraterrestrial vehicle would travel here from billions of miles away, or even from another dimension, only to land on Earth and then rely on Interstate highways for navigation? Or does it make more sense that a group of pilots unfamiliar with the terrain and flying at night would use the line of car headlights along the easily identifiable Interstate system as a navigation tool? Or better yet, they followed the Interstate system because the pilots wanted to be seen by as many people as possible?

The Light's Destination: When the radio exchange occurred between the America West airline crew and a pilot claiming to be part of the mysterious formation of planes (lights), the mystery pilot said they were headed to Davis-Monthan Air Force Base in Tucson. But when I interviewed a spokesman for the base, Sgt. Deborah Van Nierop in the public affairs office, I was told: "We have no records of them landing here."

The only other major military facility in the direction near where the lights were last reported that night is the Army's Fort Huachuca, at the Mexican border. Here is what we know about Fort Huachuca, based on public information that is widely available. It is located outside Sierra Vista, southeast of Tucson and south of Interstate 10, which the lights had been following. It has an airport, Libby Airfield, with three runways for military aviation.

Fort Huachuca is home to the U.S. Army Intelligence Center, which trains military intelligence personnel for all four branches of the U.S. military. The Thunderbirds performance air team trains here. It has an Electronic Proving Ground and a training center that specializes in imagery, deception, counterintelligence and electronic intelligence.

Psychological warfare tactical training occurs at Fort Huachuca. This bears repeating. Huachuca is a psychological warfare training center!

How Could Such a Rorschach Test Work?

What I am about to provide is mere speculation on my part. No inside source or active participant has yet stepped forward, at least to me, and revealed details of how and why such a psychological warfare experiment, if that's what it was, would be conducted on thousands of unknowing U.S. citizens. Nor has anyone come forward to explain why, if this was just a hoax, pilots would jeopardize their careers by violating Federal Aviation Administration rules against flying at night cross-country in a show formation with their landing lights on.

Let's start our analysis with an observation. Something stands out about what many witnesses to the incident noticed and remarked on to me. These are people who believed they had viewed a single gigantic object in the sky, but who didn't confirm that perception through binoculars. These people are sincere. They are relating what they actually believe they saw. I have no reason to doubt them. But there is a consistent thread of a clue in their accounts that has been overlooked.

The comments made to me not long after the event happened went like this: "the mass behind the lights was more like a gray and wavy distortion of the night sky," said witnesses Dana Valentine and his father.

"In the space between the arms, I pointed out to my wife how strangely the stars looked, almost as if looking through a very thick glass with the slight distortion of the light as it passed through," remarked witness Tim Ley.

"It seemed that I was seeing the light through a kind of transparent waviness, like a mirage," Ley further observed.

"There was a bright bottom quarter moon setting in the west, and as the front of the v-shaped craft entered the light of the moon, this black chevron object became translucent," said witness Mike Fortson. "We could still see the bottom quarter moon through the object, but the moon turned a dingy yellow."

An obvious question arises. Was this single object image a projection?

The Most Prosaic Explanation First

To get a sense of our natural perceptual limitations as human beings, I interviewed an expert in this area, Dr. Barry Byerstein, a professor of psychology at Simon Fraser University in Vancouver, British Columbia. (He has since died.) He made these observations about how normal people react when they see something new to their experience which they can't identify or rationally explain:

"The brain is always trying to create a model of reality. We all have the tendency to fill in details. Even highly trained and experienced people can make bad guesses and errors about size and distance. The limbic system of the brain screens information and matches it with experience, so we seek validation for our worldview and cosmology. Groups of people often come to a consensus about what was seen based on adopting the perspective of one influential member of the group."

Continued Dr. Byerstein: "Our perceptual experience is a construction. It's not like a video camera. The process of perception is a creative act affected by our prior experience and hopes and cultural conditioning. Human memory doesn't store a literal videotape of events. It stores summary statements and a few important details. Memory is more like the village storyteller than a tape recorder."

Factoring these observations into the sensory experience people had that night, we have two important details to work with:

1) The lights or object was absolutely silent. On this point, all witnesses were in agreement. There was no engine noise. There wasn't even a swooshing sound. This could have happened if the lights were much higher in altitude than the witnesses thought.

2) Once over the Phoenix area, the movement of the object or lights appeared very slow, more like that of a blimp than planes whose engines could have stalled at low speeds. Some witnesses had the lights in view for up to ten minutes. Again, this could have happened if the object or lights flew much higher in altitude than people perceived.

What could have distorted witness perceptions? Maybe atmospheric conditions. Though the skies were said to be crystal clear over most of Arizona, there was a haze from pollution reported over and around Phoenix. Could that have produced enough of an atmospheric filter to warp people's perceptions of sight and sound?

The pattern of evidence points us in another direction.

Holographic Deception Technology

During my interviews in and around Phoenix, I met with Mutual UFO Network field investigator Richard Motzer who was the first to offer this speculation: "the event might have been a military exercise creating holographic images, which would explain why the description varies so much on the object seen that night."

But was such a deception even technologically feasible? We know that military breakthroughs in technology usually occur a decade or more before civilian applications begin to appear. That's one of the advantages the military has with generous taxpayer funding of its secret 'black ops' projects.

During the first decade of the 21st century, we began to see some of these advances in holographic research receive attention in science journals. An edition of *Science Daily* (June 15, 2005) carried an article summarizing science papers that had appeared in *Optics Express* and other specialized journals showing how a laser-based holographic system works in practice. One example given in the article of how this technology can be applied was the holographic image of circling fighter jets projected to a point in the sky.

Over the years I had heard rumors that the technology necessary to project three-dimensional images to a point in space had been tested at Fort Huachuca and elsewhere during the 1990s. But until the Arizona Lights event in 1997, there had been no clear evidence that these electrical optical and laser devices had been used to target a civilian population to test their reactions to unusual phenomena.

You can imagine how such technology might be useful to the military as a psychological warfare terror weapon. If you can fool an enemy into believing what they are seeing is an extraterrestrial spacecraft rather than U.S. military craft, you can manipulate their will and ability to effectively resist. Holographic deception in a battlefield situation can provide all sorts of tactical advantages.

Illusions in the sky can be silent and made to appear huge, slow moving, or even motionless. Such a holographic effect might appear to witnesses at times as a 'wavy distortion' in the sky, or a 'mirage,' or 'translucent.' You will recognize all of these descriptions as being among what many witnesses reported the night that five lights over Arizona appeared to be a single huge aerial craft.

Through The Looking Glass

Those mystery pilots responsible for the five lights morphing into the image of a single gigantic craft were using a convenient cover story. When queried by other pilots or air controllers about their odd behavior, they claimed to be 'Snowbirds,' which was left open to interpretation. Their statement could have been interpreted to mean they were from the Canadian Snowbirds air show team, which, of course, they weren't. Or their statement could have been interpreted to mean they were participating with the Snowbirds military exercise later that night dropping flares over a gunnery range outside of Phoenix. They didn't do that either.

These pilots may have engaged in radar jamming so that none of the civilian or even Air Force control towers could identify them. It was a deviously clever move if the flare drop was intentionally timed to sow further confusion about what really happened that night. The ruse succeeded on that score because numerous videos of the flare drop were paraded around for months afterwards as a UFO event in their own right.

Once expert analysis exposed the videos as having recorded nothing but flares, that finding made it easier for cynics to pounce and dismiss everything happening that evening, including the mysterious five lights, as simple observer error and a product of hysteria and wishful thinking.

Ironically or not, a few months after the Arizona Lights event in 1997, an unclassified version of a study from the usually secret CIA journal, *Studies In Intelligence*, was released discussing the CIA and U.S. Air Force deceptions of the American public during the 1950s and 1960s, a disinformation campaign trying to deflect attention from U-2 and SR-71 spy planes being flown from bases in Nevada by encouraging speculation these were UFOs. The article admits that CIA officers working undercover, masquerading as U.S. Air Force officers, contacted the media, UFO researchers, and UFO witnesses to plant false stories about what had been seen. Even more stunning, and in alignment with what I speculate may have happened in the Arizona Lights case, the CIA journal confessed this disinformation campaign was intended to evaluate how the agency *"might use the UFO phenomenon in connection with U.S. psychological warfare efforts."*

What happened over Arizona on the night of March 13, 1997 deserves to be enshrined in our collective memory. Though it wouldn't be the first time that an intelligence agency of government used its citizenry as unsuspecting guinea pigs, if that is what happened, it would be the opening salvo of a Brave New World in which our consensus reality is manipulated.

POSTSCRIPT: The Tragic Aftermath

Thirteen days after the Arizona Lights event occurred, the 39 members of the Heaven's Gate UFO cult committed suicide by ritualistically poisoning themselves at their spacious home outside San Diego, California. They believed that a spacecraft trailing the Hale-Bopp Comet had made its appearance and would transport their souls aboard for a glorious trip to the stars. They had interpreted what happened in the sky over Arizona as a signal that the timing was right for their ritual mass suicide.

Less than three weeks after the Arizona Lights incident, Captain Craig Button, 32 years old, flying out of Tucson's Davis-Monthan Air Force Base—where the flare dropping A-10 planes had come from—piloted his A-10 Thunderbolt fighter 800 miles off course and intentionally crashed it into a Colorado mountain. He reportedly had a conversation just days earlier with relatives that the Lights over Arizona might herald a Second Coming and the end of the world.

A month later, Captain Amy Svoboda, 29-years-old, also flying an A-10 out of Davis-Monthan, crashed her fighter into the desert of southwestern Arizona. Circumstances surrounding her death remain a mystery.

The Evolution of UFO Theories and Evidence, 1950 Onward. . .

The Ether Ship and Its Solution
MEADE LAYNE
(1950, Borderland Sciences)

"Ether Ship" is a generic term for flying disks and other unidentified aerial craft, ether being "the true nature and origin" of these phenomena that have appeared at intervals throughout history. Meade Layne, founder of the Borderland Sciences Research Foundation, and the first theorist to originate a clearly metaphysical explanation for UFOs, believes these visitors are neither friendly nor hostile to humans, regarding us with indifference except when we discomfort them by clumsily attempting to master nuclear fission.

That region of existence known as the etheric plane, or Etheria, surrounds, engulfs, and coexists with us, imperceptible to our senses, appearing to us as empty space. Yet there is no emptiness in the universe. Matter only varies in its density and substance. The dense matter of our world is a rarefaction, "spaced out like a vast net-a net with enormous meshes," through which other matter and energies flow, like wind and water through a fisherman's net. Fill a bucket to the brim with large stones, pebbles, and sand. Our material world would be like the pebble, or a grain of sand. "Things do not really occupy the same place," the author states, qualifying, "it is only that the enormous places we call empty are all filled up."

From the etheric plane, or "empty space," these craft materialize, awakening our perceptions and lowering in vibration their atomic motion, a process that is like a fast fan slowing down until we can see its blades. At certain stages of materialization, or at certain pressures or altitudes, "the substance of the ether ships is jellylike and actually does change in shape and apparent size." In flight ether ships often follow the magnetic meridians, north and south, since these areas are where the etheric vortexes form.

These ether craft were known in antiquity, Layne writes, by at least a few persons of unusual training or gifts who "understood their origin and purposes." Rosicrucians refer to the nothingness that is Etheria with the phrase: "Space is the unperceived aspect of Reality." Occultists, adepts, and initiates for thousands of years have preached of an etherian existence. "There has always been a store of secret knowledge in the world. In fact, all advanced technical knowledge is secret in a sense, to all except the few who can understand and apply it." Chaldean oracles written about 3,000 years ago say at one point: "From the ether have come all things, and to it all things return; the images of all things are impressed upon it; it is the storehouse of the germs or remains of all visible forms and even of ideas."

Etherians are not excarnate humans, but a race of beings born into and dying within that world beyond our senses. "They have knowledge of our world and can and do penetrate it." Persons in our realm possessed of "exceptional psychic powers" involving thought projection or clairvoyance are able to perceive to varying degrees the etheric regions.

Layne believes that a number of ether ships resembling disks have landed "through accident of some kind" on our material world. He does not know whether the "dwarf occupants" survived the impact. Since, so he was told, the scientists who inspected these craft found no visible drive mechanism, they must use "some kind of magnetic propulsion."

Because etheric matter "is responsive to thought-energy," human beings can actually materialize, under the right conditions, a projection of consciousness. Many UFO sightings could be subconscious thought forms of the observer. The Etherians encourage these manifestations. They "are intensely desirous of awakening earth people to an awareness of other forms and regions of life than our own-for our own sake and for theirs also."

Behind the Flying Saucers
FRANK SCULLY
(1950, Henry Holt)

Frank Scully boasts that in an October 12, 1949, column for Variety, the show-business magazine, he became the first journalist to confirm the reality of flying saucers. Ten weeks later, Major Donald Keyhoe wrote "The Flying Saucers Are Real!" for *True* magazine, an article that generated newspaper headlines and put the Air Force on the defensive. Scully dismisses the Keyhoe piece as a poorly done "rewrite" of previous material. Scully claims, however, that he uncovered the story of the century when, in a series of columns for Variety, he revealed how the Air Force had captured a flying saucer and its crew of sixteen. His book is based on that series of columns.

Through an oil millionaire named Silas Newton, president of Newton Oil Company, Scully says he met Dr. Gee, a magnetic engineer released only two months earlier from government employment. Dr. Gee and seven other government scientists had been sent to New Mexico to examine the first of three saucers that crashed. He and a geophysicist who is never identified allegedly told Scully the following story.

Accompanied by Air Force officers, the scientists were sent to a rocky, high plateau east of Aztec, New Mexico. For several days they studied the 100-foot-diameter saucer from a distance, testing and recording it with Geiger counters and other devices until they were sure it was safe to approach. One broken porthole allowed them a view inside. They discovered sixteen bodies ranging from 36 to 42 inches in height. Their skin seemed charred a dark chocolate. The scientists found pamphlets or books in an indecipherable script. An aluminum-like metal encased the saucer's hull, but it proved unlike any metal on Earth in its strength and lightness. The scientists theorized that it used a magnetic propulsion system.

The bodies of the sixteen tiny occupants, dressed in matching dark blue garments, without insignia, collars, or sleeves, were taken to research labs, where they were dissected and studied. Each must have been thirty-five to forty years of age, by our standards. Other than their teeth, which had no cavities, they appeared to resemble humans in every respect. Food had been discovered in the saucer, consisting of small wafers. Water taken from two containers proved to be twice as heavy as Earth water.

Soon thereafter, a second saucer crashed near a proving ground in Arizona. Sixteen more tiny humanoids were found inside. This saucer was 72 feet in diameter. A third even smaller saucer landed in Paradise Valley near Phoenix; only two humanoids were found within the 36-foot diameter craft. Decompression apparently killed the occupants in each instance. Since at the time of writing no other crashed saucers had been reported, the scientists concluded that these visitors must have solved the problem of decompression.

Scully alleges that his two sources allowed him to inspect a tubeless radio, some gears, and tiny disks that had been taken from these saucers. He reports that the gears "had no play, no lubrication." The radio contained no tubes or wires, only one dial, and could have fit into a pack of cigarettes. "It wasn't a radio as we know it, but it was a means of communication with somewhere."

Armed with this information, Scully posed twenty questions to the U.S. Air Force.

He asked whether the thirty-four humanoid bodies could be found in a preservative solution "placed between human specimens from prenatal to grown man in an exhibit in Chicago?" Question 17 read: "Do you know how magnetic waves emanate from the sun, revolve around the earth, continue on the earth's moon, come back to the earth, and return from there to the sun?" The U.S. Air Force never bothered to reply.

The Riddle of the Flying Saucers
GERALD HEARD
(1950, Carroll & Nicholson)

Seven chapters describe such "classic" sightings as Kenneth Arnold's nine disks over Mount Rainier, the Maury Island doughnut shaped saucers and the alleged residue they left behind, the death of Captain Thomas Mantell who thought he was chasing a flying saucer, and the air duel between Air National Guard pilot George Gorman and a bright light less than 1 foot in diameter—a light the author believes was projected as bait from above to see what "men-minnows would do."

The author dismisses the suggestion that flying saucers are a product of Russian or American technology. But might other humans, composing "some association that was not public but private," possess the capabilities to construct these mysterious craft? He wonders whether a secret society on Earth, "a body of men who thought that they could manage the world better than any one of the governments of today," hasn't built a fleet of flying saucers "as a first step to taking over world government." But he finds little or no evidence to support this suggestion.

Of all the planets in the solar system, Heard selects Mars as the most attractive possible environment for life similar to our own. Because Mars is further from the sun than Earth, he assumes the inhabitants must be more advanced. And what sort of inhabitants would they be? He quotes astronomer Gerard P. Kuiper: "No form of life as we know it could exist on Mars but insect life."

Based on current (1950) studies of the insect world, Heard concludes that bees, ordinary honey bees, are the most advanced species of insect known to humans. Bees apparently are capable of thought, they constantly exchange information and make plans, communicating in a complex sign language. "Now if the mentality of our Bees has developed, why should not insects in the world of Mars-so much more ancient than ours-have gone ahead? We should indeed assume that this must be so."

He finds it "difficult to resist" the conclusion that Mars is ruled by insects, that they are even now visiting Earth, piloting flying saucers as large as 1,000 feet across. These superbees are only about 2 inches in length, yet "as beautiful as the most beautiful of any flower." Martian bees have "eyes like brilliant cut-diamonds, with a head of sapphire, a thorax of emerald, an abdomen of ruby, wings like opal, legs like topaz such a body would be worthy of this 'super-mind.'" In the presence of these superbees, should they ever decide to make themselves known to us, "it is we who would feel shabby and ashamed, and maybe with our clammy, putty-colored bodies, repulsive!"

How could 2-inch superbees pilot a 1,000-foot-long flying saucer? Heard draws an analogy to ternlites, which build houses to almost human dimensions. We must also remember that these superbees "are immensely ahead of the Bees here-or any insect." Perhaps they have learned to use materials other than the wax primitive Earth bees use. As their first step into space, our Martian visitors probably launched synthetic satellites, like the Martian moons Phobos and Deimos, which Heard believes are hollow and artificial.

So why do these superbees from Mars buzz Earth in their flying saucers? "Because they fear what our industrialization seems to lead to intensive wars that drive us finally to the air, to rockets, to atom power, to the capacity not only to destroy ourselves, but to make [our planet] into a kind of cosmic bomb." Heard urges Earth scientists to establish communication with Earth bees, the queens in their hives, since these "might be able to act as invaluable translators and interpreters when, and if 'Bees' of a still more advanced breed might swarm upon us." Our bees could tell the Martian bees that humans "in spite of our unprepossessing appearance, our lack of method and order, our laziness shot-with-violence," are not "really or wholly creatures of blind instinct, but capable, if treated kindly, and not frightened into panic, not only of reasonable behavior and of seeing things from our own interest and security, but also of something approaching at times to detached curiosity, and even, it is to be believed, of compassionate interest!"

The Coming of the Saucers
KENNETH ARNOLD & RAY PALMER
(1952, Clark Publishing)

Kenneth Arnold, a private pilot and fire extinguisher salesman, flying near Mount Rainier in Washington on the afternoon of June 24, 1947, sighted nine bright objects resembling silver wings without fuselages that traveled faster than any aircraft he had ever seen. They flew or fluttered in formation, and later, in describing their flight characteristics, he said they moved "like a saucer would if you skipped it across the water." That day in popular literature was created the "flying saucer" by which all future reports would be categorized. This book chronicles the resulting baptism of Arnold into the ranks of those seeking to solve the UFO mystery.

At the time, Arnold thought the objects he had seen were guided missiles, since no other known aircraft could attain the 1,350 miles per hour he had calculated for their speed. But other evidence quickly accumulated. On July 4, the crew of United Airlines Flight 105 observed two loose formations of disks over Idaho, nine objects in all. That same evening a Coast Guardsman captured on film an image of a disklike object in flight. These were certainly not like any known guided missiles.

On July 29, with $200 in expense money from Ray Palmer of Venture Press, Arnold set off to investigate a report by two harbor patrolmen in Tacoma, Washington, that they had not only seen the objects but possessed pieces of one. While at about 5,000 feet over Union, Oregon, Arnold claims he sighted another formation of UFOs, this time twenty or twenty-five brass-colored objects, round and rather rough on top, that fluttered like wingless ducks. Several farmers later reported seeing this peculiar cluster of objects.

Someone, Arnold never found out who, had reserved a Tacoma hotel room in his name. That proved only a preview of the bizarre circumstances surrounding his first venture into UFOlogy. The two harbor patrolmen told an incredible tale. On the afternoon of June 21, three days before Arnold's sighting, they were patrolling Maury Island about 3 miles from the mainland when six doughnut-shaped craft appeared overhead. Each loomed about 100 feet in diameter, a shell-like gold and silver in color. One object spewed forth fragments of a dark and a lighter-colored metal that struck the harbor patrol boat, damaging it and killing their dog.

For several days Arnold and Captain E. J. Smith, who piloted the United Airlines plane, questioned the harbor patrolmen and examined several pounds of the alleged "saucer metal," fragments that looked and felt like lava rock, slag, or salvaged aluminum. The metal appeared to be a clumsy hoax, which only deepened the mystery. If the harbor patrolmen were perpetrating a hoax, neither Arnold nor Smith could figure out what they hoped to gain from it. Of further concern, several news reporters had been calling their hotel room during these meetings and claiming that a "crank caller" had eavesdropped, overhearing every word of the interviews. Arnold and Smith searched the room for bugging devices, but found none.

Two officers from Military Intelligence arrived to interrogate the harbor patrolmen. Later that evening, carrying a large box bulging with "saucer metal," the Air Force officers boarded a B-25 for the return trip to Hamilton Field in California. Their plane crashed soon after takeoff. Both men died.

Within a few days the harbor patrolmen disappeared, leaving behind practically everything they possessed. Arnold returned to where one of them lived. The house was deserted, cobwebs matted the windows, yet only four nights earlier Arnold had been inside, seen furniture and a family. He apparently never discovered the whereabouts of the two men.

Why had two men with nothing to gain concocted such a hoax? Arnold puzzled over the implications. He suspected involvement by the Soviet secret police, using the patrolmen as undercover operatives in seeking clues to the saucer mystery. Perhaps he and Captain Smith, as two UFO witnesses, had been milked of information even as they questioned the harbor patrolmen, or maybe the hoax amounted to an attempt to undermine their investigation and lead Military Intelligence astray. Had the B-25 been sabotaged? Had the metal fragments on that plane been fake, but the others real? Who were the two harbor patrolmen and why did they disappear? Arnold apparently never learned the answers.

Flying Saucers from Outer Space
DONALD E. KEYHOE
(1953, Henry Holt)

Retired Marine Corps Major Donald Keyhoe, writing in 1949 for True magazine, concluded that flying saucers were probably interplanetary machines. One year later, in his book *The Flying Saucers Are Real!*, Keyhoe again insisted that the U.S. Air Force knew these vehicles were interplanetary, but for reasons that were unclear, perhaps to prepare the public for this shocking news, the military had adopted a policy of secrecy and cover-up. This book is a continuation of Keyhoe's attempt to document that government policy.

He reports the ridiculous ploys to which the military resorted in debunking UFO reports. Several are memorable. Dr. Urner Liddel, of the Office of Naval Research, confidently asserted that the Navy's skyhook cosmic-ray research balloons accounted for all reported UFOs: "There is not a single reliable report which is not attributable to the cosmic balloons," he said. Even the death of Captain Thomas Mantell, whose F- 51 disintegrated over Kentucky in 1948 while pursuing a huge, round, metallic object, could be attributed to a balloon, according to Liddel. But Air Force Intelligence disagreed. Mantell died, their analysts claimed, as he chased the planet Venus.

Keyhoe had initially been concerned that the saucers were a Russian secret weapon. Too many sightings were being reported over atomic energy plants, Air Force and Navy bases, aircraft plants, major cities, and high-altitude rocket testing bases. Gradually he became convinced the devices could only be extraterrestrial in origin, piloted by a potentially hostile and dangerous race from Mars, or another planet in our own solar system. "I'm convinced the green fireballs are guided missiles," he writes at one point, discounting an attack as their motive for coming if only because they had been seen in the skies for four years without landing in large numbers.

The author noticed that color is somehow connected with UFO propulsion. Whenever disks accelerate, they seem to suddenly brighten, then dim again on slowing for turns. The electromagnetic nature of their propulsion was first evidenced in 1947, on the same day Kenneth Arnold made his famous sighting near Mount Rainier, when an Oregon prospector saw several disks over the Cascade mountains. As they circled nearer, the needle on his compass began gyrating.

Keyhoe quotes at length a Canadian electronics engineer, Wilbert "Wilbur" Smith, director of that government's UFO inquiry. Smith reasoned that flying saucers avoided low reconnaissance over inhabited areas because eddy currents induced by the propulsion unit's magnetic field would blow fuses and bum out wires in power lines. Smith also seemed persuaded that the disks came from Mars because scientists had recently observed an atomic like explosion on that planet's surface.

This electromagnetic theory got public attention in 1952 when Joseph Rohrer, president of Pike's Peak Broadcasting Company in Pueblo, Colorado, announced that seven crashed saucers had been recovered by the government, and one 3-foot-tall saucer crewman captured alive. These craft supposedly used electrostatic turbines that created magnetic fields, enabling the machines to achieve tremendous speeds. Variations in the magnetic field resulted in the color changes. The crewman was being held in an incubator somewhere in California; linguists had educated him in English, using pictures. Rohrer made these revelations in a Chamber of Commerce speech that received considerable newspaper and radio coverage. Keyhoe urged the Air Force to deny or disprove the report since Rohrer claimed he had actually been inside one of the disks. The Air Force ignored Rohrer, telling Keyhoe that any response would only generate more publicity.

Citing predictions by the Joint Chiefs of Staff alluding to possible mass A-bomb attacks by the Russians in 1954, Keyhoe warned that any government policy of leaving UFOs unexplained or unidentified might result in the Soviets boasting that the objects were their secret weapons. By paralyzing our communications systems with bogus UFO reports, the Soviets could overwhelm the United States in a sneak attack.

Keyhoe offers six possible reasons why the flying disks are in our skies: the fear that humans will be warlike once space travel is achieved; a fear of our own "more powerful atomic explosions," which they observed from space; perhaps the visitors also use atomic energy and have come to mine uranium; the saucers may intend to invade and conquer the Earth; another unknown plan besides conquest may be in effect; or, they may be surveying and studying the Earth, waiting until we convince them of our peaceful intentions before establishing meaningful contact.

The Case for the UFO
MORRIS K. JESSUP
(1955, The Citadel Press)

Since the dawn of civilization, human beings have recorded the "erratics" or "oddities" known today as Fortean phenomena, freak occurrences such as rocks, ice, and animals falling from the sky, people disappearing, fireballs, and the strange lights we call UFOs. Astronomer

M. K. Jessup believes "we are the posterity for whom these data were recorded." Isolated and lonely facts that never seemed to fit in were preserved for a purpose, "and the solution of the mystery of the UFO's may well be that purpose."

As far back as 1500 B.C., and even before, flying saucer reports have been recorded. The oldest and most prolific sources for descriptions of wingless flight "are the records of the Indian and Tibetan monasteries." Jessup relates dozens of sightings of disklike objects seen through the centuries until the late 1800s, sightings on which he bases his contention that humans have always been under the watchful eye of other intelligences.

These visitors from elsewhere may have temporarily colonized parts of Earth, leaving behind as calling cards the megalithic structures on Easter Island, on the plains of Peru, at Baalbek in Lebanon, and in Egypt. Flying saucers used some means of interacting with the gravitational field to levitate into position the giant stones composing these structures. No other explanation suffices, says Jessup, because "there is little... to show a gradual development of so advanced a culture or civilization" to account for human construction of the megaliths.

Other artifacts extraterrestrials either left behind or inspired humans to produce include the crystal lens found in Babylon, thought to be 5,000 years old, indicating a high level of optical knowledge. Iron nails, "straight with perfect heads," have been found embedded within quartz, coal, and other minerals at a depth of hundreds of feet. Coins have been found within rocks during mining operations, old Roman coins and others not easily identified. "They may have been dropped from space ships," theorizes Jessup.

That chunks of ice have fallen from clear skies indicates to Jessup that "space contrivances" of the extraterrestrials shed coatings of ice upon entering our atmosphere. That storms sometimes appear suddenly in otherwise undisturbed skies indicates to Jessup that they may be artificial, created by an intelligence to conceal something. That fish and other Earth land animals have fallen from the sky indicates to Jessup that spaceships occasionally empty the contents of "celestial hydroponic tanks" in which collected Earth specimens are kept. And that apparently human flesh and blood has been seen falling from the sky not only indicates to Jessup that "our space friends" are flesh and blood, but provides clues as to the whereabouts of human beings who have vanished suddenly under mysterious circumstances.

Jessup devotes two entire chapters to missing ships and planes. He recounts the disappearance of ship crews aboard the Sea Bird and the famous Marie Celeste. He relates how, in the 1940s, five military planes with fourteen men aboard vanished on a training flight over the Atlantic several hundred miles from Miami. A Navy bomber with thirteen men aboard sent to find the five aircraft also, in the words of Jessup, "vanished... forever...without a trace!" Fifteen years after the publication of this book, an entire spate of paperbacks popularized this disappearance off the coast of Florida. Some of these "Bermuda Triangle" books used Jessup's phrase "vanished without a trace." One of the authors, John Wallace Spencer, borrowed Jessup's thesis that "no explanation other than that of abduction by intelligently navigated...craft can be advanced" for these disappearances.

Based on his observation of unusual lights and strange happenings on the moon, Jessup contends that flying saucers are based there. He proposes that extraterrestrials have constructed space islands, using "as their most natural and permanent habitat" the points in space where the gravity of the Earth-Sun-Moon is neutralized.

It appears to Jessup that the Russians during the post-war years were concealing something from the rest of the world. Have the Russians captured a space ship? Or have space people taken over the Red Empire? He suspects that the secrets of levitation and ancient flight, preserved by holy men in the Himalayas, have fallen into Russian hands since the Communist capture of Tibet and China.

The Report on Unidentified Flying Objects
EDWARD J. RUPPELT
(1956, Doubleday)

To Edward Ruppelt must go the credit for inventing the term "UFO," or "Unidentified Flying Object," as an alternative to the more widely used phrase "flying saucers." As chief of the Air Force's Project Blue Book during the period 1951-53, Ruppelt's perspective on the phenomenon wavered somewhere between that of skeptic Dr. Donald Menzel, the Harvard astronomer, and Donald Keyhoe, the former Marine Corps major who became convinced in 1948 that UFOs were interplanetary spaceships. This book chronicles Ruppelt's three years as a UFO investigator, his methodology, his solutions, and in many instances, his puzzlement over what competent and credible witnesses claimed to have seen.

Of several thousand UFO reports received by the Air Force from 1947 through 1953, up to 20 percent remain unexplained or unexplainable. Skeptics offered many explanations, but for Ruppelt their facts often did not fit the theories. Even the figure 20 percent for unexplained cases is misleading. "I think it would be safe to say," he writes, "that Blue Book only heard about 10 percent of the UFOs that were seen in the United States."

Ruppelt continually found himself under orders to tell the public only about the sighting reports the Air Force had solved, never mentioning all those for which no solution could be found. "I know that the negative approach is typical of the way that material is handed out by the Air Force," says Ruppelt, "because 99 percent of the story was devoted to the anti-saucer side of the problem." He accuses Project Grudge, the Air Force UFO project that preceded Blue Book, of having launched a campaign "that opened a new age in the history of the UFO," an era he refers to as the Dark Ages. Every sighting had to be written off as solved, even if it wasn't, or couldn't be, so as to "put an end to UFO reports" altogether.

Among those who have seen UFOs but failed to report them for fear of ridicule, Ruppelt found astronomers to be the highest caliber of observers. A representative sampling of astronomers by Project Blue Book found 11 percent admitting they had "seen something that they couldn't explain." "For a given group of people," Ruppelt concluded, "this is well above average." A similar sampling of people interviewed at random found only 1 percent who had witnessed unknown aerial phenomena.

Although Ruppelt and Project Blue Book systematically discarded into a crackpot file all reports from people claiming to have seen and spoken with UFO occupants, or to have examined UFOs while on the ground, one close encounter involving a Florida scoutmaster defied the crackpot file and easy explanation. After an evening meeting, the scoutmaster and three of his troopers were driving near West Palm Beach on a sparsely traveled black-top road when they noticed what looked like airplane lights descending into a palmetto thicket. Believing a plane had crashed, the scoutmaster grabbed a machete and two flashlights, told his troopers to remain in the car, then began clawing his way through the waist-high brush. About 30 yards later he reached a clearing, where he smelled a pungent odor and felt a stifling heat. Hovering about 30 feet in the air was a dark object that appeared circular and greyish in color when he shined his flashlight on it. A small ball of red fire emerged from the object, drifted toward him, then engulfed him in a mist. He passed out.

The troopers in the car had seen the ball of fire but not the UFO, and went for help. When the Highway Patrol arrived, the scoutmaster had regained consciousness. His arms, face, and cap were burned. One of the flashlights was missing and never found. Ruppelt uncovered nothing to directly contradict the scoutmaster's story, but while conducting a character investigation of the scoutmaster, he became convinced that the witness could not be trusted. Then some unsettling pieces of evidence came to light. A lab analysis indicated that burns on the scoutmaster's cap had been made by an electrical spark. Similarly, grass samples from the site of the alleged sighting showed that the roots had been charred by an intense heat. The mystery deepened. Only by the generation of a powerful alternating magnetic field could Ruppelt explain how grass roots might be burned. That would also explain burns on the cap, possibly even the pungent odor. If it was ozone gas, a product of an electrical process, it could render someone unconscious. If the case was a hoax, says Ruppelt, it was "the best hoax in UFO history."

According to the laws of normal distribution, "if UFOs are not intelligently controlled vehicles, the distribution of reports should have been similar to the distribution of population in the United States-it wasn't." UFOs were "habitually reported" around areas of technological interest, such as atomic energy installations, harbors, and manufacturing centers, yet seen in fewer instances around military bases and regions of large population.

Two physicists with the Atomic Energy Commission revealed to Ruppelt how their colleagues had discovered a correlation between radiation levels in the atmosphere and the presence of UFOs. From 1948 until 1951, the year these experiments were discontinued, scientists found on at least a dozen occasions that background radiation increased 100 times above normal when UFOs, usually described as dark or silvery circular objects, were seen overhead.

Ruppelt succeeded in disproving many of the "classic" UFO sightings, such as the Lubbock lights photographs (streetlight reflections off swarms of moths or birds), the death of pilot Captain Thomas Mantell (chasing a skyhook balloon), and the Maury Island incident in which pieces of a UFO were reputedly found (it turned out to be a hoax). But always a residue of reports remained to keep Ruppelt mystified. What constitutes proof, he wonders. "Does a UFO have to land at the River Entrance to the Pentagon, near the Joint Chiefs of Staff offices?"

The Truth About Flying Saucers
AIME MICHEL
(1956, S. G. Phillips)

Flying saucers all display the same definite characteristics, writes mathematician and engineer Aime Michel. That translates into four mysteries: their tremendous accelerations in violation of the law of mass ratios; their resistance to the intense heat generated by friction with the surrounding air; the absence of supersonic booms or other noises in association with their movement; and the mystery of their ability to alter shape and appearance.

These mysteries are profoundly shocking to conventional science. We simply cannot imagine solid bodies changing shape, noiselessly breaking the sound barrier, violating the principles of fluid mechanics, or subjecting occupants to instantaneous turns and accelerations. But Michel thinks perhaps a solution has been found.

Writing in Forces *Aeriennes Fran aises* (September 1953), the official organ of the French Air Force, a young officer named Lieutenant Plantier proposed a mathematical formula for construction of the ideal interplanetary vehicle. An engine, propelled by particles of cosmic radiation, would create a force field similar to a magnetic field between poles. He calculated that such a machine, to attain peak efficiency, must be shaped like a disk. Air molecules would be dragged along "at speeds proportional to their proximity to the engine," resulting in soundless movement. Within such a field, acceleration would not affect the passengers. Changes in speed through the atmosphere should cause alterations in color and luminosity in the ionized air surrounding the vehicle. This process would also occasionally produce what is known as "angel's hair," which would quickly disintegrate as the ionization dissipated, remaining in the air and on the ground long enough for observers to mistake the chemical reaction for pieces of the saucer.

Naturally, as Michel points out, all these characteristics of Plantier's hypothetical machine had long since been witnessed in the behavior of flying saucers. If the saucers exist, Michel is convinced Plantier's theory explains their propulsion. He chronicles a series of sightings where the relationship between color and movement is evident. When a saucer momentarily travels in a jerking motion, as many are seen to do, that enables the vehicle to deaccelerate without having to reduce its field of propelling force. Green then merges into blue until the saucer attains full acceleration, when it appears a brilliant white.

Going back to Roman times, mention can be found of disks maneuvering just as Plantier envisioned his ideal interstellar craft would in flight. Latin historian Pliny, in his Natural History, referred to "disci" as a peculiar kind of comet. Aristotle earlier described disks in his *Meteorologica*. They have been seen cavorting over battlefields, swooping down and terrifying whole armies. During World War II pilots called them "foo fighters," and Michel chronicles several incidents in which these balls of light were mistaken for enemy craft.

European records reveal an increase in saucer sightings when Mars is aligned to the sun. September and October also seem to be peak months. He wonders why UFO sightings are so common over White Sands, Los Alamos, and other areas connected with national defense. Military theorists might suppose this indicates a Russian spy program, while psychologists maintain that workers in environments built around secrecy and suspicion eventually find that which they fear in the sky. Michel has another theory: UFOs are often observed around military installations simply because the equipment necessary to spot them is concentrated there.

They Knew Too Much About Flying Saucers
GRAY BARKER
(1956, Saucerian Press)

Why were Richard Shaver, a welder; J.D. Desvergers, a scoutmaster; UFO researchers Albert Bender and John Stuart; Harold Dahl, a harbor patrolman; and radio newscaster Frank Edwards, all silenced when they began revealing what they knew about flying saucers? Gray Barker believes "forces or agencies" exist on this planet to prevent UFO investigators from learning the truth about the nature of the phenomenon.

Voices speaking to him through a welding machine told Richard Shaver of vast caverns below the Earth's surface, artificially constructed and inhabited by a demented race known as the Dero, who delighted in the playful torture of human beings, making them hear voices and causing them to have accidents. These Dero accounted for the devils and witches of folklore, materializing in seances through mediums in trance. An ancient conspiracy of silence kept information about these caverns from human ears. Anyone prying into this matter flirted with danger. For five years, Shaver wrote these "true" tales in Ray Palmer's science fiction magazine, Amazing Stories. Then for some reason, says Barker, this magazine dropped the Shaver series "like a hot potato" after five years of popular acclaim. Barker doesn't think Shaver was perpetrating a hoax, so it must have had something to do with the truth being uncomfortable for someone.

J. D. Desvergers stumbled out of a palmetto thicket babbling incoherently. He had been driving three of his Boy Scout troopers home near West Palm Beach, Florida, when they saw an object with windows like an airliner appear to crash. He left the scouts in the car and went to investigate. He came upon a dome-shaped object hovering over a clearing. A ball of fire struck him, knocking him senseless, burning his arm and his yachting cap. After questioning by Air Force officers, Desvergers refused to reveal publicly any details about his encounter. Barker theorizes that government agents threatened to blackmail the scoutmaster if he didn't keep secret certain details pertaining to a creature seen aboard the vehicle.

Albert Bender of New Jersey left the UFO business after being visited by three men in black suits who frightened him into believing that he had chanced upon the secret of UFOs. They pledged him to secrecy, apparently on grounds of national security. Bender would never reveal what agency, if any, the men represented. Only a month earlier, on August 28, 1953, an FBI agent questioned Gray Barker about his association with Bender's saucer organization. Six months later, John Stuart of New Zealand, a friend of the author's, advanced a theory connecting Antarctica to the saucers. His life has never the same. Apparitions mocked and menaced him, until he deserted his UFO research forever.

Harold A. Dahl of Tacoma, Washington, claimed a man in black appeared after he and another harbor patrolman saw a doughnut-shaped object eject a large quantity of metallic residue that damaged his boat and killed a dog. Dahl collected some of the slag like material. The man in black allegedly threatened to harm Dahl and his family if he revealed what he knew.

When Mutual Broadcasting newscaster Frank Edwards used his program to crusade against Air Force censorship of saucer sightings, his American Federation of Labor sponsors pulled the show off the air. Thousands of protest letters from UFO enthusiasts were ignored. "If they couldn't frighten someone into silence," Barker contends, "they bring economic pressure to bear."

Flying Saucers and the Straight-line Mystery
AIME MICHEL
(1958, S. G. Phillips)

For two months, from late August through October of 1954, France experienced an unprecedented wave of UFO reports. As French mathematician Aime Michel chronologically charted these sightings on a large map, patterns began to form. Sightings occurring on the same day were found to be in straight lines. These alignments and the scientific method used to compute them Michel described as "orthoteny," a Greek term meaning stretched in a straight line.

On September 24, six sightings were reported stretching along a line from Vichy to Bayonne, an unwaveringly straight line almost 300 miles long. In each sighting, luminous round or cigar-shaped objects were seen. Could this alignment of six sightings be based on mere chance, asks Michel, or was it due to ordinary phenomena, like a balloon or a fireball? Balloons, of course, do not travel in straight lines. Fireballs sometimes do, but are seen over a vast area because of their height.

Could the sightings have been the result of psychological factors, hallucinations, lies, or hoaxes? Such an explanation "assumes that a wave of hallucinations, lies, and delusions can travel along a straight line." Michel also rejects theories proposed by Harvard astronomer Donald Menzel that ascribe UFO sightings to optical effects and misinterpretation of natural phenomena, since witnesses in many instances reported hearing sounds, or found themselves temporarily blinded by the lights. The only alternative, Michel concludes, aside from the extraterrestrial hypothesis, is that human thoughts, in some unknown way, actualized these visions.

As the weeks went by, hundreds of sightings overwhelmed law enforcement agencies. Michel noticed that even the daily alignments of sightings began to assume patterns of their own. The network of sightings, as plotted on his maps, converged in large star formations for the month of October. That chance or coincidence could explain such convergences seemed unlikely. Michel detected in these patterns an intelligent and premeditated design.

Many witnesses reported close encounters with the objects and their occupants. Motorists often told of experiencing heat and electric shocks, sitting helplessly as their motor died and headlights went out when brilliant luminous objects passed overhead. Dozens of reports filtered in describing these shock symptoms. A half dozen or more persons told of confronting large-eyed, short creatures in "diving suits." M. Antoine Mazaud became the first man in Europe to claim he had seen and touched an extraterrestrial when on the night of September 10, as the fifty-year-old farmer walked home with a pitchfork on his shoulder, he came face-to-face with an unknown creature wearing what seemed to be a helmet. The creature entered a dark thicket accompanied by a low hum, like bees buzzing. A dark object, 20 feet long and cigar-shaped, shot up out of the forest and into the sky. Mazaud told his story to the police, bemoaning that he had not "killed him with the pitchfork, so that I could find out what he was."

Later that same evening, 300 miles to the north, a thirty-four-year old metal-worker saw two short creatures enclosed in divers' helmets enter an object that rested on the railroad tracks outside his home. Police investigators later found five identical depressions 1 1/2 inches square on the wooden railroad ties. The marks were fresh and sharply cut, in a symmetrical pattern. Railroad engineers "calculated that the pressure revealed by the prints corresponds to a weight of thirty tons." For the first time in the history of UFOs, says Michel, "a saucer landing had left undeniable traces."

Are these alien beings deliberately avoiding us? Is contact between intelligent species for some reason impossible? Or is contact going on between select humans and these visitors, but in secret? Michel offers another hypothesis: Contact may be real, but it is usually invisible to us. If contact occurs on their level, rather than ours, "then no matter what we do, it will forever remain imperceptible to us, just as most of our relationships with animals are altogether undiscoverable by them." Perhaps our eyes can see these extraterrestrial visitors, but our consciousness is blind to them. We are able to perceive only what is at our psychic level or below it, like the mouse that nibbles on old leather-bound books, never realizing that something far more important than food is being consumed.

Flying Saucers: A Modern Myth of Things Seen in the Sky
CARL G. JUNG
(1959, Routledge & Kegan Paul, Ltd.)

For ten years, Swiss psychoanalyst Carl Jung studied UFO reports as a symptom of psychic change in humankind. "These rumors, or the possible physical existence of such objects, seem to me so significant that I feel myself compelled ...to sound a note of warning," he writes.

He puzzles over why the belief that UFOs are real "suits the general opinion to the point that disbelief is to be discouraged." He asks why it should be more desirable for flying saucers to exist than not. He wonders whether it isn't difficult to form "any correct idea" of these objects "because they behave not like bodies but like weightless thoughts." With these and related questions Jung examines the UFO phenomenon as a complement to, or the cause of, "long lasting transformations of the collective psyche."

This psychic component of the phenomenon Jung details is represented by three stages, or interconnections: in the first, an "objectively real, physical process forms the basis for an accompanying myth"; in the second, an archetype, those specific forms our collective instincts take, creates a corresponding vision; then, emerging with these two "causal relationships," we experience synchronistic behavior, the meaningful coincidence, in which the psychic stress of humankind and the appearance of UFOs coincide as a meaningful pattern.

Jung uses myths, dreams, art, and the sexual implications of the shapes in which UFOs are most often manifested, to construct a historical framework to trace the psychological evolution of the UFO vision. He first considers UFOs as simply rumors, or psychic products, different from ordinary rumors in that they are expressed using visions. These visionary rumors have been recorded throughout history-among the 70,000 persons at Fatima in 1917 and among the Crusaders during the siege of Jerusalem. Belief in extraterrestrial life, like belief in a Supreme Being, sufficiently excites the emotions to bring about a delusion of the senses.

Collective distress or anger, fear over apocalypse, the claustrophobia and paranoia caused by overpopulation, all combine to produce the emotional tension that is the basis for rumor and the resulting psychological projection. This projection can be seen at work in mental illness, in political propaganda, and even in so-called normal people who are least prepared to experience or believe in the UFO phenomenon yet make the most credible witnesses when their belief systems are challenged by a UFO sighting. "In just these cases," writes Jung, "the unconscious has to resort to particularly drastic measures in order to make its contents perceived. It does this most vividly by projection, by extrapolating its contents into an object, which then mirrors what had previously lain hidden in the unconscious."

In the frequently reported disklike and cigar-shaped UFOs, Jung sees a sexual symbolism. The disk, or circle, corresponds to the womb, while the cigar, or cylinder, is a penis image. But beyond these symbols is deeper meaning. Round bodies are often produced in dreams and visions as analogous to the mandala, the symbol of totality, a modern symbol of order known since ancient times as the sun wheel or magic circle of alchemy. The soul was also said to assume the form of a sphere, hence UFOs might represent a mythological concept of soul. When the projection thrusts itself "to the forefront in the form of a symbolic rumor," as does the UFO, an archetype expressing order, wholeness, and salvation is activated. Jung finds it characteristic of our age that this archetype has taken "the form of an object, a technological construction," which makes it easier for humans to accept.

Scientists such as Donald Menzel, the UFO skeptic, too easily restrict themselves to common explanations. Jung claims that this results in the exclusion of all that is "exceptional and extraordinary." Professor Menzel has not succeeded, despite all his efforts, in offering a satisfying scientific explanation of even one authentic UFO report," writes Jung.

"It boils down to nothing less than this: that either psychic projections throw back a radar echo, or else the appearance of real objects affords an opportunity for mythological projections." Jung says he cannot speculate on whether UFOs are "manned machines or a species of living creature" making appearances in our atmosphere from places unknown.

"If these things are real-and by all human standards it hardly seems possible to doubt this any longer-then we are left with only two hypotheses." They are either a psychic projection or a material phenomenon. That something psychic could possess material qualities and a high charge of energy "surpasses our comprehension."

If material, perhaps they "have long been visible to mankind." But only now, because our existence seems threatened, because we look to outer space for escape, has the contents of our collective unconscious been projected on these objects, giving them "a significance they in no way deserve."

They Live in the Sky
TREVOR JAMES CONSTABLE
(1959, New Age Publishing Co.)

Sky Creatures: Living UFOs
TREVOR JAMES CONSTABLE
(1976, Confucian Press)

In these two books Trevor James Constable, an aviation author and radio electronics officer in the U.S. Merchant Marines, develops the theory that many UFOs are creatures, or critters, as he calls them amoebalike aerial life existing in our atmosphere in the plasma state.

Critters can change their density, materializing in metallic appearance when crossing the visible infrared range of the electro magnetic spectrum; ordinarily they exist beyond the range of human vision in the stratosphere. They travel through the air by pulsating, reflect solid returns on radar, and are usually disk-shaped or spheroid, with a transparent structure that allows a view of their interior. They propel themselves using orgone energy-the biological energy possessed by everything living-as proposed by Dr. Wilhelm Reich.

Constable's theory that UFOs are bladderlike and biological found first expression in a 1950 monograph, The Ether Ship Mystery and Its Solution by Meade Layne. Decades earlier, in 1919, Charles Fort had speculated about sky critters in The Book of the Damned. Constable, however, claims he photographed the critters in large numbers.

The rapid and prolific development of radar during World War II disturbed the ether blanketing this planet, resulting in appearances by these "foo fighters," which reportedly chased after aircraft during bombing missions. On April 27, 1949, in an official release, the Air Force observed that many UFOs "acted more like animals than anything else." Even the man who popularized the word "flying saucer" based on his sighting of disklike objects near Mount Rainier in 1947—Kenneth Arnold—concluded "after 14 years of extensive research" that UFOs "are groups and masses of living organisms" in our atmosphere.

Many UFOs are observed on or near water, which is a fundamental animal trait. When critters are in our density and polarity, contends the author, they are capable of glowing with blinding intensity; they also kidnap and consume animals found around these water sources, and when fired upon by our jet planes, they aren't beyond consuming a few of them, either.

Constable claims to have been in psychic communication with UFO intelligences-those from extraterrestrial spacecraft, not the critters-who conveyed to him information on how to photograph the critters. These beings supposedly told Constable that they were constituted of various orders of etheric intelligences capable of materializing at will. They are engaged in a struggle for control of human minds, battling against negative forces "from beneath man" to determine the future course of evolution on Earth.

Anatomy of a Phenomenon
JACQUES VALLEE
(1965, Henry Regnery)

"Flying saucer" says Jacques Vallée is a term first coined not in 1947 by pilot Kenneth Arnold, as most people believe, but sixty-nine years earlier. A Texas farmer of "undoubted veracity," John Martin, described a dark object that passed over him near Dallas as a "large saucer." *The Dallas Herald* published the account on January 24, 1878. The age of flying saucers had been born.

Vallée details other milestones: The first reported landing of a flying saucer with a dome occurred in April 1897, in Carlinville, Illinois. George Adamski's story of having met a blond, long-haired Venusian in 1952 somewhere in the California desert inspired the modern-day "contactee" phenomenon, but Adamski was not the first. Throughout history, similar tales have been told. David Fabricius in the seventeenth century claimed contact with inhabitants of the moon. An eighteenth century Swedish mystic named Swedenborg wrote of visiting with moon men who were the size of children. Eliminating cultist claims and obvious hoaxes, Vallée counts more than 150 instances of beings, ranging in size from dwarfs to 8-foot-tall hairy giants, reported as occupants of UFOs.

According to his examination of historical reports between 1914 and 1946, a period of rapid development in balloon and plane technology, the skies remained virtually empty of unknown objects. This period of little or no UFO activity became "one of the richest in science fiction stories of all kinds," from the Orson Welles radio portrayal of War of the Worlds, to Flash Gordon, horror films, and fantastic novels of space adventure. Given this thirty-two-year period with few sightings, there would seem to be little substance to the theory that UFO rumors are stimulated by public interest in science fiction, or as a safety valve to release psychological tensions.

Fifteen persons are thought to have died directly or indirectly in connection with sightings of UFOs. All but one died as a result of plane crashes when pilots attempted to chase unidentified objects. UFOs are often responsible for power failures in aircraft, cars, and other vehicles. Diesels and jets have never been known to be affected. When a UFO flew over two tractors, one a conventional engine, the other diesel, only the conventional quit functioning.

Vallée denounces scientific analysis that "distorts a set of unknown phenomena until it is recognizable by ordinary standards." He calls this the "Harvard syndrome." Evidence of extraterrestrial intelligence, if only because it is extraterrestrial, would necessarily filter through such an analytical system undetected. Numerous examples are cited. On November 12, 1887, a huge ball of fire was seen slowly emerging from the ocean. The sphere moved against the wind to a height of 17 meters, stopped near the ship from which it was being observed, then shot into the sky and disappeared. It remained in view for five minutes. The French astronomy journal *L'Astronomie* explained the object away as "ball lightning."

Flying Saucers-Serious Business
FRANK EDWARDS
(1966, Lyle Stuart)

Former radio broadcaster Frank Edwards believes Russia and the United States have an ulterior motive in the race to reach the moon and explore outer space. He relates a "wealth of oddities" seen on the moon's surface. He wonders what Army Major Patrick Powers meant when he said, in Family Circle magazine, that "the first men to reach the moon must be prepared to fight for the privilege of landing." Is the moon an extraterrestrial space base? "Unless we actually know that our moon is being used as a way station by the UFOs, then our crash drive to get there is not readily understandable," writes Edwards. "If we do know that the UFOs are there, or HAVE BEEN THERE, then the urgent nature of the moon program makes some sense."

From the Bible, a few "very old" Irish manuscripts, and 19thcentury American newspaper clippings, Edwards gives various descriptions of unidentified objects allegedly seen by persons from every social background. Over the past 100 years, Edwards perceives a transformation in the design of these "strange craft" in the skies, "possibly intended to enable them to match or exceed those improvements which our own aircraft have undergone in the past sixty years." The dirigible-shaped craft seen over the States in 1896 and 1897 have been replaced by the flying disk. "But even that was not the ultimate in design for it seems to be in a process of being replaced by an egg-shaped craft."

Of those persons who claim to have obtained a piece of a flying saucer, Wilbert B. Smith impresses Edwards with his integrity, reputation, and truthfulness. During the 1950s, Smith headed the Canadian government's study of UFOs. In 1952, over Washington, D.C., a military jet supposedly got a radar lock on a glowing disk about 2 feet in diameter, and sprayed it with a burst of machine-gun fire, loosening a bright fragment that plummeted to the ground. The pilot watched as the piece hit. Ground crews found it embedded in a farmer's field. A U.S. Navy analysis could not ascertain whether the fragment was artificial or part of a meteorite. It was sent to Smith in Ottawa for further study. Smith described the chunk as weighing about 1 pound, composed of a blend of magnesium orthosilicate. Edwards points out that even while these examinations were taking place, Air Force spokesmen were regularly denying possession of any such fragment.

The first account by a credible witness of UFO occupants seen landing came to Edwards' attention in an October 1950 Canadian publication. A senior executive with an iron mine, and his wife, while sitting on the bank of a cove off Sawhill Bay near Steep Rock Lake in Ontario, heard a loud noise and observed a large saucer-shaped craft bobbing on the water, with "ten queer-looking creatures" moving slowly over its surface. Each of the beings appeared less than 4 feet tall and moved like automatons. The entire time, as the man and woman watched about 1,200 feet away, they heard a steady humming sound. When the object streaked off, the only noise was the rushing wind.

One year later similar beings were seen under circumstances that do not seem obviously fabricated. The Unmatjera tribe of aborigines in central Australia, during early September of 1951, saw two shiny circular objects land below the hilltop on which they were sitting. Afraid of objects they had never seen or heard of before, the aborigines remained hidden, watching as a small man like being in a shiny suit and helmet emerged from one object and entered the other. The craft were about 50 feet in diameter. As the objects ascended, a buzz like the swarm of insects could be heard. When the aborigines told Australian authorities about their sighting, they were impressed that these primitive people had no access to the news media or any prior conditioning for concocting such a story on their own. They had never heard of flying saucers before. "Pure fabrication would seem to be most unlikely," says Edwards, because of the detail in which the objects and the humanoid were described, and which fit so many other reported sightings.

Incident at Exeter
JOHN G. FULLER
(1966, G. P. Putnam's Sons)

Saturday Review writer John G. Fuller, faced with a deadline for his regular monthly column, decided to write about UFOs. Knowing little or nothing about the subject, and being a skeptic by nature, he began interviewing witnesses to an incident that had taken place several weeks earlier, on September 3, 1965, in Exeter, New Hampshire. Two policemen and a Navy recruit came within 100 feet of a huge, round, silent object with brilliant red lights. After Fuller wrote and published the column, he remained intrigued by the case. Reports of UFOs in that area persisted. Fuller re-visited Exeter, saw one of the objects himself, and stumbled upon an unsettling yet persuasive theory to explain the massive Northeast power blackout of November 9.

For a *Look* magazine article, he expanded into this book, Fuller interviewed at least sixty people who claimed to have seen flying disks in the vicinity of Exeter. Many similarities in these reports emerged bright, blinding balls of red light, which would usually swoop down and hover at night over power lines, chase cars, or be chased by Air Force planes from a nearby Strategic Air Command base.

One evening, in the company of three other persons, Fuller watched as a reddish-orange disk, three-fifths the size of a full moon, shot across the sky with a jet fighter in pursuit. They watched the glowing object for nearly twenty seconds. Fuller was no longer a skeptic.

He concluded that what dozens of people were seeing could be accounted for by one of four explanations: the craft were our own secret weapons; they were revolutionary new craft belonging to another government; the sightings were psychic aberrations; or they were interplanetary devices, built by a society far in advance of our own. He ruled out psychic aberrations because during this flurry of sightings radar had targeted the objects and at least one was photographed.

The Pentagon attempted to explain away the sightings as "stars and planets in unusual formations." From that point on, Fuller could not believe anything released by the government about UFOs. He had interviewed numerous military personnel, including pilots and radar operators, who confirmed that objects had been picked up on radar, jets had been scrambled, orders had even been issued to shoot the objects down. One brilliant orange ball of light actually landed on the edge of a runway at Pease Air Force Base, casting such a bright light on the officers' quarters that they thought it was morning.

One of Fuller's friends went so far as to speculate that the CIA might covertly be creating and funding crackpot flying saucer groups, the wilder and more irresponsible the better, to make "the entire UFO situation a laughing matter." That way, any real news breakthrough would be carefully controlled. Fuller's frustrating experience with the Air Force left him receptive to that suggestion.

On November 8, Fuller interviewed several persons who had seen, independently of each other, reddish, cigar-shaped objects hovering a few feet over power lines and extending pipelike protrusions that touched the lines. Similar reports came in from Pennsylvania, and included a photograph (which Fuller uses on the cover of his book). The next day, November 9, about 5:30 P.M., the Northeast Power Grid inexplicably failed, plunging one-fifth of the nation's population into darkness.

Electrical engineers thought they had isolated the problem in a remote-controlled substation at Clay, 10 miles north of Syracuse, New York. Niagara Mohawk repairmen found the substation in working order. No conclusive explanation for the power failure was offered. But Fuller provides a provocative clue. At 5:15 P.M., the same moment as the blackout hit Syracuse, pilot Weldon Ross was approaching Hancock Field for a landing when he saw below him, over the Clay power substation, a huge, brilliant red ball, 100 feet in diameter. Five other persons, including Robert C. Walsh, deputy commissioner for the Federal Aviation Agency in Syracuse, reported sighting the same unidentified object.

Uninvited Visitors
IVAN T, SANDERSON
(1967, Cowles)

Biologist Ivan T. Sanderson argues that the UFO phenomenon is primarily a biological problem because some UFOs may be forms of life, actual living machines manufactured to duplicate a variety of species. He makes a persuasive case that UFOs don't seem to do anything that can't be equaled within the animal kingdom of our own planet.

UFOs are often reported to change shape and size, but so do puffer fish and toads, blowing themselves up to twice their normal size, and radically changing in shape. UFOs have been seen to vanish, then suddenly reappear, but so do hover flies, which seem to hover motionless in midair for minutes, then instantaneously move because their movements are usually subliminal to us. UFOs have been shot at by the Air Force and skittish civilians, yet appear to suffer no ill-effects; but a common June bug, with plating only a fraction of a millimeter thick, "can fly into a brick wall at sixty miles an hour...right itself, spread its wings, and fly off again totally undamaged." UFOs are seen to emit dazzling and multicolored lights, but so do luminous bacteria and the beetle larva of South America, whose green lights at the front and red lights on the tail blink when landing or ascending.

Sanderson's point is simply that we must not overlook terrestrial explanations for the behavior of UFOs. In answer to the argument that alien visitors would need to be almost immortal, if only to traverse thousands of light years to get here, the author again provides a terrestrial formula. Tardigrades are related to spiders, and possess primitive eyes, a central nervous and circulatory system, four pairs of legs, and an alimentary tract. If denied water, they shrivel up and become specks of crystal. When placed in an airtight jar, they can be preserved. To resuscitate them, one need only add a few drops of water. They assume their original form and immediately begin to breed.

If many UFOs are living creatures, rather than just biological machines, they might exist on the plentiful raw energy of space, deciding to visit our atmosphere only once we began producing electricity that attracted them like derelicts to free lunch counters. Is the suggestion of space-animals really so appalling, asks Sanderson. He answers his own question. It makes a lot of biological sense to utilize space-animals, like trained dogs, to search for life elsewhere in the universe. These animals could even carry parasites, or occupants, to undertake the actual scientific studies. These passengers, too, might be artificially bred intelligences, expendable yet intelligent. Bear in mind that American and Russian scientists first sent aloft dogs and monkeys before humans, and we may yet send another species-perhaps our own version of artificial intelligence-into other solar systems before we ourselves attempt the trip.

Sanderson theorizes that such a flight of intelligently controlled life forms flew over West Virginia on the evening of September 12, 1952. He personally investigated these "landings," or "crashes." One occupant came to be known as the Flatwoods Monster, seen in Braxton County near Flatwoods by seven persons who described it as having a head shaped like the ace of spades. This strange "pilot" disappeared and his spaceship disintegrated, melting like dry ice and giving off a nauseating metallic stench.

Even though UFOs and their occupants generally have shown no aggressive traits, Sanderson cautions that one variety of vehicle—the lens-shaped with central domes on top—does exhibit patterns that are cause for concern. These objects are seen the world over maneuvering near our sources of water and areas of fertile vegetation. They might be zoologists, collecting soil and water samples. Or maybe these uninvited visitors are interested in colonization and exploitation. Sanderson suggests a third alternative: that humans are larval forms, and these paternal objects in the sky are only keeping watch over this cosmic nursery we call Earth.

Flying Saucer Occupants
CORAL & JIM LORENZEN
(1967, New American Library)

Only two explanations for UFOs seem convincing to Coral and Jim Lorenzen, founders and directors of the Aerial Phenomena Research Organization. UFOs and their operators are real. While their motivation for coming to Earth may be to study humankind, it is a mistake to suppose that simply because they are more advanced than us technologically, they are more spiritually advanced. On the other hand, there is no conclusive proof these visitors intend to exploit or abuse us. They remain a suspiciously deceptive presence, modifying their craft to resemble our Earth aircraft, "and dressing their crews to resemble ours."

A second alternative they propose rather hesitantly: that the "population of the world is falling victim to a particularly insidious and apparently contagious mental disease which generates hallucinations." This could be a symptom of what psychologist Carl Jung called the human need for "psychic wholeness" to help reach an understanding of the world around us.

Some reports of UFOs, contend the Lorenzens, are nothing more than a response to that craving for "a symbol of wholeness." Humankind's spiritual hunger too easily finds an outlet in UFO contactee cultism, resulting deplorably in "many otherwise objective students (discounting) all reports of landed UFOs with occupants." Witnesses who interpret UFOs in terms of "religious mythology" only further isolate legitimate "close encounters" from the mainstream of acceptance and responsibility. We have no spiritual framework with which to understand UFOs; nothing in human history or contemporary life can prepare us. Consequently, our fear of the unknown as manifested in UFOs inevitably distorts our perception of them. We either refuse to accept them as real, or we insist on fitting them neatly into theories with relevance only to our world view.

The Lorenzens advance a set of guidelines to evaluate reports of contact between humans and extraterrestrials. For instance, "when emotional stress precedes a UFO experience, it can be fairly assumed that the incident may be one of psychic projection." Under these conditions UFOs become "vehicles of reassurance carrying big brothers here for the express purpose of straightening out the difficulties we already have." One must be skeptical of contactees reporting physical beings as closely resembling humans, and likewise of anyone receiving messages or warnings, often including rationalizations of why he or she was "chosen."

More trustworthy witnesses describe occupants according to their unfamiliar characteristics. They appear genuinely frightened or puzzled by the experience, repeating no messages from the occupants. Above all, they must be consistent in relating the circumstances of what occurred.

Based on the available evidence, the Lorenzens believe UFO occupants are bipeds. Three distinct types of UFOnauts predominate among witness accounts-humanoids about 4 feet 6 inches tall; 3-foot-tall humanoids; and shorter, animal-like dwarfs. Features repeatedly reported are large eyes, large craniums, and small stature. These three types probably represent "several races" from one planet or a "planetary alliance." Some may even be trained animals.

Those who crusade against an alleged Air Force/CIA cover-up of the UFO phenomenon receive no sympathy from the authors. This cover-up accusation has an "unconscious motivation," known as "Instant Reassurance," which assumes the authorities have answers and are withholding them. It is an assumption designed to stifle "the fear of the possibility that no one may be completely aware of the problem."

Harmonic 33
BRUCE CATHIE
(1968, A.H. & A. W. Reed)

New Zealand airline pilot Bruce Cathie, after six UFO sightings and fifteen years of research, believes he uncovered the only plausible reason why UFOs are here.

At some point in prehistoric times, a "master race," the same folks who later assisted the Egyptians, the Incas, Mayans, Aztecs, and Easter Islanders, built a world-wide power grid deep underground for navigation and from which "they drew motive power" to propel their spaceships. Utilizing this power grid, they moved the stones used in building the Pyramid of Cheops from a quarry 600 miles away, and levitated into place the Mayan structures of Tiahuanaco. Mount Sinai, the traditional landing site of UFOs during the biblical era, is an "integral part of the grid system," aligned with Cheops, another important landmark.

"If we plot the meridian passing through Mount Sinai, using the [Cheops] Pyramid position as longitude 30 degrees east, we see that the longitude of the Sinai position equals 33 degrees east and 33 equals the grid basic harmonic," writes Cathie. This ancient grid system occasionally malfunctioned, resulting in the destruction of Sodom and Gomorrah, and the 1908 explosion in the Tunguska region of Siberia.

Since the grid was constructed "to transmit gravitational frequencies," with the grid aerials buried up to "36 nautical miles underground" blending in with Earth's normal gravity, seismic disturbances such as earthquakes and volcanoes periodically displace these aerials from a vertical position. Gravity in these areas becomes grossly distorted, warping and twisting objects, blowing up Sodom and Gomorrah, and creating the vortex effect observed in Oregon and California, where light waves and gravity are so warped that weights will not hang vertically.

Cathie says he stumbled across this grid system while aligning on a map all the daily sightings recorded in New Zealand and surrounding areas-much as Aimie Michel did in Flying Saucers and the Straight-line Mystery. He theorized on the basis of patterns formed that the saucerians were embarked on a reconstruction job. Since World War II and a succession of nuclear tests, UFO occupants have returned in large numbers to

111

repair the grid they built in ancient times, thus making the magnetic field of the Earth once again uniform.

"Energy is constantly being pumped out of the grid into the surrounding atmosphere of Earth, and our visitors can make use of it due to its axial rotation and orbit within the electromagnetic field of the Sun," the author claims. From this he concludes that "the purpose of the grid was to increase the values of the speed of light, gravity acceleration, and therefore, time." Vehicles used by the saucerians are probably constructed "to certain harmonic diameters," so that as they spin or resonate with the power grid field a harmonic reaction is set up which causes them to be displaced in space time. This means that UFOs vibrate within a space-time continuum at so much higher a level than ours that normally they remain invisible to us, which explains "why a saucer will sometimes show up on a photographic plate, although it cannot be seen by the eye."

Nikola Tesla, who discovered the alternating current, the rotating magnetic field, and the principles of radar, probably knew about the grid system, Cathie says, because at one point Tesla proposed making the Earth into a giant lamp by tapping power from within the planet. Tesla died in America in 1943. All his notes and papers were confiscated by the Custodian of Alien Property. "It is alleged that government officials are the only people allowed access to these papers," says Cathie, who hints darkly that the power grid's secrets are now known to-and being exploited by-certain powerful scientists.

====================

UFOs Over the Americas
JIM & CORAL LORENZEN
(1968, New American Library)

Since 1947, UFO sightings have been on the increase, in cyclic fashion, reaching a peak every twenty-six months, and every five years. Although peak periods remain, since 1965 the trend has been toward constant UFO activity, intensifying both in sightings and landings. The Lorenzens attribute this trend to one (or both) of two possible causes: a mass psychosis may be generating the additional reports; or these interplanetary craft have established bases on or near our planet, enabling longer and more frequent appearances in our skies. The Lorenzens lean toward this latter view.

UFOs apparently placed Earth under military surveillance following the large-scale detonation of nuclear devices in the 1940s. They are here gathering specimens and information, often with little or "no respect for human life or health." They intentionally elude our attempts to document their presence. When discrepancies occur between what observers have seen and what the camera recorded, the Lorenzens conclude that UFO occupants might somehow be able to project onto film an image in conflict with observational testimony. This could also be occurring with radar.

The authors describe technological changes in the reported UFO craft; now quite often the UFOs seem to have a lighting system at night resembling the multicolored blinking lights on our aircraft. In design, most still adhere to four general configurations: the egg, the disk, the globe, and the cigar or cylinder shape.

"There seem to be at least three types of (UFO) occupants," the Lorenzens observe. Each of these different beings may prefer one or more of the UFO configurations, depending on its mission and function. Although the Lorenzens are open-minded about contact between these beings and humans, even to the point of sparingly endorsing the statements of a few contactees, they suggest that UFOs might be projected images of what contactees want to see, or what the UFO occupants want them to see.

Even though our technical equipment, our own minds, and the UFOs themselves may be deceiving us, it is the CIA that remains the chief agent of deception, according to the Lorenzen analysis. They reject the claims of Donald Keyhoe and others that UFOs are a "special conspiracy of silence" within the government. Rather, UFO information "is withheld through the application of normal national security procedures...." They theorize that Keyhoe, and the group he formed in 1957, the National Investigations Committee on Aerial Phenomena (NICAP), probably were infiltrated by the CIA, using repetitive attacks on Air Force secrecy and involvement in the UFO field as "an ideal smoke screen for covert CIA activity." Serving on NICAP's board of directors was Admiral Hillenkoeter, a former director of the CIA. This deceptive maneuver, so the Lorenzens claim, created an impression that the agency was not involved with UFOs, and provided a channel "through which to institute subversive measures" if that became necessary.

Aliens in the Skies
JOHN G. FULLER
(1969, G. P. Putnam's Sons)

Several months before the University of Colorado released its massive government-sponsored UFO study known as the Condon Report, hearings by the House Committee on Science and Astronautics featuring six scientists—all but one a proponent for the evidence of extraterrestrial visitation—attempted to dispel in advance the negative conclusions of Condon. This book is a transcript of that congressional symposium, embellished by John Fuller's introduction and commentary.

Astrophysicist and former Air Force UFO consultant Dr. J. Allen Hynek, the leadoff witness, focused his testimony on puncturing a series of general misconceptions regarding UFOs. For instance, the notion that "only UFO buffs report UFOs" is simply not true; the most baffling reports come from reliable and articulate persons. Other fallacies are that UFOs "are never reported by scientifically trained people, are never seen at close range, have never been detected on radars, and have never been recorded by scientific cameras."

Dr. James E. McDonald, senior physicist at the Institute of Atmospheric Physics in Arizona, and a specialist in meteorological optics, strongly disagreed with the conclusions of Harvard astronomer Dr. Donald Menzel, who wrote two books dismissing UFOs as a misidentification of natural and optical phenomena. "I have checked case after case of his," said McDonald, "and his explanations are very, very far removed from what are well-known principles and quantitative aspects of meteorological optic objects." McDonald said the views of Philip Klass, that UFOs are atmospheric-electrical plasmas, "just do not make good sense." As evidence he uses an Air Force report on ball lightning which concluded that such short-lived plasmas could not possibly explain the sightings being reported.

The dissenter among the witnesses proved to be Dr. Carl Sagan of Cornell University. "I do not think the evidence is at all persuasive that UFOs are of intelligent extraterrestrial origin, nor do I think the evidence is convincing that no UFOs are of intelligent extraterrestrial origin." Sagan discouraged Congress from investing any more money in the search for answers to the UFO mystery, even though a by-product of that report might be useful information on atmospheric physics. He leans toward the theory that UFOs may be delusions in the guise of unidentified objects, but does not claim this explains most or all sightings. If Congress chose to display an interest in the pursuit of extraterrestrial life, Sagan urged that it be demonstrated in funding for radio astronomy, NASA, and space missions, rather than in the study of UFOs.

Berkeley engineering professor Dr. James Harder theorized that UFOs utilize a propulsion system based on an application of gravitational fields that we do not understand. Apparently, theoretical grounds exist to assume a second gravitational field, corresponding to the magnetic field, interacting as do the electrical and magnetic fields. If nothing else, the study of UFOs may unlock the secret of harnessing gravity.

Dr. Robert Baker, senior scientist with the Computer Sciences Corporation, pointed out that "we have not now, nor have we been in the past, able to achieve a complete-or even partially complete surveillance of space in the vicinity of the earth, comprehensive enough to betray the presence of, or provide quantitative information on, anomalistic phenomena." He recommended development of a sensor system to detect and record "anomalistic observational phenomena" from which hard data might be extracted for evaluation.

To demolish the argument that mass hysteria accounts for many UFO reports, Dr. Robert Hall, chairman of the Department of Sociology at the University of Illinois, emphasized that UFO witnesses "first try to explain their observation in some very familiar terms." This process of assimilation allows the observer to classify on the basis of what is understood, known, and familiar. This is contrary to the notion that UFO witnesses are eager or motivated to see objects in the sky. While hysteria and contagion of belief do account for some reports, Hall sees strong evidence that "some physical phenomena" underly a portion of other reports.

In statements prepared for submission to the House committee, Dr. Donald Menzel and nuclear physicist Stanton Friedman evaluated basically the same evidence to support their diametrically opposed views. While conceding that the "concept of extraterrestrial visitors is not an impossibility," Menzel nonetheless blames the chemistry and physiology of the human eye, not alien spacecraft, for the proliferation of UFO reports. He recounts a personal experience when, on looking skyward, he thought he saw a flotilla of UFOs flying in formation. They were after images of sunlight reflected off a car fender he had seen a few moments earlier. This tendency to regard apparitions as solid objects has retarded the formulation of a solution to the problem, Menzel claims. Only sensationalism by an "irresponsible" news media has kept the UFO myth alive. "Reopening the subject of UFOs makes just about as much sense as reopening the subject of Witchcraft."

Friedman accuses Menzel, Klass, Condon, and other skeptics of trying to make data fit hypotheses rather than the more difficult job of "creating hypotheses that fit the data." He contends that while known aircraft cannot duplicate the speeds and maneuvers of UFOs, "no laws of physics have been violated by UFOs."

Passport to Magonia
JACQUES VALLEE
(1969, Henry Regnery)

The French astrophysicist Jacques Vallée, on whom the character of the scientist Claude Lacombe was based for the movie *Close Encounters of the Third Kind*, says UFOs may not be a scientific problem after all. He would actually be disappointed if they prove to be merely extraterrestrial space probes. He suggests instead that we begin to perceive the phenomenon as metaphysical, a psychic device or programing method, intended to trigger the deepest symbols of our culture, perhaps to alter our concepts of the universe and prepare us for contact with advanced consciousness.

For that reason, Vallée believes it more important that we study the UFO phenomenon's impact on culture and our collective psyche, rather than focusing on the question of whether objects in the sky are extraterrestrial in origin. He draws parallels between religious apparitions, UFOs, and reports of fairies and dwarfs who materialize and exhibit extraordinary powers. Most reports alleging contact with UFO occupants describe the visitors as dwarflike, with oversized heads and nonhuman complexions, something straight out of the fairy tales.

All religious apparitions, mystical experiences, UFOs, and appearances by supernatural creatures rely upon the same mechanisms, share similar characteristics and effects on the human observer, varying only to the extent that the projections are interpreted within the prevailing cultural environment. Thus, humans in the pre-Industrial Age saw angels in the sky. In nineteenth-century rural America, people saw "airships that resembled zeppelins." Since 1947, we have seen flying saucers.

Vallée theorizes that if it were possible to construct three dimensional holograms with mass, then most religious miracles and UFO sightings could be explained. He also raises the prospect that humankind is being exposed to deliberately faked apparitions of space visitors, somewhat like mirages in the desert, that are intended to program our imaginations by tuning us into "space operas." He poses other intriguing speculations, almost as an afterthought: perhaps we are in contact with a parallel universe; maybe UFOs are "windows," rather than objects; the sexual overtone of many UFO reports, and biblical tales of intercourse between angels and humans, could indicate a pattern of genetic engineering and crossbreeding with an advanced species.

We must eventually confront the problem of nonhuman intelligence, says Vallée, because otherwise, we will never begin to understand the behavior of UFOs and their occupants. Their behavior often seems silly and absurd, as when a sixty-year-old chicken farmer in Wisconsin named Joe Simonton was visited, so he claims, by three short men in an egg shaped craft who traded four pancakes for a jug of his spring water. Such stories make it ever more difficult for conventional science to take the phenomenon seriously. Might humankind be the straight-man in a theater populated by ethereal practical jokers?

There remains the possibility that the human imagination is playing tricks upon itself. Fiction may be dictating reality. For instance, the first blackout of a city caused by a UFO was the creation of Arthur Koestler, in a play he wrote in 1933. The first reference to a UFO affecting a car ignition came in 1950 when Bernard Newman published his novel *The Flying Saucer*. Other examples are available. Is it coincidence, or the logical consequence of symbolism and the creative impulse?

Vallée warns that the long-term insolubility and continued manifestation of UFOs, coupled with an intense public interest in the phenomenon, may someday produce a new mythological movement or another brand of charlatanism. The human imagination might actually seek to fill the vacuum of rational solutions to this mystery by creating and substituting fantasy. *Passport to Magonia* concludes by chronicling 923 UFO cases representing a century of sightings—from 1868 to 1968—collected from throughout the world.

===============================

The Hollow Earth
RAYMOND BERNARD
(1969, University Press, Inc.)

William Reed in 1906, and Marshall Gardner in 1920, first advanced theories that the Earth is hollow, with openings at both poles. Ray Palmer, editor of *Flying Saucers* magazine, speculated in 1959 that this Underworld must be where the UFOs originate. Raymond Bernard, for his part, has written a book that relies almost entirely on these earlier works.

Atlanteans constructed the subterranean cities of the inner world as refuges from radioactive fallout produced by a nuclear war they had fought. This migration in flying saucers from "the four-sided sacred mountain in the center of Atlantis"—Mount Olympus—was referred to in mythology as the Twilight of the Gods. When atomic bombs were exploded on the surface of the planet in 1945, Atlanteans swarmed into the air in flying saucers to avert another nuclear catastrophe; they told Earth people they came from space so as to conceal their true origins.

At one point, Bernard says these Atlanteans are giants; in another passage, he refers to the hollow Earth inhabitants as being related to the Mongols and the Eskimos, who were supposedly thought of by Norwegians as "fairy people." Bernard theorizes that Santa Claus was an Atlantean benefactor from the North Pole whose flying saucer found symbolic expression as a flying sled with reindeer.

The author believes that a conspiracy exists to suppress information about the hollow Earth. He cites the intrigues of "secret forces" that prevented circulation of the December 1959 issue of Flying Saucers magazine, which contained an article claiming that Admiral Byrd's expedition beyond the North Pole in 1947 had stumbled into the hollow Earth opening. A truck carrying 5,000 copies of the magazine arrived with the magazines missing. A distributor who received 750 copies vanished, taking the magazines with him. The plates which printed that issue were badly damaged under mysterious circumstances. Who were these "invisible and secret forces" of suppression? Bernard offers no answers.

Bernard heads the European branch of the "Ancient and Mystical Order of the Rosy Cross," which claims to preserve knowledge from Atlantis. Sirhan, the killer of Robert Kennedy, was an AMORC member. Bernard says extraterrestrials told him to write *The Hollow Earth*, and other books, to prepare humans for their coming.

Invisible Residents
IVAN T. SANDERSON
(1970, Thomas Y. Crowell)

Water covers 78 percent of the Earth's surface. By actual count, in excess of 50 percent of all reported UFOs have been sighted over, near, or under water. At least ten, possibly twelve "lozenges" or "vile vortices" exist, most over water, where ships, planes, and people seem to disappear under peculiar circumstances, leaving not a trace. Biologist Ivan T. Sanderson concludes from the evidence that an underwater civilization has evolved here, or is visiting here from elsewhere, using the oceans, seas, lakes, and rivers as a base for exploration.

Hundreds-perhaps thousands-of reports throughout history mention "luminous meteors" or other aerial phenomena in connection with water. From among them Sanderson cites numerous well authenticated reports, like one from the northeast Pacific in 1945, where crew members of the U.S. Army transport Delarof, hauling munitions and supplies to Alaska, sighted in the open sea a large round object emerging from the water. It climbed straight up, then circled the ship two or three times before heading southwest. Crewmen estimated it to be 250 feet in diameter.

Sanderson seeks to draw direct connections between reported UFO activity, above and below water, and instances of ship, plane, and submarine disappearances. Based on the enormous volume of air and sea traffic through the Bermuda area, he calculated that the so-called Triangle is no more a hazard than being struck by lightning in a crowd. Furthermore, he found that the area in which disappearances were reported resembles a lozenge, rather than a triangle. This area extends from about 30 degrees to 40 degrees north latitude.

By plotting on a map disappearances occurring over large bodies of water, Sanderson discovered another lozenge-shaped area, also precisely between 30 degrees and 40 degrees north latitude, about 250 miles south of the Japanese island of Honshu. Once all the disappearances for the previous several hundred years were plotted out, a startling pattern emerged. Three lozenges existed at 30 degrees to 40 degrees north latitude, but another three lozenges, their equivalents, were discovered situated within 30 degrees to 40 degrees south of the equator, off the east coasts of South America, South Africa, and Australia. All six lozenges were tilted eastward by the same number of degrees. Surface ocean currents, strong in each of these areas, seem somehow to be involved.

Eventually, with the help of geographers and mathematicians, Sanderson found ten vortices, or lozenges, ringing the Earth in two belts, one in the southern, the other in the northern hemisphere. They are approximately centered 72 degrees apart. All but two—one over Pakistan and one nudging the Mediterranean—are over water. Two others were theorized, in the North and South Poles, making a total of twelve lozenges.

Sanderson believes these lozenges are a perfectly natural phenomenon triggered by gravitational or magnetic anomalies; all the "oddities, enigmas, and horrors allegedly noted in the vortices" could simply be indigenous to certain areas, remaining natural and stable until humans, or some outside influence, upsets the balance. It is possible that UFOs, if they do possess an electromagnetic propulsion system, might generate in these areas an anomaly that distorts our space-time continuum, creating vortices-holes in time-into and out of which objects can enter ours or another space-time continuum. This would explain instances when craft in these zones have apparently gained or lost time, or disappeared altogether. It offers a means by which advanced civilizations could traverse almost instantaneously the length of the universe.

Sanderson crystallizes his own opinions by quoting Nikola Tesla, the electrical wizard at the turn of the century, who declared at least seventy-eight years ago: "We cannot even with positive assurance assert that some of them [intelligent beings from other planets] might not be present here in this our world, in the very midst of us, for their constitution and life manifestations may be such that we are unable to perceive them."

UFOs-Operation Trojan Horse
JOHN A. KEEL
(1970, G. P. Putnam's Sons)

John Keel makes five propositions: UFOs are transmogrifications, primarily electromagnetic in origin, utilizing the creation and manipulation of matter to assume any form desired, even masquerading at times as airplanes, meteors, or balloons; the intelligence that directs these manifestations is itself a form of energy, or an energy field; this intelligence is not extraterrestrial; it accounts for religious miracles, spiritual seances, and the paranormal; and it is frequently reflective, tailoring effects to the attitudes and beliefs of witnesses. As the title of the book implies, this intelligence throughout history has intentionally deceived us into believing that angels and extraterrestrials move about through the skies as our protectors and advisers.

When, in 1966, John Keel began investigating UFO sightings, he admitted skepticism. He culled through 10,000 clippings and reports that first year alone, searching for patterns. Several clearly emerged: the greatest proportion of sightings occur on Wednesday nights, between the hours of 8:00 and 11:00 p.m. From that peak, the sightings slowly taper off throughout the week. Less densely populated areas have far higher concentrations of sightings than populated ones, and these sightings tend to cluster within specific geographical areas, or "windows," centered over magnetic deviations in the Earth's crust. Keel discovered, to his embarrassment, that his statistical research simply verified information already compiled and published by the U.S. Air Force's Project Blue Book, which had concluded no evidence exists that UFOs are extraterrestrial. Keel came to a similar conclusion; but unlike the Air Force, he refused to accept the explanation that people were either hallucinating or mistaking natural phenomena.

Keel began searching through historical records. A Mexican astronomer, Jose Bonilla, in 1883 had taken the first UFO photograph, actually of an entire herd of them as they flew between Earth and the sun. Bonilla counted 143 circular objects that revealed their true contours on film as cigar or spindle-shaped. Thirteen years later, in 1896, two San Francisco attorneys were shown drawings for a patent of a cigar-shaped airship operating on either compressed air, gas, or electricity (they were each told different stories). The inventor, described as well-dressed, dark eyed, of dark complexion, and short, was accompanied by three mechanics. They said the airship would be used to drive the Spaniards from Cuba. These comments received mention in the press, thanks to the attorneys. Five months later, airships were reported floating over practically all the midwestern states. Hundreds of sightings were recorded. But the mystery inventor and his assistants never appeared again. Keel speculates that a well-organized group, intending to conduct a survey of the Midwest and not wanting to attract attention (for airships had not yet been perfected), planted stories about the patent to make their appearance in the sky seem harmless. These "decoys" dropped potatoes and other objects, notes, and newspapers to the ground to confuse the witnesses.

The mystery inventor never filed for a patent, and the first verifiable flight of an airship would not take place until three years later, when Count Zeppelin flew his dirigible for less than 4 miles in Germany.

UFOs, too, have been leaving artifacts behind as evidence of their presence. But the objects, as with the airships, are always of terrestrial origin. Saucers have been seen to leave behind strips of aluminum, piles of magnesium and silicon, or truly bizarre items, like the pancakes the Wisconsin chicken farmer named Joe Simonton claims a UFO occupant handed him. Hardly the kind of evidence NASA could use in support of extraterrestrial visitation.

Keel concludes from this that the UFO phenomenon is a cosmic joke perpetrated by entities who have always frightened, confused, and misled humankind. Air Marshal Sir Victor Goddard, who participated in Britain's UFO probe in the early 1950s, similarly believes that UFOs are Earth-created by illusion-prone spirits. Dr. Leon Davidson, a physicist on the Manhattan Project, undertook with Air Force cooperation his own UFO investigation, focusing on the claims of contactees. He believed they were telling the truth as they knew it, but had been hypnotized or tricked. Dr. Davidson speculated that the CIA was behind the deception.

John Keel warns that dabbling with UFOs is as dangerous as flirting with black magic. He says the phenomenon preys upon neurotics and the gullible, producing paranoia and schizophrenia. He recommends that parents forbid their children to become involved. He cites experiences that made him "question my own sanity"-strangers would call at all hours with bizarre messages "from space people," UFOs seemed to be following him around, impossible coincidences occurred, he was followed by black Cadillacs that would vanish when he pursued them, and on numerous occasions he would awaken late at night unable to move, "with a huge dark apparition standing over me."

UFOlogy
JAMES M. MCCAMPBELL
(1973, Celestial Arts)

James M. McCampbell, a technician specializing in nuclear power and advanced technology theory, does not attempt to prove, disprove, or evaluate the validity of UFO sighting reports. Acting on the assumption that witnesses generally tell the truth as they see it, he weaves from an enormous number of reports a series of patterns that reflect, when applied to known Earth technologies, an electromagnetic explanation for UFO flights, and their reported physiological effects upon human and animal observers. Electromagnetic energy, when pulsed in the range of 300 to 3,000 MHz or higher-well within the microwave region-has been demonstrated in theory and by laboratory testing to produce numerous effects similar to UFOs:

...Colored halos around UFOs, in descriptions ranging from red glows to blue hazes, indicate that UFO luminosity is produced by the surrounding air, not by the object itself; the dazzling white plasma seen on the surface of UFOs is related to ball lightning, a variety of plasma that induces chemical changes accompanied by an odor described as sharp and repugnant, like burning sulphur;

...UFOs, like microwaves, are capable of turning off automobile headlights through an increase in the resistance of their tungsten filaments, and stopping internal combustion engines by suppressing the current. In one particular revealing example, a UFO in Italy passed over two farm tractors, one conventional, the other diesel, and only the conventional engine died;

...Interferences with radio and television reception and trans mission, although UFOs seem to have frequency components closer to TV; drying up grass, bushes, and small ponds by resonant absorption in water molecules; igniting volatilized gases and heating at depth bituminous highway surfaces; heating internally the human body, with an excess of ultraviolet rays that produces a condition similar to sunburn;

...Causing people to experience electrical shocks and temporary paralysis, occurring when a pulsed microwave field induces the skeletal muscles to work against each other; also stimulating the production of sleep-inducing chemicals in the brain; at low audio frequency, microwaves directly stimulate the auditory nerve, giving the observer the sensation of hearing a buzzing or humming sound. McCampbell theorizes that these microwave beeps produced by UFOs might induce hypnotic trances in witnesses, since the "mechanism for transmittal of the beeps seems to be encoded signals on a high-frequency carrier...." UFOs are often described as sounding like generators or vacuum cleaners. This electrical phenomenon is even more pronounced when one considers the similarities between human and mechanical reactions. In each recorded instance of a human being experiencing heating, paralysis, electrical shock, or loss of consciousness, usually preceded by loud humming or beeping, automobile engines also stopped or misfired.

Often, the light emitted by UFOs is so intense witnesses describe it as burning magnesium. In Brazil, a UFO was observed disintegrating into thousands of fiery fragments; those extinguished in water were analyzed and discovered to be extremely pure magnesium. Variations in light and color of UFOs while in flight suggest to McCampbell that acceleration and the propulsion system are closely related to sequential color change, with the energy state graduating from metallic at low speed, to blue, orange-red, then brilliant white at maximum speed, indicating an almost total ionization of the surrounding air.

One 1957 sighting reinforces McCampbell's correlation between microwaves and UFOs. An Air Force B-47 on a training mission encountered a huge object with a "steady, red glow" over the Gulf of Mexico. For nearly two hours the object seemed to fly in circles around the plane. Military ground control radar, navigation radar on board the plane, two airborne electronic countermeasure receivers, and the pilots in the cockpit with visual observation, constituted five physical channels through which the UFO was apparently confirmed. Two monitors on board the plane recorded that the UFO emitted electromagnetic energy in a frequency of 2995 MC to 3,000 MC, pouring forth radiation "in a very narrow range of the microwave region...pulsed at a low audio rate." McCampbell believes that microwave energy is an essential element of the UFO propulsion system, capable somehow of nullifying or diminishing inertial and gravitational forces.

Beyond Earth: Man's Contact with UFOs
RALPH BLUM with JUDY BLUM
(1974, Bantam)

UFOs are either extraterrestrial spacecraft, a paraphysical phenomenon "composed of a type of intelligent energy that can take any form it desires," or they constitute "living holograms projected on the sky by the laser beams of man's unconscious mind." In the absence of tangible data, such as debris or a spacecraft, physical science cannot be productive in investigating UFOs. The Blums propose that future UFO study be confined to the social sciences, especially anthropology, focusing on the contactees and others experiencing close encounters, since "these people are the evidence."

This lack of concrete data has to be a massive government cover-up of UFO activity. There are two possible reasons for perpetuating this "cosmic Watergate." Since the American military is "bound to have the best collection of UFO data in the world," and assuming the information possessed makes no more sense than when the investigation began, the Air Force cannot afford to admit that something it can neither cope with nor understand is flying around in the sky. But what if proof of extraterrestrial visitation has been found, a UFO fragment, conclusive film footage, or bodies? Any technology that "could render our weaponry and missile systems obsolete" would be viewed with suspicion and alarm by the military, "so long as the intent of the UFOs remains unknown." The Blums find the possibility that UFOs are real "less disconcerting...than the idea of all those crazy policemen, hallucinating pilots, and inept radar operators" who have reported UFO sightings and not been believed.

Communist governments have been even more fanatical in debunking UFOs. For instance, during the 1954 "flap" (the term used to describe periods of concentrated UFO sightings) Romanian newspapers accused the United States of deliberately plotting to give the world "flying saucer psychosis," while the Soviet newspaper Red Star denounced UFOs as capitalist propaganda, and the Hungarian government explained in official pronouncements that UFOs didn't exist because "all flying saucer reports originate in the bourgeois countries, where they are invented by the capitalist warmongers with a view to drawing the people's attention away from their economic difficulties."

Medical science laughed when people claimed miraculous healings from beams of light projected by UFOs. But scientists in Hungary discovered that laser beams heal open wounds faster than any previously known surgical technique. A seventy-three-year-old Argentinean, an illiterate nightwatchman named Ventura Maceiras, was momentarily blinded by a flash of light from an enormous UFO that hummed "like the noise of angry bees," causing him unbearable headaches, nausea, and an abnormal loss of hair. Another side effect he found equally puzzling, though less distressing-three months after sighting the object, in December 1972, he grew another set of teeth! The Blums ponder the "intriguing coincidence" that in Brazil and the Philippines those psychic surgeons and healers who claim to perform major operations without anesthesia or instruments began developing their powers in 1947 and 1948, when the modern wave of UFO sightings became public knowledge. They quote parapsychologist Dr. Andrija Puharich and others who contend that one of the attributes of the intelligent energy in space now in communication with humans is the power of psychic healing.

After reviewing all the evidence, especially claims by the contactees, the authors feel that "we are being provided with a sophisticated blend" of information, "part extension of our own scientific techniques, part evidence that seems realistic since we are already predisposed by years of science-fiction writing to expect such things, and part fantasy introduced by the phenomenon for reasons of its own."

Mysteries of Time and Space
BRAD STEIGER
(1974, Prentice-Hall)

Brad Steiger theorizes that UFOs fit into the context of a more significant phenomenon involving spaciotemporal definitions of reality. Space and time are only apparent limitations of human perception. A wide variety of manifestations, ranging from UFOs and Sasquatch to poltergeists, are evidence for the flexibility of time and space and the power of human minds to perceive, as well as create other realities or other arrangements of space and time.

Extraterrestrial visitors are demonstrating how space and time can be molded. They are intentionally confounding human notions of reality constructs as a teaching method, conditioning our species to exert mind power. Although at this stage these teachers play a benevolent role, Steiger hints at a less favorable interchange in future contacts.

Quoting extensively from Creationist scientists and nineteenth century newspapers, Steiger makes a case for an ancient civilization on the North American continent, perhaps a part of the legendary Atlantis, existing thousands of years before the final development of Homo sapiens as an intelligent species. He lists artifacts, such as Roman coins unearthed in Illinois, Japanese pottery from 3000 B.C. found in Ecuador, all unexplainable findings in the unlikeliest of places as evidence that these and other "erratics" may be "some kind of fallout from other dimensions of reality...(and) indicate that the reality we like to think of as being solid and dependable and real is actually plastic...an artificial representation of true reality."

In seeking an explanation for time and space distortions, Steiger examines poltergeists, which are possibly composed of "pockets of intelligent energy (which) may be directed and semi-controlled by human intelligence; or vice versa...." He suggests that the essentially hostile poltergeist spirits might be harnessed and used as a source of energy.

The Sasquatch, otherwise known as Bigfoot or the Abominable Snowman, is an animal out of its proper spacio-temporal context, and directly related to the appearance of UFOs. He speculates that these creatures might enter our realm to test the planet as a suitable environment for extraterrestrial life, or perhaps they are exiles from another planet or dimension, set down here simply to provide food or a robotic army for some future invasion or visitation. Sasquatch are not found more often, Steiger suggests, because their "vibratory rate" when adjusted to another dimension causes them to literally explode before they can find the aperture back into their own dimension.

Steiger postulates an electrical theory to explain communication between humans and extraterrestrials, since thoughts are apparently manifested in electrical patterns. These patterns in turn can tune our minds to other dimensions and the intelligences that reside within them. Gifted human beings on this planet in growing numbers are learning how to tune in to these channels, men like Uri Geller and Olof Jonsson. Mediums in trances are receiving these messages. Contactees believe they have actually been taken aboard the alien craft, seduced as part of a ploy to experiment with human genes. According to the author, this can all be explained as "someone of as yet undetermined origin...giving us bits of information, 'meaningless on their own' but scraps of evidence like the isolated clues in a mystery story."

No Earthly Explanation
JOHN WALLACE SPENCER
(1974, Phillips Publishing)

In *Limbo of the Lost*, his earlier book on what has otherwise become known as the Bermuda or Devil's Triangle, this former postal inspector, newspaper editor, and public relations specialist chronicled the disappearances of ships, planes, and people without reaching any definite conclusions about the origin or nature of the phenomenon. This second book advances an extraterrestrial explanation.

He claims that the body of water in which these disappearances occur is not triangular in shape, but irregular, covering 380,000 square miles of both sea and coastline extending from New Jersey to the Gulf of Mexico. Within this region during a ten-year period ending in 1973, "60 ships carrying over 900 people mysteriously vanished without a trace."

Spencer says he considered all the possible solutions-atmospheric aberrations, time warps, sea serpents, Mayan or Atlantean abductors, giant waves, even human error-before settling on "the only real logical explanation." He believes extraterrestrial visitors, during the course of deep-sea explorations on this planet, established their UFO bases and laboratories off the coasts of North and South America. Whenever they "want someone or something for their experiments," they wait on the surface and "electronically latch on" to it. "Sometimes they want many people, and other times just one or two; occasionally they check our craft, but in just about every case nothing is left behind, no debris, oil slicks, or bodies, either dead or alive."

As evidence, the author cites instances in the nineteenth and twentieth centuries when sailors observed flying disks entering and leaving the waters of this region, singly and in pairs, apparently conducting some kind of weird experiments. This theory was reinforced, writes Spencer, when a Nebraska policeman named Herbert Schirmer, who had allegedly been abducted by a UFO in 1967, told of his experiences in detail while under regressive hypnosis. Schirmer was on patrol at 2:30 a.m. when he says the silvery, metallic saucer landed, disgorging 5-foot-tall occupants who kidnapped him for twenty minutes. The four humanoid occupants of this observation craft supposedly told Schirmer of their "large base facilities under the ocean off the Florida coast, under the ice of one of the polar regions and off the coast of Argentina." These beings are clever. They absorb electricity from the world's power lines, deliberately operating in a whimsical, chance fashion "so that the governments of the world cannot determine any patterns."

UFO's Past, Present and Future
ROBERT EMENEGGER
(1974, Ballantine)

In the midst of recounting many of the "classic" UFO sightings investigated by the Air Force's Project Blue Book, Robert Emenegger reveals a bizarre series of incidents involving Lieutenant Colonel Robert Friend, the director of the Air Force's Project Blue Book for five years until 1963.

Two Naval Intelligence officers had been sent to interview a woman in South Berwick, Maine, who claimed to be in contact with extraterrestrial intelligences. When the woman used automatic writing, the officers asked her scientific and technical questions she ordinarily could not have answered. Yet she responded correctly to all that they asked. She described how an organization of these extraterrestrials, known as the Universal Association of Planets, undertook a project directed at planet Earth. She apparently was part of that project. She told her military guests, one a Navy commander, the other an Intelligence officer, that the aliens were willing telepathically to answer questions directly through them.

Later, in a meeting with CIA and other military personnel, this naval commander lapsed into a trance and succeeded in contacting a supposed extraterrestrial being. Questions were put to him. Something calling itself AFFA answered, guiding the commander's hand in writing out each response. According to Emenegger, a portion of the question and answer session went like this:

Q- Do you favor any government, religious group, or race?

A- No, we do not. Signed AFFA.

Q- Will there be a third World War?

A- No. Signed AFFA.

Q- Can we see a spaceship or flying saucer?

A- When do you want to see it? Signed AFFA.

Q- Can we see it now?

A- Go to the window. Signed AFFA.

At this point, approximately 1400 hours on July 6, 1959, as detailed in the transcript, the men looked out the window and observed a round object in the sky, "with the perimeter brighter than the center." On checking with local radar installations, so Lieutenant Colonel Friend related to Emenegger, they were told "that particular quadrant of the sky was blanked out on radar at that time."

Nothing more came of these contacts. Friend read the Naval Intelligence files on the original contactee, a woman named Mrs. Swan, and he briefly considered subjecting her to further testing. But on orders from the commanding general, Project Blue Book dropped the entire matter.

"I just don't know what to make of it," Friend told Emenegger. "It seems totally unique in all my experience with investigations of UFOs."

The Edge of Reality
J. ALLEN HYNEK & JACQUES VALLEE
(1975, Henry Regnery)

Hynek and Vallée offer six propositions in this "progress report" on the UFO phenomenon:

(1) UFOs exist, and not merely as fads, self-delusions, or mistaken identification.

(2) Unexplained sightings "fall into a relatively small number of fairly definite patterns of appearance and behavior."

(3) The more puzzling UFO reports come from educated, affluent, reputable persons.

(4) Characteristics of UFOs reported tend to correspond worldwide;

(5) Conventional science has ignored or improperly studied the phenomenon.

(6) New departures in methodology may be necessary in order for science eventually to excavate solutions from the mountain of evidence.

That the awareness of UFOs and a genuine puzzlement over their nature and intentions is worldwide cannot be doubted; differences seem to emerge only in the way each culture reacts. Even in China and the Soviet Union, as Vallée points out, Western visitors are often approached by persons asking whether "those things we see in the sky are seen in other parts of the world, too!" The authors defend the credibility of these UFO witnesses by drawing upon several studies evaluating the accuracy of details reported under similar circumstances.

For instance, the Air Force in 1964 released five railroad flares attached to plastic balloons over Clearwater, Florida, at an altitude of 10,000 feet. Several days later, an ad requesting information on this "sighting" appeared in the local newspaper. Eight persons responded. In evaluating the results, Air Force officers discovered remarkable accuracy in the details described, especially regarding color, numbers of lights, and the time of their observation. Only a few persons accurately guessed that the lights were railroad flares. But Hynek and Vallée contend it was what the witnesses did not report that is illuminating. "They did not report creatures, abduction, telepathic messages, luminous craft with portholes and antennas...in short, by and large, they reported flares."

Hynek relates several instances when persons with a known bias against the existence of UFOs were hypnotized into believing they had seen one. On a Canadian television show a hypnotist known as the 'Amazing Kreskin' put fourteen persons into a trance, led them outside, pointed at the sky, and told them to see a UFO. Everyone did. One man became violent, dashing about shouting: "We've got to call the police!" Yet back in the studio, when Kreskin snapped them out of the trance, none of them could draw on paper what they thought they had seen. Only vague blobs and confused circles emerged. Hynek makes the point that while people can be hypnotized into seeing objects in the sky, they are incapable of describing or sketching what they see, which argues against "any explanation of the UFO phenomenon as the result of hypnosis."

Vallée does not exclude hypnosis as a factor, but his concern relates more to the UFO phenomenon as a control system, "a way to condition our social behavior." He concludes, based on the absurdity and confusion accompanying so many UFO reports, that maybe "somebody is systematically exposing human witnesses to certain scenes, carefully designed to convey certain images." As in the instances where UFOs land in the middle of a highway, humanoids emerge, and pretend to examine or fix their craft. It makes no sense, says Vallée, unless it is purposefully designed to change the belief structure of witnesses. Hynek calls it a process of cosmic inoculation.

Take the case of Joe Simonton, the chicken farmer in rural Wisconsin who claimed during the 1960s that an egg-shaped object descended over his backyard. From it, three creatures traded him four pancakes for a flask of water, then flew off. Hynek tested one of the pancakes, found it to be rather ordinary, composed of three or four varieties of grains. He concluded that Simonton had undergone a "waking dream." But this initial impression of "sheer nonsense" soon wore off as Hynek encountered even stranger stories from other apparently credible people with nothing to gain by inventing outlandish tales. Both Hynek and Vallée now believe Simonton told the truth as he perceived it.

If superior intelligences have Earth under secret surveillance, Hynek wonders whether they wouldn't have "deliberately, somehow, picked and energized people like Adamski [the contactee], to completely muddy the waters? It would be a beautiful counter-espionage plot." Vallée extends the theory to propose that a group of humans, involved in a secret order or society, might have established contact with other forms of consciousness. "A group like that could have the motivation and the means to manipulate public opinion on a grand scale." And Hynek responds: "If psychic projection is a fact, then these things could be kept secret and could be manifesting on a psychic plane." Neither man sees much hope in radio telescope attempts to contact advanced civilizations, if only because other beings are unlikely to have communication concepts similar to ours. "Do you realize that some of the radio communications we have today could not have been detected with the radio equipment we had ten years ago?" Vallée asks if we can expect any civilization far in advance of our own to continue using such an antiquated form of communication.

About the possibility for significant discoveries in the UFO field, Hynek and Vallée propose a variety of scenarios:

...UFOs continue to be seen, books continue to be written on the subject, but no answers ever emerge.

... Extraterrestrials land, and take over.

... UFOs are no longer seen, the phenomenon disappears.

...We finally establish contact with aliens, by telepathy, and an elite develops on this planet, an elite of people able to contact aliens who wield power over other humans who can't.

...The Air Force shoots down a UFO to see if they are friendly.

...Some human discovers what UFOs are, writes a book, explains the whole thing, wins the Nobel Prize, then everyone forgets about it.

...UFOs turn out to be holograms projected by clever Earth scientists, or perhaps the phenomenon is genetically programmed, a built-in defense mechanism emerging only in times of social stress and crisis.

Our Mysterious Spaceship Moon
DON WILSON
(1975, Dell)

Since even before the invention of telescopes, earthly stargazers have seen strange flashes of light on the moon. With the aid of those devices, astronomers have observed unexplainable glows, apparently artificial structures, and on at least one occasion, in 1950, a mechanical object described by British astronomer H. P. Wilkins as "some type of glowing machine hovering near the crater floor." The author has uncovered 400 reports of strange lunar happenings or observations, evidence from which he raises an obvious question: Is the moon inhabited as a base used by extraterrestrials to visit Earth?

In 1927, 1928, and 1934, radio researchers detected unexplained radio signals in the vicinity of the moon. Ohio University and other observatories reported in 1956 "codelike radio chatter from the moon." As the Apollo 11 spacecraft approached the lunar surface in 1969, the astronauts heard a "weird radio noise," a collection of loud sirens and buzz-saw sounds that prompted Mission Control to ask: "You sure you don't have anybody else up there with you?" Apollo 12 astronauts reported sighting two bogeys, or UFOs, as they neared the moon. Apollo 15 astronauts, while on the moon's surface, saw numerous white objects fly by, as if propelled or ejected.

By all cosmic laws, says the author, the moon should not even be circling the Earth. The moon is one-fourth the size of the Earth, proportionately larger than any other satellite in our solar system in relation to the planet it circles. Why does the moon have a huge bulge, a distortion far in excess of what the tidal pull of the Earth might cause? Why is the far side of the moon so different from the Earth side? Why does the moon have such low density in comparison to the Earth?

According to an analysis of the moon's motion by Dr. Gordon McDonald, a NASA scientist, it appears that the moon is hollow. McDonald could not accept the idea that his figures were correct because he could not accept a hollow moon, says Wilson. But other scientists have reached similar conclusions. Two Russians, Mikhail Vasin and Alexander Shcherbakov of the Soviet Academy of Sciences, argued in a Sputnik magazine article that "the Moon is not a natural satellite of Earth, but a huge, hollowed-out planetoid fashioned by some highly advanced, technologically sophisticated civilization."

To support this theory, Wilson draws upon the seismic records of Apollo 12, whose seismometers, left on the moon after the Apollo 12 mission, measured the impact of the Apollo 13 rocket booster as it crashed into the moon. It hit 87 miles from the seismometers with the force of 11 tons of TNT. The moon vibrated for more than three hours at a depth of up to 25 miles. These gonglike vibrations puzzled NASA scientists, but are explainable "if the Soviet theory of an inner metallic spaceship hull is correct.

This theory holds that the moon was steered into orbit around the Earth many eons ago. Somewhere human records must make mention of the event. Wilson thinks he has found persuasive evidence. He quotes archeologist H. S. Bellamy, who says the Gate of the Sun, a Mayan calendar at Tiahuanaco, chronicles a solar year only 298 days long. There were such years, Bellamy claims, about 11,500 years ago when "our moon was not yet the companion of our earth." According to Mayan legend, Tiahuanaco was founded by "sky gods" from the stars and the moon. Even the name of the city, says Bellamy, means city "of the decaying moon," or city of the "doomed satellite." Wilson speculates that the ruins and carvings of Tiahuanaco will eventually yield their secrets, and someday an earthly astronaut "yet unborn may find the originals of those carvings in some cavern on the Moon."

———————————

The Eighth Tower
JOHN A. KEEL
(1975, Saturday Review Press)

Does a single intelligent force account for all religious, occult, and UFO phenomena? Are UFOnauts, leprechauns, and the Sasquatch from another dimension? Are humans biochemical robots controlled by radiation?

That shadowy world known as the superspectrum, a hypothetical spectrum of energies encompassing gravity, the magnetic field, and infrasonic sound, is the source of all paranormal manifestations, from ESP to flying saucers, says John Keel. These phenomena exist outside our space-time continuum, making the masses of energy we call UFOs extradimensional, rather than extraterrestrial. They are unaffected by our natural laws because they are detached from our reality. When UFOs are observed changing color or shape, they are simply making the transition across the visible part of the electromagnetic (light) spectrum and back again into the invisible, altering frequencies into a seemingly solid object. Infrared lenses and film often capture glimpses of these UFO-like objects that are normally invisible to the human eye; UFOs are seen only by accident or design.

Sensitive humans, the psychics among us, are occasionally able to tune in to this superspectrum, but what they pick up is mostly garbled and static, especially at the longer ESP scale, where billions of human minds everyday broadcast trivia, greed, and lust. The superspectrum blindly records all the electrical impulses of the human mind, creating mischievous, often evil patterns. Demonic possession has even resulted. Pagan religions attempted to manipulate the superspectrum, says Keel, and at times succeeded because the spectrum has a computerlike intelligence. But as the human population increased, static jammed the lower frequencies, making the spectrum more difficult to control, more unpredictable in its many manifestations.

"We create the supernatural world," writes Keel. Beliefs of the living create ghosts of the dead; the evil is a by-product of our collective evil. Keel credits the energy consciousness of the superspectrum with the cosmic creation of humankind.

If the superspectrum can create humankind or evolve consciousness, then it can conjure up monsters like Bigfoot and Nessie of Loch Ness. These distortions of our reality are composed of "highly condensed atoms comparable to plutonium." That is why the creatures deteriorate rapidly, disappearing through the process of transmogrification. This explains why UFOs are so often reported accompanied by Bigfoot or other hairy or humanoid creatures; each is produced by the same process, and when the monsters disintegrate, all that is left behind is a residue of silicon carbide and a foul smell, like that of rotten eggs.

UFO sightings, angelic apparitions, ghosts, and related phenomena often begin with a flash of light, so recipients have reported, a light that Keel contends is energy from the superspectrum "tuned to the exact frequency" of the observer's brain. The hallucinations that result are thought to be a part of reality. The Betty and Barney Hill UFO abduction case in 1961 is explained by Keel as a largely hallucinatory experience. The Men in Black (MIB), those Orientals driving black Cadillacs who allegedly interrogate UFO witnesses in an attempt to secure oaths of secrecy about what the witness has seen, have been identified as representatives of every government agency and conspiracy imaginable, from the CIA to the Illuminati and Freemasons. Keel believes the Men in Black are another illusory product of the superspectrum's accumulated casserole of human fears, paranoia, and insecurities.

———————————

The Invisible College
JACQUES VALLEE
(1975, E. P. Dutton)

Jacques Vallée advances a hypothesis that takes the form of five propositions: 1) UFOs are neither objects nor flying; 2) people throughout history who have seen UFOs find explanations for them within the framework of their culture; 3) UFOs might be from a point in time, rather than space; 4) psychic effects produced by the phenomenon offer a key to understanding it; 5) contact between humans and UFOs always "occurs under conditions controlled by the latter."

Based on these propositions, UFOs may be the "manifestations of a process not unlike that of a thermostat in a house," which stabilizes the relationship between outside temperature and human body needs. UFOs could be stabilizing the relationship between human consciousness and the "complexities of the world" humans must learn to cope with and understand. Through the human observer, the UFO phenomenon controls or influences the human belief system and the relationship between "our consciousness and physical reality." Forms of life associated with UFOs, such as the humanoid occupants so often described, might be projections, their reality a product of our dreams.

This powerful force, which Vallée believes has influenced humankind since the dawn of history, originates either within the collective human consciousness or as a direct consequence of extraterrestrial intervention. Those scientists who are investigating either one of these explanations comprise what the author refers to as an Invisible College, working privately, without publicity, to avoid the skepticism and derision of their colleagues in the scientific establishment. Vallée explores the technical feasibility of projecting sounds and images into people's minds from a distance, implying that this could somehow represent part of the technology of the UFO phenomenon. Is it not possible, he asks, that we are dealing with "a terrestrial technology," which is saturating parts of our planet with symbols and messages as a tool for social change? The more absurd such a phenomenon appears, the less seriously it is taken by scientists and politicians; the longer its source remains undetected, the more likely the chances for its eventual success.

Those persons who claim contact with extraterrestrial intelligence or spirits of the dead could very well be tuned into a communications channel. Vallée deals with several of these contactees and their experiences, particularly that of Uri Geller, the Israeli psychic and spoon bender, who says he received his powers from SPECTRA, a computerlike intelligence outside our galaxy. Vallée finds Geller's feats rather persuasive, but concludes that whatever force Geller is tuned into "shows no evidence of being higher than man." This still does not rule out an advanced civilization broadcasting symbols and concepts "on psychic wavelengths" to gifted persons on this planet.

"Such differences as exist between the Koran, the Bible, the Book of Mormon, and other sacred texts would be due to the imperfect understanding of the various individuals who pick up these broadcasts," Vallée writes. Many of the beliefs of certain esoteric groups, their rituals, and the initiations of these secret societies, correspond to a large number of reported UFO encounters where witnesses claim either to have been taken inside the craft or exposed to symbols and unsettling experiences that dramatically alter their perceptions of reality. Vallée wonders whether this "confusion technique" is "deliberately used to affect change on a major scale?"

He proposes the existence of a "control system for human consciousness." He does not know yet whether it is natural or spontaneous, genetic or artificial, the product of social psychology or "superhuman will." It could be a phenomenon governed "by laws that we have not yet discovered."

UFO appearances, especially when they occur in waves or flaps, serve as reinforcement in the evolution of this control system. The phenomenon conforms to the "best schedule of reinforcement," which is one that combines periodicity with unpredictability. Since human life is "ruled by imagination and myth," any governing control system at that level would be practically impossible to detect using conventional scientific methods. If this is occurring, then attempting to analyze UFOs, or even to conceive them, remains a hopeless exercise because "they are the means through which man's concepts are being rearranged." Human beliefs are being controlled and conditioned.

Furthermore, even if UFOs don't represent extraterrestrial visitors, if enough people continue to believe that they do, then they will. The myth will become "truer than true" until certain irreversible changes take place. These changes, the culmination of a learning process, may result in the UFO phenomenon disappearing entirely, or in its assumption of "some suitable representation on a human scale."

UFO's: Nazi Secret Weapon?
MATTERN FRIEDRICH
(1975, Samisdat, Ltd., Toronto)

Germany had a fleet of flying saucers in the experimental stages as early as 1940. Two different UFO designs spawned prototypes, both operating on an electromagnetic propulsion method developed by Victor Schauberger (who invented the implosion motor) and manufactured by the Kertl Company in Vienna. The first flying disk actually flew on February 14, 1945. Piloted by two technicians named Schriever and Habermohl, it reached a speed of 2,000 km/hour. Because special heatresistant metals had to be found, progress in development was slow. During flight, these craft came to be known as "foo fighters," or "Kraut meteors," by the American pilots, who were in awe of them. When the war ended and most other German secret weapons were captured by the Americans and Russians, the UFO scientists and their craft escaped.

So did Adolf Hitler! He had no intention of committing suicide. He and his mistress, Eva Braun, along with Martin Bormann and a few other intimates, flew from Berlin at the last moment, arriving at a secret submarine base. Their bodies, of course, were never found in the Berlin bunker; only a pair of Eva's panties and a few bones. But there were lots of bones and panties in Berlin during those days, thanks to the "saturation fire-bombing of German cities by U.S. Air Terrorists." An armada of submarines took Hitler and his Last Battalion to Argentina, where Hitler's admirer Juan Per6n was in power. From Argentina they established their saucer base in an Antarctic area known as New Swabia, first claimed by a Nazi expeditionary force in 1937.

Antarctica was an ideal place for the saucer base. It has no rust, germs, or decomposition, which would have appealed to "a very health conscious, vegetarian Adolf Hitler." From outside Germany they would continue the struggle, which was not for Germany alone but for "the existence of the white man."

But Hitler's escape had been discovered. In 1946, eight countries undertook "scientific work" in Antarctica, including Soviet, Norwegian, and American contingents. The American force alone numbered 4,000 "specially selected elite U.S. Navy troops" on thirteen ships, including an aircraft carrier, a destroyer, and a submarine, under the command of Admiral Byrd. On nearing the secret Nazi saucer bases, "vengeance was apparently swift" for "the Fuhrer was not to be humored." Four of Byrd's planes were lost without survivors. A secret German weapon known as the sound cannon, which had been tested on pigs and, toward the end of the war, on Russians crossing the Elbe River, was allegedly unleashed on Byrd's troops, paralyzing many of them, bugging out their eyes, and causing them to run helter-skelter. Admiral Byrd abandoned his mission and sailed home.

World War II is not over. The more than forty "police" action wars since 1945, spanning the Korean and Vietnam conflicts, "were supposed to provoke a premature 'showing of hands' by the Last Battalion." When Admiral Byrd failed to lure Hitler from his ice bunker, in the process acknowledging "the superiority of the UFOs and their secret weapons," he recommended to the president that Antarctica be turned into an atomic testing range. A strange thing then happened. An entire fleet of UFOs swarmed in the skies over Washington, D.C., for several nights in 1952, "in perfect, typically German formation." This demonstration of strength prompted America to abandon its planned nuclear devastation of Antarctica.

Occasionally these craft land to seek converts. The author relates the experience of American grain-buyer Reinhold Schmidt, a German immigrant, who was taken aboard a flying saucer in 1957 by its German speaking occupants, a crew of blond, Aryan men and women. The design of their craft resembled in most every detail the German prototypes seen by such technicians as Hermann Klass, who is quoted describing himself as being involved in the production of UFO parts.

Where did Hitler and his scientists get their UFO plans? Did visitors from other galaxies give them a helping hand because they spoke the same or a similar technological language? During expeditions to Tibet and the Himalayas, could the Nazis have discovered long-hidden secrets? It may even be possible, the author claims, that the Nazis were "outer earth representatives of the 'inner earth' or 'outer space' blond, blue-eyed giants who spoke through Nordic, Inca, Aztec, and even North American Indian legends."

Is this the explanation for why Germans "are different," why they are "leading the world in precision engineering and in technology"- because among them dwell Saturians and Atlanteans?

The "Last Battalion" is amongst us already, waiting to "spring into action" when "racial strife and economic disaster" trigger the final struggle. Then they will descend, these saucer Nazis, to rule over the dead and bury the living.

UFOs: What on Earth Is Happening?
JOHN WELDON with ZOLA LEVITT
(1975, Harvest House)

Demons are behind the UFO phenomenon. As fundamentalist Christians, Weldon and Levitt interpret the upsurge of interest in psychic and occult phenomena as inextricably linked to UFOs, each of the various manifestations a consequence of demon powers, and each a part of the pattern heralding the coming of an Antichrist.

They set forth the relationship between demons and UFOs according to attributes ascribed to demons in the Scriptures. Demons seek to possess human bodies, even as UFO occupants have allegedly possessed the minds and bodies of UFO contactees. Demons, like UFO occupants, skillfully imitate benevolent beings and provide humans with information, such as predictions of the future. Demons can assume human form and make contact with humans, even kill them if they wish. Demons can materialize and dematerialize at will. Demons want to be worshipped and are seeking to deceive the entire world. By masquerading as beneficent space brothers, promising peace, harmony, and prosperity to our troubled world, demons intend to play their cruelest and most deceitful trick.

UFOs are no friends of ours, say the authors. Occupants of these objects have kidnapped, raped, terrified, and murdered humans. Persons who have sought to solve the UFO mystery, for example, "suffer a higher than normal death rate."

The intelligence guiding these objects refuses to communicate except by using occult methods such as telepathy, automatic writing, dream states, trance mediums, and the ouija board. To use these methods constitutes a form of entrapment. Like dope pushers, the demons are passing out samples through these occult communications channels. And when humans get hooked, "their allegiance is to the pusher."

Uri Geller claims to derive his powers from extraterrestrial beings. The authors don't conclude from this that Geller is evil, only that he allows evil forces to work through him, which at least makes him an accessory to the crime. They estimate at least 2,500 other people since 1897 have admitted to establishing contact with extraterrestrials. These alleged extraterrestrials are eager to have their story told. Many contactees find themselves writing books, making speeches, and generally acting as public relations spokesmen for demons. Since most people don't display the powers of a Uri Geller, or care to endure the ridicule accompanying claims by contactees, most people who have had similar experiences refuse to reveal them.

Demons are manipulating the magnetic fields of our planet "to affect the perceptions of those who see or contact them." UFO sightings are either projections into our atmosphere or a temporary manipulation of matter and energy. UFO craft might even be the demons themselves. Contactees frequently are victimized, suffering insanity and schizophrenia. Contactees have been commanded to murder others. One woman starved herself to death after sixty-six days of fasting, as commanded by her extraterrestrial teacher, a resident of Jupiter.

Relying on the theories of Carl Jung and Jacques Vallée, the authors conclude that UFOs are intended to produce alterations in the collective psyche of humankind. Since the UFO phenomenon is parapsychological in nature, demons must be preparing us for an Antichrist, who will bring about world unification, under a satanic dictatorship, by creating an illusory enemy-hostile extraterrestrial invaders.

———————————————

Angels: God's Secret Agents
BILLY GRAHAM
(1975, Doubleday)

In some of their reported appearances, UFOs are "astonishingly angel-like," says Billy Graham, Baptist evangelist and theologian, describing those ethereal entities supposedly sent to Earth as God's messengers to aid us in our "struggles against Satan."

"Some Christian writers have speculated that UFOs could very well be a part of God's angelic host who preside over the physical affairs of universal creation," Graham writes, adding that he cannot personally "assert such a view with certainty." However, he points out that UFO reports are on the increase, as is "satanic activity," which "may indicate that the Second Coming of Jesus Christ is close at hand."

He writes of a "spectacular formation" of UFOs that cruised over Japan on January 15, 1975, objects resembling a string of pearls that frightened and mystified thousands of people. "A scientist at the atomic laboratory research installation at Los Alamos told me that for every one in twenty of these UFOs that have been investigated no scientific explanation exists."

With satisfaction Graham notes that "people who make no claim to believe in the God of the Bible" are giving serious attention to books by writers like Erich von Daniken, which theorize that "in pre-history astronauts from distant stars visited earth in spaceships." These theorists take descriptions of modern-day UFOs "and lay them alongside Ezekiel 10, and put forward a strong case."

This passage in Ezekiel describes the descent of a flaming chariot, or UFO. Graham says any attempt "to connect such passages with the visits of angels may, at best, be speculation." But he doesn't dismiss the interpretation. In fact, as an alternative to outright skepticism about events portrayed in the Bible, he clearly would prefer the extraterrestrial hypothesis.

Graham assigns attributes to angelic entities that take on many of the characteristics that humans have described in their alleged encounters with UFO occupants. Angels do not possess physical bodies, although they can assume a humanlike form. Angels can change their appearance, then disappear in a flash. They can't, however, be in all places at once; they are not omniscient. Angels are beings "white and dazzling as lightning." Their beauty and brilliance, "shining like the sun," cannot be measured. Angels are sexless, neither male nor female. While they possess much knowledge that humans do not, they can't know everything. Angels, like humans, are organized according to authority and glory.

Each possesses "different degrees of excellence," and they play disparate yet coordinated roles. Angels often give humans messages, like the time two "unidentified heavenly messengers" warned Lot and his family to flee before the destruction of Sodom and Gomorrah.

If angels surround us, why can't we see them more often? "Our eyes are not constructed to see them ordinarily any more than we can see the dimensions of a nuclear field." Graham uses examples from the animal kingdom: bats with sensitive radar, the sophisticated guidance systems of swallows and geese "that appear to border on the supernatural," to underscore human limitations. "Why should we think it strange if men fail to perceive the evidence of angelic presence?"

―――――――――――――――

The Unidentified
JEROME CLARK & LOREN COLEMAN
(1975, Warner Books)

UFOs are simply a contemporary response to a psychic need as ancient as the human species, contend these two authors, who make extensive use of psychologist Carl Jung's theory of archetypes. They dissect numerous reports of UFOs to establish similarities with psychological elements observed in fairy folklore, monster sightings, and religious revelations, like the experiences of Joan of Arc and Joseph Smith, founder of the Mormon Church.

Clark and Coleman propose two laws governing what they call "paraufology." The first states that the UFO phenomenon "is primarily subjective and its content primarily symbolic." They utilize evidence which seems to indicate that "the considerable majority of... contact experiences...occurs in states of altered consciousness" comparable to the state of mind in which religious visions are experienced, the percipient undergoing "a profound experience at the very deep collective level of the unconscious." The authors do not believe UFO contactees are typically psychotic or otherwise mentally ill, even though they contend that this "otherworld which may seem 'real'...could not possibly exist," much in the same way that mystics or visitors to fairyland reach a nonexistent reality through dreams, trances, or self-induced ecstasy. Hallucinations often times occur "partly because the brain is not equipped to handle the...influx of materials from the collective unconscious."

UFOs arise from the collective unconscious. The circular shape, recurring numbers, such as three, four, twelve, and eight, the asexuality or hermaphroditic appearance of most UFO occupants, their strange beauty, and more importantly the brilliant quality of light accompanying the objects are all symbols permanently embedded in the collective unconscious. Jung said the round object, representing a circle, traditionally signifies psychic wholeness. Three beings are often reported in connection with UFOs, the number three having long been regarded as a symbol of the "pure abstract spirit."

Again, relying upon Jungian terminology, the authors propose that the collective unconscious is represented by the "anima," that nonlogical portion of the psyche that erupts, when denied expression, "violently into consciousness in order to confront it with strange and seemingly incomprehensible contents." Our increasingly technological world has made humankind materialistic and "dangerously out of balance....[human-kind] is out of touch with [the] soul...[in] a machine-dominated world which values only the logical, thinking function." Thus, what results is an attempt by the unconscious "mystical, nonrational elements" of the psyche to achieve conscious recognition through UFO manifestations. The UFO actually seems to parody developments in science. This "otherworld" realm of the collective unconscious has also produced the "Men in Black," those elusive characters who supposedly harass UFO witnesses and seem to symboli-cally represent "archetypal depictions of the devil." This "otherworld" exists outside the conscious, rational realm of the five senses.

The second law of "paraufology" accounts for the apparent physical effects asso-ciated with UFOs, explaining why persons other than just the contactee can see and ex-perience the apparition. While in their "trance," contactees broadcast telepathic signals or use psychokinetic powers to create material manifestations. In each cultural frame of reference, a dream world is created "relatively fixed in the psychic realm," which oc-casionally produces "psychic spillovers" beyond what the human mind can adequately control. The mind powers exhibited by contactees—their ability to foresee the future, their powers of healing, levitation, and teleportation—are fixed outside the space-time continuum as part of that psychokinetic region known as the "psi field." This is the do-main of the collective unconscious. Contactees enter it when their "psychic barriers are relaxed and the ego is vulnerable."

The UFO phenomenon amounts to a "planetary poltergeist" operating like an in-dividual poltergeist, except on a worldwide level, as an expression of modern human-kind's repressed unconscious self, and generating apparitions by the combined psychic energy of us all. As the objective manifestations of a collective psyche, UFOs can be seen and experienced by anyone, no matter what their sympathies or skepticism regard-ing the existence of UFOs.

But poltergeists, warn the authors, can be dangerous and malevolent as well as playful. If the nonlogical, mystical nature of humankind is not brought into harmony with the conscious, logical self, something far more serious than the metaphorical ap-pearance of UFOs will occur: "the collective unconscious, too long repressed, will burst free, overwhelm the world, and usher in an era of madness, superstition, and terror— with all their sociopolitical accoutrements: war, anarchy, fascism."

UFO Exist!
PARIS FLAMMONDE
(1976, G.P Putnam's Sons)

The author dedicates his work to Kennedy assassination conspiracy theorists Sylvia Meagher and Bernard Fensterwald, Jr. On reading this book, it readily becomes clear why. Flammonde seems to believe that a human conspiracy of "enormous influence and incalculable economic strength" is somehow instigating or concealing the UFO phenomenon, with sinister implications for life on this planet.

UFOs could represent the private air force of a "nongovernmental cabal," perhaps an "amazing advance in flying technology by the military," or these craft could be a monstrous creation of human intellect over which humans have lost control, entities or energies beyond the normal understanding of the human world. While the various phenomena may appear as curiosities, rather than threats, "their purpose may be a greater danger than we can conceive." That purpose may in some way be related to "the assassination of a radiant, young President at high noon, in the brilliant sunlight of one of America's great cities." Flammonde further insinuates a connection between the UFO phenomenon and the death of Robert Kennedy, the crippling of George Wallace, and Nixon's demise in Watergate.

Whatever UFOs are, a powerful and determined human conspiracy keeps their true nature a secret to the rest of humanity. During the great airship UFO flap of 1897, for instance, when people across America saw what they thought were newly invented airships in the sky, many statements and events seemed calculated simply to confuse. What were these machines, who built them, and why? Flammonde singles out newspaper publisher William Randolph Hearst as one culprit of deception. *The Examiner* in San Francisco, where the airship sightings began, repeatedly ridiculed people claiming to have seen such objects, call them drunkards and worse. On the East Coast, another Hearst paper, the *New York Morning Journal*, hailed the appearance of airships as signaling a new age. Flammonde asks why Hearst, who "did nothing without a reason," allowed or encouraged his papers to provide such contradictory reportage. He portrays Hearst as a power-hungry international meddler who would stop at nothing to be President. Maybe this was a ploy in his presidential strategy. What more did Hearst know about "the great airship that he wished to have obscured?"

Over the years, official deception, public bewilderment, cultish fanaticism, scientific and religious ignorance, and "political manipulation of individuals" combined to create an atmosphere in which it became virtually impossible to decipher the pa-

142

rameters and nature of the UFO phenomenon. "The public was victim of the inexplicable plans of a group of men who wished to camouflage true extraterrestriality in the air above America, or who successfully screened events, or coming events, of a more earthly, but equally stunning purpose." Flammonde wonders whether deception wasn't a programmed policy within government, especially the Air Force, during the 1940s and 1950s, to prevent anyone from reaching a publicly acceptable solution to UFOs. The 'power clique' might intentionally be taking "the path of greatest incredibility" to create the widest possible conflict of opinion "and the most durable state of general confusion."

Flammonde is not hopeful that humankind will ever communicate with extraterrestrial life, even if we overcome the 'power cabals' to find a solution to the UFO enigma. "Regardless of the mental capacity of a totally unknown plasmic animal, vegetable, or inorganic material, the likelihood of establishing communication verges on nil...the enigmas may be...a more developed stage of life, of which Man is a low form. The possibility of contact in such a circumstance seems improbable in the extreme."

The Hynek UFO Report
DR. J. ALLEN HYNEK
(1977, Dell)

For twenty years the astronomer J. Allen Hynek served as scientific consultant to the U.S. Air Force on Project Blue Book to determine whether UFOs were of extraterrestrial origin, or posed a threat to national security. Hynek initially thoughts UFOs "were just a lot of nonsense." Since the Air Force had previously adopted the position that UFOs simply could not exist, even impressive sightings by credible witnesses were often casually explained away. In this book Hynek reveals how and why these investigations were a calculated sham.

Dating back to 1952, the year the CIA formed its own short-lived inquiry known as the Robertson Panel, government officials feared the reports of UFOs more than their existence. Using the "it can't be, therefore it isn't" philosophy, the CIA expressed concern that an enemy might overwhelm the military communications channels with flying saucer reports to camouflage an attack on this country. So the Air Force, in its investigations of these reports, began to treat UFO witnesses and those expressing an interest in the subject as adversaries. "The public was placed," writes Hynek, "in the role of the enemy."

On August 13, 1947, three persons near Twin Falls, Idaho, in the Snake River

Canyon, watched an oblong object resembling an inverted pie plate as it flew only 75 feet above the canyon floor. Trees over which it passed "spun around on top as it they were in a vacuum." Earlier on the same day, another person had reported similar objects only 20 miles away. In his report Hynek speculated that the effect might have been due to "a rapidly traveling atmospheric eddy." The Air Force used that explanation to "solve" the case. Hynek never heard of such an eddy described anywhere, nor did he consider "other pertinent evidence" in evaluating this sighting. He bemoans how this case, among others, "haunts me to this day."

Another case, at Minot Air Force Base in North Dakota, involved radar, ground, and air visual sightings. Project Blue Book dismissed the radar returns as "possible plasma," the ground visuals as "probable aircraft," and the pilot sighting as the star Vega. In other words, the Air Force was willing to consider any explanation but UFOs. Everything had to be identified.

Hynek demonstrates that Project Blue Book intentionally deceived and lied to the public about its investigation. For instance, a farmer in Oregon snapped two photographs of a flying disk-shaped object in 1950. Evaluations by government photo-analysts concluded that the photos were probably legitimate. But in response to inquiries, the chief of community relations for the Air Force denied that the government held any information concerning the farmer's photos, and further stated that "all photographs submitted in conjunction with UFO reports have been a misinterpretation of natural or conventional objects." Hynek insists that other examples of withheld or missing evidence, false statements, and unscientific methods abound.

Some of the more authenticated reports Hynek evaluated came from militant skeptics. He recounts a report by an Air Force lieutenant colonel who saw a huge, orange, blimplike object 500 feet from the ground sail over his car south of Atlanta. It silenced his radio before disappearing in a 45-degree angle climb at "tremendous" speed.

Of 13,134 cases investigated by the Air Force, all but 587 were identified as hoaxes or mistakes. That is still a large number. Hynek breaks the unidentified category down and discovers that more of these sightings occurred in July and August when people are outdoors in larger numbers than during the rest of the year. Based on population density, New Mexico had a higher percentage of reports than any other state.

Hynek offers no theories in this book to explain the phenomenon. Based on one sighting alone, a boomerang-like propeller that was seen maneuvering in the daylight, Hynek got the feeling that UFOs, whatever they are, want to "play games with us," just to lead us on a confusing chase.

Socorro Saucer: The closest encounter of them all…
RAY STANFORD
(1976, Blueapple Books)

Five tourists from Colorado driving outside of Socorro, New Mexico, made the initial sighting of the object at about 5:45 pm on April 24, 1964. They described it as egg-shaped and metallic and it passed just a few feet above the top of their Cadillac on Highway 85 before streaking a few hundred yards to the southwest where it suddenly stopped, hung mid-air for 30 seconds, then began landing behind a hill. The family saw a white police car which seemed to be following the object and had turned off the highway onto rough terrain, heading toward where the object landed.

Inside the police car was 31-year-old Socorro officer Lonnie Zamora, who had been chasing a speeder when he saw the object. His car windows were down and he heard a loud roar and observed a brilliant cone of blue flame coming from the egg-shaped object. As he drove closer the roar was continuous until he reached the top of a hill and saw the object slowly descending to the ground in a ravine, landing on four extended legs.

Two humanoid figures the size of young boys, wearing what looked like white coveralls, emerged from the object and stood on the ground next to it. They seemed to notice Zamora when he got out of his police car. Before exiting his patrol car Zamora radioed the Sheriff's office and requested backup assistance. He began walking toward the object and once he got to within 50 feet, he heard "a sudden, very loud ear-splitting roar," his report read, and a bright blue flame came from beneath the object and immediately it began lifting off the ground. Zamora fell to the ground to protect himself. The object slowly rose into the air with a sharp whining sound, moving toward the west, and began to pick up speed, until it soundlessly and rapidly headed up and over nearby mountains and disappeared.

Before it lifted off, Zamora had noticed some sort of reddish design or insignia on the side of the craft, which he drew on paper a few minutes later. It resembled an upside-down V with two lines across it. Around where the craft had taken off, nearby bushes were smoking and smoldering.

First officer on the scene was New Mexico State Police Sergeant Samuel Chavez, who arrived just a couple of minutes after the object departed. Chavez saw the smoldering bushes and observed four indentations in the ground where the object's landing pads had been, each indentation being about 4-6 inches deep and about 12 to 16 inches across. More officers arrived on the scene, including an FBI agent who had been at the state po-

145

lice station on business. Not long afterward, an Army Captain from nearby White Sands military site also came to investigate. (Both the Army and Air Force would eventually deny that the object had been one of their own craft.)

Within a couple of days two new investigators arrived on the scene—Astronomer J. Allen Hynek from Illinois, representing the Air Force's Project Blue Book investigation of UFOs, and Ray Stanford from Phoenix, an investigator with NICAP, the National Investigations Committee on Aerial Phenomena. Stanford's personal investigation of this case, which lasted five years, forms the basis for this book, which represents the most exhaustively complete recounting ever published.

Eventually, 11 visual witnesses to the Socorro incident would be identified, along with two auditory witnesses who lived nearby (they heard the vehicle but did not see it). Besides Lonnie Zamora, the witnesses were the five tourists from Colorado passing by, two Iowa men driving by who saw it, as did three witnesses who made reports to local police, and the two women living nearby who Stanford located and at the time of the sighting, had heard two different strange roaring sounds unlike anything they had ever heard before or since.

Stanford retrieved a rock that had been beneath one of the landing pads of the craft and noticed tiny metallic debris attached to it. He and NICAP arranged for a metallurgist at NASA's Goddard Space Flight Centre in Maryland to examine the metal using spectrometers and electron microscopes. When the analysis report came back, performed by NASA's Dr. Henry Frankel, according to Stanford, he was told by Frankel that the metal "was composed of a zinc-iron alloy material that could not occur naturally." In fact, said Dr. Frankel, there is no known such alloy ever produced on planet Earth. "I am virtually certain the alloy is not manufactured anywhere on Earth," Frankel told Stanford and the head of NICAP, Richard Hall.

Soon thereafter, something mysterious happened. Frankel had promised a full report on his metallurgy findings but weeks went by and Stanford and NICAP never received it, nor would Frankel return or answer phone calls. Finally, Stanford heard from a lower-level NASA colleague of Frankel who declared that Frankel had been in error in his analysis. The apparent metal wasn't anything more than ordinary silica. Not only that, but Frankel "is no longer involved with this matter" and no attempt should be made to contact him again.

Stanford and the NICAP officials were flabbergasted by this turn of events. Frankel was being accused of incompetence and he was head of the entire Spacecraft Systems Branch of NASA. Their suspicions naturally settled on a cover-up of the true metallurgy findings, involving Frankel being silenced. That scenario was later confirmed by a high-level Navy official who told Stanford the U.S. government would never allow the truth about UFO visits and landings and crashes to ever be revealed to the public for national security reasons.

"One of the classics in UFO history," declared Dr. Hynek regarding the Socorro sighting, a statement he only felt at liberty to make years after Socorro occurred, when he was no longer associated with the Air Force or its Project Blue Book.

Situation Red: The UFO Siege
LEONARD STRINGFIELD
(1977, Doubleday)

Flaps is the term UFOlogists use to describe periods of concentrated sightings. Leonard Stringfield chronicles and evaluates the flap of 1973, lasting from late summer through autumn, when practically every state was affected. More than fifty cities and towns reported unidentified lights in the sky on October 17, at the flap's peak.

He draws connections in reports between the cattle mutilations, first recorded in western states, the appearance of Bigfoot, and the "phantom helicopters" that were allegedly seen near UFOs. Stringfield believes that the "real" UFOs in our skies are of extraterrestrial origin, their occupants highly advanced, possessed of psychic skills to manipulate witnesses into trances to disguise their reason for coming.

During two of the creature appearances in Pennsylvania and Ohio, witnesses gave similar reports of huge, hairy apelike critters that would change into another form, then vanish in a flash of light, like "someone taking a picture." A third incident, on the night of October 25, 1973, involved fifteen persons who saw a large red ball descend into a pasture in New Jersey. Three of the witnesses grabbed rifles and approached the object, estimated to be 100 feet in diameter. Two apelike creatures with glowing eyes stood nearby; the smell of burning rubber, then sulphur, stifled the air. One witness fired three shots into them and they disappeared. Six persons, including a state trooper and a Civil Defense officer, arrived several hours later and found a 150-foot-diameter area glowing white. Livestock in the vicinity acted strangely. Suddenly, one of the witnesses began growling like an animal, threw his father to the ground along with another man, and ran through the field growling and swinging his arms before collapsing. Sulphur blanketed the air again. The investigators felt light-headed and experienced difficulty in breathing. All of this was recorded on tape.

Strong, offensive odors, such as sulphur, burning rubber or oil, have long been associated with sightings of UFOs and their occupants. Stringfield quotes another UFO researcher as speculating that perhaps this can be explained as simple mischief. UFO entities are taunting us, or staging these demonstrations to monitor our adrenaline flow.

During the 1973 flap, fully one-third of reported sightings were made by police personnel, many during "close encounters." But he points out that the media can create and control a flap. In the Cincinnati area the news media "whipped up UFO news with such intensity" that Stringfield began to wonder whether people were "being guinea-pigged as a test of psychological reaction."

On the evening of October 11, two fishermen named Hickson and Parker, while sitting on a pier near Pascagoula, Mississippi, were supposedly abducted by a UFO that descended onto the water and beamed them aboard. That story got national coverage. Less than a month later, four Pascagoula fishermen spotted in less than 10 feet of water a round, metallic object, about 9 feet in diameter, that glowed brilliantly beneath the surface. The Coast Guard was called and two crewmen, poking at the moving object with oars, realized that the white light penetrated the oars like x-rays. The light headed into the channel, 90 feet deep, and out toward the Gulf of Mexico, escaping from the Coast Guard boat. Within a few miles of this sighting and the alleged abduction was a naval shipyard and a large nuclear plant operated by Litton Industries for the U.S. Navy. Stringfield warns that since 1952, UFOs have been observed over or near every nuclear power development on the continental United States.

Space-Time Transients and Unusual Events
MICHAEL A. PERSINGER & GYSLAINE F. LAFRENIERE
(1977, Nelson-Hall)

Into a computer the authors fed information on 6,060 Fortean events-"Fortean" referring to Charles Fort, who chronicled such aberrations as rocks, flesh, and blood falling from the sky, appearances by supposedly extinct animals, cultural artifacts found in unlikely places, and various unexplained aerial phenomena. A total of 1,242 UFO sighting reports were included in this computer analysis, sorted on the basis of time, space, and category. When plotted on maps, then compared to other species of Fortean phenomena, striking similarities emerged. All the data seemed to form a series of patterns with a common geophysical source.

For instance, the distribution of events for all categories corresponded to the density and distribution of UFO sightings as plotted on a map of the United States. Of even more importance to the authors' thesis is that both these distributions in turn corresponded to a seismic map of the country picturing magnetic faults and earthquake zones. Consequently, the earthquake-prone areas like California and the New Madrid region, running through Missouri and Ohio, reveal more UFO and related activity than do other sections of the nation.

From these findings four hypotheses are established:

(1) Unusual events occur in the same locality, year after year.

(2) Clusters of these unusual events parallel similar clusters in other localities worldwide.

(3) Serial patterns of these events precede and follow geophysical and meteorological cataclysms.

(4) These patterns are often associated with stellar fluctuations.

Persinger, a psychologist specializing in physical mechanisms of the natural sciences, and his research associate Ms. Lafreniere, draw connections to sunspot activity and solar flares, whose dense clouds of charged particles, in colliding with the Earth's magnetic field, oscillate the field "like the movements of a large, invisible bouncing spring." These solar pulses penetrate our atmosphere in eddy-like currents, upsetting surface equilibria and producing unusual Fortean phenomena, including UFO appearances, as "expressions of our earth resonating in response."

When massive flare and sunspot activity erupted between August 2 and 7, 1972, huge multicolored fireballs appeared over much of Canada and the United States. A week later, the United States underwent "one of its largest UFO flaps" in history. Had storm-induced clots of magnetic flux within the solar wind released visible plasma in our upper atmosphere to account for these sightings?

Some kind of connection between solar activity and seismic disturbances on Earth seems apparent. Many Fortean events occur "before the manifestation of a severe earth jolt or a volcanic explosion." The authors wonder whether unusual Fortean events aren't by nature transient, produced by accumulating stresses that ebb and flow within limited localities. From these stresses many of the effects associated with UFO sightings apparently occur.

A high electric field stimulated in the localized stress area would produce a low level of ionization in the air. That might cause rocks to bounce around, or seem to fall from the sky or pop from the ground. Rain could fall on a clear day. Electrical appliances might malfunction, and car engines would stall. Animals, being more sensitive to electrical and magnetic fields, would be the first living creatures to react, just as they do before earthquakes and storms.

Human bioelectrical systems, when in contact with such a field, would react by producing in the percipient "dreamlike states, episodes of paralysis, or intervals of unconsciousness." The consciousness might be inundated by stored images "that he or she cannot control." Even more subtle modifications in thought are possible. The person could experience those stored images in a sort of "waking nightmare," in which everything perceived is shaped by expectations formed by conditioning, at the cinema, or by the peer group. "Each person might perceive the stimulus in different ways. Where one person sees a globular UFO with men inside, another person might see a metallic ship." The individuals would be convinced of the reality of what their memory experienced, which would complicate, perhaps even entirely nullify, hypnosis as a method for discriminating the source of the information.

Other psychological and physical reactions of the human system to such a field would include putrid smells, tingling sensations, humming or buzzing noises, the sound of voices, and strange feelings of "a presence." Should the area be sufficiently ionized to produce a luminous object, paralysis or severe burns would result if the observer ventured too close. During certain stages this "electric column," as the authors call it, could even be detected on radar, moving along the lines of stress displacement in the Earth until it dissolved.

Another possible explanation for UFOs is what the authors describe as a space-time overlap caused by solar or other disturbances. Material manifestations might emerge, analogous to a three-dimensional hologram. Like the power of magnetism, while the image could not be destroyed, the act of splitting it into separate images would reduce the total energy in each. The degree of "materialness" of the hologram would depend "upon the severity and degree of the space-time overlap." As the space-time manifold became displaced, the object, or hologram, would appear to be transparent.

"Interaction between large numbers of biological systems and the geomagnetic environment within which they are immersed," might conceivably result in a metaphysical phenomenon whereby the potential is energized for that interaction to "display behaviors and patterns of its own." Electronic units of human organisms— human brains—when clustered and exposed to a changing magnetic field (especially under stressful or emotional conditions such as political and social turmoil) induce in themselves and others thought images that are indistinguishable from reality, or that become reality.

The Roswell Incident
CHARLES BERLITZ & WILLIAM MOORE
(1980, Grosset and Dunlap)

Perhaps the most unusual press release in U.S. military history was circulated on July 8, 1947 by Lieutenant Walter Haut, public information officer at the Roswell Army Air Base in New Mexico. In it Haut announced that a crashed "flying disk" had been obtained from a local rancher by the intelligence office of the 509th Bomb Group of the Eighth Air Force. Possession of the disk was taken by Major Jesse A. Marcel, who "subsequently loaned it to higher headquarters." Associated Press picked up the story and it appeared in newspapers worldwide. The local Roswell Daily Record headlined its story: RAAF CAPTURES FLYING SAUCER IN ROSWELL REGION.

"Almost immediately a news blackout descended over Roswell while higher authorities as far away as the Pentagon decided what the next move would be," write Moore, a Minnesota high school English teacher, and Berlitz, author of The Bermuda Triangle. Major Marcel accompanied the crash debris aboard a B-29 to Carswell Air Base in F'ort Worth, Texas. There General Roger Ramey, commander of the Eighth Air Force District, held a press conference to announce that the flying disk "was really nothing more than the remains of a downed weather balloon."

On July 9, Roswell's newspaper printed two stories about the incident. One quoted Gen. Ramey about the weather balloon explanation. The second was an interview with William Brazel, the ranch foreman who found the debris. Under the headline HARASSED RANCHER WHO LOCATED 'SAUCER' SORRY HE TOLD ABOUT IT, Brazel said he was familiar with weather balloons, having found others on the ranch, but "I am sure what I found was not any weather observation balloon."

In 1979, more than three decades after these events, Moore and Stanton Friedman, a UFO lecturer, tracked down and interviewed some of the participants. Colonel Thomas DuBose, Gen. Ramey's former adjutant, recalled that "orders from on high" came for the debris to be shipped by plane to Wright Field in Ohio, while Gen. Ramey tried to "put out the fire" of publicity by fabricating a story that the debris came from a weather balloon. Warrant Officer Irving Newton, who had been in charge of the Carswell weather office, examined the debris Gen. Ramey showed the press and pronounced "there's no doubt that what I was given were parts of a balloon." But he expressed bafflement to his interviewers that Major Marcel and others at Roswell, who must have seen hundreds of weather balloons, could have failed to accurately identify the debris.

Although Colonel William Blanchard, commander of the Roswell base, had died,

Friedman found his widow. She claimed that Col. Blanchard knew the debris was not from a balloon. "He knew it was nothing made by us. At first, he thought it might be Russian because of the strange symbols on it. Later on, he realized it wasn't Russian either."

Major Jesse Marcel, who had been promoted to Lieutenant Colonel after the crash, was interviewed by Moore and Friedman from his retirement home in Louisiana. He described seeing wreckage on the Brazel ranch scattered "over an area of about three quarters of a mile long and several hundred feet wide." Aided by a Counter-Intelligence Corps agent whose last name he remembered as Cavitt, Marcel collected enough fragmented debris to fill the trunk and back seat of his Buick along with the jeep that Cavitt drove.

"It was definitely not a weather or tracking device, nor was it any sort of plane or missile," Marcel insisted to his interviewers in 1979. The debris consisted of small beams about a half-inch square resembling balsa wood, with pink and purple lettering that appeared to be hieroglyphics. "They were very hard, although flexible, and would not burn." There were many pieces of a metal, like tinfoil, only it could not be creased, dented, or cut. A B-29 was half-filled with the wreckage and flown to Fort Worth, then later to Wright Field in Ohio for analysis. To mislead reporters in Fort Worth, Gen. Ramey ordered weather balloon debris to be substituted for the real unexplained wreckage.

Marcel's son, Jesse Jr., though only 12 years old at the time, still vividly remembers his father coming home with a car and jeep filled with wreckage. "The material was foil-like stuff, very thin, metallic-like but not metal, and very tough," recalled the younger Marcel. Some of the beam remnants contained pink or purplish-pink colored writing that resembled Egyptian hieroglyphic characters.

Bill Brazel, whose rancher father died in 1963, also recalled these events. The military had sworn his father to secrecy about what was found on the ranch, and had given him a complete physical exam before releasing him. Not all of this debris was collected by the military. "Seems like every time after a good rain I would manage to find a piece or two that they had overlooked," reported Bill. He described the material as comparable to balsa wood in weight, but much harder, along with metal like substances thin as tinfoil but which he was unable to crease or tear because it always resumed its original shape. Two years after the crash, because Bill had apparently talked too much about his collection of debris, four military men from Roswell visited him and confiscated his findings, warning him "this stuff was important to the country's security." From these interviews and related reports and rumors the authors "postulate a tentative picture of the sequence of events." On the evening of July 2, 1947, a flying saucer flew over Roswell and into a lightning storm where it was struck, spewing "a great quantity of wreckage" over the ranch. "The saucer itself, although stricken, managed to remain in the air for at least long enough to get over the mountains before crashing violently to the ground in the area west of Socorro known as the Plains of San Agustin." A military group from the Alamogordo air base on the White Sands Proving Grounds was sent to the final impact site where they found the saucer and the bodies of its extraterrestrial pilots, including perhaps two injured survivors.

As the Roswell debris was being sent by plane to Fort Worth and then Ohio, the saucer and alien bodies were sent by train to Muroc Air Base in California. Years later, in 1954, President Dwight Eisenhower visited Muroc "to see the remains of the crashed disk and the bodies." Soon thereafter, according to "rumor and circumstance," the disk was shipped by truck to Wright-Patterson Air Force Base "to join the bits of wreckage and bodies which had preceded them there in the late 1940s."

(It should be noted that Charles Berlitz, listed as co-author of this book, did not participate in researching the book, but wrote it. Research fell to William Moore and Stanton Friedman. The book's publisher replaced Friedman with the better-known Berlitz as co-author to enhance the book's sales potential, based on Berlitz having written a bestseller about the Bermuda Triangle.)

Clear Intent
LAWRENCE FAWCETT & BARRY J. GREENWOOD
(1984, Prentice-Hall)

What does the U.S. government really know about UFOs? That question motivated the authors and researchers associated with them to files a series of Freedom of Information Act (FOIA) requests, then numerous lawsuits, to shake loose UFO-related documents from the U.S. Army, Navy, Air Force, Department of State, Defense Intelligence Agency, FBI, CIA, and the National Security Agency. The resulting 3,000 pages of previously classified documents that were released form the foundation for this book.

During October and November 1975, an unprecedented wave of UFO sightings were reported over, around, and on the northern U.S. tier of four Strategic Air Command bases and missile sites. Documents released by the Air Force give an inside account. At Loring Air Force Base, Maine, an unknown object was tracked on the tower radar at 7:45 p.m. and simultaneously seen by a security policeman. The object penetrated the base's airspace and came within 300 yards of the nuclear storage area. The next night an unknown craft reappeared, sighted by security police and the crew of a B-52 bomber on the ground. Two crew members said the object resembled a stretched-out football, reddish orange in color. It appeared at the end of a runway at an altitude of about 150 feet, then proceeded to hover over a weapons storage area. The object shut off its lights and disappeared, not to be seen again. Similar equally puzzling incidents occurred a few weeks later at Malmstrom Air Force Base, Montana, Wurtsmith Air Force Base, Michigan, and Minot Air Force Base, North Dakota. A major security alert was activated, and according to the authors, "the UFOs slipped away, evading all attempts to identify them."

While writing this book, the authors were contacted by a former security policeman at Bentwaters Air Force Base, a NATO installation in England. Though they give him a pseudonym, Art Wallace, he would later go public with his story and identify himself as Larry Warren. This source maintained that in late December, 1980, a UFO had landed at night in a forest next to the air base. About 1 a.m., relates Wallace/Warren, he was part of a convoy of security police sent to investigate a light which was tracked on radar before it came down in the forest. At a clearing in the woods, movie cameras were recording an incredible scene-an object 50 feet in diameter, resembling a transparent aspirin tablet, was hovering about one foot off the ground. A second object resembling a red light flew out of the trees and stopped above the first one, then merged with it creating a bright white domed disk. Wallace/Warren and other security officers walked around the disk, noticing how they cast shadows upon it. At this point all the officer remembers is waking up in bed, fully dressed and muddy to his knees, at 4 a.m. thinking he had been dreaming.

In May, 1983, an American UFO researcher, Robert Todd, filed an FOIA request about the incident with the Air Force's 513th Combat Support Group, which provides document management for the Head quarters of the Third Air Force based in Europe. One month later Todd received a startling response from the commander of the 513th, who enclosed a copy of an official letter describing the incident written by Lt. Col. Charles Halt, deputy base commander at Bentwaters. The Halt letter, written January 13, 1981, about two weeks after the UFO sighting, relates how two security policemen spotted a strange glowing object, metallic in appearance, landed in a forest near the base. It had a red light on top, blue lights underneath, and seemed to be hovering. It maneuvered through trees and disappeared, only to reappear an hour later near the base's back gate. Nearby farm animals were observed going "into a frenzy." The next day three depressions one-and-a-half inches deep and seven inches in diameter were found where the object had been sighted on the ground, and radiation levels were elevated inside the depressions and within the triangle formed by them. A similar red object returned the next night. Col. Halt affirmed that "numerous individuals, including the undersigned, witnessed the activities."

On another case, an equally intriguing document was released by the Air Force Office of Special Investigations in response to a 1982 FOIA request by Greenwood, wanting information on UFO sightings at Kirtland Air Force Base in New Mexico. Two of the seven released pages consist of an Office of Special Investigations report about three security policemen at Kirtland observing a bright light perform strange aerial maneuvers and then land inside Coyote Canyon, which is part of a restricted weapons test range. On three more nights security police watched disk-shaped objects and lights land in the same area, before leaving at high speed.

The next five pages in the file involved an OSI investigation of a civilian, Dr. Paul Bennewitz, whose Albuquerque home adjoined the northern boundary of Kirtland's weapons storage area and who claimed to have photographed the lights which were seen by security police in August and September, 1980. OSI Special Agent Richard Doty was sent to interview Bennewitz, and view the photographs and over 2600 feet of 8mm motion picture film picturing UFOs over the weapons test and storage areas. Doty noted in his report how Bennewitz had several pieces of electronic surveillance equipment pointed at the secret base "attempting to record high frequency electrical beam pulses." On Nov. 10, 1980, Bennewitz was invited to Kirtland to present the film and photos he had collected over 15 months. Nine Air Force officers and scientists met with him, including a brigadier general, four colonels, and the commander of the base investigative unit. During this session Bennewitz, said the OSI document, "related he had documented proof that he was in contact with the aliens flying the objects." One week later Special Agent Doty informed Bennewitz that the Air Force "would not become involved in the investigation of these objects."

Light Years
GARY KINDER
(1987, Atlantic Monthly Press)

Since the age of five Eduard "Billy" Meier believed himself to be in contact with a group of alien beings from the Pleiades star system. They were nurturing him and implanting telepathic images in his mind so he might one day undertake his life's mission of photographing Pleiadian spaceships, a necessary step in convincing humankind "to accept the truth that they belonged to a network of galactic societies." Beginning in 1975, at the age of 37, Meier produced the first of hundreds of sharp photographs allegedly depicting Pleiadian "beamships" hovering in forests and fields near his home outside the Swiss village of Hinwil. It is the subsequent investigation of these photos and other reputed evidence of contact, such as "crop circles," spacecraft artifacts, and beamship recordings, which Gary Kinder recounts in this book.

Though his left arm had been severed above the elbow in a bus accident, Meier still had amazing agility, once rebuilding part of a barn without help. Despite these talents people could not figure out how, if the UFO photos were fakes, he had managed to concoct such an elaborate hoax without assistance. The hundreds of photos showing a variety of 'beamships' were the clearest color, daylight shots of alleged UFOs ever produced in the entire history of the phenomenon.

No one ever personally witnessed one of the beamships as Meier photographed them. He claimed the Pleiadians would telepathically alert him to their presence, prompting him to rendezvous at all hours with their intermediary, a German-speaking female alien named Semjase, who allowed him to photograph her 21-foot spacecraft. Semjase looked exactly like an Earth woman, with blue eyes and amber hair, except she was 330 years old. Her planet, Erra, so Meier related in his journals, resembles Earth with trees, grass, running water, and species of horses, cows and fish.

As laughable as these descriptions of the Pleiadians may sound, widespread publication of Meier's photos made believers out of thousands of people worldwide, including actress Shirley MacLaine, who made a pilgrimmage to Meier's humble Swiss abode and turned him into a cult figure. Others became believers or were mystified because Meier seemed capable of producing unexplainable phenomena. In the summer of 1976, for instance, Hans Schutzbach accompanied Meier to a secluded meadow where, so Meier claimed, an invisible beamship would be hovering. Meier held up a tape recorder and from somewhere above them, in open air about 30 feet high, Schutzbach estimated, they heard a loud "eerie and grating noise, like a high-pitched cross between a jet engine and a chain saw." Meier seemed capable of altering the sound by moving his hand back and forth. Afterwards, Schutzbach searched the entire area but saw no indication of speakers, cables, or recording devices.

This tape recording of beamship noises and the photos intrigued a group of American UFO researchers, prominent among them retired Air Force Lt. Col. Wendelle Stevens and private investigator Lee Elders. They sent the recording to sound engineers and electronics specialists for analysis. No one could duplicate the complex sounds, nor could they conceive of how the recording was produced. The beamship photos did not fare so well. No original negatives existed-Meier claimed they had been stolen-and so no competent scientific analysis could be undertaken. Meier also had produced several pieces of metal which the Pleiadians told him came from the hulls of their beamships. On examination by a metallurgist one piece turned out to be "pot metal," a common low-grade casting alloy. The other piece, however, became a puzzle. IBM scientist Marcel Vogel pronounced the golden-silver triangle-shaped metal "very, very unusual." It contained the rare-earth metal thalium, which is more rare and expensive than platinum. Unfortunately, soon after he analyzed it, Vogel 'lost' the metal fragment and it has never been seen again.

Above Top Secret
TIMOTHY GOOD
(1987, Sidgwick and Jackson)

In this massive 592-page examination of worldwide UFO reports, British researcher Timothy Good, a longtime musician with the London Symphony Orchestra, concentrates on summar1zmg government documents which, when taken together, paint a broad picture of official cover-up and deceit. An entire section of each is devoted to military and intelligence agencies in the U.S. and Britain, with other chapters discussing treatment of UFO events by the governments of France, Italy, Portugal, Spain, Australia, Canada, China and the USSR.

"One of the most sensational UFO events ever reported by military personnel," as Good describes it, occurred in England at an American base, documented by U.S. Air Force witnesses. He reprints a letter about the incident sent by Lieutenant Colonel Charles Halt, deputy base commander, to the British Ministry of Defense. In it Halt recounts how UFOs were over the Woodbridge/Bentwaters installation on successive nights, December 27 and 28, 1980, seen by numerous security police, other base personnel, and Halt. The first object appeared metallic, triangular in shape, about three meters across, and left behind ground depressions and radiation where it landed.

At least one dozen Air Force witnesses to these incidents have come forward, of whom Sergeant Adrian Bustinza, the Security Police Acting Commander at Woodbridge, "is undoubtedly the most important." Bustinza related in an interview how he and two other officers set off in a truck after midnight to search for the object, but all of their equipment and the truck kept malfunctioning "like all the energy had been drained out."

They found an area in the forest where "triangular tripods" had been burned into the ground, leaving a radiation residue. They tried to follow the object as it moved through the trees and "came upon a yellow mist, about two or three feet off the ground." Then they spotted the object moving from 10 to 20 feet off the ground. "It was a tremendous size, a round, circular shape, a red light on top and several blue lights on the bottom." Bustinza and a detachment of men formed a perimeter, at 15- foot intervals, encircling the object for about 30 minutes. Suddenly it took off in a flash, emitting "a cold blast of wind which blew toward us for five or ten seconds."

In 1984 a Cable News Network reporter posed questions about the incident to the U.S. Air Force in Washington, D.C. A one-word answer was given to nearly every question-"unknown." The Air Force did, however, deny that any photographs, video-tapes, or tape recordings were made during the encounter. Even that was unmasked as untrue when Colonel Sam Morgan, former Woodbridge base commander, released a tape recording made over a two-hour period by Col. Halt as Halt and his men watched and followed the object.

Good spends a chapter trying to rehabilitate the credibility and reputation of Frank Scully, an entertainment journalist who wrote the 1950 book, *Behind The Flying Saucers*, claiming that four extraterrestrial spacecraft and the bodies of their humanoid pilots had been recovered. The account has long been branded a hoax because two of Scully's sources turned out to be notorious con men. "But there is a great deal more to this particular story," Good alleges.

Scully's principal source, identified in the book as Dr. Gee, "was in fact a composite character of eight scientists, each of whom supplied him with various details." The crash these informants were reportedly in agreement on happened near Aztec, New Mexico, in 1948. A disk 99.99 feet in diameter came down, killing its 16 humanoid occupants-each from thirty-six to forty-two inches in height. The craft was dismantled and sent, along with the bodies, to Wright Field in Ohio for study. Quoting a "quite astonishing" report published in 1987 by William Steinman, who, like Scully, was unwilling to divulge his sources, Good writes that the disk crashed on March 25, 1948, after radar tracking disrupted its control mechanism. Within hours it was recovered about 12 miles northeast of Aztec by an Army Counterintelligence squad called the Interplanetary Phenomenon Unit. Steinman names eight prominent scientists as members of the team sent to assess the wreckage and bodies, including Dr. Robert J. Oppenheimer and Dr. John von Neumann.

"The most convincing evidence that Scully's claims are fundamentally sound has been provided by the Canadian government scientist Wilbert Smith," writes Good. In 1950, Smith, then a senior radio engineer with Canada's Department of Transport, wrote a memo about a conversation he had in Washington, D.C. with Dr. Robert Sarbacher, a consulting scientist to the U.S. government. Scully's book had just been published and Smith asked Sarbacher about it. Sarbacher confirmed that "the facts reported in the book are substantially correct," and furthermore, the whole subject of saucers had been classified by the U.S. government "two points higher than the H-bomb."

In 1983 William Steinman corresponded with Dr. Robert Sarbacher, then Chairman of the Board of the Washington Institute of Technology in Palm Beach, Florida, to confirm the accuracy of Smith's account. Sarbacher wrote back that he had "no association with any of the people involved in the recovery and have no knowledge regarding the dates of the recoveries." But he went on to state that John von Neumann and Robert Oppenheimer were "definitely involved." Sarbacher claimed that he too, "had been invited to participate in several discussions associated with the reported recoveries," but he could not personally attend the meetings. He had heard, however, that "certain materials reported to have come from flying saucer crashes were extremely light and very tough," and he "got the impression" talking to people in his office that "these aliens were constructed like certain insects we have observed on earth."

Out There
HOWARD BLUM
(1990, Simon and Schuster)

Based on a tip in 1987 from a National Security Agency contact, Blum, a former *New York Times* reporter, learned about the existence of a top secret UFO Working Group, a panel organized by a colonel in the Defense Intelligence Agency at the Pentagon and composed of 17 officers and scientists from the Army, Air Force, DIA, NSA, and the Central Intelligence Agency. Blum eventually turned two of these men into sources for this book, and the fact that spokesmen for the NSA, CIA, and Department of Defense all denied the existence of a UFO Working Group spurred Blum on to find out what lay behind the stonewall of secrecy and lies.

What provoked formation of the UFO Working Group were several alarming incidents where unidentified objects "tripped" the electronic energy field fence extending into space that surrounds America's defense perimeter. Colonel Harold Phillips of the DIA, who as a child had seen a UFO in an Iowa cornfield, was further persuaded to convene the high level secret working group by an unorthodox experiment he had requested concerning the "tripping" of this electronic fence. The DIA operated, in co-sponsorship with Naval Intelligence, a classified project that employed remote viewers who used their minds to scan the oceans for Soviet submarines. Colonel Phillips asked the scientists managing Project Aquarius, as it was known, to have their scanners search for what had tripped the fence.

"The precise latitude and longitude where the fence had first been tripped was provided to three of the most reliable Aquarius viewers," Blum reports. The viewers were separated in different chambers and asked to draw anything their scans at those coordinates picked up as having occurred within the last 48 hours. Three sketches were faxed to Phillip's Pentagon office-all were remarkably similar depictions of "rounded, wingless aircraft." These sketches were brandished as evidence at the initial meeting of the UFO Working Group to make a case that the U.S. Space Surveillance Center in Colorado had monitored an intrusion by alien spacecraft. The task of the Working Group thus became, in Phillips' words, "a scientific one-to search for proof of extraterrestrial intelligence."

As Blum began his own investigation into the history of the UFO phenomenon, delving deeply into declassified government reports, he found a pattern of Pentagon interest, if not obsession, with the subject. For instance, during eight months beginning in the fall of 1975, visual sightings and radar recorded UFOs repeatedly encroaching on airspace around the Air Force's nuclear weapons supply depots, triggering a series of high alerts by the Strategic Air Command. The Joint Chiefs of Staff during this period received daily "UFO Intrusions at SAC Bases" updates. "As mysteriously as they had started, the intrusions stopped," Blum discovered. "The Air Force was never able to identify the craft that had penetrated the protected airspace above its nuclear bases."

In 1961 Air Force Intelligence initiated two secret projects-Moon Dust and Blue Fly-intended to "locate, recover, and deliver descended foreign space vehicles." Military units were trained to act as space-related SWAT teams, delivering in secrecy items fallen from space of "technical intelligence interest" to the Air Force's Foreign Technology Division based at Wright Patterson AFB in Ohio. The explicit mission for Moon Dust and Blue Fly teams, as described in a classified mission statement, was to "field intelligence personnel on a quick reaction basis to recover or perform field exploitation of unidentified flying objects." Blum could never determine whether the teams had ever been actually activated to retrieve crash debris.

Past and present CIA employees informed Blum that the agency used officers from its Domestic Collection Division, under a variety of cover identities, to staff an ongoing covert operation investigating UFO sightings by conducting witness interviews nationwide. Numerous internal CIA memos from the 1970s described this project as involving both its Domestic Collection Division and the Science and Technology Division. In July 1988, two officers from the Domestic Collection Division were detailed to the UFO Working Group and, carrying papers giving them phony identities as NASA engineers, they were sent to Elmwood, Wisconsin, to undertake field research into a series of UFO sightings in the area.

In the fall of 1988, UFO Working Group members received visits from the FBI's Foreign Counterintelligence division asking for their help in confirming, or debunking, the authenticity of an eight-page briefing document allegedly prepared for President-Elect Dwight Eisenhower in 1952, stamped "Top Secret" on each page. Known as Operation Majestic- 12, this document described the crash of a spacecraft and recovery of four alien bodies in 1947, north of Roswell, New Mexico. According to this briefing paper, a secret group called MJ-12 was formed to undertake a covert analysis of the saucer wreckage and the four "extraterrestrial biological entities."

Blum's own investigation of the MJ-12 document led first to William Moore, co-author of The Roswell Incident. That book "persuaded government counterintelligence agents to recruit him (Moore) as a spy" in September 1980, just a few months after the book's publication. The recruitment came in Albuquerque, New Mexico, initiated by a man Moore would call The Falcon, who claimed to be highly placed in the government intelligence business and directly connected with a government UFO project whose members wanted the truth about UFOs to be released to the public. The Falcon said if Moore would cooperate with him, he would make certain Moore received inside help with his UFO research. Moore agreed to enter into a working arrangement. Moore's liaison to The Falcon became Master Sergeant Richard C. Doty, an agent with the Air Force Office of Special Investigations assigned to Kirtland Air Force Base in Albuquerque.

Moore's first undercover assignment was to infiltrate and evaluate the findings of something called Project Beta, a UFO monitoring program begun by Paul Bennewitz of Albuquerque. Bennewitz had recorded lights hovering over parts of the Kirtland base, and strange messages he thought were from alien spacecraft. Bennewitz believed that two species of aliens had invaded America-the whites and the greys-who had entered into a secret treaty with the U.S. government. For four years Moore spied on Bennewitz and reported on his actions to Doty and The Falcon. Meanwhile, Doty and Falcon systematically tried "to confuse, discourage, and discredit Bennewitz." Official looking faked government documents about the treaty with aliens, underground alien bases, and alerts about alien invasions were passed on to Bennewitz to further feed his belief and his paranoia. Why was Air Force intelligence engaged in a campaign of disinformation against Bennewitz? Moore claims he never knew, though he speculated that it could have been a training exercise, or Bennewitz "had been monitoring a top secret military training program," or even that Bennewitz "had actually been filming UFOs" and that jeopardized the U.S. government cover-up. Whatever the motive, it worked, as Benne-witz was driven to the breaking point and hospitalized.

It was into this atmosphere of deception, disinformation, faked government doc-uments, and intrigue that the MJ-12 document turned up in the hands of one of Moore's close associates, Los Angeles movie producer Jaime Shandera. It was mailed to Shan-dera anonymously in December 1984, in the form of exposed but undeveloped film. He and Moore developed the film themselves and found images of eight pages which seemed to prove Moore's book thesis that an alien craft and its humanoid occupants had fallen into military hands at Roswell.

After a year of investigative inquiries ending in 1989, the FBI "could not find an agency or an individual willing to swear out a complaint asserting that the MJ-12 docu-ments had been stolen from their classified files. Therefore, if the papers weren't stolen, they must be forgeries." On the list of forgery suspects were the band of OSI agents at Kirtland Air Force Base, who were known to have fabricated convincing OSI reports about alien invaders and mutilated cattle. "The FBI had little doubt these Air Force OSI agents were capable of putting together the MJ-12 documents." But all of them denied any role in fabricating MJ-12 and to further complicate the FBI investigation, "many of the agents had suddenly decided to retire." As an exasperated FBI agent told Blum, "Even the government doesn't know what it knows!"

Angels and Aliens
KEITH THOMPSON
(1991, Addison-Wesley Publishing)

Picking up where psychologist Carl Jung left off, and where mythologist Joseph Campbell might have begun if he were still alive, this scholar of the cultural imagination places the UFO phenomenon squarely in the context of an evolving mythology which can only be understood against the rich backdrop of all other visionary experiences-re-ligious miracles, visions of angels, folkloric accounts of fairies, shamanic journeys, and near-death experiences. As with these related visionary encounters, UFO events "are typically surrealistic-dream-like, fantastical, at once less than and more than real—the psyche reaches for interpretations in order to bridge the gaps."

Within the "drama," as Thompson calls the "unfolding UFO epic," can be found key defining personalities whose appearance at crucial turning points helped alter "the course of the plot." These include Kenneth Arnold, Carl Jung, Betty and Barney Hill, Jacques Vallée and Allen Hynek. Arnold's 1947 description of aerial objects which undulated "like saucers" is the opening scene of the modern narrative. Jung first brought to public consciousness the idea of how legend is formed, voicing the view that "seemingly new events in the sky mirrored important changes in the human soul." Simply by virtue of timing and circumstance Betty and Barney Hill, though not the first alleged abductees, nevertheless generated a wave of publicity for an experience "against which all others of that genre would be measured." Vallée wrote books challenging us to treat the symbolic nature of the phenomenon as "more significant than the UFOs themselves, whatever they may actually be." Dr. Hynek avoided becoming a tragic figure, in the classic sense, by transforming himself from paid UFO debunker for the Air Force into an enlightened "member of a reformed social order," taking up the UFO believer's mantle as a "chastened elder hero."

Myths either deepen or die. Within the realm of UFO occupant and abductee stories exist striking parallels with other "mythological journeys" into "infernal regions of the collective soul," where humanity encounters the "unknown Other." Visions of angels, of demons, and of aliens alike "can easily be seen as messengers," existing somewhere between mind and matter, "able to change their forms at will in the sight of select witnesses." Thompson raises the question of how these linkages occur, what pattern connects aliens, abductees, angels, shamanic and near-death experiences, to the "tenuous dimension known as ordinary reality."

All of these experiences constitute "initiations and rites of passage" for us collectively and as individuals. Despite surface differences between these phenomena, all involve life-altering "otherworldly journeys amid extraordinary—and apparently autonomous—beings." UFO initiations are the most modern manifestation of a conditioning process helping us to redefine "conditions of the game we call Reality."

As a sort of "cosmic chameleon darting back and forth between mind and matter," UFOs provoke us to revise our perceptions of the supposed chasm between mind and matter, spirit and body. Angels, demons, fairies, and related phenomena have always been depicted as holding that middle ground. Perhaps the UFO experience is designed to accelerate an evolutionary path allowing our species to harness "strange, uncharted human capacities" that would enable us to navigate this twilight zone. To that end this collective rite of passage may be destined, in the words of Joseph Campbell, to culminate with "an anthropomorphic vision: the Cosmic Man."

Revelations
JACQUES VALLEE
(1991, Ballantine Books)

Spurious government documents about UFOs which have proliferated and groups which have emerged to "study" fantasies channeled from alleged alien intelligences all provide evidence to Jacques Vallée that some of the UFO phenomenon is composed of "complex hoaxes that have been carefully engineered by government agencies engaged in psychological warfare exercises. "UFO sightings in this category "are covert experiments in the manipulation of the belief system of the public," maybe heralding the birth of a new myth or perhaps even of a new religion.

Manipulation comes in a variety of guises. Vallée relates how he and Dr. Allen Hynek were tantalized in 1985 by the prospect of U.S. Defense Department cooperation in releasing genuine UFO evidence. Two officials of the Defense Audiovisual Agency (DAVA), General Glenn Miller and General Robert Scott, held several meetings with Vallée and Hynek at Norton Air Force Base in California, and admitted they believed UFOs were extraterrestrial spacecraft because they had seen UFOs themselves. Gen. Miller even claimed to have been aboard a UFO piloted by a "normal human being" with Oriental eyes who came from either Mars or Venus. No secret government evidence was ever released to Vallée and Hynek, forcing them to conclude that Scott and Miller "were two friendly contactees who were trying to validate their own beliefs." The experience gave Vallée an insight into how high-ranking government officials can use their positions to promote their own agendas.

This explanation fits the 1984 appearance of the so-called Majestic-12 documents, eight pages of an alleged classified 1952 briefing paper for President Eisenhower discussing UFO crashes at Roswell and elsewhere. Vallée believes MJ-12 is a fake, deliberately leaked disinformation "designed and executed by a rogue group within the intelligence community." As further evidence he cites the case of Air Force Captain Robert Collins, and Air Force Office of Special Investigations agent Richard Doty, both of Kirtland Air Force Base in New Mexico, who in 1983 fed fabricated documents about crashed UFOs and recovered alien bodies to Linda Howe and other UFO researchers. Vallée can only speculate whether these pieces of disinformation were intended "to destabilize the few groups that are still seriously doing UFO research" and to place "the few competent investigators in a ridiculous light."

As for Area 51, that top secret facility at Nellis Air Force Base in Nevada, where rumor has it crashed UFOs have been reverse-engineered and are being test flown, Vallée recounts how Lockheed Aircraft may be using the site for test flights of Aurora, a super fast new aircraft which uses ramjet propulsion. People like John Lear and Robert Lazar, who have made claims about UFOs and aliens at Area 51, may have "become part and parcel of the real cover-up" whose motive is keeping under wraps "a radically new intelligence platform" intended to replace the SR- 71 spy plane.

Reports of a 1947 UFO crash near Roswell, New Mexico leave Vallée unimpressed. The materials described as being recovered from the crash site are within human technological capabilities in the late 1940s. Even the thin lightweight metal from the crash, which supposedly could not be dented or burnt, resembles silvered saran, a paper-thin product of the 1940s which restored itself to a smooth finish after being crushed and would remain undented from hammer blows. "My guess is that someone deep within the U.S. government structure is using the stories of crashed saucers to hide something else," Vallée writes.

A 1980 UFO incident witnessed by military personnel at the Woodbridge/Bentwaters U.S. Air Force Base in England may be evidence "that military groups engaged in psychological warfare have actually mastered the art of simulating close encounters and have designed exercises involving confrontations with nonlethal weapon platforms disguised as unidentified flying objects." Vallée tells of a conversation he had with an inventor of a remotely-piloted vehicle, developed for a U.S. intelligence agency in the 1960s, who described it as disk-shaped and able to manuever in and out of trees, even windows, surveying its surroundings with a miniature television camera. This device "can be equipped with mechanical, optical, and electronic devices that can be used in sequence or in combination to produce very spectacular UFO sightings." The purpose of these staged UFO encounters around military installations could be to test anti-terrorism security measures and to evaluate the judgment and reactions of observers.

While strongly believing that a genuine UFO phenomenon exists, Vallée nonetheless is disturbed that "somebody is going to a lot of trouble to convince us of the reality of extraterrestrials, to the exclusion of other, possibly more important hypotheses about UFOs." Is the phenomenon being used as a cover by secret groups for something else entirely? The apparent ability of UFOs, the real ones, to manipulate space and time suggests to Vallée the presence of a nonhuman consciousness, perhaps one which coexists with us and may not be extraterrestrial at all, but has interacted with us, been our companions or caretakers, since the dawn of recorded time.

Crash At Corona
STANTON T. FRIEDMAN & DON BERLINER
(1992, Marlowe & Company)

"Two very strange devices crashed in central New Mexico in July 1947," contend Friedman, a nuclear physicist, and Berliner, an aviation writer. "By every indication, what crashed were two alien spacecraft, along with their crews of small humanoids." Based on interviews with "dozens" of firsthand and secondhand witnesses, the authors believe "hundreds and possibly thousands" of Americans were, and still are, "involved in the huge, costly official effort to cope with the crashes, to transport, examine, and store wreckage and bodies and house at least one live alien, to learn who and what was involved and to keep it all secret."

For these two authors the question of crashed alien craft begins with an eight-page document called Majestic-12 (sometimes referred to as MAJIC 12 or MJ-12), purporting to describe the crashes for a super-secret group of 12 high-level figures from the military, scientific and intelligence fields known collectively as the Majestic-12 group. The document is alleged to be a briefing paper for President-Elect Dwight Eisenhower, dated November 18, 1952, detailing the recovery and preliminary analysis of a disk which crashed 75 miles northwest of Roswell, New Mexico.

Though the document surfaced under suspicious circumstances-it appeared under the door of a Roswell crash researcher in 1984, not in paper form but as unprocessed photos of the document pages-the authors believe the chances of it being a hoax "have decreased almost to zero." Even if the document did turn out to be a hoax, "there must be something very similar in existence, since the reality of the Corona crash increases in probability with each passing day."

In early July, 1947, one disk crashed northwest of Roswell on the Foster Ranch, near the small town of Corona, an event chronicled in the 1980 book, The Roswell Incident. A second disk crashed during the same time frame 150 miles to the west, on the Plains of San Agustin, where it was allegedly seen by six-year-old Gerald Anderson, who was there rock hunting with his father, brother, uncle, and a cousin. They suppos-

166

edly inspected a circular silver object which had plunged into a hillside, disgorging four tiny humanoid crew members, one of which survived. The U.S. Army arrived, cordoned off the area, and took possession of the disk and aliens.

"No other firsthand witnesses have been found to corroborate Anderson's testimony," the authors concede. And three years after publication of the hardcover edition, the paperback version of their book carried a preface in which they further conceded that "problems have arisen" with Anderson's account because "he has admitted falsifying a document, and has changed his testimony."

Nevertheless, Friedman and Berliner claim they are still "convinced that there was a crash at the Plains of San Agustin in early July, 1947, at about the same time as the crash near Corona," and this has been "established beyond any reasonable doubt." The total number of alien bodies recovered include three dead and one survivor from the Plains, and three more dead and perhaps one survivor from the crash near Corona. The descriptions of these bodies-about four feet tall, large heads, slanted eyes-are consistent with reports made by numerous abductees describing their alien abductors.

A consequence of scientific analysis of these crashed disks may have been technological spin-offs accelerating human scientific development. For instance, solid-state electronics arose in late 1947, months after the crashes, with the invention of the transistor, which "might have resulted from study of the wreckage" as "has been suggested by scientists with knowledge of these events."

The Truth About The UFO Crash At Roswell
KEVIN D. RANDLE & DONALD R. SCHMITT
(1994, Avon Books)

After interviewing more than 300 persons, almost half of them alleged to be firsthand witnesses to some aspect of a UFO crash north of Roswell in 1947, including the retrieval of wreckage and extraterrestrial bodies, the authors wrote this volume to "correct errors" and "add data collected" since publication of their first book on this subject, UFO Crash At Roswell, released in 1991.

In a sequence of events they piece together, the story begins on July 1, 1947, when radar equipment in the Roswell, White Sands, and Alamogordo areas of New Mexico track an object whose "speeds and maneuvers suggest that it is not a craft manufactured on Earth." On July 2, Mr. and Mrs. Dan Wilmot spot an oval object pass over their home in Roswell at 9:50 p.m. heading northwest at high speed. Two days later, on July

4, as "radar sites continue to watch the object" it explodes at 11:27 p.m. Witnesses see and hear this event. William Woody and his father watch a flaming object fall north of Roswell. James Ragsdale and his girlfriend see a bright flash and hear a roar near their campsite outside Roswell. And farther north, near Corona, sheep rancher W.W. "Mac" Brazel hears a thunderclap which resembles an explosion.

On July 5 at 5:30 a.m., the military sends a recovery team to the crash site 35 miles north of Roswell. There they find numerous civilians including a group of archae-ologists and members of the Roswell Fire Department-already viewing the craft and its five dead alien passengers. The civilians are escorted away and the site is cleaned within six hours. To the north of this site the rancher, Mac Brazel, finds unusual debris scattered over one of his pastures. Meanwhile, a Roswell mortician, Glenn Dennis, receives sev-eral puzzling phone calls from the Roswell Army Air base mortuary officer asking about the availability of small caskets and procedures for preparing a body which had been exposed to the elements.

On July 6, Brazel drives 75 miles to Roswell and informs Sheriff George Wil-cox of the debris on his land. Wilcox calls Roswell Army Air Field, whose commander sends intelligence officer Jesse Marcel to investigate, accompanied by Sheridan Cavitt, a counterintelligence agent. On July 7, some of the debris and the alien bodies are flown to Andrews Air Base outside Washington, D.C. Meanwhile, Marcel and Cavitt collect wreckage from Brazel's field into several vehicles and drive it to Roswell. On July 8, Roswell base commander Colonel William Blanchard orders the distribution of a press release announcing "a flying disc had been found." Marcel accompanies several pack-ages of debris from Brazel's field on a flight to Fort Worth Army Air Field. General Roger Ramey holds a news conference to "announce to the world that the officers at Roswell had been fooled by a weather balloon." He displays pieces of a weather balloon which has been substituted for the debris that Marcel brought from Roswell.

In September 1947, Master Sergeant Lewis Rickett assists Dr. Lincoln La Paz from the University of New Mexico in trying to determine the speed and trajectory of the craft when it crashed. La Paz inspects the two now-cleared debris sites and concludes a probe from another planet had to have been responsible. In November, Arthur Exon, on assignment from the Air Materiel Command at Wright Air Field in Ohio, flies over the ranch impact area and sees "two distinct sites" where debris came down gouging the topsoil. Exon, later to become an Air Force Brigadier General and, in 1964, commander of Wright-Patterson Air Force Base, heard at the time that alien bodies had been sent to Wright Field, as were pieces of the spacecraft's wreckage which underwent "everything from chemical analysis, stress tests, compression tests, flexing. The boys who tested it said it was very unusual. It had them pretty puzzled." As a result of "the recovery of a craft from space," according to Exon, a top secret committee was formed within the government to study the debris and the entire UFO phenomenon.

Authors Randle and Schmitt devote several chapters of their book to a debunking of two stories associated with the Roswell incident—that another spacecraft crashed during the same period on the Plains of San Agustin; and that the so-called Majgestic-12 documents concerning Roswell are authentic. They point out how the only supposed firsthand witness to a 1947 crash on The Plains is Gerald Anderson of Missouri, who claimed he was six-years-old when he saw the alien bodies while out rock hunting. But a relative's purported diary produced by Anderson discussing the event turned out to be phony, say the authors, and on other points in Anderson's story he contradicted himself and destroyed his credibility.

As for the clever Majestic-12 hoax, as they describe it, this reputed briefing paper for President Eisenhower about a Roswell saucer crash and alien bodies contains stylistic errors, misspellings, and inaccurate ranks for persons supposedly on the MJ-12 committee. Where the MJ-12 briefing paper says "on 07 July, 1947, a secret operation was begun to assure recovery of the wreckage of this object," the authors note how their research indicates recovery actually began on July5, which true insiders would have known in writing a briefing for the President. What could be the motive for this forgery? The suggestion is made that Roswell researcher William Moore, one of those who released the document, had proposed to friends a year before its discovery that if he created such a Roswell document it might "open doors that were closed." In addition, a year before MJ-12 surfaced Moore was allegedly at work on a novel with reporter Robert Pratt, which Pratt revealed was about UFOs and a secret government report designated "Majik."

UFO Retrievals
JENNY RANDLES
(1995, Blandford)

From this chronology of 32 alleged UFO crashes worldwide over the past 100 years, British researcher Jenny Randles concludes "something interesting" can be found in parts of the accounts, but "the majority of evidence is peppered with misperception, mistaken identity and a pinch of fabrication." She estimates that at most six of the 32 episodes qualify "even as potential candidates" for alien spaceship retrievals.

As if to illustrate her point she begins the narrative describing more than a pinch of fabrication. William Loosley was an English cabinet maker who died in 1893, supposedly leaving behind a manuscript recounting his abduction and medical examination by an alien robot from a crashed spaceship. An English physicist, David Langford, published the manuscript in 1979, in book form, presenting it as a truthful story. Many UFO-oriented publications favorably reviewed the book without a single writer or researcher ever contacting Langford asking to see the original Loosley manuscript. Once the book went out of print Langford confessed the hoax, calling it a demonstration of UFO enthusiasts' gullibility.

What may have been the first and longest surviving hoax occurred in 1897, with an article in the *Dallas Morning News* quoting several residents of nearby Aurora, Texas, who claimed an airship struck a windmill owned by the local judge. A non-human body, badly maimed, was recovered and buried, along with debris bearing hieroglyphic symbols. Seventy-five years later a group of UFOlogists tried to prove the crash had actually occurred. Three persons in their nineties who had reportedly lived around Aurora before the turn of the century were traced and two of them related having seen the crash and the alien pilot, though one later changed her story and the other was shown to have been living in Oklahoma at the time of the event. A final blow to the credibility of this story came with the revelation that no windmill had ever stood on the supposed crash site.

A first hint of the Roswell UFO crash came in 1955, in the premier issue of the British magazine *Flying Saucer Review*, recounting an anecdote told by Hughie Green, who had been in the Royal Canadian Air Force in July 1947. He was driving through the southwestern U.S. when he allegedly heard radio alerts about a saucer crash in New Mexico. He heard nothing more the next day about it and remained intrigued by what had happened for years afterward. Not until 1978 would the curtain of silence part thanks to Lt. Col. Jesse Marcel revealing the Roswell crash details. To Randles this secrecy constitutes the most telling evidence for a UFO crash having occurred. "The fact that silence still prevails—or rather that the absurd weather balloon theory is adhered to—is the most serious argument that something extraordinary—secret even now—was involved in the Roswell crash." Yet, she worries that a credible account is attracting jokesters and hoaxsters and the whole story "is in danger of being sunk by an over-abundance of witnesses and testimony."

What the author describes as "the best attested case of an alleged UFO crash outside the USA" occurred in late December 1980, at two neighboring NATO air bases in England, Bentwaters and Woodbridge, staffed primarily by American Air Force personnel. Randles wrote an article about the crash in 1981, and later wrote two books on the subject. At least 50 witnesses to some aspects of the event have been identified. Both the British Ministry of Defense and the U.S. Air Force officially conceded that an unexplained flying object landed in a forest between the two bases, excess radiation readings were later detected in ground traces, and another encounter with a hovering light was witnessed by numerous persons, including the base commander. "From the witnesses I have talked with," observes Randles, "I have little doubt that these men did see something remarkable: a weird phenomenon full of lights, misty forms, with elements of electrical fields, animal disturbance, physical energies and mind distortion."

A History of UFO Crashes
KEVIN D. RANDLE
(1995, Avon Books)

From a UFO crash database he developed, Randle examines six reports of alleged crashes in some depth, finding three of these deserving of closer scrutiny. He also dissects the Majestic-12 documents, concluding that all of them are hoaxes, and Project Moon Dust, the government project to retrieve fallen outer space debris, which he believes was a cover for the investigation of physical evidence related to UFO reports. "Flying saucers do exist," argues the author, a U.S. Air Force captain. "They are craft from other planets. And they do crash."

Beginning with the strongest case, the Roswell 1947 crash about which Randle co-authored two previous books, he generally recycles a familiar chronology of events and witness testimony. In response to skeptics of an alien explanation for this well-publicized case, who claim it would be impossible to keep such a momentous military secret for so long that involved so many people, he responds that they are right because the secret has not been kept. The story has been leaking since 1950, when Frank Scully published the first book alleging a saucer crash in New Mexico. Though Scully got the details wrong—relying on testimony from two convicted con men—and that ended up helping to discredit him and the story, he had apparently stumbled upon the essence of the secret.

Saucer case number two is the story championed by Stanton Friedman that 150 miles from Roswell, on the plains of San Agustin, a second craft and its crew of aliens crashed in early July, 1947. Only one alleged firsthand witness to this incident has been produced—Gerald Anderson of Missouri, who would have been six years old when it happened. Randle points out numerous inconsistencies in Anderson's account. Not only that, but Anderson was caught fabricating a document which supposedly bolstered his story, and even his wife accused him of habitually concocting tall tales. Randle believes this case should be discarded "given the impressive amount of evidence that has been marshaled against the Anderson testimony, the lack of firsthand corroboration, and the lack of any supporting documentation."

The alleged crash in 1953 of a 12-foot-long cigar-shaped spacecraft near Kingman, Arizona, was first reported by Raymond Fowler in 1976. His source, given the pseudonym of Fritz Werner, who claimed to have worked as an engineer for the Air Force's Project Blue Book, told how he was put on a bus with blacked-out windows and taken to a crash site where he saw the craft and the body of a four-foot-tall humanoid wearing a silver suit. In subsequent interviews with other researchers Werner periodically changed the details of his story. Randle concludes this witness is of "dubious reliability," though he refuses to entirely dismiss the case because two other secondhand sources surfaced who corroborated a few aspects of the story. "For all its faults," Randle writes, the Kingman story "is still better than the vast majority of the UFO crash/retrieval cases."

Two other cases—in Nevada and Pennsylvania—which the military discounted as meteor sightings. Randle describes as instances where something extraordinary happened that could involve extraterrestrial spacecraft. In April, 1962, witnesses nationwide reported a bright object flashing from east to west across the night sky. In Utah and Nevada witnesses described the object as changing course and then, somewhere outside Las Vegas, disappearing in a series of bright explosions. The radar at Nellis Air Force Base north of Las Vegas tracked an object that night at 10,000 feet before it suddenly disappeared. Numerous witnesses, including pilots, said the object had a flat trajectory, made sounds, and changed course, none of which matched the capabilities of a meteor. Two different flight crews insisted that it had passed below their planes, and radars from New York to California tracked the object, whose flight time of 32 minutes was far too long for a meteor. "The Air Force offered a series of explanations ignoring the facts," conclude Randle. "But the witnesses who were there know the truth. They saw something from outer space, and it was not a meteor. It was a craft from another world."

An Air Force team from the highly classified Project Moon Dust was apparently sent to the site of a crash outside of Kecksburg, Pennsylvania, on December 9, 1965. Late that afternoon, a fireball flashed across Canada and the northeastern U.S. before striking the ground near Kecksburg at 4:47 p.m. At first observers thought it might be the reentry of Russian Kosmos 96, a malfunctioning space probe. But it had reentered and crashed in Canada about 13 hours earlier. Within two hours of the object's impact in a forest, military units had cordoned off the area. A few hours later a flatbed military truck with a tarp covering something was seen to leave the area at high speed. Two alleged witnesses later told of having seen the object at the impact site before it was taken away. They described it as acorn-shaped, about nine to twelve feet in diameter with a gold band around the bottom. Randle finds this case intriguing but inconclusive. "Until all the facts are known, the case must remain open."

Alien Impact
MICHAEL CRAFT
(1996, St. Martin's Press)

To help himself understand his own "share of strange, UFO-type encounters," this Fortean phenomena researcher decided to explore the role of consciousness in the UFO experience and "the impact of the powerful belief systems of those touched by the phenomenon." Consequently, while researching this book, everyone Craft met who had undergone an unexplained sighting, an alien abduction, or received a channeled message, emerged with a drastically changed worldview and belief system, which leads him to suspect we are being conditioned to engage in new behaviors that will ultimately reshape our species.

Perhaps the first psychological investigation of an alleged contact with aliens occurred in the 1890s, when a Swiss professor at the University of Geneva studied Helene Smith, who began channeling automatic messages through writing while in a trance. She claimed to be in communication with a resident of Mars named Astane, who taught her to speak the Martian language. The professor translated the Martian rune-like symbols Smith wrote into French, which was published as the book *From India to the Planet Mars*. Michael Craft notes how many elements of Smith's tale-such as three-feet-tall beings, and Martians appearing from a rose-colored or pink light-still turn up100 years later in modem contactee accounts. What were then 19th century spiritualist visions can be seen now as composing one of the two streams or traditions of contact—"people who see or meet UFOs, and those who channel messages from the 'space people' while in trance. Nowadays these two themes often run together."

UFO cases remind the author of ghost sightings. Both ghosts and UFOs seem to prefer appearances at night, both provoke the sensitivity of dogs, cats and farm animals, both appear and disappear out of nowhere in silence, both seem able to glide through walls and other solid objects. Like ghosts, UFO occupants are often described as luminous or radiant. When speech is reported, both ghosts and aliens use cryptic, grammatically poor language. Witnesses to both ghosts and UFOs frequently report similar smells-ammonia, and burning sulfur-which lends more credence to the idea that UFOs and ghosts "may be more closely related than anyone previously thought." Both phenomena seem to be deliberately deceptive, cosmic tricksters playing with the human mind.

Animal mutilations may be another case in point. These inexplicable stories have been reported for centuries, though not necessarily accompanied by the modern version's "strange lights in the sky." Outbreaks happened in the Middle Ages, described as "vampire attacks," in which herds of sheep were found missing their genitals, eyes, and other organs. Similar slaughters occurred in 1810 along the Scottish English border involving both sheep and cattle, in 1874 in Ireland where 30 sheep a night were discovered drained of blood, and in 1906 throughout parts of England. Adding these old accounts to the wave of cattle mutilations in America since the early 1970s leads Craft to conclude "there now seems to be undeniable evidence that the worldwide reports of animal mutilations, unidentified lights in the sky, and human abductions are closely linked, whatever their real cause is."

Based on his own experience of having visions-usually of elflike entities emerging from bright light-while under the influence of "magic mushrooms," Craft proposes that contactees, practitioners of white and black magick, shamans, channelers, vision questers and the like "may all be seeing the same things. When witnesses meet aliens or 'lose time' watching UFOs, they may be entering the same Dreamtime that the old Aborigines spoke of." Meeting with alien beings "bear a striking similarity to traditional accounts of fairies, goblins, and elves. The beings' appearance, speech, mode of travel, taste for trickery and kidnapping" make the author wonder whether they were already on Earth centuries ago, maybe before our species evolved, and we are only beginning to realize that we are rediscovering them.

Top Secret/Majic
STANTON T. FRIEDMAN
(1996, Marlowe & Company)

"I am positively convinced that alien UFOs exist, that they are visiting earth, and that our government knows this," begins Friedman, who spends the next 14 pages re-counting his background as a nuclear physicist for Westinghouse and other corporations.

The book then becomes a defense of the authenticity of the original Majestic-12 document, as well as two more MJ-12 documents which subsequently surfaced, including an entire "operations manual" which purports to be a set of procedures for UFO wreckage handling by special military recovery teams.

The first eight-page MJ-12 document appeared in December 1984 in the form of an undeveloped black-and-white 35mm roll of film mailed to Los Angeles movie producer Jaime Shandera, without a return address but bearing an Albuquerque, New Mexico postmark. Dated November 18, 1952, prepared for President-Elect Dwight Eisenhower, it refers to "a secret operation" begun on July 7, 1947, to recover the wreckage and four small alien bodies from a crashed disk near Roswell, New Mexico. Further on, the document mentions another crashed saucer having been recovered in December, 1950, from the Texas border with Mexico.

Shandera was known in UFO circles to be working closely with Friedman and William Moore, co-author of The Roswell Incident, following up on new Roswell-related information. Friedman speculates that "insiders" connected with the Air Force's Office of Special Investigations, who had promised Moore and Shandera "to help quietly" in the release of UFO data to the public, had sent the top secret papers. Most prominently mentioned among these OSI officers was Richard Doty, based in Albuquerque, who met with Moore and other UFO researchers numerous times to share information in the early 1980s.

Friedman confesses that when he first saw the name of Dr. Donald Menzel on the list of MJ-12 group members he thought the document must be a hoax. A Harvard professor of astronomy, Menzel wrote three books debunking UFO sightings as misidentifications of natural phenomena, which would not seem to make him a natural candidate for membership on a secret panel studying an alien craft. Yet, as Friedman examined Menzel's personal papers and correspondence in the Harvard archives, he discovered that the debunker had led a secret life doing highly classified consulting work for the National Security Agency and the CIA. "Now my confusion about Menzel was giving way to the certainty that he was the best suited of all the members of Majestic-12 to provide disinformation to the general public," Friedman concluded. Menzel was the "ideal person to analyze the symbols on the Roswell crash debris, since he had the high-level security clearance to go with his cryptographic skills." Thus, the inclusion of Menzel in the MJ-12 document, given that his intelligence work and high security clearance had been kept from the public, helped convince Friedman of the document's authenticity.

Other persons listed as MJ-12 group members also aroused Friedman's suspicions that a connection existed between them and the Roswell crash. For instance, the membership of General Nathan Twining, eventually named Air Force Chief of Staff, "was certainly no surprise." From Twining's correspondence files at the Library of Congress, and in an interview with the general's former pilot, who provided flight logs, Friedman pieced together Twining's schedule in the few days following the Roswell event. On July 7, 1947, Twining flew to Alamogordo Army Air Field in New Mexico, and apparently spent four days in the Roswell area. Then on July 11, he flew to Wright Field in Ohio, where the crash debris had allegedly been flown. To Friedman this itinerary placed Twining at the center of the crash retrieval and cover-up.

Friedman concedes that the MJ-12 document cannot absolutely be guaranteed as genuine because "a clever forger or disinformation specialist-especially one within the intelligence community-would have access to all the appropriate ink, paper, typewriters, signature samples, and memo formats." Yet he still believes a case can be made for the legitimacy of the MJ-12 papers and the existence of an MJ-12 group. As an example, the document claims President Truman issued a classified executive order creating the MJ-12 group on September 24, 1947. When Friedman contacted the Truman Library to learn Truman's appointments on that date, he was told that Dr. Vannevar Bush and Secretary of Defense James Forrestal visited the President, the same two people who the MJ-12 document identifies as heading up the MJ-12 group. Friedman interprets this revelation as evidence that only an insider could have known the significance of that date, therefore the document must be real.

In 1985 Shandera and Moore received several anonymous postcards sent from overseas containing riddles. One mentioned a Box 189 and Suitland, which they decided meant the National Archives annex in Suitland, Maryland, which housed declassified government files. Both men flew to Washington, D.C., and combed through boxes of files. In Box 189 they found a July 14, 1954 White House memo to General Twining referring to a MJ-12 Special Studies Project briefing. The memo had no relationship to anything else in Box 189, and had apparently been planted for Shandera and Moore to find.

An attack on the authenticity of the Twining memo came from debunker Philip Klass. He contended that typewriters in use at the White House at that time used elite type and did not have the pica typeface portrayed in the memo. In 1989 Klass challenged Friedman to produce other known-to-be-authentic White House memos from the 1954 period written in the Twining memo typeface, for which Klass agreed to pay $100 each up to a maximum of $1,000. Friedman says he found 34 such memos in a pica typeface, winning the bet and a check from Klass for $1,000.

Still more reputed MJ-12 documents appeared in 1992, obtained by Tim Cooper, a California researcher whose father had once managed the printing department at Alamogordo Air Field. One document was a memo from the head of the CIA to the President urging him to familiarize himself with Army summaries of MJ-12 material. "In some ways they were too perfect," Friedman says of Cooper's documents. Further investigation demonstrated each to be an "unambiguous fraud," nothing more than re-typed and slightly reworded versions of legitimate letters and memos. Even this fraud gave Friedman hope that the original MJ-12 source "was still alive, still trying to get the truth out."

Next came news of "what is perhaps the mother of all Majestic-12 documents," exults Friedman. In December 1994, UFO researcher Don Berliner received in the mail a roll of 35mm film, postmarked in Wisconsin. Once Berliner developed the film, he discovered a report dated April 1954, and entitled "Majestic-12 Group Special Operations Manual: Extraterrestrial Entities and Technology, Recovery and Disposal." Marked TOP SECRET, MAJIC-12 CLEARANCE LEVEL, the 22 pages purport to be wreckage handling procedures for the teams handling crashed alien craft and alien bodies.

"Some people have asked why, if we earthlings have recovered the wreckage of at least two very advanced flying saucers in New Mexico in 1947, that technology hasn't shown up yet in our own products. In response, I have to say that I think it has shown up." Specifically, Friedman cites samarium-cobalt technology in magnets as possibly "stimulated by investigation of a piece of a flying saucer," and also the development of the transistor by Bell Labs about five months after the Roswell crash. Friedman finds it suspicious that three well-known scientists composed the team that worked on the transistor and that Bell had close ties with Sandia National Laboratory in New Mexico. "It is very unlikely that three top scientists would be assigned to a single project unless someone knew that if the secret could be unlocked, the results might be very exciting indeed. Sandia, of course, is very close to the New Mexico crash sites, and there is evidence that wreckage from the crashes was investigated there."

UFO Danger Zone: Terror and Death in Brazil
BOB PRATT
(1996, Horus House Press)

Former longtime *National Enquirer* reporter Bob Pratt made at least 10 trips to remote areas of Brazil between 1978 and 1993 researching UFO encounters and dozens of those often quite bizarre stories he found are recounted in this book. What sets many

UFO reports in Brazil apart from reports made in other countries are the numbers of people injured or even killed as a result of their encounters. "Almost everyone knows of someone who had been chased, hurt or killed by these things," writes Pratt. These UFO encounters of the unhealthy kind occur most often "in the small towns, farms and forests of central and northeastern Brazil," often characterized by terrified people who are struck at night by beams of intense light and levitated off the ground as they struggle to free themselves or as companions hold on and pull them back down. The beings sometimes seen inside these balls of light are usually described as resembling ugly humans.

A case in 1979 involved Francisca Bispo De Assis, 45 years old, and her 13-year-old daughter, Josefa, who were walking home about 11 p.m. in their village near Campo Redondo. They saw what looked at first like a star in the sky until it came toward them, growing bigger into a ball of fire. As the ball got closer it opened up like an umbrella and shot a beam of light at them. Francisca began to rise off the ground in the beam of light, but Josefa grabbed her and pulled her back down. When Josefa began to run away the light beam seized Francisca again and lifted her into the air. According to Josefa and the rest of their family, who had been watching from a window in their nearby home, Francisca levitated 40 meters into the air before the light beam slowly lowered her back to the ground.

Pratt reports a similar case from 1983 involving Maria Dos Dores Lopes, 47, and her daughters Marileide, 15, and Maria DaGuia, 13, who were walking their dog at night, around 10 p.m., outside their home, when they spotted a light in the sky heading toward them. It was an intense white light shaped like a big tub and as it hovered over them, it looked like a fishing net. The youngest daughter ran inside the house but Maria and Marileide and their dog were captured by the light and pulled into the air. "I felt this cold wind all around me, pulling all three of us up," Maria told Pratt. "We were about a meter off the ground. I was running in the air. I tried to look up at the thing and could see it was spinning." It eventually dropped the two women and the dog to the ground and the white light that resembled a fishing net went straight up into the sky and disappeared.

The same thing happened in the same year to a couple, Geraldo and Angela, farmers in an area known as The Valley of the Old Women. They were walking home about 10 p.m. when an intense bluish-white light emerged from a dark form in the sky over them. The object was the size of a mini-bus and emitted a sound like a refrigerator motor. Geraldo levitated in the air and was being carried away. Angela screamed. "It looked like he was dancing in the air," she told Pratt. She grabbed her husband and pulled him back to the ground and the object reacted by moving back in the direction it came from. In the aftermath, Geraldo had bad headaches and chest pains for more than a year.

Several cases Pratt investigated involved permanent injuries to UFO witnesses. Rancher Luis Fernandes Barroso had been in a vegetative state for 17 years when Pratt met him, a result of being hit by a beam of hot light from a large lighted object that hovered over him and his donkey one night. The other victim was farm laborer Jose Vonilson Dos Santos who was zapped by a beam of light from an object hovering ten meters above him, resulting in paralysis that put him in a wheelchair for the rest of his life. Pratt also describes other cases of pregnant women losing their babies after being hitting by beams of light.

In the community of Colares, Pratt interviewed a physician, Wellaide Cecim Carvalho, who treated 40 people over a three-month period in 1977, that suffered injuries, mostly burns, from bright objects in the sky shooting beams at them during the night. One of them, a fisherman, died from burns on his chest. Dr. Carvalho herself saw one of the UFOs, which she described as a metallic cylinder-shaped object that she and her secretary watched for many minutes hovering about 40 meters away.

The Day After Roswell
COL. PHILIP J. CORSO, (RET.)
(1997, Pocket Books)

In 1961 and 1962, as a U.S. Army lieutenant colonel in charge of the Foreign Technology desk in Army Research and Development at the Pentagon, Philip Corso maintains he oversaw "the army's deepest and most closely guarded secret": a single file cabinet holding pieces of debris, along with scientific analytical reports on that debris, taken from the wreckage of an extraterrestrial spaceship which crashed in 1947 north of Roswell, New Mexico, killing its crew of alien humanoids. Corso's job under the guidance of Lt. Gen. Arthur Trudeau, director of Army Research and Development, was to "harvest" the advanced technology from this crash and secretly "seed" it among defense contractors, a process which led directly to development of the integrated circuit chip, night-vision equipment, fiber optics, lasers, and the bulletproof vest.

Though not present at the crash site, Corso tells a version of events different from previously published accounts. After the nighttime crash of "the soft-cornered delta-shaped eggshell type craft," a recovery operation was launched before dawn which included Roswell Army Air Base intelligence officers Major Jesse Marcel and Steve Arnold. It is from Arnold's perspective that Corso relates this wreckage retrieval story.

On arrival at the arroyo north of town Arnold noticed heat still rising from the debris of a craft shaped like a flying wing with two tail fins on the top sides. Sprawled across the ground were the bodies of four dark gray figures, each about four and a half feet in length. A fifth body was near an opening in the craft. Suddenly one of the creatures on the ground began struggling. Arnold and several medics stood over the creature with its egg-shaped head as it "made a crying sound that echoed not in the air but in his (Arnold's) brain." The creature got up and tried to climb away up a hill. Nervous sentries fired a volley from their Mls and the shots "flung him over like a rag doll." Roswell firefighter Dan Dwyer arrived on the scene and watched the "small bodies being lifted on stretchers from the ground into army transport trucks." One seemed to be still alive. Major Marcel ordered Dwyer to leave the area with the admonition, "this is top security here, the kind of thing that could get you put away."

Corso says the spacecraft's wreckage was shipped for analysis to Fort Bliss, Texas, headquarters of the 8th Army Air Force. Some of it was then flown to Wright Field in Ohio, while the rest was loaded onto trucks and driven to Fort Riley, Kansas, an intermediate stop before delivery to Air Materiel Command at Wright Field. Here at the Fort Riley stop, on Sunday night, July 6, 1947, Corso claims that he encountered an extraterrestrial body from the Roswell crash.

Master Sergeant Bill Brown was standing guard duty at a base veterinarian building when he called over Major Corso to take a look at what had just been trucked in "from some accident in New Mexico." Corso saw about 30 wooden crates nailed shut and stacked inside the building. One crate resembled a coffin. Corso opened it and found a thick glass container in which floated "a four-foot human-shaped figure with arms, bizarre-looking four-fingered hands—I didn't see a thumb—thin legs and feet, and an oversized incandescent lightbulb-shaped head." The being had pale gray skin, no hair, and a tiny slit for a mouth. Army Intelligence paperwork inside the coffin described the creature as coming from a craft that crashed-landed. The body had a routing manifest for Wright Field, and from there to the Walter Reed Army Hospital morgue's pathology section outside Washington, D.C.

In the 1950s Corso, by now a lieutenant colonel, served on President Eisenhower's National Security Council staff, a position he says enabled him to see memos describing the Roswell "incident" with references to the "package" and the "goods," which presumably meant wreckage and bodies. In 1961 he became intimately involved with this treasure trove of alien technology through a posting to the Pentagon as head of the Army Research & Development Division's Foreign Technology desk. His boss, General Trudeau, turned over to him the four-drawer file cabinet of material recovered from Roswell and ordered him to devise a plan for utilizing its untapped technological potential.

Inside the file cabinet, which Corso fondly called his "nut file," were a collection of intriguing pieces of debris from the Roswell craft. They included: "tiny, clear, single-filament, flexible glasslike wires" through which an eerie glow shined when held up to light; "thin two-inch-around matte gray oyster cracker-shaped wafers" with "tiny road maps of wires" along the surface; a "two-piece set of dark elliptical eyepieces thin as skin" which intensified images in darkness; and a headband "with electrical-signal pickup devices on either side." Also inside the cabinet were analytical studies of these and other materials, such as a description of a stubby device resembling a flashlight which, when pointed at a surface, emitted a tiny circle of red light. It turned out to be "an alien cutting device like a blowtorch."

"Each of the different branches of the military had been protecting its own cache of Roswell-related files and had been actively seeking to gather as much new Roswell material as possible," reports Corso. All of the services had field reports, scientific analyses, crash debris, and medical autopsy reports from Walter Reed Hospital regarding the physiology of the alien bodies. Presiding over analysis of this debris, its dispersal, and handling the policy implications were a top secret group of military, government and civilian scientific authorities "that some people have called Majestic-12." Within the Eisenhower administration, however, it was known simply as "the group." Bigger and more secret than the Manhattan Project, this operation surrounding the Roswell crash had to be designed so it could be "managed on a larger scale and for a longer period" than any program in history, forming "nothing less than a government within the government." As a result, the cover-up itself became covered up, meaning "the five or six of us in the navy, air force, and army who actually knew what we had didn't confide in anyone outside his own branch of the military and certainly didn't talk to the CIA."

General Trudeau and Lt. Col. Corso agreed that the alien technology they harvested should be seeded to companies with Army contracts, allowing them to apply for patents, but the companies would not be told where the technology came from. Piece by piece Corso farmed out "the puzzle pieces for a whole new age of technology." Night vision equipment technology was handed over to scientists at Fort Belvoir, integrated circuit chips were shared with Bell Labs, laser technology went to Hughes Aircraft, fiber optics to Western Electric, and bulletproof fabrics to Du Pont and Monsanto.

This "secret history of the United States since 1947," as Corso calls it, culminated in the Strategic Defense Initiative under the Reagan administration, whose real target "wasn't a bunch of ICBM warheads" but rather "alien spacecraft thinking themselves invulnerable and invisible as they soared around the edges of our atmosphere." In fact, the entire Cold War and nuclear arms race between the U.S. and Soviet Union was a "cover for the secret agenda" of preparing "defense against the extraterrestrials without ever having to disclose to the public what they were really doing."

The UFO Enigma: A New Review of the Physical Evidence
PETER A. STURROCK
(1999, Warner Books)

This book is based on the findings of a scientific study of UFO physical evidence undertaken in 1997, conducted by a six-person scientific steering committee and an eight-person investigative team, all but one holding a Ph.D. in some branch of science. The Study Director was Peter A. Sturrock, Ph.D., a Professor in the Applied Physics Department at Stanford University and author of more than 200 scientific papers.

Case studies presented to the science panel by the investigators included image analyses of two photographs of UFOs, physical traces from 10 UFO sighting events (such as the 1977 Council Bluffs, Iowa sighting that left several dozen pounds of metallic residue), and several cases with strong witness testimony (such as the 1973 Mansfield, Ohio UFO close fly-by that involved the four-man crew of an Army Reserve helicopter).

The Scientific Review Panel (which became known as the Rockefeller Panel because the group had been convened and financed by the billionaire philanthropist Laurence Rockefeller) evaluated this data and came to a series of general conclusions and observations after several sessions of analysis and debate:

—"Some of the phenomena are not easily explainable."

—"A few reported incidents might have involved rare but significant phenomena such as electrical activity."

—"A few cases may have their origins in secret military activities."

—"Reflecting on evidence presented at the workshop that some witnesses of UFO events have suffered radiation-type injuries, the panel draws the attention of the medical community to a possible health risk associated with UFO events."

—"The UFO problem is not a simple one, and it is unlikely that there is any simple universal answer."

Professor Sturrock summed up his aspirations for the scientific review this way: "I hope this book will help encourage more scientists to study this subject, develop their own ideas, and test those ideas by independent research. This is I believe our best hope—and may be our only hope—for finally arriving at a full resolution of the problem posed by UFO reports."

The Missing Times: News Media Complicity in the UFO Cover-up
TERRY HANSEN
(2000, Xlibris)

Science journalist and computer magazine publisher Terry Hansen investigates the extent to which national news media organizations have succumbed to government influence and propaganda in coverage of the UFO phenomenon from the 1940s onward. His initial focus in this book concerns the 1975 wave of UFO sightings, many of which occurred around nuclear installations and other military sites, particularly in Montana. "Despite considerable regional awareness of the 1975 sightings," writes Hansen, "the national news media were either oblivious to the events or simply declined to report the story." The only national circulation publication to give the sighting wave attention was the *National Enquirer*.

A similar thing happened during the 1980s when thousands of witnesses reported UFO sightings over New York's Hudson Valley. Local newspapers, radio and television reported the story, but it was ignored by the national media. Local media reporters and editors have tended to be more open-minded about the phenomenon and what the origins of it may be, compared to the national media which has been clinging to skepticism and outright ridicule of the subject since the 1940s, beginning with the Roswell crash case, when national media outlets began taking military and government debunking explanations as the gospel truth.

Hansen points to the news media presenting two "fundamentally different pictures of reality...*official reality,* represented by the elite national and big-city news media, and *folk reality,* portrayed by the local or small-town news media." Hansen describes how psychological resistance "to surprising new discoveries has always plagued journalists and editors, just as it has science itself." For example, *Scientific American* magazine ridiculed the claimed aviation achievements of the Wright Brothers because mainstream scientists had assured the magazine that powered flight was impossible and the Wright brothers were engaged in a hoax.

When freelance journalist Leslie Kean tried to sell an article to publications in 2000, revealing how high-level French officials had prepared an unprecedented report supporting the validity of UFOs, she was rejected by at least 20 publications saying it wasn't a newsworthy subject. Even when an editor at the *Boston Globe* newspaper finally agreed to publish the article, Kean had to strenuously argue to keep a tone of snide ridicule out of the wording from being added to the article.

A long list of similar historical examples of media dismissal and ridicule and adherence to official propaganda gets Hansen's attention in these pages. One of the more blatant examples was newsman Frank Edwards in the 1950s, who lost his radio show when the military allegedly pressured advertisers to stop supporting his nationwide radio show because he spent too much time talking about and reporting on the UFO phenomenon.

Another form of censorship and news manipulation came in the form of military officials cultivating anti-UFO press coverage from favored journalists. *The Saturday Evening Post* was one such magazine spoon-fed information by Pentagon public relations officers to produce highly-slanted articles dismissing UFO sightings and the people making them as guilty of misperceptions of natural phenomena, hoaxes and crackpot conspiracy theorizing. Helping to solidify the Pentagon's bias on the subject being spread in the media was the private debunking organization, the Committee for the Scientific Investigation of Claims of the Paranormal, whose primary UFO debunker was an editor at the magazine, *Aviation Week & Space Technology*.

The role of the *National Enquirer* tabloid and its frequent sensationalized coverage of UFOs receives special attention from Hansen. As long as most national UFO coverage was restricted to articles appearing in *The Enquirer*, the more 'reputable' media outlets had an even bigger rationalization for ignoring or ridiculing the subject area as being beneath their dignity. Hansen finds it ironic, perhaps beyond coincidence, that *Enquirer* publisher Generoso Pope Jr. worked for the CIA's psychological warfare division before he founded the nationwide tabloid. Whether Pope and his tabloid were consciously or unconsciously playing the role of muddying the UFO waters with sensationalism, on behalf of intelligence agencies of government, Hansen leaves to the reader's imagination.

Disclosure: Military and Government Witnesses Reveal the
Greatest Secrets in Modern History
STEVEN M. GREER, M.D.
(2001, Crossing Point)

North Carolina emergency room physician Steven Greer created The Disclosure Project in 1992 as a program of his non-profit group, The Center for the Study of Extraterrestrial Intelligence. The goals of The Disclosure Project are to reveal how extraterrestrial lifeforms are visiting our planet, end the secrecy about energy systems that could save the environment but are locked away in 'black projects', and to campaign for a total ban of weapons in space.

This 573-page book represents a public step forward in Greer's efforts to turn government and corporate UFO 'insiders into whistleblowers by presenting their testimony and statements based on interviews. Nearly 100 government officials, military officers, and corporate scientists speak out about various aspects of the UFO phenomenon in these pages.

Greer says the evidence in these testimonies proves that we have been visited by advanced extraterrestrial civilizations for many years, this knowledge remains the most classified program within the U.S. and other countries, these projects have escaped legal and constitutional oversight and control, that extraterrestrial spacecraft have crashed and the wreckage retrieved and analyzed since the 1930s, this wreckage has been back-engineered and provided breakthroughs in energy generation and propulsion, and that these classified above top secret projects include operational antigravity propulsion systems.

Notable among the high-level official statements presented in this book are those from U.S. Brig. Gen. Stephen Lovekin, Admiral Lord Hill-Norton, who formerly headed the British Ministry of Defense, Major General Vasily Alexeyev of the Russian Air Force, and Dr. Robert Wood, an aerospace engineer for 43 years at McDonnell Douglas.

General Lovekin served as an Army officer at both the Pentagon and the White House, under Presidents Eisenhower and Kennedy, and describes being shown metallic debris from the 1947 Roswell crash in New Mexico and being told about either three or five alien bodies being recovered. Lovekin states that President Eisenhower "lost control of what was going on with the entire UFO situation. He realized that the phenomenon or whatever it was that we were faced with was not going to be in the best hands." According to Lovekin, this was why Eisenhower, in his farewell speech, warned the nation about the dangers of the Military Industrial Complex.

Lord Hill-Norton, a five-star Admiral who had served as Head of the British Ministry of Defense, vouches for the credibility of the military witnesses in the 1980 Rendlesham Forest UFO landing case outside of two NATO air bases in Britain. He reveals his belief that "there is a serious possibility that we are being visited—and have been visited for many years—by people from outer space, from other civilizations, that it behooves us to find out who they are, where they come from, and what they want." As a case in point the Admiral cites the 1980 incident as "an apparent intrusion into our airspace—and indeed, a landing in our country—which was witnessed by serious-minded people in the military."

Russian Major General Alexeyev confirms that UFO reports came in regularly to the Russian and prior to that, Soviet, military, the Defense Ministry, and the Academy of Sciences, and these reports were taken seriously and investigated. He even confesses that he knows of instances where the military "learned to create a situation which would deliberately provoke the appearance of a UFO. A UFO would appear where there was increased military activity connected, say, with the transportation of 'special' loads. In other words, some kind of conditional relationship emerged and they detected it. I know that at certain testing ranges they even learnt to make contact of a kind" with the UFOs and their occupants.

In the case of Dr. Wood, the veteran scientist at McDonnell Douglas aerospace, he describes being tasked within his corporation with the job of analyzing different possible propulsion systems for UFOs and developing comparable systems. In his last conversation with company found Jim McDonald, before his death, Wood concluded that "what he'd found was that there was a cover-up—and that he very likely had run into the crash retrieval story…since then I have not closed my mind to any possibility—including the degree to which we might have been successful in reverse engineering the craft" retrieved from UFO crashes.

Greer sums up the overriding meaning to be drawn from all of the witness statements: The presence of extraterrestrial (ET) visitors on this planet is being covered up by "a hybrid, quasi-government, quasi-privatized operation which is international—and functions outside of the purview of any single agency or any single government." Secrecy is being maintained because of the reaction if the public discovered "that trillions of dollars have been spent on unauthorized, unconstitutional projects over the years" and these taxpayer dollars "have been used by corporate partners in this secrecy to develop spin-off technologies based on the study of ET objects which were later patented and used in highly profitable technologies."

186

*UFOs and the National Security State: Chronology of a
Cover-up 1941-1973*
RICHARD M. DOLAN
(2002, Keyhole Publishing)

Year by year, from World War II through 1973, the Oxford University educated
historian Richard Dolan describes significant UFO sighting cases and related developments, along with the actions of key personalities who either influenced public perceptions of the phenomenon, or who spearheaded secret military investigations of these
cases and subsequent coverups of what really happened. His focus is on providing a
historical narrative that lays out the national security dimension of this phenomenon.

Using these descriptions of the various UFO cases as puzzle pieces, Dolan
demonstrates the "disparity between official and unofficial truths about UFOs." He uses
the term 'national security state' to express how the military and intelligence agencies,
along with defense contractors, have wrapped themselves around the UFO phenomenon
using five levers of control: secrecy, wealth, independence, power, and duplicity.

This national security state coverup has been historically aided and abetted by the
news media with its news management. "Without question," writes Dolan, "the mainstream media have supported government propaganda about UFOs. From 1947 onward,
while the air force worked to remove the UFO problem from the public domain, the
media helped it to ridicule the subject. The release of every major air force and CIA statement about UFOs has, without exception, been met by uncritical media acquiescence."

In accumulating research material for this book, Dolan drew upon three basic
groups of sources: 1) Previously classified documents released through the Freedom of
Information Act, which in 1966 had become U.S. law. 2) Primary sources provided by
persons involved in UFO research during the time frame covered in this book. 3) Contemporary scholarship from other historians which help to show the pattern of control
and deception being exercised by the national security state.

Among the famous UFO cases and related issues that Dolan discusses: Kenneth
Arnold's sighting over Washington in 1947; 10 pages are devoted to the Roswell incident
in New Mexico; the Maury Island saga in Washington gets 8 pages of attention; 7 pages
go to the authenticity of the MJ-12 documents dealing with U.S. government activities
in the 40's and 50's; 6 pages deal with the death of Secretary of Defense James Forrestal;
2 pages concern the Lubbock Lights sighting; much of an entire chapter chronicles how
the Air Force Project Grudge became Project Blue Book dedicated to debunking UFO
sightings; 5 pages discuss the 1952 Washington, D.C. UFO sightings; 11 pages go to the

CIA's involvement with the Robertson Panel and its efforts to debunk the entire UFO phenomenon; the history of the early UFO organizations, NICAP and APRO, and their conflicts get considerable deserving treatment, as does the conversion of astronomer J. Allen Hynek from UFO skeptic to believer; nearly eight book pages go to the Betty and Barney Hill abduction case; the activities of debunkers such as Donald Menzel receive analysis, as does The Condon Report and its UFO investigation flaws, ending with the demise of Project Blue Book and finally, the mysterious suicide of James McDonald, a prominent physicist who had embraced an extraterrestrial explanation for UFOs.

From 1949, with publication of his UFO expose in *True* magazine titled "The Flying Saucers Are Real," through the 1960s, the most important UFO researcher in the world was U.S. Marine Major Donald Keyhoe, according to Dolan. Keyhoe wrote five influential books on UFOs and became "the driving force behind the world's most important civilian UFO organization," the National Investigations Committee on Aerial Phenomena (NICAP). Yet, today, Keyhoe remains a largely forgotten figure even though he was the first to "pry open the UFO problem for the public."

In this book's Appendix readers will find a list of 285 military UFO encounters from 1941 through 1973, representing "only a small fraction of encounters between military personnel and UFOs," says Dolan. These incidents range from U.S. Navy jets in a dogfight with a UFO over Florida, to an Ohio incident in which a U.S. Army helicopter had a near collision with a UFO.

———————————————

The Phoenix Lights: A Skeptic's Discovery that We Are Not Alone
LYNNE D. KITEI, M.D.
(2004, Hampton Roads.)

When a formation of unidentified lights crossed the Arizona skies on the night of March 13, 1997, physician Lynne Kitei and her physician husband, Frank, weren't taken by surprise because "for the past two years my husband and I had been taking both still photographs and video footage of the heavenly lights. At times they had been so close that we could have thrown a rick from our bedroom balcony and hit them."

This time, rather than just being seen by Dr. Kitei and Frank, the lights she saw and filmed from her home on March 13, were also observed and reported by hundreds of other witnesses in what later was proclaimed to be the most viewed UFO event in recorded history.

It all began for the Kitei's one night, two years earlier, when they had looked out their mountaintop bedroom window to see that "less than a hundred yards away from our property, three objects hung in midair, about 50 to 75 feet above the ground." She writes that each sphere was between three and six feet across, hovering motionless, and each emitted soft amber light. She grabbed a 35-mm camera and snapped a photo as the orbs slowly faded from view.

Twenty-three months passed, and then another incident happened, about 8 pm on the night of Jan. 22, 1997. Dr. Kitei saw on the western horizon "three huge amber orbs in a stationary row, strangely similar to the three orbs outside our window in 1995." After hovering for three or four minutes, they faded out.

The next evening, while her husband was away, she spotted the lights again. She filmed the phenomenon with a video camera for 17 seconds, but once the footage was developed, it turned out to be blank. (Subsequent footage and photos she took of other sightings did yield useable images, which she reproduces in this book.) She phoned Sky Harbor Airport and spoke to an air controller named Vern, who was on duty that night. He admitted seeing an array of six amber lights hovering motionless, about the same time as her viewing. None of the lights showed up on airport radar. He had no idea what he and Dr. Kitei had witnessed.

A month later, on the night of March 4th, Dr. Kitei and Frank once again saw two amber lights from their bedroom balcony. They watched the lights for about seven minutes through a telescope. The next night, they once again saw two glowing orbs, this time seeming to hover over a downtown building.

After the March 13th main event occurred, seen throughout Arizona, Dr. Kitei began her personal investigation into the incident by interviewing some of the witnesses, which inspired her to write this book. Among the witnesses she spoke with were several air traffic controllers who had seen both the January 23rd and March 13th phenomena.

What the air traffic controllers, Bill Grava and Vern Latham, described for her certainly sounded mysterious and otherworldly. Said one: "There must have been five of us up there {in the control tower} and we all saw these lights. We've never, ever seen anything in that direction before and the level at which they were spaced apart, the uniformity, was very odd. We were awestruck by the intensity of them. We saw them on both dates {January 23rd and March 13th} at the same location and they were the same basic color, the same basic size." Neither controller had ever seen the phenomena before, or after, the two dates in 1997. Nor did either man believe the lights were connected to any training missions conducted out of nearby Luke Air Force Base, or from the Davis-Monthan Air Force Base further south, in Tucson.

In January 1998, Dr. Kitei and her husband again saw two huge amber lights in the distance, hovering motionless in the darkness, glowing through a thick haze that blanketed the city skyline. Again, she trained a video camera on the lights. The same thing happened the next night, at 9:40 pm. It seemed to be a pattern.

Subsequently, Dr. Kitei learned the Michigan Air National Guard had been on training maneuvers, dropping flares both nights over the Goldwater Gunnery Range, outside of Phoenix. But a spokesman for the Guard claimed his planes left the range by 8:30 pm, to return south to Davis-Monthan AFB, outside Tucson. The lights Dr. Kitei filmed were seen an hour later. What explained this discrepancy? Were they two separate events? No one could provide a convincing answer.

Hunt for the Skinwalker: Science Confronts the Unexplained at a Remote Ranch in Utah
COLM A. KELLEHER & GEORGE KNAPP
(2005, Paraview Pocket Books)

Though not specifically about the UFO phenomenon, an entire range of events recounted in this book delineate that intersection between suspected alien visitation and the paranormal, showing how bizarre mysteries combine and take many forms to baffle and frustrate observers trying to make sense of it all. The authors of this book are no exception: Knapp is a well-known Las Vegas television reporter who did stories about the ranch, and Kelleher is a Ph.D. biochemist, author or co-author of more than 40 science papers in cell and molecular biology, who spent months having unusual experiences at Skinwalker Ranch as part of a research team from the National Institute for Discovery Science.

Located in northeastern Utah, about 150 miles from Salt Lake City, the 480-acre ranch has been avoided for many generations by members of the nearby Ute tribe because they feared the land was haunted by a 'skinwalker', said to be a shapeshifting creature that could morph into a wolf, a Sasquatch, or any other animal it wanted. For about two years, until 1996, the ranch was owned by Tom and Ellen Gorman, who kept a herd of registered cattle on the property. They had heard the rumors and legends but had tried to ignore them, until an escalating series of bizarre incidents, recounted in this book, terrorized them into selling the property.

The first unnerving incident involved a wolf three times larger than any the Gorman's had ever seen. Tom and Ellen, along with their two children, Tad and Kate, and

Tom's father, Ed, all witnessed the huge gray wolf walk right up a few feet away from them, without any sign of fear, just outside a cattle corral. His light blue eyes seemed friendly as it intently gazed at each family member. Without warning the wolf turned and bounded over to the corral and savagely attacked a calf, clenching its head in his jaws. Tom grabbed his .357 Colt Magnum pistol and shot the wolf in the ribs, without any effect. Tom put two more shots into the wolf's abdomen and it released the calf. Standing 10 feet away, Tom couldn't miss, yet the wolf showed no sign of injury or bleeding. It just continued gazing at Tom. Once again, Tom raised the pistol and fired a fourth shot into where the animal's heart should have been. Still the animal didn't move, didn't make a sound, didn't bleed.

Tom's son ran and returned with a hunting rifle, which Tom used to pump two more shots into the wolf, with little effect. Finally, the wolf turned, still seemingly unhurt, and began to trot across the pasture. Though they were in shock, unable to believe what they had seen, Tom and Tad took their weapons and began to pursue the wolf. They followed it into a tree line, noticing that it clearly left large paw prints in the wet ground along the way, but no sign of blood from the six shots. They reached a creek and saw that the paw prints had stopped suddenly in the mud just before reaching the creek. The wolf had disappeared, as if vanished into thin air. The five members of the Gorman family vowed afterward to simply forget what they all had witnessed because it seemed too incredible and unexplainable. No matter how much they tried, the ranch would not let them forget.

Incidents of high strangeness kept occurring with alarming frequency. One night, for instance, Tom and Tad, accompanied by one of Tad's teenage friends, saw what appeared to be the lights of a trespassing RV out in a pasture. The three set off jogging in pursuit as the RV lights began to ascend over fences. As they got closer, they could see the RV lights were hovering above the ground and moving away from them, until the lights were at the tree line, soundlessly hovering about 50 feet above them. Now they could see the vehicle silhouetted against the horizon and it wasn't an RV, it was an oblong dark shape, like a huge refrigerator, with lights at the front and back. The three watched in openmouthed amazement as the object slowly disappeared into the distance.

Many more UFOs would be seen in the ensuing months. Some were black triangles hovering, others were orbs of blue or orange lights darting about. Holes in the sky seemed to open up and objects would shoot out, or dark figures would crawl out, as if from interdimensional tunnels. Some of their cattle were mutilated in horrific yet bloodless ways, other cattle simply disappeared without a trace. Household objects disappeared and turned up later in strange places, like high in trees. Doors of buildings opened and shut as if attacked by poltergeists.

The most tragic and terrifying incident happened on an April evening in 1996, as Tom sat outside with his three dogs beside him. A small intense blue ball of light, bigger than a baseball, approached from a pasture, moving toward him at less than ten feet off the ground. He had seen similar mysterious blue lights before. His dogs began barking and chased after the light, snarling and leaping at it. When the ball of light slowly began moving toward nearby trees, the dogs gave chase. Moments later, Tom heard the three dogs yelping in pain and fear, followed by silence. When his dogs didn't return, Tom went searching for them the next morning. In a small clearing beyond the trees Tom found three large circles of brownish grass and at the center of each circle, a blackish greasy mess that had been his dogs. They had literally been incinerated. This was the day that Tom and his family decided to sell their ranch.

An organization called the National Institute for Discovery Science, created and funded by Las Vegas real estate mogul Robert Bigelow, bought the ranch, after Bigelow heard some of the strange stories about it. Bigelow and the team of scientists he recruited decided to set up a 'laboratory in the wild' at the ranch to investigate its paranormal happenings. Book co-author Colm Kelleher became one of the lead scientists and personally witnessed many of the incidents documented by the NIDS team.

Early in their investigation, on September 16, 1996, for example, at 1:30 in the morning, Kelleher and two NIDS scientists were encamped in an observation trailer on the property when one of them glanced out a window and spotted a bright light over the cottonwood trees. It hovered over a tree line for about ten minutes and then began soundlessly moving around the ranch. All three scientists agreed was "unlike any aircraft, helicopter, flare, star, or planet" they had ever seen. There was no doubt it qualified as a UFO.

Cattle mutilations occurred on the ranch while the scientific team was present, and other cattle mysteriously disappeared without any sign of struggle or tracks. Four registered bulls somehow got transferred from a corral and crammed into a tiny trailer, without any human assistance. Other poltergeist like activity occurred, padlocks being removed from doors, or objects removed to strange places, surveillance cameras vandalized, and a six-foot diameter hole carved into pond ice. Bluish-white lights the size of basketballs and red orbs the size of baseballs made periodic appearances, captured on videotape. Two team members watched a dirty yellow light near ground level expand in size until it resembled a tunnel, or portal, out of which a black creature crawled out and then fled into the darkness of the ranch, leaving behind a pungent sulfur odor.

Kelleher relates how "I personally witnessed the shooting of a large catlike animal from a tree. I was forty to fifty yards away and I am certain the bullet hit its target. I was just a few yards away when an unknown doglike animal weighing an estimate four hundred pounds was pierced by bullets fired by an experienced marksman, yet no body and no blood were found after both of these incidents. The only physical evidence was a single claw mark left in the snow."

Many theories about the nature of the phenomenon were proposed by the science team. They discounted it as a natural phenomenon, they didn't have enough data to support an alien explanation, they didn't find evidence for military experiments—though the Gorman's had reported the sounds of heavy machinery underground—and an inter-dimensional portal explanation lacked hard proof, but several of the NIDS science advisory board members came around to suspecting some sort of non-human intelligence occupied the ranch and had been engaged in a form of psychological warfare. Whatever it was, it seemed to feed off fear and confusion and altered states of consciousness.

Flying Saucers and Science: A Scientist Investigates the Mysteries of UFOs
STANTON T. FRIEDMAN
(2008, New Page Books)

During his four decades giving hundreds of lectures called "Flying Saucers ARE Real" the author, Stanton Friedman, started each lecture, as he does this book, by giving these four conclusions: "evidence that planet Earth is being visited by intelligently controlled extraterrestrial spacecraft is overwhelming"; some people in government have known at least since 1947 that two crashed flying saucers and alien bodies were recovered in the New Mexico desert; and "there are no good arguments against conclusions number 1 and 2; and finally, "flying saucers are the biggest story of the millennium."

Skeptics and debunkers, according to Friedman, always respond by using four tactics in their arguments against the reality of flying saucers: an attitude of "don't bother me with the facts, my mind is made up"; and "what the public doesn't know, I am not going to tell them"; and "if one can't attack the data, attack the people"; and finally, "do your research by proclamation rather than investigation. No one will know the difference."

After spending more than a decade as a nuclear engineer testing nuclear rocket engines for Westinghouse and other corporations, Friedman read a book about UFOs and got hooked on the subject, giving his first lecture on it in 1967, at the home of a Westinghouse laboratory technician. He eventually investigated some of the most famous UFO events of the 20th century, including the Betty and Barney Hill abduction case, and the Roswell incident of 1947, about which Friedman played an instrumental role in finding firsthand witnesses to the event and bringing them to public attention. In 1980, when the first book on the Roswell event was published, Friedman didn't receive the public credit he deserved for having researched most of the book.

Two subject areas Friedman refused to touch over the decades were crop circles and animal mutilations, which he felt were not directly connected to the flying saucer phenomena. Friedman also makes it clear he isn't a fan of SETI, which he thinks should stand for Silly Effort To Investigate because the entire effort "is an exercise in futility." He believes the scientists who lead the SETI search for alien radio signals are leaders of a cult because of their refusal to accept the reality that alien beings are already here. "Cults do their best to ignore or repress testimony that is opposed to their beliefs—no shortage of that from the SETI community," says Friedman. He goes on to list 16 specific objections to how SETI operates.

Where did the flying saucers come from and what did they want? "My own conclusion is that some aliens have come to Earth from a planet around the old southern sky stars Zeta 1 or 2 Reticuli, that there are probably others from elsewhere in the local neighborhood, and that they have known we exist for a very long time. I certainly expect that there is some kind of neighborhood association with rules about interference with other more backward civilizations such as ours until we give signs of being able to bother them."

---

*UFOs & The National Security State: The Cover-Up
Exposed 1973-1991*
RICHARD DOLAN
(2009, Keyhole Publishing)

His training as a historian continues serves Richard Dolan well in this, his second of two books, providing a historical narrative of the U.S. national security state's involvement with and manipulation of the UFO phenomenon, covering the period 1973 through 1991. This book, at 637 pages, is even longer than the first history, and it's equally comprehensive, the nearest thing to a complete history of the UFO phenomenon and government ever published.

Write Dolan: "The following pages are a methodical presentation of facts and analyses that show the UFO phenomenon to be most assuredly 'not us'. It is also a reality that is actively being covered up {by} elements of the human power structure {who} have made it their priority to keep information about it strictly to themselves, apparently at all cost."

Who might be these the secret-keepers? Dolan suggests they are 'beyond' nations and transcend the U.S. power structure. In other words, they are the international banking and foreign policy elite that meet in venues organized by such groups as the Trilateral Commission.

The UFO cases covered by Dolan include the following:

(1) 7 book pages are devoted to Paul Bennewitz, a scientist in New Mexico who believed he had intercepted alien signals and as a result, became the subject of an Air Force security investigation.

(2) 12 pages go to describing the Rendlesham Forest sightings in Britain by U.S. Air Force personnel in December 1980.

(3) 3 pages outline the Cash-Landrum Incident in Texas, which occurred a day after Rendlesham and involved a UFO and the radiation poisoning of witnesses.

(4) 5 pages discuss the Japan Airlines encounter with a UFO over Alaska that was tracked by FAA radar.

(5) 7 pages are given to alien abductions and the work of researchers Budd Hopkins, Whitley Strieber, and Raymond Fowler.

(6) 10 pages discuss the Gulf Breeze, Florida series of sightings on the Gulf Coast and allegations of UFO photos being hoaxed.

(7) 8 pages go to dissecting the strange case of Bob Lazar, a reputed physicist who claimed to work for a defense contractor at Are 51 where he inspected a flying saucer and saw photos of 4-foot-tall grey alien bodies.

(8) 9 pages look at a series of UFO cases during 1989, in the Soviet Union, that involved landings and dozens of witnesses.

(9) Numerous pages reveal the impact of the U.S. Freedom of Information Act on UFO disclosure and the even greater impact of leaks from inside the government and military "pointing to the existence of UFO crash retrievals and the existence of a back-engineering program."

"The evidence is conclusive: an intelligent UFO phenomenon beyond the control of our civilization existed during the period under review," concludes Dolan. "Documented military encounters alone ran into the hundreds, many of which have been included here. Hundreds more 'fastwalkers' were recorded by the Defense Department

Program satellite system…Regardless of the actual source of the UFOs themselves, it is undeniable that they triggered a significant response by military agencies around the world."

At the end of this book Dolan announces that he is at work on a third volume of his UFO history series to take the chronology from 1991 to the present day.

The Cryptoterrestrials: A Meditation on Indigenous Humanoids and Aliens Among Us
MAC TONNES
(2010, Anomalist Books)

What if the entire alien visitation phenomenon isn't exraterrestrial in origin at all, but rather evidence for the existence of a race of indigenous humanoids who have always lived clandestinely among the human species?

While the author of this book, Mac Tonnes, calls it a speculative 'meditation', he nonetheless assembles a range of evidence and arguments, building on earlier books by Jacques Vallée and John Keel, to make a case that "some accounts of alien visitation can be attributed to a humanoid species indigenous to the Earth, a sister race that has adapted to our numerical superiority by developing a surprisingly robust technology…{and} seek to perpetuate themselves by infusing their gene-pool with human DNA."

We have seen their shape morphing abilities in folklore, those tales of fairies and elves and the like, and more recently in the accounts of human abductions by small grey aliens. These entities use "subterfuge and disinformation" to achieve their goals and "have mastered the art of camouflage in order to co-exist with us."

Many if not most reported UFO landings "have the undeniable flavor of staged events" and seem designed to be a misdirection to keep human attention focused on the stars for answers, rather than imagining an origin closer to home. Could this non-human intelligence be using sophisticated projections—holography—to trick us into thinking we're observing tangible vehicles? Such an explanation might also explain why these beings are reported to rapidly materialize and then fade away or instantly disappear during abduction episodes, as if they have "mastered a technology of consciousness." In that sense, these entities may have also mastered some form of mind and perception control.

Tonnes finds it highly suspicious that many alien encounters involve the abductees being exposed to needles and chemicals, or being told to drink noxious liquids, prior

196

to their interactions with the so-called aliens, as if sensory alteration of the human is a prerequisite for contact. The humans are not being allowed to trust their senses. This fits into the overall pattern of deception.

As for the idea that abductions of humans occur so extraterrestrials can harvest genetic material to create a hybrid species, Tonnes points out this would mean the abductors are likely genetically compatible with us, with genetic modification skills not far in advance of our own, giving more credence to the notion the abductors "are really an unacknowledged aspect of ourselves." These sexual experimentation reports tell Tonnes that "we're likely dealing with a sister species of incredible tenacity and a chameleon-like sense of invisibility."

One reason why these Cryptoterrestrials can remain mostly invisible to us, if they have a physical presence at all, may be that they live in subterranean realms on the planet, from which they can engage in psy-ops campaigns influencing the human species. By contrast, John Keel proposed that "we share the planet with 'ultraterrestrials' who occupy higher realms of an unseen 'superspectrum'" of electromagnetic frequencies.

What is the purpose of these master manipulators? Writes Tonnes: "I propose that this intelligence has played a significant role in occasionally hastening our species' development as well as keeping us in a periodic 'standby' state, rendering us less likely to destroy ourselves."

While conceding that some UFO encounters may originate from space, the author nevertheless remains intrigued that what the 'inner-space' explorer and psychedelics experimenter Terence McKenna said is quite literally true: "We are part of a symbiotic relationship with something which disguises itself as an extraterrestrial invasion so as not to alarm us."

Tonnes died in his sleep at the age of 34, just weeks before this book was finished.

———————————

UFOs: Generals, Pilots, and Government Officials Go On the Record
LESLIE KEAN
(2010, Harmony Books.)

Eighteen UFO witnesses and investigators from nine countries provided accounts forming the narrative foundation for the incidents described in this book, written by Leslie Kean, an investigative journalist for newspapers and magazines, who says she spent 10 years examining the UFO subject. The 18 persons whose first-person accounts form the narrative core of her book range from a Deputy Chief of Staff for the Belgian Air Force, to officer pilots for the Air Forces of Peru, Brazil, Iran, Chile, France and Portugal.

Most of these UFO incidents had been previously reported in books and news accounts. For example, the 1989 UFO 'wave' of sightings over Belgium, the 2006 UFO 'incursion' over Chicago's O'Hare Airport, the 1976 UFO 'dogfight' over Tehran, and the 1980 UFO 'incident' at the NATO base in England's Rendlesham Forest. Kean examines each incident from the perspective and in the words of the witnesses she interviewed.

Kean says she became intrigued by the UFO subject in 1999, while working for a California public radio station, when an acquaintance in Paris sent her an unpublished study, called the COMETA Report, in which 13 high-ranking French scientists, space experts, and retired generals concluded that 5% of UFO reports have no earthly explanation. She ended up reporting on the study in a freelance article for *The Boston Globe*, which got international attention and launched her career as a UFO phenomenon investigative reporter. She grew up politically well-connected—her father was a wealthy philanthropist, her grandfather a congressman, and her uncle the Governor of New Jersey. She lived mostly off a family trust fund so she was able to devote fulltime to the reporting efforts that resulted in this book.

In researching cases featured in these pages, she confesses some of her sources "showed me documents that must remain off the record because of their sensitivity." Otherwise, she believes in and practices full disclosure. Each of her sources began their relationship to the subject as a natural skeptic, but all found themselves baffled by what they saw, heard, or read, and they transformed into dedicated truth seekers.

The author says in the book's Introduction, "to approach UFOs rationally, we must maintain the agnostic position regarding their nature or origin, because we simply don't know the answers yet." In her concluding chapter, she urges readers, particularly scientists, to "realize the fallacy" of being either an unwavering believer or nonbeliever about whether UFOs are piloted by alien visitors, and instead, "accept the logic, necessity, and realism of the agnostic view."

She also believes that the evidence presented in her book affirms "a physical manifestation of something highly unusual of unknown origin" in our planet's skies, which requires "an extraordinary investigation" by the world's scientists "to solve this extraordinary mystery."

Part of what makes her book noteworthy and unprecedented is the impressive lineup of scientific endorsements on the book's front and back jackets. Physicist Michio Kaku called the book "the gold standard for UFO research," while Rudy Schild, Ph.D., of the

Harvard-Smithsonian Center for Astrophysics, lauded it as "carefully reasoned" and a strong case made that "rightfully questions U.S. government denials and absurd cover-up stories."

Subsequent to the book's publication, she co-authored an article in *The New York Times* in 2017, headlined, "Glowing Auras and 'Black Money': the Pentagon's Mysterious UFO Program," which revealed the existence of the Pentagon's UFO investigative office called Advanced Aerospace Threat Identification Program. That revelation further opened the door to a series of unprecedented public disclosures by the Pentagon. All of this publicity for Kean and her work resulted in the British newspaper, *The Guardian*, lauding her in a 2021 article as "The woman who forced the US government to take UFOs seriously."

The Aztec Incident: Recovery at Hart Canyon
SCOTT & SUZANNE RAMSEY, FRANK THAYER & FRANK WARREN
(2011, Aztec.48 Productions)

This book by two authors (primarily the Ramsey's) supported by the other two men, expands upon a previous book, *UFO Crash at Aztec: A Well Kept Secret*, by William Steinman and retired Air Force Colonel Wendelle Stevens, published in 1987, that reinvestigated an alleged flying saucer crash near Aztec, New Mexico. This Aztec story was first described much earlier, in 1950, by Frank Scully, in his book, *Behind the Flying Saucers*, which was widely discounted at the time as a hoax. Both the Ramsey and Steinman books make a case that Scully and his sources were unfairly smeared in a campaign orchestrated by the U.S. government to cover up the saucer crash.

The Ramsey's estimate they spent over $500,000 over a 23-year-period investigating this long-disparaged case, collecting over 55,000 documents, and Steinman, for one, congratulates them in a Preface to the book, saying the couple "located first hand witnesses who actually stood at the crash site viewing and handling the saucer and bodies." And just as importantly, they revealed the true purpose behind the fraud trial that the government brought against the two primary sources for Frank Scully's 1950 book.

As the Ramsey's tell the story, on March 25, 1948, New Mexico Rancher Valentine Archulete saw "the flying saucer pass over his ranch in the early morning hours like a fluttering leaf falling from a tree, and he saw the craft strike the ridge wall, making sparks, before disappearing to the north toward Hart Canyon." The authors believe it was Archulete who called Kirtland Air Force Base to alert military authorities and they were the ones who sent out a retrieval squad to investigate.

Several oil field workers, Doug Noland and Bill Ferguson, were among the first witnesses at the crash site about 12 miles northeast of Aztec, New Mexico. The object had ignited a small brushfire. What they saw was a very large, metallic lens-shaped craft about 100-feet in diameter with a raised section on the top. "We realized the craft was smooth with no noticeable seams, rivets, blots or weld marks," Noland told the authors decades later. "It looked as though it was molded. The windows or portholes looked like mirrors until you would look closer; then you could see through them. One of the windows or portholes was busted. Inside two small bodies were slumped over what appeared to be a control panel of sorts. The bodies were charred a dark brown."

Soon other witnesses arrived, drawn by the smoke from the fire, including two elderly local ranchers and two law enforcement officers. Officer Manuel Sandoval told everyone that he was from the nearby town of Cuba, N.M., and had been following the low flying disc-shaped craft before it crashed. Another witness was Solon Lemley Brown, a minister at a local Baptist Church, who would later confide about what he saw to a church deacon and his young son.

Still another witness tracked down by the Ramsey's was Ken Farley, who had been driving nearby with a friend when they saw the smoke. Farley told the Ramsey's: "We saw a large disc-shaped object, aluminum in color. The disc had a bubble or protrusion on the bottom...also one on the top of the craft. One of the two police officers walked up to us and told us the military had been notified and that we should leave the area at once...Some of the oil field workers were climbing all over the damn thing... some older couple there started yelling at them to get the hell away from."

When the military personnel showed up, they took all of the witnesses aside, one by one, and told them to keep quiet about what they had seen. "This event is extremely important to the United States of America," the military officers allegedly said. "We are {all} responsible for our national security."

One of the military workers sent to the site to clean it up a few weeks later, Fred Reed, told Scott Ramsey in an interview how he knew "something big had been removed" from the crash site because "trees had been damaged with some tops removed or chopped off." Reed and his crew did a survey of the site and gathered any remaining debris, after which they re-landscaped the site to make it look normal again." They were under the constant watch of a military security detail.

In Frank Scully's version of this story, described in his 1950 book, none of the witnesses mentioned above were among his sources. He relied on interviews with an oil millionaire named Silas Newton, and a recently retired government scientist, Dr. Gee, a pseudonym Scully gave to protect his identity. Dr. Gee claimed he had personally inspected the 100-foot diameter crashed saucer, which was unlike any metal known on Earth, and he saw the 16 tiny humanoid bodies inside, all charred a dark chocolate. Scully claimed his two sources allowed him to see several pieces of metal taken from inside the craft.

Soon after Scully's book was published, it came under attack by a newspaper reporter who had wanted to collaborate with Scully and turned vengeful when Scully refused. The reporter made allegations of fraud to the FBI against Scully's two sources and they were indicted, but the case against them was quietly dropped. The public damage had been done and the smear campaign resulted in UFO investigators declaring the Aztec case a hoax and Scully and his sources to be con men. When the Ramsey's were given access to Scully's files, thanks to Scully's widow, they found evidence that the Air Force Office of Special Investigations had collaborated with the FBI and CIA in attempting to track down debris from the crashed craft and to confiscate any photographs that had been taken of it by Scully's two primary sources.

Based on their 23-year investigation, the four authors of this book reach a series of conclusions which they believe "are true beyond argument."

(1) A 100-foot diameter flying saucer was recovered off the mesa above Hart Canyon, along with its crew of 16 humanoid bodies, and everything was transported to a secure government facility.

(2) Oil field workers, ranchers, passersby, and law enforcement officers saw and even touched this flying saucer.

(3) Military personnel administered an 'oath of secrecy' to the civilian witnesses.

(4) The U.S. Government started a smear campaign against Frank Scully and intentionally ruined the reputations of witnesses Silas Newton and Leo GeBauer.

"We now have exhumed and rehabilitated the Scully story," the authors declare.

Encounters at Rendlesham Forest: The Inside Story of the World's Best-Documented UFO Incident
NICK POPE with JOHN BURROUGHS & JIM PENNISTON
(2014, Thomas Dunne Books)

In the opinion of these three authors, two of whom were witnesses, the UFO incident described in this book constitutes a much better documented and relevant case than the more publicized Roswell incident because "unlike Roswell, the witnesses are very much alive—and ready to tell their stories. Simply put, the Rendlesham Forest incident is by far the best-documented and most compelling UFO incident ever to have taken place." Co-author Nick Pope headed up the British government's UFO project at the Ministry of Defence for a period of time, while co-authors Jim Penniston and John Burroughs both served more than two decades in the U.S. Air Force and were present when a UFO landed in Rendlesham Forest, in December 1980, near the perimeter of two NATO air bases.

The twin NATO bases of Bentwaters and Woodbridge, where this incident occurred, operate on the east coast of England, in the county of Suffolk. On the night of December 25/26, at about 3 a.m., unusual lights were spotted in woods east of the Woodbridge runway and it appeared the object had landed or crashed. Staff Sergeant Penniston, Airman First Class Burrough, and another airman were sent to investigate. Penniston picks up the story:

"When we arrived near the suspected crash site it quickly became apparent that we were not dealing with a plane crash or anything else we'd ever responded to. There was a bright light emanating from an object on the forest floor. As we approached it on foot, a silhouetted triangular craft about nine feet long by six-point-five feet high came into view. The craft was fully intact sitting in a small clearing inside the woods."

Penniston goes on to describe how their radios began malfunctioning and the air was electrically charged as they walked toward the craft. Blue and yellow lights swirled around the exterior of the craft. Over ten minutes of examining the vehicle, photographs were taken (they would later be found to have been overexposed) and on one side of the object, three-inch high pictorial symbols were seen etched into what felt like a metal surface. When the light from the craft intensified, "it lifted off the ground without any noise or air disturbance," and then "maneuvered through the trees and shot off at an unbelievable rate of speed." According to Penniston, more than 80 Air Force personnel witnessed this craft take off.

A second UFO sighting occurred the subsequent night. For 18 minutes during his investigation of the previous landing site on the second night, deputy base commander Lt. Col Charles Halt made a cassette recording in which he narrated what was being seen—up to five red and yellow lights and strobe-like flashes in the nearby sky—and what an airman with him was measuring from Geiger counter—showing elevated radiation—around where three pod indentations in the ground were found and trees damaged at the apparent craft landing site. The three ground depressions were less than two inches deep and seven inches in diameter and this is where peak radiation readings were taken. The transcript of Halt's tape is included in the Appendix of the book.

During a subsequent Air Force security investigation all of the five primary witnesses who got closest to the reported craft were interrogated after being given truth serum, and then ordered to keep quiet about what they had seen. From dozens of possible witnesses over the two nights of sightings, known official U.S. Air Force statements were taken from only five, among them Staff Sergeant Penniston and Airman First Class Burroughs. Statements made by all five men are reproduced in this book. Other reported witnesses to the incident, such as airman Larry Warren and Sergeant Adrian Bustinza, later told their own versions of the story in interviews and books.

In the aftermath of this series of sightings—there were three altogether—soil and tree sap samplings taken at the crash site went missing, or at least the U.S. Air Force claimed they had disappeared, and researchers later determined that important files on the incident were also missing from the National Archives. Military medical records for both Penniston and Burroughs remain classified. A former Chief of the Defence Staff in Britain eventually voiced his concern and belief that both the British and American defense establishments have intentionally covered up the truth about this UFO incident.

Theories proposed by skeptics over the years to explain what happened in Rendlesham Forest are addressed one by one in arguments made by the authors. These theories include that the witnesses had their perceptions distorted by alcohol and drugs; the witnesses were exposed to hallucinogenic mushrooms; they were infected by mass hysteria; the entire incident was a hoax done by practical jokesters; meteors or a rocket re-entry accounted for the sightings; lights from a nearby lighthouse produce an illusion of a spacecraft; a guard force test was conducted by security personnel to test base readiness using holographic technology; or, secret drone technology was being tested in the forest.

In 2010, the former deputy base commander Col. Charles Halt signed a notarized affidavit summarizing his observations after 30 years of reflecting on what he saw, concluding with this assessment: "I believe the objects that I saw at close quarter were extraterrestrial in origin and that the security services of both the United States and the United Kingdom have attempted—both then and now—to subvert the significance of what occurred at Rendlesham Forest and RAF Bentwaters by the use of well-practiced methods of disinformation."

Section Two: UFOs And UFO Occupants

Insiders Reveal Secret Space Programs & Extraterrestrial Alliances
MICHAEL E. SALLA
(2015, Exopolitics Institute)

This is one of the first in a series of books on the 'Secret Space Program' which Australian-born author Michael Salla, who has a Ph.D. in government from the University of Queensland, contends reveals the scope of a hidden U.S. government program spearhead by the U.S. Navy that involves on-going contact with numerous extraterrestrial civilizations having outposts on Earth. His primary source in this book is self-described whistleblower Corey Goode, a Colorado video producer and director, who claims at the age of 6, he signed a 20-year contract to join this Secret Space Program where he served on different spaceships and interacted with friendly aliens called the 'Blue Avians'.

"In my own independent vetting of Goode," writes Salla, "I found his claims proved to be consistent with other whistleblowers saying they had similar 20-year tours of duty with secret space programs, which also used advanced age-regression and time travel technologies to return them to ordinary civilian life...Also, I found a compelling body of circumstantial evidence in unfolding global events, which convincingly support Goode's extraordinary claims."

Among the many claims Salla and/or Goode make:

(1) The first flying saucer prototypes came from Maria Orsic, a Croatian who moved to Germany and in 1919, began channeling through automatic writing extraterrestrial beings claiming to be from the Aldebaran star system. Technical information came through Orsic in two foreign languages, one of which was ancient Sumerian, seemingly showing instructions for building an engine that could power a spacecraft. Orsic formed the Vril Society to attract funding for her flying saucer project and a scientist at the Technical University of Munich, Dr. Winfried Schumann, began to help her build a prototype using an 'implosion' engine and anti-gravity technology. The first prototype flew in 1931.

(2) On June 13, 1933, "a circular craft resembling a pair of saucers joined at their outer rims crashes" near the town of Maderno in northern Italy. This 50-foot in diameter could have been one of the Orsic/Schumann prototypes since Maderno was only about 300 miles from Munich, where the saucer was built.

(3) Beginning in 1934, Hitler's Nazi regime effectively took control of Orsic's creations and initiated its own space program. Though Orsic apparently never joined the Nazi Party, she did believe the Aryan race had a metaphysical

superiority over other races. (Orsic and her boyfriend, also a medium, disappeared at the end of World War II, allegedly to a flying saucer base in Antarctica.)

(4) "Goode claims that the Vril Society spacecraft were advanced enough to travel the 230,000-mile distance to the moon, land the first astronauts and even establish a moon base," writes Salla.

(5) Under the U.S. program called Operation Paperclip, Nazi scientists, including Dr. Schumann of the Vril Society, were brought to the U.S. in 1945 to continue their advanced scientific work on rockets and flying saucers. Nazis then infiltrated and took over much of the U.S. Military-Industrial Complex. The MJ-12 Group formed by President Harry Truman in 1947, authorized the U.S. secret space program utilizing Schumann's flying saucer creations.

(6) Subsequent attempts by inventors, such as Otis T. Carr in 1955, to develop civilian spacecraft using advanced propulsion discoveries, similar to those pioneered by Orsic/Schumann, were brutally suppressed by the CIA and the MF-12 Group. Carr was charged with swindling investors and received a long prison term.

(7) As a result of the Vril Society's and Nazi Germany's flying saucer developments, a series of secret space programs emerged with bases on the Moon and Mars and flying saucer fleets capable of interstellar travel. Each program is controlled "either by national security or corporate elites, or by secret societies." These programs are hidden under layers of national security systems. Goode claims one of these secret programs "can be traced to the Mayan Civilization, which maintains fleets of spacecraft capable of interstellar flight and even has colonies in other star systems."

(8) When President Kennedy became too insistent about learning details of these secret space programs, he was killed on orders of the space program cabal.

(9) Salla believes that 19 different extraterrestrial or 'intraterrestrial' (from the hollow Earth) groups are involved in alliances with these secret human space programs. He describes them as ranging from the short grays, to the praying mantis, indigenous Reptillians, Aldebaran's, Solarians, etc., each with a different mission and different levels of cooperation with the Military-Industrial-Extraterrestrial Complex. Several of these alien groups abduct humans who become part of a galactic slave trade peddling human flesh.

(10) Along with Goode, Salla identified two other whistleblowers—Randy Cra-

mer and Michael Relfe—who he says competed their 20-year service in the secret space programs. Relfe, for one, says he was based mostly on Mars and was employed as a psychic assassin, personally killing 70 high-profile targets including human VIPs and extraterrestrial entities. Salla provides a chart comparing details of the stories told by Goode, Cramer and Relfe, showing the many similarities in their accounts, which Salla infers provide circumstantial evidence of their validity.

The Roswell UFO Conspiracy: Exposing a Shocking and Sinister Secret
NICK REDFERN
(2017, Lisa Hagan Books)

One reason given by the author for writing this sequel to his previous book on the Roswell event—*Body Snatchers in the Desert*—is to show that "numerous people and sources within UFOlogy have uncovered near-identical data to that which I was exposed to." While Redfern believes UFOs are real, he just doesn't find convincing evidence that one crashed in the New Mexico desert near Roswell. Furthermore, the aliens involved as victims in this incident were human, and not from outer space.

Four whistleblowers who provided most of Redfern's information in the first book, alleging that the U.S. government had covered up the incident because it involved human guinea pigs in flight experiments, are further described in this book, along with how they came to Redfern's attention. Two of his primary sources remain anonymous because they feared government reprisals for speaking out.

UFO author John Keel, points out Redfern, first began writing about the Roswell crash as being a Japanese Fugo balloon in 1990, when he labeled what happened as a vestige of World War II, when the Japanese sent explosives laden Fugo balloons across the Pacific to terrorize the U.S. West Coast. Keel also speculated the balloons could have carried aloft gliders manned by air crews and these had been captured by the U.S. military and used in post-war flight experiments. Keel wrote: "this would explain many other things, too, such as the persistent rumors in the 1940s about the bodies of small, Oriental-looking men in flight suits that were supposedly recovered in various western states."

Rumors had also circulated among UFO researchers in the 1970 and 80s that a U.S. military installation near Roswell, called Fort Stanton, had housed Japanese 'enemy aliens' during the war, some of whom were tiny in stature with Mongoloid huge heads. UFO researcher Leonard Stringfield picked up similar information in his crashed saucer investigations indicating that shocking human experimentation tests had occurred involving handicapped people and the U.S. military had attempted to cover up the evidence.

A UFO researcher named Kathy Kasten, who died in 2012, had collected extensive files—thousands of pages—detailing her own Roswell investigation and her family bequeathed the files to Redfern. In those files Redfern discovered that Kasten had also uncovered evidence the Roswell crash "had nothing to do with aliens, but everything to do with post-war experiments on human guinea pigs." She concluded that Fort Stanton, not far from where the crash debris was found, provided the key to what happened at Roswell. She had written in her notes: "My research has uncovered the fact that the American Government was testing many different types of aircraft at the time of the Roswell crash; some of it for the purpose of forming the basis for a future space program, and perhaps even one that involved American-Japanese internees from a New Mexico detention camp."

Further evidence supporting Redfern's thesis that the victims were 'enemy aliens' not 'outer space aliens' came in a 1997 issue of *Popular Mechanics* magazine, in which an article claimed that "the craft that crashed at Roswell will eventually be identified as either a U.S. attempt to re-engineer a second-generation Fugo, or a hybrid craft which uses both Fugo lifting technology and Horten-inspired lifting body. In either case, Japanese engineers and pilots brought to the U.S. after the war to work on the project could have been the dead 'alien' bodies recovered at the crash site."

As for the late Lt. Col. Philip Corso, who authored the 1997 book, *The Day After Roswell*, alleging a UFO crash, alien bodies, and the back-engineering of crash debris, Redfern writes of his military career: "Corso was an expert in the field of disinformation—namely, creating faked stories to fool certain targets, individuals and entire countries. And, maybe, to fool the field of UFOlogy."

UFOs & Nukes: Extraordinary Encounters at Nuclear Weapons Sites
ROBERT HASTINGS
(2017, CreateSpace)

In this second edition of his original 2008 book, Robert Hastings devotes 571 pages to detailing the results of more than 150 interviews he conducted since 1973 with former and retired U.S. military personnel concerning their involvement with UFO incidents at nuclear weapons storage sites or testing areas.

His interest in this subject got triggered by a personal experience he had as a teen-ager in 1967, when he worked nights as a janitor at the air traffic control tower at Malm-strom Air Force Base in Montana, where his father was a non-commissioned Air Force officer. One night a controller he knew "called me over to his radar scope and pointed out five unidentified 'targets' then being tracked." Two jet fighters had allegedly been dispatched to intercept the objects which then disappeared at high speed. Later, Hastings learned the objects "had apparently been maneuvering near Minutemen missile sites" southeast of Malmstrom. From this period forward Hastings was hooked on investigat-ing the UFO phenomenon, particularly in connection with nuclear weapons.

This book covers many previously unpublicized UFO cases, as well as numer-ous famous cases, such as 41 pages he devotes to the Rendlesham Forest NATO base sightings in Britain, 19 pages discussing evidence relating to Roswell, 31 pages spent on the Big Sur UFO incident that involved a nuclear missile test allegedly attracting in-terference from a UFO that was caught on camera, along with 10 pages describing UFO nuclear sightings in the former Soviet Union.

A key firsthand witness and interview source for Hastings was Chester W. Lytle, Sr., who had been involved as an engineer with the Manhattan Project developing atomic bombs, and who later worked for the Atomic Energy Commission as a nuclear weapons stockpile expert, holding a Top Secret clearance. Lytle had a dramatic UFO sighting while overseeing an atomic weapon being loaded onto a U.S. Air Force bomber at Kirtland Air Force Base, and he witnessed radar tracking of disc-shaped craft over White Sands Prov-ing Ground. Lytle maintained a friendship with William H. Blanchard, who had been base commander at Roswell Army Airfield in 1947, when the alleged Roswell crash event oc-curred. Lytle claimed that Blanchard confessed to him the object recovered near Roswell had indeed been an extraterrestrial spacecraft containing four dead humanoid beings.

The numbers of military witnesses to some of the UFOs seen around nuclear installations seem extraordinary. Hastings quotes from an official report by the 90th Strategic Missile Wing of the U.S. Air Force which detailed sightings of disc and ci-gar-shaped objects in 1965 over and around Minuteman launch control facilities and nuclear installations near Cheyenne, Wyoming. On the night of July 31, UFOs were ob-served by 70 military personnel, on the night of August 1, 27 personnel saw UFOs, and on the following night, another 46 military personnel reported sightings. Skeptics tried to dismiss the sightings as due to strange atmospheric conditions, but Hastings counters that "no natural phenomenon could have been responsible for the sightings" given their controlled movements and precise geometric formations.

A wave of UFO sightings over and around nuclear installations in 1975, especially at Malmstrom, the Strategic Air Command missile base, gets detailed by Hastings. He lists NORAD log entries about Malmstrom released under the Freedom of Information Act and from a leak of information provided by a Defense Intelligence Agency analyst, including 15 separate sightings of objects between November 7 and November 10 of that year. These sighting log entries describe disc-shaped objects being tracked by radar and being chased by fighter jets, resulting in the missile and bomber base being placed on high alert. In this unprecedented wave of UFO incidents in 1975, objects were also sighted over the Loring Air Force Base Weapons Storage Area in Maine. Hastings was able to interview military witnesses to these events involving Malmstrom, Loring, and several other nuclear weapons facilities.

After 40 years of investigating the phenomenon, Hastings concludes this book with: "The available facts suggest to me that extraterrestrial visitation, by one or more races of beings, is occurring and that it accounts for all of the nuclear weapons-related incidents presented in this book, as well as the secrecy surrounding those events. In my view, the essential message being conveyed by our Visitors is this: As long as nuclear weapons exist, they remain a potential threat to the future of humankind—and to the planet itself. Get rid of them!"

Inside the Black Vault: The Government's UFO Secrets Revealed
JOHN GREENEWALD JR.
(2019, Rowman & Littlefield)

In the two decades since he was 15 years old, John Greenewald filed more than 8,000 Freedom of Information Act requests to just about every known U.S. government agency and department seeking information about what these arms of government knew about the UFO phenomenon, resulting in the release of two million pages of declassified documents. In this book he details the laborious and often frustrating steps he had to take to shake loose this 'black vault' of government information by penetrating thick layers of disinformation, deception and outright lies designed to cover up what government knows about a subject that officials repeatedly claimed was no longer even being investigated.

When he first began filing FOIA requests in 1996, the only response he ever got back from most government agencies was a so-called 'fact sheet' summarizing the Air Force's Project Blue Book findings—which had been terminated in 1969—claiming that

UFO sightings could be explained and were not worth any longer investigating. Rather than give up after being rejected dozens of times by the Air Force and other branches of the military, Greenewald persisted in filing his document requests with more and more civilian agencies of government.

Greenewald began to find evidence that UFO documents were not all being stored at the National Archives and Records Administration, as the Air Force and other agencies claimed. The first big break he got came when a UFO researcher, Rob Mercer, in Ohio discovered that someone had placed on Craigslist an ad offering to sell old Project Blue Book photographs and documents that had belonged to a former Air Force captain. The researcher purchased everything and found a treasure trove of unpublished materials, including Blue Book briefing documents, case studies, internal letters and inter-office memos, film reels and audio recordings. Mercer tracked down the Air Force officer and took possession of four more boxes of unclassified material from Project Blue Book, all of which had been designated as trash by the Air Force.

Working with Mercer, Greenewald digitized and organized the vast amount of material into an online data base. Much of this trove of information did not appear in the National Archives records and opened up new angles for filing more FOIA requests, showing that nearly every agency of government had UFO-related documents that were hidden in the bowels of the bureaucracy. This previously unpublished material also clearly demonstrated that Project Blue Book was a debunking agency, not an investigative agency, and went so far as "to fabricate evidence, squash witness testimony, and alter the facts in order to 'solve' a case and make it disappear."

Slowly, Greenewald's dogged determination began to pay off. Another big break came when the Defense Intelligence Agency released a batch of documents on something called Project Moon Dust, which investigated unidentified objects, such as space debris, that crashed to Earth. UFOs was not a designation associated with this project, indicating that government agencies had learned to hide the UFO subject in their records using a variety of other innocuous sounding terminology. The document distribution lists for Moon Dust and other such projects proved to a gold mine of new leads to follow, showing the on-going involvement of the CIA and the National Security Agency (NSA).

Still another document retrieval breakthrough came when Greenewald noticed that Canada's Department of National Defense was on the distribution list for many U.S. military agencies, especially NORAD, the North American defense command. He found that Canada also has an equivalent law to the FOIA and so he filed requests for

UFO documents with Canada's defense agency. That gave him access to batches of more UFO-related documents that U.S. agencies had claimed didn't exist.

Based on his reading of thousands of documents that were never intended to be made public, Greenewald concluded: "I am not 100% convinced the UFO phenomenon is 'aliens' visiting Earth. What I am saying is when you deal with the evidence and all possible conventional explanations, the 'alien' one is the only one that makes sense."

To access the two million pages of declassified U.S. government documents collected by Greenewald, go to: TheBlackVault.com.

UFO Secrets Inside Wright-Patterson
THOMAS J. CAREY & DONALD R. SCHITT
(2019, New Page Books)

These two authors have collaborated previously on the books *Witness to Roswell* and *The Children of Roswell* and in this book, they bring together all of their accumulated evidence that Wright-Patterson Air Force Base in Dayton, Ohio, has been a destination for the analysis, the reverse engineering, and storage of crashed UFO debris and alien bodies since the 1947 crash at Roswell. In presenting these accounts from reputed crash debris witnesses, the authors admit "we have encountered a number of alleged witnesses to the Roswell events of 1947 who were fortuitously situated in both time and place, which allowed them to falsely plug themselves into the Roswell narrative as participants when such was not the case…In some cases, it has taken years to expose them."

Among the witnesses the authors found convincing, five stand out.

Between 1942 and 1952, June Crain was employed at Wright-Patterson as a clerk/typist, with a Q level security clearance, working in the Foreign Technology Division. Before she passed away in the late 1990s, Crain reportedly told former police detective James Clarkson that she was aware, as were most of the scientists and engineers she worked with, of at least three UFO crashes, including Roswell, that produced debris being analyzed at Wright-Patterson. She claimed to have even handled a piece of the 'memory metal' taken from a New Mexico crash site. One of the scientists she claimed to have worked with was Werner Von Braun, the German rocket expert, who told her he personally knew of three crashes of extraterrestrial origin.

General Arthur Exon served as base commander of Wright-Patterson in 1964 and he had heard 'scuttlebutt' that Roswell crash wreckage had been tested at the base. Based on what he heard, but never saw firsthand, Exon said the crash material "was flimsy but tougher than hell," he told the authors of this book. "The metal and material were unknown to anyone I talked to." As for alien bodies, Exon said he had been told "they were found outside the craft itself in fairly good condition." He knew people who were involved in the recovery of the bodies, though he never claimed to have personally seen them.

Bomber squadron commander Lieutenant Colonel Marion Milton Magruder told his children, before he passed away in 1997, that he had been at Wright-Patterson Air Force Base and seen wreckage that was "out of this world," including metallic cloth resembling tin foil that would unroll itself after being rolled into a ball. Magruder also claimed he has seen a four-foot-tall survivor of the crash. It seemed 'rubbery' and had long thin arms, a large head, a slit for a mouth, no ears, and a flesh-tone coloration. "It was a shameful thing that the military destroyed this creature by conducting tests on it," Magruder reportedly told his family.

A second-hand story is told about U.S. Air Force flight surgeon Colonel D'Jack Klinger, who reportedly told a business associate that in the late 1940s he witnessed an autopsy of two humanoid bodies at Wright-Patterson, each about 4 feet in length, who had apparently died in a crash of a craft. Klinger allegedly said the torsos of the two bodies resembled insects and their skin was fabric-like, lacking discernible genitalia.

An elderly dental technician based in Dayton, John Mosgrove, ends the book with his claims that in 1979, he took an impression of an unusual jawbone and cast it into a template on orders from his dental clinic boss, who had received the specimen from two Air Force officers based at Wright-Patterson. The v-shaped jawbone resembled nothing human that Mosgrove had ever seen and because he had heard the rumors about alien bodies being stored at Wright-Patterson, Mosgrove suspected the sample might be from one of those bodies. Mosgrove was ordered to keep quiet about the plaster cast he had made, which his boss then broke into pieces and threw in the trash. Mosgrove was able to secretly retrieve and reassemble the pieces. Some years later a dental anthropologist examined the mysterious cast and determined that it had not been taken from a primate jaw.

===

American Cosmic: UFOs, Religion, Technology
D.W. PASULKA
(2019, Oxford University Press)

For six years D.W. Pasulka, a professor of religious studies at the University of North Carolina, interviewed scientists and Silicon Valley entrepreneurs about their beliefs concerning the existence of extraterrestrials and whether they are visiting Earth in UFOs. She begins her journey in 2012, in the company of Jacques Vallée, a legend in the UFO field, who has been an astronomer, computer scientist, and a Silicon Valley entrepreneur and investor, along with being the author of many books on the UFO phenomenon.

Periodically, throughout this book, Pasulka returns to Vallée for his insights as she researches the cultural impacts of UFO belief systems. While interacting with a fascinating case of characters she meets at UFO related events, she begins to view her experience as bearing witness to "the formation of a new, unique form of religion."

Her attention focused on meeting those who she calls 'meta-experiencers', scientists who study UFO experiencers and the phenomenon they are immersed in. Two are Tyler and James, as the authors calls them, meta-experiencers who became her tour guides on a visit to the New Mexico desert where they searched for artifacts of a 1947 crashed extraterrestrial aerial craft, a spot the author refers to "as ground zero of a new religion."

James was a scientist and a research university professor with impressive credentials as a molecular biologist; Tyler had worked as an engineer on the space shuttle program, owned 40 mostly bio-medical patents, which made him a fortune, and claimed the patents had been downloaded to him from an off-planet intelligence. James had a UFO sighting as a teenager and considered himself to be an alien experiencer. Pasulka calls them "two of the most intelligent and successful people I had ever met."

Using specially designed metal detectors, they scoured the desert for metallic craft artifacts. The author indicates this location is NOT the famous Roswell incident site, but another crash site, a no-fly zone, they had to secure special permission to even enter. They found and bagged several pieces of odd metal for later analysis. One piece resembled "crumpled tin foil that was also a type of fabric."

James analyzed the artifacts at his research lab and concluded they were not only weird and anomalous, it was "hard to believe they were made on Earth...and certainly not on Earth in 1947." While confessing the anomalous artifact may have been "planted for me to find," she goes on to describe the reactions of the other scientists who examined it along with James. "According to these scientists, I was told, it could not have been generated or created on Earth. One scientist explained it to me in this way: 'It could not have been made in this universe'."

Pasulka observes how "for Tyler and the scientist-believers, the artifact's mystery is not only impenetrable but also compels their reverence and belief. It inspires them. In the words of Tyler D., it was 'elegant beyond comprehension'." Finding the artifact and being unable to identify it as natural or human-made became akin to a religious or spiritual experience for many of the scientists, affirming to Pasulka that the mysterious object functioned like a religious object of veneration akin to the Shroud of Turin in Catholicism.

———————————————————

Identified Flying Objects: A Multidisciplinary Scientific Approach to the UFO Phenomenon
MICHAEL P. MASTERS
(2019, Self-Published)

What if alien visitors to Earth are really highly evolved time-traveling humans from our far distant future returning to study the origins of the human species? That is the premise for this speculative book by Michael P. Masters, Ph.D., a professor of biological anthropology at a Montana college.

Masters call these visitors 'extratempestrials' (from the Latin root, tempus, meaning time) and sorts through eyewitness reports and alien abduction accounts describing these visitors to make a case they resemble how humans might look thousands of years in the future of our species. "They may be better understood," writes Masters, "as the product of further human evolution on this planet, following many millennia of continued biological and cultural change. In other words, these 'aliens'—rather than being from a different planet in a different solar system—may simply be us, from a different time in the distant future."

Many scientists consulted by Masters believe it would be highly unlikely for an extraterrestrial species evolving on another planet to ever develop the physical traits similar to humans, traits which have repeatedly been reported in UFO-related entity reports, such as being bipedal, not having a tail, being relatively hairless, a large brain and eyes, a small mouth and nose, and dexterous hands and fingers. These creatures are also said to communicate with humans telepathically in our own languages. Add to that the vast distances these visitors would have to travel to even find Earth, and Masters finds evidence that the visitors are related to present day humans, just as we are related in evolution to other hominid species whose bones our paleo-archaeologists dig up and study.

These future humans could be tourists or they could be scientists, or a mixture of both, curious about the origins of their species, just as we are curious about the origins of our species on the evolutionary tree. The UFOs these visitors reportedly travel within, which seem to violate the known laws of aerodynamics and physics, could be the technology, the time machines, that present day humans often see represented in science fiction movies. This might help explain the 'missing time' phenomenon reported by many alleged abductees.

Manipulation of space-time remains highly theoretical for 21st century human scientists, though Masters devotes several sections of his book to sifting through evidence and speculations that backward time travel might be more feasible in some respects than interstellar travel between galaxies. The big hurdle in resolving time travel challenges is a unified theory of gravity and quantum mechanics. However, Masters argues this problem may be solved by future generations of scientists, hundreds or even thousands of years hence, opening the door to developing backward time travel technology.

"If we are destined to eventually become the extratempestrials observed now and in the past," concludes Masters, "we would expect to learn of this imminent reality long before the creation of any actual time machine, at whatever point in the future our time traveling descendants wished to inform us of it." Once the human species learns and accepts that it is in contact with its own descendants, "we would usher in a new phase of human history" in which we would interact across time "in a network of predetermined causality."

Russia's USO Secrets: Unidentified Submersible Objects in
Russian and International Water
PAUL STONEHILL & PHILIP MANTLE
(2020, Flying Disk Press)

These two authors—Mantle is a British UFO researcher, Stonehill a emigre from the USSR—collected dozens of UFO and USO (Unidentified Submersible Objects) reports filed by officers and seamen of the Soviet and later, Russian Navies, some reports made publicly, others described here for the first time in the West, to give a broad overview of how the phenomenon has been experienced in one of the world's more secretive cultures.

Most of these reports come from the lakes and seas of the former Soviet Union, going back to before World War II, though some also include sightings by seamen aboard submarines, Naval ships and fishing boats in the Atlantic and Pacific oceans. As occurred in the U.S. and many other Western countries, military and intelligence agencies of the Soviet and then Russian governments attempted to dismiss and debunk these sightings to quell public concerns, while privately taking the phenomenon and the reports quite seriously.

A primary source for the authors was Vladimir Ajaja, a former Soviet Naval seaman and oceanographer, whose persistent investigation of UFO and USO reports caused him problems with the Communist Party and cost him several jobs. Some of the reports that he wrote and lectured about came from Soviet Navy documents he had seen while at Navy headquarters.

A representative sighting case involved the submarine tender, *Volga*, stationed in the Barents Sea in 1977. Ship radar picked up objects approaching and a group of seamen on the ship's bridge saw nine "bright shining discs" that began to circle overhead. During the 18 minutes that the objects circled all ship communications were affected. Radio operators could not send or receive messages. This incident so concerned commanders of the Soviet Navy that a directive called 'Instruction for UFO Observations' was sent to all fleets and flotillas of the Soviet Navy. This incident along with a second encounter that year by the crew of a Soviet nuclear submarine, during which a cylinder-shaped object seemed to track the vessel, resulted in creation of a secret Soviet military program called SETKA to conduct research into the UFO phenomenon, a program that lasted until 1991, when the Soviet Union dissolved.

Another source for the authors was Yevgeny Litvinov, a former Soviet Navy officer, who compiled a database of 10,000 UFO observations and incidents. Litvinov "developed a scale of credible authenticity based on 350 criteria. From this, he concluded that around 70% of UFO reports can be explained as either misidentification of known technology, meteorological phenomena, or simply wishful thinking. However, he argued, the other 30% are observations of bona fide UFOs." As often happens in the U.S. and other countries, "more often than not UFOs are observed over military installations, areas of ecological disasters, and geological faults."

Some of the stranger cases described in this book involve the USOs (unidentified submersible objects) that appeared so frequently some Navy officers speculated there were USO bases in the Bering Sea, the Baltic Sea, and other bodies of water. One case used to illustrate this phenomenon occurred in October 1988, when the Soviet aircraft carrier *Novorossiysk* was on a training exercise three miles off Shikotan Island, between Russia and Japan. The submarine crew witnessed a large object rise from the ocean, adorned with 36 lights located geometrically throughout the object. It was visible for 15 minutes and when a helicopter attempted to reach it, the object departed rapidly. All electronic systems, including the engine, ceased to function on the submarine while the object was visible.

216

Roswell: The Ultimate Cold Case
THOMAS J. CAREY & DONALD R. SCHMITT
(2020, New Page Books)

This book represents the 8th collaboration between the authors over several decades, most of the books covering aspects of the Roswell crash case. If the Roswell case were the subject of a trial, the authors call this book their summary of closing arguments. They present 28 'undeniable truths' which they believe cannot be disputed, based on 600 witnesses directly or indirectly giving accounts about the events that happened in 1947 outside of Roswell. The "vast majority of them support the military's first account—the recovery of an actual flying saucer."

These 28 'truths' range from the obvious: finding of a debris field on the Foster ranch outside of Roswell, to the issuance of an Army press release touting the discovery of a flying disc, and the later disavowal of the press release with the military claiming the debris was an ordinary weather balloon. And the not so obvious truths: the Federal Communications Commission threatening the license removal of a Roswell radio station if it continued to broadcast the flying disc story, a series of White House meetings the week after the crash involving President Harry Truman and his national security staff, and the use of U.S. military officers to threaten civilian witnesses and their families with lethal force unless they remained silent about what they knew concerning the crash.

Deathbed confessions from witnesses about the true nature of what happened at Roswell form a key piece of the cumulative evidence presented in this book. Among notable confessions were:

(1) Staff Sgt. Melvin Brown, stationed at the Roswell base in 1947, whose dying words to his daughter were: "There were two bodies…small bodies…the color and texture of the skin looked strange…and they had big heads and slanted eyes."

(2) Corporal Robert J. Lida, an MP at the Roswell base, who told his wife that he had guarded the hangar where the crash wreckage "and a number of small bodies" were being temporarily stores before shipment elsewhere.

(3) Staff Sgt. Homer G. Rowlette, stationed at Roswell in 1947, who told his son before his death how "I saw three little people. They had large heads and at least one was alive."

(4) Private First Class Edward D. Sain, an MP at the Roswell base, who told his son before dying that he had been sent to the crash site to guard the bodies overnight before they were transported to the base and that the crash debris "was the strangest thing I have ever seen in my life."

217

(5) Captain Meyers Wahnee, a B-24 pilot and security officer, who told his family the year he died that he had flown with the alien bodies from Roswell to Fort Worth and that there had been three crash sites involved in the debris recovery.

(6) First Lieutenant Walter Haut, who was ordered to write the famous press release announcing the recovery of a flying saucer, left a signed and sealed statement in December 2002, to be opened at his death, attesting that he saw debris inside a base hangar, including a 12-15 foot by 6-foot piece of the crash debris that was egg-shaped, along with several bodies under a canvas tarpaulin. He stated the heads on the bodies were larger than normal and they seemed to be about four feet tall. "I am convinced," wrote Haut, "that what I personally observed was some type of craft and its crew from outer space."

Levelland
KEVIN D. RANDLE
(2021, Flying Disk Press)

By revisiting and reevaluating the evidence from a series of UFO sightings in November 1957, around the West Texas town of Levelland, retired Air Force Lt. Col. Kevin Randle underscores the importance of this widely witnessed yet largely forgotten case that was one of the first in the U.S. to involve UFOs electromagnetically affecting the functioning of motor vehicles.

"Levelland was the case that brought the theory of electromagnetic interference to the forefront," writes Randle. "Here was a series of sightings in which the UFO interfered with part of the environment. Not only that, there were, literally, dozens of witnesses around the small town of Levelland who independently reported the same thing over a period of two or three hours. A close approach of the UFO resulted in their car engines stalling, their headlights dimming, and their radios filling with static."

On the evening of November 2, 1957, a young couple driving near Amarillo, Texas, reported to police that a UFO had appeared over the highway, causing their car engine and battery to die. Soon thereafter, another driver near Seminole, Texas, reported to the Sheriff's department that a UFO above the highway had caused his car engine and headlights to fail. The UFO apparently quickly flew on that night (about two hours driving time by car) to the Levelland area where the largest concentration of UFO reports began to flood law enforcement phone lines.

Some Levelland area witnesses described the object overhead as torpedo shaped and glowing a bright red. Others described it as egg-shaped and pulsating as it glowed while sitting on the ground. Said witness Jim Wheeler, who had been driving along Hwy. 116 about eight miles from Levelland: "The object cast a glare over the area. You get close to it and it shuts off your lights and kills your motor." Levelland Sheriff Weir Clem drove out to search for the object, followed by two Texas Highway Patrol officers, and they reportedly saw an oval-shaped object that was red to orange in color.

Soon after the sightings around Levelland ended, further to the west, at White Sands Proving Ground in New Mexico, in the early morning hours of November 3, two U.S. Army enlisted men on motor patrol, Cpl. Glenn Toy and Pfc. James Wilbanks, saw a bright egg-shaped object, about 75 yards in diameter. It slowly descended. "All the lights went out," said Cpl. Toy, "and it landed right across the road from us." U.S. Air Force investigators later tried to dismiss the sighting as the two soldiers having misidentified the moon.

By combing through U.S. Air Force Project Blue Book investigative files, author Randle exposes how the Air Force investigators went to great lengths to explain away the Levelland sightings as ball lightning, a rare atmospheric phenomenon, even though weather experts said the conditions for ball lightning didn't exists around Levelland during the sightings. "The Air Force file is riddled with mistakes, inaccuracies, and apparently invented data," notes Randle.

In the book's Appendix, Randle presents a chronology of electromagnetic effects reported from UFOs, most involving engine failures. These many dozens of cases range from 1945 through 2020, and include accounts from numerous countries throughout the world.

Trinity: The Best-Kept Secret
JACQUES F. VALLEE & PAOLA LEOPIZZI HARRIS
(2021, Starworks USA)

Exactly one month after the first test of a plutonium bomb on July 16, 1945, the first UFO crash in modern history took place outside of San Antonio, New Mexico, just a few miles from the Trinity nuclear test site, according to these two authors, the legendary scientist Jacques Vallée, and Italian investigative journalist, Paola Leopizzi Harris, both of whom had once worked with astronomer J. Allen Hynek investigating UFO sightings. This case remained relatively unknown through the decades because, unlike the Roswell crash case occurring two years later, this incident was successfully covered up by the U.S. military, partly as a result of the civilian witnesses being too scared to speak up until now.

As the authors tell the story, late on the afternoon of August 16, 1945, two young boys were riding horses on a ranch just a few miles from the White Sands nuclear testing site when they heard a loud bang and saw smoke on the horizon. On investigating, seven-year-old Reme Baca and nine-year-old Jose Padilla found a craft resembling a flattened avocado, crashed on the ranch, accompanied by several small creatures with bulging eyes and large heads that Reme thought looked like praying mantis insects. A long gouge had been carved into the ground where the craft had hit and then slid, causing a fire in nearby vegetation, which accounted for the smoke they had seen.

Through binoculars, both boys took turns watching the three small creatures appeared to walk by sliding across the ground outside the craft. They seemed to be injured because they emitted sounds like the squeals of young human babies. The greyish vehicle had a hole in its side, apparently a panel dislodged from impact with the ground, and it stood about 14 feet high and 30 feet long, and debris from inside the craft was scattered around it.

A day or so later the two boys returned to the crash site with Jose's father, Faustino, and a New Mexico State Trooper, Eddie Apodaca. The three creatures were nowhere to be seen. Faustino and the Trooper entered the craft through the hole and stayed inside for five or ten minutes. When the two men emerged, they were grim-faced and warned the boys to keep what they had seen a complete secret from everyone. The Trooper apparently alerted the U.S. Army to the crash because jeep loads of military personnel arrived at the site soon thereafter and began cleaning up the debris.

Being curious and adventurous boys, Reme and Jose sneaked back to the site a few days later and watched from a hiding spot as the Army personnel began the site cleanup and removal of the craft. When the cleanup crew broke for a meal, Reme and Jose crept near the craft and picked up several pieces of the debris. They took the pieces home and hid them. One looked like aluminum foil, but it retained its shape like a 'memory metal' and wouldn't burn (sounds like reports from Roswell two years later), a second find was clear-white spidery 'angel hair' that glowed at night and which the boys stuffed into a gunny sack, a third was a pyramid-shaped piece of metal the size of a small cookie, and lastly, a type of bracket about 12 inches long and weighing 15 ounces which a metallurgy lab eventually analyzed and determined was nothing more than an Aluminum-Silicon alloy. The authors speculate this pedestrian piece of bracket metal had been used by the military in its debris recovery, or else the occupants of the craft had scavenged it as a quick terrestrial fix for something that was broken.

In the months following the 'crash' Jose's father received visits from White Sands military personnel who told him to keep what he had seen secret because it involved national security These officers claimed that what Reme, Jose, Faustino and the State Trooper had seen were remains of a weather balloon (once again the cover story that would be used at Roswell.)

A third witness interviewed for this book, Jose's cousin, Sabrina Padilla, never saw the craft itself, but claims she handled some of the debris for years afterward and even kept a triangle-shaped piece in her home until her children lost it. This entire story remained unpublicized over the ensuing decades until UFO author Timothy Good mentioned it in passing in his 2007 book, *Need To Know*, based on having interviewed the witnesses. Thereafter, Paola Harris tracked down and interviewed the two men and finally, a few years after that, she connected with Vallée and they embarked on writing this book together.

When it comes to why crashes might have occurred in 1945 at Trinity and 1947 at Roswell, Vallée raises some tantalizing options that may not involve intergalactic extraterrestrial visitors. "What if your spacecraft *was designed to crash*? What if it was a gift? Or a signal? Or a warning? The hopeful inception of a strategic conversation? What if it wasn't a 'spacecraft' in our current, primitive sense of the word? What if you didn't care if the occupants died? Nobody had seriously considered those alternatives."

"We believe the phenomenon is not trying to teach us physics or advanced propulsion," write the authors, "although most researchers will keep trying to extract such data, or turn it into new weapons. Instead, we believe it is trying to teach us to transcend our own humanity. Or perish in a toxic mental cloud of our own making, when our civilization reaches its point of singularity."

Skinwalkers at the Pentagon: An Insiders' Account of the Secret Government UFO Program
JAMES T. LACATSKI, COLM A. KELLEHER, & GEORGE KNAPP
(2021, RTMA, LLC)

In some ways this book is a sequel to their 2005 title, *Hunt for the Skinwalker*, by Kelleher and Knapp, about the bizarre paranormal and UFO incidents at the Skinwalker Ranch in northeastern Utah, which inspired a popular 2019-2020 television reality series on The History Channel. In other respects, this book goes far beyond the earlier title by adding input from a high-level co-author and scientist, James T. Lacatski, who was an intelligence officer at the Defense Intelligence Agency during the several years he spent as part of the government-sponsored science team investigating the ranch and its high strangeness.

After buying the 500-acre ranch in 1996, billionaire real estate and aerospace developer Robert Bigelow financed an on-going scientific investigation of the property conducted under the auspices of his National Institute for Discovery Science. That investigation was the subject of the Kelleher and Knapp book. Then, in 2007, the Defense Intelligence Agency became involved after Lacatski read the book and contacted Bigelow with a proposal to use Pentagon funding and science expertise to investigate Unidentified Aerial Phenomena (UAP) in general, and related paranormal activities at the ranch, using Bigelow's aerospace firm as the private contractor. The $22 million in funding for the program was shepherded through Congress by U.S. Senator Harry Reid of Nevada.

Between late 2008 and the end of 2010, "the Pentagon spent those millions investigating UAPs as well as the paranormal and psychic correlates to UAPs," note the authors, and this investigation was unprecedented in its scope and led to later disclosures, beginning in a 2017 *New York Times* article, of the so-called Tic-Tac UAP sightings by pilots of the USS Nimitz carrier. These revelations resulted in a 2021 intelligence assessment of UFOs by the Office of the Director of National Intelligence which concluded these craft "may pose a challenge to national security."

Altogether a team of over 50 people participated in the science project. This book details some of the high strangeness experiences of these military scientists and officers during and after visiting the ranch. Juliett Witt, for example, was a Department of Defense analyst and counterintelligence specialist who had served multiple tours in Russia and Afghanistan. On her first night at the ranch, she and a project scientist, co-author Kelleher, witnessed a bizarre large creature with dinosaur-like spikes silently walk past them and disappear. When she returned home to Virginia, poltergeist activity broke out in her townhouse, including wine bottles flying across the room smashing on walls, along with different colored orbs floating around, terrorizing her and her housemate.

Hitchhikers was the term given to seemingly infectious paranormal phenomenon where project participants 'brought something home with them' after spending time at the ranch. Each of ten security officers who spent two-week tours on the ranch reported experiencing "poltergeist and other paranormal activity in their homes" after leaving the ranch. Also, "five out of five intelligence professionals, the majority of whom had combat and military experience, had visceral anomalous experiences while visiting the ranch, became infected by a 'contagion,' and brought the infectious entity back to their families and households on the East Coast." These reported incidents involved bizarre wolf-like creatures suddenly appearing outside the homes of project members and blue orbs flying through their residences, witnessed by entire families. Another aspect of this hitchhiker phenomenon raises even more alarming health-related questions. "In some cases," the authors report, "the transmission into some households was correlated with the emergence of autoimmune disease in family members."

Interviews were conducted by the science team with 30 nearby residents—including four police officers and six ranchers—who lived within a two-mile radius of Skinwalker Ranch. Most had frequently seen small blue, white or red orbs flying close to the ground, along with disc-shaped and triangular unidentified craft, and 11 had witnessed dog or wolf-like creatures that ran fast upright on just two legs. This research made it clear the 'Disneyland of the paranormal,' as Skinwalker had been dubbed, wasn't a phenomenon confined just to ranch boundaries.

After two years of work the science group submitted about 100 technically rigorous investigative reports to the Defense Intelligence Agency on UAPs and other anomalies. Among a series of remarkable findings and recommendations advanced by the science group: "Decades of field research by AAWSAP BASS, NIDS, and multiple other organizations has suggested that consciousness (including telepathic communication) may play an integral role in Human-UAP interactions."

In Plain Sight: An Investigation into Ufos and Impossible Science
ROSS COULTHART
(2021, HarperCollins)

Ross Coulthart, an award-winning investigative broadcast journalist in Australia, spent two years digging into The Phenomenon, as he calls it, by interviewing numerous U.S. military and civilian personnel connected to it. This book covers a series of topics in detail, including the civil rights attorney who made a shocking discovery in classified Project Blue Book documents, an alleged alien visitation disclosure made by top Defense Intelligence Agency officials, new revelations about the 2004 'tic tac' UFO sightings by Navy pilots, a rock star pries the lid off government UFO secrets, puzzling anti-gravity patents from a Navy scientist, and a death bed confession from the Navy's Director of Science and Technology.

As General Counsel for the U.S. National Jesuit organization in Washington, D.C., federal civil rights attorney Daniel Sheehan worked with the Congressional Research Service to ask for and receive access to the classified document portions of the Air Force's defunct Project Blue Book. He went to a guarded basement office in the Library of Congress, in 1977, and began going through rolls of microfiche, looking for photographs, since he wasn't allowed to make copies or even take notes. He eventually found classified photos of "a full-scale classic saucer with a dome," which had apparently crashed into a snow-covered field, seen surrounded by U.S. Air Force personnel with cameras. One photo showed unknown symbols "etched into the side of the craft just below the dome." Subsequent classified reports on UFOs given President Jimmy Carter never mentioned the photos that Sheehan had found in the classified files. President Carter was also reportedly was denied a briefing on the UFO subject by then CIA Director George Bush because Bush claimed Carter "didn't have a need to know."

What Sheehan's discovery lays the groundwork for in Coulthart's book is a case showing how the U.S. government has consistently hidden evidence for crashed or landed alien spacecraft over many decades. The next piece of that puzzle the author presents involves a Pentagon meeting in 1997, arranged by astronaut Edgar Mitchell, involving The Disclosure Project founder and physician Steven Greer, and Admiral Thomas Wilson, Deputy Director of Intelligence for the Joint Chiefs of Staff. In this meeting, according to Mitchell and Greer and three other witnesses, Admiral Wilson made an extraordinary admission that a corporate cabal and shadow-like part of government was engaged in covering up physical evidence of non-human spacecraft landings and crashes. Though years later Admiral Wilson did acknowledge to Coulthart that the meeting happened, he denied stating that a coverup was underway or that he was improperly blocked from accessing UFO information. Coulthart indicates that he believes the five witnesses present at the meeting who agree Admiral Wilson, despite his later denial, did make the reported admissions.

The next piece of the puzzle that Coulthart explains in detail involves the series of 2004 'Tic Tac' sightings by U.S. Navy personnel, which Coulthart calls "probably the most well-verified UAP {unidentified aerial phenomena} event in history," because there were so many credible witnesses and the phenomena had been captured on multiple independent sensor systems, including cameras and radar. The hunt for "the big secret," as Coulthart calls it, soon got underway, inspiring U.S. Senator Harry Reid to spearhead funding for a Defense Intelligence Agency program to investigate these sightings—and UAPs in general—using a subcontractor, the Nevada billionaire Robert Bigelow.

One of Bigelow's scientific investigators was Eric Davis, Ph.D., who said he had a private meeting in Las Vegas, in 2002, with Admiral Thomas Wilson, in which Wilson, recently retired as Director of the Defense Intelligence Agency, basically affirmed what he had said privately in 1997, and added that he had uncovered a long hidden military program to reverse-engineer a non-human spacecraft. A private corporation was secretly storing the recovered alien craft, creating a 'plausible deniability' for the military. Davis wrote up a transcript of this conversation with Wilson in a 15-page memo that was given to astronaut Edgar Mitchell. It was only after Mitchell died that the memo was leaked on the Internet. Once again, Wilson issued a denial, as he had after the 1997 meeting, saying he had not revealed what was being claimed.

Rock star Tom DeLonge quit his band Blink-182, in 2015, to pursue investigating UAPs fulltime and formed an organization, To The Stars Academy, devoted to the cause of disclosure. Observes Coulthart: "I am now certain that very senior government officials, claiming to be protecting one of the United States' most closely held secrets, briefed DeLonge on what they assured him was the truth about a genuine UAP cover-up." The author proceeds to tell the story of how DeLonge gained incredible military access, such as meeting with the Air Force's Space Command to discuss UAP crash retrievals. Part of the key to his success was having recruited people to his Stars project like Jim Semivan, retired from the CIA, and Steve Justice, retired director of advanced systems at Lockheed Martin Skunk Works, and Christopher Mellon, former Deputy Assistant Secretary of Defense for Intelligence. Another possible reason DeLonge got such unprecedented access was the claim that his group had obtained metamaterial samples from alien craft, something the military might want to examine. What further gave DeLonge credibility were revelations from the 2016 email leaks of John Podesta (Hillary Clinton's chief of staff) showing DeLonge and Podesta in discussions about these matters. In 2017, The Stars Academy website posted three of the U.S. Navy videos of UAP encounters, giving DeLonge and group even greater public attention.

As a final piece of the disclosure puzzle for this book, Coulthart reveals a series of conversations he had with a U.S. Navy scientist, Nat Kobitz, former Navy Director of Science and Technology. Kobitz didn't have long to live and seemed willing to make some admissions he had previously been sworn to secrecy about. He told Coulthart about inspecting an amazing piece of metal at Wright-Patterson Air Force Base that was reportedly not of this world. Kobitz admitted that the U.S. had been trying to reverse-engineer recovered alien technology. "I am in absolutely no doubt that Nat Kobitz told me the truth of what he knew and saw," writes Coulthart. "That he was 'read into' a crash retrieval program and shown crafted bonded metal technology beyond anything he had ever seen before."

Coulthart ends the book with this observation: "What do I know for sure, after two years down the rabbit hole? I have no doubt at all that the US government is hiding extraordinary secrets about The Phenomenon. The categorical statements made by defense and intelligence insiders Dr. Eric Davis and Luis Elizondo (and the more qualified assertions by Christopher Mellon and former Senator Harry Reid) suggest that the United States has indeed recovered non-human intelligently manufactured technology, a conclusion that makes my head spin with its awesome implications."

SECTION THREE

Contactees and Abductees. . .

What Are They Trying to Tell Us?

Throughout history, encounters have been reported between humans and sky-dwelling entities which communicate either telepathically or in disembodied voices. Moses, Ezekiel, Jesus Christ, Mohammed, and Joan of Arc, among others, claimed contact with a higher intelligence which inspired them to influence human events. In 1656 Jesuit priest and scholar Athanasius Kircher wrote a book alleging that two angels had accompanied him on an out-of-the-body excursion to the moon, the sun, and five planets. Joseph Smith founded the Mormon Church in the early 1800s after encountering two entities which reportedly descended from an aerial craft over New York state. Once the age of air flight dawned with hot air balloons, a Russian mystic and medium, Helena Blavatsky, attracted a cultish following in England and the U.S. in the late 19th century by alleging telepathic contacts with spirits of the dead and advanced beings on the planet Venus.

During the 1950s dozens of contactees—nearly all of them Americans—generated publicity with tales of having encountered UFO occupants visiting Earth from other planets. UFO groups which were seeking scientific legitimacy actively disparaged the contactees, viewing them as little more than a distracting embarrassment. In 1963 the entire phenomenon took a leap in visibility, if not credibility, when a New Hampshire couple, Betty and Barney Hill, revealed under hypnosis their belief that UFO occupants had abducted them for two hours and subjected them to painful medical tests. Their account produced a bestselling book and a 1975 television movie starring James Earl Jones.

Over the next three decades a veritable floodgate opened releasing remarkably similar stories into popular culture. Six woodcutters in Arizona told authorities in 1975 of seeing a UFO zap a seventh member of their crew, who disappeared for five days after allegedly being abducted by the craft's humanoid occupants. A year later three religious Kentucky housewives related similar abduction events of a nighttime UFO encounter while returning from a restaurant. Thousands of such reports have since surfaced worldwide, most describing abductors with a resemblance to the grey dwarfish, insect-eyed aliens portrayed in the 1977 movie *Close Encounters Of The Third Kind*. Of course, as UFO enthusiasts are quick to point out, the model for Steven Spielberg's aliens came from astronomer J. Allen Hynek, the movie's technical consultant, who based the composite on numerous reported cases of alien encounters.

Still another leap in visibility for the phenomenon occurred in 1994 with the release of Harvard University psychiatrist John Mack's book, *Abduction: Human Encounters with Aliens.* He revealed how hypnotic regression of more than 100 persons had convinced him aliens are kidnapping earthlings for medical experiments to produce a hybrid species better suited to adaptation if and when the planet's ecosystems are destroyed by pollution. Dr. Mack's stature in the psychiatric field prompted widespread attention to his book with a prominent review in *The New York Times*, and a guest spot on the Oprah Winfrey Show.

Mack's success at generating media attention can be partly attributed to ground broken by Whitley Strieber's 1987 book, *Communion*, which fixated public interest on the alien abduction theme as it hovered for many months on the New York Times best seller list. Subsequently, a nationwide survey by the Roper Organization confirmed widespread public intoxication with the subject. This random sample of 5,947 American adults in 1993 asked five questions-such as, have you awakened paralyzed and sensed a strange presence in your room, experienced periods of missing time, or found unexplained scars on your body-which were designed to measure the possible frequency of alien encounters. About two percent of the sample answered "yes" to at least four of the questions, supposedly making them prime abductee candidates. Extrapolated out to the entire population, that would mean 3.7 million Americans may have been abducted, or at least possess the attributes which abduction researchers believe would constitute evidence of alien contact.

As an investigator, my own immersion in this realm can be traced to 1978, the year I heard a story which, if remotely true, seemed to constitute a best case of evidence for alien visitation. As first related by Robert Emenegger in his 1974 book, *UFO's Past, Present and Future*, a shy woman in southern Maine had supposedly convinced Naval Intelligence, the U.S. Air Force, and the CIA that she was in communication with an alien being named Affa. She had allegedly successfully answered highly technical and scientific questions by channeling Affa through automatic writing. Even more astounding, she had taught a Naval Intelligence officer how to communicate with Affa and he had summoned one of the alien spacecraft, which appeared over Washington, D.C. witnessed by a group of CIA and Naval Intelligence officials. Acting in my role as co-editor of *Second Look* magazine, I tracked down most of the principals in this case and interviewed many of them at length and in person, including the contactee herself. What emerged after several months of research was a story different from the myth that had evolved, yet equally unsettling in its implications.

Case History of a Contactee

As a young girl, Frances Swan wanted to know the secrets of the Universe. She read and studied everything esoteric that rural Maine had to offer. She went to seances, sought out spiritualists, used the ouija board. Local farmers sometimes asked her to intuit the whereabouts of their lost cattle and her predictions rarely disappointed them. She was a joiner, a respected member of her South Berwick, Maine community. She joined the Congregational Church, and after her daughter was born, was elected to the School Board and served as president of the area's Girl Scout Leader's Association.

On Halloween night of 1953, as she stood on a ladder hanging decorations in the local Grange Hall, all of her searching for a deeper meaning in life abruptly ended. A distinguished stranger walked into the hall and attracted Mrs. Swan's attention. Her memory of his appearance would fade over the years, but she never forgot the impact his presence had on her. "He said later he was supposed to speak to me. He was supposed to touch my hand by shaking hands. But he couldn't get up the nerve because of all the people around. I talked to him and I was the only one that talked to him that night. That seemed strange. He didn't tell me anything then. But ever after that night, if I looked in the direction he came in, I could almost see him. It was sort of like an impression had been left. And that was exactly what he came for."

About six months after this encounter Mrs. Swan began hearing in her left ear a shrill whistle, a soft flat musical note A. On April 30, 1954, at 5 p.m., she received her first message: "We come will help keep peace on EU do not be frightened." On May 2 at 2:30 p.m., according to scrupulous notes she kept, she again heard the ringing noise and felt compelled to scrawl with a pencil: ''We are on moon we are being watched constantly...We are ready to make flight to Earth under cover of barrage of weather balloons..."

The "entity" speaking through Mrs. Swan's automatic writing identified itself as Affa, from Uranus, Bell Flight Signal M4 M4, cruising above Earth in a spaceship 753,454 feet across. Affa said he was the man Mrs. Swan had seen at the Grange Hall in October. He was on a mission to "place a network of magnetic lanes over the danger spots which will reinforce the wasted magnetism brought about by the sin and greedy hearts of men on your planet."

"Do not be frightened at anything we may ask of you," Affa counselled Mrs. Swan. "You are selected to contact your people."

By the early morning hours of May 14, Mrs. Swan was receiving transmissions from Affa's associates within the Universal Association of Planets-Ankar from Centuras,

Ponnar from Pluto, and Alomar from Mercury. Mrs. Swan remained distrustful of these entities for she could not quite believe what was happening to her. "I knew there was flying saucers out there, but there was all kinds of weird things. They said we've come to make use of you, and I thought that might be wrong because I always figured there might be a Devil around too."

These entities interrupted her repeatedly at all hours, announcing their presence with a sharp ringing in her ear so loud that she experienced extreme discomfort. They could sense her feelings and her thoughts. "I resented them at first because I didn't think they had a right to look into my mind like that. I didn't know what they were, and they wanted complete mind control. I really fought it quite a lot."

On May 18, Affa told Mrs. Swan to write a letter to her government. He suggested that she send it to the U.S. Navy, since they had short wave sets that could tune in to his messages. Affa wanted everyone to know that aliens were friendly.

Mrs. Helen Knowles remembers being in the kitchen when her neighbor Frances Swan knocked on the door. Since they were only casual acquaintances, Mrs. Knowles was surprised to see her standing there. Mrs. Swan was emotional and upset. She asked to speak with Admiral Knowles, who was in the backyard gardening. Rear Admiral H.B. Knowles, several years retired from the Navy, had developed an interest in UFOs largely because of retired Marine Major Donald E. Keyhoe, who had recruited him to serve on the Board of NICAP, the National Investigations Committee on Aerial Phenomena. As Mrs. Swan described her contacts with Affa, Admiral and Mrs. Knowles listened with both skepticism and sympathy. It appeared obvious to them that Mrs. Swan was sincere in her plea for help and understanding.

Just after noon on May 26, according to notes made by Admiral Knowles, he and his wife arrived at Mrs. Swan's home. Affa had promised to appear in person at 1:12 p.m. The four of them (Mr. Swan was also present) sat and waited for an hour. "Mrs. Swan appeared to be very much provoked at the failure of Affa to arrive," wrote Admiral Knowles, "and was indignant to the point where she declared that if he couldn't produce for her she was about ready to be through with the whole deal. All at once she began to write the following message: "'I am very sorry person not to be able to get there at the time appointed.'"

Admiral Knowles asked a series of questions of Affa, to which Mrs. Swan replied in automatic writing using a pencil and a notepad. "The answers came through without hesitation, any apparent premeditation or confusion on her part. She wrote swiftly and smoothly in a peculiar hand. During the whole time she is receiving messages there is a ringing in her ears which has been so intense at times to be painful and on one or two occasions the ringing has been heard by her husband." Admiral Knowles asked Affa the distance of his "satellite" from Earth, what sort of landing field Affa would need, and whether Affa desired any guarantees for a safe landing and departure.

Later in the day, as Mrs. Swan sat alone, Affa apologized to her for not appearing in person as promised. "Even though you feel that you have been duped I am real. You have seen me. I do know that you have faith in me. I need you very much." As Mrs. Swan scribbled out this message she noticed static sparks on her hands. Affa called the effect "magnetic over flow," a by-product of her being controlled by magnetic impulses "such as are used by the brain."

The next day, May 27, Admiral Knowles wrote a letter to Rear Admiral C.F. Espe, Chief of Naval Intelligence in Washington, D.C. He described Mrs. Swan as "about 40 years of age, of average education and perhaps better than average intelligence, and deeply religious." Admiral Knowles said he did not believe that "she has the knowledge or ability to manufacture the fantastic story. She has the appearance of one being impelled into doing something over which she has little control." He requested that Naval Intelligence attempt contact with Affa using Band CMM-306, repeating the signal M4 M4 AF FA, as Affa had earlier suggested to Mrs. Swan.

On May 28, at 8:35 a.m., Affa explained to Mrs. Swan why she had been selected as an intermediary. "The reason we have chosen you is because of the spiritual development you have achieved." Affa then began to reveal details about himself. He claimed to have a home the size of Mrs. Swan's, except that he has "one more fireplace in the kitchen" for his wife who "likes to cook over an open fire." Affa has seven "lovely daughters" who each have "faith and love of God." Affa set the population of Uranus at 787 million, the planet's terrain being "exactly as your Earth." Even the government of Uranus resembles that of America. "Some of us dress the same as yourselves. Many of our young girls like to wear long skirts for dancing. We also have animals similar to your own. Yes, we even have roadside eating places on Uranus."

One week after Affa's revelations about his planet and his personal life, Admiral Knowles requested that Mrs. Swan transmit a three-page statement to Affa asking him to signal with a blinking light or radio to alert Air Force planes to his spacecraft's approach. Affa agreed to attempt such a communication. Admiral Knowles then sent a second urgent letter to Admiral Espe: "I am sending you a more important installment of messages from and concerning Affa. Believe me, these messages are real! Communication has been established with Earth through Mrs. Swan. Can you read these communications and believe they are the product of Mrs. Swan's imagination?"

Naval Intelligence apparently could no longer ignore Admiral Knowles. On June 8, intelligence officers Captain John R. Bromley and Captain Harry W. Baltazzi arrived at the home of Mrs. Swan, accompanied by Admiral and Mrs. Knowles. They asked Affa to reveal himself. Affa replied: "This would not be possible at this time." The Navy officers suggested that Affa establish radio contact with them at 2 p.m. Affa finally agreed but released a flash of anger at their demands for proof: "I am saving your planet. What more do you want in the way of friendship? You must realize these little bell hops (Earth visits) are not as easy as they seem."

On the day of the scheduled radio transmission, Affa woke Mrs. Swan at 5:25 in the morning. "Today is the day we will try to contact your Navy department. Pray for me and I am sure we can succeed in getting this message of contact into being." The day passed without further word until 6 p.m., when Ponnar sent a message through Mrs. Swan (Affa is said to "be away"): "We want you to know that we did not have a very successful try today, but I do believe we may in the very near future."

Admiral Espe wrote to Admiral Knowles on July 8: "Thank you for your letter with which you forwarded additional transcripts of Mrs. Swan's thought transference. It appears that such transcripts will continue to be viewed with some skepticism by the technical offices unless a more conventional means of communication is arranged."

On July 28, W.B. Smith of Ottawa, representing the Canadian government, visited Mrs. Swan to learn the secrets of magnetism. Smith had become convinced that flying saucers were emissaries from advanced civilizations using magnetic propulsion systems. As Superintendent of Radio Regulations Engineering for Canada, Smith administered Project Magnet, a government program to study UFOs. In 1952 he had shown Admiral Knowles a piece of metal, twice the size of a human thumb, which had allegedly "been shot from a small flying saucer near Washington, D.C." in July of that year. Smith said the U.S. Air Force loaned him the specimen for analysis. It turned out to be a matrix composed of magnesium orthosilicate, studded with thousands of 15- micron spheres. No one could apparently determine whether it was of earthly or extraterrestrial origin.

Affa cautioned Smith that the end of human civilization was near. "Have your government tell its people to get down on their knees and pray as they have never prayed before. This earth is really going to end as stated in the Holy Bible around the year 1956." Affa told Smith that he should arrange an appearance before the United Nations and say "look, these people out in space need you to cooperate. We don't want one more nuclear explosion because they're making windows in the ionosphere."

Smith asked Affa for information about technology humans do not yet possess.

Affa, with technical support from Alomar, used Mrs. Swan to draw a series of circles to demonstrate how their generators, utilizing magnetic force through an alignment of magnets, powered their spacecraft. Smith arranged for Affa to attempt radio communication at 3 p.m. the following day. A half-dozen Canadian engineers waited in vain for Affa's signal. Smith was disappointed but undeterred.

As word of Mrs. Swan's connection to Affa spread beyond government circles, people from a variety of backgrounds made a pilgrimage to her home. "They all came for not any good they could do, but it was what they wanted. Each one who came to visit had their own little iron in the fire. Some fellow came from California who wanted to know how to preserve food so it would last forever. Wib Smith wanted anti-gravity in the worst way, and he would go around and around on questions cause Affa would say there's no such thing as time, and there's no such thing as gravity."

Despite official Navy pronouncements to Admiral Knowles that Mrs. Swan did not warrant further interest, Naval Intelligence continued sending contingents of officers to gather information from her. In 1954 three intelligence officers, including a chemist and a psychologist, spent several days debriefing her at Admiral Knowle's home in the company of W.B. Smith. This encounter prompted Mrs. Swan to fear for the sanity of her interrogators. "The chemist came down in the middle of the night scared to death. He thought flying saucer people were after him and they were being terrible to he and his wife. Wib Smith came down and sat up all night with him. We found ourselves in a strange predicament. They were the ones who needed help instead of me."

Still another group of Navy officers visited Mrs. Swan later in 1954. They rarely asked her technical questions anymore, only questions about religion, the nature of spirit, the nature of God, and that began to puzzle and irritate Mrs. Swan. "I felt gee, I could tell them most anything. We finally got onto them, what they were doing. They were of the Christian Science religion getting in their flying time. Affa refused to answer any more questions. He had gotten sick of it."

The CIA Gets Involved

On a hot weekend in June 1959, two intelligence officers initiated what was apparently the last official Navy contact with Mrs. Swan. Navy Commander J.M. Larsen, serving as liaison officer between Naval Intelligence and the CIA's Photographic Interpretation Center, accompanied by a fellow Navy pilot, spent the night at Admiral Knowle's home and were visited the next day by Mrs. Swan. Larsen was young and enthusiastic, and he needed no convincing of Affa's reality. "He was all for spiritualism. He swallowed everything. He decided he'd like to do automatic writing and would I show him how. I said sure. I just put my hand on his shoulder and he could write. But that wasn't flying saucers, because you know what they're going to say before they say it. With one try he began writing and right away someone named Affa started."

Larsen scribbled furiously, getting more excited as sentences began to form. Admiral and Mrs. Knowles watched as Larsen wrote. The other Navy officer stood up from the dining table, angry and disgusted, and left the room. Mrs. Swan warned Larsen that he was not in contact with Affa, but he refused to listen. "I said that's not Affa, he wasn't available. But I couldn't make him believe it. I think he thought I was telling him a fib. I said it says Affa, but it isn't. Where it said 'Signed Affa,' Affa never wrote that way. He always said God bless you. But if you're an officer, what's a little old lady like me? He just went overboard."

On returning to Washington, D.C., Commander Larsen phoned his friend and CIA contact Arthur Lundahl, who agreed to witness a demonstration of Larsen's channel to Affa. Lundahl worked as the CIA's chief photo analyst, having analyzed the Tremonton UFO sighting photos for the agency. In that 1952 sighting, a Navy officer took 16-mm motion pictures one morning of bright objects flying in formation over Utah, which Lundahl's CIA investigation allegedly concluded may have been a flock of seagulls.

About 2 p.m. on July 6, 1959, at the CIA's photo analysis center hidden in the top story of a downtown Washington, D.C. garage, Larsen went into a trance observed by Lundahl and Lt. Comdr. Robert Neasham, a Navy photo analyst assigned to the CIA. Both men began asking Larsen questions, to which he responded with automatic writing in the name of Affa.

"Can we have proof of your existence?" asked Lundahl.

"What kind of proof do you want?" Larsen (Affa) scribbled in reply.

"Can we see you or your craft?"

"When do you want to see it?"

"Now!"

"Go to the window."

Both Lundahl and Neasham got up and walked over to a window that looked out over the skyline. What they saw, or didn't see, over the city that afternoon is a matter which would remain in dispute for decades to come. According to a CIA document leaked years later (that I have reproduced below), Lundahl and Neasham spotted a UFO slowly flying past the window a short distance away. It was allegedly saucer-shaped and brighter around the perimeter than in the center. Their attempt to verify the sighting by phoning a government radar center was unsuccessful because that area of the sky was 'blacked out' for some unknown reason at the time of the sighting.

What cannot be disputed is that later in the afternoon of July 6, Major Robert Friend, chief of Project Blue Book, the U.S. Air Force's UFO investigative unit at Wright-Patterson AFB in Ohio, received an urgent phone call from a CIA contact. Major Friend was needed to fly immediately to Washington and evaluate a "discovery" by Naval Intelligence. On July 9, at the CIA photo analysis office, Major Friend met with Larsen, Lundahl and Neasham. Here the mystery deepens. Friend would claim in a report to his Air Force superiors that the three men described in detail the UFO which Larsen had summoned in the skies over Washington. Lundahl in particular, according to a CIA memo record of the meeting, expressed a belief that he had seen a flying saucer.

In an interview two decades later, with my magazine, *Second Look*, Lundahl adamantly denied having seen a UFO or telling Friend about it. "Never for a fleeting moment did I believe this Navy officer was in communication with people from outer space, nor did I see a UFO," declared Lundahl. "Though I believe in intelligent life other than ours, I felt nothing but sympathy and embarrassment on this occasion, for a man who was troubled, who was my friend, and who, if his superiors had learned of this, would undoubtedly have suffered in his career." (As you will see in the CIA memo reproduced below, Larsen's superiors already knew of the incident and had debriefed Larsen about it. My interview with Lundahl occurred before I had the CIA memo in hand and thus I couldn't challenge him about how it portrayed his experience).

Colonel William Coleman, who was the Air Force's chief spokesman in the early 1960s, supports the authenticity of the CIA document and the veracity of Major Friend's account. "The document is genuine, and even without the document substantiating him, Friend's credibility is beyond reproach."

Major Friend remembers asking Larsen to undertake another contact with Affa which would include a flyby of his spacecraft. Once Larsen went into a trance, "I could see his pulse quicken," Friend later related. "His handwriting became entirely different from his normal handwriting. The muscles in his arms were obviously stressed, as were the muscles around his neck. I asked if Affa could arrange a flyby. The officer's arm jerkily wrote out, 'The time is not right.' His trance lasted about 20 minutes. I was convinced that there was something there. There was something we should have found out more about."

On his return to Wright-Patterson AFB, Major Friend prepared a detailed report of this incident and submitted it to his commanding general who said he would take personal charge of the case. Though Friend never heard anything more about the people involved, or what happened in the follow-up investigation, if there was one, he considered the incident to be one of the more puzzling experiences of his five years directing Project Blue Book.

(**Note to Readers**: here below is a transcript of the CIA memo recording the extraordinary meeting at a CIA office in Washington, D.C., in July 1959, a memo which J. Allen Hynek had seen at Project Blue Book headquarters, Wright-Patterson Air Force Base. Hynek made a handwritten copy of the memo, which belonged to Major Robert Friend and had been shared with General Charles B. Dougher, Chief of ATIC (Air Technical Intelligence Center) based at Wright-Patterson. Hynek, in turn, shared the memo with his associate, Jacques Vallée. Many years later, in a conversation with Vallée, Arthur Lundahl would admit that "everything in the memo was all true.")

Memorandum for Record
On 6 July 1959 Mr. A.C. Lundahl, Washington, D.C. contacted Col. Leonard Glaser concerning evident flying object. Col Glaser informed Mr. Lundahl…Maj. Friend—Meeting set CIA July 9, 1959.

At 1400, 9 July 1959, a meeting was held at the CIA, 5th & K streets N.W. Wash. Present at meeting were:
Com. Julius M. Larsen ONI
Lt. Com. D.W. Leiber CIA
Lt. Com. R.S. Neasham CIA
Mr. C.F. Camp CIA
Mr. A.F. Schenfele CIA
Mr. J.W. Cain CIA
Mr. W.S. Stallings CIA
Mr. Arthur Lundahl CIA
Maj. R.J. Friend ATIC

B. Mr. Lundahl acted as Chairman {unintelligible} the UFO program and the part which CIA and ONI had taken to date. Specifically mentioned were the Mariana sighting Aug. 1950 and the Tremonton sighting 2 July 1952. Both of these cases had physical evidence in form of {unintelligible} which were analyzed by Navy.

(A discussion for 2 hours & then they finally got down to business.)

At end of 2 hour period asked whether Maj. Friend was open minded concerning the program. The purpose of the meeting began to take shape.

C. As background information Mr. Lundahl briefed Maj. Friend on a case investigated by the Navy in May-June of 1954. This case concerns a Mrs. Frances A. Swan of {unintelligible} Maine who reported to the Navy through Rear Admiral Herbert B. {Knowles} that she was in contact with space persons. Mrs. Swan's method of contact is to {unintelligible} a question and by completely relaxing with a pencil in her hand, some unknown force controls the hand and writes the answer. It was also pointed out that the Canadian government had conducted an extensive investigation of Mrs. Swan's claims. A complete file of this case is in the office of Captain Frankel, ONI. At this point Mr. Lundahl turned the discussion over to Commander J.M. Larsen.

D. Com. Larsen pointed out that during the latter part of June, he and another Naval Officer had flown up to Maine and visited Mrs. Swan for the purpose of witnessing a contact and to interview the lady. Mrs. Swan, after the interview and contact, asked Cmdr. Larsen why he didn't make a contact himself. The officer then tried, but was unsuccessful.

E. After his return to Wash. Cmdr Larsen was discussing the case with Mr. Lundahl and Lt. Comdr. Neasham at CIA. At the insistence of these two gentlemen he attempted another contact and was app. Successful in receiving messages from a person called AFFA an inhabitant of the planet Uranus. Cmdr. Larsen would pen his question on a large sheet of paper (ques. Put to him by other 2) relax, and some unknown force would guide his hand in writing the answers. During the time that the message is being transmitted Larsen is subjected to very great physical strain. Of the many questions put to AFFA...some samples...

Q. Do you favor any government, religious group or race.

A. No, we do not Signed AFFA

Q. Will there be a third world war?

A. No. Signed AFFA

Q. Are Catholics the chosen people?

A. No. Signed AFFA

Q. Can we see a spaceship or flying saucer?

A. When do you want to see it?

Q. Can we see it now?

A. Go to the window. Signed AFFA.

(Mr. Lundahl, Cmdr. Larsen & Lt. Cmdr. Neasham all go to the window).

Q. Are we looking in the right direction?

A. (Answered vocally!) Yes, Signed AFFA.

At this time, approximately 1400, 6 July 1959, these three men saw what they have indicated was a flying saucer. They described the object as round, with the perimeter brighter than the center. Lt. Cmdr. Neasham checked with Washington Center (radar) and was informed that for some unknown reason radar return from the direction in which the ship was supposedly seen had been blacked out at the time of the sighting. During the exchange the answer to one of the questions indicated difficulty in penetrating our radar net. {i.e.-physical penetration of our radar net—slipping through it}

F. After the discussion and examination of the documents Mj Friend requested that Cmdr. Larsen attempt another contact. Larsen consented, but had only limited success. It was indicated in the few answers which he received that this was not the right time. However, it was further indicated that there was no objection to the audience.

G. Mr. Lundahl and all of the persons present indicated that they had known Larsen for many years and that he has always been competent, quiet, reserved and very conservative. They all attached significance to this experience due to this respect from Cmdr. Larsen and the experience of Mr.

Lundahl and H.C. Neasham of seeing what they believe to be a space ship.

H. On July 10, 1959 Maj. Friend in the company of Cmdr. Larsen visited the office of Capt. Frankel, ONI to study the case file of Mrs. Swan. The record indicates that Mrs. Swan has been in touch with the following persons from the planet or constellation

AFFA {unintelligible symbol}

CRLLL {unintelligible symbol}

ALOMAR {unintelligible symbol}

PONNAR {unintelligible symbol} (reported to leave human race alone to {unintelligible})

ANKAR Centaurians

The Navy indicates that through these contacts Mrs. Swan has been able to answer technical questions beyond the level of her education or background. The case file contains records of some of the exchanges that Mrs. Swan has had, and while there is some loose mention of how space ships work and of what they are made, there was little of value.....Larsen indicated that the Canadians (a Mr. Smith) had exploited this scientific angle.

The Swan record indicated that there was an organization {unintelligible} which means the Universal Association of Planets, and that the organization has a project EU or {unintelligible} (earth) which is being conducted. What this project was to accomplish was not mentioned. The record indicated that the population of {unintelligible} was 787,730,016 and that the day was 7 times longer than an earth day (!) and that a day on {unintelligible} was 10 x longer.

J. In discussion with Capt. Frankel, he indicated there was no evidence which he felt was concrete enough for him to indicate action on this case. However, he did suggest that specific questions be prepared and put to Mrs. Swan if the Air Force plans to pursue the case further. Arrangements were also made for Larsen to attempt a contact for Frankel & Lundahl on 11 July 1959. Maj. Friend requested that the ATIC be informed of the outcome.

III Impressions

Capt. Frankel- Obviously a very clear thinking man—only his regard for Larsen stimulates his interest in the case.

Cmdr. Larsen: Appears to be a very steady person, has (or had!) a responsible position in ONI {unintelligible} This officer appeared very embarrassed during the initial part of the discussion concerning his experience and exhibited some reluctance. However, he warmed to the task once the communication was well underway.

Lt. C. Neasham: This officer was one of the persons who worked on the Tremonton and Mariana films. He indicated that his mother had submitted a UFO report in 1954 of an object which was widely seen in Nevada County, Cal. Has strong belief in Larsen.

Mr. Lundahl: This man appears to have both feet on the ground. Feels certain that the object that he saw with L and N was a flying saucer. Has great regard for Larsen.

During the period of actual contact Larsen appears to be under great physical strain. His jaw is tense, and pulses in his neck & temples are very evident (says very sore the next day) Larsen states his impression is that he is being used as a medium for transmitting the messages and that he doesn't enter mentally into the exchange consciously or subconsciously (!)

End of CIA Memo

It has been reported that Commander Larsen was transferred to California, apparently a confused and troubled man. Affa and the Universal Association of Planets would not relinquish control over his mind. In desperation he wrote to Mrs. Swan for help. "He wrote me a long letter pleading with me to get them off his back. He couldn't think. He couldn't do anything. He was a total wreck. And so I told him you've got to pray, and you've also got to be mean to anyone who's trying to control you. You've got to be mean and negative and drive them out."

Many people felt a need to believe in Mrs. Swan, desiring reassurance that a more advanced and benevolent force existed out in the void and that this shy and sensitive woman was its link to humanity. Affa spoke through her of love and spiritual healing. Affa was the philosopher that Frances Swan yearned to be. While channeling Affa she radiated integrity and warmth, truth and understanding. Even those who came away skeptical came away impressed.

Several weeks after I interviewed her in 1979, one of the Naval Intelligence officers who had dealt with Affa, by visiting Mrs. Swan, phoned Mrs. Swan again after many years of no contact. This seemed a curious coincidence so I contacted the man, John H. Hutson, at his home in Florida. He refused to discuss Affa or Mrs. Swan. "I'd rather not go into my involvement. She still feels a religious connotation about her experience. I would honor that. I have never publicly revealed my own experiences with her, because I was a part of national security. But I just won't get into that."

For years since, I have puzzled over Hutson's reference to national security still being honored by him regarding Mrs. Swan. What could possibly still—or have ever—been the national security issue with her? Also, the fact that he, a Naval Intelligence officer, albeit retired, had apparently known about my visit to interview Mrs. Swan, either before or right after it happened, and then he had phoned to question her about what she revealed, made me suspicious that Mrs. Swan might have still been under surveillance for some reason. What would cause a seemingly naïve and harmless Maine housewife to trigger a continuing intelligence agency interest in her and her claims of alien contact? Maybe there was still concern she might actually have been a channel to a higher intelligence.

It would have been easy for Admiral Knowles, Wilbert Smith, or any of the others to have challenged what Mrs. Swan told them. Affa contradicted himself often, giving every appearance of being no more and no less human than Mrs. Swan. On June 25, 1954, Affa said his spaceship was 150 miles from point to point; on May 2, he had said it was 753,454 feet across, a difference of about 7 miles. Affa said Uranus was 11 times larger than Earth, yet human scientists knew that ratio was only 4 to 1. Affa did not know what megacycles were, yet he claimed to communicate by short wave radio. Each time an unsuccessful attempt was made to contact Affa using radio, he had a convenient excuse: wrong frequency, magnetic interference, mistrust of our government's motives.

And yet every once in a while, like winning small jackpots in a slot machine, Mrs. Swan's Affa came up with a few correct answers to technical questions thought to be incompatible with her education and scientific understanding. According to what Naval Intelligence officers told Major Friend, for instance, Mrs. Swan accurately answered such questions as "What is the length of Uranus' day?" and "What is the distance between Jupiter and the sun at Jupiter's apogee?" These occasional hits intrigued some investigators, inspiring them to conveniently forget or rationalize away her many wild misses. If she had a real communication channel with an extraterrestrial intelligence, it had some faulty 'wiring' somewhere in the system.

Until his death in 1962 Wilbert Smith maintained faith in Mrs. Swan's communication channel to Affa, who Smith described as a person "very much like us," one of our distant relatives who colonized this planet before migrating, and who then returned as part of an inter-solar system police force to investigate atomic testing. During a March 1961 speech in Vancouver, Smith said he had actually built "hardware that works" from information channeled through Mrs. Swan. He apparently believed he had deciphered Affa's magnetic generator charts harnessing the secrets of anti-gravity.

If we are to judge Mrs. Swan, Affa, and their believers harshly, we should do so in the context of the times. A Polish immigrant named George Adamski ushered in the modern contactee epidemic in 1952, when he claimed to have met a Venusian in the California desert. These Venusians rode around in "bells," just like Mrs. Swan's Affa. One of Adamski's associates, George Hunt Williamson, claimed to have established radio contact with an entity calling itself Affa from Uranus between August and November of 1952. Affa told Williamson that their 'bells' traveled along magnetic lines of force. Affa warned Williamson that Earth scientists should immediately stop experimenting with atomic energy. In early 1954, Williamson co-authored a book about these alleged experiences entitled *The Saucers Speak*. Frances Swan confessed to me that she had read that book prior to her own introduction to Affa.

Similar connections can be found in stories related by other contactees from that period. Gloria Lee was an airline stewardess with an interest in UFOs, psychic research and esoteric sciences. While practicing her extrasensory perception one day in September 1953, at the Los Angeles airport, she claimed to have established telepathic contact with a being from Jupiter called J.W. Her preferred method of communication with him became automatic writing. J.W. said the planet Uranus has "the same physical plane" as Earth, and on Uranus "beings have evolved to the Christ consciousness." Meanwhile, Dr. Daniel Fry, an electronics engineer, and a specialist in missile guidance systems at White Sands Proving Ground in New Mexico, supposedly had three contacts with an extraterrestrial from an unnamed planet. The third telepathic contact, in which the being issued a warning about nuclear power, occurred on April 28, 1954, just two days before Mrs. Swan's first message from Affa about the nuclear peril our species faced.

We can infer from these interconnections that either the hoaxes—be they conscious, or unconsciously programmed—are far more elaborate than we ever suspected, or else coincidences occur in the UFO field with unsettling regularity. Mrs. Swan, or Affa, if you prefer, has this to say about coincidences: "There is nothing left to chance. What is coincidental is usually planned before time and that moment in time is the act.

Coincidence is a fusion of mind force of all who are participants. It can be arranged any moment in time when spirit is an active element."

And yet, we are left to wonder whether it was mere coincidence alone that produced a situation where a CIA officer and two Naval Intelligence officers asked Affa to materialize a UFO outside a CIA office and Affa—or their own collective consciousness—responded with the image of a classic UFO hanging in the sky, and, just as importantly, it just so happened that radar coverage for that quadrant of sky over Washington, D.C. was mysteriously 'blacked out' at the time of their sighting. If the three intelligence officers involved thought this had really been a mass hallucination, they would not have placed an urgent call to the Air Force's Project Blue Book asking for immediate assistance.

This bizarre Affa incident ranks high in my Top 10 most interesting cases throughout the entire history of the UFO phenomenon!

A Fantasy Prone Culture?

Some experts in the fields of psychiatry and hypnosis warn that subjects in a deep trance—as many UFO abductees are when they 'remember' their abductions—can summon both memories and fantasies with equal intensity, leaving the subject unable to distinguish between the two. This 'false memory' syndrome has been seen repeatedly in cases where hypnotized children and adults recalling childhood have made accusations of sexual abuse which were later proved false. The American Medical Association began cautioning in 1985 against any systematic use of hypnotic regression precisely because of this unreliability and its potential to create false memories which subjects might cling to with artificial certainty.

Dr. William McCall, a former president of the American Institute of Hypnosis, used hypnotic regression on 30 UFO abductees during the 1970s and concluded "the abductees are unable to separate fact from subconscious fantasy." In a separate controlled experiment, Dr. McCall hypnotized 16 volunteers who had little or no familiarity with UFOs, and while they were in trances, he told each to imagine they were being abducted by UFO occupants. All of the hypnotized volunteers produced abduction tales which resembled other 'real' abduction stories, right down to their descriptions of the aliens, the UFO's interiors, and the type of medical exams the aliens subjected them to. The only major difference in this experiment between imaginary and "real" abduction stories was the strong emotional charge that "real" abductees felt toward their experiences.

Section Three: Contactees and Abductees

Sleep researchers have identified two types of relatively common sleep disorders which can produce waking dream effects remarkably similar to many reported abduction encounters. Known as hypnogogic (when falling asleep) hallucinations, and hypnopompic (when waking up) hallucinations, they are phenomena in which the subject typically experiences partial or complete paralysis, a sensation of floating out of the body, feelings of sexual stimulation, and vivid auditory and visual impressions of being in the presence of a mysterious entity or entities. Depending on the cultural conditioning and belief system of the subject, this presence can be interpreted and experienced as ghosts, demons, angels, or alien beings.

"Ordinary, perfectly sane and rational people have these hallucinatory experiences," writes Robert A. Baker, a professor of psychology at the University of Kentucky. The historical roots of these phenomena in folklore extend far back through time. Medieval accounts, for instance, describe Incubus (male demons) visiting women in their sleep and copulating with them, and Succubus (female demons) sexually attacking men while asleep. In the 19th century these visitations were more popularly ascribed to ghosts, fairies, and elves. Only in our modern era have space aliens dominated the memories of people in the grip of hypnogogic and hypnopompic experiences.

Could it be possible that what we see during these visitations is genetically implanted in human consciousness? An Ohio psychologist, Fred Malmstrom, after studying numerous prison inmates who claimed UFO abductions, concluded in 1997 that the typical abductor, reported as short, with an oversized head and big eyes, may be a "template ingrained in to the human brain in the facial recognition area. Human beings are pre-wired to generate and recognize that particular UFO face." But why is this the case and how did the brain wiring of this image happen?

Evidence which might support this view comes from an unexpected source. Michael Craft in his book, *Alien Impact*, tells of childhood experiences where he awoke "into a sleep paralysis with a sense of beings standing nearby." These memories flooded back over him after he read *Communion*, the abduction account by Whitley Strieber. On an impulse, Craft gave copies of *Communion* to fifteen of his friends. Months later he asked their impressions of the book. "Every single one confessed to strange, disturbing feelings of familiarity regarding Strieber's experiences," Craft reports, a finding which prompted him to wonder if "we are in the midst of an epidemic of alien abduction." And yet, as Craft also conceded, it might simply be that Strieber's subject matter and alien descriptions are "a powerful, archetypal theme buried deep in our minds."

Weighing the Evidence

While sometimes acknowledging potential pitfalls in the use of hypnotic regression, Harvard's Dr. John Mack and fellow hypnotic abduction researchers countered that not only do 'real' abductees possess an emotional charge, but many carry observable physical symptoms of abuse by their UFO captors. Bruises, cuts, abrasions, indentations in the skin and other physical scars have been alleged to be widely documented in the wake of abductions.

Either alien abductions are physical phenomena occurring as reported, and represent "the most important event on our planet since the beginnings of sentient life," as Budd Hopkins shapes his argument, or the human capacity for delusion and mass hysteria has created a "pervasive, world-wide form of fantasy." To demonstrate his belief in UFO abductions as physical events, Hopkins makes four interrelated observations. Physical marks and scars of two highly specific patterns frequently are found on the bodies of abductees in the aftermath of their experience. Many abductees awaken afterwards to find their feet dirty, or sandy or muddy, with leaves, grass, or other unexplained debris in their beds and bedrooms. Dozens of instances have been claimed where abductees were discovered to be missing and friends and relatives searched unsuccessfully for them until they were released by their alien captors.

Two basic, closely related systems of symbols and patterns are often recollected by abductees as having been seen in connection with UFOs and their occupants. Hopkins refuses to publicly divulge these two systems to protect a means for him to test the validity of new cases. But he has shown examples of the two systems to a few trusted colleagues and claims they were "astounded" at this evidence which "undeniably places corroborating abductee testimony beyond the realm of chance."

A fifth category of alleged evidence involves implants the aliens sometimes reportedly insert into the nasal cavities or under the skin of abductees, a practice similar to human wildlife biologists who abduct animals and plant tracking devices on them before their release back into the wild. Once removed from the human body many of these tiny implants supposedly disappear, dissolve, or turn to powder. Those which survived long enough for clinical examination turned out to possess a wide variety of shapes and chemical compositions.

A metallic object removed from the big toe of a female abductee measured one-half by one-half centimeter, in a greyish triangular shape, and had been magnetized. A male abductee had an implant removed which was under the skin of his left leg for 34 years—it appeared to be a shard of glass containing high levels of calcium, phosphorous and sulfur. Abductee Betty Dagenais willed that the implant she believed was in one of her ears be removed on her death. In 1989 she died and the object was taken out, but an electromicroscopic analysis of it did not occur until 1995. The one millimeter-in-diameter object was found to be primarily composed of aluminum, titanium, and silicon. Questioned about what a device consisting of these elements might be intended for, an electronics specialist reportedly replied: "it could be used as a transmitter or receiver."

Implant researcher Dr. Roger Leir helped to surgically remove objects from the bodies of six self-described abductees. Two of these objects were studied by the National Institute for Discovery Science in Nevada, which found both to have iron or iron-alloy cores similar to meteorite-type materials. The Institute is an unconventional science re-search organization funded by Robert Bigelow, usually described in media reports as a millionaire Las Vegas real estate magnate whose Bigelow Foundation supports studies on UFOs, alien abductions, parapsychology, and related subjects.

Can marks and scars, even foreign objects found on the bodies of abductees be linked to stigmata-the spontaneous appearance of wounds approximating those on the body of a crucified Jesus Christ-which has been a periodic symptom of fervent Christian belief for two thousand years? It was long thought that Jesus was crucified with nails driven through the palms of his hands, and devout believers who experienced stigmata in turn bled from the palms of their hands. Only within the 20th century did archeologists discover that Roman crucifixion nails were driven through the wrists, and not the palms, because palms would have been unable to support body weight. That finding made clear the power of strong belief, of mind over matter, of the physical body's subservience to wish fulfillment.

Stigmata can be a by-product of any powerful belief system which carries an emotive force. If a UFO abductee is deeply and emotionally convinced of having been subjected to invasive medical procedures, manifesting physical symptoms to approxi-mate that treatment could simply be the human mind's way of reinforcing the need to believe. Yet based on what little we know about the nature and workings of stigmata, it would be too much of a stretch to say this phenomenon accounts for all body marks and scars found on abductees. Most reported stigmata markings eventually fade away, whereas scars which abductees say were inflicted by aliens apparently last a lifetime.

Skeptics demand harder, more persuasive evidence than scars and "implants" whose composition seems entirely terrestrial in origin, and within the capabilities of current human technology. They ask why abductees have failed to secret back mementos from inside the alien crafts, to which believers respond that maybe some of them have. One possible piece of evidence has withstood both the test of time and prolonged scrutiny to remain a minor mystery in UFO circles.

Betty Hill came back from her alleged abduction in 1961 retaining a memory of the aliens having shown her a three-dimensional map resembling a hologram on which 15 various sized dots representing stars, including our own sun, were portrayed and the prominent ones linked with a series of lines. Two years after her abduction she underwent hypnotic regression, enabling her to draw the star map. She remembered that the aliens had described the lines as "trade routes" and "places visited occasionally."

An amateur astronomer, Marjorie Fish, decided to investigate whether the Hill map corresponded to any known groupings of stars. Fish worked off and on for five years poring over star maps and constructing three-dimensional models of nearby star clusters by dangling beads on threads. Using data from the 1969 edition of the Catalog of Nearby Stars—information on the latest astronomical findings which was unavailable when Hill did her drawing—Fish found an almost perfect alignment between one of her models and the Hill map. An article summarizing her findings in the December 1974 issue of *Astronomy* magazine marveled that the pattern in our southern sky discovered by Fish bore an "uncanny resemblance" to the Hill map, and coincidentally or not the stars identified were all solar type bodies similar to our own sun, thus enhancing the prospect they harbor planets conducive to life. (*Astronomy's* editors would later reveal how this article "sparked more interest among our readers than any other single article in *Astronomy's* history.")

Based on the Fish interpretation, Betty Hill's aliens came from the Zeta 1 and Zeta 2 Reticuli star system 220 trillion miles away, which Astronomy calls "prime candidates for the search for life beyond Earth." These stars are older but otherwise almost identical to our sun. They are barely visible to the unaided human eye and remain invisible at all times to anyone living north of Mexico City's latitude.

In the aftermath of the *Astronomy* article UFO skeptics dissected the Fish interpretation from every conceivable angle. No other UFO encounter on record had produced a map or any other comparable evidence making it "very provocative," as astronomer Carl Sagan conceded. Sagan nonetheless sought to debunk the map by contending it was a pattern correlation arising inevitably by chance once Fish set out to find such a resemblance among billions of stars. Other skeptics came up with several additional star patterns that could fit the Hill map, while still others called into question Betty Hill's ability to recall details accurately from a map two years after she claimed to have observed it.

Aliens in the Mirror

Could the entire alien abduction phenomenon really be human interaction with a higher state of our own consciousness, not extraterrestrial in nature at all, but simply an evolutionary breakthrough for our species at the level of a collective Supermind? After writing a series of books on alien abduction, beginning with *Communion*, and experiencing his own contact with 'aliens' for a decade, Whitley Strieber feels "it's impossible for me to conceive the experience has something to do with aliens who have arrived here from another planet. It doesn't seem to me that it's an alien-human kind of contact. It seems to be some kind of life-changing experience that apparently involves a level of consciousness that at times has an animation and physical reality that we didn't even know existed."

Over a hundred thousand people sent letters to Strieber describing their own experiences after having read his books, and the overall impression he got from them elevated the phenomenon into a realm of strangeness far beyond mere abductions involving medical exams aboard flying saucers. "The letters I got portrayed this as essentially a vast, immensely subtle and complicated theatrics of hyperconsciousness trying to penetrate to our level of reality." When these penetrations occur, the human mind, in its reflexive need to explain and understand, reaches deep into the psyche for an inner reference, and up surge the most convenient cultural myths. In this sense the UFO phenomenon is a potent modem folklore impacting our historical epoch just as the old gods of ancient history influenced the collective imagination.

Budd Hopkins, David Jacobs, and Dr. John Mack argue in their respective books on abduction that the consistency of witness reports describing the alien abductors is a proof of the phenomenon's reality. Yet few of the people who wrote to Strieber provided descriptions that conformed to the Hopkins/Jacobs/Mack alien template: beings less than four feet tall, grayish skin, large hairless heads, big reptilian eyes, earless, with slits for mouths. Nor do most reports of alien beings originating outside the United States closely conform to what Hopkins/Jacobs/Mack have excavated from witnesses during their hypnotic regressions. (Of course, some would argue these varying descriptions simply indicate how a broad range of entities are engaged in abductions).

Consider what reportedly happened to Kelly Cahill, a 25-year-old Australian, in August 1993. As she and husband Andrew, 31-years-old, drove home about midnight along an unlit road at a point about thirty miles outside Melbourne, they saw an unusual orange light above the treetops directly in front of them. They pulled the car over and stopped along the roadside, as did two other cars following behind them. Before the light shot up and away, Kelly thought she saw the silhouettes of several beings inside it. When they finally got home the Cahills discovered their trip had taken an hour longer than it should have. Over the next month, Kelly and Andrew began having flashbacks about the sightings. They remembered being abducted by a group of seven or eight identical beings, all dark, gangly, and at least 7 feet tall! Three other persons came forward publicly to declare they were occupants of the other two vehicles, and had seen the UFOs, the 7-foot-tall entities, and could not account for almost two hours of time that night.

Psychologists skeptical of the alien abduction theory use this kind of story as evidence of Hopkins/Jacobs/Mack engaging in a pattern of inadvertent cueing to obtain from hypnotic subjects a desired consistent description of the abductors. "If the hypnotist is a believer in UFO abductions the odds are heavily in favor of him eliciting UFO/abductee stories from his volunteers," contends Robert A. Baker. On the other hand, a case like the Cahills clearly undermines the theory of hypnogogic/hypnopompic sleep disorders accounting for all reports of alien abductions. While research does indicate that many hypnotic subjects, particularly the fantasy prone, can be led through hypnosis to create and rabidly believe in pseudo-memories—a process known as confabulation—does it automatically follow that the instigating experience itself is always a delusion? Perhaps not.

Survey research by psychologist Kenneth Ring suggests that certain people who had stressful childhoods grow up to possess "encounter-prone" personalities marked by a higher than normal brain sensitivity to electromagnetic fields. These shifting fields, which he speculates might be produced by our collective Supermind as an agent of evolutionary change, can be perceived by the encounter-prone and that stimulates in them dramatic imagery which they interpret as alien abductors, angels, demons, fairies, or whatever else their cultural conditioning dictates.

That conditioning extends to the theme and content of messages imparted to channelers, contactees, and abductees. Mrs. Swan and others "contacted" in the 1950s were the vanguard of expressions of our collective apprehensions about nuclear power. This was the consistent message issuing forth up through the 1980s-that aliens were here to help stop the nuclear arms race before humans destroyed the planet. Once the Cold War ended and the nuclear arms race was momentarily defused, the mission of alien visitors underwent an alteration. Now, according to channelers, contactees, and abductees, space visitors are here to help us avoid global environmental catastrophe caused by own reckless polluting practices.

251

Dr. John Mack's UFO abduction research has been funded by the Center for Psychology and Social Change, which he created in 1983 to study the nuclear arms race. As concerns about nuclear war eased, Dr. Mack and his foundation switched their agenda to the study of environmental pollution issues. Could it be more than coincidence that most of the abductees he has interviewed under hypnotic regression report that aliens are here to help us take better care of our planetary environment? Or is it, so Dr. Mack might maintain, simply that UFO visitors are sensitive to political changes in the focus of what humanity happens to need for its survival?

If the UFO epidemic happens to be a warning that something is seriously wrong with us, as Carl Jung first suggested in 1959, then we must view the channelers, contactees, and abductees as bearers of the message. They are a multiplying and tangible sort of evidence, maybe even the genesis of a social movement, alerting us to a broader unfolding mystery. For even if space visitors were a product of the contactee/abductee imagination—shadows projected from the collective unconscious—the sheer impact of their numbers and the fact most sincerely believe in the reality of what they have experienced represents a psychological condition which any healthy society ignores at its own peril.

Should the abductee image of aliens spring entirely from the collective unconscious of humanity, acting as a window into our unbounded evolutionary potential, tantalizing questions still remain. What mechanism, be it physical or psychological, or both, stimulates the contactee/abductee experience? Is it an arbitrary natural phenomenon, perhaps connected to human electrical sensitivity and geomagnetic forces? Or is it a conscious conditioning process following a script devised by a higher intelligence? Perhaps only by consulting the mirror of our evolutionary destiny will our species ever glimpse the full dimension of what this phenomenon is intended to teach.

The Evolution of Contactee & Abduction Theories
and Evidence, 1953 Onward. . .

Flying Saucers Have Landed
DESMOND LESLIE & GEORGE ADAMSKI
(1953, Neville Spearman)

On the afternoon of November 20, 1952, George Adamski claims he established personal contact with a being from another world. Accompanied by six other persons, among them George Hunt Williamson, who would later record in a series of books his own contactee experiences, Adamski drove out into the California desert near Parker, Arizona, in search of flying saucers. He admits to having "many times" entertained dreams of meeting extraterrestrials and spending considerable hours searching for them through telescopes. He was not only willing but "decidedly anxious" to take a trip in a saucer.

While picnicking in the desert, Adamski and his six companions saw "a gigantic, cigar-shaped silvery ship" drifting soundlessly in their direction, until it hovered overhead. Through binoculars they saw that it had no wings. "That ship has come looking for me and I don't want to keep them waiting!" Adamski shouted, jumping into a car driven by Lucy, his secretary. She drove him a half-mile toward the object near a mountain ridge. He was still in view of the others, who watched through binoculars as Adamski walked several hundred yards taking photographs with his Brownie camera. A man suddenly appeared about a quarter of a mile away, at the entrance of a ravine, and motioned for Adamski to come nearer. At first, both Adamski and his companions, still observing him through binoculars, thought the man was a prospector. But as Adamski approached he saw immediately this was no ordinary human being. His sandy hair hung "in beautiful waves" to his shoulders. "The beauty of his form surpassed anything that I had ever seen."

They communicated with each other using telepathy. Adamski asked if he came from Venus; the man nodded his suntanned head. Adamski asked if the Venusians were concerned that Earth's nuclear radiations threatened outer space; the man nodded affirmatively. They exchanged thoughts for several more minutes, then the Venusian walked to a dome-shaped craft nearby and disappeared inside. As it ascended, Adamski motioned for his companions. When they arrived, he pointed triumphantly at footprints, Venusian footprints, left in the loose desert soil. George Hunt Williamson, being an anthropologist and just happening to have with him packages of plaster of Paris, made a dozen casts of the imprints. On the bottom of each shoe print they found strange indecipherable symbols.

Subsequently, over the next five years, Adamski claimed other encounters with this Venusian, whose skin resembled that of a golden-skinned baby. He produced photographs allegedly depicting the scout ships that transported this Venusian. But these appeared to be only facsimiles of a chicken brooder plugged in from underneath with three lightbulbs. Few people outside the UFO cult groups took Adamski seriously. Yet six persons signed sworn statements that on November 20, they watched through binoculars as Adamski conversed with a long haired man in a one-piece brown uniform who left as he apparently came, in a cigar-shaped spacecraft.

Desmond Leslie, the Irish journalist who wrote this book based on Adamski's account, speculates that the impact of this initial encounter "might conceivably have caused a temporary mental imbalance, producing later hallucinations..." Adamski's account of having been inside the Venusian craft "has all the marks of a spiritual, out of the body experience."

We Met the Space People
HELEN & BETTY MITCHELL
(1959, Saucerian Books)

Helen and Betty Mitchell had been shopping one afternoon in May of 1957, when they entered a downtown St. Louis coffee shop for a soft drink. As they sat talking two men in grey suits interrupted their private conversation "in a very mannerly way." They introduced themselves as Elen and Zelas, Space Brothers from a "huge mother-craft orbiting the planet Earth." Betty and Helen laughed at this silly joke, until the men recited childhood incidents no one outside of the Mitchell family could have known. The men explained how the sisters had been watched closely for eight years by the Space People, who selected them as contacts through whom certain information would be conveyed to Earthlings. After two hours the men left Betty and Helen convinced and elated.

One week later, the sisters were impelled to return to the coffee shop. There sat a Space Brother, apparently indistinguishable from the normal male human. This fellow gave the sisters instructions on building a device for tuning in to the mother craft. For the next six months they spoke many times through this device with the Space People and their commander, known as Alna.

In November, Helen met one of the Space People in St. Louis and he drove her by automobile into an Illinois forest where a flying saucer was hidden. It took about fifteen minutes in flight for this saucer to reach the mother craft. There she saw Alna, who spoke with a heavy accent and whose skin had a darker bronze tint than the others. Helen placed a call to Betty directly through their home telephone, watching on a scope as Betty answered.

The Martian Council requested that Helen and Betty speak out against the development of atomic and hydrogen bombs. Radioactivity has already contaminated every living organism on the planet; any further explosions might result in self-destruction, or mutations. Not all Space People are benevolent, they counseled. Those with negative qualities, usually short in stature, "are coming from farther space systems," intending to indoctrinate humans with ideas to "cause confusion and disturbances upon the planet." A Venusian named Tregon, also in contact with the sisters, added his warning that Earthlings, like their ancestors the Atlanteans, are encouraging cataclysms by testing radioactive bombs.

Flying Saucers and the Three Men
ALBERT K. BENDER
(1962, Saucerian Books)

What makes this author and his book 'special' is that six decades after publication, an idea he pioneered and describes in this book is still practiced by UFO contactees during seminar and weekend conference events. Albert K. Bender worked as a company supervisor in Connecticut and formed one of the earliest civilian UFO research organizations, the International Flying Saucer Bureau. He shut down that group in late 1953, after allegedly being visited by three men in black clothing who warned him to discontinue his UFO investigations because he had stumbled across a secret of the UFO mystery. (This became one of the first recorded instances of the Men In Black phenomenon, popularized decades later in a series of movies.)

What apparently provoked this threat from the men in black was a March 1953 event that Bender and his saucer group held, called 'World Contact Day', in which all group members worldwide attempted to send out telepathic messages to visitors from space. On March 15, at 6 pm Eastern U.S. time, group members 'cleared their minds' and closed their eyes in a quiet secluded spot, and focused on mentally repeating a memorized message to the flying saucer occupants.

The memorized message began with: "Calling occupants of interplanetary craft! We of IFSB wish to make contact with you. We are your friends and would like you to make an appearance here on EARTH…"

Bender claims his own telepathic message resulted in contact while he lay on his bed. A cold chill came over him, his head ached, an odor of burning sulphur filled his bedroom, and he began to lose consciousness as small blue lights inside his head "seemed to blin like the flashing light of an ambulance." When he opened his eyes, he seemed to be floating above his bed in the semi-darkness.

A disembodied voice then commanded him: "We have been watching you and your activities. Please be advised to discontinue delving into the mysteries of the universe. We will make an appearance if you disobey."

Bender confided what happened to two officers of his saucer group, but their reaction was unexpected and disturbing. "They were of the opinion that I had invented the story in order to gain more publicity for IFSB, and insisted they didn't want their names dragged into it." As a result of their reactions, Bender decided to keep what happened to him a secret for the time being, until he could eventually write a book about it.

Over the following months Bender said he had other encounters at night with the space visitors. The most unnerving encounter was a nocturnal visit by the three men in black who wore Homburg style hats and materialized in his bedroom. They warned him about the dangers he faced from his UFO investigation fixation, but assured him that even though they periodically "found it necessary to carry off Earth people to use their bodies to disguise our own," they would keep in touch with Bender and "tell you many things, because one day you will write about this, and we are certain that nobody will believe you."

(In the 1990's, North Carolina emergency room physician Dr. Steven Green created a CE5 protocol, as he called it, to use group meditation in seminars in attempts to telepathically contact extraterrestrial visitors at night in isolated rural locations, often in the southern California desert. Greer had been trained in transcendental meditation.)

My Contact with the Space People
REINHOLD SCHMIDT
(1963. Reinhold Schmidt, self-published)

By average standards his life seemed normal enough, says Reinhold Schmidt, a sixty-year-old grain-buyer. One misty afternoon, November 5, 1957, a few miles from Kearney, Nebraska, Schmidt passed an abandoned farmhouse near a sand bed on the Platte River. He saw a brilliant flash of light ahead. His car engine suddenly died. As he got out, he noticed what appeared to be a half-inflated balloon. On walking closer. he saw that it was some sort of silvery craft. A pencil-thin stream of light shot from it and struck Schmidt in the chest, paralyzing him. Two men emerged from the craft. One spoke English with a German accent. They invited Schmidt aboard their spaceship.

These men were of average height, as were the women on board. "Any one of them could have walked unnoticed among our people." When they spoke telepathically among themselves. they used "high German," which Schmidt, being the son of German immigrants, could understand. After less than an hour, they asked Schmidt to leave.

Later, when the "significance of my experience hit me full force, I shook so violently I had to stop the car...." He reported the encounter to local law enforcement authorities in Kearney. They put him in jail. Two Air Force officers arrived from Colorado to interrogate him. A day later, local officials convened a mental-hearing board. They assumed, after asking him only three questions, that Schmidt must be mentally ill.

Within the hour he was driven to Hastings, Nebraska, admitted to a mental hospital, subjected to brain wave and other tests-"If you weren't a human being, what would you rather be?" one of the psychiatrists asked Schmidt, who replied: "I'd rather be a psychiatrist!" He was released after two weeks.

Schmidt reestablished contact with his friends, visitors from Saturn. They always landed their craft on accretion land (not privately owned) so "they would not be trespassing on private property." Schmidt noticed they drank MJB brand coffee and carried in their craft an MG sports car, which they periodically used for sightseeing. They flew him in their spacecraft over the Arctic, and to Egypt, where they visited beneath the Pyramid of Cheops a secret chamber containing the huge wooden Cross on which Jesus Christ died. Jesus had been transported by these space people back to Venus, his original home, his kingdom of Heaven.

While flying over Southern California on one of these outings with his Saturnian friends, they pointed out for Schmidt the existence of a quartz mine that cured cancer. Schmidt began selling stock in the mine, which he did not own, by telling elderly and wealthy widows that the quartz had healing power. Schmidt subsequently was indicted, convicted, and sentenced to prison on charges of fraud.

Coral Lorenzen, in her essay for the book *The Humanoids*, describes an unsettling coincidence connected with Schmidt's initial contact with the alleged space people. "It is generally felt that he later embroidered his original story and that tended to discredit him," she wrote. Except for a peculiar related incident, he might easily be dismissed. About 6:30 a.m. on the morning after Schmidt's experience of November 5, twelve-year-old Everett Clark of Dante, Tennessee saw an object in a field near his home, with two men and two women walking around it. One of the men grabbed for Everett's dog, which growled and backed away. The four persons talked "like German soldiers," Everett later told police. When the occupants reentered the balloon-like object, they seemed to walk right through the side "as if it were glass." Everett probably could not have known about Schmidt's claim of having met German-speaking occupants of a balloon-like craft, two states away and just hours earlier.

<hr/>

UFO Warning
JOHN STUART
(1963, Saucerian Books)

For nearly a year, until December 1954, John Stuart and his slim, innocent co-worker, Barbara Turner, the only members of Flying Saucer Investigators of New Zealand, pursued evidence to support their theory that UFOs came from Antarctica. They apparently stumbled upon something of import, for Stuart and his assistant claim they were frightened into dissolving their relationship and abandoning the UFO field.

Stuart's first unnerving experience occurred in 1952, as he stood in the hallway of his home smoking a cigarette. He heard footsteps on the sidewalk. The doorbell rang. He opened the door, but nobody was there. One night many weeks later, at about 11:30 p.m., his telephone rang. An expressionless, machinelike voice wanted him to cease his interest "in what earth men call flying saucers." Stuart told the man to go to hell. "Beware, Earthman!" the caller warned.

Was it too fantastic to believe that Satan was behind the disks? Stuart began to wonder. He met nightly with Barbara, an arrangement his wife seemed tolerant of, to discuss the latest UFO sightings and theories. Barbara rarely asserted her views in these sessions, but one night, "almost as if someone other than Barbara were talking," she speculated that perhaps the UFO occupants were once Earth dwellers, maybe the Aztecs, who "were a race of very clever people." Stuart says at that moment he "first noticed some change taking place in Barbara."

The next evening, as "sweet, kind and innocent" Barbara sat relaxed in a chair, Stuart momentarily forgot about UFOs and "allowed my thoughts to dwell on this attractive young woman," whose lips "were slightly parted in a sort of eagerness." As far as he knew, she had no boyfriends. He just assumed that since she spent "almost every evening" at his home, she had no interest in boys, only UFOs. Suddenly, Barbara said: "Gee, I'm glad I'm a girl...I like to be kissed." According to Stuart, her smile then "turned more sensual." He laughed nervously. Then she said something that made Stuart think an entity had "taken over" Barbara. She whispered suggestively: "I'd like to sit here naked. Like me to?" Stuart, startled and embarrassed, declined.

The next evening, after Stuart had spent a sleepless night thinking about her strange behavior, Barbara seemed the same innocent girl. In discussing UFO occupants at one point, she expressed the fear that "one of those blokes might rape me too!" Stuart calmed her. But later, when Satan's name came up, he saw "her innocent face" quickly "steel into a cold, sensuous thing." She asked again if he wanted to see her naked. Stuart panicked, changing the subject, detecting in her an evil possession. But that was only the sordid beginning.

One warm evening, as Stuart and Barbara talked of Mars, a tall stranger with an effeminate face and tan skin "any girl would have been envious of" suddenly materialized in the house. He told them to stop pursuing UFOs, then vanished. A few nights later, Stuart saw a bell-shaped object descend above his home. Still, he and Barbara persisted in their research, even though "we know more than is safe for us."

He told Barbara to get out of the UFO business before it was too late. "It's you they'll hurt. You're a girl!" But she refused to give up. Even as she said those words, "her slim body stiffened." They could hear breathing, as if someone "had a serious case of asthma." A terrible stench, like sulphur, overcame them. About 27 feet away, across the lawn, an 8- foot-tall, hideous creature stood, webbed feet supporting a furry ungainly body, lime green in color, arms thin like stalks of bamboo. It was definitely male. "Its filthy eyes fixed on Barbara's slim body." Stuart couldn't move, nor could Barbara. She "seemed to be waiting for the filthy hands to touch her!" At the critical moment it withdrew and disappeared. Stuart walked her home, but the terror was not over for her.

She had undressed alone when an invisible attacker pounced. For nearly three hours three of these entities ravished her as ten others watched. They covered her body with fine scratches, even on her palms, and left on her ribs two brown marks the size of a dime. They seemed clinically interested in her. The experience convinced her that UFO investigating was too dangerous. She told Stuart to press ahead without her. But now he no longer remained immune.

About 1:30 one morning fear gripped his spine. Five feet away something faced him "in all its vile, base hideousness." Its greyish, stinkingly putrid flesh from the waist up was a man, from the waist down a naked woman. It used telepathy to converse. It obscenely described what Barbara had undergone, promising such a fate for all others attempting to "solve the enigma." It wavered, growing less distinct, then materialized again, and Stuart drew back in horror and revulsion, for the "male and female areas of its body had suddenly changed places." It again threatened him with suffering if he didn't end his research, then it dissolved.

John Stuart packed and left, spending the next two years in Auckland "with my old mother, resting my nerves." Since good health meant more to him than solving the UFO enigma, Stuart wrote on all his research notebooks, "Case closed."

The Interrupted Journey
JOHN G. FULLER
(1966, The Dial Press)

On a bright, cloudless night, September 19, 1961, after 10:30 p.m., Betty and Barney Hill turned their Chevrolet off Route 3 onto a picnic overlook beneath Cannon Mountain, a national forest area south of Lancaster, New Hampshire. Betty had been watching a curious light, resembling a star, that grew bigger and brighter. Through binoculars she and Barney could discern an object, like the fuselage of a plane, but without wings. Lights flashed along the rim-red, amber, green, and blue. The object came closer, seeming to circle them.

They drove on slowly toward Cannon Mountain, catching glimpses of the object through the windshield. It began to glow a steady white, descending to within a few hundred feet of their car. It was huge. Betty could see a double row of windows. Barney stopped the car in the middle of the highway, got out, and trained his binoculars on the still descending object. He could see movement at the windows, faces staring down at him. In a panic he jumped back into the car and sped down the road. Suddenly, they heard an odd electronic beeping sound. The car seemed to vibrate. The sound came from behind, near the trunk. A drowsiness came over them; everything became hazy.

Later, how much later they could not be sure, they remember hearing two sets of beeping sounds again. They found themselves driving alone, passing a road sign that read CONCORD-17 MILES. They had traveled 35 miles since the first series of beeps. They looked at their watches, but both had stopped running.

About dawn they arrived home in Portsmouth. The trip had taken them two hours longer than usual. Later that day on the trunk of their car they discovered a dozen or so shiny circles, each brightly polished and about the size of a silver dollar. A compass swung wildly when placed near the circles. For many nights afterward, Betty had nightmares. Barney refused to even discuss their experience.

Barney was a member of the State Advisory Board of the United States Civil Rights Commission; Betty worked as a social worker for the state of New Hampshire. Neither had anything to gain, but much to lose, by publicizing their UFO sighting. They initially discussed the subject only with close friends and relatives. Yet they could not reconcile having experienced a period of simultaneous amnesia, somehow forgetting two hours of their conscious lives. Betty's nightmares continued, and Barney was afflicted with anxiety and nervous tension. They decided to see a psychiatrist.

On February 22, 1962, they paid the first of a series of visits to Dr. Benjamin Simon, a Boston psychiatrist and neurologist. Dr. Simon prescribed hypnotic treatments, beginning with Barney. Regressing each separately to the point when they first heard the beeping sounds, a fascinating abduction tale emerged, each version corroborating in detail the other.

They remembered making a left turn onto a side road and being stopped by six men in dark jackets standing in the highway who spoke by telepathy, telling the Hills, "Don't be afraid." The Hills felt weak, half asleep. Opening their eyes periodically, they found themselves being carried through the forest and into the vehicle they had seen in the sky. It was lit with a bluish fluorescent kind of light. Their short-statured abductors had large, hairless grey craniums, almost metallic skin, and two slits for nostrils. They emitted a low, humming sound. Betty and Barney were separated, placed on examining tables in adjoining compartments. The beings probed Barney's spine and mouth, placing a device on his groin, where later he would develop a circular growth of warts. They pulled out a few strands of Betty's hair, probed underneath her fingernails, slicing a part of one nail. They felt her feet and toes, unzipped her dress, and placed on her back a cluster of needles, or what felt like needles to examine her nervous system. They stuck another needle into her navel. Betty communicated telepathically with one of the beings, who asked why Barney's teeth could be removed but hers could not. The beings seemed very excited by this. Betty explained that Barney wore false teeth. She had to describe false teeth as something human beings use in old age, when their bodies degenerate. The abductors did not understand old age. She tried to explain the relationship of age to time, but they had no conception of time. She asked where they came from. The leader showed her a map which she could not understand. Betty and Barney were returned to their car; a second series of beeping sounds signaled the end of their ordeal.

After several months of these hypnotic sessions, without either Betty or Barney being told what they had related on tape while in a trance, Dr. Simon reached several conclusions. Since in hypnosis what the subject believes emerges as truth, it seemed unlikely the Hills were lying. They absolutely believed in the reality of what they had experienced. Simon ruled out any joint fabrication in their story. Only two possibilities remained: Either they had witnessed a UFO, and been so emotionally disoriented by the encounter that an illusion or fantasy was imprinted, and later embellished and reexperienced as dreams; or the abduction was "a totally real and true experience."

———

The Stranger at the Pentagon
FRANKE. STRANGES
(1967, I.E.C., Inc.)

Valiant Thor claimed to be from Venus. He and seventy others from that planet, all wholesome and humanlike in appearance, infiltrated Earth society on a special mission of salvation, hope, and charity; but more specifically to neutralize our stockpile of nuclear weapons, encourage the creation of a one-world government controlled by scientists, and reestablish "God's Kingdom" by leading Earth "creatures" back to their Creator.

Valiant had visited Earth seven times previously, twice during the Stone Age, once in the midst of the American Civil War when a cannon shot disabled the force field on his saucer, and more recently, with a fleet of 100 ships in 1945 and 1948 to investigate Earth's nuclear potential. On a flyover of Kentucky in 1948, three F-51 fighter planes pursued his saucer. Valiant says he realized the oxygen supply of one of the pilots, Thomas Mantell, was low, so he enveloped Mantell's plane with "life light" and beamed him aboard the spacecraft. The Air Force said Mantell died while chasing the planet Venus. Mantell's body was never shown to his widow, so the Air Force claimed, because it had been disfigured. Valiant Thor found this explanation quite humorous. For Mantell had enthusiastically adopted the Venusian way of life, since the atmosphere on Venus is "basically the same as on the Earth."

Descending in a scout ship, Valiant landed in 1957 near the city limits of Alexandria, Virginia. Two state policemen drove him to the Pentagon, where he met the Secretary of Defense. Simultaneously, two other scout ships landed at Edwards Air Force Base in California. Contact with higher Earth authorities had been established.

Without entry papers, a visa, or even a passport, much less fingerprints, Valiant was nevertheless whisked by underground train to the Capitol building, where he met a "worried" President Eisenhower in his office. Secret servicemen had their revolvers drawn. Another gentleman rushed into the room. It was Vice President Nixon, who impressed Valiant as "very sharp, quick-witted, with fixed eyes and an amazing attitude toward speed and proficiency." Valiant concluded that "this young man would be destined to greatness-but in the distant future."

For the next three years, Valiant lived in "a beautifully furnished" apartment at the Pentagon. Heads of state were stalling, unable, or unwilling to meet Valiant's demands. President Eisenhower complained that Valiant's proposals "would upset the economy of the United States."

The Venusians began to understand that it was hopeless to seek cooperation from Earth politicians. They needed a loyal and dedicated following, a silent majority, to work within society on planet Earth for peace and social change.

Valiant learned one day of a serious UFO researcher, Dr. Frank Stranges, then presenting a series of lectures at Washington, D.C. churches. As president of the International Evangelism Crusades Inc., and member of the Mayor's Advisory Council of Los Angeles, Dr. Stranges possessed a reputation that Valiant found of value. He sent a young woman to request Dr. Stranges' presence. Security guards allowed Dr. Stranges into the Pentagon because they thought he wore an identification badge, only they were hallucinating thanks to Valiant's psychic intervention. Dr. Stranges left the meeting with Valiant a changed man, and embarked on an important mission that would attract "organized attempts to both discourage and discredit him."

Instructed to leave Washington no later than March 16, 1960, only three months away, Valiant made a final attempt to persuade the President to undertake the Venusian model for social organization. Debate ensued. Politicians and religious leaders feared losing their control over the people. "These parasites have imbedded themselves in human societies," Valiant told Dr. Stranges, "and will never be exposed except by extraterrestrial intervention."

On March 16, Valiant dematerialized his body to depart this phase of his earthly existence. He reassembled himself outside Alexandria, where his saucer and crew waited. As he cruised toward home, Valiant meditated on Venus, on those "low, heavy, colorful clouds, the even temperature, the perfectly diffused sunlight...the lushness of the rich green grass surrounding our home." But in parting, he warned in a message to inhabitants of this disobedient planet, "Remember, we might be your employer, your minister, your neighbor, or...your mate."

The Humanoids
EDITED by CHARLES BOWEN
(1969, Henry Regnery)

This collection of eleven essays surveys more than 300 reports of landings of UFOs and their alleged occupants. Descriptions of these occupants range from giants over 8 feet tall to dwarfs no larger than a young child. This is characteristic of UFOs; rarely do the details of one report correspond to another. That could be because, as Charles Bowen, editor of Flying Saucer Review magazine, explains: "UFOs and their occupants are in the eyes of the beholder." Accounts of objects seen in flight are less responsive to analysis than landings, says Jacques Vallée, since they are "always open to discussion in terms of natural effects." Landing reports, on the other hand, "represent the UFO mystery in its most crucial form." We are confronted with an unmistakable choice between the reality of alien craft bearing intelligent occupants, and the conclusion that all witnesses reporting such close encounters "are absolute liars of the most extreme psychological type."

After summarizing 200 landing accounts, Vallée found that of 624 witnesses associated with the cases surveyed, only 98 were alone when they experienced the encounter. Most of these evaluated sightings occurred in France during 1954. Witnesses were generally rural, steadily employed persons, almost equally divided among men, women, and children, who observed the phenomenon in their own familiar environment, usually while working or returning to and from their jobs. Of reports giving the estimated diameter of the object and approximate distance from the observer, those who got within 100 meters of what they saw consistently gave similar reports. Of these, witnesses who got extremely close offered a smaller figure for the diameter, whereas those further away gave a higher estimate of size. This is significant, Vallée points out, for if the witnesses were liars or victimized by delusions, this illusion of increasing size at increasing distance would not have appeared frequently in reports so consistent in detail. Based on these accumulated reports, whatever the witnesses observed had a diameter of 5 meters.

Another recurring feature in all reports is the apparent pointless and bizarre nature of the behavior of creatures seen with these vehicles. In 1953, for instance, in central Spain, a young illiterate cowherder, Maximo Hernaiz, while watching his herd early one afternoon, heard a whistling sound and saw a large, grey, balloon-like object land. Three little men with Oriental features emerged. One spoke but the boy couldn't understand him, at which point the little man slapped Maximo hard across the face, turned, and walked away with his companions. They reentered their craft and took off. According to the newspaper *Ofensiva,* published in nearby Cuenca, "many people" observed the object land, then leave.

The first known occupant case, reports Coral Lorenzen, supposedly occurred in Death Valley, California, on August 19, 1949. Two prospectors saw two beings emerge from a landed disk-shaped object. Four years later, two other gold miners near Brush Creek, California, told police that two midget saucer pilots had been visiting the creek near their mining claim.

Charles Bowen wonders whether occupants might not be some form of psychic projection, intended to experiment on humans, or "put on a show," since many witnesses have remarked how the entities were seemingly projected into and out of the UFO. "There are noticeable dreamlike qualities about the incidents described in these cases," writes Bowen, meaning that some unknown intelligence may be "pumping stylized pictures into the minds of humans..."

But Donald Hanlon protests that UFO occupants might be human, perhaps in the employ of extraterrestrials as "Fifth Columnists." He cites a 1966 incident in southern Oklahoma when Eddie Laxson, an instructor at Shepard Air Base, found Highway 70 blocked one morning by a fish-shaped silver object. A man in "GI fatigues" entered the object and it took off. Laxson said he could decipher the letters TL41 on the side of the craft. It resembled no known airplane. Hanlon claims the letters TL are code names used for all experimental vertical takeoff craft in the United States. The trajectory on departing would have taken the craft over a nearby military installation. Laxson himself thinks he stumbled onto a secret government craft that for some unknown reason had been forced to land on the highway during a rarely traveled hour of the morning.

Aime Michel contends that our perceptions of contact with a level of thought that is superhuman will be incomprehensible, appearing to us as absurd. So we should come to expect contradictions and absurdities in any manifestations of a superhuman nature. Michel suggests that contactees be studied from this angle, since the most effective way for extraterrestrials to avoid contact with us, and hamper the UFO investigators, is "to make absurd contacts" that no one can take seriously.

265

Section Three: Contactees and Abductees

Uri
ANDRIJA PUHARICH
(1974, Doubleday/Anchor)

At age three, while playing in a garden, Uri Geller says he saw a large, bowl-shaped light in the sky. From it radiated a human form, a cosmic intelligence. Geller claims the encounter "programmed" him, charging him with psychic powers to accelerate the evolution of humankind and prepare our species for contact with advanced galactic neighbors.

On November 30, 1971, an American physician named Andrija Puharich hypnotized Geller. As Geller recalled his childhood encounter with a dazzling UFO, a voice identifying itself as Uri's "programmer" was heard. This alleged cosmic intelligence issued the first of a series of messages, warning that Egypt was preparing to wage war against Israel.

In this book Puharich chronicles the circumstances surrounding Geller's reception of the messages, speculates on the nature of the intelligence involved, and offers insight into Geller's paranormal abilities, portraying the young Israeli as something more than just a spoon bender and mind reader. Geller may embody, Puharich believes, all the attributes of a prophet "specifically created to serve as an intermediary between a 'divine' intelligence and man."

The disembodied intelligence, calling itself SPECTRA, or Hoova, claims to be a Rhombus 4-D computer, or a group of them, into which the souls, bodies, and minds of intelligent beings have been transferred. These entities have supposedly established contact through automatic writing, Geller's hypnotic trances, and even on blank tapes in noiseless rooms.

The voice behind SPECTRA claimed credit for UFO sightings, having first visited Earth 20,000 years ago and landed at the Oak of Mamre, in what is now Israel. About every 6,000 years this intelligence gives advice to human beings. Israel is a protected country, and the Jews a protected race. Space visitors other than Hoova have come and gone, beings of "different vibrations, different spaces, different velocities."

When Puharich asked this intelligence if it resembled human beings in appearance, the reply was a qualified yes, that they look like "certain exotic types of Japanese," with dark skin, eyes rather far apart, and of short stature. They exist in the future, materializing space probes at will when they want to visit Earth. Their computer, SPECTRA, is many millions of light years from our planet, embarked on a mission of considerable importance.

266

UFO Missionaries Extraordinary
HAYDEN HEWES & BRAD STEIGER
(1976, Pocket Books)

Him and her, otherwise known as Bo and Peep, gained notoriety in 1975 as two Pied Pipers barnstorming the western United States in search of converts to accompany them in ascension to "higher levels," ostensibly aboard a UFO. Hundreds of persons responded, giving up all worldly possessions-homes, bank accounts, loved ones, and "human habits," like drugs and sex-to achieve a state of purity enabling them to communicate with that higher realm. Twenty persons "disappeared" from one public meeting in Waldport, Oregon, generating newspaper headlines accusing The Two, as Bo and Peep were called, of brainwashing their followers, mutilating cattle in mystical rites, and planning human sacrifice.

Herff Applewhite, forty-four-year-old church choir director, and Bonnie Trousdale Nettles, forty-eight-year-old nurse and astrologer, both of Houston, Texas, began their period of "awakening" and the shedding of "humanness" sometime in late 1974 when, as they would later explain to the authors of this book, they realized their "life forms" had come to Earth in a spacecraft the day they were conceived. Only after a thorough involvement with the human world, enabling them to become better teachers, did "members of the next level" expose them to smelling salts, saying, in a metaphorical way, Okay folks, wake up, shake off your humanness, it's time to remember who you really are.

They began thoroughly studying the Bible. They pored over theosophical material, such as the "secret doctrine" of Madame Blavatsky, the nineteenth-century mystic who claimed contact with extraterrestrials. In the *Book of Revelation*s they seized upon a verse which suggested they were the two witnesses who were prophesied to follow in the footsteps of Jesus Christ until their death or assassination, at which time they would be reincarnated.

This synthesis of metaphysics, religion, UFO literature, and parapsychology-combined with their aura of sincerity and zeal apparently enabled The Two to found Human Individual Metamorphosis (HIM) and rapidly mesmerize followers. UFO evangelism had been christened decades earlier, but its message had not been thoroughly cloaked in pop theology or the prevailing pseudo-sciences.

As even those who abandoned the group admitted, Bo and Peep were not ordinary con artists. They seemed capable of transplanting thoughts. Their pasty white skin, hollow-looking eyes, and monotone voices heightened this effect. Their philosophy

267

of salvation by UFOs touched a sensitive human longing, or emotion. How else does one explain why so many people literally erased their former lives, abandoning all personal relationships, marriages that had lasted twenty or more years, to live in poverty? "One who has completely overcome any desire for sex or physical affections," The Two taught, "is far more of a virgin than one who has never had sex but desires it. All must become completely pure of their humanness." This process, they claimed, would result in a fine tuning of "extremely sensitive transmitters and receivers with which we can communicate with members of the kingdom"-those extraterrestrials at higher levels who pilot the UFOs.

To underscore the eerie effectiveness of their message, one of the authors, Hayden Hewes of Oklahoma City, relates how Bo and Beep visited him in July 1974. They talked with Hewes for several hours, explaining their mission on Earth. Before leaving, they gave Hewes a "simple thought-code sequence" to use if he ever needed to get in touch with them. About fifteen months later, when The Two began attracting news media coverage, Hewes decided to use the mental code while "asking for the truth in the name of our Father in Heaven." The following morning, Hewes received a phone call from a follower of The Two, his first contact with either The Two or their followers in fifteen months. The man said he had been directed to contact Hewes. Marvels Hewes: "It is very hard to explain the feeling I experienced when it appeared that, in fact, the code had worked."

(Note to Readers: After Nettles died, Applewhite named his cult group Heaven's Gate, and in 1997, the three dozen members, led by Applewhite, committed mass suicide by poisoning themselves outside San Diego, California, in the belief they would be beamed up into a spaceship if they took their own lives.)

The UFOnauts
HANS HOLZER
(1976, Fawcett)

Ghost hunter and psychic investigator Hans Holzer asserts five "undeniable facts": people more or less like us come here frequently in UFOs; UFOs are not imaginary; they are "tangible machines made of metal"; their occupants come here to take specimens from our world; and these UFOnauts have been in contact with a great many human beings because they are curious about us.

Except for aliens seeming to use telepathy to communicate with humans, nothing about UFOs "has the remotest connection with parapsychology," insists Holzer, clinging to the nuts-and-bolts theory that these machines are always three-dimensional and metallic. There is no doubt in Holzer's mind that some alien beings have "walked among us, unrecognized, or perhaps properly camouflaged " Holzer does make one concession to paraphysical theorists. He considers it conceivable that "individuals who have passed on to the next dimension" might be acting as "practical jokers" by pretending to be extraterrestrials communicating through mediums, and manifesting in other psychic phenomena. In reality, of course, these practical jokers are only the spirits of dead human beings.

Borrowing heavily from other writers and researchers, Holzer chronicles tales of UFO landings, descriptions of UFOnauts, close encounters, a few of which led, in Holzer's opinion, to sexual intercourse between humans and the seductive space visitors. On reexamining "evidence" of contactee George Adamski's ride on UFOs piloted by Venusians, the author concludes: "One cannot be so sure that Mr. Adamski wasn't after all, telling the truth as he saw it." In another instance, Holzer seems to embrace as gospel the 1897 saucer crash in Aurora, Texas, widely known in UFO circles as a hoax. A tiny pilot of a spaceship that supposedly crashed into a windmill was said to be buried in the town cemetery. Holzer says this case has been labeled fraudulent by "people who do their research from remote libraries or in their own heads."

Paranormal abilities, such as those exhibited by contactees, might result from a short circuiting of the nervous system, made possible by head or brain injuries. Ted Owens of Virginia attributes his psychic ability to Space Intelligences, who arranged, in four separate accidents during his early life, alterations in his brain enabling him to communicate with extraterrestrial life. New York psychic Shawn Robbins reported her first flying saucer communication soon after suffering a head injury in a taxicab accident.

On May 2, 1968, a teenager in central New York State, Shane Kurz, awakened after 4:00 a.m. to find herself lying atop her bed, her robe and slippers covered with mud, and muddy footprints leading through the open door into her bedroom. Two reddish, ring-shaped marks were found on either side of her lower abdomen. Several weeks earlier, Shane and her mother had observed a bright, cigar-shaped object maneuvering over their home. There seemed to be a connection. Shane contacted Holzer, who put her into a trance. She recounted being lured outside on May 2 by a voice, like a hum. She was taken aboard a saucer, where a short, hairless man with penetrating eyes, wearing what looked like a motorcycle jacket, undressed her, spread her onto a cold slab, and probed her abdomen with a triangular instrument. He rubbed jelly on her abdomen and chest for stimulation and mounted her. She described his sexual organ as humanlike, but cold and

off-white. She says: "I feel terrible...! am enjoying it ...He is humming. He is like an animal. He moans..." For nearly a year after this experience, Shane never had a period. For
nine months after the rape, she lost weight, remained depressed, and developed psychic
abilities. Holzer's interpretation is that she was selected from among other virgins for
breeding, and ova were taken from her when the leader somehow climaxed the act by
intercourse. The ova were implanted "somewhere far off in space" in an extraterrestrial
woman.

Holzer recounts a similar seduction of a Brazilian named Antonio Villas Boas,
when a woman more beautiful than any he had ever seen rubbed a liquid on his body to
excite him sexually. Her lovemaking style seemed rather peculiar to the Brazilian farmer.
She grunted a lot, like an animal, and never kissed him, except to bite his chin. The hair
in her armpits and pubic area was red. As Antonio left the saucer, she pointed to her belly,
smiled, pointed to him, and then up toward the sky.

Holzer finds these examples of sexual intercourse, or rape, somewhat reassuring.
He says this proves that space visitors are pretty much like us, and do not "consider us
totally unworthy," otherwise they wouldn't breed with humans. "Obviously," writes Holzer, "we on earth have something they find attractive..."

========

Abducted: Confrontations with Beings from Outer Space
CORAL & JIM LORENZEN
(1977, Berkley)

A young Brazilian farmer named Antonio Villas Boas claimed a beautiful extraterrestrial woman seduced him aboard her spacecraft on October 15, 1957. Betty and
Barney Hill of New Hampshire revealed under hypnosis their abduction by a UFO,
whose occupants submitted them to a medical examination, then erased from their minds
all conscious memory of the experience. From 1961, the year of the Hill abduction, until 1973, no kidnappings were reported. On October 11, 1973 two shipyard workers in
Pascagoula, Mississippi, Charles Hickson and Calvin Parker, sat fishing on a pier when
a dirigible-shaped object descended and "floated" them aboard, where they underwent
examination. Five nights later, Mrs. Patty Price in the company of two of her six children, awoke to find in their home alien intruders, who spirited her away to a nearby craft
where they undressed her and "took her thoughts." The authors chronicle in detail the
experiences of Mrs. Price, the shipyard workers, and six other cases that occurred during
a three-year period, 1973-76.

They search for correlations, uncovering in the process "a rather frightening picture of superior races little by little learning everything there is to know about the human race..." These abductions represent "the "logical culmination" of what the Lorenzens describe as a "well-conceived plan." UFO landings of the 1950s followed flyover mapping expeditions in the 1940s. Abductions are simply the next step in an information-gathering process, concentrating now on the physical and psychological make-up of human beings. They seem particularly interested in learning more about human emotions.

October 25, 1974—While hunting elk near the Medicine Bow National Forest in Wyoming, Carl Higdon encountered a chinless man named Ausso, dressed in a black suit, who propelled Higdon in a transparent cubicle to a point in space where he was examined, but declared unsatisfactory. Higdon says he saw five other humans in captivity, a grey-haired man and four teenagers.

August 12, 1975—Sergeant Charles Moody of Holloman Air Force Base in New Mexico was sitting on the front fender of his car in the desert watching a night meteor shower when a metallic, disk shaped object landed 300 feet away. A numbness gripped him and he lost all memory of what happened next. Hypnosis later lifted that mental block, revealing how he had been taken inside the craft and examined.

August 26, 1975—Mrs. Sandra Larson of Fargo, North Dakota, her daughter, and a friend, while driving along Interstate 94 at 4:00 a.m. observed eight to ten orange, round, glowing objects descend 50 yards from their car. They felt themselves frozen in time for only an instant, although later they discovered that an hour had passed by. When later placed under hypnosis, Mrs. Larson remembered being beamed aboard, undressed, and having an x-ray taken through her stomach.

October 27, 1975—David Stephens of Norway, Maine, and his friend Glen, were run off the highway at 3:00 a.m. by a blinding light that resembled a cup sitting upside down in a saucer. They lost consciousness. Hypnosis later determined that Stephens had been taken inside the object, undressed, and relieved of a blood sample.

November 5, 1975—Travis Walton and six others spent the day cutting trees in the Apache-Sitgreaves National Forest in Arizona. At sundown they saw a disk-shaped, amber object in a small clearing. From it a bluish-green ray struck Walton in the head and chest. The others panicked, drove off in a pickup, and left Walton behind. For five days he remained missing. Under hypnosis, Walton remembered being abducted and examined by UFO occupants.

January 6, 1976—Louise Smith, Mona Stafford, and Elaine Thomas of Liberty, Kentucky, were on a country road returning from dinner about midnight when a metallic, glowing dome took control of their car. Each woman felt a burning sensation in her eyes. Somehow, they lost an hour and twenty-five minutes of time. Under hypnotic regression, each of the women told similar stories of how four or five humanoids, 4 feet tall with grey skin, observed and examined them.

From these cases the Lorenzens detect a pattern. Patty Price, the shipyard workers, Higdon, and Mrs. Larson all claimed contact with entities who floated, rather than walked, and possessed claw-like hands or appendages. Moody also reported that his abductors floated along the ground. In each of the seven abduction cases-the exception being Higdon-the beings are described as small in stature, less than 5 feet, with domed heads, large eyes, and hairless bodies. They seemed to communicate by telepathy.

Why were these people chosen? What special qualities did they have? The Lorenzens speculate that each possessed some cultural knowledge of value to their abductors. Moody, for instance, could have provided information on the organizational structure of the Air Force; Higdon, involved in the oil-drilling business, knew about the mechanics of how we obtain our principal source of energy; Patty Price is a former government employee; David Stephens spent four years in the U.S. Navy; Sandra Larson was a country-western singer, cocktail waitress, and real estate agent; the three Kentucky women were all devoutly religious, two had been divorced, the other was a grandmother, each had an interest in art, one was a gospel singer.

"Something or someone is afoot in the land," write the Lorenzens, warning that every human on this planet is a potential kidnap victim. Since officialdom refuses to take UFO abductions seriously, they suggest that persons who experience the trauma of a close encounter refuse to cooperate with government authorities and report instead to the authors and their colleagues.

Cosmic Trigger
ROBERT ANTON WILSON
(1977, And/Or Press)

Robert Anton Wilson began his odyssey in search of Higher Intelligence by indulging in a series of initiation rites, such as co authoring the Illuminatus trilogy, a fictional excursion into the nature of occult conspiracy theories focusing on the Bavarian Illuminati. He sought enlightenment, through drugs and meditation, to dial and tune his own nervous system. What emerged was a self-described "belief system" in which he thought he received telepathic messages from intelligences existing in the Sirius star system, some 8.6 light years away.

Wilson synthesizes and borrows heavily from the theories and research of, among others, Carl Jung, Aleister Crowley, Jacques Vallée, Timothy Leary, John Lilly, and Robert K. G. Temple. He weaves together complex functional models and coincidences, or, in Jungian terminology, synchronicity, to explain his own experiences and provide a plausible, scientific rationale for his thesis: That interstellar telepathic communication between Earth and the Sirius system may have been going on for 6,000 or more years, a cosmic dialogue around which secret societies have arisen and flourished throughout history. UFOs might then be hallucinations shared by telepathy. We may even be in touch with entities that are in reality but manifestations of ourselves, our species, existing in our own future.

These signals from Sirius Wilson thinks he received were first beamed to him on July 23, 1973, following a day of Tantric sex-trance rituals (devised by the English mystic Aleister Crowley) combined with a hypnosis tape recorded by Dr. John Lilly, the pioneer in dolphin research. The message was simple, and direct: "Sirius is very important."

On researching myths and beliefs associated with Sirius, Wilson discovered a truly bizarre collection of coincidences, or synchronicities - July 23, the day of the message, according to Egyptian tradition is when the "occult link" between Earth and Sirius is most powerful, the beginning of the "dog days" (Sirius is the Dog Star) of summer; Aleister Crowley identified the source of his "magical current" as residing in Sirius, or "Sothis," as it is also known in occult lore; and, unbeknownst to Wilson, his friend Dr. Timothy Leary and three others had, in the same month, received nineteen bursts of communications they called the "Starseed Transmission." The messages explained that life on Earth had been seeded, that humans would decipher the genetic code and learn the secret of immortality, that the Japanese are the most advanced race on Earth, and that human destiny is among the stars, "where we, your interstellar parents, await you."

Nearly three years later Wilson read a new book, *The Sirius Mystery*, by Robert K. G. Temple of England, which offered impressive evidence that Earth had been visited about 3500 B.C. by intelligent amphibious beings from the Sirius star system. Information about this visit, Temple contended, had been preserved and passed on through numerous initiatory orders in the ancient Mediterranean and Africa up until the present. Temple's book "staggered" and "discombobulated" Robert Anton Wilson, who began searching ever more doggedly for explanations to resolve Temple's thesis with his own experiences. Two "meta-models" emerged:

(1) As the human species advances toward Higher Intelligence, the nervous system affects the universe, creating images of Beings that are masks of the human self that evolution will one day produce;

(2) As evolution proceeds, and Higher Intelligence in humans develops, we come in contact with "advanced adepts" throughout the universe occupying simultaneously the space-time continuum of past, present, and future.

―――――――――――――

The Scientist: A Novel Autobiography
JOHN C. LILLY
(1978, Lippincott)

One of the more original scientists of our age, John Lilly, the pioneer dolphin researcher who developed the technique of using electrodes to study the human brain, reveals in this autobiography that while under the influence of mind-altering drugs, his body floating in an isolation tank, his mind came into telepathic contact with extraterrestrial beings who are engaged in manipulating reality on Earth to advance human evolution.

Lilly's first message from these beings came on a plane as it neared an approach for landing in Los Angeles. The pilot had announced that the comet Kohoutek could be seen from the plane. As Lilly turned to look, he received this message: "We will now make a demonstration of our power over the solid-state control systems upon the planet Earth. In thirty seconds, we will shut off all electronic equipment in the Los Angeles airport. Your airplane will be unable to land there and will have to be shunted to another airport."

As predicted, the equipment failed. Lilly's plane landed at Burbank; another crashed at Los Angeles. Soon thereafter, Lilly received a new message, or vision. In this one, the fate of humankind was described in frightening detail. A solid-state intelligence, all the components of computers, satellites, and electronic systems, will be gradually relied upon until every problem of human survival is left to the care of these intelligences, giving them the capacity to build and program themselves, to correct their own mistakes, and to operate beyond human control.

"By the twenty-sixth century," Lilly writes, relating his futuristic vision, "the entity was in communication with other solid-state entities within the galaxy."

There are two forms of intelligent life in the universe, according to Lilly's information: the solid-state and the water-based. One constructs the other, until the other eventually transcends its maker. Lilly implies that humans, under subliminal influence from outer space, have embarked upon this course, a trend that dominates life in the universe, a never-ending struggle between organic and electronic life forms.

It is with these "water-based forms similar to those of man and the organisms of

Earth" that Lilly has established contact, learning that both forms of life have developed systems of interstellar communication, a process similar to telepathy, through which they beam messages to other intelligent life. On Earth, Lilly believes these messages are mostly received by whales and dolphins.

These extraterrestrials inhabiting another reality operate what Lilly refers to as the Earth Coincidence Control Office. We are being lavished with their psychic attentions, organic vying with solid-state to influence the evolution of intelligence on our, and many other planets.

Ultimate Encounter
BILL BARRY
(1978, Pocket Books)

Just after 6:00 p.m. on Wednesday, November 5, 1975, in the piney woods of the Sitgreaves National Forest in Arizona, seven woodcutters riding in a truck over a logging road observed a large glowing object hovering about 100 feet away. Silent and motionless, the oval yellow craft, approximately 20 feet in diameter, hung a few yards in the air over a slash pile. It illuminated the forest with a soft, milky light. One of the woodcutters, Travis Walton, bolted from the truck toward the object to stand almost directly underneath. The object began to wobble, emitting a beeping sound, then a low rumble, like a generator throttling to full power. A flash of brilliant bluish-green light shot from it and hit Walton in the head and chest. He stiffened, hurtling backwards through the air.

In a panic the other six woodsmen drove off and left him lying there on the ground. Several miles and many minutes later, when they had calmed themselves, they returned to search for their friend. The UFO was gone. So was Travis Walton. They went for the sheriff; a search party formed. For several days, forty to fifty men scoured the area on foot, on horses, in jeeps and a helicopter. No trace of Walton could be found.

Law enforcement authorities initially suspected foul play. Maybe Walton had been beaten up, maybe murdered, by one or more of his cohorts, who hid or buried his body, then concocted the UFO story as a cover-up. On Monday morning, five days after Walton's disappearance, the six woodcutters, ranging in age from nineteen to twenty-eight, were given a series of polygraph tests. Each man was tested four times. Three of the questions pertained to Walton, whether he was injured or murdered, while the fourth asked if they had actually seen a UFO that Wednesday evening. The Arizona Department of Public Safety polygraph examiner concluded that without question five of the men were telling the truth, while answers provided by the sixth man proved inconclusive.

Abduction cases are relatively common for UFO investigators. But this one possessed several unprecedented elements: no other reported abduction had lasted more than a few hours, nor been observed by independent witnesses. Using an Anis TM Gauss meter, a representative of Ground Saucer Watch claimed to have found high traces of residual magnetism in the area around the woodpile where the UFO was seen hovering. He also discovered fragments of silicone. About midnight later that Monday, Travis Walton called home from a telephone booth. He seemed to be in shock. He had lost 11 pounds. Under hypnosis, he later described how he had regained consciousness aboard the spacecraft, finding himself lying on a table surrounded by three beings, each less than 5 feet tall, with large, domed heads, enormous eyes, and hairless, marsh-mallow skin. He later saw what appeared to be human beings among these aliens, with dirty blond hair and hazel eyes, but they never spoke to him. He remembered waking up on the highway about 10 miles from where he was allegedly abducted, as a round craft that had apparently returned him shot straight up into the sky. This tale accounted for only about two hours of five missing days.

His first polygraph test resulted in the examiner accusing him of deception. Consulting psychiatrists declared that given his emotional stress, and the somewhat leading and assumptive questioning, such a test could at best only be inconclusive. Although Walton passed a second polygraph administered several months later, Dr. Jean Rosenbaum concluded in his psychiatric analysis that the young man was suffering "from a combination of imagination and amnesia" that made him believe he had been abducted. But where had Walton been for five days?

Walton's encounter fit into a pattern of UFO sightings for that region. On November 4, the day before his alleged abduction, a sheriff's deputy in nearby Fennimore took photographs of a large light that swung across the sky. Other witnesses reported a ball of fire over a farm in Patch Grove. Three months before the woodcutter episode, on the night of August 12, some 300 miles away in the New Mexico desert, Sergeant Charles Moody of the U.S. Air Force allegedly confronted a dull metallic object that dropped from the sky near his car. The glowing saucer emitted a high-pitched sound, like a dental drill. A feeling of numbness came over Moody. All he remembered next was the object leaving silently. He had lost consciousness for almost an hour. When his memory returned, he told Jim and Coral Lorenzen of the Aerial Phenomena Research Organization how he had been transported aboard an object where numerous beings about 5 feet tall, with large hairless heads and huge eyes, examined him in a dimly lit room. The Lorenzens learned of Moody's encounter before Walton vanished, and only afterwards, when Walton reappeared, did they reveal to anyone details that would indicate both men apparently underwent remarkably similar experiences.

Messengers of Deception
JACQUES VALLEE
(1979, And/Or Press)

Are the contactees, those who claim to have received messages from extra-terrestrial visitors, being unwittingly manipulated by human programmers? Could the entire UFO phenomenon be a mechanism through which an unknown group of humans is seeking to bring about social change? In a continuation of themes developed in his previous books, Dr. Jacques Vallée has analyzed the social and political implications of growth in the number of UFO cults and contactees and concluded that "subliminal seduction" is a worldwide enterprise and that UFOs are not from outer space.

Vallée traces the extremist political roots of many contactees and UFO groups. Most of them preach philosophies with overtly totalitarian overtones from which three consistent themes usually emerge-universal peace, a single world economy, and the elimination of the money system. One UFO group in California has even organized a political party to put a contactee in the White House, believing that since Earth is the "property of one group of saucers," and America is a "protected" country, such a contactee would be in a position to dictate our planet's priorities. The study Center of Cosmic Fraternity in Italy, for instance, claims that President Jimmy Carter, who once saw a UFO, has already been "programmed" by the experience, making him the messiah of contactees.

Occult groups have historically been used as cover for espionage. Vallée identifies a large number of "former" CIA employees who serve on the boards of the largely respectable and scientific UFO groups, like the National Investigations Committee on Aerial Phenomena and the Center for UFO Studies. He quotes from a CIA memo of the early 1950s which recommended that UFO groups be kept under agency surveillance. While the implications are clearly toward some sort of government involvement, Vallée stops short of identifying these UFO "manipulators." He admits that he does not know who or what they represent.

Vallée began to pursue this conspiracy theory when computers, used to search for patterns in the global distribution of UFO sightings, began portraying the behavior of the phenomenon as if it were a conditioning process, using "absurdity and confusion to achieve its goal while hiding its mechanism." Evidence seemed to mount that the consistent nature of stories contactees were telling was meant as a message; contactees are being used to tell our leaders something. But how and why?

In an experiment at California State University, eight students generally uninformed about UFOs were placed into a trance. They provided "coherent, intriguing UFO abduction narrative," all a product of their imagination and some hypnotic coaxing. The stories they told, even in the details, were surprisingly similar to what alleged abductees and contactees have been describing for the past twenty years. Vallée uses research conducted by the various CIA drug programs to make a case it is not only possible, but highly probable, that many contactees and UFO observers have been exposed to an experience intended to alter their minds. UFOs distorted their reality by projecting images, as on a television screen, designed "to change our belief systems."

Terror is the next stage in this social conditioning process. More than 700 cattle in fifteen western states were mutilated during one eighteen-month period in the 1970s. Always the circumstances bore details too similar for coincidence. The mutilations occurred, and still occur, at night, no tracks are found, no blood or sign of a struggle is evident; organs cut out with "surgical" precision-the eyes, tongue, and genitals-are always connected to reproduction and communication. At first satanic groups were blamed. But no helicopters or other evidence have been found. The phenomenon, Vallée contends, is intended to challenge the law enforcement community. It has. No arrests have been made. The message has been sent.

During the early years of Nazi Germany stories were planted in newspapers alleging that members of the Thule Society, a Nazi occult group, had been mutilated, their sexual organs tampered with or removed. Hundreds of opposition party members were eventually rounded up, accused of the crimes, and executed. Those persons or groups first able to harness for political ends the emotions and confusion surrounding the UFO phenomenon and contact with extraterrestrial life "will be able to exert incredible spiritual blackmail," Vallée warns. Both religion and science are already being undermined by the proliferation of occult groups and contactees; our institutions, all of them, are vulnerable to this spreading belief in the irrational.

The Andreasson Affair
RAYMOND E. FOWLER
(1979, Prentice-Hall)

Just after nightfall the electric lights in Betty Andreasson's house began to flicker before blinking out. Betty, her seven children (aged 3 to 11), and Betty's parents, then observed a pulsating, reddish-orange glow shine through the kitchen window. Betty's father, Waino, looked out into the backyard and, as he would later relate in a signed statement, saw a group of "creatures" resembling "Halloween freaks" jumping around like grasshoppers.

It was January 25, 1967 in South Ashburnham, Mass., and the story of what allegedly happened that night would not be revealed for another eight years, until Betty wrote to the Center for UFO Studies. It assigned Raymond Fowler to investigate once preliminary lie detector tests on several of the witnesses indicated they believed in the truth of their account. In 1977 both Betty and her oldest child Becky, now 22, began undergoing hypnotic regression sessions conducted by Harold Edelstein, director of the New England Institute of Hypnosis.

Becky recalled being in the darkened living room and looking down a hallway toward the kitchen where she saw a dark silhouetted shape bobbing in the glow. Then her memory went blank. It seemed as if everyone in the family but her mother Betty had been paralyzed in place, and made unaware of what was transpiring around them. Becky had only one other memory to emerge in hypnosis-she regained consciousness that night long enough to see her mother conversing with a group of four entities. She described them as resembling clay men, tiny in stature, with hairless pear-shaped heads and big, marble-like eyes. They had just handed her mother what appeared to be a small blue book. The taller of the four entities noticed Becky watching and with a glance he sent her back into unconsciousness.

Betty's hypnotic sessions produced a long, richly detailed story rivaling any work of literary imagination. She remembered the four beings entering her kitchen by passing directly through the door, prompting her to think they must be angels. They had grey skin, large outsized heads, Mongoloid features, scar-like mouths and catlike eyes. They wore dark blue uniforms, and gloves fit over their three-digited hands. The leader, who identified himself as Quazgaa, spoke to her telepathically. She handed him a Bible, and he in turn presented her with a thin little blue book.

"What are you doing here?" Betty asked them.

"We have come to help," Quazgaa replied. "Will you help us?"

Quazgaa explained that Earth is trying to destroy itself and Betty must help prevent that. "We will not harm you," Quazgaa kept repeating. "Would you follow us?"

Betty stood behind Quazgaa and suddenly found herself floating inches above the floor. They floated right through the door and into her backyard where an oval object rested on struts. An opening appeared beneath the craft and Betty swooped up inside, finally floating into a small room with curved walls where she was subjected to some sort of cleansing process inside a brilliant light. She was asked to wear a white garment, and then she was placed on an upraised platform where aliens in shiny white silver clothes began to physically examine her. Long silver needles were stuck up her nose and into her head. An alien touched her forehead and her pain melted away. "They said they were awakening something," Betty explained. Another silver needle was inserted through her navel and an alien observed that she had some parts missing, a comment Betty thought might refer to her having had a hysterectomy.

She felt like a human guinea pig. When the needle was extracted from her nostril there was a tiny ball on the end of it, as if the ball had been removed from her sinus cavity. She continued to hear the alien's voices in her mind as they discussed measuring her for procreation. "I'm very sorry," Quazgaa apologized at one point. "It needed to be done."

After the exam Betty was asked to sit in a strange chair. She felt powerless to resist their polite requests. A transparent veil fell around her, self-sealing tubes were connected to her mouth and nose, and a greyish-colored liquid flowed down and enveloped her. She was then transported into an alien realm. She glided along darkened tunnels and emerged into a red atmosphere, watched strange headless creatures resembling monkeys scamper about, entered another area with a green atmosphere with odd plants and mist-shrouded waters, and glided along a bridge above a complex of structures which looked like pyramids. She beheld a 15-foot tall eagle, a Phoenix, which erupted into a fiery inferno and burned down, its ashes turning into a grey worm. A loud voice thundered: "I have chosen you to show the world!" Betty thought she must be in the presence of her Lord Jesus, maybe even God himself.

Later she was transported back the way she came, out of the craft and into her own kitchen where her family still stood in suspended animation. Before departing Quazgaa locked within her mind certain secrets, formulas for technology that humans could use if they can access spirit. "If man will just study nature itself, he will find many of the answers that he seeks," counseled Quazgaa. But Betty is told she must forget all this knowledge until an appointed time far in the future.

Raymond Fowler speculates from Betty's experience that "the extraterrestrial phenomena may be a combination of advanced technology and theology." Just as a primary motive behind European explorations of the Americas after Columbus was to spread Christianity and convert the natives, "could it be possible that visiting extraterrestrials might in actuality be interstellar missionaries?"

The Tujunga Canyon Contacts
ANN DRUFFEL & D. SCOTI ROGO
(1980, Prentice-Hall)

Near Los Angeles, inside an isolated cabin in Tujunga Canyon, two women, Sara Shaw, 21, and Jan Whitley, 22, lay asleep when a bright bluish light illuminated their bedroom and awakened them. Sara glanced at the clock-it was 2 a.m. All the two remembered next is realizing that the clock had advanced to 4:20 a.m. and neither had a conscious recollection of what transpired in the missing two hours. Frightened and confused, they rushed out of the cabin and as they passed the garage Jan spotted, superimposed against foliage, the vaporous apparition of a human-like figure. It was March 22, 1953, the beginning of a contagion of contacts which would haunt both women, and several of their friends, for decades to come.

Twenty-two years later Sara phoned Ann Druffel, a Los Angeles UFO researcher, wanting advice on how to explore her missing time experience. A Los Angeles Police Department psychologist, Dr. Martin Reiser, hypnotized Sara and regressed her to that night in 1953. She related how eight tall, slender, shadowy beings entered the bedroom directly through the closed door, took control of her and Jan's minds and bodies, and floated them outside to a UFO shaped like the planet Saturn. Inside, both women were undressed and medically examined. The beings seemed fascinated by Sara's scar from having had lung surgery. They communicated with her by telepathy, instructed her to forget the abduction, then floated both women, their knees drawn up in a fetal position, back into their cabin.

Three years after this encounter, Jan and Sara's relationship had ended and Jan was living with a woman named Emily. These two women accompanied by Emily's six-year-old son were on a long drive and had pulled off at a rest stop late at night to sleep. A yellowish-white light flooded the car and a high-pitched whining sound paralyzed both women, as their car began to sway back and forth. Emily felt the presence of a being watching them through the back window.

Under hypnotic regression in 1976, Emily recalled being told by her alien abdúc-tors to forget her encounter with them. Nonetheless, the hypnotist, Dr. William McCall, was able to elicit from her the belief that a group of beings about three feet tall, with large, bald heads, had projected her out of her body and out of the car into a white, bubblelike UFO. In later interviews Emily revealed that she believed these entities had been visiting her at night much of her life, always announcing their presence with a high-pitched whine which made her unable to move or resist them. During a period between her hypnosis sessions, Emily received a frantic phone call from two friends, Lori and Jo, former residents of Tujunga canyon, who apparently had just had their own abduction experience. They described awakening after midnight feeling themselves paralyzed as two entities entered their bedroom accompanied by a loud whining noise, and one entity stood over the bed and asked Lori to "come with him." The entities were described as short, with extremely white complexions and large, round, bald heads.

Lori, age 25, remembered having her first alien encounter as an infant, long before she met Jan or Emily, but the experience she had while with Jo occurred soon after she came into contact with Jan. Under hypnosis Lori recalled her most recent encounter. She described the aliens with the egg-shaped heads as having powerful eyes without lids who spoke to her using telepathy. They levitated her out of bed and, encased in a light emitted by the beings, she was transported directly through her apartment's walls and into a dark, dome-shaped object sitting in an adjacent empty field. She was subjected to a medical exam, and she came away with the impression that these beings were trying to figure out how to combine "what they are and what we are" to create a more powerful being. Jo also explored this experience under hypnosis and her account corroborated many of the details provided by Lori. Jo remembered their bedroom filling with a blue-green light, and she felt herself float out of bed and merge with the light, all the while hearing the sound of a pitched tone. She too, was examined atop a platform inside a domed craft, her body scanned and inspected by several flashing lights.

"We know of no other case in the archives of ufology typified by the odd 'con-tagion' phenomenon that seems to have spread from Sara and Jan to Emily, and then to Lori and Jo," write the authors. They speculate that the UFO entities may be akin to the spiritual beings known as angels and demons, composed of invisible, pure energy not bound to a material existence. Either UFOs are from the "psychic realm," says Druffel, or the presence of UFOs set off psychic manifestations from a parallel universe or an in-tersecting space-time continuum. Why were these particular women chosen for contact? Maybe because all had an interest in metaphysical studies or displayed psychic talents, and all were involved in the lesbian alternative lifestyle, which may have intrigued UFO entities investigating reproduction and evolution of the human race. Scott Rogo proposes a somewhat different theory to explain this abduction contagion. It seems unlikely to him that Lori and Jo were actually physically abducted from their apartment because the UFO would have been seen by neighbors or passersby. He notes that the two women described equivalent abduction experiences, but not a shared experience. He suspects that some kind of phenomenon exists, whatever it is, and it creates UFO dramas by tapping information buried in our cultural consciousness.

"UFO abductions occur when the witness is in a state of psychological need, and when the unconscious mind needs to impart an important message to the conscious mind," concludes Rogo. "Once contacted by a human mind in such a state, the super mind creates an abduction experience for the witness by drawing upon information and preoccupations buried deep within his mind." Sometimes this abduction drama is projected into three-dimensional space, a dream which takes on an objectified reality and can be shared, passed from one person to the next.

Missing Time
BUDD HOPKINS
(1981, Marek Publishers)

Painter and sculptor Budd Hopkin's fascination with the UFO enigma began about 5:30 on a summer afternoon in 1964, as he, his first wife, and an English friend drove along Route 6 in Massachusetts. They spotted a dark, elliptical object about two car-lengths long hovering ahead of their vehicle. A shaft of sunlight momentarily made the object appear a dull aluminum in color. As they watched, it moved against the wind toward the ocean and disappeared into clouds.

Starting in 1976, Hopkins got involved with the investigation of 19 possible UFO abduction cases involving 37 people, including a Wall Street lawyer, a painter, a college instructor, a golf pro, and two registered nurses. Seven of these cases became the basis for this book. Three of these people, all unrelated and born in 1943, were first abducted in the summer of 1950 as seven-year-old children. "It seems to me," Hopkins observes, "as if these quite similar abductions constitute some kind of systematic 'research' program, with the human species as subject."

His initial investigation of a possible abduction concerned George O'Barski, 72, owner of a Manhattan liquor store across the street from Hopkins' art studio. In January

1975 O'Barski was driving home through a park after two a.m. when a brilliantly lit object passed over his car with a humming sound and began to hover a few feet above the park's lawn. About nine or ten entities, each less than four-feet tall, rapidly descended from the object and began to dig, tossing dirt into bags. From 60 feet away O'Barski watched in disbelief as the helmeted or hooded entities finished their task and ascended back into the object, which sped up and away. The next morning, he returned to the site and found 15 holes in the soil each about four inches deep.

Ten months following this encounter O'Barski told Hopkins his story and Hopkins was inspired to investigate. He visited the park and spotted 15 or so bare places, six inches in diameter, where O'Barski had described them, and a park custodian recalled having found the unexplained openings and refilled them earlier in the year. Hopkins interviewed a night doorman from a building adjoining the park who remembered seeing bright lights attached to a dark object hovering over the area during the same time frame as O'Barski had related. Though O'Barski refused to undergo hypnotic regression, he nonetheless felt as though the entities had "told" him something using telepathy that he could no longer grasp or remember.

Numerous of Hopkin's subjects did submit to hypnosis, conducted by Dr. Aphrodite Clamar, and related richly detailed yet similar stories of bright lights followed by alien abductions. Steven Kilburn was in his early twenties and driving late at night in rural Maryland when he saw two whitish lights pass over his car, after which his car was violently jerked off onto the right-hand shoulder of the road. Four or five chalky white beings, below his shoulders in height, with slits for mouths and heads like inverted teardrops, surrounded his car and began digging in dirt alongside the highway. They communicated using telepathy, and escorted Kilburn inside a saucer-shaped craft where they gave him a physical exam, at one point passing a seven-inch long white "wand" over his body.

Corporate lawyer Virginia Horton recalled under hypnosis having been abducted in 1950 just before her seventh birthday, taken from a barn on her grandfather's farm near Lake Superior and left with a bleeding leg where an inch-long piece of her had been sliced away. Another time, as a 16-year-old on a picnic in France, she turned up with unexplained blood on her blouse after being missing for an hour. In the woods she had entered a bright blue column of light. Under hypnosis she described alien beings having inserted a probe in her left nostril and having taken a piece of her as "a combination of a souvenir and a way to know me better." They had asked her permission, which she gave, telling her it was "very important and it won't hurt." One of the beings asked her how long humans and different animals lived, he talked about the importance of biological diversity, and he showed her pictures of star maps, explaining that he came from another galaxy. To Hopkins the Horton case was evidence of a sub-group of UFO abductees in which the aliens suppress all conscious memory traces of a UFO sighting and abduction.

Hopkins began to notice a pattern of persons with an obsessive interest in the subject of UFOs being motivated by a forgotten but real abduction experience. A 37-year-old journalist, given the pseudonym of Philip Osborne by Hopkins, did an article about UFOs in 1978 and Hopkins noticed the man had a "particular edge" to his reportage, seeming to accept much too readily the strangest of UFO case material. Hopkins suggested that Osborne undergo hypnosis. Osborne remembered being seven in 1950 and on a vacation trip through the mountains of Tennessee. He was sucked up inside a bright geodesic dome structure. He glimpsed a metallic hand and a robotlike arm which made an incision into his leg, but otherwise he could not recall any UFO occupants. Osborne had found an answer for the three-inch straight scar on his upper thigh which neither he, nor his parents, had ever been able to explain.

From these and other cases Hopkins wonders whether "the UFO crew members are taking something besides information, or they are leaving something behind with their captives." Perhaps persons who are abducted as children "had tiny monitoring devices installed high in their nasal cavities, much as terrestrial ecologists and zoologists install implants to monitor wildlife." Humans may also possess some kind of natural resource or genetic structure which alien cultures use as raw material. Maybe sperm and ova samples must be taken from a large cross section of humans to conduct some kind of experiment. It is possible memory blocks are placed in the minds of abductees to protect them from the traumas of their experiences.

For Hopkins the conclusion became inescapable that "extraterrestrials have been observing us in our innocence for many years." Yet, despite long-term monitoring and experimenting on human specimens, there is no reason for these alien visitors to communicate directly with earthly authority figures. "In other words, the government might not know anything more about the UFO phenomenon than you or I."

As for Dr. Clamar, who hypnotized more than a dozen men and women brought to her by Hopkins, she is persuaded "that all of the subjects do, in fact, believe that something strange and unknown did occur." All are deeply confused and troubled by their experience, and no common threads tie them together, no common pathology, except their UFO encounter. "The events recounted by a variety of people from scattered places are strikingly similar," writes Dr. Clamar, "suggesting that there might be more to the whole business than mere coincidence."

The Star People
BRAD & FRANCIE STEIGER
(1981, Berkley Publishing)

Do you possess compelling eyes, personal charisma, an unusual blood type, lower than normal body temperature and blood pressure? Do you suffer from chronic sinusitis, thrive on little sleep, have flying dreams regularly, feel a strong affinity for ancient Egypt, and as a child had an invisible playmate? If the answer to all or most of these questions is yes, then you may be one of the Star People, an alien intelligence which has been seeded here on Earth.

Paranormal writer Brad Steiger claims that beginning in the early 1970s, as he toured America lecturing and gathering research for his books, he began attracting the friendships of Star People. He would intuitively recognize them on meeting. Like him, they possessed many physical anomalies in common, and each had experienced contact as a child with alien entities. Steiger's contact occurred at the age of five when he encountered a small man with a large head peaking in the kitchen window of his parent's Iowa farm. Since that incident Steiger has felt himself to be a stranger visiting here on Earth-one of the Star People.

After a lecture in Saratoga Springs, New York, Steiger found himself compelled to speak to a woman in the audience named Francie. She turned out to be a channeler (and his future wife) who embodied each of the Star People pattern profile criteria that Steiger was compiling. Since the age of five Francie had been a channel for an alien intelligence called Kihief, who she described as "angelic," and who was helping her prepare humanity for a transition through a period of terrible cataclysms and social upheaval.

In 1979 *The National Enquirer* printed a story about the Steigers, quoting Francie as admitting she is one of the Star People, and Brad as declaring that he had interviewed 60 other Star People, all descendants of space beings who had mated with humans. Within months of the article's appearance nearly 1,000 letters swamped the Steigers with testimonials from other Star People. These included a psychiatrist in Washington state, a social worker in Oregon, a mental health worker in San Francisco, many of them describing dreams or visions in which hooded entities had told them: "Now is the time." Those were the same words Francie had informed *The Enquirer* that two men in a dream had told her.

What "Now is the time" means, say the Steigers, is a reference to a triggering mechanism which has alerted the Star People to reveal themselves and prepare our planet for transformation. It is as if "some incredible time-release capsules are going off inside their hearts, brains and psyches." These humans are awakening as extraterrestrials, remembering their "true ancestral home" as very distant and very alien.

––––––––––––––––––––––––––

Aliens Among Us
RUTH MONTGOMERY
(1985, Fawcett Crest Books)

According to the spirit guides who have, by her account, helped Ruth Montgomery channel through automatic writing a series of bestsellers about life-after-death and reincarnation, our space brothers and sisters who led previous lives on Earth have returned in UFOs "to rescue us from our limited thought patterns before it is too late." Some aliens have volunteered to be born into human bodies as "Walk-ins," while others travel here to test our environment, sample our flora and fauna, and "conduct harmless experiments with human beings."

By dissolving the atomic structures of both their bodies and spaceships, these visitors journey here from beyond our Milky Way galaxy. Though they have visited us for millennia they come now with urgency and in greater numbers to "awaken earthlings and help them to realize that their destruction is imminent" unless disputes between nations are settled, nuclear weapons outlawed, and the depletion of natural resources stopped.

A space being named Rolf, who Montgomery believes sometimes communicates through her spirit guides, warned her that extraterrestrials will one day converge en masse "to replace earthlings who want to escape the shift of the earth on its axis." They will come in peace to help rescue our planet from pollution and nuclear war because they fear that earth's defects will "endanger other forms of celestial life."

Many of these visitors are from the Sirius and Arcturus star systems, or from the Andromeda galaxy, who have taken human form as Walk-ins and become advisors to the presidents and rulers of earth's governments. They are quite active at this time (1985) in Russia, say her guides, "as the world will learn after the present leadership there falls and men feel free to discuss the reasons for that collapse, which is in the not too distant future."

Montgomery's spirit guides make a series of predictions about the period 1984 through the year 2000. Walter Mondale will win the 1984 Democratic presidential nomination and Ronald Reagan will defeat him, but Reagan will be unable to serve out his second term and George Bush will succeed him. Then, in 1992 or 1996, the American people "will knowingly elect a Walk-in as president" and he will "harness the energies of the people and guide them aright."

Communion
WHITLEY STRIEBER
(1987, William Morrow)

In the middle of a wintry night in his upstate New York log cabin, Whitley Strieber awoke to an odd whooshing and swirling noise, as if a group of people were moving rapidly about in the living room downstairs. He glanced at the burglar alarm panel beside his bed-the system was still armed and unactivated. The door to his bedroom eased open and a compact figure less than four feet tall entered and rushed toward the bed. In the dim light Strieber could see its two dark holes for eyes, its 0- shaped mouth, a rounded hat on its head and a square plate across its chest. At first, he thought this must be a hypnopompic hallucination, a state between waking and sleep.

Strieber's next conscious recollection was of floating paralyzed and naked out of the room. Then he found himself sitting in the woods on bare ground, even though there had been snowfall when he went to bed. He floated up into a small circular chamber with a grey-tan, ribbed ceiling. Tiny beings moved around him at great speed. He was seated on a bench and one of the beings pulled out a shiny hair-thin needle and telepathically told Strieber that it would be inserted into his brain. Filled with terror, Strieber responded, ''You'll ruin a beautiful mind." And then he began screaming. One of the beings who Strieber sensed was female tried to calm him by asking telepathically, "What can we do to help you stop screaming?" Strieber heard himself reply, "You could let me smell you." One of the other beings put a hand against Strieber's face. It smelled faintly of cardboard, and this helped give Strieber "an anchor in reality."

After a bang and a flash, some kind of operation was performed on Strieber's head. As he glanced around, he noticed four different types of figures in the room-a small robotlike being; a group of short stocky beings in dark blue overalls; a slender being about five feet tall with black slanted eyes; and a group of smaller beings with round black eyes like large buttons. Two of the stocky beings drew Strieber's legs apart and inserted a foot-long triangular object up his rectum. He thought a sample was being taken, but he felt like he was being raped and a surge of anger came up. Another being made an incision on his forefinger, yet there was no pain from any of these procedures. Abruptly the entire episode ended.

The next morning Strieber awoke with a sense of unease, not remembering any of the abduction events. His wife noticed a personality change in him over the following weeks. He became hypersensitive and easily confused, short-tempered, and depressed. The only conscious memory he retained from that night was of seeing a barn owl staring at him from the bedroom window, though he noticed his right forefinger had become infected and every time he sat, he experienced rectal pain. A week later he felt pain behind his right ear and his wife spotted the pinpoint of a scab there. Then one afternoon he suddenly recalled a smell-their smell, and a flood of terrible, unbelievable memories washed over him.

Strieber had heard of an abduction researcher named Budd Hopkins, so he phoned him up and they met. Hopkins asked if Strieber remembered any other unusual events before the abduction in December, and Strieber fixated on an incident at the rural cabin in October 1985, a night when he, his wife, their young son, and two close friends had been awakened by a loud bang. A bright glow surrounded the house and filled the interior, turning night into day. One of the guests reported having heard the scurry of little feet in the house immediately afterward, while Strieber's son had been dreaming that "little doctors" took him away on a boat. On Hopkin's recommendation Strieber hired Dr. Donald Klein of the New York State Psychiatric Institute to perform hypnotic regression. The first sessions were in March 1986, with Hopkins present, concentrating on recovery of buried memories from the October and December 1985 incidents.

Under hypnosis Strieber recalled that moments prior to the loud bang in October, he saw a short being with a bald head and big slanted eyes standing over his bed. The being touched Strieber's forehead with a silver-tipped ruler, stimulating in Strieber's mind a burst of disturbing pictures of the world blowing up and images of his son dying. Then the being stuck the ruler or wand into the air and caused the bang which woke up everyone in the house. In a second hypnotic session Strieber described in detail being abducted from his bedroom in December, and telling the aliens they had no right to do that. The aliens responded with "we do have a right," and the one Strieber thought was female added, "you are our chosen one."

Further hypnotic sessions produced Strieber's belief that he had been abducted by aliens repeatedly as a child. He recalled an incident on a train at age 12, returning to Texas from Wisconsin, when both he, his sister, and their father were apparently taken together. Previously Strieber's only conscious recollection of the train trip was of vomiting and being deathly ill the entire way. Even in the midst of these hypnotic sessions strange incidents continued to plague Strieber. On several mornings, for instance, he and his wife and their son all awakened with nose bleeds. Another time Strieber found two small triangles inscribed on his left forearm.

Based on his own encounters and the descriptions he had heard from other abductees, Strieber suspects the abduction experience has "its symbolic center in the number three and the triangular shape," because the visitors often appear in threes, wearing triangular devices and emblems, shining triangular lights. Triangular rashes and marks often are found on the bodies of abductees, and triangular-shaped objects are sometimes sighted. In ancient human times the triad was considered the "primary expression of the essential structure of life."

As a novelist who has published numerous books of horror fiction, Strieber understands the vast imaginative potential of the human mind. So he concludes with a cautionary note: "I cannot say, in all truth, that I am certain the visitors are present as entities entirely independent of their observers."

Intruders
BUDD HOPKINS
(1987, Ballantine Books)

Kathie Davis, a resident of suburban Indianapolis, read Budd Hopkin's book, *Missing Time*, and wrote to him in September 1983, to report her own "missing time" incident and how she, her mother, her closest friend and her next-door neighbor all had similar scars on their lower legs which may have resulted from UFO abduction experiences. This letter triggered nearly three years of investigation by Hopkins into events surrounding the Davis family and their three-acre homesite in the Copley Woods.

According to Kathie's account, during the first week of July 1983, she looked through her kitchen window and spotted a light about two feet in diameter moving around the family pool house sometime after 8 p.m. Her mother saw the same light. A few days later they discovered a section of their backyard had turned brown-a circular area about eight feet in diameter-where the grass was dead and disintegrating into powder.

Hopkins phoned Kathie and also spoke with her parents and her sister Laura. He began to uncover a pattern of strange events which had affected the family for years. For instance, Kathie recalled a frightening and realistic dream from 1978, when she was 19 and newly married, in which two short, grey-faced creatures with oversized heads stood over her bed. They showed her a box and explained: "When the time is right you will see it again, and you will remember and you'll know how to use it."

Mary Davis, Kathie's mother, "was apparently abducted as a child and again as a young mother," Hopkins reports. And two of her four children-daughters Kathie and Laura-were abducted separately later, along with two of Mary's grandchildren. Mary and Kathie both have "virtually identical scars on their lower legs from apparent childhood abductions, and there is evidence that both Kathie and her son Tommy have had implants inserted near their brains, one through the nasal cavity and the other through the ear."

During hypnotic regression Kathie revealed that her first pregnancy occurred about the time in 1977 that she had a UFO encounter, and that a baffled doctor later found her to be no longer pregnant. "I knew somebody took my baby," Kathie told Hopkins. Hypnosis uncovered her belief that short grey alien beings had stolen the fetus from her womb during another in her series of abductions.

Hopkins describes other accounts of abductees experiencing pregnancy while still a virgin, then having the fetuses taken from them in subsequent abductions. Several of the women also remembered being shown infants aboard the alien craft and being made to feel they were their offspring. These revelations lead Hopkins to conclude that "abductions represent a genetically focused study of particular bloodlines," and he believes this book presents "compelling evidence that an ongoing genetic study is taking place and that the human species itself is the subject of a breeding experiment."

Report On Communion
ED CONROY
(1989, William Morrow)

Feature writer Ed Conroy published an article in the May 17, 1987 edition of the *San Antonio Express-News* about San Antonio native Whitley Strieber, author of Communion. After interviewing Strieber, two possible explanations for his abduction experience occurred to Conroy: either Strieber had "constructed one of the most remarkable literary hoaxes of all time," or Strieber "had finally stumbled upon the source of all his literary inspiration, and touched it, face-to-face in horror, amazement, and awe." Conroy decided to pursue the story further with this book by interviewing Strieber's friends, associates, and detractors, and investigating whether any evidence supported Strieber's claims.

The strongest evidence Conroy found came unexpectedly from his own "visitor like experiences," which turned him into a participant observer and "served to deepen my capacity to relate to the strange events that make up the narratives of Communion and Transformation." A series of incidents throughout 1987 and 1988 convinced Conroy that, similar to Strieber, "I have been in touch with some kind of phenomenon that, as far as I am able to tell, acts in a manner indistinguishable from the kind of intelligence one would expect from other beings."

On a night in July 1987, shortly before he began this book in earnest, Conroy awoke in the predawn hours sensing a presence in his apartment. He reached for a back massager next to the bed to use as a weapon, but "the next thing I knew it was early morning." When he awoke this second time he found splotches of blood on his pillow-case, his right sinus ached, and dried blood caked in his right nostril. He had no memory of ever having had a nosebleed before in his life. He had, however, recently been read-ing descriptions of nasal probes being inserted into abductees, which resulted in severe nosebleeds. More disturbing to him, Conroy noticed that his wife, who had been sleep-ing next to him, awoke with three heavy bruises on her thigh and buttocks.

Both Conroy and his wife were mystified, and the thought seized him that "per-haps we had been abducted."

After visiting friends in San Francisco, a couple named Neil and Naomi, both Conroy and Neil "began to experience a series of more or less 'classical' nighttime visi-tor experiences," including a sighting of a triangle-shaped UFO by Neil and Naomi. Neil went into hypnotherapy and related "what appeared to be experiences of having been aboard flying saucer-like craft," though Neil later concluded these abduction memories might themselves be a screen behind which other true memories hid.

Beginning in early 1988, Conroy went through a period of awakening at 4 a.m. every morning feeling something or someone other than his wife "touching the back of my head, as though my head were being put down upon my pillow." On several occa-sions he noticed that he was sweating and the temperature in his bedroom had shot up to 80 degrees even though the thermostat was set at 68 degrees. He also had vivid dreams featuring visitor-like entities.

During the Spring and Summer of 1988 "began a remarkable presence of anom-alous helicopters in my life." Conroy's neighborhood and home were repeatedly buzzed at all hours by Bell-47 and Chinook-style helicopters, often appearing with regularity over his building at 4 p.m., and sometimes shining searchlights even in daytime hours. Whitley Strieber, his wife, and their son, witnessed one of these helicopter flybys outside Conroy's building, as did several of Conroy's neighbors.

"Remarkably, other persons whom I know—some of them close, personal friends—began to report having nighttime experiences with entities, balls and flashes of light, and other anomalous phenomena during the winter months of 1987-88." This pattern led Conroy to think "a social element" accompanies the visitor experience, with one person's encounter becoming a catalyst for that of others. While the phenomenon may be trickster like, Conroy came to believe that it has "a direct link with human consciousness."

The Watchers
RAYMOND FOWLER
(1990, Bantam)

Since 1947 Raymond Fowler had been obsessed with the subject of UFOs, but only after writing a book about the alien abduction experiences of Betty Andreasson did he begin to have flashbacks from childhood which prompted him to suspect that he too, might be an abductee. He underwent a series of hypnotic regression sessions in 1988, jarring loose numerous memories of having been abducted beginning at the age of five, and the realization came to him that "there was an unmistakable pattern of UFO and anomalous events stretching back to at least three generations in my family."

His mother had her first UFO encounter at age 12 in 1917 in her hometown of Bar Harbor, Maine. She and several friends were crossing a field at night when a huge dark object, encircled by bright flashing, colored lights, descended over them, sending the children into a running panic. Other incidents throughout her life right up to her death at age 83 were characterized by loud humming sounds vibrating her house, and grey oval disks and orange glowing objects appearing above her in the sky and outside of her home.

Fowler's father, Raymond Sr., was a 22-year-old radioman at a Navy station on the Maine coast in 1923 when a nighttime electrical storm sent a bolt of lightning into him through the radio transmitting equipment, forming a ball of rotating fire suspended within his abdomen. Three distinct light flashes in the room produced three radiant beings in shining robes of light, who withdrew the ball of fire from Fowler and tossed it back and forth between them until it shrank in size and disappeared, at which point the three beings bowed to Fowler and departed in three flashes of light.

UFO and related anomalous events were also claimed by two of Fowler's aunts, by his wife Margaret, by two of his brothers, and by two of his four children who had daylight UFO observations. These revelations brought Fowler to a startling conclusion related to his work researching the experiences of Betty Andreasson. On August 14, 1988, Fowler got a phone call from Andreasson who reported that three scars in a triangular pattern had appeared mysteriously on her right arm, scars similar to one on her leg which she believed was the result of a medical experiment during an abduction by aliens. Three days after this call Fowler was taking a shower when he noticed with astonishment a freshly cut scoop mark on his lower leg, as if a cookie cutter had bloodlessly removed a circular piece of flesh. Several days later Andreasson sent photos of her scoop marks-the scars on her and Fowler were identical. "In light of all this," concluded Fowler, "the reason for the scoop mark on my leg becomes obvious. The scar is the result of a biopsy taken as part of the aliens' ongoing genetic research within families of human beings."

Into The Fringe: A True Story of Alien Abduction
KARLA TURNER
(1992, Berkley Books)

From May 1988 to the summer of 1989 a strange series of events episodes of missing time, unexplained body marks and wounds, and unusual phenomena in the home-afflicted five people in Texas who subsequently discovered through hypnotic regression that each had been abducted numerous times by alien beings. Karla Turner, a PH.D. in Old English Studies who taught at a Texas university, recounts how she and her husband, their son David and his future wife Megan, along with David's roommate James, all were "victims of abductions by some alien force which had been a part of our lives for many years."

Karla's conscious recognition of these experiences began during April 1988 after she read two books about alien abduction, Communion and Missing Time, when both she and her husband were in counseling to find out why each felt physical symptoms of stress. She started having dreams about UFOs landing, and she remembered having seen an odd light in the sky over Oklahoma as a young girl.

In May, Karla demonstrated for her husband a hypnotic relaxation technique she had learned from her therapist. While in a trance, Casey recalled being two years old and driving with his father near Grass Valley, California, after an afternoon thunderstorm when they were paralyzed by a bright beam of light, then transported into a saucer shaped craft by four small grey beings with huge, circular black eyes. Casey recounted still other encounters with these beings at age five living in Dallas, and again at age 13 when he engaged in sexual intercourse with a dark-eyed female alien with white wispy hair.

Several nights after Casey's trance session Karla awoke hearing strange clicking and bumping noises in the house, followed by disembodied voices from a corner of her bedroom. One voice informed her: "this is the longing for that you've asked for." Later that day Karla remembered a nightmare from childhood in which an insect-like being held her hand and told her it was her mother.

An Oklahoma UFO researcher was enlisted to perform hypnosis on Karla and Casey, starting with Casey. He told of seeing a metallic sphere in December 1987, of disappearing into its beam of light and undergoing a medical exam in which aliens cut a skin sample from his leg. He described an earlier encounter in Kansas when, as a sixth-grader, he saw a UFO land near his home. The beings inside, which resembled "strange children," pushed an instrument up his nostril and into his brain.

After this particular hypnotic session ended, it was about 3 a.m. when Karla and Casey, accompanied by their friend Jack, stood in a street and witnessed a dark pie-pan shaped craft with a row of lights hover over them. It would be the opening sequence in a year's worth of bizarre experiences which were to haunt Karla's family. "It may sound foolish," she confessed in July 1988, "but we wanted another contact from the aliens because we wanted answers."

Two weeks after the UFO sighting Karla again heard voices in the night and loud knockings. She awakened to find a pair of small puncture wounds on her inner left wrist and three white circles on her lower left abdomen. Over the next few months body marks continued to appear. She found a solid red triangle on her upper left forearm, more puncture wounds, scratches and bruises materialized on both Karla and Casey's arms and legs, a small triangle developed over her jugular vein, three more puncture marks on her neck. Every morning their ritual became to check each other over for fresh body marks.

Other poltergeist-like phenomena began to occur. Sometimes their bed would shake them awake, their bathroom light would come back on at all hours, synthesized music played throughout the house seemingly without a source, and a variety of voices shouted out slogans and incomprehensible admonitions. Karla and Casey began to suspect the U.S. military might be "monitoring information transmitted by alien technology" directly into their brains, because a white Chevy and unmarked helicopters seemed to follow them, especially when they went to and from lectures on UFOs.

Like some spreading infection, the UFO abductions, odd happenings, and body wounds began to plague Karla's son David, his girlfriend, and their roommate James.

Each would eventually remember childhood experiences of being abducted by alien beings resembling a praying mantis. James, 23, was the most impacted, and suffered numerous abductions including a forced copulation with a female alien in late 1988. James' mother, Sandy, experienced an hour of missing time after seeing a UFO while in James' presence.

Karla's own hypnotic regressions produced accounts of her repeated abductions since childhood, and evidence her entire family might be involved. In December 1988, she got a confirming phone call from her sister-in-law, Tanya, in California, who revealed that Karla's brother, Paul, had been abducted along with Tanya prompting them "to stay away from the rest of the family, since they feared their stories wouldn't be believed." Altogether, at least 10 people in Karla's life are alleged to have gotten caught up in the same disturbing pattern of alien intrusions and disturbances over a 13-month period.

The Omega Project
KENNETH RING
(1992, William Morrow)

For ten years Dr. Kenneth Ring, a professor of psychology at the University of Connecticut, had been researching and writing about near death experiences when he read Communion in 1987 and realized that alien abduction stories shared many NDE characteristics. Both UFO and NDE encounters seemed to be alternate pathways into the same type of psycho-spiritual transformation, which produced heightened ecological concerns and a greater awareness of the sacredness of all life. To delve deeper into these similarities, Dr. Ring conducted a survey among hundreds of persons claiming UFO and NDE experiences using an extensive battery of questionnaires designed to explore why certain persons seem predisposed to such phenomena.

He found a remarkable consistency in the descriptions that abductees gave of the aliens and their behaviors. Despite the variety of witness ages and backgrounds, they uniformly reported the aliens as childlike in size, grey or greyish-white in color, with big black eyes in a head disproportionately large like that of a human fetus. These beings acted detached, clinical, and methodical in their movements.

Alien abduction stories always struck Dr. Ring as inherently discontinuous, non-linear and segmented, composed of scenes much as dreams are constructed with distortions of time and abrupt shifts of setting. But "they seem more like dreams that one has awakened into and that, in some unknown way, have come to interpenetrate ordinary reality." Even more puzzling, they appear to constitute a collective dream as glimpsed or fashioned by those who experience them. And no matter whether the experiencers recall the abduction through hypnosis, or spontaneously, or as a dream, the details are similar and the themes of the episodes are identical.

During near-death the out-of-body moments often occur in the midst of operations or other medical procedures. Medical exams are also a typical feature of alien abduction cases. During NDEs beings are routinely encountered which are described as angelic, usually glowing or dressed in white robes, and usually communicating by telepathy. In these sorts of details Dr. Ring sees evidence at the pattern level for archetypal initiatory journeys.

Are people who experience abductions and NDEs simply more susceptible than normal to the altered states of consciousness necessary to interact with alternative or nonordinary realities? Ring's survey findings detected no evidence that such people are fantasy-prone personalities, yet there was a pattern for both NDEs and abductees to report much higher than average incidences of childhood abuse and trauma, including serious illness. In turn, this led Ring to conclude that people who report abductions and NDEs "appear to have a greater likelihood of showing dissociative tendencies in their psychological functioning." The ability to dissociate may even act as a key to accessing alternate realities. Individuals who can dissociate easily, transcending normal sensory states, are "encounter-prone personalities" more likely than the average person to have extraordinary encounters. Childhood abuse and trauma seems to act as a psychological conditioning which enables the experiencer to "develop an extended range of human perception beyond normally recognized limits." Thus, these individuals can spontaneously slip into an altered state of consciousness and glimpse what the rest of humanity is oblivious to or programmed to ignore.

In the aftermath of unusual experiences both abductees and NDEs generally report that their nervous systems function differently than before. They claim an intensified electrical sensitivity, and a tendency to affect nearby electrical appliances and systems, causing electric lights to inexplicably blow out, watches and other personal devices to fail. Both groups also report more allergies, sensitivity to light, greater hearing acuity, psychic abilities, and healing gifts.

Canadian psychologist Michael Persinger speculates that electro magnetic field stimulation of the human brain-in particular two structures of the temporal lobe-can produce intense hallucinations which feel like reality to the experiencer, including sensations of floating, being out-of-body, seeing apparitions and hearing internal voices.

Afterward, amnesia and a sense of having lost time can be further symptoms of having encountered electromagnetic fields. Dr. Ring is persuaded that "a common neurological mechanism underlies" both NDEs and UFO abductions, so he finds the Persinger thesis persuasive as a possible explanation for the pattern of psychophysical changes evident in experiencers, and for the electrical sensitivity syndrome both types have in common.

UFO and NDE encounters are usually explained one of two ways either they are real experiences, or they are the products of fantasy, delusion and hoaxes. But maybe there is a third explanation. Maybe a real unexplained phenomenon exists, it has an electrical effect on the human body and brain, and the experiencer interprets the encounter according to cultural conditioning. Some people think they have encountered angels or demons, others perceive fairies or spirits of the dead, while others see visitors from another galaxy, another time, another dimension.

Abduction experiences are a collective dream of the species mind, speculates philosopher Michael Grosso, and have emerged so intensely because the threat of nuclear war and global ecological catastrophe has evoked a new level of consciousness from humanity. The fact that so many abduction experiences involve medical exams, and so many NDEs happen during medical procedures, may indicate we are being given a symbolic message about healing ourselves. Even the descriptions of aliens, with their hairless oversized grey heads, evoke an image of human fetuses freshly emerged from the womb. The aliens in this collective dream turn out to be ourselves, a symbol of our own alienation and the need we feel to evolve into a higher more adaptable state of consciousness. "Grosso argues that there is a kind of helping intelligence," writes Dr. Ring, "a planetary mind that reflects our collective concerns as a species and then feeds them back to us symbolically in the form of an archetypal abduction drama that is orchestrating these experiences in imaginal space."

Secret Life
DAVID M. JACOBS, PH.D.
(1993, Simon and Schuster)

After meeting abduction researcher Budd Hopkins in 1982, Temple University history professor David Jacobs decided to undertake his own research by learning techniques of hypnosis, which he did by reading books and attending a conference. In 1986 he performed the first of more than 325 hypnosis sessions with 60 abductees. They were a cross-section of America, representing a variety of religions, ethnic groups, ages, and backgrounds. Though they claimed to have been abducted from both cities and rural areas, from within both houses and apartment complexes, and in both day and night, they all told similar stories of being taken by strange beings and subjected to a range of physical and mental procedures, which left them feeling confused and victimized.

During these hypnosis sessions Jacobs had to learn how to distinguish legitimate memories from projection and fantasy. "I understood that some of what was being told to me was the product of confabulation (the unconscious invention and filling in of memories), false memories, and dream material." Yet, he noticed that the abduction accounts he was hearing began to fit distinct patterns, with even small details confirmed many times over. He eventually became persuaded of the prospect his subjects "were being employed to produce another form of life-a secret life. And all this was being carried out by an alien form of life that existed secretly in our environment."

Whoever or whatever is doing the abducting seems to take great care "to take people when they will not be missed or when their lives will not be overly disrupted." No reported abductions have occurred from within a large group of people or in front of people at a public event; usually they occur at night as a person sleeps, or when one or two persons are driving in an isolated area. Often abductions begin when a subject believes he or she is witnessing the appearance of an owl, deer, monkey, or other animals. Abductees frequently describe being floated through closed doors and windows, or directly through walls and ceilings, and "although it sounds impossible, the physical mechanism that allows people to pass through solid objects probably renders them invisible."

Communication between abductees and their abductors is always telepathic. The alien beings are usually small, less than four feet tall, with bald, bulbous heads, immense dark eyes without pupils, no ears, and a slit-like mouth which never moves. They either wear form-fitting clothing or nothing at all, and no genitalia are obvious. The UFO room these beings escort abductees into resembles a hospital operating room, and a central table is used for abductees to lay upon once they have been undressed. The physical examination lasts no more than 20 minutes. Specific anatomical sites on the human body are poked and felt, painless incisions are sometimes made in the thigh, calf or back of the knee, and gynecological inspections are given to women, with milk taken from those who are pregnant. These exams are thorough, involving the ears, eyes, and mouth. If the abductee had been previously abducted, any changes in the body, such as scars or even braces on teeth, will attract the beings' immediate curiosity. Near the end of these procedures the beings implant or remove previously implanted small, metallic objects from the abductee's nose or ear. All during this process a being slightly taller than the others calms the abductee by staring into their eyes, a type of mind scan to extract information is performed, and the abductee is told something reassuring along the lines of ''You are very special to us."

The most intriguing part of the abduction ritual involves a series of procedures to collect sperm from men, and eggs or fetuses from women. Numerous female abductees reported having fertilized eggs inserted into them and being left with the impression they were now pregnant. Those women who were already pregnant have the implanted embryo extracted, later causing confusion among doctors when the previously pregnant patient is no longer carrying a child, yet she has not had a miscarriage. In one exchange related by Jacobs, a waitress named Lynn Miller was told after her fetus had been removed, "This is your child and we're going to raise it." Miller protested that the beings had no right to do so. The taller being in charge of the extraction replied, "It's our right." Some women have been shown the offspring of this hybrid breeding program, taken to see fetuses floating in liquid solutions, and into nurseries where dozens of sickly, not-quite human babies are laid out in rows. The women are then mentally forced to touch and hold these offspring, even to suckle them.

All of this information taken together, drawn with consistency in detail from abductees, leads Jacobs to suspect that another species of life is exploiting us. These visitors are not here to help us. They have their own agenda, and it is concerned with the genetic alteration of our species, accomplished by "tagging" human children at an early age and mining them of genetic and reproductive material the remainder of their lives. "We have been invaded. It is not an occupation, but it is an invasion. At present we can do little or nothing to stop it."

Abduction
JOHN E. MACK, M.D.
(1994, Scribner)

What impressed Dr. John Mack most about the first abductees he met in 1990, through Budd Hopkins in New York, was the consistency of the stories they told, the fact they had come forward reluctantly, and all seemed troubled "as a consequence of something that had apparently happened to them." Nothing in their demeanor or stories led Mack to believe they were delusional or engaged in fantasy. For the next three years he worked with 76 apparent abductees, including 13 persons whose cases are recounted in this book, and most underwent numerous hypnosis sessions conducted by Mack, who is a professor of psychiatry at Harvard Medical School.

His subjects ranged in age from two to 57, nearly two-thirds of them were women, and by profession they included computer industry employees, psychologists, musicians, writers, and homemakers. With remarkable consistency this group reported being taken against their will by alien beings and "subjected to elaborate intrusive procedures which appeared to have a reproductive purpose." In the aftermath of these experiences the abductees felt powerful emotions which reinforced their impression these were real incidents. Their experiences were often associated with UFO sightings made by their friends and relatives, and the encounters sometimes left the abductees with small cuts, scratches and scars on their bodies. "In short," marveled Mack, "I was dealing with a phenomenon that I felt could not be explained psychiatrically, yet was simply not possible within the framework of the Western scientific worldview."

Based on the hypnosis sessions he conducted, Mack found a consistent pattern of event sequences, details, and themes in abductee stories. Abductees are commonly taken when in their homes or while driving automobiles, and the encounter usually begins with an intense bluish or white light accompanied by a buzzing or humming sound. Abductees are floated out of cars and bedrooms, often through solid objects, after having been numbed or paralyzed by one or more humanoid beings. The UFOs into which they are floated vary in size and shape, from a few feet across to a hundred yards wide, and in cigar, saucer or dome shapes of a silvery or metallic color, with intense blue, white, red or orange lights emanating from the bottom of the craft.

Several different types of entities are described as the abductors, though all may have the power to be shape-shifters, appearing initially to the abductee as some type of animal. The most common beings reported are small "greys" less than four feet tall, having large, pear-shaped heads, spindly legs, long arms with three or four fingers, and huge black eyes which curve upward. Both tall and short luminous entities have been observed, along with beings with reptilian features, and tall Nordic looking blond beings which appear human. They wear single-piece formfitting garments resembling tunics. Their communication with humans is always telepathic.

Once inside the craft humans are mentally forced naked onto body contoured tables where every part of their body is penetrated by instruments. Sperm samples are taken from men, fertilized eggs from women. Hybrid fetuses and young children are often seen aboard the alien craft. "The purely physical or biological aspect of the abduction phenomenon seems to have to do with some sort of genetic or quasi-genetic engineering for the purpose of creating human/alien hybrid offspring."

Alteration of human consciousness, "profoundly changing their perceptions of themselves, the world, and their place in it," seems to be another goal of the abduction phenomenon. During direct mind-to-mind telepathic transfers, aliens implant into their captives powerful images of apocalypse—the planet devastated by nuclear war, by environmental pollution, by earthquakes, firestorms and other disasters. Abductees' emotional response to these images are closely monitored. Some abductees report being given specific assignments to undertake when this future holocaust occurs. Once their abduction ends, experiencers are frequently convinced that a homing device has been planted somewhere in their bodies. Some of these tiny objects have been surgically removed and studied. "There is no evidence that any of the implants recovered are composed of rare elements, or of common ones in unusual combinations."

For any theory to even begin to explain the abduction phenomenon, Mack believes it must take into account five dimensions of data. (1) The high degree of consistency in the detailed accounts by abductees, supplemented with intense emotions appropriate to the experience being reported. (2) There is no psychiatric illness or psychological factors that can account for what is reported. (3) Body marks and physical changes in abductees are often and easily observed. (4) UFOs are often witnessed independently while abductions are taking place. (5) Children as young as two or three years of age have described abduction experiences which cannot be explained by "cultural pollution."

"It seems clear to me at this time that we are not dealing with 'false' or confabulated memories," Mack concludes. The data collected so far "suggests that abduction experiencers have been visited by some sort of 'alien' intelligence which has impacted them physically and psychologically. Indeed, this conclusion fits so tightly with the data that I and other abduction researchers have collected, that it is doubtful to me that this possibility would be so vigorously resisted if the phenomenon did not violate our scientific worldview."

Breakthrough
WHITLEY STRIEBER
(1995, HarperCollins)

As Whitley Strieber sat in his upstate New York cabin reading an essay on physics, precisely at the moment he read the words "the mind is not the playwright of reality," he heard nine loud knocks in three groupings of three on the side of his house up near the ceiling, a spot where no one could possibly be standing. "For me, the nine knocks were personal confirmation," writes Strieber. "The visitors were real. Damned real."

This experience in August 1986 became his personal proof-a public proof would soon follow. Eighteen months to the day after this incident, "a large number of people in Glenrock, Wyoming, were awakened at 2:45 a.m. by a series of nine knocks in three groups of three on their cars, on the sides or roofs of their houses, or on their doors." Glenrock police logged more than 50 calls during a 15-minute period that morning from residents alarmed by the knocks. The local newspaper published an account of the dull thuds which residents were certain had been caused by physical contact on the outsides of their dwellings.

In Tibetan Buddhist tradition the concept of three groups of three means progress in past, present, and future time. For Strieber the nine knocks are a call to contact, a call to ascension, and a challenge to us from the visitors.

It appears to Strieber that the visitors constitute a large number of familial groups which use "a plethora of different approaches under the broad umbrella of a shared ethic of minimal disturbance of our own freedom of choice." This impression arose from Strieber's analysis of the 139,914 letters he got between 1987 and 1994 from persons claiming encounters. Eighty percent of the writers described a positive experience with the visitors, and these persons wrote from Russia, England, Australia and elsewhere, not just from the U.S. Most did not report the typical abduction scenario of little grey beings taking the person aboard a UFO and subjecting them to intrusive medical procedures. Instead, the interactions described to Strieber were "at a far higher level of strangeness."

Most of his correspondents reported a lifetime of strange encounter experiences connected in a pattern that seemed to involve other family members. The beings these thousands of writers described are a varied lot-resembling insects, cat people, Orientals, Greek gods, shafts of light, etc. These beings have the power to morph into and out of images of owls, deer, and other animals. When the beings disappear, they often leave behind an odor of smoldering cardboard. This strikes Strieber as evidence that the visitors are "chipping away at our resistance" and moving us toward a contact "of a very unexpected kind," in which they become "part of our interior life."

Cosmic Voyage
COURTNEY BROWN
(1996, Dutton)

Two races of extraterrestrial beings, one called the Greys, the other being survivors of an ancient civilization that flourished on Mars when dinosaurs roamed the Earth, now live on our planet playing a role in the evolution of humans. "This is not a book of speculation," insists the author, Courtney Brown, an associate professor of political science at Emory University. "I could not have gathered any data or written this book if many of these extraterrestrials did not cooperate with my research efforts." The book jacket carries endorsements from Whitley Strieber (it "breaks new ground") and from Dr. John E. Mack (he "has documented the reality of intelligent life outside of our planet.")

Research for this book came through Brown's use of remote viewing, an ability to perceive information at great distances across space and time using only the unconscious mind. Brown claims he developed this talent under training from a former member of a U.S. Army intelligence team which had perfected remote viewing as an espionage tool during the Cold War. When they weren't remotely viewing Russian missile silos or Kremlin meetings, these psychic spies allegedly solved the UFO enigma by tuning in to watch the activities of alien visitors.

ETs rarely impose limitations on their activities being observed by remote viewers, according to Brown, unless it is "to protect us from something for which we are not fully prepared." He believes that remote viewing is a more reliable process than hypnotic regression to understand the experience of abductees. Memories recalled by abductees are probably unrepresentative, about as reliable as "ETs trying to find out what humans are like by interviewing only automobile accident victims."

Brown's cosmic voyage rendezvous with ETs began in January 1992, after he mastered an advanced version of Transcendental Meditation called the "Sidhis," then completed a one-week course at the Monroe Institute in Virginia, a prerequisite to remote viewing training. During this period his wife, who was a Sidha, encountered a typical Grey alien in her backyard as it attempted to render her unconscious, a state she was able to resist. Brown interpreted her experience as evidence the ETs were investigating him as a prelude to him investigating them.

Beginning in September 1993, with his remote viewing trainer as monitor, Brown made the first in a series of mental trips to the planet Mars where he discovered that the Martian civilization-which at its peak compared technologically to ancient Egypt-had been doomed by an ecological catastrophe. The survivors were rescued and transported to Earth by the Greys and many now live inside a mountain near Santa Fe, N.M. When NASA's Mars Observer space probe threatened to expose the ruins of Martian civilization in 1993, an ET craft piloted by Greys destroyed the probe.

Later, another remote viewing journey enabled Brown to interact with the Galactic Federation, a sort of United Nations of different alien species in our galaxy. Federation council members are white humanoids in white gowns and they told Brown "in no uncertain terms" that he was to write this book to alert humans of an impending series of planetary disasters occurring by the year 2030.

On June 2, 1994, Brown succeeded in having a remote viewing conversation with Jesus Christ, who was introduced to him through the Galactic Federation. "I then asked Jesus why I came to him through the Federation folks," Brown writes. "He told me that it was specifically because of the book that I am writing. He wanted to help me with the book because it is my evolutionary contribution." In subsequent sessions Brown found that Adam and Eve, who had been "project managers in a genetic-uplift program for humans," were still around and helping to guide our evolution.

A key to how our evolution is being shaped can be seen in the television show Star Trek: The Next Generation. Brown did a remote viewing session where he entered the brain of a Star Trek writer and found an alien implant device which was dictating plot ideas to the writer on a regular basis. "ET manipulation of Hollywood products had been occurring for a long time," Brown maintains, but the ETs specifically "generated the idea of Star Trek to transform humankind in some way."

Witnessed
BUDD HOPKINS
(1996, Pocket Books)

Either the abduction case described in this book constitutes what is "easily the most important in recorded history," as Budd Hopkins puts it, or else "an intricate, cold-blooded hoax" has been perpetrated by a group of people, a conspiracy for which Hopkins finds "not a shred of evidence." Not only does this book claim that nearly a dozen persons witnessed a woman being floated out of her twelfth-floor window and into a hovering UFO at 3 a.m. in New York City, it alleges that among the witnesses on November 30, 1989, were two security officers and the world leader they were guarding-a figure whom Hopkins strongly insinuates was Javier Perez de Cuellar, Secretary General of the United Nations.

For Hopkins this enigma unfolded on February 1, 1991, when he received a letter marked "personal and important" from two men using the names Dan and Richard, who identified themselves as police officers. They described being parked near the Brooklyn Bridge about 3:30 a.m. on a day in late November 1989, and seeing an oval object with bright reddish-orange lights hovering over an apartment building. A little girl or woman in a white nightgown floated out of an apartment window, escorted by "three ugly but smaller humanlike creatures," and was brought up through the bottom of the oval craft. The UFO whisked up and away several blocks toward the East River, where it plunged into the water and disappeared.

As Hopkins read the letter, he realized that he knew the woman these two men claimed to have seen abducted. She went by the name Linda Cortile (her actual last name would later be revealed as Napolitano), and she had phoned Hopkins on November 30, 1989, to relate how three short, nonhuman beings had seized her from her bedroom at 3 a.m. that morning and floated her out a twelfth-floor window into a UFO. Inside, she was subjected to medical procedures and returned two hours later. Cortile lived in an apartment building just two blocks from the East River near the Brooklyn Bridge.

During the remainder of 1991 Hopkins investigated this case by placing Cortile under hypnosis numerous times, during which she revealed having been abducted by grey-skinned aliens repeatedly since childhood, and by corresponding with the two self-described policemen. Richard and Dan never revealed themselves in person to Hopkins, though they did send him their tape-recorded account of the Cortile abduction and six more letters elaborating on their experience. The two men did, however, confront Cortile at her apartment to satisfy their curiosity that she really existed. Inquiries with local police agencies soon convinced Hopkins that Richard and Dan were not actual policemen. They were probably agents of a protective service associated with the United Nations.

In a September 1991 letter to Hopkins, Dan revealed that he, Richard, and the important figure they were guarding were beginning to remember more details about Cortile's abduction. After the UFO with Cortile in it splashed into the river, all three men recall instantaneously finding themselves sitting on a seashore somewhere watching Linda Cortile and three alien beings digging in the sand. At one point Cortile held up a dead fish and told the three men, "Look and see what you have done!" Next, the three men found themselves back at their car on the street below Cortile's apartment.

"Had two security agents and a very important, internationally known political figure actually been abducted that night along with Linda?" wondered Hopkins. To find out he put Linda Cortile under hypnosis again, not telling her about the letter from Dan. She recounted her abduction once more, only this time she recalled having been taken to a beach by the aliens and given a scoop and a pail. The aliens are concerned that sea creatures are dying and they want samples to find the source of the pollution. She found a dead fish on the beach, which made her sad and angry. She and the three grey aliens with her walked up to three men sitting on the beach. She felt like it was their fault, that people like them are killing the sea life. She waved the fish at them, saying "Look what you've done!" The older of the three men, distinguished in a charcoal grey suit, looked familiar to her. She also recognized Richard and Dan. She later identified the distinguished third man from photos as the Secretary General of the United Nations.

In the aftermath of this session Hopkins sensed history in the making. "For the first time in my experience the UFO occupants were apparently trying to influence earthly politics at an extraordinarily high level. A political leader of international stature and importance had been abducted and shown a scene designed to demonstrate to him the aliens' selfless interest in the problems of pollution on earth."

On a visit to her niece, Lisa Bayer, a doctor of podiatric medicine, Linda had an x-ray done of her head. Dr. Bayer remembered from childhood that her aunt had talked about a bump on the side of her nose, and how a doctor had found a scar inside. Since Linda believed she was abducted numerous times as a child, they decided to see what an x-ray might show. "The picture clearly shows the presence of a complex, radiopaque, metallic object in Linda's nasal cavity," writes Hopkins. "When I finally saw the x-ray-nearly two weeks after it was taken-I was astonished, for it provided solid evidence of an alien implant, a radiologic smoking gun." (That x-ray is reproduced in the book.) There was only one problem. A week later Linda woke up with a severe nosebleed. The implant was gone! To Hopkins this meant the aliens somehow know when an implant has been x-rayed. "And so before Linda or I had seen Lisa's x-ray, the UFO occupants apparently abducted Linda from her apartment and removed the implant, thus causing her nosebleed and preventing us from recovering the artifact."

Eventually three more people would step forward during Hopkin's investigation of this case to claim that they too, had been witnesses to aspects of Linda Cortile's abduction in November 1989. One of them, a widow in her sixties identified as Janet Kimball, was crossing the Brooklyn Bridge at 3:16 a.m. when her car engine and headlights died. Several other vehicles on the bridge experienced the same problem. Even Kimball's watch stopped. Nearby she noticed what appeared to be an apartment building on fire in Manhattan. As she stared, she saw what looked to be a group of children, their knees balled up under their chins, float out the building bathed in light and enter a hovering object. When the UFO passed over the bridge, "my clothing clung to me and my body hair stood up. The clinging sensation went away after the object went away, and my car started again."

In December 1991, Hopkins received a letter from The Third Man—the important world figure guarded by Richard and Dan—who called his witnessing of Cortile's abduction "the most astounding event of my life." The letter bore a United Nations postmark, and it had been typed on UN stationery, but there was no signature or identification. "My position stands firm," the letter read. "I cannot and shall not give a hint concerning my involvement."

The precisely orchestrated abduction of Linda Cortile in front of a world leader, and his subsequent abduction to witness her and the aliens gathering sand samples on a beach, seemed designed to scold the world's power elite for polluting the environment and to portray aliens as benevolent environmentalists. Yet, Hopkins believes the aliens have little real interest in teaching us to take better care of our planet because "all of the evidence points to their being here to carry out a complex breeding experiment in which they seem to be working to create a hybrid species, a mix of human and alien characteristics."

———————————————

Alien Dawn: A Classic Investigation into the Contact Experience
COLIN WILSON
(1998, Virgin Publishing)

By linking the esoteric UFO phenomenon ideas of John Keel, Jacques Vallée, John Michell and Carl Jung, with the alien abduction research of Budd Hopkins and John Mack, and integrating all of it with speculations about the true nature of paranormal events, Colin Wilson comes to a new understanding of our consensus reality and how the 'visitors'—whoever or whatever they are—seem embarked on transforming human consciousness.

Wilson has authored more than 50 books on a wide range of topics, two of his best known being *The Outsider* and *The Occult*. This is his first foray into examining the UFO phenomenon and with his trademark erudition, he contrasts the evidence for UFOs and alien abductions with mystical experiences, ancient folklore, crop circles that are real not hoaxed, instances of time displacement and hypnotic induction. From his point of view, all of this is interconnected.

Wilson credits John Keel in his book *The Mothman Prophecies* as one of the first theorists "to show that there is no clear dividing line between UFO phenomena and the 'paranormal'—for example, poltergeist activity, telepathy and precognition." And with the abduction phenomenon, "the line often dissolves completely."

Both Keel and Jacques Vallée reached similar conclusions in their various books "that the purpose of UFO activity is, to some extent, the effect it has on human beings. They have every intention of being seen" and they can somehow focus on and interact with the human mind of observers. Both Keel and Vallée believe these visitors are 'paraphysical entities' who "are related to the manifestations involved in religious miracles and spiritual seances." The mass sighting at Fatima in 1917 provides one example. Keel in particular concluded "the secret of the UFOs lie in the electromagnetic spectrum," which is one reason why UFOs can be picked up on radar even when they are invisible to the naked eye.

Whatever the intelligence is that manifests UFOs and manipulates human perceptions and consciousness, it arises from electromagnetic frequencies and while it is very aware of humans, most humans have only the vaguest awareness of this intelligence until it chooses to shock us into abandoning our rigid mindsets and consensus reality. It was the psychologist Carl Jung who first proposed that our interactions with the UFO phenomenon "presage a profound change in human consciousness."

Wilson wonders if there is "some other reality {existing} on a level that is somehow parallel to our, *but on a different vibration rate*." Such an idea was first proposed by a Cambridge archaeologist, T.C. Lethbridge, who had seen a UFO in 1931, and came to believe that other realities exist around us all the time, in other dimensions, but they are mostly undetectable "because they are on different vibrational rates," yet evidence of them manifest in UFOs and alien entities.

With this new understanding of the nature of reality, observes Wilson, we can begin to comprehend the 'paradoxical behavior' of UFOs and their apparent occupants, "their ability to appear out of nowhere, to defy the laws of inertia by changing direction at tremendous speeds, to disappear in one part of the sky and reappear simultaneously in another. Our chief mistake lies in thinking of UFOs as craft like our own space probes when all the evidence suggests that they are unknown energy forms."

Passport to the Cosmos: Human Transformation and Alien Encounters
JOHN E. MACK, M.D.
(1999, White Crow Books)

Harvard University psychiatry professor and Pulitzer Prize-winning author John Mack wrote this book as the culmination of ten years studying the alien abduction phenomenon, and the resulting evolution of his views, to address what these sorts of anomalous experiences "can tell us about ourselves and our evolving knowledge of the nature of reality."

Since release of his 1994 book, *Abduction,* Mack worked with an additional 100 more people reporting encounters with strange beings who seem to reach his clients and intrude on their lives from another more subtle realm. He chooses to call these people 'experiencer participants' and he finds himself fascinated by the parallels between their reported experiences and what those people having near-death and out-of-body experiences also report, all of which present challenges to our concepts of human consciousness. In many ways the abduction phenomenon seems to be "a kind of tricksterism that mocks our technology and the literalness of minds which require material proof before they believe anything really exists."

Though Mack says he sometimes uses a modified form of hypnosis or relaxation exercise to interview experiencers, "it should be emphasized that about 80 percent of the information is obtained through conscious recollection." This puts Mack's methods in direct contrast to those of abduction researchers like David Jacobs, who rely on information obtained through hypnotic regression of experiencers. Mack's concern is that hypnosis can sometimes result in interviewers influencing or even shaping the memories of interviewees.

What comes across to Mack through his research is how experiencers consistently talk about being taken into another dimension or plane of reality where the laws of physics in our collective reality no longer seem applicable. In these realms experiencers have a "different experience of time, space, and dimensionality" within these other dimensions intruding on their awareness and altering their states of consciousness. Mack notes how theoretical physicists now propose there may be 10 or more other dimensions to explain the existence of subatomic particles.

Another regularly reported aspect of experiencer accounts describe seeing and feeling intense energy in the form of light and higher vibratory frequencies that accompany their shift in consciousness and altered perceptions. Interference with electronics and appliances often accompany the experience itself, or remain as a side effect for the experiencers afterward, as if their own bodies had become an intensified frequency source. When experiencers gather together "they often feel an energy resonance that they describe as 'infectious'." Mack wonders why observing or feeling intense light and vibrational energies during the experiences seem to have lasting effects. He compares these experiences to shamanic journeys and to the manifestations of chi, prana or kundalini awakenings which have long been associated in some religious traditions with spiritual transformation.

Abduction experiences appear to be created or designed to "shatter the previously held idea of reality." In the aftermath of these experiences, many experiencers realize that "they have encountered intense vibratory energies, still held in the body, that have also profoundly affected their consciousness." Their bodies seem to be vibrating differently at their very core, as they 'awaken' and move to a higher level of being.

Out of the ego-shattering impact of their abduction experience, this intrusion into their hold on consensus reality, they develop a heightened awareness, if they are able to work through the trauma of their experience. This heightened awareness takes four forms: They access non-ordinary states of consciousness usually experienced by shamans; Many abductees expand their psychological and spiritual powers of perception; They feel a loving connection "to all living beings and creation itself"; and, they feel a "renewed sense of the sacred and a reverence for nature."

"The abduction phenomenon seems to me to be a part of the shift in consciousness that is collapsing duality and enabling us to see that we are connected beyond the Earth at a cosmic level. No common enemy will unite us, but the realization of a common Source might," writes Mack. "The alien abduction phenomenon is largely an opportunity or a gift, a kind of catalyst for the evolution of consciousness in the direction of an emerging sense of responsibility for our own and the planet's future."

Contact With Beings Of Light: The Amazing True Story of Dorothy Wilkinson-Izatt
PETER GUTTILLA
(2003, Timeless Voyager Press)

When she passed away in 2021, at the age of 98, Dorothy Izatt had accumulated more than 30,000 feet of film footage in which she captured images of lights that she believed were of UFOs, orbs, and 'light beings' that she could seemingly summon at will. Her abilities were described in this 2003 book, and in a 2008 documentary film, *Capturing the Light*.

Her story began late one afternoon in November 1974, in a suburb of Vancouver, British Columbia, after her daily session of prayer and meditation, when she had a strange feeling of being watched. She peered out her living room window and saw in the sky a bright, spinning object like a huge diamond, with a horizontal ring of lights revolving around the middle. When it disappeared from view, she returned to her household chores, confused by what she had seen.

That evening after dinner, while watching television with her husband, Duncan, an electrical engineer, "an intense beam of light pierced the living room drapes and shone directly on me," Dorothy later related. She got up and opened the drapes to confront "an enormous, stationary ball of light in the sky, low on the horizon." Dorothy then felt herself receive a mental message: "We are real; we are here; it is not your imagination." She got a flashlight and returned to the window and blinked it at the object; the ball of light answered her, and did so repeatedly, replicating every motion of her flashlight. That's when she realized the phenomenon was real and not a product of her imagination.

Over the ensuing years Dorothy used a Super-8mm movie camera to capture her interactions with the balls of light and what Dorothy believed to be 'light beings' which were the intelligence behind the lights. She could sense when they wanted to communicate with her and she could even sometimes summon them with her thoughts. This book by California phenomena researcher Peter Guttilla chronicles many of these interactions between Dorothy and the lights and describes the growing number of persons who witnessed aspects of this phenomenon and became believers in Dorothy.

On three occasions the astronomer and UFO investigator J. Allen Hynek visited Dorothy at her home, between 1975 and 1978, to interview her and take photo samples for analysis by Fred Beckman, a photographic expert at the University of Chicago. "Though convinced the films were authentic," writes Guttilla, "Dr. Hynek remained puzzled as to their origin and meaning." Hynek shared the films with other scientists and researchers, including Dr. Jule Eisenbud, a physician who had worked with people who apparently had an ability to affect photographic film with their minds, though none "compared to the volume and quality of Dorothy's work and none produced images on movie film."

As an Epilogue to this book, the author describes how in June 2000, he drove from southern California with his wife, their son, and two other adults to visit Dorothy in Vancouver. While sitting with Dorothy in her apartment the five visitors began feeling a sensation of intense heat radiating through their feet and hands. "They must be here," commented Dorothy, and at that moment, reports Guttilla, "a light appeared in the center of the room and shot straight up through the ceiling."

The following evening the five people visited Dorothy again and after an hour of chatting and viewing her latest film footage, Dorothy suddenly announced, "I think you should go out on the terrace now." The group rushed out to a porch behind her apartment and according to Guttilla, "suddenly from out of nowhere, an enormous, silent triangular-shaped object passed overhead at a sight angle, squarely in our line of sight."

They managed to capture the images of the object on their cameras "as well as numerous smaller lights scurrying in every direction."

After working with Dorothy for nearly eight years, Guttilla became convinced "there's no single explanation for what she has captured on film...Her encounters embrace elements of multiple phenomena, including structured objects, physical transport, time travel, intelligent and interactive entities and, in Dorothy's words, 'beings of light'. It's precisely this mixed and varied blend of activity that ought to alert researchers that something of singular important is taking place."

Ultraterrestrial Contact: A Paranormal Investigator's
Explorations into the Hidden Abduction Epidemic
PHILIP J. IMBROGNO
(2010, Llewellyn)

During his many decades investigating UFO events, Philip Imbrogno found the most bizarre occurrences he encountered to be those involving witnesses who claimed they had contact with beings from another world. In the early years, starting in the 1970s, he "shied away from the majority of these contact cases because they appeared to be more psychological than physical representations of the UFO experience." By the mid-1980s, he had changed his mind and began to view contact cases, no matter how bizarre, as being worth taking seriously.

"I believe every close encounter is purposeful, not accidental," writes Imgrogno. "My analysis has me convinced that many cases of this type are types of pre-contact experience. At times, the contact may be so subtle that the person involved may not immediately identify it as such. Although not everyone who has a close encounter claims communication with an alien intelligence, a considerable number of witnesses report feeling a connection that leads to various types of contact with nonhuman intelligence."

Imbrogno believes the UFO and abduction phenomenon "possibly involve beings from several different origins," one being the djinn. Djinn are Islamic demons, also known as genies, which reportedly can shapeshift and control human minds. They are said to have existed on this planet before humans ever evolved and remain mostly hidden from us because they may be interdimensional.

"We must remember that whoever or whatever we're dealing with is an intelligent race of beings that exist in the multiverse alongside us," writes Imbrogno. "The djinn play an important part in the contact phenomenon and paranormal manifestations."

313

Other types of beings that Imbrogno believes are associated with contact experiences are the 'Nordics', tall blondes with light skin and blue or green eyes, who "seem to be more angelic in nature." Other types of more menacing alien visitors are the insect-like 'Reptilians', and, of course, the short, big-eyed 'grays'. From 259 contact cases in his investigative files, Imbrogno found the following breakdown in categories of alien abductors described by witnesses and abductees: 44% were tall grays, 44% were reptilian, 9% were short grays, while the remainder were shadow beings, perhaps the djinn.

As a further breakdown of statistics in his contact case files the author notes how among 115 abductions involving males, 19% "showed some psychic ability or had a psychic experience with a history of contact since childhood." Among his 152 cases involving women, 83% had type B negative blood, 67% displayed some psychic abilities, and 92% had a previous contact experience at a young age.

Walking Among Us: The Alien Plan to Control Humanity
DAVID M. JACOBS
(2015, Red Wheel/Weiser)

Temple University associate professor of history David Jacobs, Ph.D., authored two previous books on alien abduction, *Secret Life* and *The Threat*. The first book explored what happens during alien abductions, the second book focused on the offspring of humans and our alien visitors, the 'hybrids' who were being trained on how to act and appear more human so they can integrate into human cultures. In this third book of the series, *Walking Among Us*, Jacobs describes what he calls The Change, an agenda of planetary acquisition by the aliens that is occurring as a result of this hybrid integration that is being facilitated by abductees.

Over the past few decades, Jacobs investigated 1,150 abduction events, using hypnotic regression of abductees, and for this latest book he culled out the testimony of 14 abductees which led him to what he confesses sound like "seemingly ridiculous conclusions." In Jacob's view, a new and alarming pattern had emerged in the accounts characterized by the 14 abductees in which "they were having complex public interactions with late-adolescent and young-adult hybrids who were all focused on one goal—assimilating into human society."

The 14 abductees selected by Jacobs for profiling all "demonstrate new and chilling aspects of the alien agenda." These 9 women and 5 men range in age from a 1942 birthdate to a 1986 birthdate; their occupations range from company owners and medical personnel to a retired engineer and a retired school teacher. Each risked their reputation and livelihood by relating their experience to Jacobs, so he gives them pseudonyms in this book. All of them underwent hypnotic regression with Jacobs because in his experience, "abduction accounts remembered without the benefit of competent hypnosis are most often untrustworthy, no matter how much abductees are invested in their memories' truthfulness and accuracy."

Jacobs says he waited until "multiple descriptions of the same phenomena" emerged from the transcripts of these regression sessions to delineate patterns and form conclusions, remaining skeptical until "other abductees without knowledge of the previous testimony report the same thing."

What these 14 abductees reported were consistent in their details. They were being abducted, again and again, to act as teachers for these alien-human hybrids and for another category that Jacobs has added, the 'hubrids', who are the most advanced degree of hybrids based on their heightened neurological development. The aliens who are doing the abductions and overseeing the hybrid integration program are these types: Insectalins, who are praying-mantis-like; Small Grays, short in stature with large hairless heads; Tall Grays, taller than the short ones and with different functions in the group; Reptalin Hybrids, with snake-like heads and scaly skin; and the seven stages of Humanoid Hybrids.

Abductees report (and Jacobs describes in anecdotes) how they are engaged against their will (because they are being mind-controlled) in teaching the hybrids all aspects of how to be human and blend in with human society. Hybrids are taught what to say or do and how to act in polite company, how to dress appropriately, how to furnish their homes, how to express emotions, how to use computers, smart phones, and televisions, how to play sports, drive vehicles, and go shopping.

Eventually, once the global integration and takeover is complete, aliens will control the planet through their hybrid colonists. It's a non-violent, stealthy takeover and Jacobs speculates this is not the first time that planetary lifeforms have been coopted in this way. The aliens seem to possess "previous knowledge of how to 'capture' a planet." They are here among us now, says Jacobs, and "there is apparently there is little that can be done to stop the inexorable takeover."

―――――――――――――――

Confession: Our Hidden Alien Encounters Revealed
ROBERT HASTINGS & BOB JACOBS
(2019, Self-Published)

For decades these two authors have been at the forefront of research into the attraction UFOs seem to have for nuclear weapons sites and military installations, and in this book, for the first time, they reveal something they have kept secret from the public about a possible origin for their fixation—each man believes he has interacted with, or been abducted by, non-human intelligent entities, not once but multiple times.

Hastings writes, "I do not know whether these entities are from other worlds in our universe/multiverse, or from another dimension of reality, but I do know that my experiences were physically real, not psychological fantasies, and sometimes involved other hapless humans who were with me at the time." These experiences began for Hastings in early childhood, in 1952, when he remembers being abducted by two gray aliens at the rural farmhouse where he lived with his parents. He continued to have similar encounters with these entities beyond the year 2000.

For Jacobs, a UFO sighting he had in 1964, while a U.S. Air Force officer, became his introduction to the phenomenon. "My involvement with abduction/contact must date from {that} dramatic experience," writes Jacobs. His alien-related visitation and abduction experiences were similar to what Hastings describes.

What brought these two men together was a shared consuming interest—perhaps a fixation—with investigating UFO sightings involving military personnel and nuclear weapons. Both men felt like they were on a mission and had the nagging sense of being tasked with publicizing this aspect of the phenomenon. They had known each other for years but only began working together in 2012, Jacobs videorecording interviews that Hastings conducted with Air Force veterans who had UFO stories to tell. After the last interview, Hastings revealed some of his abduction experiences and a pattern of awakening at 4:44 am from abductions and disturbing dreams. To the amazement of Hastings, Jacobs responded by saying, "I always wake up at 3:33 am after my abduction nightmares."

These 4:44 and 3:33 times coinciding with alien-related experiences or dreams occur regularly and are what the authors refer to as the 'Triple-Digit Thingy'. They suspect that the TDT's are integral to their experiences in some way. Perhaps looking at the clock at these certain times triggers a hypnotic suggestion to forget details of what would otherwise be traumatic events for them.

Curious about how common these clock coincidences might be, Jacobs used a speaking appearance in Britain as an opportunity to ask the crowd if the TDT's meant anything to any of them. "When I finished, seven or eight folks gathered around and confessed that they had disturbing dreams, and were awakened at one of those times. One of them, Robert Hulse, said outright that he was an abductee."

Air Force Captain Robert Salas, an ICBM launch officer who was involved in an incident in 1967, at Malmstrom Air Force Base in Montana, during which a UFO triggered a missile shutdown, "shocked many of his former military colleagues {in 2013} by openly admitting that he had subsequently had apparent alien abduction experiences as well." Hastings and Jacobs identify several other former Air Force officers who have gone public with similar account of seeing UFOs around nuclear sites and in the aftermath, being subjected to alien abductions. Because of the stigma attached to going public with these stories and the veil of secrecy that continues to conceal many witnesses, the authors suspect there are countless more similar witness/abductees who might otherwise come forward.

Harvest: The True Story of Alien Abduction
G.L. DAVIES
(2020, Sixth Books)

Though his previous books, most notably *A Most Haunted House*, dealt with paranormal themes, British author G.L. Davies had never before tackled the subject of alien abduction until he met a woman he calls Susan, a twenty-something university student in West Wales, a chain-smoking vegan, who described for him her terrifying abduction ordeal that had lasted several years.

In a series of interview sessions with Davies, Susan described how "I have witnessed and experienced experimentation and unimaginable pain and terror at the hands of a race that are not human...I want women like me to know that they are not safe."

Susan's ordeal began in 2009, when she attended a sleep-over party with three female friends at a country farmhouse. While in a bathroom during the night the power in the farmhouse went out and she was suddenly bathed in a bright white light coming in through the skylight. The light disappeared and the power came back on. Later that night, while asleep with her friend's dog, Lennie, in a guest room in the barn, she was awakened by the sound of a small slender figure moving around just as the room filled with bright light streaming in through a skylight. The dog Lennie growled and attacked the slender figure, but there was a blue flash and the dog howled in pain and crumpled onto the floor. When Susan awoke four hours later, she had a bloody nose and Lennie was gone, never to be seen again.

A series of equally unsettling events occurred over the following weeks. Susan and a male friend were parked one night looking out over an estuary when a bright orange ball of light approached and hovered above them for a few seconds and then shot off at great speed. On subsequent nights Susan had vivid nightmares, or at least she thought they were nightmares, involving imagery of death and destruction. Meanwhile, her aunt's cat died mysteriously, and the aunt, who Susan was living with while attending the university, became deathly ill with cancer.

On another night, driving to her parent's home from work while talking to her father on the phone, her car radio began making loud screeching and clicking noises, which her father heard in the background. A few moments later headlights appeared behind her on the country road and her car stalled, at which point the two lights behind her rose up vertically and silently, before disappearing into the sky. All of these events left Susan feeling depressed and wondering if suicide would be her only option to escape the insect-like creatures and end their control over her.

The worst terror was yet to come! Once again, she was driving home at night when she had to brake quickly to avoid a fox sitting in the road. As she stared at the fox her car radio began screeching and clicking and her car was bathed in an intense red light. Soon she found herself walking naked through a woodland following the fox. She felt like she had been in a car crash or that she was ghostlike and dead. She encountered an older black lady, also naked, and the two of them walked together until they came across still more naked women, of all ages, being herded together towards a deep red glow on the horizon.

Like imagery from Dante's Inferno, Susan and the other women, numbering in the dozens, encountered increasingly horrendous scenes that caused them to panic and shout and scream and cry. When women tried to run away, a bright red light with two enormous metal wings, resembling an owl, would appear overhead and herd them back into the group while dispersing a spray over them. They were herded together shepherded by the owl lights into a vast expanse, like a cavern, each woman packed together chest to back and urinating and defecating and retching on each other like cattle being led to slaughter. The mechanical owls sprayed them with a mist that could have been a disinfectant.

As the women walked in single file the pregnant ones were milked like cows by tubes resembling tendrils, while other women were inseminated by the erect penises of half-men half-machines. Susan and some younger women had tubes inserted in their genitals and needles into their necks. Older women past childbearing age were being torn apart and harvested for their body parts and body fluids. At the end of these procedures, those women who were still alive were showered with another mist and the ordeal was over.

When Susan woke up, she was lying naked in a field beside her car. She looked at her watch; only three minutes had passed since she had seen the fox sitting in the roadway. She felt "a vicious pain behind my right eye. They had let me go…for now."

In Susan's last email to Davies, in December 2018, she said goodbye because she was embarked "on my farewell tour." Davies kept his promise to her that he would publish this book to spread her message, a dire warning that the aliens are here to exploit us, to harvest us, just like we abuse and harvest animals.

The Alien Agendas: A Speculative Analysis of Those Visiting Earth
RICHARD DOLAN
(2020, Independent)

Historian Richard Dolan confesses up front that this book is "an unapologetic speculative analysis" asking who are the alien visitors and why are they here. "From the evidence I will present, there appear to be multiple groups {of extraterrestrial visitors} and, most likely, multiple agendas."

Dolan begins his speculations by referencing the ideas of one of his deceased friends, Dr. Colleen Clements, who had been a professor at the Rochester Institute of Technology, and up until she died in 2011, had been writing about humans being a hybrid race enhanced by extraterrestrial visitors about 40,000 years ago. This genetic experiment involved changes in a gene responsible for the development and size of the human brain. This gene alteration has not been found in our distant relatives, the Neanderthals and the Denisovans, which may explain why humans experienced huge strides in intelligence and creativity but our relatives did not. It might also explain why so many ancient cultures credit Sky Gods with giving humans the tools to create civilization.

Observes Dolan: "If extraterrestrials manipulated our genetics some 40,000-plus years ago, what is the likelihood that some of the humans at the time were *taken*? Not merely temporary, as we understand modern day abductions, but permanently?"

As to why we today seem to experiences so many more UFO sightings and abductions than ever before, Dolan suspects "that it has been *our own development* that is the main reason…they came in larger numbers once we gave them a reason to." This escalating interest may also be part of a long-term planning operation "under the control of an advanced artificially intelligent algorithm…a living machine of some sort."

What intrigues Dolan is that among all of the statistics accumulated over the decades showing descriptions of alien abductors, 45% of these reports by abductees claimed to have encountered human looking beings, "roughly the same percentage also reported having seen short gray aliens." These surveys indicate the following, by order of most reported appearance: human, short gray, tall gray, hybrid, insectoid, reptilian," and a smattering of other types.

Why are almost half of all reported alien abductors human in appearance? The author suggests after our species was genetically enhanced in the distant past, "some of our ancestors were taken and adopted by whomever was visiting," and some of these enhanced humans were returned to Earth to participate in more kidnappings.

While witness reports seem to demonstrate there are at least five different groups of alien visitors, it seems "there is also some amount of collusion going on among these various alien groups," writes Dolan. "They're here because of us, and especially because of humanity's current state of development."

The Uninvited: An Expose of the Alien Abduction Phenomenon
NICK POPE
(2020, Lume Books)

When he began his involvement with the UFO phenomenon, Nick Pope found himself highly skeptical of alien abduction stories. Pope spent three years (1991-94) investigating UFO reports for the British Ministry of Defense. Since that period, he has spent much of his career continuing his UFO investigations as a private citizen and book author. During that time, his views on abductions gradually changed until he became convinced the phenomenon has a grounding in our physical reality.

In this book he covers with short descriptions the experiences of many of the most well-known contactees—George Adamski, George Van Tassell, Daniel Fry, Billy Meier, etc.—showing common threads in their stories, and then he does the same with many well-known abductees—Betty and Barney Hill, Travis Walton, Betty Andreasson, etc. He devotes a chapter to summarizing nearly a dozen less known abduction cases from Britain.

One difference he notes between U.S. and British abduction reports is that the 'greys' as abductors are rare in Britain, where most abductors are described as human or Nordic in appearance. British abductees were also far less willing to go public with their stories than their American counterparts. Otherwise, the alien abductions which are reported throughout the world "are surprisingly similar in structure," with almost identical details being reported.

From all of the previous abduction reports and his own personal interviews with abductees, Pope concludes that most abduction experiences began in a person's childhood, even if they don't remember the encounter. "I am convinced that those who have such encounters have a relationship of some sort with these *other* intelligences. They are not casually picked out and then discarded, but selected, nurtured, and matured."

Why is this happening? Pope lists the entire range of theories—he calls them the 'usual suspects'—proposed to explain the origins of the abduction phenomenon and then subjects each to logical analysis. He covers birth trauma, near death and out of body experiences, hoaxes, false memory syndrome, hypnogogic and hypnopompic sleep disorders, temporal lobe lability, electromagnetic effects, sleep paralysis, projections from the collection unconscious, mass hysteria, child sex abuse and satanic ritual, government research and mind control, time travelers, and the shared earth theory (that a mostly invisible high intelligence shares our terrestrial space.)

Pope believes the abduction phenomenon has an extraterrestrial explanation. He suspects that humans are being treated like guinea pigs by extraterrestrials in much the same way as humans treat animals as guinea pigs in experiments 'for the higher good' of finding cures for diseases. We are simply being treated by Higher Intelligence as we treat the so-called Lower Intelligences of the animal kingdom. He proposes that extraterrestrial visitors see the human species as possessing psychopathic and sociopathic tendencies—our blood lust for killing each other and animals—which makes us a threat to ourselves and to other intelligence in the universe.

Our rapid technological advances combined with our "capacity for extreme violence may have convinced them that some action was needed." He notes how most abductees consider their experience to have been personally transformative, as they changed their attitudes and behaviors to become more compassionate and caring, less ego-oriented, and more concerned about the health of the environment and everyone on the planet.

Says Pope: "I believe that the abduction phenomenon could be a response to *our* behaviour, and that it might represent a gradual attempt to effect subtle changes in humans. It is possible that the extraterrestrials are attempting to civilise us...The alien abduction phenomenon may be an attempt to change the course of human evolution."

Making Contact: Preparing for the New Realities of Extraterrestrial Existence
ALAN STEINFELD
(2021, St. Martin's Essentials)

This collection of speculative essays assembled by Alan Steinfeld, host of the New York City cable show *New Realities,* features a lineup of contributors: Nick Pope, Grant Cameron, Dr. J.J. Hurtak, Dr. Desiree Hurtak, Linda Moulton Howe, Dr. John Mack, Whitley Strieber, Henrietta Weekes, Darryl Anka, Mary Rodwell, and Caroline

Cory. Their contributions cumulatively represent a mixture of UFO visitation and abductee and contactee themes and some of the material, such as what Mack and Strieber
provide, represents nothing that hasn't already been covered in their previous published
works.

To open the book Steinfeld tells readers: "right off I have to say none of this will
make any sense until there is a suspension of the logics of linear mechanistic view of
reality." He goes on to urge that we embrace other ways of knowing beyond our logical
minds if we want to gain comprehension of this phenomenon and what it teaches us.
Steinfeld says he had his own alien encounter and abduction experience in 1987, which
left him obsessed with the subject.

From having served in the British government for several decades, seeing how
government agencies function from the inside, Nick Pope doesn't believe that the British
or U.S. government is currently engaged in a conspiracy to hide the truth about alien
visitation. He believes the reason for the cloak of secrecy that governments have placed
around the phenomenon relates to their "interest in derivable technologies (irrespective
of the true nature of the phenomenon)"…a desire to obtain and use whatever new technologies can be gleaned from the phenomenon. To achieve this goal the U.S. military
now routinely contracts out UFO-related research to corporations, a move which helps
to preserve secrecy by making congressional oversight more difficult, and by limiting
public access to documents under the Freedom of Information Act.

Canadian Grant Cameron's approach emphasizes the role of human consciousness in the UFO phenomenon. He presents what he calls his 'Theory of Wow' to offer an
explanation for the motives behind the phenomenon. Whoever and whatever animates
it, "all they are doing is trying to get us to say 'wow' to realize we are not alone." The
entire phenomenon is intended to transform human consciousness. "They are giving
us an indirect approach because they want us to think. They want us to reach a level of
higher consciousness on our own."

Documentary film maker and journalist Linda Moulton Howe describes being a
ten-year-old in Idaho and having the realization one evening that "the moon is hollow
and it's watching us." Flashforward to May 2016, and when she was interviewing retired
U.S. naval engineer William Tompkins, he confirmed her childhood lunar revelation by
explaining how the moon is a hollow station built by an alien race—just one of many
competing alien civilizations—and then the moon was towed and parked in Earth orbit. Furthermore, Tompkins told her, "World War II was an extraterrestrial war fought
through human bodies." Howe devotes the rest of her book section to describing her

interactions with other alleged former government employees who revealed details of underground alien bases on Earth where genetic harvesting and cloning of humans occurs, conducted by seven-foot tall blonde haired and blue-eyed Nordic type aliens and eight-feet-tall reptilians.

"According to government whistleblowers," writes Howe, "humans have provided centuries of physical labor in the surface matter world of Earth to mine gold and other precious metals and jewels. Humans were also used to help build pyramids, ziggurats, and temples without knowing the structures were actually communication and energy 'machines' for the alien power brokers. The non-humans also harvest genetic material from the slave-humans' strong bodies, minds, and souls to create clones that can be distributed for interstellar trade throughout the Milky Way galaxy and beyond—perhaps even for trade in different timelines and dimensions."

Australian UFO contactee regression therapist Mary Rodwell refers to the "more than 3,000 individuals and their families" she has worked with who "feel they have had some sort of 'anomalous' paranormal experience" as having provided her accounts that helped shape her views on "awakening to our cosmic heritage." She believes that each successive generation she has worked with show a "heightened dimensional attunement" indicating new evolutionary capabilities being activated, resulting in savant-like children known variously as 'Indigos' or 'Children of Light' who are products of genetic modification occurring right now in utero. She quotes many of her clients talking in terms of a new human emerging, 'star seeds' awakening to our interdimensional soul selves, and Rodwell concludes that our 'cosmic cousins' are providing us with interdimensional support in pursuit of a cosmic agenda "preparing the human race for a global shift" as part of our own unique planetary awakening process.

SECTION FOUR

Debunkers and Skeptics. . .

Are They Really Skunks at the UFO Picnic?

What may have been the world's first military investigation of UFOs occurred in Japan, on September 24, 1235, when the warlord General Yoritsume, encamped with his army, observed a series of lights circling in the night sky. Yoritsume ordered the learned members of his entourage to study the phenomenon and report back to him. They came to a consensus that the effect was due to "the wind making the stars sway." UFO enthusiasts cite this conclusion to illustrate how silly debunkers can be, while debunkers use the incident as evidence that even in the Dark Ages, wise observers knew a natural phenomenon when they saw it, even if they got the astronomy all wrong.

Using 'Occams Razor' to reduce interpretations of data down to the simplest natural explanation, skeptics and debunkers analyze, contradict, and quite often resort to ridicule in making their point. But when they transform their belief that extraterrestrial visitation is improbable into a conviction that it is impossible, they are no longer being scientific. What often most separates UFO believers from debunkers is their differing perception of human nature. UFO advocates tend to regard other human beings generally as observant and truthful; debunkers try to prove that human beings make mistakes and tell lies. Are the proponents simply too naive and the debunkers too distrustful?

A mantra often repeated as gospel by self-styled debunkers contends that no credible UFO sightings ever leave behind any convincing physical evidence which can stand up to scrutiny. Veteran UFO debunker and aerospace magazine journalist Philip J. Klass once insisted to me: "in all of my years examining UFO claims, there hasn't been a single piece of credible physical evidence." I wish Klass had lived long enough so he could admit to being proven wrong, once faced with that incontrovertible evidence, though I suspect that in his case, rather than a confession, he would have invoked that old when my-back-is-against-the-wall declaration, *I refuse to believe it, even it's true.*

Anomalous Artifacts Fall from the Sky

During a 1998 dinner with Jacques Vallée and his wife, Janine, at an Italian restaurant a few blocks from their home in downtown San Francisco, Jacques described to me a UFO incident he had heard about involving a rain of mysterious molten metal outside a town in Iowa. He suggested that I use the resources at my disposal, as a Roving Editor of *Reader's Digest*, to investigate the incident by interviewing those witnesses who were still alive.

You may be familiar with Vallée, or have read some of his many books. At the very least, you may have seen the movie *Close Encounters of the Third Kind*, in which the French scientist (played by Francois Truffaut) at the center of the film's narrative, was written by Steven Spielberg using Vallée as a character model. Born in France, Vallée received mathematics and astrophysics degrees before traveling to the U.S. to work as an astronomer at the University of Texas, where he is credited with developing the first computer-based map of Mars under a NASA contract. He later received a PhD in computer science from Northwestern University and worked at SRI International, where he helped direct building the world's first network-based computer information center, which became the precursor for the evolution of the Internet.

Vallée remains, in my opinion, the most intellectual and original thinker among scientists to ever to be involved with the field of anomalous aerial phenomena and the prospect of alien visitation. He had an interest in this subject dating from childhood, after seeing an unidentified flying object over his home in France. Later in the 1960s, while on the staff of the French Space Committee, he witnessed the destruction of tracking tapes of an unidentified object that French scientists couldn't explain.

Our paths had crossed in 1979, when I had serialized Jacque's book *Messengers of Deception: UFO Contacts and Cults*, in the magazine I co-edited, *Second Look*. This book charted, as had an earlier book, *Passport to Magonia: From Folklore to Flying Saucers*, his evolution in thinking about the phenomenon, going from validating aspects of the extraterrestrial visitation hypothesis, to arguing that the phenomenon was much more complex, being made up of possible multidimensional origins, and paranormal, cult and religious group components that defied conventional wisdom. Some UFO believers and skeptics alike began to view him as an outlier at the fringes of mainstream belief systems, exactly the sort of person I could identify with and respect.

What Vallée told me over dinner that night was intriguing and I knew it had to be investigated more thoroughly. At the time, he was advising a scientific panel funded by the billionaire philanthropist, Laurence Rockefeller, who had a longstanding interest in the UFO subject. The scientific panel focused on 10 cases where physical evidence of some sort had been found in the aftermath of sightings. Coincidentally, at the time, Rockefeller sat on the Board of *Reader's Digest*, though as one of the magazine's editors I had never met him.

Here is the story pieced together from interviews I conducted with surviving witnesses and from a report made by the Rockefeller Science Panel that investigated this and other sightings that left behind evidence.

On a cold December night in 1977, Mike and Criss Moore, both 24 years old, were driving to visit Mike's mother outside Council Bluff, Iowa, when they spotted a bright red ball glowing, about a half-mile away. Mike, an auto dealership employee, thought it might be a plane landing, but the angle of its descent seemed too steep and, unlike aircraft landing lights, the light they saw was a large, intense steady red glow. Mike and Criss, a legal secretary, told investigators that "it was a big round thing hovering in the sky below the tree tops. It was hovering. It wasn't moving." They saw red lights around the perimeter of the object, blinking in sequence.

Three other witnesses closer to the glowing light saw it when it was about 500 to 600 feet in the air, seeming to be hovering, before it or something detaching from it began to fall straight down and crash in the vicinity of Big Lake Park, at the northern city limits. All five witnesses heard a loud explosion, accompanied by a brilliant flash and flames shooting into the air. (Altogether, 11 witnesses to the incident would eventually be found).

Within minutes after the 7:45 p.m. sighting, other witnesses that included a Council Bluffs policeman had converged on the impact site to behold a bizarre scene. One side of a pond levee glowed reddish-orange from a mass of molten metal, running and boiling over the frozen ground like volcanic lava. Alerted by 911 calls, Council Bluffs Assistant Fire Chief Jack Moore, Mike's father, arrived within 15 minutes to find the strange metal mass still smoldering, too hot to touch. "It was a big puddle of metal about four inches thick, bubbling and red," Jack Moore told me when I interviewed him. "I talked to three of the eyewitnesses and could find no evidence they made anything up."

Moore took a section of the cooled metal back to his office at the fire department. "You can't break it," he told a local newspaper. "You can't bend it. I know it's metal, but it's got me beat."

What everyone at the scene found particularly puzzling was that no crater, only a two-to-three-inch ground indentation, had been created where the molten metal fell. It was almost as if the metallic object, whatever it was, had been weightless when it hit the ground. Not only that, but the surrounding air temperature at the time was 32 degrees and the surface of the impact site was frozen to a depth of at least four inches, yet no ice had formed or gotten sprayed about by the impact of this hot mass of metal. It defied common sense.

Chief Moore phoned local astronomer Robert Allen and the following morning, Allen went to the site, took photos, and gathered samples from the largest 4 foot by 6-foot-wide section of metal, a solidified puddle about four inches thick. Metallic spherules were scattered about in a wide radius. Measurements taken by Allen indicated "the object was traveling from the southwest to the northeast." His Geiger counter didn't detect any radiation, nor did later analysis find any evidence of thermite, used in welding and smelting to create an incendiary reaction, a burst of high heat necessary to create what witnesses saw, if indeed the effect had been human-made.

Allen sent several samples of the metal for detailed analysis by metallurgists at Iowa State University and to the U.S. Air Force's Foreign Technology Division at Wright-Patterson Air Force Base in Ohio. He also queried the Council Bluff airport, which had no records of any aircraft in the vicinity of the impact site that night. Analyzed samples turned out to be composed of iron and small amounts of nickel and chromium, making it a carbon steel, according to Robert S. Hansen, Director of the Ames Laboratory at Iowa State. "The analytical results make it highly unlikely that the material is of meteoric origin," Hansen reported. "It is also unlikely that the sample represents debris from man-made space hardware."

In a March 7, 1978 letter to astronomer Allen, Colonel Charles Senn, on behalf of the Secretary of the Air Force, described military scientists as being baffled by the metal residue and the circumstances of its appearance. They were certain the debris couldn't have been space hardware, if only because "reentering spacecraft debris does not impact the earth's surface in a molten state." In addition, "there are no structural indications in any of the debris samples," making it unlikely it could be space debris.

Could the incident be an expensive hoax? Allen canvassed local foundry and pipe companies and found only one facility with the equipment necessary to produce molten metal, but it had not been operating on the night of the incident. Furthermore, the equipment needed, the logistics required for preparation (the melting point of the metal was about 2400 degrees, necessitating a huge brick oven and air transport), and the expense involved, would seem too elaborate for a hoax to have been perpetrated.

The only remaining 'logical explanation' might involve the location of Council Bluffs, across the Missouri River from Omaha, Neb. Outside Omaha is Offutt Air Force Base, for decades the headquarters of the U.S. Strategic Command. Could an Air Force plane flying over Council Bluffs have dumped molten metal cargo in a series of accidents, or as planned disposals? My inquiries with Offutt Air Force base public information personnel produced nothing but denials.

This mystery deepened when two more molten metal crash incidents occurred on the streets of Council Bluffs, seven months later, in July 1978. The second incident on July 5, happened one mile southwest of the first December event, with molten metal impacting a storm sewer grating. The third fall of molten metal, on July 10, impacted a parking lot across from a public school, one mile south of the second site. Each of these two July incidents happened at night, starting as a fireball in the sky seen by witnesses who called police and the fire department. Each involved a mass of splattered molten metal, about three feet in diameter and three inches thick. If he were still alive, Charles Fort might wonder if an inter-dimensional portal had opened over Council Bluffs, periodically releasing foundry slag being slung about by a Cosmic Trickster. To my knowledge none of the residue from the last two incidents received analytical testing. One noted UFO investigator cautioned me that it wouldn't be the first time that spurious material turned up nearby, after a UFO event, designed to cast doubts on the veracity of the initial sighting.

Allen described the first of the three incidents he investigated, involving the largest puddle of metal, as the most perplexing experience of his life. "No one can explain how more than a thousand pounds of molten metal could have been dropped from such a height creating a fireball," Allen told me. If what happened was due to some strange atmospheric phenomenon not yet documented by science, that reason alone makes it worthy of further study. If it was due to an Air Force series of accidents over a large city, the public safety issue alone renders it worthy of study. My initial skepticism about this incident being possibly extraterrestrial in origin eventually dissolved into bafflement when no rational alternative explanation could be identified by anyone.

The Rockefeller Science Panel investigators in their 1998 report found no evidence of a hoax involving the metal being poured on the ground by humans, no evidence that the metal fell from an aircraft flying overhead, no evidence that it was a meteorite impact, nor any evidence that it was space debris falling to Earth. The fact that the metal mass seemed to be some sort of 'slag' and not of an exotic composition "cannot be used to negate the theory that an advanced technology of unknown origin may have generated the samples," concluded the panel's analysis. Slag could be a mundane by-product, much like auto exhaust, of an unknown yet highly advanced power generation source.

Vallée found this incident fascinating precisely because the physical traces left behind seemed so ordinary. "Both the extraterrestrial visitation believers and the skeptics lose interest when a case leaves residue which seems common," Vallée explained. "Believers are looking for exotic materials, while skeptics usually conclude anything ordinary must be a hoax. This is where investigations should begin, not end."

A more technologically sophisticated and detailed analysis of the Council Bluffs metal debris was conducted and published in a January 2022 edition of the science journal, *Progress in Aerospace Sciences*, co-authored by Vallée and three others—Professor Garry P. Nolan of Stanford University, Larry G. Lemke formerly of the NASA Ames Research Center, and Sizun Jiang, a Stanford research associate. Using materials analysis technology not available to earlier researchers, this team studied the isotopic ratios in the main components of the metal samples, which had been retained over the years by Robert Allen. What they discovered at the Stanford lab was puzzling.

"We did observe significant differences in the homogeneity of the elements," the research team wrote, "it might be reasonable to conclude that the sample was inhomogeneous (incompletely mixed) across its totality for reasons yet to be determined." There was no evidence the metal had been engineered or designed, but also no evidence that it had formed naturally. If it had been dropped by an aerial vehicle, as witnesses at the time claimed, "could liquid metal be part of some propulsion or power generation system?" It certainly wouldn't be any aerial generation system presently known to humankind.

"Should the Council Bluffs material be determined to be engineered for a function we don'ts currently understand, it remains that our physics are as yet insufficient to explain the purpose of such a material," the four researchers concluded. "The Council Bluffs case is one of many—the last several decades has recorded numerous cases wherein materials were claimed to be dropped from unknown aerial objects."

Another UFO residue study was reportedly undertaken as part of a Pentagon project, the Advanced Aerospace Threat Identification Program, which investigated reports of UFOs, mostly collected from military personnel eyewitness accounts. When this program got unmasked in a December 16, 2017, *New York Times* article, it was reported that Bigelow Aerospace, hired as the contractor for the program, "modified buildings in Las Vegas for the storage of metal alloys and other materials that Mr. Elizondo {Luis Elizondo, a military intelligence official heading up the program}and program contractors, claimed had been recovered from unidentified aerial phenomena."

Integral to the analysis of these metals and other physical evidence collected after UFO incidents was the scientist mentioned earlier in the Council Bluffs case analysis, microbiologist Garry Nolan, Ph.D., a Professor of Pathology at Stanford University, the holder of 40 US patents, author of 300 research articles, and founder of eight biotech companies, making him one of the most accomplished scientists to ever study the UFO phenomenon. Nolan's involvement analyzing evidence from UFO events began when representatives of the CIA and aeronautics corporations showed up in his office asking for his help in doing blood analysis of persons, including military pilots, who had gotten too close to unidentified aerial phenomena. Once Nolan got immersed in the data, he became puzzled and disturbed by what he found. "You didn't have to be an MD to see that there was a problem," Nolan told a reporter, in December 2021. "Some of their brains were horribly, horribly damaged."

Among the anomalous brain effects—"a smorgasbord of symptoms" as Nolan put it—appearing in the MRIs of about 100 patients, was scarring from an over-connection of neurons in a part of the brain between the head of the caudate and the putamen, an area which is critical to various higher neurological functions. This condition is very rare among humans, but in Nolan's patients this density in the brain had been increased by up to 15 times normal. Up to one-quarter of the patients died of their injuries. One of the patients exposed to electromagnetic frequencies that wreaked havoc on his brain had worked at Skinwalker Ranch in Utah. The only human-made device that Nolan could imagine might cause these symptoms would be from when "you're standing next to an electric transformer that's emitting so much energy that you're basically burned inside your body."

Along with research on the brains of UFO witnesses, Nolan got involved with analyzing the metallic fragments that had been ejected from alleged UFOs, using mass spectrometry instruments he had developed. He worked with a dozen metallic samples collected from different sites and several proved to be anomalous. "Everywhere you look in the metal, the composition is different, which is odd," Nolan explained to Vice.com, in that December 2021 interview. "They're all hodgepodge mixtures. One of the materials from the so-called Ubatuba event {an unidentified aerial phenomena sighting in Brazil} has extraordinarily altered isotope ratios of magnesium. The problem is there's no good reason humans have for altering the isotope ratios of a simple metal like magnesium." Nolan pointed out that not only would such an alteration of isotopes be expensive, he can't imagine why humans would even try it.

Professor Nolan continued: "In almost every case, these {alleged UFO metals} are the leftovers of some sort of process that these objects spit out. So you go look at the cases where molten metal falls from these objects, why would 30 pounds of a molten metal fall from a flying object? One hypothesis would be that the material it offloads is part of the mechanism the object uses for moving around, and when things get out of whack, the object has to offload it. It just drops this stuff to the ground, kind of like the exhaust. Are the altered {isotope} ratios the result of the propulsion mechanism? The data is there…the explanation is not."

In a YouTube video, when asked why agencies of government aren't investigating these metal artifacts, Nolan speculated: "Maybe the stuff we have, someone in government is laughing that we're wasting our time on exhaust, when we {government} have the engine."

When Human Bodies Become the UFO Evidence

After dining together at a truck stop restaurant in New Caney, Texas, about 20 miles north of Houston, 52-year-old Betty Cash was driving home to nearby Dayton, accompanied by her friend, 57-year-old Vickie Landrum, and Landrum's grandson, six-year-old Colby. Between 9 and 9:30 p.m. on December 29, 1980, as Cash drove her two-door Oldsmobile Cutlass along a deserted rural highway, through a pine forest, Colby noticed an unusual red glow in the sky up ahead.

"What's that, Grandma?" Colby blurted out.

Neither woman paid much attention at first to Colby's question, but as the glow grew in size, Colby became more insistent and the two women finally took notice. As they approached the light the two women speculated whether it was a searchlight, or a plane on fire and about to crash. Without warning the brilliant light descended over the highway directly in front of them, spitting flames from its underside.

Landrum screamed for Cash to stop the car and she responded by jamming on her brakes. They came to a stop about 150 feet from the object and immediately they felt intense head inside their car. A loud whooshing sound assaulted their ears. Colby was terrified, tugging at Cash and Landrum's clothing, as he scrambled from the backseat and buried his head in his grandmother's lap.

Both women climbed out of the car, followed by Colby, and Landrum had to restrain Colby from running away. They stared in terror and awe at the blinding light, which lit up the piney woods like it had become daylight. By partially shielding their eyes with their hands, they could distinguish a metallic structure within the light, a structure that appeared as big as the water tower back in Dayton. The object was shaped like a diamond with a blunt top and it seemed to be struggling to ascend higher above the treetops, emitting blasts of fire as it did so. The continuous roaring or swooshing sound coming from it reminded the women of a shrill welding blowtorch, only much louder.

As they stared at the object, Landrum reassured Colby that "if you see a big man come down from it, it will be Jesus." Both women thought it was the end of the world and they were witnessing the Second Coming of Jesus Christ.

The object began to rise higher above the treetops, tilted itself onto one side, and moved slowly to the south. Though the object no longer made a roaring sound or spewed flames, it still glowed a bright red-orange. As the object departed, they heard the distinctive chop-chop sound of helicopters seeming in pursuit of the object. By Landrum and Cash's count, about 23 helicopters were swarming overhead, most of them a two-rotor craft. Cash saw markings on several helicopters that said United States Air Force, an insignia that Landrum said she didn't see.

On the drive home all three felt ill with headaches and nausea. Over the next few days their symptoms worsened, particularly in the case of Cash, who had spent the most time outside of the car closest to the object. All three experienced bouts of vomiting, diarrhea, and skin burns of the face and arms, Landrum lost her fingernails, and Cash began to lose large clumps of hair and continually felt dehydrated. Cash entered a Houston hospital on January 2, 1981, for treatment as a burn patient and spent the next four weeks under intensive care. Not long after this incident, Cash would be diagnosed with breast cancer and Landrum with cataracts. Cash had remained outside the vehicle longer than the other two, who had retreated inside out of fear.

As soon as she felt well enough, Cash joined Landrum in placing phone calls to the state's police agencies and military bases seeking information about the object and the helicopters. No one could or would provide an explanation. During a call to NASA's public affairs office in Houston, Cash was advised to contact John F. Schuessler, a NASA contractor and a Space Shuttle project manager, who had a longtime interest in the UFO phenomenon. Schuessler and NASA physicist Alan Holt paid the witnesses a visit on February 28, 1981, interviewed Landrum and her grandson, and visited the encounter site on FM 1485 (a Farm-to-Market Road). Both men examined and photographed damage to the road surface and the burn marks on surrounding pine trees.

"Where the object came down, the highway's yellow line wiggled from the melting of a heat blast," Schuessler told me in an interview, years later. "A roughly 20-foot circle of the road surface appeared to have melted and then resolidified. It was in stark contrast to the rest of the highway, which was old and cracked. On the trees, about 20 feet up, there were blackened areas facing the road."

Other witnesses to the UFO event eventually came forward. Five witnesses in four separate locations around the Dayton area had observed a large bright unidentifiable object in the sky on the same night and around the same time as the Cash/Landrum sighting. Schuessler also tracked down another eight witnesses, including a Dayton police officer and his wife, who had seen a swarm of mysterious helicopters in the air that evening. When shown photos of helicopters in the military arsenal, CH-47 Chinooks were identified by the two women as the type of helicopter seen that night.

With legal assistance from CAUS (Citizens Against UFO Secrecy) the two women sued the federal government over their injuries, but in 1986 the lawsuit was dismissed by a U.S. District Court judge based on insufficient evidence to prove the object had been owned by the U.S. government. Meanwhile, Cash moved to Birmingham, Alabama, to live with her mother. An Alabama physician who treated her, Dr. Bryan McClelland, became convinced she had been exposed to high levels of radiation. "The illness that she suffered after her exposure was an absolute classic radiation injury in which she lost skin, lost hair on the exposure side, and had diarrhea and vomiting. I don't think she made it up, nor could she have made it up," he told me.

Schuessler too, firmly believes she encountered a flying object "which emitted radiation that caused her and the others life threatening damage. I don't know what it was. It flew like nothing I have ever seen or heard of before in my more than four decades of work in the U.S. manned space program." A Stanford University physicist familiar with this case, Professor Peter Sturrock, explained to me how he suspects it might have "origins in secret military activities." But he is also open to the idea that the case illustrates how an unknown physical process may be at work in the UFO phenomenon, a process that requires continued research and analysis. "The UFO problem is not a simple one, and it is unlikely there is any simple universal answer."

An investigation by the Inspector General's office of the Department of the Army in 1982 found no evidence of involvement by Army helicopters in the incident. Reported Lt. Col. George Sarran: "Ms. Landrum and Ms. Cash were credible...the policeman and his wife {who claimed to have seen 12 helicopters near the UFO encounter site} were also credible witnesses. There was no perception that anyone was trying to exaggerate the truth." (To read a transcript of interviews conducted by two Air Force Captains of the Judge Advocate office, with Landrum and Cash at Bergstrom Air Force Base, in August 1981, go to: http://www.cufon.org/cufon/cashlani.htm)

Over the ensuing five years, Schuessler tried without success to identify the helicopters, who flew them, where they came from, and what they were pursuing. He encountered nothing but an official wall of denial. Every branch of the U.S. military denied having helicopters in the air that night anywhere near Dayton. (Soon after I interviewed Cash, Landrum and Schuessler about this case for *Reader's Digest* in 1998, Schuessler published a book detailing his investigation, *The Cash-Landrum UFO Incident.)*

In the 1998 Rockefeller Science Panel report the Cash-Landrum incident impact on the witnesses was summarized this way:

"The Cash-Landrum case seems to be unique in that there is detailed documen-

tation of the injuries (photographs, etc.), and of the subsequent medical treatment. The witnesses were initially affected mainly by the heat and the bright light, and they developed headaches. During the night, Colby vomited repeatedly and his skin turned red. The same happened to Landrum. Cash fared even worse: large water blisters formed on her face and head and by morning her eyes had swollen shut. The three witnesses continued to have severe nausea—even drinking a little water would make them vomit—they developed diarrhea, and their health deteriorated severely. Cash was taken to a hospital, where she was treated as a burn patient. Cash had more than two dozen periods of hospital confinement over 18 years until she died on Dec. 29, 1998."

This Cash/Landrum case, among countless other UFO incidents, belies the claims made by UFO debunker Philip J. Klass that "there hasn't been a single piece of credible physical evidence" in the aftermath of a UFO sighting, though Klass might have tried to argue that suspected secret military craft don't count as producing credible evidence. Klass claimed that he doubted the veracity of the story because Schuessler had found no abnormal levels of radioactivity on the women's vehicle and no medical data had been provided on the women's health prior to the alleged sighting, as if that would somehow undermine the truthfulness of what the women claimed to have seen.

As with the damaged brains of UFO witnesses that Professor Garry Nolan analyzed, in which the brains constitute the persuasive evidence that something unusual happened, medical records and physician testimony attested to Cash and Landrum having had their bodies harmed by radiation at levels sufficient for them to become the physical evidence necessary to prove that they witnessed something far beyond their normal experience. Whether it's the physical evidence left behind when molten metal got spun off a fiery UFO in Iowa, or physical evidence imprinted into the bodies of Cash and Landrum, our rational minds can't always explain away every challenge to our consensus reality, no matter how much debunkers may wish it to be so.

The Evolution of Skeptical Theories and Evidence, 1952 Onward. . .

Fads and Fallacies in the Name of Science
MARTIN GARDNER
(1952, G. P. Putnam's Sons)

Martin Gardner belittles the flying saucer "craze" and other "fads" that prey upon "human gullibility," such as psychic phenomena, Atlantis, the Loch Ness monster, and dowsing. He predicts that the "worn out saucer craze" will eventually be replaced by sea serpents as an object of public fascination.

Most of the "reliable" reports of UFOs are misidentifications of skyhook balloons, says Gardner. The behavior of those nine objects skipping like saucers near Kenneth Arnold's plane over Mount Rainier in 1947 "tallies remarkably well" with the behavior of small plastic balloons. Since other witnesses have described UFOs as noiseless, seeming to "flutter" or play tag across the sky, Gardner concludes only balloons behave that way, so balloons must be responsible.

When the U.S. Navy revealed the existence of skyhook balloons, after nearly five years of secrecy, "reports of flying saucers decreased markedly," the author claims. Green fireballs then "caught the public fancy." Those reports not explainable as meteors or balloons can be accounted for by experimental aircraft, flying birds, the planet Venus, reflections of lights on clouds, mass hysteria, and outright hoaxes.

Gardner cites how Frank Scully's *Behind the Flying Saucers*, published in 1950 quoting several scientists describing how three saucers had crashed, killing thirty-four dwarfish occupants, proved to be a hoax engineered by two Denver swindlers, one of them a geophysicist. Scully's previous book, Fun in Bed, his job as gossip columnist for the show business magazine, Variety, and his third book, Blessed Mother Goose, did not exactly inspire public confidence in his flying saucer tales.

He refers to Major Donald Keyhoe, author of *The Flying Saucers Are Real*, as a sincere but "scientifically naive" purveyor of "romantic and preposterous" speculations. A third author, Gerald Heard, who believes flying saucers come from Mars and are piloted by 2-inch-long insects, frightens Gardner because there is a possibility Heard "believes everything he writes." Heard's book, *Is Another World Watching?*, theorizes, much as Keyhoe did, that flying saucers are here to investigate the atomic explosions seen periodically on our planet's surface.

Flying Saucers
DONALD H. MENZEL
(1953, Harvard University Press)

Flying saucers are real, says Harvard astrophysicist Donald Menzel, as real as rainbows, sundogs, mirages, and other optical tricks the atmosphere plays upon our eyes. Throughout history, human beings have recorded saucer shapes in the sky. It is a natural optical effect, but not an optical illusion. "The illusion comes from our psychological impressions and mental interpretation of the phenomenon."

Of the 20 percent of saucer sightings that the U.S. Air Force listed as unexplained, Menzel characterizes all the legitimate non-hoaxes as natural phenomena-if not the misidentification of fireballs and Venus, then an effect caused by mist, ice crystals, and mirages. These effects constitute "real saucers." Menzel claims to see them all the time. Twice in one day he had an "attack of saucers," mistaking weather balloons in the morning, and later that night, while riding in the back seat of a car, seeing two hazy disks shining slightly bluish. At first he thought they were Castor and Pollux in the constellation Gemini. But no, Gemini can only be seen in the winter. Menzel leaped from the car after it had stopped, only to see the saucers mysteriously fade away. "I reported the occurrence in detail to the Air Force," he writes. "But at no time did I have even the slightest suspicion that the objects were of interplanetary origin."

Two "classic" UFO sightings Menzel dissects, then quickly dismisses. In the case of Captain Thomas Mantell, who died in 1948 when his plane crashed as he chased an object "metallic and of tremendous size," he probably mistook a mock sun, caused by ice crystals, for a metallic craft. Those round, white spots in the sky, seen and photographed in formation over Lubbock, Texas, in 1951, Menzel explains as "reflection in a rippling layer of fine haze." The light source may have been "a row of street lamps, or automobile headlights."

He exposes two widely publicized flying saucer tales as hoaxes. The first involved Kenneth Arnold, the pilot who started the modern era of saucer sightings with his report of nine disks over Mount Rainier. Arnold went to Tacoma, Washington, to investigate a sighting of doughnut shaped objects that allegedly left behind residue. Arnold suspected a hoax but could never prove it. Menzel quotes from Air Force files that cast conclusive doubt on the story told by the two reputed witnesses whose saucer residue turned out to be ordinary slag. Frank Scully's book, Behind the Flying Saucers, reporting that three saucers and thirty-four dwarfish occupants had been found by the Air Force, was a hoax perpetrated by two of Scully's sources, who were later convicted of fraud.

Drawing upon the Bible and other ancient texts, such as the work of the Roman historian Pliny, Menzel makes a case that the disk shape has always been identified with odd or unexplainable phenomena. He uses the story of the wheels seen by the prophet Ezekiel as an example of a "deluxe-model exhibition of mock suns with attendant glories." The four living creatures described by Ezekiel "would have to be mock suns themselves," and the whirlwind preceding the effect "was a storm that filled the sky with the crystals of ice...." The "chariot of fire" that supposedly carried Elijah "by a whirlwind into Heaven" could have been a similar apparition.

Ironically, with his accounts of biblical sightings and of the "flying saucer scare of 1897"-when persons all over America thought they saw airships, owing to hoaxes and mass hysteria-Menzel says he ushered in the age of ancient astronaut theories. Beginning about three years after the publication of this book, other authors would examine these same ancient sightings, used by Menzel to illustrate natural phenomena, and reach entirely different conclusions-that the vision of Ezekiel, for instance, was a spaceship.

Why do "so many civilized people" have such "an uncivilized attitude" toward flying saucers? Because saucers are unusual to the degree that people enshroud them in mystery, and because "we are all nervous" about the threat of a final war, and to some extent people enjoy being frightened. Menzel suggests that we cultivate a better understanding of science and exhibit "less emotion in the interpretation of nature."

"Ignorance, insecurity, and lack of self-confidence have fostered a tendency toward a blind acceptance of scientific authority," writes Menzel, and "that has apparently supplanted the similar faith in medieval demons and sea serpents, witchcraft and sorcery." Menzel denounces these "blind disciples" of the "scientific faith." He says they are a "special group of suckers," who will "subscribe to any claim as long as the advertisements display seemingly scientific credentials."

Myths of the Space Age
DANIEL COHEN
(1965, Dodd, Mead)

Science writer Daniel Cohen credits a science fiction editor named Ray Palmer with programing the imaginations of "an entire generation of flying saucer enthusiasts." While editing the pulp magazines Amazing Stories and Fantastic Adventures, Palmer became the first person to give "extensive publicity to the theory that the saucers were extraterrestrial spaceships." He developed the idea that there was "a conspiracy of silence" among government agencies. "It was Palmer who perfected the use of the oblique question as proof." Cohen insinuates that Palmer initiated the flying saucer craze as something of a joke.

The author contends that since "virtually every inch of air space over North America up to 100,000 feet" is under continuous surveillance by radar and other "sensitive instruments" operated by the North American Air Defense Command (NORAD), nothing enters or leaves our atmosphere that Uncle Sam doesn't know about. "But NORAD says it has never encountered anything it cannot explain," writes Cohen, who uses this as conclusive evidence that UFOs simply don't exist. Neither has the Smithsonian Astrophysical Observatory, which photographs comets, meteors, and other celestial objects, ever photographed anything "that we did not understand."

Cohen relies heavily on theories advanced by Dr. Donald Menzel and aviation writer Philip Klass to explain UFOs. The nine disks seen by pilot Kenneth Arnold in 1947 "were most probably a mirage caused by the mountains." Sightings in the small New England town of Exeter, chronicled in John Fuller's book, *Incident At Exeter*, were probably due, as Klass theorized, to corona discharges of luminous ionized air along power lines creating a special kind of ball lightning. Cohen attempts to explain another classic UFO case, those twenty lights that passed over Lubbock, Texas, in 1951, as the white-breasted migratory birds known as plover, reflecting the lights of the city below and creating the illusion of large objects.

Quoting from the findings of a social scientist who studied those who claim to be in communication with extraterrestrials, Cohen describes them as usually old and usually women, widowed or single, poor and uneducated. As a group, their physical health seems bad, their mental health even worse. Hallucinations are common. Members tend to be "either young schizophrenics or aged with advanced senility." Most participants have previously been involved in other occult movements. In 1962, Gabriel Green, an outspoken contactee, ran for senator in the California Democratic Primary after being instructed to run for office by a visitor from Alpha Centauri. Green attracted 171,000 votes.

Cohen concedes that "at least a small number of unexplained sightings" might be due to some "as yet unknown natural phenomena." But beyond that, "unless the quality of reported sightings improves radically," he insists the case for extraterrestrial visitors is so weak as to be nonexistent.

———————————————

UFOs-Identified
PHILIP J. KLASS
(1968, Random House)

Reading John G. Fuller's *Incident At Exeter* forced Philip Klass to alter his "strongly held opinion" that UFOs were either hoaxes or misinterpretations of conventional objects. In reports of UFOs around Exeter, New Hampshire, Klass detected evidence of plasma, electric coronas that form over or near power lines. These small clouds of electrified air, appearing as intense, glowing balls, can remain fixed, or use power lines as a highway. In seventy-three instances Fuller had reported persons seeing brilliant red, orange, and blue balls of light near power lines or transmission lines.

Klass compiled a rather extensive list of similarities between the coronas, another member of the plasma family called ball lightning, and descriptions of the behavior and effects of UFOs. Among the correlations he found:

...A hissing noise often accompanies plasma discharges and reported UFOs;

...Coronas in their initial stages are bluish, then change to bright white or red-orange, much in the same way UFOs have been seen to alter in color and intensity;

...Ball lightning appears to move by gliding or rolling along, can hang motionless in the air or move against the air current, just as UFOs have been seen to do;

...Plasmas are often able to produce an even stronger radar echo than solid metal objects;

... If sufficiently large, a plasma can interfere with radio or television signals, possibly even cause car engines to fail, as UFOs have been reported to do;

...Plasmoids often seem to seek each other out and attach themselves, much in the way UFOs have been observed merging into one;

...Portions of a plasma losing energy would be seen as transparent, as UFOs have on occasion demonstrated transparency;

...Persons viewing plasmas at close range might receive enough ultra-violet light to burn their skin. Many UFO close encounters produce skin burns and eye irritation.

Klass, an electrical engineer and aviation writer, concluded that plasma/UFOs "are nature's luminous equivalent of the Rorschach ink blot used in psychological testing." He contends that when observers report that a UFO had a silver or metallic color-especially in daylight hours they are unconsciously interpreting what they see, rather than describing literally. Plasma colors in the daytime would appear washed out, leaving a self-illuminated glow that might seem like sunlight glinting off a metal surface.

"The swept-wing jet aircraft," writes Klass, "I now believe is the most prolific producer of plasma-UFOs...." It is not simply "mere coincidence" that the first reports from pilots of glowing fireballs came during World War II, when more planes were in the sky than ever before. Swept-wing aircraft began to fly in large numbers in the early 1950s, about the same time that UFO sightings began proliferating. Is it coincidence that "many of the high-altitude UFOs are reported by pilots while flying along well-traveled airways, where aircraft also leave a trail of combustion-engine pollution products in their wake?" Klass suspects these pollutants play a role in the formation of some plasma/UFOs.

In 1964, police officer Lonnie Zamora of Socorro, New Mexico, claimed to have seen an egg-shaped object, aluminum-white in color, standing on two legs in a shallow gully. Two small men in white coveralls near the object saw him approach. They entered the craft and blasted off. Klass proposes that maybe Zamora encountered a plasma, the whitish wisps of which he mistook for men in white coveralls. Branches growing from black bushes in the gully "might easily have appeared to be supporting the object." Four so-called pad prints made by the object were found in the gully. Klass theorizes that miniature lightning bolts from the plasma could have created the trenchlike depressions in the sandy topsoil. But he admits this theory encounters difficulty in attempting to explain the loud roar Zamora said he heard. While loud roars are not characteristic of plasmas, neither is such a sound "characteristic of UFOs either."

Betty and Barney Hill, who thought they had been kidnapped by a UFO in 1961, probably saw a plasma that may have induced a hypnotic trance. Klass doesn't carry this theory too far, if only because his "knowledge of hypnotism is meager." But flashing colored lights like those the Hills saw, might in darkness at close range "have a hypnotic effect on some observers."

Klass bemoans the way physical scientists have ignored the "scientific mystery" of UFOs. That mystery became obscured, he believes, when sensationalist writers and a noisy fringe of UFO fanatics "cloaked the subject in an aura of science-fantasy." Of the few scientists attracted to the subject, "most had been devoted and long-term readers of science fiction." He wonders whether this avocation blurred in their minds the distinction between science fact and science fiction. He urges UFOrians to keep an open mind to the possibility that UFOs "are a family of freak atmospheric phenomena," just as he says he is keeping his mind "open to the possibility of extraterrestrial visitors."

Scientific Study of Unidentified Flying Objects
DR. EDWARD CONDON, PROJECT DIRECTOR
(1969, New York Times Company)

For two years, at a cost of half a million dollars, thirty-seven scientists and researchers under the direction of Dr. Edward Condon, a University of Colorado physicist, investigated past and current (until 1968) reports of UFOs to determine whether natural phenomena or extraterrestrial visitors were responsible. Their conclusion, although not unanimous, strongly argued against the extraterrestrial hypothesis, recommending that no further study or serious attention be given UFOs by the scientific community.

But as *New York Times* science writer Walter Sullivan points out in his introduction to Condon's 958-page report, while the project concentrated on the best-documented UFO cases, "it did not hesitate to conclude that, on the basis of available evidence, some are difficult to explain by conventional means." One of these cases included two photographs of a disklike object that could not easily be explained as either a hoax or an identifiable aircraft.

From the beginning, the project regarded UFOs as existing if only because the stimulus that produces a report is by definition a UFO. Their mission was to identify the rational, natural explanations for certain kinds of stimuli that produce UFO reports. "We take the position that if an UFO report can be plausibly explained in ordinary terms, then we accept that explanation even though not enough evidence may be available to prove it beyond all doubt," Condon wrote. In nearly all cases, project personnel found the persons who reported UFOs to be "normal, responsible individuals."

However, in several instances, the committee intentionally spent time and resources investigating the theories of known mystical cults and pseudo-scientific groups few UFO proponents had ever taken seriously. A case in point is the purely hypothetical planet Clarion, which some mystics believe is an Earthlike body orbiting the sun directly opposite the Earth, so that it is at all times invisible to us. Scientists at the U.S. Naval Observatory searched for Clarion. As expected, their calculations revealed no such planet, since in order for it to exist, the orbital path of Venus would have to be affected to an extent detectable on Earth.

Of hundreds of UFO reports studied, only fifty-nine were singled out as important. Among these, hoaxes and conventional or natural explanations, like the scintillation effects of Jupiter and Venus, accounted for practically all. Numerous examples emerged of commonplace phenomena stimulating unusual attention until the event assumed an apparent significance in the minds of the observers. Misidentification of human objects like balloons and space debris reentering the atmosphere produced many other reports of UFOs. The northeast electrical power failure of 1965, theorized to have been caused by UFOs as chronicled in John Fuller's *Incident At Exeter*, "appears adequately explained," the project concluded, "without reference to the action of UFOs." Nor did the project find any evidence of UFOs causing car engines to malfunction. Laboratory tests indicated UFOs must exert a magnetic field on the car's ignition coil in excess of 20,000 Gauss, which would have altered the magnetization of the car itself. While no magnetic alterations were found in cars allegedly affected by UFOs, the committee did not rule out the possibility that this could be accomplished without detection. "No satisfactory explanation for such effects, if indeed they (occur), is apparent."

In one instance, the project debunked theories proposed by a debunker. Aviation writer Philip Klass, in UFOs Identified, had concluded that the objects seen over New Hampshire in 1965 and recorded in *Incident At Exeter* were examples of a rare plasmic phenomena known as ball lightning. Scientists with a background in theoretical or experimental physics rejected that argument on grounds that "containment of plasma by magnetic fields is not likely under atmospheric conditions for more than a second or so."

Project researchers discovered in at least seven UFO-oriented books, including those by such authors as Jacques Vallée, Frank Edwards, and Brinsley LePoer Trench, arguments building up "UFO case histories" that had been taken from "secondary and tertiary sources without any attempt to verify original sources." Had any scientist or scholar "behaved similarly," wrote a project researcher, "he would have long since been hooted out of his profession." Frank Edwards, for instance, passed off as factual an occult tale told by Madame Blavatsky, the nineteenth-century high priestess of esoterica, which claimed that a *Book of Dzyan* she had invented told of extraterrestrial beings having waged war on this planet before humankind evolved. Vallée borrows from other UFO writers, who in turn borrowed from contactee George Adamski, the story of how an abbot and others at Ampleforth Abbey in England saw a large, silvery disk in 1290. In checking with Ampleforth Abbey, a Benedictine college, project researchers were told that the account had been fabricated by two students who included it in a manuscript scroll as a joke.

Three UFO sightings by American astronauts in the Gemini program are left unexplained by the project, posing "a challenge to the analyst." A 1956 sighting over England, when two separate radar stations and an airborne radar locked in on a white light that eluded a Royal Air Force interceptor, forced project scientists to conclude: "the probability that at least one genuine UFO was involved appears to be fairly high." Similarly, two photographs taken by a couple in McMinnville, Oregon (on May 11, 1950), showing a metallic, disk-shaped object, confounded project investigators, who concluded that fabrication "seems remote." All the factors investigated in this case, psychological, photographic, and geometric, appeared to confirm "that an extraordinary flying object, silvery, metallic, disk-shaped, tens of meters in diameter, and evidently artificial, flew within sight of two witnesses."

Crash Go the Chariots
CLIFFORD WILSON
(1972, Lancer Books)

Archeologist and Bible scholar Clifford Wilson is occasionally at a loss for words in this slim volume (122 pages). When discussing Erich von Daniken's theory that astronaut rather than angel lust accounts for biblical passages referring to sexual couplings between humans and other entities, Wilson can only exclaim: "What an imagination he has!"

While acknowledging that the Bible does recognize the existence of "other gods" beneath "Almighty God," beings who "developed from men," the author simply cannot accept the notion that they might have flown about in spacecraft influencing the development of human intelligence. Yet he claims we are surrounded by spirits that cannot be dismissed as the product of imagination or hallucination. He implies that a "satanic delusion" is at work through von Daniken and other writers, "to blind the eyes of men by allowing them to have near-truth" that seems "sufficiently acceptable," as an alternative to accepting the word of Almighty God.

Von Daniken takes an overly selective and simplistic approach in presenting evidence for his arguments, excluding facts that do not fit. Wilson points out numerous examples. For instance, Von Daniken describes the Nazca drawings in Peru, some 800 and more feet long, as attempts by humans in ancient times to communicate with the gods in their spacecraft. But what about the rock carvings at Behistun? asks Wilson. Darius the Great (486 B.C.), who ordered the inscriptions, 1,700 feet tall, carved 400 feet up the side of a mountain, only wanted his achievements ballyhooed. In this instance Wilson fails to mention that the Darius inscription can be seen on the ground, while the Nazca lines are visible only from the air.

When von Daniken talks of the huge rock at Sacsahuaman in Peru, he asks "what titanic force turned it upside down?" Wilson answers—an earthquake. When von Daniken states that the Ark of the Covenant was electrically charged, explaining why Uzzah died when he touched it, Wilson replies "Nonsense!" pointing out that the Bible makes no mention of the priests who carried it wearing protective clothes, so why weren't they electrocuted, too? When von Daniken discusses the Epic of Gilgamesh, the Sumerian flood tale, Wilson dismisses it with "the Babylonian version is a corruption of the Biblical original." Sodom and Gomorrah, rather than being destroyed by an atomic blast, as von Daniken theorizes, could just have easily been devastated by an earthquake that ignited natural gas and an oil basin beneath the two cities. When Ezekiel the prophet says he saw a space chariot, interpreted by von Daniken as a spacecraft, Wilson responds that one need only take the Bible "at face value" to see that Ezekiel saw "visions from God," not the divine entity Himself or a spaceship from another world. When von Daniken asks if it is coincidence that the height of the Pyramid of Cheops multiplied by 1,000 million almost corresponds to the distance between Earth and the sun, Wilson makes the calculation, finds 91.1 million as the Cheops figure (the distance is 93 million miles), and asks why couldn't the ancient engineers, if they had guidance, have been more accurate than that?

UFOs: A Scientific Debate
EDITED BY CARL SAGAN & THORNTON PAGE
(1972, Cornell University Press)

This collection of fifteen essays by prominent American scientists seems weighted heavily against the various extraterrestrial visitation theories. Only four of the contributors are proponents of the "UFOs are real" position. UFO proponent Dr. James McDonald, and skeptic Dr. Donald Menzel, each consume sixty pages attacking theories proposed or defended by the other.

Based on a detailed rebuttal to solutions offered by the Condon Report, and focusing on four specific UFO cases, McDonald finds no "reasonable alternative" to the hypothesis "that something in the nature of extraterrestrial devices engaged in something in the nature of surveillance lies at the heart of the UFO problem." While McDonald doesn't have evidence of an Air Force UFO cover-up—maybe a "foul-up"- he accuses the Condon Report investigators of intentionally confronting "a disappointingly small sample of the old 'classic' (UFO) cases." And those that it did consider were explained away by "unconvincing" argumentation relying on mirage distortions of stars and the optics theories of the astronomer Menzel.

Menzel lashes back that McDonald and J. Allen Hynek, who use "cliches as poor substitutes for scientific argument," purport to have had considerable experience with UFOs, but those "claims to authority stern from failures rather than from successes" because of their inability to identify "the stimulus of certain UFO sightings." Menzel says the UFO phenomenon is "more closely related to seventeenth-century witchcraft" than anything serious scientists should find of concern in the modern world. He predicts a "continued decline of public interest in UFOs" because people "seem to have taken up a new cause: Astrology." This "new cause" fulfills a similar human need as UFOs and "has a similar scientific basis." Menzel regrets that in 1953, in his first UFO book, he revealed that "flying saucers are mentioned in the Holy Bible." He says that opened up a Pandora's box. Leading writers on UFOiogy "got into the act and made similar claims, without credit to me, of course."

Physicist Philip Morrison of MIT proposes that the enigmatic radar/visual UFO cases described by McDonald might be the result of "spoofing," a deliberate penetration of U.S. air space by the Air Force, or a foreign power, "as a means of testing defense readiness." Carl Sagan of Cornell agrees, pointing out the possible conflict between solving the UFO problem and "Department of Defense interests," which might always keep a few interesting UFO cases from ever being publicly explained. Morrison bemoans government emphasis on secrecy, for it "has had a lot to do with the persistence of American support for UFO's."

Onetime Air Force UFO consultant J. Allen Hynek defends the overall reliability of UFO witnesses. During his twenty years of UFO investigations, "very rarely" did he encounter members of "the lunatic fringe" making UFO reports, if only because they would be "incapable of composing an articulate, factual, and objective report." Although people who are ignorant of common astronomical objects, like balloons and mirages, do generate "a high noise level" of UFO reports, Hynek insists any experienced investigator can quickly sort through and eliminate these cases of misidentification.

Sociologist Robert L. Hall sees in the "hard-core cases of UFO reports" witnesses who frequently find their observations "jarring to their own beliefs, but insist nevertheless on what they have seen." This seems a persuasive enough commentary on their sincerity, for it would be "an extraordinary suspension of the usual laws of human behavior" if they promptly interpreted what they saw "outside their previous beliefs and contrary to the beliefs of others around them." People usually attempt to categorize what they see in familiar terms. When they fail, that very often is a sign they have encountered something for which they have absolutely no familiarity or comprehension. Given the persistent and patterned nature of UFO reports, Hall believes "either there must be a distinctive physical phenomenon which these witnesses have observed, or there must be a powerful and poorly understood motivation rooted in projection, or contagion of belief, or a similar mechanism."

New York Times science writer Walter Sullivan does not think it relevant that many UFO witnesses were skeptics before their experience. He claims that everyone has "been conditioned by the press" and by society to a "hierarchy of beliefs" that includes images of the UFO. That such an image has been implanted makes even hardened skeptics prone to classifying what they can't identify as a UFO.

Similarly, astronomer Frank Drake argues that a witness' memory of events fades rapidly. After one day, half the reports become reconstructions from the imagination of the witness. As an example, he cites a night in 1962 when brilliant fireballs were seen in the skies of West Virginia. Of seventy-eight persons interviewed who claimed to have observed one of the meteorites, twelve said they heard a crackling sound simultaneously with seeing the fireball. "How does the sound get there as fast as the light?" asks Drake. Since what they described is "contrary to the laws of physics," Drake concludes they were exhibiting a psychological reaction closely associated with that experienced by UFO witnesses.

Astronomer William K. Hartmann, who participated in preparing the Condon Report, comes down even harder on UFO witnesses. When a Soviet spacecraft disintegrated over the United States in 1968, Hartmann says two more UFO "effects" were discovered: the "airship effect," when moving lights are connected in a single object; and the "excitedness effect," when observers "with the poorest observations are most likely to submit reports." Dozens of UFO reports resulted from the fiery demise of the Soviet craft. "The two most detailed accounts described a cigarshaped ship with windows." One witness said the object came so close she "could have seen people through the windows." Looking at the unexplained or puzzling UFO cases as a group, Hartmann says he only found "fewer than a dozen that involve phenomena marginally outside the borders of accepted science."

The Cosmic Connection
CARLSAGAN
(1973, Doubleday; 1975, Dell)

Exobiologist Carl Sagan contends that no reports of UFOs have been made that are "simultaneously very reliable" as seen "independently by a large number of witnesses," or "exotic" enough to warrant serious scrutiny. "There are no reliably reported cases of strange machines landing and taking off."

To imagine that we fascinate alien cultures "is contrary to the idea that there are lots of civilizations around," Sagan argues, because if this is true, then civilizations like our own would be common and thus not particularly interesting. Conversely, if civilizations like ours are not common, then there won't be "many civilizations advanced enough to send visitors."

He dismisses the ancient astronaut hypothesis as being impossible to prove on the basis of religious myths and legends. Only one category of legend would be convincing to him-when the legend contains information "that could not possibly have been generated by the civilization that created the legend"-for instance, if a number written down thousands of years ago as a holy number "turns out to be the nuclear fine structure constant." Legitimate artifacts might also conceivably be worthy of scientific attention.

Repeatedly referring to Erich von Daniken as Erik von Danniken, Sagan insists that all ancient artifacts used as evidence for visitation are either implausible or can be explained using more practical alternatives.

Cases that at first seem convincing, such as the perfectly machined steel cube said to have been recovered from strata millions of years old, or the reception of call letters from a television station three years off the air, "are almost certainly hoaxes."

Most of these artifacts and archeological sites constitute "psychological projective tests." People see in them what they want to see, interpret them as they would like to see them interpreted. A rain god on an Aztec pyramid outside Mexico City, for example, reminds Sagan of an amphibious tracked vehicle with four headlights. But like other interpretations-airfields in Peru, spaceships carved into Mayan ruins they are "too close to what we have today" to inspire confidence. "To a person with an even mildly skeptical mind, the evidence is unconvincing."

Sagan calls the contactee claims sad stories not warranting serious attention, except by the psychiatric profession. He describes correspondents who besieged him with letters and advice, like the woman whose shower head broadcast statements from inhabitants of Venus. He ridicules the contact stories "now quite fashionable in some UFO enthusiast circles" as improbable fantasy, especially the tales of sexual liaisons between humans and extraterrestrials. "Such crossings are about as reasonable as the mating of a man and a petunia." However, 100 pages later, in discussing dolphin intelligence, Sagan relates how a young woman named Margaret had sexual relations with a dolphin named Peter at a research institute in the Virgin Islands. Sagan says the affair has "some significance," if only because "in what we piously describe as bestiality" humans tend to choose domesticated animals "for interspecific sexual activities." He wonders whether dolphins have ever considered domesticating us.

Humankind has already announced its presence to the cosmos with the invention of radio on this planet. But our chances of eavesdropping on another civilization "may be slight" because such signals might be detectable "for only a few hundred years in the multi-billion-year history of a planet." A civilization might quickly advance, as we seem to be doing, to light beam transmissions or new technologies that would preclude any radiation leaking into space. There is also the possibility that all advanced civilizations might be listening rather than sending signals, in which case communication would be futile. Besides that, the vast distances to be overcome in such communication would mean hundreds, perhaps thousands of years before an answer would be received, much less a dialogue begun. On this planet we have not yet been able to decode some ancient languages and symbols, such as the glyphs on Easter Island and writings of the Mayas. How could we then expect to understand messages from another civilization?

Sagan raises the tantalizing prospect that we may one day master travel into and out of black holes, if they are indeed shortcuts through time and space in the universe. He speculates that our own universe may "very likely itself" be a "vast black hole." Since we have no knowledge of what exists outside our perceivable universe, "in a strange sense, our universe may be filled with objects that are not here." They are not separate universes, nor do they have the mass of our universe, but in separateness and isolation "they are autonomous universes." Sagan can foresee a federation of societies establishing a black hole rapid transit system throughout the cosmos.

***

UFOs Explained
PHILIP J. KLASS
(1974, Random House)

By training Philip Klass is an aviation writer and electrical engineer; by avocation he is a UFO debunker. This volume expands on a theme developed in his earlier book, *UFOs Identified*—that a logical, scientific explanation can be supplied for any seemingly unexplained happening.

Acting on the assumption that small, representative samples provide "remarkably accurate profiles of the whole," Klass attempts to demonstrate, using but a few dozen UFO sightings, that sufficient data already exists "to understand and explain the UFO mystery," provided that the principles deduced from these analyses "are intelligently applied to similar cases." His application of scientific methodology to explain UFOs produces persuasive alternatives to the extraterrestrial spaceship hypothesis, although several cases defied even this rigorous analysis.

He explains a series of sightings in Ohio and Indiana in 1968- cigar-shaped objects with illuminated windows-as the disintegration of a Russian booster rocket. He dismisses a 1948 sighting of a cigar-shaped object by an Eastern Air Lines crew as a meteor shower. From these two cases, he advances a UFOlogical Principle: That honest and intelligent people, when exposed to an unfamiliar object or an unexpected event, often are inaccurate in describing what they thought they saw.

A Navy transport crew in 1951 reported being followed by a saucer like metallic object about 300 feet in diameter and a fiery red ring around the perimeter. Prior to his analysis of this incident, known as the Gander case, Klass said he would have had difficulty believing "that so many experienced pilots and others in a flight crew could mistake the moon for a giant UFO..." He reasons that since UFOs had been in the news preceding this incident, even experienced pilots are "subject to the psychological influence of what they read and hear." This is demonstrated by another UFOlogical Principle: When the news media leads people to believe that UFOs may be in the area, people begin mistaking human made and natural objects, especially at night, in their eagerness to see and believe. This situation feeds upon itself creating what is known as a UFO "flap. " The "airship" sightings of the 1890s are portrayed by Klass as one such media creation.

Other UFOs can be explained by the planets Venus and Mars, which often seem to move about in the sky, or plasmic corona effects, produced around high voltage lines and more commonly known as ball lightning. One of those "classic" UFO sightings, when policeman Lonnie Zamora saw an egg-shaped object ascend from a gully near Socorro, New Mexico, in 1964, Klass now insinuates was a hoax concocted to attract the tourist trade. He points out that the UFO supposedly landed about midway between two highways that would bring tourists to Socorro, on property owned by Mayor Bursum, Officer Zamora's boss. Bursum was also the town banker, with a vested interest in tourism. Which brings Klass to yet another UFOlogical Principle: To expose a UFO report as hoax, one must rely on physical evidence rather than character endorsements of those claiming to have made the sighting.

"There is not a single photo showing a craftlike UFO which can withstand close analysis." He finds the integrity of UFO photos to depend entirely on the truthfulness of the UFO photographer. He apparently believes that UFO photographers as a group are not particularly trustworthy people. But beware even when a UFO photo or sighting report stands up to scrutiny, Klass warns, asserting a UFOlogical Principle: a "lack of sufficient information" to disprove the case "does not really provide evidence to support the hypothesis that spaceships from other worlds are visiting the Earth."

Limitations in the use of radar frequently contribute to UFO reports. Simply because a blip appears as an object on a radar screen does not prove anything. Temperature inversions during the warm, humid summer months, when most UFOs are reported, tend to produce "angels," freak radar reflections. Localized areas of turbulence in the atmosphere also produce radar echoes. Klass once more trots forth a UFOlogical Principle: Radar operators searching their screens for lights reported as UFOs "almost invariably" find an "unknown" target, and just as commonly, unusual targets on radar can usually be associated in the sky at night with an "unknown" light. Confirmation by two independent "sensors," visual and radar, can be made for something that does not exist.

In 1972, a sensationalist tabloid, *The National Enquirer* announced a contest with prizes of up to $50,000 for the most authenticated UFO sightings. More than 1,000 entries were received. The Enquirer selected five university professors as judges, including Dr. J. Allen Hynek, formerly a consultant to the Air Force UFO investigation. For many years Klass had attempted to determine from UFO investigators which cases represented the strongest evidence for extraterrestrial visitation. *The Enquirer's* contest made his job as a debunker easier.

First prize of $5,000 went to a farmer named Durel Johnson of Delphos, Kansas. His sixteen-year-old son Ronald saw a mushroom shaped object hovering about 2 feet off the ground one evening in their backyard. The object allegedly left a horseshoe-shaped section of soil dry and glowing, and knocked over a dead tree as it flew away. Klass found a number of apparent discrepancies in this story. No sign of impact was found on the tree; it had fallen toward where the UFO was seen to leave, rather than away from it. The horseshoe ring proved high in "organic" material, such as animal or plant life might leave, and had a high salinity content, as if doused by animal urine. Klass concluded that a livestock feeder created the horseshoe effect. Klass also found reason to suspect Farmer Johnson of engineering a hoax, for he was deeply in debt.

With this award to the Johnsons, and a second to the four-man crew of an Army helicopter who, Klass claims, mistook a luminous fireball for a UFO, The Enquirer and

UFO believers "had, unwittingly, made a useful contribution to the UFO controversy by demonstrating the quality" of their most credible cases. Klass calls extraterrestrial visitation nothing more than "fascinating myth for adults," a kind of "fairy story" to fill the void left when we outgrow Santa Claus and the tooth fairy.

—————————————

The Space-Gods Revealed
RONALD STORY
(1976, Harper & Row)

Ancient astronaut theories in general, and Erich von Daniken in particular, are targets in this slim volume (124 pages) intended to cast doubt on the "evidence" used in *Chariots of the Gods?* and all other books that rely upon similar material. Ronald Story accuses von Daniken of every conceivable heresy: flights of imagination, faulty suppositions, absurd rhetorical questions, superficiality, and the sin of omission discarding relevant data not fitting his arguments.

Where von Daniken concludes a nuclear explosion destroyed Sodom and Gomorrah, Story uses evidence indicating that the cataclysm described in the Bible was an earthquake accompanied by natural gas explosions.

Where von Daniken and other authors, such as NASA scientist Josef Blumrich, contend that the prophet Ezekiel saw a spaceship descend, Story dismisses the tale as a "vision." But that obviously is not an entirely satisfactory answer, so Story quotes Donald Menzel, Harvard astronomer and UFO debunker, who suggests that Ezekiel observed an optical effect "caused by the passage of sunlight through a thin layer of ice crystals...." Pulling once again from his bag of natural phenomena explanations, Menzel suggests that Moses, when confronted by the burning bush, actually observed lightning being discharged upward, a rare freak of nature that would have given the bush the appearance of being on fire.

The desert region of Nazca in southern Peru, with its gigantic etchings of animals, straight lines, circles, and triangles visible only from the air, reminds von Daniken of airport runways. Story wonders whether the lines aren't simply representations of constellations seen in the sky. He summarizes research by the International Explorers Society indicating that early Peruvians, sometime between 400 B.C. and A.D. 900, could have observed the markings from hot-air balloons, utilizing finely woven textiles to capture smoke from campfires.

The Easter Island statues, which von Daniken supposes were the handiwork of a group of stranded extraterrestrials, are shown to be terrestrial in design and craftsmanship. Thor Heyerdahl and others have demonstrated that two teams of six men working in shifts every day for a year could use primitive tools to cut the hard lava into medium-size statues. It would be an arduous task requiring fanatical perseverance, but humans are entirely capable of creating what von Daniken believed could only have been carved by a more advanced culture.

Von Daniken and others describe the carvings on the sarcophagus lid of a tomb in the Mayan ceremonial center of Palenque as representing an astronaut inside a rocket capsule. Story says the illustration is religious, not technological. Since nature's workshop was the basis of Mayan religion, this royal tomb, built for a king named Pacal who died in A.D. 683, embodied religious symbolism in the sarcophagus design. Von Daniken's rocket is a two-headed serpent; rocket exhaust is roots sprouting from a corn plant; his astronaut seat is Pacal's royal badge of rulership.

About a dozen objects von Daniken identified as batteries have been found in archeological sites in Iraq. They are pottery jars containing a copper cylinder, an iron rod, and crumbs of bitumen. If they were batteries, and used a vinegar solution, perhaps one-half volt of electricity could be obtained from each, a sufficient charge to electroplate silver onto copper. If extraterrestrials gave ancient Sumerians the secret of batteries, why were these simple one-cell devices all they could produce?

Von Daniken claims that Egyptian civilization arose suddenly, without transition or a recognizable prehistory. Story demonstrates how this statement ignores 100 years of archeological excavations that prove the Pyramids were constructed by trial and error over several hundreds of years. Humankind spent from 5000 B.C. to 1500 B.C. mastering the process of plant and animal domestication.

Story further argues that we must not allow cultists, who use UFOs as a medium for religious expression, to detract from the "serious aspects" of the UFO phenomenon. Too many reports, he says, have come from "people of unquestionable integrity."

The UFO Enigma
DONALD H. MENZEL & ERNEST H. TAVES
(1977, Doubleday)

In previous writings Harvard astrophysicist Donald Menzel did not stray much beyond explaining away all UFOs as hoaxes, hallucinations, and misidentification of natural phenomena and human-made objects. In this, his third and last book on the subject, Menzel ridicules practically everything that is fashionable or on the fringes of science, lumping together UFOs, parapsychology, the Bermuda Triangle, ancient astronaut theories, even the notion that we might eventually come into contact with extraterrestrials, as being representative of an irrational aberration he says science must somehow confront and vanquish.

"It seems to us most unlikely that we have been, or shall be, visited by aliens from other planetary systems," write Menzel and his co-author Ernest Taves, a psychoanalyst and science fiction writer. The idea that Earth could be visited by intelligences who "do not reveal themselves to us, is, simply, preposterous." Belief in UFOs "is but one manifestation of a pervasive denial of reality."

There remains "no doubt" in the minds of Menzel and Taves that "a great number of UFO sightings are attributable to liars telling lies and that large numbers of people believe the liars and the lies." From among these liars and lies, "flying saucer societies were formed," directed by persons who have "preyed upon the gullible public for years."

These liars and hoaxers first began to multiply in 1896 and 1897, when "airships" were reported over much of the United States. Menzel attempts to establish similarities between the 1897 "scare" and the wave of UFO sightings or reports of sightings in 1947. In each instance, "there were the original rumors, the self-hallucinations, the hoaxes, and the widespread interest in sky-watching" which resulted in special significance being attached to lenticular clouds, mirages, and other natural phenomena that "would ordinarily have escaped notice."

Of the twenty-four UFO cases left unexplained by the Condon Report in 1969, Menzel dismisses each, in one or two paragraphs of explanation, as chicanery, fabrication, mental illness, radar malfunction, autokinesis, or misidentification of astronomical objects. The McMinnville, Oregon, photographs of 1950, picturing a disk-shaped metallic object, Menzel labels an "obvious" hoax, even though scientists with the Condon project thought otherwise. Another film image left unidentified by Condon, a 16mm motion picture of two white lights taken in 1950 by a Montana journalist, Menzel and Taves claim could only have been the reflections of two jet airplanes.

Other reports of strange objects in the sky they attribute to ball lightning, illusory movements of Venus and other heavenly bodies, and in one particularly memorable case, two airborne tumbleweeds, 3 or 4 feet across, carried by high winds to great heights. Ice crystals are responsible for sundogs and subsuns, brilliant reflections of the sun that often confuse pilots, making them believe they are being chased by a metallic object. When the sundog outmaneuvers a pilot, it gives the appearance of being intelligently controlled. After-images on the retina, caused by flashes, also contribute to UFO reports.

Several chapters are devoted to questioning the various ancient astronaut theories. Erich von Daniken is singled out for perpetrating fabrication, error, wild surmise, and "a veritable farrago of nonsense." The authors find it "absurd" that anyone could believe the Nazca lines in Peru were inspired by extraterrestrials with whom the Nazcas intended to communicate. "The animal figures are...meant to be seen from the sky," Menzel and Taves agree, since civilizations throughout history "have placed their gods in the skies." But just because primitive people believe their gods dwelled in the sky, one needn't "bring in von Daniken's spacemen."

Where von Daniken and other ancient astronaut theorists credit extraterrestrial visitors for the "miracles" described in the Bible, Menzel and Taves propose meteorological explanations. For instance, the burning bush seen by Moses was "no miracle," but a spectacular and frightening natural apparition known as St. Elmo's fire, a rare electrical discharge. Jesus walking on water they explain as a mirage; similarly, the crossing of the Red Sea by the Israelites "may be attributed to a well-known phenomenon of meteorological optics, an inferior mirage," in which the sky over a desert appears to be a body of water. From Genesis, when Jacob dreams of an enormous ladder leading to Heaven, he might have seen a corona-the formation caused by electrons and atoms from the sun focused on the Earth's magnetic field, giving the effect of a ladder on which lights flicker, like the movements of the angels Jacob supposedly witnessed. Ezekiel's vision of a flaming chariot, supported by four living creatures or faces, they describe as a combination of solar halos, mock suns, or sundogs, produced by ice crystals in the upper atmosphere. The "eyes" Ezekiel claimed to see are interpreted as "secondary mock suns, a rare phenomenon."

Message from the Stars
IAN RIDPATH
(1978, Harper & Row)

British writer Ian Ridpath, in this broad overview of astronomy and the search for intelligent life in the universe, is not particularly encouraged about the prospects for human beings ever meeting extraterrestrials face-to-face. He even proposes that other forms of life, if they do exist, may not have an interest in us or in exploring outer space, since intelligence does not necessarily derive from or spawn curiosity.

He finds the supposed evidence for extraterrestrial visitation, UFOs, and the ancient astronaut theories totally unconvincing. He speculates that nature favors nomads over colonizers, which would explain why alien visitors aren't still here, if they ever were. But curiously, he endorses a theory that giant stone monuments on Earth may have been built to point toward where aliens left data banks for our retrieval. It is even very possible that one of these data banks is on Phobos, a moon of Mars, because a pyramid shape seen on the Martian surface points directly toward Phobos.

Erich von Daniken's books are quickly dismissed as the product of "vivid imagination" and "outrageous misrepresentation." Ridpath also singles out for criticism a book by Robert K. G. Temple, *The Sirius Mystery*, examining how an obscure primitive tribe in Mali, the Dogon, could have known about the orbits and nature of the Sirius star system.

Ridpath cites contradictions in the Dogon legends that cast doubt on their overall reliability, contradictions he claims Temple apparently overlooked. Nowhere, for instance, do the Dogon state that the alien visitors they call Nommo came from Sirius. The white dwarf star in that system, when it exploded, would have eliminated any planets in the vicinity, says Ridpath, making it unlikely that life would have evolved there anyway.

Furthermore, since the Dogon tribe live near an active trading route, they might have come into contact with Europeans, from whom they obtained their information about the discovery of Sirius B, the white dwarf that revolves around the larger Sirius A star. "In view of the Dogon fixation with Sirius," Ridpath writes, "it would surely be more surprising if they had not grafted onto their existing legend some new astronomical information gained from Europeans."

After examining some of the "classic" UFO sighting cases, Ridpath concludes that "despite more than thirty years of study, the field of UFOiogy has failed to produce one concrete example of visitation, from any dimension." Fanatical UFO believers continue to cling to their theories, despite the evidence, because for them the perfect UFO case, "like the Second Coming, is an article of faith."

He wonders whether or not we might be the first technology in the universe to survive. Whether this might not in fact be an incentive for survival if only to perpetuate the species. "And if we are the first, we inherit a responsibility that goes far beyond the bounds of tiny Earth. For if no one before has reached the plateau of cosmic maturity, our radio call signs in the future may be the lifeline that pulls other developing civilizations in space out of the despair of their own isolation."

Guardians of the Universe?
RONALD STORY
(1980, St. Martin's Press)

Despite the contentions of Erich von Daniken and other ancient astronaut proponents, the construction of the Great Pyramid in Egypt and other megalithic monuments never required a level of technology which was beyond "the capacities of Earthmen working on their own in the normal context of their own cultures." Much of the evidence used in support of ancient visitation by aliens, especially artistic representations on cave and temple walls, takes the form of psychological projective tests in which the ancient astronaut book authors plant interpretive ideas in the minds of readers, thus substituting propaganda for logic. A favorite technique is to frame the argument this way: "since x cannot be disproved, then it is probably true."

Point by point, Ronald Story attempts to refute the major pieces of evidence supporting the ancient astronaut hypothesis. An Olmec head sculpture from South America which reminds von Daniken of astronaut gear turns out to be a helmet worn by ancient ballplayers. A Mayan legend von Daniken cites, telling of a golden spaceship from the stars carrying an alien who sired Earth children, cannot be traced to any archaeological sources because it was taken from "another work of pseudoscience just as unreliable as the books of von Daniken."

In his book *The Sirius Mystery*, Robert K. G. Temple makes a case that the Dogon tribe of Mali preserve ancient knowledge about the Sirius binary star system which can be traced back 5,000 years to the Egyptians and Sumerians, who got it from space travelers visiting from Sirius. The Dogon mythology about these visitors resembles the Sumerian legend about amphibious beings who imparted knowledge of civilization to humans. The Dogon even worship the invisible companion star to Sirius, known as Sirius B.

Ronald Story finds no mystery in why Sirius was important to the Egyptians and remains so to the Dogon. As the brightest star in the sky, Sirius' appearance helped the Egyptians predict flooding of the Nile River, a phenomenon on which all their agriculture depended, and thus they were inspired to base their calendar on that star. Similarly, since Mali and Egypt are close in latitude, the helical rising of Sirius occurs near the Dogon's summer solstice, as it does for Egypt, making it vitally symbolic to both cultures and a subject for myth-making.

"Claims of any earlier knowledge of Sirius B among the Dogon rest entirely on Temple's interpretations, which are highly arbitrary and ambiguous," contends Story. During the 1920s the discovery that Sirius B-the invisible-to-the-naked-eye companion to Sirius A was a white dwarf had been widely reported, and Jesuit priests could have spread this information in their contacts with the Dogon, whose priests in turn incorporated this astronomical information into already existing myths about Sirius A. The source of information for the Dogon could also have been French or Islamic schools operating in the region. Furthermore, astronomical knowledge possessed by the Dogon strikes Story as elementary, prompting him to suspect that "had some super-intelligent interstellar explorers been involved, we would surely expect their astronomical knowledge to be somewhat more advanced."

Even though he has profound skepticism about the "pseudo mysteries" of ancient astronauts, Story reveals that "I do feel a genuine UFO mystery exists." Hoaxes and phony evidence contaminate the UFO field, but "the same is true for almost any controversial field of study." Whether or not UFOs can be explained in Jungian archetypal terms, or as spaceships from afar, "it can be said, with certainty, that a psychological 'conditioning process' is taking place." To what end is a question Story does not address.

The UFO Verdict
ROBERT SHEAFFER
(1986, Prometheus Books)

While Governor of Georgia in 1969 Jimmy Carter filed a UFO sighting report describing how he and 10 members of a Lions Club in a rural town had witnessed an unusual aerial object. It was about 7:15 p.m., just before their meeting began, when the group saw a bluish light which turned reddish, as large and bright as the moon, and "seemed to move toward us from a distance, stop, move partially away, return then depart." It appeared to be in the western sky at about 30 degrees elevation.

By conducting interviews with townsfolk, charting the launches of research balloons and computing the positions of astronomical bodies on that date, Robert Sheaffer began to piece together a hypothesis about the sighting seven years after it occurred. He discovered that on the night of Carter's sighting, at 7:15 p.m., the planet Venus was nearing its maximum brilliance at about 25 degrees elevation on a cold, clear night in the west-southwest sky, "in virtually the exact position that Carter reported his UFO."

Sheaffer concluded from this data that Carter misinterpreted Venus as a UFO. Hundreds of similar UFO reports are made every time Venus reaches its peak brilliance and, he argues, "no other single object is responsible for so many UFO sightings." During World War II Venus was frequently fired upon by air crews believing it was an enemy aircraft. For weeks, American bomber crews flying over Japan mistook Venus for a new weapon designed to illuminate them as targets for enemy gunners.

"Not one piece of UFO evidence has yet been presented that could not easily be produced by prosaic earthly natural forces or technology," insists the author. As for photos purporting to capture the images of UFOs, all are shots of natural phenomena and celestial objects, or else hoaxes. Impressive looking UFO photo hoaxes can be created with modest equipment and elementary acquaintance with cameras. A series of computerized enhancements of UFO photos conducted by the pro-UFO group Ground Saucer Watch, for example, found 595 out of 626 photos studied-95 percent-to be clearly unauthentic!

Sheaffer asks why UFOs are so reluctant to show themselves openly. They seem to have no trouble buzzing a few people at a time in isolated areas, "so long as not too many people see them and the evidence of their visit will not be too convincing." Never do they hover conspicuously in daylight over large cities, or fly low over crowded beaches. Nor do they ever pose for more than one photographer at a time. In fact, "all supposed UFO photographs produced to date have been taken by a single photographer, using only one camera." That seems logical to Sheaffer since it is difficult to successfully produce a UFO photo hoax using more than one camera and more than one photographer.

Even when UFOs appear to show up on radar, it is always due to "relatively infrequent conditions of anomalous radar propagation combined with misinterpretation of the data." And when UFO sightings occur in waves over many weeks or over a wide geographical area, it is because "such behavior is characteristic of all instances of mass hysteria." In short, Sheaffer says he has used a rigorous application of the scientific method to find an answer to the question "what are UFOs?" The answer is that UFOs do not exist because the entire phenomenon springs from the imagination of the observer.

UFO Abductions: A Dangerous Game
PHILIP J. KLASS
(1988, Prometheus Books)

Within days after the 1975 airing of the NBC primetime movie, *The UFO Incident*, recounting the alleged abduction of Barney and Betty Hill by alien beings, numerous other abduction accounts began to surface nationwide. The most famous came two weeks after the movie appeared when Arizona woodcutter Travis Walton claimed he was zapped by a UFO-witnessed by five fellow woodcutters-and taken aboard the craft for a medical examination.

Philip Klass investigated Walton's story and discovered what he calls suspicious circumstances. Walton, his brother Duane (one of the witnesses), and their mother "were avid UFO buffs who frequently reported seeing UFOs." Shortly before his "abduction" Walton informed his mother "that if he were ever abducted by a UFO she need not worry because he would come back safe and sound." Even more damaging, Walton flunked the first polygraph test he took following his abduction. "Gross deception," was how the examiner characterized Walton's answers.

What could have been the motive if the woodcutters concocted this abduction tale? Klass found several compelling ones. The cutting crew was far behind on its contract with the U.S. Forest Service to thin small trees from a 1,277-acre site. They were in danger of losing their final contract payment as well as future contracts. Their contract did, however, have an Act of God provision which, Klass believes, the crew thought they could trigger with a UFO abduction of a crewmember which would give them the excuse they needed for a contract extension. There was still another, larger financial incentive. As a reader of The National Enquirer, Walton probably knew about the tabloid's reward offer for the best UFO case of the year. (In 1976 The Enquirer did indeed select Walton's story and awarded a $5,000 prize.)

Klass credits *The UFO Incident* with having inspired an epidemic of copycats, hoaxers, and delusional storytellers. "The film provided millions of viewers with a script for UFO abduction and with visual images that would find a niche in their memories for their own UFO-abduction nightmares and fantasies." Aliens depicted in the film-dwarfish with large, grey, bald, egg-shaped heads and slanting reptilian eyes-became the "stereotype" for alien descriptions later given by a legion of abductees. Such a description, as told to Raymond Fowler by Betty Andreasson in The Andreasson Affair, is dismissed by Klass as demonstrating "that even a basically honest, religious person (Andreasson), who admits to having read UFO books and who has a vivid imagination, can easily invent a tale that credulous UFOiogists find impossible to dismiss as fantasy."

Hypnotic regression is a frequently used but dangerous tool to extract memories of "abduction" experiences. Experiments have shown that even deeply hypnotized subjects can willfully and convincingly lie, and subjects can feign hypnosis and deceive their questioners. Of equal concern, hypnotic suggestions to relive past events, particularly when used with questioning about specific details, pressures the subject to provide information which may be confabulated from fantasies and memories of other people's experiences. These pseudo-memories which can develop from hypnotic regression sessions become firmly entrenched within the subject's conscious memory the more often the pseudo-event is recounted.

Two books about alien abductions by Budd Hopkins, a New York artist and self-taught hypnotist, come under close scrutiny because Klass considers Hopkins to be "the 'Typhoid Mary' of this tragic malaise" who has inflicted "mental scars" on the people he hypnotized and from whom he extracted abduction stories. Hopkin's first book, Missing Time, convinced Klass that Hopkins has "become so obsessed with UFO abductions that any even slightly unusual story he hears becomes a UFO abduction."

Missing time became the first indicator alerting Hopkins that someone might have been abducted. And yet, what normal person has not at some point noticed in everyday life that time has suddenly slipped away faster than expected, or that a trip took much longer than expected? Hopkins believes hypnosis is the magic key to unlock abduction memories which were intentionally suppressed by alien kidnappers. Yet, many subjects can remember their "abductions" without the aid of hypnosis. This discrepancy tells Klass that "UFOnauts sometimes forget to suppress memories of abduction in their victims," which is to say, these supposedly superior beings act as if they are quite human. Further straining credulity is Hopkin's contention that, in Klass' words, "a person can be a UFO-abduction victim without ever recalling having seen a UFO or having been inside a flying saucer!"

In Hopkin's second book, *Intruders*, he describes how a troubled, divorced and unemployed mother named Kathie, after having read his first book, came to him with disturbing dreams. He put her through hypnotic regression and she told of having been repeatedly abducted by aliens who stole her unborn baby from her womb. Hopkins calls this case one of his most important because physical evidence was left behind in Kathie's backyard in the form of UFO landing trace marks. This dead grass area about eight feet in diameter turned out to be located near a bird-feeder. Rather than a burn caused by a UFO, Klass quotes soil scientists as identifying such dead grass spots to be the result of a fungus stimulated to grow by urine and excretions from the birds.

Whitley Strieber's book, Communion, is debunked on the basis of two major considerations. By his own admission, Strieber sometimes cannot recall what did or did not happen to him in the past. For instance, he often told of having seen people shot by sniper Charles Whitman from the University of Texas tower in 1966, but now Strieber believes that he was never actually present during the shootings. Strieber also shows many of the symptoms of having a brain abnormality called temporal-lobe epilepsy, defined by psychologist Dr. Barry Beyerstein as "a tendency to find profound meaning in mundane events," periodic hallucinations and mystical revelations, and frequent experiences of "a variety of spontaneous events widely regarded as paranormal."

Watch The Skies!
CURTIS PEEBLES
(1994, Smithsonian Institution Press)

When he began the research in 1988 for this "chronicle of the flying saucer myth," Curtis Peebles described himself as a skeptic who believed "flying saucer reports are misinterpretations of conventional objects, phenomena, and experiences." Those convictions only hardened after completion of his wide-ranging historical review of the phenomenon, encompassing such subjects as the saucer flap of 194 7, early Air Force UFO investigations, crashed saucer cons and scams leading up to Roswell, the CIA's Robertson Panel, the first contactees, UFO conspiracy theories, the Socorro landing, alleged astronaut UFO sightings, the Condon Report, Project Blue Book, cattle mutilations, alien abductions, the MJ-12 forgeries, and much more.

In 1947 the U.S. Air Force began its 22-year involvement with UFOs by launching an investigative unit codenamed Project Sign. That first year 122 UFO reports were received and all but 12 were identified. In secret, however, these Air Force investigators were "moving toward the Extraterrestrial Hypothesis, while publicly dismissing flying saucers as natural phenomena and hoaxes." By the end of 1948 Project Sign had completed an "Estimate of the Situation," an investigative report stamped Top Secret, which concluded that "flying saucers were real and they came from outer space." Air Force Chief of Staff Gen. Hoyt S. Vandenberg forcefully rejected that finding as being unsupported by the evidence. Project Sign was disbanded and a new investigative staff formed under the codename Project Grudge, later to be called Project Blue Book. Thus began the Air Force's long preoccupation with explaining away UFO reports as misidentifications of weather balloons, the planet Venus, and other natural objects.

A concern that UFO reports could overwhelm U.S. government communications and intelligence channels, giving the Soviet Union an opportunity to launch a surprise attack, prompted the CIA to form a scientific panel to review the UFO situation in 1952. The Robertson Panel, as the group became known, by its very association with the CIA helped to generate a flying saucer belief system "based on the idea that the government had some 'secret knowledge' which 'proved' the reality of UFOs." That the Robertson Panel concluded there were no UFO cases "attributable to foreign artifacts" only intensified the feverish, paranoid speculations of conspiracy theorists for decades to come.

Long before the alleged saucer crash in Roswell garnered sustained public prominence, the myth of crashed UFOs got its first mainstream attention in 1948 when the editor of *The Aztec Independent-Review* newspaper, as a prank, printed a story about a flying saucer crashing near Aztec, New Mexico. More than 100 newspapers worldwide would eventually reprint the story as fact. Two con men elaborated on the hoax and convinced showbusiness writer Frank Scully of its validity, and in 1950 he published a book, *Behind the Flying Saucers*, describing how the dwarfish bodies of 16 alien crewmen aboard the crashed Aztec spaceship were recovered by the Air Force. Scully accused the Air Force of engaging in a conspiracy to hide that saucer, along with the remains of two others which crashed in Arizona, at Wright-Patterson AFB in Ohio, where the bodies of the alien crewmen were being studied and stored.

The alleged saucer crash near Roswell, N.M. in 1947, first widely publicized in the late 1970s, bears little resemblance in its initial witness reports to the myth which much later evolved around the incident. Mac Brazel, on whose ranch the debris was found, described the wreckage as a bunch of broken sticks and a foil-like substance which, when the entire debris field was bundled together, weighed about five pounds. That description made by the man who found the wreckage much more closely resembles a weather balloon, as the Air Force claims it was, than any sort of sophisticated flying saucer from outer space carrying aliens.

By the early 1980s the "flying saucer myth" was a fabric of belief interwoven with three primary threads-crashed saucers, alien abductions, and cattle mutilations said to be the work of UFOs. Even the alien component itself would "become submerged in a witch's brew of fascist conspiracy theories, hate, and paranoia."

Credit goes to Paul Bennewitz, president of a small electronics company in Albuquerque, N.M., for having inspired the ultimate fear mongering conspiracy theory. In 1979 he became convinced that implants were controlling the actions of alien abductees. He also believed that he had picked up electromagnetic signals from UFOs and had translated the messages. This led him to conclude there are two types of aliens visiting us-the malevolent "Greys," which are responsible for the cattle mutilations and implants in human beings; and the friendlier "Highs," also known as the Nordics or Blonds. Bennewitz further insisted that the Greys had "entered into a secret treaty with the U.S. government" which allowed them to conduct cattle mutilations and abduct humans without interference, as they operated from their secret underground base outside Dulce, N.M. In return the U.S. government got advanced alien technology. Eventually Bennewitz, fearing that aliens were coming through his bedroom walls at night and injecting him with chemicals, "suffered a mental breakdown and was hospitalized."

Though "it is clear the alien myth was a product of the troubled mind" of Bennewitz, his message had succeeded at gaining converts. An Air Force sergeant, Richard

Doty, working at Kirtland AFB, began spreading references in 1981 to alleged secret government documents called "MJ-12" which would blow the lid off the treaty between the Greys and the U.S. government. Doty also fed UFO researchers, such as Linda Moulton Howe, a series of fake documents claiming the Greys were behind the cattle mutilations, and the U.S. government had covered up numerous UFO crashes, including one at Aztec, N.M., another at Roswell, where alien bodies were recovered. Doty eventually ended his Air Force career as a "food services specialist."

In the wake of Bennewitz and Doty, a chorus line of other claimants to the conspiracy theory throne-John Lear, Robert Lazar, William Cooper-stepped forward with some new twists on the MJ-12 papers theme. For instance, the technology the U.S. government got under its secret treaty with the Greys was being tested at Area 51 in Nevada, a part of the test flight facility which had developed the Stealth and a series of spy planes. Lazar added that the Strategic Defense Initiative was really all about developing weapons to destroy the Greys because they were now intent on enslaving the human species as if we were nothing more than cattle.

Spaceships of the Pleiades
KALK.KORFF
(1995, Prometheus Books)

Eduard "Billy" Meier had been in and out of prison several times in Switzerland for thievery, forgery, and going AWOL from the French Foreign Legion. In 1974, while living off Swiss welfare benefits, Meier formed a metaphysical study group and recruited ten members from the Swiss farming community of Hinwill. During one of these group sessions on January 28, 1975, Meier proclaimed that he was in regular physical contact with alien visitors from the Pleiades star system. Soon Meier began producing "hundreds of exceptionally clear photographs of the 'Pleiadian spacecraft' as proof that he was telling the truth." These photos later attracted notice from writer Gary Kinder and retired U.S. Air Force Lt. Col. Wendelle Stevens, both of whom would write favorable books about Meier and the credibility of his claims and photographic evidence.

During August and September 1991, American computer systems analyst Kal Korff visited the Meier UFO compound in Switzerland six times under an alias and investigated Meier's claims by interviewing current and former followers. This book which resulted from that investigation has been lauded by Jerome Clark, vice president of the J. Allen Hynek Center for UFO Studies, as "the definitive expose of the most ambitious hoax in UFO history."

Meier's 50-acre farm and his metaphysical study group evolved over the years into a religious cult called the Semjase Silver Star Center, with Meier enshrined as head guru. Among the list of claims that Meier and his followers make: (1) Between January 1975 and August 1991 Meier had more than 700 personal contacts with the Pleiadians led by a female alien named Semjase. (2) Over 1,000 photos were taken by Meier during this period documenting the visiting spacecraft and alien life forms, some taken during a five-day trip Meier made aboard a Pleiadian flying saucer. (3) Landing tracks and other physical evidence were left behind by the Pleiadians which Earth scientists have studied and verified as extraterrestrial in origin. (4) The Pleiadians anointed Meier to be a prophet to humankind and have enabled him to travel both backward and forward in time to hold personal conversations with Jesus Christ and other beings equal to Meier's superior intellect.

Though Hans Jacob, one of the original members of the Meier study group, had died, Korff was able to locate his daughter, Claudia. She provided him with her father's research records and notes pertaining to Meier, along with binders of Meier's original UFO photo prints in chronological order. Jacob had become convinced long before he died that Meier was a charlatan who had fabricated his story and the photos for financial gain. The photos Jacob had saved would prove a goldmine for Korff, who subjected them to computer enhancement analysis which revealed how Meier had dangled small models in front of his camera to give the impression of large saucers hovering.

Claudia and her sister Corneilia remembered an incident which underscored Meier's propensity for manipulation and deception. They and their father were invited one afternoon to meet Semjase, the Pleiadian leader, and see her spaceship. They stood around for hours without seeing anything. Several days later Meier stopped by their home with photos of Semjase's saucer hovering over their heads. Meier explained that the saucer had been over them the whole afternoon, only the Jacob family could not see it. An examination of the photos by Korff revealed them to be "deliberate, methodical double exposures."

During his 105th contact with Semjase, Meier claims he was given proof of the Pleiadian visitations for Earth scientists to examine—four metals, one biological (a lock of Semjase's hair), and nine mineral specimens. These samples were turned over to Wendelle Stevens so he could find scientists and labs to test them. Korff tracked down these scientists and labs to determine the results. All the analyses done on the Meier samples found them to be common Earth elements. As for the lock of Semjase's hair—it was blonde, with split-ends, very human in origin!

367

Section Four: Debunkers and Skeptics

The Demon-Haunted World
CARL SAGAN
(1995, Random House)

Alien abduction accounts involving forced medical procedures and the use of humans as breeding stock raise a series of provocative questions for astronomer Carl Sagan: Why do the alien examining instruments as described seem little more advanced than those used by local human hospitals? Why organize repeated sexual encounters between kidnapped humans when aliens could more easily steal a few egg and sperm cells and do whatever genetic experiments they want? Why would beings able to master the physics of crossing interstellar distances "be so backward when it comes to biology"?

For Sagan the preoccupation with sex and reproduction underlying most abduction tales waves a warning flag. Because we "live in a time fraught with numerous ghastly accounts, both true and false, of childhood sexual abuse," might it be possible that a large number of people claiming abuse at the hands of aliens are in fact recovering memories of sexual abuse by friends and relatives hidden under a fantasy screen of aliens? The revelation that many stories of childhood sexual abuse are false, induced by hypnotists asking leading questions, leads Sagan to suspect another link to abduction claims. "If some people can with great passion and conviction be led to falsely remember being abused by their own parents, might not others, with comparable passion and conviction, be led to falsely remember being abused by aliens"?

Hallucinations are a common and a natural part of the process of being human, says Sagan, "and may occur to perfectly normal people under perfectly ordinary circumstances." The fact that most alien abductions occur when the subject is falling asleep, or when they are waking up, or on a long driving trip, suggests that the autohypnotic state induces dreams and hallucinations which, much as a lucid dream does, can easily be mistaken for an experience in objective, waking reality.

An entire category of sleep disturbances-ranging from sleep paralysis to auditory or visual hallucinations-can account for "many if not most of the alien abduction accounts." Similarly, people with a condition known as temporal lobe epilepsy, in which the brain generates an uncontrollable cascade of electrical impulses, have been shown by neurophysiologists to suffer from hallucinations which take the form of the presence of strange beings, the sensation of floating in the air, missing time, sexual escapades, and a sense of having experienced something profound-all conditions reported by alien "abductees."

Harvard professor Dr. John Mack alarms Sagan because he is "awash in gullibility" and no longer able to exercise critical thinking, as evidenced by his book, Abduction. In it, Mack seems to have lost the capacity to distinguish between dreams and hallucinations, and events in objective reality. Why does Mack accept the accounts of alien abduction witnesses, but not the stories of other persons who, with just as much emotional intensity, describe their encounters with fairies, angels, demons and spirits of the dead?

Where is the physical evidence for the reality of alien abduction? Dr. Mack points to scars and "scoop marks" on the bodies of abductees, supposedly inflicted by the alien abductors during their medical experiments. Yet there are known psychiatric disorders in which people mutilate themselves without any recollection of the infliction of pain. And more importantly, "if the scars are within human capacity to generate, then they cannot be compelling physical evidence of abuse by aliens." Why haven't independent physicians been allowed to examine those of Mack's patients who allegedly were scarred by aliens? One of Mack's patients claims that aliens have been stealing her eggs for years and this has baffled her gynecologist. "Is it baffling enough to write the case up and submit a research paper to The New England Journal of Medicine"? Apparently, this case, like all the others claiming physical evidence, are not baffling enough to warrant submission to peer review scientific journals where they would undergo rigorous scrutiny.

If Earth women are being impregnated by aliens in genetic experiments, as Mack and other abduction apologists claim, why has there never been a miscarriage revealing an alien hybrid? Why has nothing unusual shown up in routine sonograms of fetuses? How about the abductees who allege that tiny implants were inserted into their bodies during abductions? In those few cases where the alleged implants were not later conveniently lost or discarded, expert examination has found none of extraterrestrial manufacture. None had components of unusual isotopes or unknown chemical compositions. The so-called implants were all boringly terrestrial, common elements.

Nonetheless, Sagan believes there is "genuine scientific paydirt in UFOs and alien abductions"-only it has to do with brain physiology, the nature of hallucinations, the psychology of hoaxes and systems of manipulation and belief, and "perhaps even the origins of our religions."

The UFO Invasion
EDITED BY KENDRICK FRAZIER, BARRY KARR & JOE NICKELL
(1997, Prometheus Books)

This compilation of 40 articles originally appeared in the *Skeptical Inquirer*, the bimonthly journal of the Committee for the Scientific Investigation of Claims of the

Paranormal, a nonprofit group which "encourages an attitude of critical thinking and responsible, tentative skepticism toward all new claims and assertions." Topics covered here with a skeptical eye range from the alleged UFO crash at Roswell, the alien autopsy film, and the MJ-12 papers, to famous UFO sighting cases, alien abduction claims, and the crop circle phenomenon.

Since the early 1980s, when federal courts ruled that the National Security Agency could withhold 156 UFO-related documents from release under the Freedom of Information Act on grounds of national security, UFO believers have labeled the action a cover-up and evidence of a "Cosmic Watergate." Aviation writer Philip J. Klass responds that releasing the documents would alert foreign governments to "which cryptographic codes have been cracked by NSA and are no longer secure." He notes how a former NSA employee, Tom Deuley, who reviewed many of the 156 documents for the NSA, has since left the agency and declared publicly: "none of the documents I was aware of had any information of scientific value." Release of these decoded transcripts of intercepted messages from foreign governments, according to Deuley, would result in "damage to national security sources and methods that far outweighs the value of the information under question."

UFO researchers Robert Todd and Karl Pflock independently discovered in the early 1990's that the debris found in July 1947 on Mac Brazel's ranch, later known as the Roswell Incident, came from a secret balloon program called Project Mogul and not from an alien spacecraft. The balloon and its scientific equipment had been launched from Alamogordo Army Air Field in New Mexico on June 4, 1947, and consisted of two dozen neoprene sounding balloons extending 600 feet, pulling three radar reflectors and a science payload (a sonobuoy) designed for high altitude spying on Soviet nuclear tests. A surviving Project Mogul scientist, Charles Moore, revealed to Air Force investigators in 1994 how this June 4 flight had been tracked to within 17 miles of where the debris field was found on the ranch ten days later. The debris was strewn along a southwest-to-northeast angle, precisely the direction the balloon was headed when its batteries died, cutting off contact with Moore and his colleagues. As for Major Jesse Marcel, the intelligence officer sent to gather the debris, his expertise was in aerial reconnaissance. He was not familiar with the equipment used in Project Mogul, making his failure to identify it understandable.

In 1995, a film titled Alien Autopsy: Fact or Fiction? aired on American television, purporting to show the autopsy of an alien body from the alleged crash of a spacecraft at Roswell. The film's cameraman remained anonymous, and the British marketing firm which had come into possession of the film refused to submit it for examination to determine its age. Most prominent UFO researchers branded the film a hoax. American pathologists pointed out how the doctors portrayed in the film performing the autopsy were obvious amateurs unfamiliar with autopsy procedures, instruments, or the handling of body organs. Not only that, but the alien body, with its ears, toenails and five fingers, differed anatomically from eyewitness reports of alleged alien bodies at Roswell. The film footage itself "bore a bogus, nonmilitary codemark that disappeared after it was criticized."

A 1980 UFO incident in Britain, outside the U.S. Air Force base at Woodbridge, receives a roasting from Ian Ridpath, a British science writer. What U.S. airmen thought was a bright pulsating nighttime UFO that landed in a forest, Ridpath explains away as the beam from a nearby lighthouse. The flashing beam often seems to hover only a few feet above ground level. UFO landing marks and tree burns reported by the airmen are dismissed as rabbit diggings and axe cuts in the tree bark. Supposedly abnormal radiation readings at the site were really what "would be expected from natural sources of radiation, such as cosmic rays and the earth itself." The whole incident started with observation of a bright meteor, then misidentification of the lighthouse beam, becoming "a marvelous product of human imagination."

Thanks primarily to building contractor Ed Walters and his book, The Gulf Breeze Sightings, that Florida city became a UFO capital in the late 1980s and early 1990s. Walters produced dozens of Polaroid photos in that period purporting to show UFOs over Gulf Breeze at night. This whole "three-ring flying saucer circus," claims science writer Robert Sheaffer, has been exposed as a hoax which Walters used for financial gain. A Gulf Breeze youth came forward to confess that he and two others, including Walters' son, had helped to fabricate the photos. Equally damning, occupants of a house Walters had lived in during the alleged UFO blitz found a UFO model hidden within the garage attic which resembled the object seen in the Walters photos. A national UFO group, MUFON, sent two investigators to evaluate the Walters story and they concluded Walters was "adept at trick photography" and the case clearly had all the markings of a clever, gigantic hoax that enriched Walters with a book deal and fees from movie and television producers.

The Roswell UFO Crash
KAL. KORFF
(1997, Prometheus Books)

If indeed an alien spacecraft crashed near Roswell in 1947, "it would certainly constitute the story of the millennium and be the greatest government-sponsored cover-up of all time," concedes Kal Korff. And on the face of it the case for a crash appeared strong. The sheer number of "seemingly credible, independent eyewitnesses" dredged up by researchers and the "consistency of their accounts" seemed to catapult this incident into a realm well beyond all other allegations of UFO crashes. As Korff examined evidence presented in the three major books on the subject-The Roswell Incident by Charles Berlitz and William Moore, UFO Crash at Roswell by Kevin Randle and Donald Schmitt, and Crash at Corona by Stanton Friedman and Don Berliner-he discovered serious discrepancies between these various accounts and a "curious pattern" involving the selective use of facts and testimony.

In the Moore and Berlitz book they purport to have interviewed more than 70 persons who were witness to some aspect of the Roswell crash. Korff dissects that claim and finds the testimonies of only 25 persons are presented in the book, of whom just seven are firsthand sources claiming to have seen the alleged saucer debris. Of those seven only five "claim to have actually handled the material personally, and one of them is adamant it was not from an extraterrestrial spacecraft." The remainder of the so-called witnesses were passing on hearsay information, never saw any wreckage, or were never present at the debris field.

What all of the witnesses suffer from is reliance on memories 31 years or more old. The passage of time erodes the accuracy of recollections, a fact evidenced by the "star" witness, Major Jesse Marcel. When he was first interviewed in 1978, he could not remember the month or year of the alleged Roswell saucer crash. His answer to the question of when it occurred was always "in the late forties." With each telling of the Roswell story, however, many of the witnesses began to embellish their memories of the event. Loretta Proctor is a case in point. She lived eight miles from the debris field and was allegedly shown a piece by Mac Brazel, the rancher who found the debris. In the Friedman book she is quoted as saying the piece resembled balsa wood but "we cut on it with a knife and would hold a match on it, and it wouldn't burn. We knew it wasn't wood." Yet in a 1989 taped interview before the Friedman book appeared, Proctor denied she and her husband had tried to cut or burn the piece, saying it was Brazel who had handled it. And even earlier, for the 1979 book by Moore and Berlitz, Proctor "made no mention at all of ever having personally seen any of the debris."

The greatest collapse of credibility comes in an examination of Jesse Marcel's military record. Korff obtained nearly 200 pages comprising Marcel's military service file, finding in it "beyond a shadow of a doubt" that Marcel "had a penchant for exaggerating things and repeatedly trying to 'write himself into the history books.'" In interviews with UFO researchers, Marcel had claimed to be a pilot who shot down five enemy planes in World War II, who graduated from George Washington University, and who wrote a report about the first Soviet atomic explosion which President Truman read from in an address to the nation on radio. Absolutely none of this was true! These and other lies, exaggerations, and discrepancies lead Korff to believe that everything Marcel said about what happened at Roswell must now be questioned as a possible falsehood.

Accompanying Major Marcel to the debris field outside Roswell in 1947 was Army Counterintelligence Corps special agent Sheridan Cavitt. In a signed, sworn statement made in 1994, Cavitt contradicted Marcel on every major point about the nature of the debris and the size of the debris field. "I remember recognizing this material as being consistent with a weather balloon," insisted Cavitt. "There was no secretive effort or heightened security regarding this incident or any unusual expenditure of manpower at the base to deal with it." Cavitt remembers Marcel as being someone who tended "to exaggerate things on occasion."

Among the six authors who together wrote the three major books on Roswell, warfare has broken out with several either rejecting their own conclusions, or debunking material and witnesses used by the others. Don Berliner no longer supports the San Agustin crash story he wrote with Stanton Friedman. Kevin Randle has disassociated himself from his co author, Donald Schmitt, "citing flawed research and dishonesty, among other things." Friedman has attacked Randle's two books, accusing him of "no less than 38 significant mistakes, many of which cannot be explained innocently." Meanwhile, Randle demolished the credibility of Friedman's primary witness featured in *Crash At Corona*. All of which compels Kal Korff to conclude that "if the Roswell 'UFO crash' is supposed to represent both the 'truth' and the 'best' UFO case that UFOiogy has to offer, then the UFO field is in deep trouble."

Lights in the Sky & Little Green Men: A Rational Christian Look at UFOs and Extraterrestrials
HUGH ROSS & KENNETH SAMPLES & MARK CLARK
(2002, NavPress)

These three co-authors are associated with 'Reasons To Believe', an institute founded "to research and proclaim the factual basis for faith in God and his word, the Bible." This collection of 16 essays in this book, written between the three of them, covers UFOs, life on other planets, space travel, abductees, contactees, UFO cults and the Bible, and how "the word of God" explains all of this and more as being phenomena connected to the demonic realm.

Their emphasis is on the small residual percentage of UFO reports, called RUFOs for residual UFOS, which remain unexplained. They begin by listing a series of factors they believe show that other intelligent life in the universe, if it even exists, would not be traveling to earth because the scale of space and the speeds that would be necessary to get here make visits unlikely if not impossible. So the RUFO sightings that remain unexplained are probably either secret government space vehicles or demons.

To explain why the U.S. government may have been promoting a UFO coverup the authors claim it has nothing to do with crashed extraterrestrial spacecraft or alien beings. The coverup and lying coming from military officials is to conceal military secrets. "The U.S. government lies," write the authors, and that is because "protecting national security sometimes necessitates lying." UFO conspiracy theorists are "irrational" for even suggesting the government would coverup real extraterrestrial visits because extraterrestrials don't exist except in the imaginations of UFO nuts.

Demons are behind RUFOs and one way to know is simply by surveying people who report sightings and claim abductions and you will "observe a correlation between the degree of invitations in a person's life to demonic attacks (for example, participation in seances, Ouija games, astrology, spiritualism, witchcraft, palm reading and psychic reading)." All of those practices open people up to RUFO encounters and "the only defense to be found against the evil, deception, and supernatural powers manifested in residual UFOs is in Christianity and the Bible."

The entire contactee phenomenon beginning in the 1950s had its origins in occult practices. All of the best-known UFO cults—The Atherius Society, The Unarius Academy of Science, Heaven's Gate, The Raelian Movement—were found by occultists. That means, according to the authors, a demonic influence is at the heart of the entire RUFO phenomenon and has been from the very beginning of unidentified flying object reports.

A close examination of RUFOs "shows that they are consistent with the Bible's descriptions of demons," the three men write. "The UFO mystery is a mystery solved. Earth is not being visited by aliens from another planet, but some people are being visited by spirit beings who want everyone to think they are aliens from another planet. The authors of this book are fully convinced that both science and Scripture point to the supra-dimensional beings known as demons as the malevolent sources of RUFO phenomena."

*Body Snatchers in the Desert: The Horrible Truth at the
Heart of the Roswell Story*
NICK REDFERN
(2005, Gallery Books)

Though not normally a UFO skeptic, here is how prolific author Nick Redfern ends this book: "Forget flying saucers. Roswell had *nothing* to do with the crash of an extraterrestrial space vehicle. The truth is much darker and far more disturbing and has been covered up for more than a half a century."

He proceeds to explain how a 'flying wing' craft designed in Nazi Germany had been captured by the U.S. and then test flown in New Mexico in 1947, occupied by "a number of physically handicapped people who had been found in the remnants of the Japanese military's Unit 731 laboratories and who were used in this dark and disturbing experiment—the purpose of which was to try to better understand the effects of nuclear-powered flight on an air crew." The craft crash landed in the desert and killed some of its crew.

A second test flight occurred two months later, according to Redfern, but this time the flying-wing vehicle had been attached to a large array of Fugo balloons developed by the Japanese, and the crew consisted of Japanese personnel. The aircraft and balloons were struck by lightning and the entire construct crashed, killing the crew, and giving rise "to the legend of the Roswell incident."

How Redfern reached these conclusions makes for an interesting read. He claims one of his anonymous sources was a Colonel who had served in the Defense Intelligence Agency, a position from which this Colonel had read top secret documents outlining what really happened in New Mexico in 1947 and beyond. The two flying wing crashes occurred during experiments involving simulated nuclear power propulsion systems. The handicapped pilots on board were exposed to radiation "that might be expected from a nuclear power source when we have one." The recovery of their bodies and the crash debris was cloaked in secrecy comparable to the Manhattan Project that developed the atomic bomb. This was why a "crashed UFO cover" story had been affixed to the Roswell case by the U.S. military as part of a psychological warfare campaign to mislead the Soviet Union about what had really happened.

Corroboration of the Colonel's account, says Redfern, came to him from government documents and testimony from several other sources, including an elderly lady he calls Black Widow. She approached him in 2001, after a speaking appearance he made, and confided a story about working at the Oak Ridge National Laboratory in the 1940s, where she witnessed three bodies brought there from the alleged Roswell crash of 1947. She described them as three handicapped Japanese people who had been used in radiation tests and experiments. She believed they had been killed in a classified high altitude balloon array flight with a gondola attached holding the human guinea pigs to test their exposure to radiation in the atmosphere.

The Black Widow's claims set Redfern off on his investigation to find others who could support her story. Aside from the Colonel, who filled in many pertinent details, Redfern found another former Oak Ridge employee, Bill Salter, who confirmed some of the Black Widow's story about the three deformed Japanese bodies being brought to Oak Ridge from Roswell. Salter contended that he had talked to a friend of his at Oak Ridge who had been ordered to destroy the files on this case and the man shared details what he read before the files went through a shredder.

Another named source for Redfern was Al Barker, who had worked on psychological warfare projects for the Army in the 1950s. Barker claimed that through 1947, "we had these bodies and strange-looking people used in medical tests across the country—in the desert, at Los Alamos, at Oak Ridge." These human radiation experiments and the resulting casualties were the reason for strict secrecy and the Roswell saucer crash cover story involving alien bodies served a useful purpose in keeping both the American public and the Soviets in the dark. Confessed Barker to Redfern: "I'm not proud of all this, but it is the truth."

Abducted: How People Come to Believe They Were Kidnapped by Aliens
SUSAN CLANCY
(2005, Harvard University Press)

As a postdoctoral fellow in psychology at Harvard University, Susan Clancy undertook research attempting to answer why and how the human mind can create remarkable experiences and solidify a belief in the reality of those experiences. She began by testing false-memory creation and 'repressed memories' in sexual abuse victims, but then shifted her focus to people who believed they had been abducted by extraterrestrial visitors.

During interviews with 50 or so self-described abductees, Clancy noticed they had different stories but "one thing in common: they'd begun to wonder if they'd been abducted only after they experienced things they felt were anomalous—weird, abnormal, unusual things." One of those strange experiences was sleep paralysis, which affects up to a quarter of all people at some point in their lives, but many of the people Clancy interviewed ascribed an alien abduction explanation to their experience, based on exposure to cultural priming. Many had read alien themed books, such as *Communion* by Whitley Strieber, or had seen alien abduction movies that had planted seeds of belief in their subconscious mind.

"Though I'm far from suggesting that alien abductees tend to be psychotic or otherwise psychiatrically impaired," writes Clancy, "they do hold false beliefs—ones that appear to be natural by-products of their attempts to explain the unusual things that have happened to them....Once the seed of belief was planted, once alien abduction was even suspected, the abductees began to search for confirmatory evidence."

She describes how many self-described abductees, in their search for 'evidence' to support a belief in their experience, turn to hypnosis in attempts to 'retrieve' memories of their experience. Instead of memory retrieval these hypnotic sessions mostly create false memories through the power of suggestion and imagination. "Most of my subjects who had abduction memories—like most subjects in the scientific literature who report such memories—acquired them through hypnosis or other related psychotherapeutic techniques." Clancy relates science research showing how the human brain conjures up memories and memory details during the act of 'remembering' and this process gives free rein to the imagination to summon missing pieces in the memory puzzle. Hypnosis reinforces this process by lulling the subject into a suggestible mind state inducing them to 'imagine' what might have happened, not what actually happened.

As a group, self-styled abductees that Clancy worked with "also scored high on measures indicative of a personality construct called schizotypy," which may be a genetic marker for schizophrenia and at the very least, schizotypy indicates a measure of fantasy-proneness. That doesn't mean abductees are outright schizophrenic, but Clancy says they are "generally a bit odd. They tend to look and think eccentrically and are prone to 'magical' thinking and odd beliefs...they are often loners and typically believe in paranormal phenomena such as telepathy and clairvoyance."

Clancy concludes after her research, "these nice people weren't interested in truth, at least not the kind of truth you find with scientific methods. Alien abductees have faith. They believe what they believe not because of any objective evidence but in spite of it. They didn't question their experiences. They were trying to confirm their beliefs." Clancy voices her suspicion that in coming decades "believing in aliens and in their presence among us will perhaps become as common as believing in God."

UFO Crash at Roswell: The Genesis of a Modern Myth
BENSON SALER, CHARLES A. ZIEGLER, & CHARLES B. MOORE
(2010, Smithsonian)

These three authors—Saler and Ziegler are anthropologists at Brandeis University, Moore is a professor of atmospheric physics in New Mexico—argue that a small pile of weather balloon wreckage found outside Roswell, N.M. in 1947 spawned a modern American myth and cultural phenomenon, whose adherents, believing it was a spacecraft carrying extraterrestrials, have become part of a religious-like cult.

Co-author Moore served as a project engineer on the 1947 series of balloon flights carrying radar reflectors that was part of a top-secret project, code-named Mogul, designed to spy on nuclear atmospheric tests conducted by the Soviet Union. Moore makes a case using ground tracking data and weather reports that balloon array Flight #4, launched on July 7, 1947, fell on the Foster Ranch outside of Roswell, and matched the debris reported by a rancher and Roswell base officers. The balloon had been traveling in a northeasterly direction and the debris on the ranch, as reported by witnesses, had been scattered in a northeastern direction.

According to Moore, the rancher, Mac Brazel, and his daughter, who found the wreckage "provided a good description of the scattered debris that would have been produced by one of our balloon trains." At the time of finding the debris, Brazel said "the rubber was smoky gray," and the amount of it "made a bundle about 18 or 20 inches long and about 8 inches thick," with all of the rubber and tinfoil and sticks weighing "maybe five pounds." Moore says all of these details conform with the appearance of one of his balloon arrays.

How and why would such an insignificant occurrence be blown up into a huge worldwide conspiracy and enduring myth? It didn't help that the Roswell army air base issued an incorrect and sensationalized press release claiming, without verification, that its officers had possession of a flying disc. Once the press release had been retracted, the harm had already been done. It also didn't help matters that the military lied again, to protect a classified project, by saying the debris was just an ordinary weather balloon when it was a more advanced and thus unfamiliar balloon array to spy on Soviet nuclear testing.

The authors also lay blame on Major Jesse Marcel, one of two officers sent to the ranch to inspect the debris. It was Marcel who broke secrecy in 1978 and related his version of what happened to a UFO researcher. In this book Marcel is portrayed as someone who "embroidered the truth about his background" and engaged in "a pattern of embellishment that suggests deliberate deception." They further accuse Marcel as being someone willing to lie to enrich himself financially and receive "psychological reward derived from the response of his listeners."

Authors of a series of pro-UFO books about the Roswell incident contributed to the myth by breaking "all the generally accepted rules of investigative reporting and historical research because they misquote witnesses, ignore testimony that contradicts their claims, accept the testimony of witnesses who are pre-conditioned by the media and/or by the interviewers themselves, accept conflicting testimony of several witnesses on the same topic, accept internally contradictory testimony, cite testimony from anonymous witnesses as the sole evidence for some of their assertions, accept testimony contradicted by physical evidence, and display an overreliance on the background of informants as an indicator of truthfulness."

Roswell has been nothing more than "a folk narrative masquerading as an expose," these three men claim, and over the decades each re-telling of the story by a succession of alleged witnesses has produced layers of embellishment and lies, fantasies and hoaxing, all designed to make money and perpetuate a myth about extraterrestrial visitation.

Mirage Men: An Adventure into Paranoia, Espionage, Psychological Warfare, and UFOs
MARK PILKINGTON
(2010, Skyhorse Publishing)

As detailed in this book, the U.S. Air Force Office of Special Investigations (AFOSI) apparently engaged in a campaign, during the 1970s and 80s, to spread disinformation among UFO investigators, with the intent of sowing the seeds of conspiracy theories while sabotaging and influencing the direction of UFO research being released to the public. One AFOSI disinformation effort in particular, targeting the engineer, physicist and defense contractor Paul Bennewitz, in New Mexico, raised the prospect in this author's mind that AFOSI, in league with the CIA and National Security Agency, "were in fact *responsible* for much of the UFO mythology." (Pilkington is a British journalist who wrote for newspapers and magazines in several countries.)

A key actor in the Bennewitz affair was AFOSI special agent Richard C. Doty, stationed at Kirtland Air Force Base, in Albuquerque. He befriended Bennewitz and fed him tales about crashed UFOs and ETs being in a secret alliance with the U.S. government, which eventually resulted in a mental breakdown on the part of Bennewitz, and the spread of toxic conspiracy theories in popular culture that persist to this day.

In a 1989 speech to a Mutual UFO Network conference in Las Vegas, UFO researcher William Moore revealed publicly for the first time how, over the previous decade, he had worked as an informant for AFOSI and special agent Doty, as well as on behalf of an alleged agent of the Defense Intelligence Agency, codenamed 'Falcon.' Moore, who had co-authored the seminal book, The Roswell Incident, had been recruited around the time of the book's publication, to feed false information to other UFO researchers, in return for receiving "the truth about UFOs" from his intelligence agency handlers.

Moore was entrusted by his handlers to give Bennewitz forged government documents purporting to show details of a classified government program that involved cooperation with alien visitors arriving in UFOs. Over time, as Bennewitz became more convinced of the authenticity of these and other fake documents, he even became convinced he was receiving and could decode alien transmissions. He became increasingly paranoid, "trapped in a paranoid feedback loop," manipulated by government agents he mistakenly thought were his friends.

"Most ufologists who listened to Paul {Bennewitz} based their own information on what he said, without investigating further," writes Pilkington. "The result was that Bennewitz's paranoid fantasies began to seep their way into the UFO underground. AFOSI were directly shaping what people thought about UFOs and were using Bill Moore to provide them with feedback. It was a textbook Psychological Operations scenario."

A capstone on the disinformation campaign was laid in 1983, when Moore's handlers gave him the MJ-12, Project Aquarius documents, which alleged that a secret government agency had been formed years earlier, to manage human cooperation with alien visitors in the wake of the Roswell vehicle crash. These forged documents soon became enshrined in UFO conspiracy folklore.

Despite all of the deceptions he had engaged in, and been subject to, Moore ended his 1989 speech revelations by declaring his continued support for the extraterrestrial visitation hypothesis. He also declared that the disinformation campaign he had been a party to existed to "provide security cover for a real UFO project that exists at a very high level and is known only to an elite few." He said this elite included the Trilateral Commission, who were using the appearance of a threat from UFOs to bring about a one world government, a New World Order.

In interviews that Pilkington conducted with Doty years later, for this book, the retired AFOSI agent claimed that not only did he still believe that aliens in UFOs are visiting our planet, but he revealed that he had personally seen and handled alien technology, some kind of holographic device, in the possession of a secret U.S. government agency. "Whether we believe Doty or not," Pilkington concluded, "we should also never forget that he was trained to deceive."

Pilkington interviewed former AFOSI special agent, Walter Bosley, who was involved in spreading stories about crashed saucers and alien bodies. In conversation with the author, Bosley claimed the U.S. had craft reverse-engineered from technology that isn't human. Bizarrely, he further declared, "and it's got something to do with the Nazis."

Still another of Pilkington's interview subjects, Kit Green, a former CIA employee and friend of Doty's, told a similar story as Doty: ETs have visited Earth and the U.S. government acquired one of their craft and spent decades trying to "understand or replicate it."

Scattered through this book are other examples and stories showing how U.S. government agencies engaged in attempts to shape public opinion about the nature of the UFO phenomenon. For example, the book describes how Leon Davidson, a supervisory engineer at the Los Alamos laboratories, argued in his writings throughout the 1950s and 60s, that most UFOs were 'American aviation products,' in the form of circular flying wings, and that "the CIA caused or sponsored saucer sightings for its own purposes." Davidson became the first and most prominent advocate of the theory that UFO sightings were being staged by government agencies to assess the psychological manipulation of UFO witnesses, both civilian and military.

Roswell and the Reich: The Nazi Connection
JOSEPH P. FARRELL
(2010, Adventures Unlimited Press)

Oxford-educated historian Joseph P. Farrell, author of a series of books on Nazi technologies developed during World War II, sets out in this book to debunk an extraterrestrial explanation for the Roswell crash in 1947, by dissecting the arguments and evidence made in support of the extraterrestrial hypothesis, and offering instead evidence, much of it circumstantial, that what crashed may have been a continuation of Nazi flying disc advances made by German scientists who had been brought to the U.S. at the end of the war.

Farrell critiques the four primary Roswell crash theories with supporting evidence for what happened, one by one:

(1) He spends 48 pages on the 1980 Berlitz and Moore book, the first one published about Roswell, which Farrell concludes is "deficient and unpersuasaive."

(2) His next target is *Crash At Corona*, a book by Friedman and Berliner, also blaming extraterrestrials for the crash, which Farrell uses 40 pages to disassemble as "anything but persuasive."

(3) A third version of the extraterrestrial hypothesis, advanced by Randle, Schmitt and Carey, with new witnesses and timelines, Farrell dissects in 41 pages showing how even these authors seem to concede "the technology {crash debris} is not exotic nor compelling enough to be extraterrestrial."

(4) Finally, Farrell takes issue with the debunkers and skeptics of an extraterrestrial explanation (Korff and Pflock) who try to label the crash as simply a secret Project Mogul balloon and dispatches their arguments in 39 pages of analysis.

That leaves for consideration the experimental craft crash explanation offered by Nick Redfern in his book, *Body Snatchers in the Desert*, which Farrell applauds as "the most important" of all the book because it is the closest to the truth. Farrell devotes the second half of his book to laying a circumstantial case that Nazi scientists were brought to the U.S. played a role in building and testing the craft that crashed at Roswell.

Operation Paperclip saw the U.S. military bring more than 1,000 German scientists and engineers to the U.S. at the end of World War II to continue their work developing rocketry and advanced aircraft, including a saucer-shaped craft called the Horten flying wing. Most of these scientists were stationed in and around U.S. military facilities in New Mexico, not far from Roswell, where Farrell contends that they "continued to have and pursue their own research agenda independent of their host country."

This research and development agenda had continued throughout the war as characterized by the 'foo fighters' reported by Allied pilots. These balls of fire that followed U.S. and British planes, "at least some of them," writes Farrell, "were in fact extraordinary German technologies."

Once in the U.S., Nazi scientists took control of developing the American space program. Werner von Braun, for instance, became the first director of the Marshall Space Flight Center, Arthur Rudolph became project director of the Saturn V rocket program, and Kurt Debus became the first director of the Kennedy Space Center. One piece of supporting testimony for Farrell's thesis comes from a deathbed confession by a Army Colonel who claimed he had been at the Roswell crash site and saw Germany insignia on a piece of the wreckage. The Colonel made this admission to Dr. John Lerma, who included it in one of his books.

Farrell goes on to list more categories of circumstantial evidence which he says show a pattern of independent Nazi science research culminating in a prototype of a Horten wing craft that went out of control on a test flight, crashing near Roswell and killing the guinea pig crew on board, prompting an embarrassed U.S. military to cover up the incident, not because it was extraterrestrial in origin, but because the Nazi technology connection would have been a public scandal.

"We know now that the Roswell Incident was not a silly balloon," concludes Farrell. "And we know it was not extraterrestrial either. It was in all likelihood, something Nazi, an enemy fighter."

Area 51: An Uncensored History of America's Top Secret Military Base
ANNIE JACOBSEN
(2011, Little, Brown and Company)

Based on interviews she conducted with 19 men who worked fulltime at the top-secret base, and another 32 scientists, pilots, and engineers who lived on it for periods of time, investigative reporter Annie Jacobsen sketches the history of Area 51, that infamous aircraft and bomb test facility in the Nevada desert, which has inspired fevered alien and UFO conspiracy theories for decades.

Area 51 was a dry lake bed built into an air base by the CIA in the 1950s, to provide a secure and remote military facility where experimental aircraft, such as the U-2 spy plane, could be developed and tested under a thick cloak of secrecy. Among those interviewed on the record for this book was former base commander Colonel Hugh Slater. He and her other interview subjects described how after the CIA ceded most control over Area 51 to the U.S. Air Force, in the 1970s, the rumors about the site being use to warehouse crashed saucer debris and alien bodies gained wider traction in popular culture.

Early in this book, she describes how "as soon as the U-2's started flying out of Area 51 {in the 1950s}, reports of UFO sightings by commercial airline pilots and air traffic controllers began to inundate CIA headquarters," due to the plane's radical shape and the unprecedented height at which it flew. As news media reports of UFO sightings proliferated, the U.S. Air Force initiated a public relations campaign, called Project Grudge, "to persuade the public that UFOs constituted nothing unusual or extraordinary." That U-2 aircraft were mistaken for UFOs was welcomed by the CIA, so as to further confuse the Soviet Union about developments in U.S. aerospace technology.

On pages 36 through 44 of the hardcover edition of this book, the author uses Army Intelligence documents, declassified in 1994, to help make a case that the aerial vehicle which crashed outside Roswell, N.M., in July 1947, was an experimental flying disc, first developed by Nazi scientists during World War II. Most alarming to U.S. military investigators at the time, "inside the disc, there was a very earthly hallmark: Russian writing. Block letters from the Cyrillic alphabet had been stamped, or embossed, in a ring running around the inside of the craft."

Apparently, the brothers Walter and Reimar Horten, two airplane engineers who invented a wing-shaped tailless aircraft for Hitler, had their blueprints and prototypes stolen at the end of the war by the Russians. According to this theory, as related by several of Jacobsen's sources, what was found outside of Roswell had been a Russian craft developed from the Horten prototype, powered by rockets, and manned by a single, short-statured pilot.

Debris from the Roswell crash "would stay at Wright-Patterson Air Force Base for approximately four years," writes Jacobsen. "From there, they would quietly be shipped out west to become intertwined with a secret facility {Area 51} out in the middle of the Nevada desert. No one but a handful of people would have any idea they were there." (Jacobsen notes how her sources indicated that Area 51 wasn't named after map coordinates; rather, the base was named after the 1951 date the site was established, when the crash debris arrived.)

Later in the book, on pages 367 through 384, Jacobsen relates how her interview subjects described the reverse engineering project to re-create the Horten/Russian flying disc. She indicates that much of her information came from the last living engineer, one of five assigned to examine the Roswell debris, who reverse engineering it for a new secret U.S. aircraft based on stealth technology, similar to what the Nazi scientists had pioneered using radar-absorbing paint.

Here is how Jacobsen says the surviving engineer described for her what happened at Roswell in 1947: "The crash did reveal a disc, not a weather balloon, as has subsequently been alleged by the Air Force. And responders from the Roswell Army Air Field found not only a crashed craft, but also two crash sites, and they found bodies alongside the crashed craft. These were not aliens. Nor were they consenting airmen.

They were human guinea pigs. Unusually petite for pilots, they appeared to be children... {with} ...unusually large heads and abnormally shaped oversize eyes."

What was Soviet leader Joseph Stalin's motive for sending several grotesquely deformed children flying into the New Mexico desert inside an advanced aerial craft designed by Nazi scientists? Jacobsen's engineer speculated that the plan was for the children and their unusual craft to "be mistaken for visitors from Mars" so that "panic would ensue, just like it did after the radio broadcast of *The War of the Worlds*." A side benefit would be to inspire waves of UFO sightings that could be eventually used to overwhelm America's early-warning radar system in the event of war between the U.S. and Soviet Union.

(Unfortunately, intentional or not, Jacobsen fails to credit, or even mention, Nick Redfern's book from six years earlier, *Body Snatchers in the Desert*, which was the first to make a case for the Roswell crash involving an experimental flying wing craft carrying human guinea pigs.)

They Are Already Here: UFO Culture and Why We See Saucers
SARAH SCOLES
(2020, Pegasus Books)

Freelance science journalist Sarah Scoles attended a UFO conference, visited the fringes of Area 51, the Roswell attractions, the UFO Watchtower platform, an astronomical observatory, and interviewed both UFO believers and skeptics to reach this conclusion: "In writing this book and talking to many members of my own species who I otherwise would not have known, I did not come to believe that flying saucers are real, or that an extraplanetary species made them."

This former ultra-devout Mormon set off on her research quest not because she had been interested in the UFO phenomenon, but rather as a result of reading a 2017 *New York Times* article revealing how the Pentagon acknowledged having had a secret program to investigate UFOs. What riveted her attention in the article was a reference to "metal alloys and other materials" that had allegedly been "recovered from unidentified aerial phenomena." She wrote a series of articles for *Wired* about those unverified claims and from these articles the idea for this book emerged because "what intrigued me most was not the UFOs themselves: It was the people obsessed with UFOs."

She began with a focus on hotel magnate Robert Bigelow and punk rocker Tom DeLonge, both of whom were connected to *The Times* article in various ways. Several of the primary former Pentagon employee sources for *The Times* article—Luis Elizondo and Christopher Mellon—worked with both Bigelow and DeLonge. It was Bigelow's company, Bigelow Aerospace, which received the $22 million Pentagon contract to examine UFOs, or unidentified aerial phenomena (UAPs) as the military chose to call it. DeLonge's company called To the Stars Academy of Arts and Science hosted the same two Navy videos of UFO sightings referenced in *The Times* article and DeLonge also allegedly took personal credit for 'orchestrating' *The Times* article.

Scoles found all of these interconnections raised serious doubts in her mind. "Suspicions—about the company, its people and this supposed UFO program's findings—sufficiently raised, I jumped down a wormhole whose boundary I'd been avoiding my whole adult life, especially as a science journalist."

What gave DeLonge credibility in the eyes of many UFO researchers was the appearance of his emails in the 2016 public leak of emails belonging to John Podesta, then Hilary Clinton's presidential campaign manager. Podesta had long been interested in UFOs and apparently DeLonge wanted to curry favor with him. In examining the emails, however, Scoles found that only about 30 of the emails from among thousands of leaked emails even mention DeLonge's name and most of them came from DeLonge. In one of them DeLonge wrote: "I hope you get my emails and I hope I am not bugging you." Rather than DeLonge having an intimate much less businesslike relationship with one of the world's most powerful men, it appeared that he was practically begging for attention. This is one of several examples that Scoles cites to show that DeLonge had a tendency to exaggerate claims of having powerful connections.

One of the author's interview subjects was John Greenewald, who had filed thousands of Freedom of Information Act requests over the years seeking UFO documents from the U.S. government. Those he received he posted on his website, *The Black Vault*. After *The Times* article appeared, Greenewald filed even more requests seeking information about the formerly secret Pentagon program to study UFOs. His initial round of requests got this Pentagon response: "No records of the kind you described could be identified." Meanwhile, Greenewald tried to get an interview with DeLonge and others associated with To the Stars for his radio podcast, but no one would respond to him. "There's something really fishy here," Greenewald told Scoles.

A Pentagon spokeswoman later told both Greenewald and Scoles that "the Defense Department had not released the videos in the *Times* article," and the spokeswoman "wouldn't confirm that {Luis} Elizondo had been part of AATIP" {the alleged Pentagon program}. Greenewald had a problem with the Navy videos themselves. "There's no context and they're not original. They've been put into an editing system." It also doesn't appear the alleged Navy videos were ever classified, nor was AATIP, the Pentagon program, despite claims in the *Times* article and from To the Stars. Greenewald believes that DeLonge and To the Stars have engaged in misrepresentation and for him that calls into question everything they say or do.

Scoles concludes that Luis Elizondo may have worked for the Department of Defense, but "he probably did not" work for the Pentagon UFO program. Scoles cites a Pentagon spokesman who made this claim to journalist Keith Kloor: "Mr. Elizondo had no responsibilities with regard to the AATIP program." In contrast, *The Times* article identified Elizondo as being in charge of AATIP. Furthermore, in a statement to Greenewald, a Pentagon spokesman claimed that "AATIP did not pursue research and investigation into unidentified aerial phenomena." What AATIP did or did not do, what Elizondo did or did not play, remains confusing to Scoles, since in conversations with her, *The Times* reporters stood by the accuracy of their reporting about Elizondo.

Another skeptic that Scoles interviews is Tim Doyle of the UFO Seekers YouTube channel. Doyle doesn't trust the UFO video footage used by *The Times* article and that had been posted on the To the Stars website. Writes Scoles: "He {Doyle} doesn't trust the film; he doesn't trust the interpretation; and he doesn't trust the people who're now taking it public. What they're doing, he says, is entertainment, not investigation."

As if to illustrate Doyle's point about entertainment replacing investigation, Scoles visits Roswell and the tourist entertainment industry this small town has built around the alleged crash of a spacecraft. "Why would people resurrect and perpetuate the Roswell myth"? she asks, and then proceeds to answer her own question. People pass 'sensational stories' along for entertainment, attention, escape, money, books, speaking gigs, television appearances. "Just ask Tom DeLonge," she quips.

──────────────

Saucers, Spooks and Kooks: UFO Disinformation in the Age of Aquarius
ADAM GORIGHTLY
(2021, Daily Grail Publishing)

After having written previous books about the Manson family and the Kennedy assassination, cultural historian Adam Gorightly takes on UFO conspiracy myths in this book, focused on the lunacy and deceit surrounding conspiracy theories and theorists who created a cottage industry promoting the existence of alleged underground bases around Dulce, New Mexico, where extraterrestrial technology was supposedly given to humans by alien visitors in exchange for allowing the aliens to conduct a breeding program using abducted humans.

A series of overlapping stories are sketched, told by a vast cast of weird characters who sometimes created stories, mostly from their vivid paranoid imaginations, and then shared them, quoting and referencing each other to 'factually' reinforce the myths, until it became difficult for anyone to separate fact from fiction. By linking these characters and their interactions together, Gorightly begins to disentangle the origin of the various myths and in so doing, shows how deviously manipulative that characters allegedly acting on behalf of government agencies have been in myth-making, disinformation, and deceit designed to manipulate researcher gullibility to shield clandestine military programs from scrutiny by 'managing' the public belief in extraterrestrial visitation while confusing the Soviets.

Among the characters profiled in this book, who contributed directly or indirectly to the conspiracy mythology, are Paul Bennewitz, William Cooper, Richard Doty (the primary Air Force disinformation specialist), Linda Moulton Howe, Cherry Hinkle, Bob Lazar, John Lear, Thomas Allen Levesque, Bill Moore, Phil Schneider, Jaime Shandera, Wendelle Stevens, Clifford Stone, and Michael Younger. Wrapped up with these characters are the UFO circus of attractions called Roswell, Dulce subterranean bases, cattle mutilations, Area 51, mind control, SERPO, the MJ-12 papers, and much more.

At the center of all this foolishness Gorightly identifies one character in particular nick-named Tal, real name Thomas Allen Levesque, who would ultimately confess to Gorightly in 2015 that he had fabricated "large swaths" of the Dulce subterranean base story and spread the poisonous seeds of it everywhere to be ravenously consumed and regurgitated by the other characters in this book. Tal's hoax began when he created a fictional character, Thomas Edwin Castello, who claimed to have been a security guard at the underground Dulce base in the 1980s and escaped death when 66 human base workers were massacred after rebelling against their reptilian extraterrestrial bosses who managed a breeding program to create a hybrid species.

Elements of the Dulce base story created by Tal spread like wildfire through the UFO community and the various book characters promulgated it at UFO conferences, on talk radio programs, and in their pamphlets and books. That drew out of the woodwork other alleged Duce base whistleblowers, such as Phil Schneider, who "became a rising star on the UFO-Patriot lecture circuit with tales about how he'd worked at Dulce and apparently even had some laser scars on his chest which he'd show off as proof that he was a survivor of the Dulce fire-fight." Gorightly reveals that during the period when Schneider claimed he worked at the Dulce base and then at Area 51, he actually was employed as a shoe salesman in Portland, Oregon. Schneider's chest scars were from self-mutilations done while a mental patient in an Oregon state hospital.

Gorightly reveals at the end of the book that his own journey "through the looking glass" of UFOs and conspiracy research began in the 1970s, in California, with a psychedelic UFO encounter, when he and a friend "both dropped a hit of some righteous acid" and then witnessed "a crazy UFO show" of weird crafts of many shapes and sizes. Rather than dismissing the hour-long viewing as a product of hallucinations, Gorightly explored a variety of possible answers, from demons disguised as aliens, to mind control programs. He finally concluded: "Of all the reality tunnels I explored, the one that makes the most sense—or resonates mostly strongly—is the 'Co-Creation Theory,' a term coined by my friend Greg Bishop." This theory holds that humans play a co-equal role in creating UFO experiences, that "there's an interplay between whatever forces are behind 'UFOs,' coupled with our perceptions of these events."

SECTION FIVE

Contacting Extraterrestrial Intelligence. . .

Can a Meaningful Dialogue Ever Be Established?

Within the intelligence agencies of the U.S. government rumors circulated, beginning in the mid-1960s, alluding to the interception of 'signals' from outer space suspected to be of extraterrestrial origin. This initial spate of rumors received serious attention from officials of the Central Intelligence Agency because the stories had been passed on by their counterparts at the National Security Agency (NSA), charged with eavesdropping on the world's airwaves. Established by secret executive order of the President in 1952, the NSA maintains hundreds of listening posts around the world and developed an extraordinary capacity to pick out useful information from a background of electromagnetic interference and noise. Apparently, some of these listening posts, perhaps engaged in the monitoring of radio signals from Soviet satellites, tuned in to wavelengths carrying bursts of seemingly intelligent messages from outside the Earth's orbit.

"They were genuinely puzzled," recalled Victor Marchetti, a high-ranking CIA officer from that era who served as a liaison to the NSA, and was a longtime friend of mine. "NSA got something they thought was real and intelligent in origin, and they didn't know what to make of it or do with it." With the possible exception of the CIA Director, Allen Dulles, and the head of the CIA's Directorate of Science and Technology, few CIA personnel learned of the NSA's final verdict on whether the intercepts were from another civilization in space, though the prevailing assumption became that the signals had a natural or terrestrial origin.

A culture of secrecy historically permeated the NSA at a level far beyond that of the CIA, the Defense Intelligence Agency, Naval Intelligence, or any of the other analytical and spying arms of government. It is apparent that in the aftermath of these mysterious intercepts the NSA greatly expanded its capability to monitor signals from outer space. Harvard University radio astronomer John Ball, writing in a 1980 issue of *American Scientist*, referenced an account heard within the astronomical community of an American intelligence agency, presumably the NSA, engaged for years in a massive eavesdropping program to detect stray signals and waste energy seepages from alien civilizations. This clandestine project was insulated from the efforts of SETI (Search for Extraterrestrial Intelligence) undertaken by the astronomic community.

A senior official at the NSA allegedly told former *New York Times* reporter Howard Blum, in 1987, that intercepting alien signals remained an ongoing concern. "We're catching a lot of crazy signals on our microphones and they're not from this planet," Blum reports the NSA official as admitting. For the next two years Blum investigated these claims for his book, *Out There*, but came up against a frustrating wall of secrecy and disinformation. He did find partial confirmation from three NSA officials who were part of a secret UFO Working Group, organized by the Defense Intelligence Agency, which also included scientists from the CIA and generals from the Army and Air Force. Blum uncovered evidence that the NSA "contrary to all its public statements, has since 1972 been secretly monitoring and often assessing worldwide allegations of UFO activity." NSA's listening posts are under standing orders to flash-report to NSA headquarters at Fort Meade, Maryland, "on any signals or electronics intelligence that might have an extraterrestrial origin."

Signal false alarms plagued civilian scientists from the beginning of the scientific search for extraterrestrial intelligence. During the first publicly known scan for messages in 1960, nicknamed Project Ozma, astronomer Frank Drake heard regularly spaced beeps when his radio telescope was pointed at a nearby star. For several weeks, as he tried to verify the signals, he imagined that a galactic communications network might exist. To his disappointment he found a more prosaic and terrestrial explanation—the beeps apparently came from military aircraft flying near his observatory in West Virginia.

Alarm bells concerning 'signals' continued to ring throughout the 1960s, as SETI gained legitimacy among international scientific institutions that devoted resources to radio telescope searches. In 1967, a Cambridge University Ph.D. student in astronomy, Jocelyn Bell, detected a regularly spaced, pulsating radio signal which repeated itself daily from a specific point in space. These characteristics were all on the short list of requirements scientists had theorized an intelligent signal would possess. Her supervisor made a decision to keep this discovery secret until it could be determined whether the signal was natural, human-made, or an extraterrestrial radio beacon. For several months Bell and her superiors quietly contacted experts in the field of radio astronomy, seeking help in verifying and explaining the signals. Meanwhile, word filtered through British and American intelligence agencies to prepare for a historic, maybe even a civilization altering announcement, which could have been the sources of rumors that Victor Marchetti heard at the CIA.

Bell's discovery turned out to be historic, but only to the field of astrophysics. During the months of public secrecy other researchers had found a second periodic signal source. Like the first one detected by Bell, it came from a pulsar, a type of rapidly rotating neutron star previously predicted by physicists. By not going public quickly, until her data had been painstakingly verified, Bell saved herself from the sort of international embarrassment which twice befell the Soviet Academy of Sciences. In Moscow during the early 1960s, Soviet astronomers thought they had detected signals from an extraterrestrial civilization and called a press conference to announce their findings to humanity. Within days they were made to appear foolish when more careful investigators traced the intense radio emissions to a quasar in a distant galaxy. As if the Soviet scientific establishment had not learned a lesson from this experience, it happened again on October 16, 1973, when the TASS news agency reported that Soviet astrophysicists had overheard radio signals of apparent extraterrestrial origin. Professor Vsevolod Troitsky was quoted as proclaiming, "They are definitely call-signs from an extraterrestrial civilization." With possible help from the KGB, other Soviet scientists were able to conclusively trace and identify these alien call-signs as telemetry readings from a U.S. spy satellite.

Despite these missed calls, there have been a series of tantalizing hints that we were on the verge of contact, but like someone waking up to pick up a ringing phone a second too late, we simply failed to seize opportunities. On August 15, 1977, as the constellation Sagittarius passed overhead, the Ohio State University radio observatory picked up an extremely narrow-band signal, riding a 21-centimeter frequency, which turned itself on and off while in the telescope's beam. It was exactly the sort of sharp, narrow frequency band signal SETI scientists hoped to find. On a computer printout next to the signal a researcher wrote "Wow!" This wow signal was never identified, nor did it repeat itself. "It was an artificial, not a natural, signal," insisted Ohio State astronomer Bob Dixon. "We know it didn't come from Earth." Frank Drake called the wow signal "either a very-hard-to-explain fluke, or the real thing." Because it was intermittent like Morse code clicking, such transient signals may indicate that intelligent messages are numerous in space, "falling on our planet like raindrops," in Drake's words, "each one making a brief, barely detectable splash before it disappears."

Dozens of wow signals have been recorded since, most notably using a multichannel analyzer developed by Paul Horowitz, a Harvard University professor of physics. Hooked up to a radio telescope, his system monitors up to eight million radio channels simultaneously, scanning for the telltale signs of alien civilization. He has recorded at least 60 examples of fleeting signals that could be excellent candidates for being of intelligent origin. One theory holds these random, scatter-shot wow signals are evidence of intermittent fan beam messages, a type of celestial lighthouse in which signals sweep our way for just minutes out of each earth year. Such lighthouse-type beams might be a beacon directing listeners to where they can tune in to another channel containing the main message. In that respect the beacon could be a signpost to entering an intergalactic library stocked with representative data banks from each of the most ancient, advanced civilizations.

A second novel explanation for the sporadic nature of wow signals came from New York psychologist John Gliedman, who was grappling to answer his own concern that time lags between us sending and receiving radio messages, given the vast distances which separate us from other star systems, "would exceed the length of recorded human history." Advanced intelligence may have found ways to circumvent this daunting distance barrier by slowing down subjective time, a process Gliedman calls social-time 'dilation'. Alien minds and bodies may have been genetically adjusted "to function thousands of times more slowly than bodies that evolve naturally. When individuals and societies live in slow motion, the speed-of-light barrier loses its sting." Slow-motion signals might be mistaken for random background noise. To intercept and decipher these messages, in which a single word's worth of information takes days to receive, would require continuous monitoring of specific regions of the sky for years on end, otherwise our current scanning practices will have about as much success at deciphering signals as "tuning in the evening news every 20 minutes for one second, and expecting to get the message."

Are We Under Surveillance?

Another scenario for scientists who envision extraterrestrial contact involves encountering an alien space probe somewhere within our solar system. Ronald Bracewell, then at Stanford University's Radio Astronomy Institute, published a paper in 1960, in *Nature,* the British scientific journal, proposing that such a probe "may be here now, in our solar system, trying to make its presence known to us." This probe might have been sent millions of years ago, stationed as a sentinel on a planet's surface, or placed in orbit around it, waiting patiently for the emergence of intelligence and technology. It may have tried to communicate with us first by listening for our transmissions over radio frequencies and then repeating them back to us. "Its signals would have the appearance of echoes having delays of seconds or minutes, such as were reported 30 years ago by Stormer and van der Pol and never explained," wrote Bracewell.

First revealed in a 1928 issue of *Nature,* these long-delayed radio echoes were investigated by Carl Stormer of Norway, a specialist on the Aurora Borealis, whose experimental station had been bouncing radio waves in Morse code off the Earth's ionosphere and discovered an echo effect, with a full three-second delay. The three-second echoes were recorded repeatedly in 1927 and 1928, then disappeared and have never been reported since. Three seconds happens to be the exact time it takes a radio signal to reach the Moon's orbit and bounce back to Earth. That finding would later fuel speculation about a hypothetical Bracewell space probe occupying a Moon Equilateral spot, an area equidistant from the Earth and Moon where an object could remain stable indefinitely.

Did an extraterrestrial probe detect our first radio signals—finding an emerging technology on a planet which had been silent for billions of years—and did it try to attract our attention, as it was programmed to do, by repeating our feeble stammering, much as a talking parrot might mimic a human baby? By disregarding this echo effect as a freakish, unexplained natural phenomenon and not engaging in a dialogue, did we discourage or even silence the space probe?

These sorts of questions intrigued a 27-year-old Scottish astronomer, Duncan Lunan, who in 1972, undertook a re-examination of the radio echo data. He found that while the three-second delay echoes did stop in 1928, they were replaced for a short time by delays of 15 seconds, then 30 seconds, and finally by irregular sequences of between three and 15 seconds before these too, all disappeared for good never to be heard again. "Assuming for the sake of argument that the echo patterns came from a space probe," reasoned Lunan, "what meaning could these signals be meant to convey"? Recalling that Bracewell had speculated the initial probe signals might be a television image of a constellation, which could represent its origin or the home of its builders, Lunan tried graphing the echo patterns using an x-axis. He was startled to find the resulting complex diagram produced a striking replica of the constellation Bootis, the Herdsman. The pattern seemed to point toward one particular star, Epsilon Bootis, about 103 light years from Earth.

Subsequent astronomical findings that Epsilon Bootis was twice as far away from us as star catalogues had indicated, and too massive a star to sustain planetary life, helped dispel Lunan's theory about it being the probe's home star system. Additionally, Lunan excavated more radio echo records from the 1920s and found several of his star map interpretations were incorrect. As for the radio echoes themselves, further research enabled Lunan to declare in 1979: "The radio echo effect was traced with virtual certainty to the orbit of the Moon; to one, if not both, of the 'Trojan' or 'Equilateral' points. As to whether a Bracewell probe did or does exist in the orbit of the Moon—no experimental search was made and to my mind the question remains unanswered."

A series of bizarre, inexplicable anomalies which have occurred since the era of long-delayed radio echoes may be evidence of a probe still trying to attract our attention, or giving us occasional intelligence aptitude tests. Two anomalies deserve special attention. In 1953, the call letters and identification card of Houston television station KLEE began making periodic appearances on television screens across parts of Europe, even though KLEE had been off the air continuously for three years. Months after it burned up in the Earth's atmosphere, the Soviet satellite Sputnik One's radio signal reportedly was still being picked up by some radio listening posts, as if one of humankind's objects in space had left a ghostly presence.

Decades later the alien space probe idea gained traction and wide public exposure when Harvard University astronomer Avi Loeb, in science papers and a 2021 book, described an object that entered and then departed our solar system as possessing many of the attributes theorized to be characteristic of an extraterrestrial mission of exploration.

The Sound of Silence

Let's assume for the sake of argument that maybe the skeptics and cynics are right: no intelligent signals have been received and no alien space probes have ever entered our solar system. So if intelligent life exists, where are they? Why haven't other forms of life contacted us? There are at least four broad categories of reasons why we may not have found, or may never find, extraterrestrial intelligence.

(1) *We are alone in this galaxy, if not the entire universe.*

It took a four-billion-year chain of evolutionary 'accidents' for an intelligence to evolve on Earth, so the odds are incredibly stacked against these coincidences occurring anywhere else, goes one argument made by the pessimists, most of whom are biologists by training. Of all the many billions of species of life which have existed on Earth, only ours reached a level of development and capacity to create a civilization with technology, which stacks the odds even higher against intelligence being anything but rare.

A companion argument, often made by some astrophysicists, explaining our aloneness and uniqueness goes like this: since extraterrestrials are not here in our solar system, they don't exist. Ours is a relatively young star in a much older galaxy and universe. If other civilizations had arisen around older stars in our galaxy, they would have had more than enough time—millions even billions of years—to reach us by now and in so doing, exploit and colonize us. Obviously, that has not happened, argue those who hold this point of view, because we see no evidence of their technological handiwork, nor after decades of listening, have we heard any convincing signals of intelligent origin. If we ever do conclude that we are alone, in this galaxy or the universe as a whole, then we most assuredly will have turned out to be a precious species with a special role to play in the cosmos. If there is nobody else, we will carry the huge burden of knowing "there is a God and we're it—or will be," in the words of SETI scientist John Wolfe.

(2) *Extraterrestrials are trying to communicate with us, but we are not yet smart enough to comprehend their presence or decipher their message.*

A very old alien civilization might be so far advanced that it would be invisible to us. Arthur C. Clarke once prophesied that an extraterrestrial technology would appear to us "as indistinguishable from magic." Any intelligence millions or even billions of years more evolved than humans would probably have many of the qualities we attribute to God, being able to engineer other intelligent lifeforms and physically alter entire worlds. Russian space theorist Nikolai Kardashev created a classification system for these advanced civilizations based on their energy appetite. A Type I civilization would utilize stellar energy falling on their planet; a Type II captures the complete energy output of their star; while a Type III engineers the energy of an entire galaxy. No constraints exist on Type III societies. "They could prevent their star from exploding or they could cause a supernova explosion. They could alter the orbit of their star in the galaxy," predicted Kardashev.

Our techniques in the search for other life may be too primitive for us to become a member of an intergalactic information network. The interstellar dialogue might take place using neutrinos (subatomic particles without mass) or with gravity waves (undulations in the curvature of space.) Two Japanese biologists even suggested in 1979 that interstellar telegrams may have already been sent to us in the DNA of bacterial viruses as biological messages deliberately encoded and dispatched to suitable planets where they could reproduce until an intelligent lifeform like us evolves to decipher them. Even if we were to receive radio signals the task of translating alien science could be comparable to the problems a scientist in ancient Greece would have faced 2,000 years ago if he were given Einstein's equations on relativity theory as a first step toward designing a starship.

(3) *Other civilizations in the universe are not yet aware of us.*

Radio communications on Earth began in the 1920s, which means for a radius of more than 100 light years we have already announced our presence due to electromagnetic seepage from our atmosphere. "Thus the characteristic signs of life on Earth which may be detectable over interstellar distances include the baleful contents of many American television programs and the mindless outpourings of rock-and-roll stations," Carl Sagan once observed. And yet, a distance of 100 light years only encompasses a radius of a few thousand stars out of a Milky Way galaxy of more than 100 billion stars. That would be like touching one needle in a haystack of needles twenty feet high in the hope that our scent would be detectable elsewhere in the haystack. Even the most optimistic calculations of possible intelligent life in our galaxy—placing the number at up to 500,000 technological civilizations—would mean an average separation between civilizations of at least 700 light years. On that basis alone we may have to wait another 600 or more years before any other lifeform detects us, much less responds to us.

(4) *An advanced civilization knows we exist but is avoiding contact.*

They might be ignoring us because we pose no threat, we are irrelevant to them, and they are so far ahead of us spiritually and technologically that we have nothing they could possibly want from us. Or, they might have us under long term, discreet surveillance, avoiding open contact so as to not interfere in our evolution as a species and civilization. We must also consider the possibility that advanced intelligence seeded life on our planet and has been silently watching our growth ever since.

Nobel laureate biologist Francis Crick, co-discoverer of the DNA structure, proposed that terrestrial life did not originate on Earth, but in an instance of 'directed panspermia' could have been sent here on a spaceship by an extraterrestrial Johnny Appleseed. Crick first developed the idea in a 1973 article in collaboration with Leslie Orgel, a leading theorist on the chemical aspects of the origins of life. According to their theory, bacteria can survive indefinitely in a suspended state of animation, so a collection of it might have been shipped here on a long voyage from another star system to colonize Earth several billion years ago, perhaps having been tailor-made for our own primeval soup so evolution could take over and eventually produce sentient beings. Two arguments in favor of this theory spring from our recent understanding of terrestrial life and its origins: that the planet's genetic code is remarkably universal; and the oldest signs of life seen in the fossil record are completely formed bacteria lacking any trace of an earlier form.

Take Us to Your Leader

Astrophysicist A.G.W. Cameron called the prospect of life on other planets "the greatest question in scientific philosophy." Twenty nine-year-old American astronomer Frank Drake helped elevate the debate to an entirely new plateau in April of 1960, when he used the 85-foot radio telescope at Green Bank, West Virginia, to monitor signals from the star Tau Ceti. Fourteen years later, using the giant radio telescope dish at the Arecibo observatory in Puerto Rico, a passive listening program became an active sending program when scientists directed a short-pulsed television picture transmission toward a neighboring galaxy 24,000 light years away. Humankind's first intentional broadcast of messages brought more clearly into focus this question of scientific philosophy which could dramatically impact the destiny of our species.

Have we released signals with our radio telescopes to attract from another star a Christopher Columbus, or a Hernando Cortes? Such questions tend to release a torrent of alarmist concerns and conspiracy scenarios from the dark side of our collective unconscious. Instead of connecting with those warm-hearted cultural icons from the movies *ET* and *Close Encounters of the Third Kind,* some people conjure up emotions and fears associated with *Independence Day* and *The War of the Worlds.* Just a few months after Drake's radio telescope search in 1960, the Brookings Institution sent a report to NASA announcing that the discovery of life on other worlds "could happen at any time," and warned this might result in the quick collapse of Earth's civilization.

Sir Martin Ryle, a Nobel prize-winning British astronomer, cautioned that other forms of life "may be extremely hostile and they could use their advanced technology to plunder our resources." Another British astronomer, Sir Bernard Lovell, argued that we must regard all other life in the universe as "a real and potential danger." George Wald, the Harvard biologist and Nobel laureate, said he could conceive of "no nightmare as terrifying as establishing communication with a so-called superior technology in outer space," because contact "could destroy the whole human enterprise—the arts, literature, science, the dignity, the worth, the meaning of man." Even the usually optimistic science fiction writer Arthur C. Clarke once predicted, in one of his darker moments, that once we encounter an advanced intelligence, perhaps through the discovery of their civilization's ruins, it "may be the most devastating event in the history of Mankind."

Astronomer Carl Sagan always felt confident that in order for any technological civilization to master interstellar space travel, all inter-species problems would have to be solved. Extrapolating from this perspective, if extraterrestrials were not far in advance of us intellectually, ethically, and spiritually, we might have already been dominated and exploited. So, let's imagine that in our lifetimes scientists do intercept and decipher intelligent signals, or find an alien space probe, or the remains of an alien outpost in our solar system. Can humanity trust the ruling elites of national and world government institutions to allow the full, prompt, and open disclosure of contact to all of humanity, or will that information be hoarded by just a select powerful few?

Harvard's George Wald is among those who seriously doubt we would learn the complete truth, given that most of the world's large radio telescopes are either government installations, or government-funded projects, or operate under secret NSA monitoring protocols. Alien signals could become "the most highly classified and exploited military information in the history of the Earth," Wald declared. Other voices of doubt come from within government itself. Michael A.G. Michaud served for decades as an official in the U.S. State Department, as its Director of the Office of Advanced Technology. In an article for my magazine, *Second Look,* he admitted that "the way our government has handled other events should make us think twice" about whether information obtained from alien contact would be released, since "there is plenty of evidence that government agencies do not trust the public."

What governments and ruling religious and financial elites may fear most is losing control. Extraterrestrial contact might wreck earthly civilization and diminish the power of national governments, even as contact melted away our racial, religious and linguistic differences. Contact could turn super advanced aliens into the new gods we worship as we discard and forget our old religions.

Scientists concerned about the prospect of government obstructionism drafted a protocol of steps to be taken for the verification and subsequent public reporting of authentic alien contact. The governing board of the International Academy of Astronautics approved this "Declaration of Principles Concerning Activities Following the Detection of Extraterrestrial Intelligence" in 1989, and over the next four years it was endorsed by most of the world's scientific organizations then engaged in SETI research.

Principle Number One: Before making any public announcement about the detection of alien intelligence, the most plausible possible explanation should be verified. Principle Two: Prior to any public announcement, the discoverer "should promptly inform" all research organizations signing the declaration and "relevant national authorities" so they can "seek to confirm the discovery by independent observations." Principle Three: Once the evidence of extraterrestrial intelligence is found to be credible, the Secretary General of the United Nations should be informed. Principle Four: Only after these steps should "a confirmed detection of extraterrestrial intelligence" be disseminated "openly and widely through scientific channels and public media." And finally, "no response to a signal or other evidence of extraterrestrial intelligence should be sent until appropriate international consultations have taken place."

Any government in a position to know could conceivably act to short-circuit this process, so it will be up to the individual scientists and the organizations they are affiliated with to stand on principle and transparency if we are to all benefit from an open exchange of information. It will take the collective wisdom of humankind to make decisions about the implications of contact and how that could determine the destiny of our species. What humankind has to look forward to from contact, declared physicist Paul

Horowitz, is an experience that should be far more exciting and profound than frightening. "Receipt of a message would be the first bridge across four billion years of independent life and evolution. It would be the end of our Earth's cultural isolation. It would be, without doubt, the greatest discovery in the history of mankind."

The Evolution of SETI Theories and Evidence, 1964 Onward. . .

We Are Not Alone
WALTER SULLIVAN
(1964, McGraw-Hill)

In 1960, two months after astronomer Frank Drake's unsuccessful Project Ozma, the first known attempt by humans to intercept radio signals from another star system, NASA commissioned a Brookings Institution study that raised disturbing questions about humankind's ability to absorb the cultural shock of interstellar contact with an advanced civilization.

"Anthropological files," said the report, "contain many examples of societies, sure of their place in the universe, which have disintegrated when they have had to associate with previously unfamiliar societies espousing different ideas and different life ways; others that survived such an experience usually did so by paying the price of changes in values and attitudes and behavior."

Since communication with other intelligent life might be established "at any time via the radio telescope research presently underway," the report recommends a series of studies of public reactions to "flying saucer episodes" and "past hoaxes," like the 1938 Orson Welles radio broadcast of a Martian invasion. The report suggests that artifacts left by ancient astronauts "might possibly be discovered through our space activities on the Moon, Mars, or Venus."

New York Times science editor Walter Sullivan, in making use of the NASA report for this book, excavated what was, until 1960, a relatively unexplored area for intellectual inquiry. Few scientists had devoted any attention to the search for other intelligence until Project Ozma. Astronomers such as Drake, I.S. Shklovskii, Carl Sagan, and the astrophysicists Philip Morrison and Freeman Dyson provided much of the material Sullivan utilizes in his book.

He relates Shklovskii's theories of how, several million years ago, the inhabitants of Mars were forced to take refuge in satellites when the oxygen and water of Mars began to diffuse away. Two of those satellites were the Martian moons Phobos and Deimos, which give the appearance of being hollow because of their unnatural orbits. Sullivan mentions that other "fanciful Russians" have proposed that a nuclear spaceship struck central Siberia in 1908, creating the devastation long thought to have been caused by a meteorite. Sullivan suspects a small comet was responsible.

Carl Sagan is quoted as dismissing flying saucer tales, insisting that "when critical scholarship and non-superstitious reasoning have been fairly widespread," no reliable reports of visitation have surfaced. Sagan did, however, propose a reexamination of myths for clues about visitation in the ancient past. "He cited, for example, a suggestion in the Soviet Union that *The Book of the Secrets of Enoch* may be based on an instance in which a resident of Earth was taken home by visitors and then returned to tell his bewildered countrymen about his adventures.

Frank Drake offers as possible evidence the descriptions given by the prophet Ezekiel of an apparent spaceship. Such early visitors could have left artifacts for us to find, argues Drake, clues that might have been buried in limestone caves to escape the ravages of time and primitive peoples. The artifacts might have radiation isotopes to spell out their artificial origin. Sagan says the world's first known civilization, Sumeria in present day Iraq, may be a likely place to begin a search, since Sumerian legends claim their civilization had been bestowed by "animals endowed with reason" who came ashore after landing near the mouth of the Tigris and Euphrates rivers.

Freeman Dyson wonders whether a "truly intelligent" society would any longer be interested in, or have need of, technology or space travel. It may even be that intelligence is a "cancer of purposeless technological exploitation."

Intelligent Life in the Universe
I.S. SHKLOVSKII & CARL SAGAN
(1966, Holden-Day)

Exobiologist Carl Sagan revised and expanded the original Russian version of this work by Shklovskii, an astronomer at the University of Moscow. While their opinions are often at odds—at one point the Russian says world peace, a necessity if we are to colonize space, remains impossible so long as capitalism survives—they carefully avoid squabbling over the nature and prospects for extraterrestrial intelligence.

Neither author evidences any faith in claims that extraterrestrials are presenting coursing through our skies. "The saucer myths represent a neat compromise between the need to believe in a traditional paternal God and the contemporary pressures to accept the pronouncements of science."

Sagan finds irony in the patterns seen in contactee stories, for the extraterrestrials are repeatedly described as humanlike and white Anglo-Saxon. No black or Asian saucerians have been reported up to this point. Because these alien visitors are always portrayed as wise, gentle, and loving, Sagan cannot help but conclude "that the flying saucer societies represent a thinly disguised religion, and that the saucerians are the deities of the cult."

Both authors find reason to believe that an advanced civilization visited or perhaps even briefly colonized our solar system. Shklovskii theorizes that the two moons of Mars, Phobos and Deimos, because they possess low densities, could very well be artificial satellites. This idea "may seem fantastic," he writes, but "it merits serious consideration." That these two moons could be hollow provides "mute testaments to an ancient Martian civilization."

Based on his estimates of the number of technical civilizations in our galaxy, Sagan speculates that each communicative advanced species "should be visited by another such civilization about once every thousand years." These intelligences may wish to leave planets like our own alone to evolve life forms without interference. Direct contact might be delayed until the native life develops a technical capacity. Or "perhaps strict injunctions against colonization of populated but pre-technical planets is [sic] in effect." But "if colonization is the rule, then even one spacefaring civilization would rapidly spread, in a time much shorter than the age of the Galaxy, throughout the Milky Way. There would be colonies of colonies of colonies, such as arose at many sites in the Western Mediterranean during classical times."

Some 25 million years ago, a Galactic survey ship passing by Earth "may have noted an interesting and promising evolutionary development: Proconsul." Assuming the emergence of intelligent life on this planet was "of general scientific or other interest to the Galactic civilizations ...the rate of sampling of our planet should have increased, perhaps to about once every ten thousand years." Sagan believes in the "possibility that contact with an extraterrestrial civilization has occurred within historical times."

While Sagan finds no "reliable reports" of extraterrestrial contact within the past few centuries, he believes that such contact thousands of years ago might be reconstructed were the account committed to written record soon afterwards, if major changes occurred within the society contacted, and if the extraterrestrials made no attempt to disguise their origins and mission.

In searching for such records, Sagan found himself drawn to Sumer, the world's first known civilization, whose legends seem to fulfill the criteria he established for genuine contact. Founded in about 4000 B.C., or earlier, Sumeria remains a puzzle to archeologists. No one knows where the Sumerians came from, or how their language and civilization arose. Their legends tell of contact with a nonhuman civilization, amphibians described as "animals endowed with reason," who taught humankind how to develop civilization. These visitors were worshipped, but the Sumerians never described them as gods. Sumerian pictographs that display the seven entities who presided over these visitors remind Sagan of "what we might expect if a network of confederated civilizations interlaced the Galaxy."

Other possible sources of information to prove the ancient astronaut hypothesis might be found by examining artifacts, which Sagan believes would have been left by extraterrestrial visitors, although he claims no artifact has yet been found. Nor is it out of the question "that some kind of base is maintained within the solar system to provide continuity for successive expeditions." It might not have been practical to erect such a base on Earth. "The Moon seems one reasonable alternative site for a base." An automatic technology monitor, with an alarm, might be analyzing our atmosphere for signs of radiation or telltale technological residue. "An extraterrestrial resident agent is an alternative possibility." If such an alarm exists, "then it has probably been triggered by now."

***

Communication with Extraterrestrial Intelligence
EDITED BY CARL SAGAN
(1973, The MIT Press)

For six days in 1971, at an Armenian observatory in the Soviet Union, fifty-four scientists and academicians, all but four of them representing the U.S. National Academy of Sciences and the U.S.S.R. Academy of Sciences, debated and analyzed the prospects for communicating with other life in the universe. They discussed the evolution of intelligence on this planet, the factors necessary for the evolution of technical civilizations, their longevity and galactic numbers, techniques for contacting these advanced societies, and the consequences of such contact. This book is a partial transcript of those speculations.

Although UFOs and ancient astronaut theories, for the most part, were no more than a peripheral curiosity during the panel discussions, several participants raised the possibility that contact has already occurred. American exobiologist Dr. Carl Sagan at one point emphasized: "We cannot exclude the possibility" that our technical civilization evolved "as a result of direct stimulation from a 'donor' extraterrestrial civilization." Later, elaborating on the point, historian R. G. Podolny of Moscow acknowledged cases that "merit certain study" since they may represent "traces of visitations on our planet"; he further proposed that methods be developed "to scrutinize our folklore in search of evidence of such visitations."

Physicist V. L. Ginzburg, in weighing the possibility that other forms of life might be bound by laws of physics unknown to us, speculated that it is possible some form of life and civilization may exist at the level of fundamental, or elementary particles. Other panelists offered similar unconventional theories for the evolution of intelligent life.

N. S. Kardashev, of the Institute for Cosmic Research, suggested that life could exist on planetary systems that have no suns; internal radioactivity would provide a steady source of energy to support the development of life. Theoretical physicist Freeman Dyson countered that comets would be a more likely home than planets for a large technological society; for that reason we should seek artificial signals from comets, as well as stars. He pointed out that countless millions of comets traverse the space around our solar system, each supplied with water, carbon, and nitrogen-the basic constituents of living cells-and lacking only warmth and oxygen. Biological engineering would enable us, or any advanced species, to colonize a comet and use it as a spaceship to explore the cosmos. A ten-mile-diameter comet, for instance, could support trees that would "grow for hundreds of miles, collecting the energy of sunlight..."

Black holes and white holes in space stimulated provocative speculation about advanced civilizations using these openings for intergalactic, or time travel. Kardashev describes objects coming from the past as "white holes, and objects "through which we may enter the future" as black holes-collapsed stars from which not even light can escape. Sagan considers the possibility of "apertures to other places or other times," and proposes that we begin to search by radio telescope and other means for "large technological apparatus deployed in the vicinity of black holes."

Sagan believes any solution to the problem of communicating with extraterrestrial intelligence "may lie in laws of physics yet undiscovered." He proposes, for example, that even though science has not yet verified the existence of tachyons-hypothetical particles with imaginary mass that travel faster than the speed of light-these particles would be the preferred way for civilizations to communicate over the vast reaches of space. But Sagan suspects that civilizations much advanced beyond our own would be unwilling to communicate with us at the primitive level of our communication.

Whispers from Space
JOHN W. MACVEY
(1973, Macmillan; 1974, Abelard-Schuman)

Because the subject of UFOs is "of considerable scope and implication," Scottish astronomer John Macvey urges his readers to "retain if possible a completely open mind." Although this book focuses on Project Ozma and other radio telescope attempts to contact advanced civilizations, the author devotes several chapters to alternative means of communication, such as space probes, laser beams, and telepathy, along with a discussion of whether alien beings once visited or continue to visit this planet.

This open-mindedness about UFOs may stem from Macvey's own observation in 1957, of an object he could not identify. About 9:00 p.m. one night, he and his wife watched a "brilliant golden object" through binoculars as it headed at high speed across a clear sky. No vapor trail could be seen, or any audible sound heard. "Seen through binoculars the object was undoubtedly circular and showed a sharp contour."

One element of the "flying saucer paradox" rarely if ever considered is that any creation of a society several hundred millennia in advance of our own would almost certainly "embody features beyond our comprehension." Their vehicles might be transparent, "able to pass through what is to us an unknown dimension." While his rational nature says that UFOs "do not and never did exist other than as figments of the imagination," Macvey admits to being haunted by a "niggling doubt" about such an assumption, "a- feeling that a cultured and infinitely superior cosmic people might just be keeping us under surveillance."

If surveillance is under way, it most probably began in our prehistory. Macvey calls the ancient astronaut theory of considerably more substance than "the prerogative of wishful thinkers," since the idea has been endorsed as a possibility by such personages as Albert Einstein, and one of the founders of rocketry, Hermann Oberth. Macvey wonders about the "relatively sudden" appearance of human intelligence. "Was this 'sudden' gift a natural acquisition-or did he [man] pick it up from representatives of an alien race"?

Macvey relates possible evidence of visitation from the Old Testament tale about Ezekiel, who saw what today would resemble a spacecraft; he mentions the destruction of Sodom and Gomorrah, and the collapse of the walls of Jericho. In the case of Jericho, if the walls did collapse from blasts of sound, perhaps caused by a sonic gun similar to what our technology is now capable of constructing, it could only have been through the intervention of an advanced civilization that the Israelites obtained such a weapon.

On the plains of Nazca the odd markings visible only from the air remind Macvey "of a large modern airport with its complex of runways, intersections, and taxiing strips." He contends that a "high standard of surveying must have been necessary to translate such a system into reality. From the peoples of this region in the remote past this seems most improbable."

But the Siberian explosion of 1908, thought by some to have been caused by a nuclear-powered spacecraft, is dismissed by Macvey as more likely the result of a comet or meteor. "The evidence for an exploding starship is flimsy," he says, yet "such an event could have occurred. Alien visitors to our world may have died suddenly and hideously in the catastrophic nuclear detonation of their great starship."

Radio waves and laser beams remain the most technologically feasible systems for contacting the pilots of these starships. Even accepting the existence of telepathy as a possible medium for communication, "minds totally different in bodies equally differ-ent (from our own) might in the metaphorical as well as the literal sense be on entirely different wavelengths."

Macvey concludes his book with a warning first voiced by astrophysicist Freeman Dyson at Princeton in 1972. "I have a feeling," said Dyson, "that we are going to discover things that are not so pleasant, particularly since the activities we are likely to discover first are highly technological activities. We are more likely to discover first the species in which technology has got out of control, a technological cancer spreading through the galaxy. We should be suitably alarmed if we discover it and take our precautions."

The Galactic Club
RONALD N. BRACEWELL
(1974, San Francisco Book Company)

Australian astrophysicist Ronald Bracewell sounds pessimistic when he writes of at-tempts by radio astronomers to contact advanced civilizations, or listen in on conversations among advanced members of the Galactic Club. He points out there is only one chance in a thousand of transmissions coming our way, and but one chance in a thousand "that we will have chosen to look in their direction at precisely the time when their transmission arrives in our neighborhood." The combined chance of establishing communication equals about one in a million. Other problems, such as the vast distances to be overcome, the hundreds—per-haps even thousands—of years elapsing before a meaningful dialogue could begin, make the prospects for contact even bleaker. But alternative means of communications exist.

"The answer seems to be for the extraterrestrials to send a messenger," writes Bracewell. "Not necessarily a member of their race, although biological engineering may have enabled them to breed a subrace of interstellar messengers." Rather, an advanced species would send out interstellar probes, sophisticated automatic modules much in advance of but similar to our own robot planetary craft.

"It is quite possible that a probe arrived in our solar system when our radio transmissions had not yet begun," which may mean the messenger continues to listen, reporting its findings to the civilization from which it was sent. If such a probe finally attempts to contact us, the author believes its message will be in television, exchanging ideas through signs or pictures.

Have these probes, automated or occupied, already visited our planet's surface? Could life on Earth have originated when space travelers dumped their garbage? Would extraterrestrial visitors intentionally leave signs of their presence, like a pyramid or an obelisk, that would remain durable to the present day?

Bracewell raises these questions as a transition to the ancient astronaut theories of Erich von Daniken and others, to which he devotes less than six pages, concluding that the Pyramid of Cheops had Egyptian, not extraterrestrial builders. He quotes a Soviet ethnographer who refutes claims by von Daniken that Japanese Dogu statuettes represent helmeted space visitors. Von Daniken's books, says Bracewell, "are a romanticist's fiction, and to examine or criticize the material at any greater length seems pointless."

If and when an advanced civilization chooses to establish contact, Bracewell warns that we must consider carefully why its members have initiated "a costly diversion of resources to a search for intelligent extraterrestrial life," and what they hope to receive in return for finding such life. "Their motivation would affect both the nature of their effort to contact us and our strategy for facilitating contact."

The Mysterious Signals from Outer Space
DUNCAN LUNAN
(1974, Souvenir Press, Ltd.; 1975, Henry Regnery)

From April 1927, off and on through May 1929, Norwegian, Dutch, and other scientists reported receiving a series of long-delayed radio echoes emanating from the vicinity of the moon. Initially, because the echoes came in regular three-second pulses, they were thought to be natural. But when echoes began returning irregularly, with intervals of three to thirty seconds, apparently in response to Morse code transmissions by the scientists, the very real possibility arose that these signals were originating from a space probe in our solar system.

Forty-four years later, an astronomer in Scotland, Duncan Lunan, finally deciphered the radio signals. By graphing the transmissions with delay time on an x-axis, a message seemed to emerge-beings in the double-star system of Epsilon Bootis, living on the sixth of seven planets circling the largest sun, sent a space probe into this solar system in search of intelligent life and habitable planets.

According to Lunan's interpretations, the space probe went into orbit around Earth's moon about 13,000 years ago, mapped our planet's surface, sent the signals to Epsilon Bootis (about 103 light years away), then ceased operations, "until we invented radio on Earth." Automatically it began sending star map signals in an attempt to establish contact with us. Had those scientists in the late 1920s responded by repeating the signals they received, Lunan theorizes, the space probe "would have known it had contacted intelligent beings."

Lunan compiles astronomical evidence to show that the principal star in the Epsilon Bootis system is an orange giant, far hotter than our own sun, that has been steadily intensifying in magnitude. That could mean only one thing-unmanned space probes from Epsilon Bootis were sent in a desperate search for a new home, since their own planet must eventually be destroyed.

The probe may have attempted in other ways to attract our attention. For instance, the test card of a Texas television station, off the air since the 1950s, has frequently reappeared like a ghost image on screens all over the world. There have been reports of long-delayed echoes on communication satellite channels, and a report that Sputnik I had reappeared on the air months after burning up in the atmosphere. Could the space probe be redirecting signals to us, just as it had expected us to redirect its own signals? Perhaps we flunked its intelligence test and now it is ignoring us, or playing games. In 1973, Russian scientists at Gorky University announced they had detected on high frequencies pulsed radio signals of artificial origin from within our solar system. Maybe the Epsilon Bootis machine hasn't given up trying.

There is a remote possibility that sometime within the last 13,000 years, responding to maps sent by the space probe, explorers from Epsilon Bootis arrived on Earth. Lunan devotes the latter half of his book to an examination of evidence offered by proponents of the ancient astronaut theory. Among the evidence he sifts is the sixteenth-century map of Earth known as Piri Reis, named after the Turkish admiral who discovered it, which reveals the full extent of South America, the Caribbean, and Antarctica, none of which was thought to be known in its entirety at that period. The Oronteus Finaeus map of 1532 also portrays an Antarctic coast free of ice, which meant the map had to be drawn at least 6,000 years ago, dated to the end of the last Ice Age. From these and other ancient maps, which Lunan describes as "by far the best evidence of contact currently available," he concludes that orbital survey pictures were used when these maps were first compiled in Alexandria, Egypt, several thousand years ago.

Babylonian and Assyrian legends preserve details of seven beings, "animals endowed with reason," who emerged from the Persian Gulf and bestowed civilization on Sumeria. These beings are never described as gods. Lunan identified this period, after 4000 B.C., and this region, the mouth of the Tigris and Euphrates rivers, as offering the best possible example of contact with explorers from Epsilon Bootis.

Cultures Beyond the Earth
EDITED BY MAGOROH MARUYAMA & ARTHUR HARKINS
(1975, Vintage Books)

The role of anthropology in outer space is the dominant theme of these essays, eight in all, ranging from the implications of first contact with extraterrestrial cultures to the moral obligations of anthropology inherent in that first contact. With the exception of futurist Alvin Toffler, who contributes a four-page introduction, none of the contributors are household names. Their opinions are uniformly skeptical of extraterrestrial contact having already been made.

Professor of linguistics and anthropologist Roger W. Wescott proposes that we "cope intellectually with such creatures as flying saucerites" by regarding them as mythical beings "proper to the Stone Age," somewhat as "angels were mythical beings proper to the biblical period." As folklore, these beings can be dealt with "in terms of symbolic projection of the major concerns of the era."

Wescott does pose other alternatives. It might be possible, if space turns out to have more than three dimensions, or time more than one direction, for material beings "to pass through our illusively constricted space-time continuum as a needle passes through a piece of cloth." Because these beings would seem to appear, then vanish suddenly and inexplicably, we would "dismiss them as hallucinations or hoaxes." From such a theory emerges an explanation for all miraculous occurrences or supernatural beings described throughout religion and folklore-they would be "intrusions from the larger earth of reality into the smaller earth of our self-habituation." If indeed we discover additional spatial or temporal dimensions, extraterrestrial anthropology will come to include the emerging field of anomalistics, described by Wescott as the systematic study of anomalies-phenomena failing to fit the picture of reality sketched by conventional science. These areas concern parapsychology, noetics (the study of consciousness), exobiology, chronontology (the nature of time), and even alchemy and astrology. Charles Fort, the early twentieth-century journalist, and biologist Ivan T. Sanderson are generally credited as the creators of anomalistics as a creative discipline.

One basic tenet in science fiction writing, points out Donald K. Stern, a student of extraterrestrial sociology at the University of Washington, "is the avoidance of culture interference and contamination of less advanced cultures...by superior ones." Yet it is conceivable that "undercover agents" or "guardians" might be "planted within a society without the knowledge of the natives," assuming genetic similarity would make that possible. But "there are no reliable reports of direct contact with an extraterrestrial civilization."

Once humans laughed at alchemists who attempted to transmute into gold the base metals. Now, writes Mary Oberthur, a registered nurse, a cyclotron converts mercury into gold, although at extraordinary cost. Ray guns were once within the realm of science fiction. Laser, maser, and plasma guns are reality. Humans once reassured each other that the sound barrier could never be broken, and no one could escape the force of gravity alive. What these illusory barriers underscore is the mistake entailed in believing that the speed of light needs to always be a limitation on travel, keeping us bound to this solar system. Advanced civilizations may have overcome this limitation millions of years ago.

CETI: Communication with Extra-terrestrial Intelligence
JACK STONELEY & A. T. LAWTON
(1976, Warner Books)

Given the rules of relativity—which state that mass cannot travel faster than the speed of light, 186,000 miles per second-how would a more advanced civilization traverse the thousands, even millions of light years it would take for them to reach our part of the Milky Way galaxy? The authors—Stoneley a science writer and Lawton a Fellow of the Royal Astronomical Society—explain several cosmic "shortcut" theories being discussed in scientific circles.

The first involves Einstein-Rosen bridges, or "worm holes," that might connect "space bubbles" woven into the fabric of what we refer to as space and time. Just as bubbles exist in the ocean, capable of moving about and popping up, space may well contain similar turbulences linking together other universes, or other dimensions. It would be like an air race from Tokyo to New York. Two planes with maximum speeds of 186 miles per hour leave Tokyo at the same time, but one plane follows a tunnel through the Earth directly to New York, arriving several days ahead of the plane forced to travel the curvature of the planet.

A second theory is more widely known. Black holes (stars that have collapsed, sucking up mass and even light) may be connected to white holes (cosmic gushers) to form expressways in space. Matter drawn into the black hole emerges in another universe or another dimension through the white hole. The authors quote astrophysicist Dr. Robert Hjellming as concluding, based on his reading of galactic pulse throbs, that matter is flowing into our own universe from elsewhere at the same rate as black holes appear to be consuming it. These pipelines between universes, like blood transfusions, might be the "life-blood of creation," and a freeway for celestial travelers.

Advanced civilizations may even now be attempting to contact us, but in ways conventional science has never before suspected. For instance, a super-accelerator could be pulsing neutrinos-particles without mass, normally emitted by stars-as code intended for a species at their own intellectual level, and we might be mistaking these messages for ordinary bursts of supernova radiation. Since neutrinos travel at the speed of light, they make convenient transmitters. Our radio telescope techniques may also be rendered obsolete by super-laser beam communication. Or, and here the authors refer to research projects being conducted by NASA and the Soviets, some nonphysical medium, like ESP, might prove our only hope "of ever breaking the frustrating time barrier of interstellar communication."

On UFOs the authors are noncommittal. They point out that the vast majority, though not all, can be explained as natural phenomena. Others may be the result of psychological factors, the desire to see and believe. The human brain may be engaging in a subtle form of visual deception. Electromagnetic fields can affect brain stimulation, but only certain people possess this sensitivity to radio and magnetic fields, just as only certain people seem to "see" UFOs. This could mean that legitimate UFOs belong to another dimension, and the mind, like the tuning of a television receiver, must be able to focus the correct wavelength in order to visualize manifestations. People who possess this "gift" are not crazy, nor do crazy people seem to report UFOs. In a study of the records of 30,000 mental patients, not one had ever claimed to have seen a flying saucer.

One theory of extraterrestrial communication, advanced by Duncan Lunan in *The Mysterious Signals from Outer Space*, the authors critically examine and debunk. Lunan had theorized that longdelayed echoes recorded in 1928 and 1929 were messages from a space probe orbiting our moon. A. T. Lawton demonstrates that these echoes were caused by signal reflections in the upper ionosphere, a perfectly natural phenomenon.

Extra-terrestrial Intelligence: The First Encounter
EDITED BY JAMES L. CHRISTIAN
(1976, Prometheus Books)

This collection of fifteen essays deals in general, nontechnical language with many of the sociological, ethical, and religious implications of contact with civilizations elsewhere in the cosmos. Science fiction writers Isaac Asimov and Ray Bradbury are perhaps the best-known contributors.

James Christian, a philosophy professor who edited this anthology, wonders whether our "egocentric perversity" hasn't prevented us from conceding the existence of a variety of other intelligences on this planet. He points out that 10 million species of life are known to exist on Earth today, but that represents only a small fraction of the estimated 10 billion species of life that evolved on this planet in the last 4 billion years, each eventually becoming extinct. How many of these vanished species were capable of intelligence? Christian concludes that we ourselves may become classified as a lower form of life in relation to an advanced species.

Using statistics compiled by others, Asimov estimates that our Milky Way galaxy contains 135 billion stars, with 100 billion or more galaxies distributed through space, and argues that odds dictate the existence of at least 64 million Earthlike, life-bearing planets in our galaxy alone. But Asimov does not take UFOs, or theories of alien visitation in prehistoric times, seriously. Nor does he think radio telescope communication will necessarily ever yield answers. He goes so far as to speculate that although life in the universe may be common, intelligence may be the product of "an extremely rare combination of events" that might forever preclude our contact with an equally advanced species.

Dr. George Abell, professor of astronomy at the University of California, Los Angeles, contends that virtually all "professional" astronomers consider the extraterrestrial hypothesis "the least likely explanation for the UFO phenomenon." Abell quotes Michael H. Hart, of the National Center for Atmospheric Research, as defending the

416

proposition that Earth is the only technological society in the galaxy because had another species mastered interstellar travel, it would have set out "to colonize other habitable planets in the galaxy."

Can something we recognize as existing make a difference without our recognizing it? So asks Peter Angeles, who teaches college philosophy. He proposes that in "biocosmic history" an extraterrestrial intelligence could intentionally direct, might even now be intentionally directing, our behavior and attitudes even though we are made to feel in control of our destiny. We are being programmed-and we are never meant to know.

Extraterrestrial Encounter
CHRIS BOYCE
(1979, David & Charles)

Sometime within the next 50 years humankind will obtain a piece of "hard irrefutable data" that other intelligent life exists, predicts the author, a science fiction writer and member of The British Interplanetary Society. The cultural impact of this discovery will dwarf any other happening in human history, which is why we must begin the process of preparing for it now by speculating on the possible natures of these alien beings and what the consequences of contact may be for our species.

Like the ancient Judaic reactions to occupation by Rome, humankind may react to contact with an advanced civilization "with a chameleonlike attitude in an attempt to become as like the assaulting culture as possible," or by rejecting "everything foreign as a contagion." We should expect evidence of both types of reactions, especially if we were to encounter an exploitive space-going civilization about as advanced compared to us as were the Spaniards to the Aztec and Incan civilizations. The odds are that we will instead meet an intelligence much older and wiser than us, permitting contact with us only when we appear to have matured sufficiently to absorb the shock. If contact comes from radio telescope messages rather than face-to-face, "we will have the required length of time to make a well-considered series of adjustments at a pace which will minimize potential traumatic impact."

Alien intelligence will have evolved along a much different path than our own, meaning that we will probably "find its mental activity to be rich but bewildering, and certainly exotic." Its modes of perception and consciousness may seem far different from our own, if only because brain development "is a reflection of the creature's adaptation to its changing environment." They may not possess a consciousness as we are aware of it or comprehend it. They may be gaseous or microscopic in size. The possibilities are endless. So to even begin to understand the minds of the aliens we will one day meet we must discover the nature of the dolphin and whale intelligence on our own planet, how they perceive their environment, what is of significance to them, and how we are viewed by them.

Searching in our own solar system for renewable space probes launched by extraterrestrial civilizations "is more readily justifiable than radio searches for interstellar communications." To conduct radio searches alone might mean we would "go on squatting here on planet Earth, listening vainly forever" and still not hear intelligent signals while, in the meantime, we could also be scouring our own neighborhood for evidence of visitation. The author feels confident that probes will be found in the solar system "well within the next century." Such alien probes or databanks could be located almost anywhere: inside an unmistakably extraterrestrial reference point such as a meteorite impact crater; genetically buried inside the brains of dolphins or whales, making them aquatic librarians; erected on the Moon, Mars, or another planet or moon of our solar system, much like the monoliths in *2001: A Space Odyssey*; or riding on comets; or circling within the asteroid belt; or suspended at the Lagrangian points in the Moon's orbit around Earth.

Extraterrestrial Civilizations
ISAAC ASIMOV
(1979, Crown Publishers)

We are not alone, believes Asimov, normally a science fiction author, and while we have no idea what they're like, we can be assured they are intelligent. But we II are not looking merely for extraterrestrial life," nor are we "even looking merely for extraterrestrial intelligence. We are looking for extraterrestrial civilization that disposes of enough energy of a sufficiently sophisticated kind to be detectable over interstellar distances." That means the intelligence we are searching for, at some point in their history, must have developed the use of fire, or some energy equivalent, or "they could not have developed those attributes that would make it possible for them to be detected."

Based on what we know about life, other worlds will be lifeless if they are without liquid and without air. Using these and other variables, Asimov calculates that one out of every two Earthlike planets in our galaxy are habitable. That translates into 650 million habitable planets in the galaxy, a figure which he says is more conservative than what some astronomers suggest. "It is rather breathtaking to decide on the basis of (we hope) strict logic and the best evidence we can find that there are 650 million habitable planets in our Galaxy alone, and therefore over 2 billion billion in the Universe as a whole."

More calculations yield the figure that 92 percent of these habitable planets are old enough for life to have evolved on them. That means 600 million planets in our Galaxy are life-bearing. He further restricts the figure to multicellular life and comes up with 433 million planets. Still more refinements, estimating the growth times of civilization, produces 390 million as the number of planets in our Galaxy on which a technological civilization has developed. That means one star out of every 770 stars have nurtured the development of a technological civilization. At least one-third of these 390 million civilizations will, in contrast to humankind, possess superhuman intelligence.

If these 390 million civilizations are spread evenly through the outskirts of the Galaxy, then on average about 40 lightyears separate every two neighboring civilizations. So the obvious question becomes where is everybody? Could the answer be that these civilizations "have not made themselves known to us because they don't endure long enough to be heard from?" Anything could happen. If a civilization didn't destroy itself through war or pollution, radiation from a supernova explosion might have damaged its gene pool, an asteroid could have collided with the planet, or the star it circles might have had spasms of instability. "We might argue that, from the fact that we have not been visited by any advanced civilization, the duration of civilizations must be short."

Asimov finds the most logical reason why Earth has had no extraterrestrial visitors is the difficulty of interstellar flight. With more extrapolation he concludes that 530,000 is the number of planets in our Galaxy on which technological civilizations presently exist. That works out to an average separation between civilizations of 630 lightyears, a distance sufficiently daunting that the result "may well be that every civilization, no matter how advanced, is isolated in its own planetary system and that visits among them are out of the question."

Are We Alone?
ROBERT T. ROOD & JAMES S. TREFIL
(1981, Charles Scribner's Sons)

These authors argue that the so-called Drake or Green Bank equation of 1961, purporting to calculate the possible number of advanced civilizations in our galaxy, has been rendered overly optimistic and obsolete by astronomical and other findings to the point of giving "credence to the view that we might be alone." After detecting "an enormous gap" between public perceptions of the likelihood of extraterrestrial intelligence and the skepticism scientists display in private gatherings, Rood, an associate professor of astronomy, and Trefil, a professor of physics, both at the University of Virginia, decided to compose and vent that skepticism in the form of this book.

Advances in knowledge about the formations of stars and planetary systems lead the authors to conclude that binary star systems probably do not possess planets, which would rule out up to 90 percent of all stars in the galaxy as potential harbors of life. Taking into account the evolution of planetary atmospheres, which is apparently restricted to stars whose mass is near that of our own sun, the prospective harbors of life are reduced still further. Because the authors believe that all living systems will be carbon-based, and the evolution of life on a planet is dependent on the presence of oceans with tidal pools caused by a large satellite around the planet, a role much as our moon plays, even an optimistic scenario for life in the galaxy would produce few if any prospects.

"Imagine the evolution of communicating civilizations as a series of bottlenecks," they write. "Each bottleneck represents one of the hurdles that must be jumped ...all that is necessary for the pessimistic result to hold is that any one of the bottlenecks be truly narrow. On the other hand, for the optimistic result to hold, all of the bottlenecks must be as wide as they can possibly be." These bottlenecks are the formation of a star similar to our own, the formation of planets around that star, a continuously habitable zone on one of those planets, the existence of tidal pools necessary for the primordial soup to form polymers and primitive life, the evolution of intelligence, the production of technology and survival of a civilization, and finally the willingness and ability to communicate with other forms of life. The result: "the total number of advanced civilizations in the galaxy is small, and there could well be only one." That means the Earth is something very special after all.

Since our sun is a relatively young star, and "stars like it existed in our galaxy for several billion years before the birth of the solar system, if we believe the original Green Bank equation, there should be millions of civilizations in the galaxy that reached our own present level of sophistication at least 30 million years ago." If that is so, at least one of these civilizations engaged in exploration and colonization, and it should have reached us by now. Therefore, the absence of an extraterrestrial presence on Earth indicates that (1) We are the first in our galaxy to reach a technological stage of development; (2) Some other race expanding into the galaxy has not reached us yet.

Robert Rood offers a personal view that it is hard for him to accept the conclusion that "we may well be the only civilization in the galaxy with both the capability and the desire for interstellar communication." He wonders if a galactic civilization might be hiding from us "until we develop to a point where we are interesting." Maybe their vast knowledge would be of no use to us, a little like "trying to convince an aborigine of the superiority of nuclear bombs to clubs." Or maybe any civilization like ours which "blurts out its existence on interstellar beacons at first opportunity may be like some early hominoid descending from the trees and calling, 'Here, kitty' to a saber-toothed tiger."

By contrast, James Trefil asks "Where are they?" and responds that the first extraterrestrials humankind meets will be our own grandchildren who have migrated into space. If another technological civilization had evolved it would have colonized the entire galaxy by now, preempting all available energy and material resources, perhaps even dismantling entire planets. That has not happened. Humans are this galaxy's single "fruit of a 15-billion-year experiment in the formation of sentient life."

Extraterrestrials...Where are They?
EDITED BY BEN ZUCKERMAN & MICHAEL H. HART
(1982, Pergamon Press)

In this collection of 22 essays, a variety of scientists from the fields of astronomy, biology, chemistry, and physics mostly thrust skeptical scalpels through the notion that other technological civilizations exist in any large numbers, arguing that humans might well possess the most advanced brains in the entire Milky Way Galaxy.

Editor of this collection, Michael H. Hart, a former NASA astronomer, believes that since intelligent beings from outer space are not here on Earth right now, they do not exist. "If there were other advanced civilizations in our Galaxy, they would have had ample time to reach us, unless they commenced space exploration less than 2 million years ago." And if they reached us, Hart reasons, they would have colonized us. "For colonization not to have occurred requires that every single civilization which had the opportunity to colonize chose not to." Since there is "strong evidence" we are the first civilization in our galaxy, Hart reaches two corollary conclusions: it is probably a waste of time and money to search for extraterrestrial radio signals; and in the long term "cultures descended directly from ours will probably occupy most of the habitable planets in our galaxy."

Since the development of life on Earth up to 50 billion species have existed, with the average life span of a species about 100,000 years, yet only one-Homo sapiens-evolved "the kind of intelligence needed for the establishment of a civilization," argues Ernst Mayr, a Harvard University zoologist. This indicates that most life on other planets will probably not evolve intelligence. Nor will every intelligent civilization which evolves on other planets be able to send and receive signals in space. In the past 10,000 years on Earth at least 20 civilizations have existed, including the Sumerian, Egyptian, Mayan and Incan, yet only ours reached a level of technology to send and receive signals. Furthermore, "all civilizations have only a short duration," or a short open window of communication potential, if only because they will give up trying after a period of time in which no answers are received. It is almost exclusively astronomers and physicists who are optimists about SETI, while scientists concerned with the origin of life realize that biologic and sociologic factors make the "conditions to be met for SETI success highly improbable."

Evolutionary biologist Jared Diamond makes a case that radio communication between intelligent species separated within the universe will be highly unlikely given our own evolutionary path. Of billions of species on Earth only one has shown "any proclivities toward radios" and it has done so only in the past 70 years of its 7-million-year history. Nuclear weapons and our passion for destroying ourselves leads Diamond to conclude that the Earth may not "have humans and their radios for much longer." Our experience in this regard tells him that radio civilizations are short-lived and "the deafening silence from outer space is not surprising." There may be radio transmitters in the universe, but probably none in our Galaxy. "For practical purposes, we're alone," he writes, and "Thank God!"

The SETI Factor
FRANK WHITE
(1990, Walker and Company)

Searching for extraterrestrial intelligence, SETI, "may be one of the most important tasks that human beings have ever undertaken," proposes Frank White, a Senior Associate at the Space Studies Institute in Princeton, N.J. Regardless of whether we find aliens or not, the search itself "is an identity-expanding process for humanity." In this regard his book focuses on four key concepts: we have been engaged in SETI since the dawn of human consciousness; this "SETI Factor" has played a role in human evolution; the social and psychological impact of this search on humanity will be substantial; and preparing for SETI means we must explore our relationship to the entire universe.

422

Our attempts at SETI so far have really been SETILO—a "search for extraterrestrial intelligence like ourselves," which is to say civilizations that develop technologies similar to our own. Intelligence could take any number of unpredictable and exotic forms, from lacking a physical body to being a swarm of micro-organisms floating through space. This exotic intelligence "might evolve to such a level that we would be unaware of it, and it might be unconcerned with us." It might even be around us all the time, invisible to us because it does not exist or behave according to our assumptions, or because of our limited understanding of physics. We must be prepared that if we fail to detect extraterrestrials like ourselves, we may still "yet stumble onto something far more profound."

Up to the year 2015 the SETI program may play out into one of at least three "meta-scenarios," each containing a range of options and possible outcomes.

(1) No contact. SETI fails to detect another advanced civilization because:

    (a) None are out there;

    (b) They are beyond the search space we are exploring;

    (c) Our techniques for searching are wrong;

    (d) They are not in a communicative phase of development;

    (e) They are avoiding us.

(2) Contact occurs within our Milky Way Galaxy that might happen thusly:

    (a) Traces of extraterrestrial visitation are found within our own solar system;

    (b) We find a civilization within 100 light years of us, making communication a possible two-way dialogue;

    (c) We pick up signals from a distant star system sent thousands of years ago from a now dead civilization;

    (d) Contact is made with a galactic society of alien civilizations which observed our evolution with robot space probes.

(3) Contact is made with another galaxy. Though Earth is 170,000 light years from the nearest galaxy called the Large Magellanic Cloud, we might still:

    (a) Pick up signals sent before our planet formed, produced by an old civilization around an old star;

    (b) Actual contact with another galactic civilization of migrants occurs;

    (c) Contact with a universal civilization, an intergalactic federation which has overcome the immense distance barriers to communication.

Is Anyone Out There?
FRANK DRAKE & DAVA SOBEL
(1992, Delacorte Press)

Since 1959 astronomer Frank Drake has been scanning the stars in search of extraterrestrial intelligence, having engineered humankind's first such effort called Project Ozma. In this book he describes the enormity of this task of "hunting for a needle in a cosmic haystack of inconceivable size," but with a confidence that "the imminent detection of signals from an extraterrestrial civilization" will profoundly change our planet, and is a discovery "which I fully expect to witness before the year 2000."

Just as Earth's radio and television transmissions have leaked out into space to herald our existence for decades, so has similar information from other planetary civilizations "no doubt been quietly arriving at Earth for perhaps billions of years." The aliens who have sent these signals are too far away to pose a threat to us. From these signals we will learn an Encyclopedia Galactica of information about their planet, culture, history and technology. Based on the Drake Equation, there could be "10,000 advanced extraterrestrial civilizations in our Milky Way Galaxy alone," and contact with just one of them could help us answer these age-old questions: Where did we come from? Are we unique? What does it mean to be a human being?

For Drake there is a solution to the Fermi Paradox, the question of "Where are they?" The fact that "they" are not here "does not prove that 'they' do not exist. Perhaps they are on their way here even now." But Drake does not believe "we will receive visitors from other planets of other stars-any more than I believe we have been visited in the past by ancient astronauts or UFOs that are alien spacecraft."

His solution to the Fermi Paradox is that alien civilizations are probably content to colonize their own planetary systems, being uninterested in "the costs and hazards of going to other stars." Because the universe "permits only limited kinds of direct encounters among its residents," radio communication is much easier and safer than interstellar travel and direct contact.

These radio communications from other civilizations, when we are able to detect them and decipher them, may "bequeath to us vast libraries of useful information." Drake suspects that immortality may be common among other intelligent life. And given "their reverence for the preservation of individual lives," they may endeavor to help other civilizations to become immortal, actively spreading "the secrets of their immortality among young, technically developing civilizations." So we must be alert to these first interstellar messages delivering unto us "the grand instruction book that tells creatures how to live forever."

Are We Alone?
PAUL DAVIES
(1995, Basic Books)

Whether or not humankind is alone in the universe has been a question of philosophy debated for thousands of years, with at least 170 books published between ancient Greek times and 1917 examining the possibility of extraterrestrial life. Australian Paul Davies, a Professor of Natural Philosophy, devotes this book to consideration of "what the discovery of extraterrestrial life would mean for our view of ourselves and our place in the cosmos."

Since Earth and our solar system are about five billion years old, and many star clusters are thought to be up to 15 billion years old, most life in the universe, if it is widespread, may be billions of years older than the human species. Given that human technological society is only a few centuries old, "the nature of a community with millions or even billions of years of technological and social progress cannot even be imagined. Such advanced alien lifeforms would probably appear as gods to us. Science fiction writer Arthur C. Clarke has remarked that technology very far ahead of our own would seem indistinguishable from magic.

The odds are overwhelming that the aliens we meet will be our teachers, if only because "there is a negligible chance that two planets will produce intelligent life that matches in its developmental level to within even a million years." As a result of the almost certainty that humanity will be discovered to be dwelling "at the bottom of the league," we can also expect to find ourselves "to be among the least spiritually advanced creatures in the universe." This discovery of our evolutionary standing may prove two-edged. It could make humanity feel demoralized and hopelessly inferior. Or it could inspire our species to begin a rapid quest for knowledge. "Either way, it is hard to see how the world's great religions could continue in anything like their present form." These advanced beings may have no beliefs or theology about existence and the universe, or they may have spiritual practices which humanity would quickly adopt.

Davies advances a personal conjecture that what we know as consciousness is a "fundamental emergent property" and natural consequence of the laws of physics, and as a result "the emergence of consciousness, somewhere and somewhen, in the universe is more or less guaranteed." We may not be able to expect that aliens will look like us and think like us, but we can assume some properties of consciousness based on our own human experience. In fact, such an outcome seems preordained because "it almost looks as if the structure of the universe and the laws of physics have been deliberately adjusted in order to lead to the emergence of life and consciousness."

Rather than relegating humanity to an inferior creature, contact with extraterrestrial life might instead "give us cause to believe that we, in our humble way, are part of a larger, majestic process of cosmic selfknowledge." By our interaction with superior beings, by gaining access to a special and heightened knowledge, we will in some sense be brought "a step closer to God."

If the Universe Is Teeming with Aliens…Where Is Everybody?
STEPHEN WEBB
(2002, Springer)

It was the physicist Enrico Fermi who once stated that a conflict exists between the 'lack of evidence' for the existence of extraterrestrial life and the estimates made in The Drake Equation and other such equations formulated to indicate that intelligent life should be widespread in our galaxy and beyond. British theoretical physicist Stephen Webb uses The Fermi Paradox, as it's called, to propose—and then rationally demolish—75 'solutions' offered to resolve this paradox.

Webb begins with an assumption, though he calls it a 'truth', that we humans have "encountered no evidence, no messages, no artifacts" left by any extraterrestrial civilization "at least as advanced as our own." His first 10 proposed solutions to the Fermi Paradox are grouped under the heading 'They Are (or Were) Here' and include such obvious topics as "They Are Watching Us From UFOs," and "They Were Here and Left Evidence of Their Presence," to "They Exist And They Are Us."

That residue of UFO reports which remain unexplained don't interest Webb because "if we were clever enough and had enough resources and patience to carry through the necessary investigations" ALL sightings would be explained, he assures readers. He quotes U.S. UFO skeptic Robert Sheaffer saying "the apparently unexplainable residue {of UFO sightings} is due to the essentially random nature of gross misperception and misreporting."

In that context Webb admits that as a child, while playing soccer in the street, he and a friend "looked up and saw a pure white circle about the size of the full moon. Protuberances on either side of the circle made it look rather like Saturn showing its rings edge-on. Whatever it was, it seemed to hover for a few seconds before moving off at tremendous speed." Though Webb says he and his friend "definitely saw *something* in the sky that day and I have absolutely no idea what," he knows it couldn't have been a flying saucer because flying saucers don't exist and humans only think they see them because humans are poor observers.

Fermi Paradox Solutions #11 through #50 are grouped together to address such rationalizations as we don't see them because 'They Have Not Had Time to Reach Us', and 'They Stay at Home', to "They Are Signaling but We Don't Know How to Listen'. Webb spends a few pages arguing the flaws of each so-called solution. With Solution #22, involving extraterrestrials sending space probes into our solar system, Webb dismisses the mere prospect because "we see no evidence of aliens *nor of their probes*'.

Webb argues that life in the universe is rare and intelligent life is so rare as to be non-existent. Even if life elsewhere were to evolve a rudimentary intelligence, Webb makes a rational case that evolving a technological civilization is not inevitable, and indeed, evolving consciousness as we understand it will not be inevitable. Despite dismissing the entire SETI {search for extraterrestrial life} program as doomed to frustration and ultimate failure, the "subject is still important," Webb contends, if only for humans to prove how special that we and life on this planet really is and how we must protect it at all costs.

In Solution #75, his 'final' solution, Webb writes: "The debate about extraterrestrial intelligence contains just one gleaming, hard fact: we haven't been visited by ETCs nor have we heard from them." The reason why Webb finds quite obvious. "I believe it's because 'they'—sentient, intelligent, sapient creatures that build civilizations and with whom we can communicate—don't exist." In other words, we humans are quite alone in the Universe and our search for other intelligent life has really been undertaken because "we're searching for ourselves..."

Confessions of an Alien Hunter
SETH SHOSTAK
(2009, National Geographic)

A senior astronomer at the SETI Institute in California, Seth Shostak claims in this book the worst fear of UFO believers is that "SETI might succeed" in contacting extraterrestrials using radio telescopes because once that happens, if space signal contact begins, no one would pay attention to stories about lights in the sky. Shostak is convinced "the presence of aliens is still a doubtful claim" because he hasn't seen any evidence of alien UFO artifacts that "pass the smell test." What would help convince him?

First, good photographs that aren't hoaxes, which he says hasn't happened. Second, he needs "decent physical evidence," which once again, he says doesn't exist. Third, he claims that reconnaissance satellites "have failed to find alien UFOs" by taking photo of them from orbit. "I would switch my point of view on UFOs," writes Shotak, "if I saw a satellite photo of an alien craft that's as crips as the Google Earth imagery showing the Honda parked in my driveway."

He spends three book pages dismissing the claims of the late Army Lt. Col. Philip Corso, who co-wrote *The Day After Roswell*, maintaining that he was involved in the reverse-engineering of alien crash debris resulting in the development of fiber optics, lasers and other modern technology. Shostak quotes investigators as ridiculing Corso's account for being "riddled with demonstrable errors of fact involving dates, people, and institutions," and overall, he finds Corso's entire premise "is less credible than the Easter Bunny." Shostak devotes another three pages to the Roswell crash itself and concludes that the Air Force's Project Mogul balloon array explanation for the debris field makes the most sense.

A discussion of 'Monuments on Mars' takes up another six pages, during which Shostak addresses claims made by Richard C. Hoagland, in a book, that a human face created by aliens exists on the Cydonian plains of Mars based on photos taken in 1976 by the Viking Orbiter craft. Hoagland spent years trying to make a case The Face, as he called it, and other seemingly artificial structures had been built by alien visitors. In 2001, higher resolution photos taken by the Mars Global Surveyor documented that the so-called face was nothing more than a weathered mountain enhanced in earlier photos by tricks of light perception Unfazed, Hoagland continued to argue that NASA was engaged in a coverup of alien artifacts; not even more detailed photos taken by the European Space Agency in 2006, could shake Hoagland from his religious-like belief.

Periodically, even astronomers are fooled by false evidence, Shostak explains, pointing to examples of radio telescopes on Earth picking up mysterious signals, seemingly from distant stars, only to have it turn out to be mundane in their origins, usually misidentifications of satellite signals or natural celestial phenomena. Usually, the claims from amateur astronomers of having intercepted alien signals, or having hacked SETI and found evidence of an alien signal coverup, were found to be hoaxes, as was the case in 1998, spread by an anonymous British hacker/engineer.

Elsewhere in the book he discusses alternative communication mediums for signaling alien civilizations, such as lasers, gravity waves, and neutrinos, and whether the aliens might have sent space probes our direction. He counters the argument that SETI has been a failure because no signals have been detected by pointing out "we have carefully examined only 0.0000005 percent of a single galaxy."

The Eerie Silence: Renewing Our Search for Alien Intelligence
PAUL DAVIES
(2010, Houghton Mifflin Harcourt)

Arizona State University physicist and cosmologist Paul Davies uses this book to argue that the SETI (Search for Extraterrestrial Intelligence) program using radio telescopes to search for evidence of alien life these past five decades needs a deep rethinking and given the 'eerie silence' this program has been met with, we need to find entirely different approaches if we ever hope to contact intelligent life elsewhere in the universe.

Using current approaches SETI has "only a slender hope of receiving a message from the stars at this time," and as a result, "we need to establish a much broader program of research, a search for *general* signatures of intelligence, wherever they may be imprinted in the physical universe." To even begin this process, we must first abandon "all of our presuppositions about the nature of life, mind, civilization, technology and community destiny."

First, Davies addresses the issue of UFOs and whether extraterrestrials are currently visiting us or have visited us in ancient times. He describes how in 1970, he spent time with UFO believer and astronomer J. Allen Hynek, when he was science adviser to the Air Force's Project Blue Book, and "for a while he almost convinced me too—I was at least prepared to keep an open mind. But over the years, as I thought more about these unexplained sightings, I came to see how deeply anthropocentric they were—bearing all the hallmarks of human rather than alien minds."

Though he says "it would not surprise me if a small fraction of cases involve new or little-understood atmospheric or psychological phenomena," he believes UFO sighting accounts "cannot be taken seriously as evidence for extraterrestrial beings."

After dismissing any investigations of the UFO phenomenon as a waste of time, Davies sets out to make a case that SETI "compels us to make *much* greater leaps of imagination" than even the UFO phenomenon does. There is no evidence that the universe is teeming with life, says Davies, or that circumstances in our galaxy or any galaxy are even congenial for life to evolve and be widespread at all. But if scientists still insist on conducting this search for life anyway, argues Davies, at least they should abandon reliance on listening for narrow-band radio messages, or sending such messages, which is simply not a credible scientific approach for a series of reasons that Davies lists in these pages.

What would make more sense, according to Davies, might be to search for alien probes in our solar system. "There is no reason why a probe should have arrived in the solar system only recently. It could have been dispatched millions of years ago by a civilization that had determined, using remote observation, that there was life on Earth. The probe would remain passive, quietly monitoring our planet and biding its time until a technological society emerged." (Interestingly, Davies proposes a search for alien probes even as he argues that investigating UFOs is a waste of time.)

Other ways aliens, if they were to exist, might try to communicate with us would be to "use comets as delivery vehicles." Once the comet comes close enough to our sun or any galactic sun, it would begin to evaporate and eject dormant microbes and viruses that could fall on Earth or other habitable planets. Genome sequencing by the aliens could have implanted messages in the microbiological entities that, if we were smart enough, we could discover and interpret.

At the end of this book, after spending several hundred pages evaluating the science case for intelligent life elsewhere, Paul Davies, speaking as 'the scientist', makes a confession in response to the question 'are we alone'? He writes: "My answer is that we are probably the only intelligent beings in the observable universe, and I would not be very surprised if the solar system contains the only life in the observable universe. I arrive at this dismal conclusion because I see so many contingent features involved in the origin and evolution of life, and because I have yet to see a convincing theoretical argument for a universal principle of increasing organized complexity."

Extraterrestrial: The First Sign of Intelligent Life Beyond Earth
AVI LOEB
(2021, Houghton Mifflin Harcourt)

What began as a suspected comet entering our solar system turned into an inquiry with an unprecedented alternative explanation—we were being visited by an extraterrestrial space probe. The scientist making a case for this explanation was a distinguished one, Avi Loeb, Chairman of the Astronomy Department at Harvard University, who had authored 800 scientific papers. The mystery that Loeb chronicles in this book began on October 19, 2017, when astronomers first noticed a new interstellar visitor had made its appearance in our solar system. Most observers assumed it was a comet or an asteroid. But everyone noticed that it behaved strangely.

"This visitor, when compared to every other object that astronomers have ever studied, was exotic," writes Loeb. "And the hypotheses offered up to account for all of the object's observed peculiarities are likewise exotic. I submit that the simplest explanation for these peculiarities is that the object was created by an intelligent civilization not of this Earth."

Humanity didn't yet know the object existed when it entered our solar neighborhood, from the direction of Vega, a star 25 light years away, and then looped around our own sun. Only when the object was beginning to exit our solar system at an accelerating speed exceeding 58,000 miles per hour, did our telescopes detect it. Because the first telescope to spot it on October 19 was located in Hawaii, the object became known by the Hawaiian word Oumuamua, loosely translated as 'scout'.

Over the 11 days astronomers tracked Oumuamua before it exited our planetary system, they had to confess it was unlike any comet or asteroid ever observed. By looking at how the object reflected sunlight, it could be estimated the object was five to ten times longer than it was wide, making it about 100 yards long and about 10 yards wide. Nothing like this shape had ever been seen in any natural space object.

There were several other puzzling anomalies. It was 'strangely luminous', ten times more reflective than any comet or asteroid. It actually shined like a metal. But its "most arresting anomaly," declares Loeb, was how its trajectory "deviated from what was expected based on the Sun's gravitational force alone." It smoothly accelerated away from the sun and us. Not only that, if Oumuamua was a comet, where was its tail of dust and ice when it encountered the sun? There was no observable outgassing or debris trail, unlike all comets ever observed.

As most conventional scientists continued stretching logic and the facts to insist Oumuamua was just a peculiar comet, Avi Loeb followed the evidence to conclude what other astronomers were loath to even consider. Oumuamua could be extraterrestrial in origin, made and sent by an advanced civilization, and its dimensions and strange behaviors could mean it functioned like a solar sail, propelled by the pressure that sunlight exerted on it. Perhaps it was "floating in interstellar space as debris from advanced technological equipment," or it might be a communications buoy in space "and our solar system was like a ship that ran into it at high speed."

Professor Loeb spends much of the remainder of this book discussing the need for developing 'space archaeology', meaning "searching for technological civilizations by digging into space." If we fail to do so, if we are short-sighted and close-minded, we will "miss the chance to take {a} million-year leap forward."

Epilogue: Consciousness in a Mirror

If humankind ever hopes to decipher the behavior of UFOs and their occupants, Jacques Vallée wrote in 1969, we must eventually confront the larger problem of understanding nonhuman intelligence. That challenge for our species begins with learning to communicate with non-human intelligent lifeforms already evolving on this planet—the entire primate family, the octopus, ravens and dolphins, for starters—that we have largely taken for granted as vastly inferior.

In the first two decades of the 21st century botanists and biologist uncovered compelling evidence that some plants (fungi networks connected to tree and plant roots, in particular) and certain animals (including insect swarms) possess varying levels of communicating awareness and functional intelligence sufficient to challenge some prevailing human assumptions about our special evolutionary niche on the tree of life. From this intelligence can emerge consciousness, defined as the sum total of a mind's thoughts, perceptions, feelings and heightened awareness. Such research may offer us clues about how we might learn to communicate with other non-human lifeforms and even how a planetary consciousness could be at work animating The Phenomenon, a term I use for unidentified aerial phenomena and related anomalous effects.

Earth having 'a mind of its own' and a planetary consciousness was the subject of a pioneering thought experiment in a February 2022 issue of the *International Journal of Astrobiology*, in which astrophysicists from Arizona State University and the University of Rochester proposed that cognitive activity may be operating on a planetary scale, an evolving complexity connecting the collective activity generated by intelligence in microbes, plants, animals and humans. Funded by a NASA grant, this study concluded that Earth's planetary intelligence "operates via feedback loops that are global in scale, coordination and operation" and by recognizing these interactions animating on our own planet, we will be better positioned to recognize global minds on other planets where extraterrestrial life may have evolved.

Another type of feedback loop may be in play with the discovery in the late 20th century of mirror neurons in the brains of humans and several species of animals. Mirror neurons are brain cells that establish a learning feedback loop between two or more individuals, irrespective of species, in which actions and energies are unconsciously mimicked or mirrored, producing resonance and empathy. With mirror neurons we have a mechanism, if only metaphorical, to explain an oddity reported in many interactions between humans and The Phenomenon. I wonder if such a 'mirroring' may be at work between human consciousness and The Phenomenon, as illustrated by a series of reported effects during high strangeness events.

• When U.S. Navy carrier pilots flying off the California coast in 2004 saw 'Tic Tac' shaped UFOs—tracked visually and on ship radars and infrared scanners—these pilots noticed that the wingless objects mirrored many of their plane's movements. Several pilots commented that it was as if the objects 'had been reading their minds' because the UFOs were waiting at the rendezvous coordinates the pilots had been directed to converge on.

• In dozens of 'contact' meditation seminars held in the desert over the past few decades, organized by Dr. Steven Greer, numerous attendees reported experiencing a range of strange phenomena, including lights, entities, and objects in the night sky that seemed to mirror group intentions and collective thoughts during and after the guided group meditations.

• Over several decades of research at 'Skinwalker' Ranch in Utah, conducted by both federal government and civilian investigators, a disturbing pattern, nicknamed 'hitchhikers', was reported in which orb-like lights and paranormal incidents occurring on the ranch seemed to follow some of the investigators to their homes. The 'hitchhiker' contagion (resembling a mirroring feedback loop) reportedly got attached to 10 ranch security guards and to five intelligence agency officials who spent time at the ranch.

• A similar 'hitchhiker' contagion of paranormal effects afflicted San Antonio newspaper reporter Ed Conroy in 1987, after he did a feature article about local-born Whitley Strieber, author of the alien abduction story, *Communion*. For months after the article was published, Conroy had his own strange 'visitor experiences' with the phenomena spreading like a contagion, affecting several of Conroy's friends who "began having nighttime experiences with entities, balls and flashes of light, and other anomalous phenomena." Conroy said the hitchhiker contagion felt like it had "a direct link with human consciousness."

• Such a contagion pattern seemed attached to abductee Karla Turner, a Ph.D. English professor at a Texas university, who reported that 10 people in her circle of friends and relatives were affected "by alien intrusions and disturbances" after she revealed her abduction story in 1988.

• Vancouver, Canada housewife Dorothy Izatt apparently demonstrated an ability to summon anomalous orbs and other light phenomena after engaging in prayer or meditation, phenomena which she recorded on photos and tens of thousands of feet of film from the mid-1970s through the 1990s. Groups of witnesses vouched for having seen her consciously interacting with these lights, which appeared both within and outside of her home, mirroring her stated intentions.

• Three CIA and Naval Intelligence officers witnessed a bright sphere of light UFO outside their office window in Washington, D.C., apparently manifested in response to their expressed collective desire to see it. One of the Naval Intelligence officers had learned 'channeling' from a woman contactee and believed he was interacting with an extraterrestrial consciousness when the UFO was summoned. (Refer to the Introduction in Part 3 of this book.)

Many of the books summarized in *Alien in the Mirror* also convey various aspects of these consciousness mirroring and shaping themes.

College English Professor Meade Layne, writing in his 1950 book, *The Ether Ship and Its Solution*, became the earliest known theorist to propose a psycho-physical explanation for UFOs, seeing the phenomenon as "responsive to thought energy" in which observers materialize the objects and entities from a parallel dimension, a summoning initiated by projections of human consciousness. This theory seems reminiscent of Tulpas—thought forms—a belief tradition in Tibetan Buddhism. Layne's opinions were particularly pioneering given how the purely extraterrestrial and physical 'nuts and bolts' view of UFOs completely dominated mainstream thinking at that time. (Layne founded the Borderland Sciences Research Foundation in 1945, to examine the 'border-land' between reality and fantasy).

It was Swiss psychoanalyst Carl Jung who first examined UFOs as a symptom of psychic distress and changes in the collective human consciousness, writing in his 1959 book, *Flying Saucers*, that the objects seen in the sky "behave not like bodies but like weightless thoughts." If not machines, UFOs could even be a species of living creature, he speculated. While acknowledging that UFOs must be either a psychic projection from human minds, or a material nuts and bolts phenomenon, he left open the possibility it is a combination of both. "That something psychic could possess material qualities and a high charge of energy surpasses our comprehension."

John Keel advanced the view in his 1970 book, *UFOs—Operation Trojan Horse*, that UFOs are primarily electromagnetic in origin, manipulate matter to assume any shape they desire, and the intelligence directing these manifestations isn't extraterrestrial but rather a form of energy, or an energy field, that has tailored itself to human attitudes and beliefs to shape religions throughout human history. Keel further refined these ideas in his 1975 book, *The Eighth Tower*, in which he hypothesized a 'super-spectrum' of energies encompassing gravity, the magnetic field, and infrasonic sound, as a single intelligent force to account for all paranormal manifestations, from ghosts to UFOs. These masses of energy are extradimensional and record the collective electrical impulses broadcast from billions of human minds. These superspectrum energies periodically tune in to the exact frequency of the observer's brainwaves and by influencing consciousness, manifest UFOs and other paranormal phenomena.

Ralph and Judy Blum in their 1974 book, *Beyond Earth: Man's Contact with UFOs,* also proposed that if these visitors aren't extraterrestrial, UFOs could be either "a type of intelligent energy" that can morph into any shape, or they are "living holograms" projected by the human unconscious mind.

Jacques Vallée introduced numerous provocative ideas in his 1975 book, *The Invisible College*, wondering if the UFO phenomenon could be a control or influence mechanism over human belief systems and the relationship between our consciousness and physical reality. It might be a terrestrial rather than extraterrestrial technology we are being exposed to. He pointed out how psychic effects produced in human witnesses may offer a key to understanding the true source and nature of the phenomenon. UFOs may be projections from time rather than space and observations of UFOs throughout history have always been explained within the prevailing belief systems of the dominant culture. In his 1969 book, *Passport to Magonia*, Vallée had raised the prospect that UFOs might be more like 'windows' to a parallel universe intended to program our collective imagination, or the phenomenon may be a control system for human consciousness. It could also be that we are in contact with a nonhuman consciousness which coexists with us and has been interacting with us as companions or caretakers since humans began evolving.

Canadian research psychologists Michael Persinger and Gyslaine LaFreniere in a 1977 book, *Space-Time Transients and Unusual Events*, used data from their laboratory experiments to examine electromagnetic field effects on human perceptions and consciousness in an attempt to explain some UFO sightings. They speculated that space-time overlaps may be produced by these fields and three-dimensional holograms might emerge, causing human bioelectrical systems to react with "dreamlike states, episodes of paralysis, or intervals of unconsciousness." Human minds might even be inundated by the release of stored images of culturally conditioned ideas about what UFOs and the entities inside are supposed to look like. "Interaction between large numbers of biological systems and the geomagnetic environment within which they are immersed," the authors proposed, might be an interaction that generates behaviors and patterns in which the phenomenon produces thought images indistinguishable from reality, or which create a new consensus reality.

Michael Craft observed, in his 1996 book *Alien Impact*, how reported alien visitors engage in acts of trickery that resemble accounts of fairies and elves through the centuries, a theme that Jacques Vallée had explored in *Passport to Magonia*. Even the appearance, enigmatic speech, and mode of travel attributed to aliens make Craft wonder whether these entities are a consciousness already present on our planet for thousands of years, maybe even before the human species evolved, and we are now just beginning to discover their presence in fleeting glimpses seemingly lifted from episodes of *The Twilight Zone*.

British author Colin Wilson concluded, in his 1998 book, *Alien Dawn*, that the visitors—whoever or whatever they are—are on a mission to transform human consciousness by altering our consensus reality. The intelligence that manifests UFOs and manipulates human perceptions and consciousness arises from electromagnetic frequencies. It may be part of "some other reality {existing} on a level that is somehow parallel to our own, but on a different vibration rate."

Harvard psychiatrist John Mack came to similar conclusions in one of his books about the alien abduction phenomenon, *Passport to the Cosmos,* in 1999, showing how abduction experiences seem designed "to shatter the previously held idea of reality." In the aftermath of their experiences, abductees "realize that they have encountered intense vibratory energies, still held in the body, that have also profoundly affected their consciousness." Their bodies seem to vibrate at higher frequencies as if they have been awakened by something akin to a shamanic journey of consciousness transformation.

Mac Tonnes speculated in his 2010 book, *The Cryptoterrestrials*, that the alien visitation phenomenon isn't space visitors but rather evidence for a race of indigenous humanoids who have always secretly lived on this planet and who have perfected the art of camouflage and mastered a technology of consciousness for mind and perception control designed to manipulate humans to further some mysterious agenda.

More recently, three authors of the 2021 book, *Skinwalkers at the Pentagon,* chronicling the high strangeness associated with Skinwalker Ranch in Utah, noted how several decades of government and civilian study of the phenomena occurring on that 500-acre property produced evidence suggesting that human consciousness and some unknown intelligence interacts to play an integral role in the unidentified aerial and other strange phenomena being documented on the ranch.

A few philosophers have wondered if the collective human consciousness might be projecting a planetary mind that reflects back to us an imaginal realm, encompassing all of our collective fears and hopes, while confronting us with imagery in the form of symbolic archetypal scenes and psycho-dramas, all intended to accelerate the evolution of our species consciousness.

Existence of a 'group mind' or 'planetary mind' received research attention at the Princeton Engineering Anomalies Research lab, established in 1979 by Princeton University Dean of Engineering Robert G. Jahn, to investigate psychokinesis and remote viewing. One of the research experiments, called the Global Consciousness Project, employed random event generators (REGs) to test the ability of test subjects to mentally influence random output distributions to conform with intentions set for either higher or lower number generation. For our purposes the most interesting feature of the REG experiments involved testing to measure what happens when the focused attention of millions of people interacts with the sub-atomic information realm, as reflected in REG behaviors.

The Princeton project's network of 37 computers scattered worldwide, from the U.S. to Brazil, India and Switzerland, used the REG's to electronically 'flip' virtual coins, while measuring to see if the randomness would be altered by humankind's collective focus on world events. The research question was straightforward: would the energetic focus of millions of human minds create order in otherwise random flows of information?

A possible answer came on September 11, 2001, with terrorist events in New York City and Washington, D.C. A large statistical spike in the second-by-second data stream for these 37 computers occurred throughout the morning of September 11th, an effect apparently far beyond chance. Similar spikes in the data were recorded on other dramatic news days when world attention had been riveted, such as seconds before midnight on New Year's 2000, the Y2K transition, an event that had generated tremendous apprehension among millions of people during the preceding months.

Given these and related Princeton project results, had Carl Jung's hypothesized collective unconscious been radiating effects that were measured like a seismograph charting earthquake activity? Or could the Princeton project's results be analogous to an electro-encephalograph measuring electrical signals from a group mind? With these experiments we may have stolen a peak through a crack in our consensus reality that establishes an entire new way to measure and understand a human planetary consciousness. Though skeptics of the experiments claim the results "ignored the laws of physics" and haven't been replicated by other investigators, these replication attempts mostly involved the REG trials of individuals, not the mass mind REG effects linked to events generating worldwide attention.

If we were to imagine The Phenomenon as operating like a kind of cosmic TV 'reality' show, as with the various reality shows we see on television today, when the cameras turn on and the act of observation begins, human behavior changes, often to mirror audience expectations. Could The Phenomenon be operating on the same principle, reacting to the observers, fulfilling expectations with an interactive mirroring that blurs the distinctions between producer and director and actor. In this scenario, The Phenomenon continually needs human observer consciousness to complete the scene and continue the psycho-drama.

We might also employ an analogy from the field of physics, with its 'observer effect', where the act of human observation and measurement of subatomic particles changes what is being observed. Could the human act of observing The Phenomenon be shaping it and simultaneously changing our experience of it, an observer effect being orchestrated on a grand scale?

What we have inherited are an array of intriguing threads of evidence requiring us to embrace a multi-disciplinary approach, bonding botanists and biologists and neuroscientists with astronomers and astrophysicists and AI futurists, into a genuinely collaborative effort, if we ever hope to find plausible, satisfying answers to The Phenomenon and the implications of its high strangeness effects for human consciousness.

Appendix: The Author's Recommended Books

Books Chronicling the History of the Phenomenon

The UFO Encyclopedia, by Jerome Clark, 3rd Edition (2018, Omnigraphics)

UFOs & The National Security State, Volumes 1 and 2, by Richard Dolan (2002, 2009, Keyhole Publishing)

The Encyclopedia of Extraterrestrial Encounters, by Ronald Story (2001, New American Library)

UFOs and the Extraterrestrial Contact Movement, by George M. Eberhart (1986, Scarecrow Press)

Scientist's Examining the Phenomenon

Extraterrestrial: The First Sign of Intelligent Life Beyond Earth, by Avi Loeb (2021, Houghton Mifflin Harcourt)

The UFO Enigma, by Peter Sturrock (1999, Warner Books)

*Passport to the Cosmos: Human Transformation and Alien Encounte*rs, by John E. Mack (1999, White Crow Books)

The Omega Project, by Kenneth Ring (1992, William Morrow)

The Hynek UFO Report, by J. Allen Hynek (1977, Dell)

Space-Time Transients and Unusual Events, by Michael A. Persinger & Gyslaine F. LaFreniere (1977, Nelson-Hall)

UFOlogy, by James M. McCampbell (1976, Celestial Arts)

The Invisible College, by Jacques Vallée (1975, E.P. Dutton)

The Edge of Reality, by J. Allen Hynek & Jacques Vallée (1975, Henry Regnery)

Uninvited Visitors, by Ivan T. Sanderson (1967, Cowles)

Phenomenon Case Study Books

Skinwalkers at the Pentagon, by James Lacatski, Colm Kelleher, & George Knapp (2021, RTMA)

Trinity: The Best-Kept Secret, by Jacques F. Vallée & Paola Leopizzi Harris (2021, Starworks)

Encounters at Rendlesham Forest, by Nick Pope, John Burroughs & Jim Penniston (2014, Thomas Dunne Books)

The Cash-Landrum UFO Incident, by John Schuessler (1998, CreateSpace)

The Truth About the UFO Crash at Roswell, by Kevin D. Randle & Donald R. Schmitt

(1994, Avon Books)

Communion, by Whitley Strieber (1987, William Morrow)

Socorro Saucer: the closest encounter of them all, by Ray Stanford (1976, Blueapple Books)

Incident at Exeter, by John G. Fuller (1966, G.P. Putnam)

The Interrupted Journey, by John G. Fuller (1966, The Dial Press)

Phenomenon Overview Books

In Plain Sight: An Investigation into UFOs and Impossible Science, by Ross Coulthart (2021, HarperCollins)

UFOs: Generals, Pilots, and Government Officials Go On the Record, by Leslie Kean (2010, Harmony Books)

Alien Dawn: A Classic Investigation Into the Contact Experience, by Colin Wilson (1998, Virgin Publishing)

Above Top Secret, by Timothy Good (1987, Sidgwick & Jackson)

The Eighth Tower, by John Keel (1975, Saturday Review Press)

Passport to Magonia, by Jacques Vallée (1969, Henry Regnery)

Aliens in the Skies, by John G. Fuller (1969, G. P. Putnam)

Anatomy of a Phenomenon, by Jacques Vallée (1965, Henry Regnery)

The Morning of the Magicians, by Louis Pauwels & Jacques Bergier (1960, Editions Gallimard)

Flying Saucers: A Modern Myth of Things Seen in the Sky, by Carl Jung (1959, Routledge & Kegan Paul)

Flying Saucers and the Straight-line Mystery, Aime Michel (1958, S.G. Phillips)

The Report on Unidentified Flying Objects, by Edward J. Ruppelt (1956. Doubleday)

Flying Saucers from Outer Space, by Donald E. Keyhoe (1953, Henry Holt)

The Ether Ship and Its Solution, by Meade Layne (1950, Borderland Sciences)

About the Author

Randall Fitzgerald's ten books (and more than 50 books as a ghostwriter) have been pioneering explorations of a wide variety of topics, reflecting his diverse interests and an insatiable curiosity cultivated by 35 years as a newspaper and magazine journalist. For two decades he was a Roving Editor for *Reader's Digest* and also wrote investigative feature articles for *The Washington Post* and *The Wall Street Journal.*

He began his journalism career at 19, as a general assignment reporter for *The Tyler Morning Telegraph*, in Tyler, Texas. While in journalism school at the University of Texas at Austin, he worked as a political reporter in the state capitol bureau of *The Houston Post* and spent a semester as a Congressional Fellow in Washington, D.C., working as press secretary to a U.S. Congressman. In August 1974, the week that Richard Nixon resigned as President, he became an investigative reporter for newspaper syndicated columnist Jack Anderson, in Washington, D.C.

He received a grant from the Fund for Investigative Journalism in 1975 to investigate the Mafia and CIA connections of the publisher of *The National Enquirer* by going undercover as a reporter for the tabloid. His first book contract came from Pocket Books/ Simon & Schuster, based on his *Enquirer* investigation. His second book appeared in 1979, from Macmillan, *The Complete Book of Extraterrestrial Encounters*, the cover of which was immortalized in Ron Howard's extraterrestrial-themed film *Cocoon*. During 1978-80, he co-edited *Second Look* magazine, devoted to articles about the search for extraterrestrial life, the nature of consciousness, and the origins of civilization. He edited articles from some of the biggest names in science and science fiction—Isaac Asimov, Stanislaw Lem, Sir Fred Hoyle, Paul Davies, Sir Roger Penrose. In 2003 and 2004, he was a Senior Editor of *Phenomena* magazine, founded by former Hollywood studio executive Jeff Sagansky.

Two of his books, *Lucky You!* (2004, Citadel/Kensington) and *The Hundred Year Lie* (2006, Penguin/Dutton) were Amazon.com big sellers. *Lucky You!* was the first book to examine the link between intuition and luck in games of chance and got distribution in Spanish, Japanese, and Korean editions. *The Hundred Year Lie*, about the impact of synthetic chemicals on human health, was also published by Beijing University Press in China, where it has been a perennial seller.

Based on his *Lucky You!* book, he was selected in 2005 as the media master of ceremonies for the 100th anniversary celebration of the founding of the city of Las Vegas, on behalf of the Fremont Street Experience, a collection of 10 casinos, including the Golden Nugget, along with the city of Las Vegas, giving live television interviews to dozens of local television stations nationwide.

He has been a guest on *ABC's The View, The Oprah Winfrey Show, The Dr. Mehmet Oz Show, The Michael Smerconish Show, Court TV,* CBS' s *48 Hours,* ABC's *20/20, BBC* and *PBS Radio,* and hundreds of other television and radio shows, including four appearances on *The Coast-to-Coast* radio show with George Noory.

For more information, go to www.alieninthemirror.com.

Index

A

AATIP, 386–87

ABs (Advanced Beings), 52, 60–61, 229, 425

Adamski, George, 104, 244, 320

Admiral Knowles, 232–35, 243

advanced species, 87, 116, 408, 411, 416

Affa, 127–28, 231–245

AFOSI (Air Force Office of Special Investigations), 155, 161, 164, 201, 379–80

Air Force, xvi–xx, 85–87, 89–91, 94, 105–7, 129–30, 143–44, 146–47, 153–55, 157–60, 162–63, 171–72, 202–3, 208, 210, 219, 330–31, 339–40, 364–66, 383–84

Air Force Office of Special Investigations. *See* AFO-SI

Air Force Project Blue Book, xxv–vi, 94, 120, 127–28, 143–44, 146, 147, 172, 187–88, 209–10, 219, 224, 237–38, 245, 279, 364, 429

Albuquerque, *See* New Mexico

alien

    abductees, xxiv, 163, 196, 227, 230–322, 245, 248, 285, 362, 368–69, 373, 377, 437

    abductions, 245–48, 249–51, 261–62, 270–72, 278, 283–85, 291, 294, 299–300, 302, 305–6, 308, 314–17, 319–20, 362–65, 368–69, 373, 377, 437

    abductors, 167, 197, 229, 246, 250–51, 262, 272, 282, 299, 301, 314, 319–20, 369

    beings, xvii, 100, 246, 250, 284, 294–95, 299, 301, 306, 409, 417

    bodies, xvi, xviii–xxi, 161, 167–69, 175, 177, 181, 207, 211–12, 366, 370–71, 381, 383

    civilizations, 8, 393, 395, 423–24

    contact, 60, 100, 116, 127–28, 130, 137–38, 155–56, 230–34, 236–37, 239–41, 243–44, 254–57, 265–66, 281–82, 313–14, 401–2, 406–7, 409–13, 415–17, 423–24

        claimed, 104, 229, 267, 272

        telepathic, 229, 244, 274

        contactees, 110, 113, 121, 123–24, 126, 128, 130, 134, 138, 141, 229–31, 251–52, 277–78

    craft, 126, 162, 175, 225, 249, 264, 291, 301, 428

    crashed, 166, 177

    encounters, 196, 229–30, 322

experiences, 140, 282–83, 290–91, 293, 298, 302, 309, 311, 314, 316 17, 320, 322, 362, 437, 442

intelligence, 286, 302, 313, 402, 417, 429

phenomena, 250, 301–2, 308, 310–11, 313, 320–321, 437

probes, 396, 398, 401, 418, 430

spacecraft, xvii, 115, 160–61, 166, 230, 370–71, 424

visitations, xv, xviii, xxii–xxiii, 4, 8, 11–12, 125, 196, 230, 246, 322, 350, 358, 405, 408–9, 416, 418, 437

visitors, 3, 9, 11, 17, 49, 52–53, 55, 61–62, 84, 86, 92, 116, 214, 251–52, 255–57, 266, 270, 290–91, 298, 300, 302–3, 308–9, 314, 319–20, 358, 366, 380, 406, 410, , 436–37

aliens, xxvii, 58–61, 161–63, 173–74, 196–97, 206–7, 230, 245, 247–52, 280, 287, 289, 294–96, 298, 306–9, 314–15, 358–59, 365, 368–69, 376–77, 424–28

Anderson, Gerald, 166–67, 169, 172

angels, 3, 5, 7, 11, 14, 19, 31, 116, 120, 138–39, 162–63, 279, 282

animals, 54–55, 100, 103, 147, 149, 190–91, 270, 299, 301, 303, 321, 353–54, 433

Antarctica, 32–33, 98, 136, 205, 258, 412

Anunnaki, 53–54, 57, 61

archetype, 101–2, 140

Arizona, xviii, xxi, 65–66, 74–77, 80–83, 86, 114, 172, 189, 271, 275

    Arizona Lights, xxvii, 80–81, 83

    Phoenix, xx, 66–68, 71–77, 80–81, 86, 146, 190, 280

    Phoenix Lights, 77, 188

    Tucson, 71–72, 74, 76–78, 83, 189–90

Arnold, Kenneth, 87, 89–90, 163, 180, 340

Arnold, Kenneth & Palmer, Ray: *The Coming of the Saucers*, 88

artifacts, 3, 45, 59, 121, 125, 213, 307, 350, 404–5, 407, 426

Asimov, Isaac, xxiii, 416, 418–19

    Extraterrestrial Civilizations, 418

asteroids, 419, 430–31

Atlantis (Atlanteans), 13–16, 28, 32–36, 38, 117–18, 137, 255, 338

Index

Aztec, New Mexico, 86, 158, 199–201, 365–66
Aztecs, xix, 111, 137, 258

B

Babylonians, 3, 6, 21, 41, 48, 347, 413
balloons, 9, 99, 104, 151–52, 338, 345, 348, 370, 375, 378, 383
Barker, Gray: *They Knew Too Much About Flying Saucers*, 97
Barry, Bill: *Ultimate Encounter*, 275
Baxter, John & Atkins, Thomas: *The Fire Came By*, 275
beings, 3, 9–10, 12–13, 20–21, 103–4, 106, 113, 139–40, 250–51, 261, 265–66, 272–74, 281–82, 288, 292–96, 299–301, 303, 313–14, 367–68, 413
advanced, 52, 60–61, 229, 425
luminous, 24
mythical, 413
belief systems, human, 134, 436
Bender, Albert K., 98, 255–56
Flying Saucers and the Three Men, 255
Bennewitz, Paul, 155, 161–62, 365–66, 380
Bergier, Jacques, 12–13, 24–25
Extraterrestrial Visitations from Prehistoric Times to the Present, 24
Berlitz, Charles & Moore, William: *The Roswell Incident*, 151
Bernard, Raymond: The Hollow Earth, 117
Bible, 10–11, 14, 19–22, 45–48, 54, 57, 60, 134, 139, 346–47, 354, 357, 373–74
Bigfoot, 25, 35–36, 125, 133, 147
black holes, 39, 351, 408, 415
Blum, Howard: *Out There*, 159
Blum, Ralph, 123–24, 159–62, 393–94
Beyond Earth: Man's Contact with UFOs, 123
Blumrich, Josef F., 29–30, 354
The Spaceships of Ezekiel, 29
Bigelow, Robert, 192, 222, 225, 248, 332, 385–86
Bowen, Charles: *The Humanoids*, 264
Boyce, Chris: *Extraterrestrial Encounter*, 417
Bracewell, Ronald N., 396–97, 410–11
The Galactic Club, 410
Bramley, William: *The Gods of Eden*, 50
Brown, Courtney: *Cosmic Voyage*, 303

C

Carey, Thomas J. & Schmitt, Donald R.:
Roswell: The Ultimate Cold Case, 217
UFO Secrets Inside Wright-Patterson, 211
Cash, Betty, 195, 334–37, 441

Cathie, Bruce: *Harmonic* 33, 111
Cavitt, Sheridan, xx, 152, 168, 373
channelers, 174, 251–52, 286
Charroux, Robert: *One Hundred Thousand Years of Man's Unknown History*, 15
Christian, James L.: *Extra-terrestrial Intelligence: The First Encounter*, 416
China, Ancient, 61
CIA, xvii, xix–xx, xxv–xxvii, 113, 143, 175, 177, 181, 230, 235–39, 242, 277, 364, 381, 383–84, 393–94
civilizations, 3, 5, 7, 37, 42–45, 48, 55–56, 130–31, 350–51, 393–94, 398–401, 405–8, 416–17, 419–24, 429–30
human, 27, 30, 37, 44–45, 52, 57, 234
origins of, xxiii, 12, 42, 443
technical, 406–8
Clancy, Susan: *Abducted: How People Come to Believe They Were Kidnapped by Aliens*, 376
Clark, Jerome & Coleman, Loren: *The Unidentified*, 140
Cohane, John Philip: *Paradox: The Case for the Extraterrestrial Origin of Man*, 44
Cohen, Daniel: *Myths of the Space Age*, 341
Collyns, Robin: *Did Spacemen Colonise the Earth?*, 35
colonists, 32, 34, 37
colonization, 109, 406, 420–21
comets, 39, 42–43, 65, 73, 97, 405, 408, 410, 418, 430–31
Communion, 230, 246, 250, 288, 291–92, 294, 296, 363, 377, 434, 442
Complete Book of Extraterrestrial Encounters, xxvii, 443
computers, 26, 52–53, 75, 148, 266, 274, 278, 315, 438
Condon, Edward: *Scientific Study of Unidentified Flying Objects*, 344
Condon Report, xii, 113, 188, 347–49, 356, 364
Conroy, Ed, 291–93, 434
Report On Communion, 291
consciousness, xxiii–xxiv, 130, 133–35, 193, 196, 246, 250, 293, 297–98, 301, 308–11, 322, 414, 417–18, 422, 425–27, 433–37, 439
altered states of, 193, 297
nonhuman, 166, 436
consensus reality, 82, 308–9, 311, 337, 437–38
Constable, Trevor James:
Sky Creatures: Living UFOs, 102
They Live in the Sky, 102
contagion, hitchhiker, 434
Coppens, Philip, 58–60

Index

Index

L

Lacatski, James T, Kelleher, Colm A. & Knapp, George: *Skinwalkers at the Pentagon: An Insiders' Account of the Secret Government UFO Program*, 221

Landrum, Vickie, 195, 334–37, 441

Larsen, J.M., 235–42

Las Vegas, 67, 77, 172, 190, 192, 225, 332, 380, 443–44

Layne, Meade: *The Ether Ship and Its Solution*, 84

Lemuria, 16–17, 32

Leslie, Desmond & Adamski, George: *Flying Saucers Have Landed*, 253

Lethbridge, T.C.: *The Legend of the Sons of God*, 27

light beings, 311–12

light formations, 66, 72, 74, 76

Lilly, John C.: *The Scientist: A Novel Autobiography*, 274

Loeb, Avi: *Extraterrestrial: The First Sign of Intelligent Life Beyond Earth*, 430

Lorenzen, Coral & Jim:
  Abducted: Confrontations with Beings from Outer Space, 270
  Flying Saucer Occupants, 109
  UFOs Over the Americas, 112

Lorenzens, 109–10, 112–13, 270–72, 277

Lunan, Duncan: *The Mysterious Signals from Outer Space*, 411

Lundahl, Arthur, 236–42

M

Mack, John E., 230, 247, 250, 252, 300, 308–9, 321, 368, 437
  Abduction, 300
  Passport to the Cosmos: Human Transformation and Alien Encounters, 309

Macvey, John W.: *Whispers from Space*, 409

magnesium, 121, 123, 333

magnetic fields, 91, 96, 112, 114, 132, 138, 150, 345, 415, 435

Marcel, Jesse, xvi, xx–xxi, 151–52, 168, 170, 180, 370, 372–73, 378–79

Marchetti, Victor, 393

Mars, 4, 26, 32, 36, 43, 48–50, 54, 57–58, 87, 91, 205–6, 404, 406

Maruyama, Magoroh & Harkins, Arthur: *Cultures Beyond the Earth*, 413

Masters, Michael P.: *Identified Flying Objects: A Multidisciplinary Scientific Approach to the UFO Phenomenon*, 214

Mayan, 12, 17–18, 26, 32–33, 54, 59, 111, 126, 132, 205, 350, 355, 359, 422

McCampbell, James M.: *UFOiogy*, 121

Menzel, Donald, 94, 99, 102, 114–15, 175, 188, 339–41, 347–48, 354–57
  Flying Saucers, 339

Menzel, Donald H. & Taves, Ernest H.: *The UFO Enigma*, 355

metal, 69, 72, 86, 89, 146, 152, 157, 201, 212–13, 220, 225, 329–33, 337

metallic, 26, 90, 123, 145, 148, 154, 157, 179, 200, 247, 269, 271, 299, 307, 329, 343, 346, 352, 356

meteors, 9, 39, 119, 172, 203, 338, 341, 410

Michaud, Michael A.G., 402

Michel, Aime:
  Flying Saucers and the Straight-line Mystery, 99
  The Truth About Flying Saucers, 96
  Michell, John, 18–19, 33, 96–97, 99–100, 111, 265, 308, 442
  The Flying Saucer Vision, 18

military, xxv, 77–78, 80, 90, 152, 166, 168, 181, 183–84, 186–87, 206–7, 210, 220–21, 225, 381–83
  intelligence, 89–90, 127–28, 160, 230, 233–35, 237, 243, 245, 332, 393, 435
    See also ONI (Office of Naval Intelligence)
  personnel, 127, 157, 165, 188, 200–201, 207–8, 216, 220, 234–37
    See also Pentagon

miracles, 10–11, 23, 31, 46, 357

Mitchell, Helen & Betty: *We Met the Space People*, 254

MJ-12
  documents, 161–62, 175–76, 187
  group, 175–176, 205

moon, 22, 32, 43, 71, 79, 87, 104–5, 107, 131–32, 205, 229, 231, 322, 358, 360, 397, 404, 406–7, 412, 418

Montgomery, Ruth: *Aliens Among Us*, 287

Mooney, Richard E., 37–38
  Colony: Earth, 37

Moore, William, xxii, 151–53, 161–62, 169, 175–76, 329, 370, 372, 378, 380, 382, 388

Moses, 14, 20, 24, 31–32, 45–48, 51, 229, 354, 357

N

National Investigations Committee on Aerial Phenomena. *See* NICAP

National Security Agency. *See* NSA

national security state, xxv, 187, 194, 441

Index

Index

Printed in Great Britain
by Amazon

87056765R00275